**Studies in Jewish and Christian Literature**

*Messiah and the Throne,* Timo Eskola
*Defilement and Purgation in the Book of Hebrews,* William G. Johnsson
*Father, Son, and Spirit in Romans 8,* Ron C. Fay
*Within the Veil,* Félix H. Cortez
*Jude's Apocalyptic Eschatology as Theological Exclusivism,* William Wilson
*Intertextuality and Prophetic Exegesis in the War Scroll of Qumran,* César Melgar
*The Past Is Yet to Come,* Barbara Isbell
*At the End of All Things,* Jason P. Kees
*Prophetic Patterns in the Passion of Jesus,* Donald Lee Schmidt
*The Obedience of Sonship: Adamic Obedience and the Heavenly Ascension in Hebrews,*
    Timothy J. Bertolet

# The Obedience of Sonship

## Adamic Obedience and the Heavenly Ascension in Hebrews

# The Obedience of Sonship

## Adamic Obedience and the Heavenly Ascension in Hebrews

Timothy J. Bertolet

Fontes

*The Obedience of Sonship: Adamic Obedience and the Heavenly Ascension in Hebrews*

Copyright © 2023 by Timothy J. Bertolet

ISBN-13: 978-1-948048-90-3 (hardback)
ISBN-13: 978-1-948048-88-0 (paperback)

Scripture quotations are from The ESV® Bible (The Holy Bible, English Standard Version®), copyright © 2001 by Crossway, a publishing ministry of Good News Publishers. Used by permission. All rights reserved.

All rights reserved. No part of this publication may be reproduced, stored in a retrieval system, or transmitted in any form or by any means—electronic, mechanical, photocopy, recording, or any other—except for brief quotations in printed reviews, without the prior permission of the publisher.

Typeset by Monolateral.

FONTES PRESS
DALLAS, TX
www.fontespress.com

εἰς Ἰησοῦν Χριστόν τοῦ κυρίου μου καὶ σωτῆρος

"...αὐτῷ ἡ δόξα καὶ νῦν καὶ εἰς ἡμέραν αἰῶνος"
(2 Pet. 3:18)

# Contents

Abbreviations . . . . . . . . . . . . . . . . . . . . . . . . . . . . . . . . . . . . . . . . . . . . . . . . . . . . . xi

1. Introduction to the Ascension . . . . . . . . . . . . . . . . . . . . . . . . . . . . . . . . . . . . 1
   Survey of Scholarship . . . . . . . . . . . . . . . . . . . . . . . . . . . . . . . . . . . . . . . . . . 4
   Proposal . . . . . . . . . . . . . . . . . . . . . . . . . . . . . . . . . . . . . . . . . . . . . . . . . . . . 13
   Argument . . . . . . . . . . . . . . . . . . . . . . . . . . . . . . . . . . . . . . . . . . . . . . . . . . . 14

2. Sonship and the Deity of Christ in Hebrews 1, Part 1 . . . . . . . . . . . . . . . . 17
   Introduction . . . . . . . . . . . . . . . . . . . . . . . . . . . . . . . . . . . . . . . . . . . . . . . . 17
   Heb 1:1–4 . . . . . . . . . . . . . . . . . . . . . . . . . . . . . . . . . . . . . . . . . . . . . . . . . . 18
      The Son as the Climax of Revelation . . . . . . . . . . . . . . . . . . . . . . . . . . 18
      Recently Appointed Heir but Active at the Creation . . . . . . . . . . . . . . . 21
      The Son as ἀπαύγασμα and χαρακτήρ . . . . . . . . . . . . . . . . . . . . . . . . 24
      Upholding All By His Powerful Word . . . . . . . . . . . . . . . . . . . . . . . . . . 30
   Heb 1:5—Sonship and the Use of Ps 2:7 and 2 Sam 7:14 . . . . . . . . . . . . . . . 35
   Functional Sonship as Revelatory of the Son's Ontology . . . . . . . . . . . . . . 39
   Conclusion . . . . . . . . . . . . . . . . . . . . . . . . . . . . . . . . . . . . . . . . . . . . . . . . 41

3. Sonship and the Deity of Christ in Hebrews 1, Part 2 . . . . . . . . . . . . . . . . 43
   Introduction . . . . . . . . . . . . . . . . . . . . . . . . . . . . . . . . . . . . . . . . . . . . . . . 43
   Heb 1:6—The Son as Firstborn and Object of Worship . . . . . . . . . . . . . . . 43
   Heb 1:8–9—Sonship and the Use of Ps 45:6–7 . . . . . . . . . . . . . . . . . . . . . 55
   Heb 1:10–12—The Unchanging One: Sonship and the Use Ps 102:25–27 . . . . . . . . 64
   Conclusion . . . . . . . . . . . . . . . . . . . . . . . . . . . . . . . . . . . . . . . . . . . . . . . . 73

4. The Adamic Vocation of Sonship in Hebrews 2 . . . . . . . . . . . . . . . . . . . . 75
   Introduction . . . . . . . . . . . . . . . . . . . . . . . . . . . . . . . . . . . . . . . . . . . . . . . 75
   Second Adam Christology: A Working Definition . . . . . . . . . . . . . . . . . . . 76
   Ps 8 in the Argument of Heb 1 and 2 . . . . . . . . . . . . . . . . . . . . . . . . . . . . . 78
   Hebrews 2:6–8 . . . . . . . . . . . . . . . . . . . . . . . . . . . . . . . . . . . . . . . . . . . . . 81
   Heb 2:8b–10—Seeing Jesus made perfect through suffering . . . . . . . . . . . . . 100
   Heb 2:11–13—Jesus' Solidarity with His People . . . . . . . . . . . . . . . . . . . . . 117
   Heb 2:14–18—Made Like His Brothers to Become a High Priest . . . . . . . . . . . . . 122
   Conclusion . . . . . . . . . . . . . . . . . . . . . . . . . . . . . . . . . . . . . . . . . . . . . . . 129

5. The Son Ascends into the Heavenly Tabernacle . . . . . . . . . . . . . . . . . . . 133
   Introduction . . . . . . . . . . . . . . . . . . . . . . . . . . . . . . . . . . . . . . . . . . . . . . 133
   Cosmology: A Throne in a Heavenly Tabernacle . . . . . . . . . . . . . . . . . . . . 134
   Ascension Texts in Hebrews . . . . . . . . . . . . . . . . . . . . . . . . . . . . . . . . . . 140
      Heb 1 . . . . . . . . . . . . . . . . . . . . . . . . . . . . . . . . . . . . . . . . . . . . . . . . . 140
      Heb 4:14–16 . . . . . . . . . . . . . . . . . . . . . . . . . . . . . . . . . . . . . . . . . . . . 141
      Heb 6:19–20 . . . . . . . . . . . . . . . . . . . . . . . . . . . . . . . . . . . . . . . . . . . 148
      Heb 7:26 . . . . . . . . . . . . . . . . . . . . . . . . . . . . . . . . . . . . . . . . . . . . . . 156
      Heb 8:1–6 . . . . . . . . . . . . . . . . . . . . . . . . . . . . . . . . . . . . . . . . . . . . . 162
      Heb 9:11–14 . . . . . . . . . . . . . . . . . . . . . . . . . . . . . . . . . . . . . . . . . . . 164
      Heb 9:23–26 . . . . . . . . . . . . . . . . . . . . . . . . . . . . . . . . . . . . . . . . . . . 180
   Conclusion . . . . . . . . . . . . . . . . . . . . . . . . . . . . . . . . . . . . . . . . . . . . . . . 187

6. THE SON'S ADAMIC OBEDIENCE LEADS TO ASCENSION .......................... 191
   Introduction .......................... 191
   Heb 5:8a καίπερ ὢν υἱός .......................... 192
   Heb 5:1–4 The Qualification of Weakness for Priesthood .......................... 205
   Heb 5:7–8b Suffering and Obedience .......................... 208
   Heb 5:5–6, 9–10 Glorification, Perfection, and Ascension .......................... 232
   Heb 10:5–9 Obedience to Establish the Second Covenant .......................... 239
   Heb 10:10–14 Christ's Sacrifice and Ascension .......................... 248
   Conclusion .......................... 250

7. CONCLUSION .......................... 255
   Summary of the Argument .......................... 255
   Contribution to Scholarship .......................... 263

BIBLIOGRAPHY .......................... 267
INDEX .......................... 287

# Abbreviations

Unless otherwise noted, the abbreviations in this book follow *The SBL Handbook of Style for Ancient Near Eastern, Biblical, and Early Christian Studies* (Second Edition; Atlanta: SBL Press, 2014).

Unless otherwise noted, quotations from the LXX are from *Septuaginta* (Alfred Rahlfs, ed; Stuttgart: Deutsche Bibelgesellschaft, 2006). The Masoretic Text quotations are from the *Biblica Hebraica Stuttgartensia* (Deutsche Bibelgesellschaft, 1997). The Greek Text of the NT is from the Nestle-Aland 28th Edition of the *Novum Testamentum Graece*.

Unless otherwise noted, quotations from the Bible in English come from the *English Standard Version* (ESV).

| | |
|---|---|
| AB | The Anchor Yale Bible |
| Add. Esth. | Additions to Esther |
| ALD | Aramaic Levi Document (e.g., 1Q21, 4Q213, 4Q214) |
| ANE | Ancient Near East |
| ANF | Ante-Nicene Fathers |
| ANRW | Aufstieg und Niedergang der römischen Welt |
| *Ant.* | Josephus, *Jewish Antiquities* |
| Apoc. Ab. | Apocalypse of Abraham |
| Apoc. Sedr. | Apocalypse of Sedrach |
| Apoc. Zeph. | Apocalypse of Zephaniah |
| Ascen. Isa. | Ascension of Isaiah |

| Barn. | Epistle of Barnabas |
| --- | --- |
| *BBR* | *Bulletin for Biblical Research* |
| BCOTWP | Baker Commentary on the Old Testament Wisdom and Psalms |
| BDAG | Danker, Frederick W., Walter Bauer, William F. Arndt, and F. Wilbur Gingrich. *Greek-English Lexicon of the New Testament and Other Early Christian Literature.* 3rd ed. University of Chicago Press, 2000 |
| BDF | Blass, Friedrich, Albert Debrunner, and Robert W. Funk. *A Greek Grammar of the New Testament and Other Early Christian Literature.* University of Chicago Press, 1961 |
| BECNT | Baker Exegetical Commentary on the New Testament |
| Bel | Bel and the Dragon |
| *BR* | *Biblical Research* |
| *BSac* | *Bibliotheca sacra* |
| BZNW | Beihefte zur Zeitschrift für die neutestamentliche Wissenschaft |
| *CBQ* | *Catholic Biblical Quarterly* |
| CHALOT | Holladay, William, ed. *A Concise Hebrew and Aramaic Lexicon of the Old Testament.* Eerdmans, 1988 |
| 1–2 Clem. | 1–2 Clement |
| *Conf.* | Philo, *De confusione linguarum* |
| *Det.* | Philo, *Quod deterius potiori insidiari soleat* |
| DSS | Dead Sea Scrolls |
| *Ebr.* | Philo, *De ebrietate* |
| EDNT | *Exegetical Dictionary of the New Testament.* Edited by Horst Balz and Gerhard Schneider. 3 vols. Eerdmans, 1990–1993 |
| *EvQ* | *Evangelical Quarterly* |
| *ExpTim* | *Expository Times* |
| *Iph. Aul.* | Euripedes, *Iphigenia Aulidensis* |
| *Fug.* | Philo, *De fuga et inventione* |
| *Her.* | Philo, *Quis rerum divinarum heres sit* |
| HNTC | Harper New Testament Commentary |
| *HTR* | *Harvard Theological Review* |

| | |
|---|---|
| HvTSt | Hervormde Teologiese Studies |
| JBL | Journal of Biblical Literature |
| JETS | Journal of Evangelical Theological Society |
| JJS | Journal of Jewish Studies |
| Jos. Asen. | Joseph and Aseneth |
| JSJ | Journal for the Study of Judaism |
| JSJSup | Supplements to the Journal for the Study of Judaism |
| JSNT | Journal for the Study of the New Testament |
| JSOT | Journal for the Study of the Old Testament |
| JTS | Journal for Theological Studies |
| Jub. | Jubilees |
| J.W. | Josephus, Jewish War |
| KEK | Kritisch-exegetischer Kommentar uber das Neue Testament (Meyer-Kommentar) |
| LAB | Pseudo-Philo, Liber antiquitatum biblicarum |
| LAE | Life of Adam and Eve |
| Leg. | Philo, Legum allegoriae |
| Mart. Pol. | Martyrdom of Polycarp |
| Mos. | Philo, De vita Mosis |
| Mut. | Philo, De mutatione nominum |
| Neot | Neotestamentica |
| NETS | New English Translation of the Septuagint. Edited by Albert Pietersma and Benjamin G. Wright. Oxford University Press, 2007 |
| NICNT | New International Commentary of the New Testament |
| NIGTC | New International Greek Testament Commentary |
| NovT | Novum Testamentum |
| NovTSup | Supplements to Novum Testamentum |
| NTS | New Testament Studies |
| OTE | Old Testament Essays |
| OTL | Old Testament Library |
| Opif. | Philo, De opificio mundi |
| Plant. | Philo, De plantatione |

| | |
|---|---|
| PNTC | Pillar New Testament Commentary |
| *Hist.* | *Histories* (of Herodotus or Polybius, e.g.) |
| Pr. Man. | Prayer of Manasseh |
| Pss. Sol. | Psalms of Solomon |
| *QE* | Philo, *Quaestiones et solutions in Exodum* |
| *ResQ* | *Restoration Quarterly* |
| *SBJT* | *Southern Baptist Journal of Theology* |
| SBL | Society of Biblical Literature |
| Sib. Or. | Sibylline Oracles |
| *SJT* | *Scottish Journal of Theology* |
| SNTSMS | Society for New Testament Studies Monograph Series |
| *Somn.* | Philo, *De somniis* |
| *Spec.* | Philo, *De specialibus legibus* |
| STDJ | Studies on the Texts of the Desert of Judah |
| T. Ab. | Testament of Abraham |
| TDNT | *Theological Dictionary of the New Testament*. Edited by Gerhard Kittel and Gerhard Friedrich. Translated by Geoffrey W. Bromiley. 10 vols. Eerdmans, 1964–1976 |
| T. Job | Testament of Job |
| T. Jud. | Testament of Judah |
| T. Isaac | Testament of Isaac |
| T. Levi | Testament of Levi |
| Tob. | Tobit |
| *TJ* | *Trinity Journal* |
| *TynBul* | *Tyndale Bulletin* |
| WBC | Word Biblical Commentary |
| *WTJ* | *Westminster Theological Journal* |
| WUNT | Wissenschaftliche Untersuchungen zum Neuen Testament. |
| *ZAW* | *Zeitschrift für die alttestamentliche Wissenschaft* |
| *ZNW* | *Zeitschrift für die neutestamentliche Wissenschaft und die Kunde der älteren Kirche* |

# 1

## Introduction to the Ascension

The purpose of this study will be to explore the ascension in the book of Hebrews. Ascents into heaven are common in both Greco-Roman and Jewish texts in the Mediterranean world. "[T]he dominant understanding of ascent in ancient Jewish and Christian literature is of a process initiated not by the visionary but by God."[1] In works on heavenly ascensions in Christian and Jewish thought, there is a tendency in scholarship to overlook or ignore Hebrews as evidence of ascension, when they are considering NT examples.[2] Although there are a few exceptions in this scholarship where

---

1 Martha Himmelfarb, "The Practice of Ascent in the Ancient Mediterranean World," *Death, Ecstasy and Other Worldly Journeys,* ed. John J. Collins and Michael Fishbane (New York State University Press, 1995), 133. For another introductory essay in this same work see John J. Collins, "A Throne in the Heavens: Apotheosis in pre-Christian Judaism," in *Death, Ecstasy and Other Worldly Journeys,* 43–58. See also John Collins, "Journeys to the World Beyond in Ancient Judaism," ch. 11 in *Apocalypse, Prophecy, and Pseudepigraphy: On Jewish Apocalyptic Literature* (Eerdmans, 2015), 178–197.

2 Paula Gooder, *Only the Third Heaven? 2 Corinthians 12.1–10 and Heavenly Ascent* (T&T Clark, 2006), in chapter 5 reviewing NT examples, she discusses only Luke-Acts and the Revelation of John. James D. Tabor, *Things Unutterable: Paul's Ascent to Paradise in its Greco-Roman, Judaic, and Early Christian Contexts* (University Press of America, 1981) mentions Acts 1:9–11 (p. 79) and relevant Pauline texts of Christ's resurrection, exaltation, and glorification (pp. 16–19). J. M. Scott ("Heavenly Ascent in Jewish and Pagan Traditions," in *Dictionary of New Testament Background,* ed. C. A. Evans and S. E. Porter [Intervarsity, 2000], 447) only lists Luke 24:50–53; Acts 1:1–12; 2:34; John 3:13–15; 6:62; 20:17; Phil 2:6–11; Eph 4:8–10; Rev 12:5 as references to the ascension; Paul's ascent to the third heaven 2 Cor 12:2–4; and Enoch's rapture (Heb 11:5), although he admits "the list grows longer if we include NT texts that presuppose the ascension (e.g., Mark 12:62)." Adela Yarbro Collins, "Traveling Up and Away: Journeys to the Upper and Outer Regions of the World," in *Greco-Roman Culture and the New Testament: Studies Commemorating the Centennial of the Pontifical Biblical Institute,* ed. David E. Aune and Frederick E. Brenk (Brill, 2012), 135–166. Leif Carlsson, *Round Trips to Heaven: Otherworldly Travelers in Early Judaism and Christianity* (VDM, 2008). On the one hand, the absence of Hebrews in Carlsson may be because he focusses primarily on ascents that are "round trips" (he does not discuss the Revelation of John), but on the other hand he does look at *Life of Adam and Eve* where

Hebrews is mentioned, these references are largely in passing.[3]

The ascension of Jesus Christ is important to the writers of the NT. As Felix Cortez writes, "Jesus's ascension stands at the foundational core of NT theology."[4] In Christian theology, the ascension of Jesus Christ refers to his return to heaven after his death and bodily resurrection. The importance of the doctrine for the early church ensured its place in the Rule of Faith.[5] In the past, this doctrine generally has been studied with respect to its historical development in the early church,[6] from the perspective of systematic theology,[7] or

---

Adam's journey does not entail a return trip. Pointing to the differences in the Latin version, he writes "Here Adam is the archetype for the sinner who does not become righteous until *after* death, at the time of resurrection" (emphasis original, 247). J. Edward Wright, *The Early History of Heaven* (Oxford University Press, 2000) discusses numerous pictures of heaven and the seven heavens in Jewish apocalyptic literature, devotes two and half pages on Paul's vision in 2 Cor 12 but makes only one passing reference to Hebrews in a list of texts (196). Himmelfarb's work is somewhat different than the overviews listed above since the work intentionally limits itself to books that are apocalypses, so there is no sustained treatment even of 2 Corinthians 12 or Hebrews (*Ascent to Heaven in Jewish and Christian Apocalypses* [Oxford University Press, 1993]). Likewise Mary Dean-Otting does not primarily discuss Christian literature but Hellenistic Jewish Literature (*Heavenly Journeys: A Study of the Motif in Hellenistic Jewish Literature* [Lang, 1984]).

3  Alan Segal, "Heavenly Ascent in Hellenistic Judaism, Early Christianity and Their Environment," *ANRW* 23.2:1375. Morton Smith, "Ascent to the Heavens and the Beginning of Christianity," *Eranos-Jahrbuch* 50 (1981): 417. Elaine Jones, "Origins of 'Ascension' Terminology," *Churchman* 104.2 (1990): 156–161.

4  Felix Cortez "'The Anchor of the Soul that Enters the Veil': the Ascension of the 'Son' in the Letter to the Hebrews" (PhD diss., Andrews University, 2008), 2.

5  Irenaeus, *Against Heresies* I.x.1. (*ANF* 1:330) and III.iv.2 (*ANF* 1:417). Tertullian, *On Prescription Against Heretics* ch. 13 (*ANF* 3:249).

6  J.D. Davies, *He Ascended into Heaven: A Study in the History of Doctrine* (Lutterworth, 1958). Henry Barclay Swete, *The Ascended Christ: A Study in the Earliest Christian Teaching*, (Macmillan, 1910). Morton S. Enslin, "The Ascension Story," *JBL* 47 (1928): 60–73. Peter Toon, *The Ascension of Our Lord* (Thomas Nelson, 1984). Joseph Haroutunian, "The Doctrine of the Ascension: A Study of the New Testament Teaching," *Interpretation* 10 (1956): 270–281. Joseph Fitzmyer, "The Ascension of Christ and Pentecost," *Theological Studies* 45.3 (1984): 409–440. Brian K. Donne, "The Significance of the Ascension of Jesus Christ in the New Testament," *SJT* 30 (1977): 555–568. Peter Toon, "Historical Perspectives of the Doctrine of Christ's Ascension Part 1: Resurrected and Ascended: The Exalted Jesus," *BSac* 140 (1983): 195–205.

7  William Milligan, *The Ascension and Heavenly Priesthood of Our Lord* (Macmillan, 1894; Wipf & Stock, 2006). James Benjamin Wagner, *Ascendit ad Coelos: The Doctrine of the Ascension in the Reformed and Lutheran Theology of the Period of Orthodoxy* (Keller, 1964). Gerrit Scott Dawson, *Jesus Ascended: The Meaning of Christ's Continuing Incarnation* (P&R, 2004). Douglas Farrow, *Ascension and Ecclesia: On the Significance of the Doctrine of the Ascension for Ecclesiology and Christian Cosmology* (Eerdmans, 1999). Douglas Farrow, *Ascension Theology* (T&T Clark, 2011). John E. Jansen, "The Ascension, the Church and Theology," *Theology Today* 16 (1959): 17–29. Nick Needam, "Christ Ascended for Us: 'Jesus' Ascended Humanity and Ours,'" *Evangel* 25.2 (2007): 42–47. Ralph Norman, "Beyond the Ultimate Sphere: The Ascension and Eschatology," *Modern Believing* 42 (April 2001): 3–15. Peter Toon, "Historical Perspectives of the Doctrine of Christ's Ascension Part 2: The Meaning of the Ascension of Christ," *BSac* 140 (1983): 291–301; "Historical Perspectives of the Doctrine of Christ's Ascension Part 3: The Significance of the Ascension for Believers," *BSac* 141 (1984): 16–27; "Historical Perspectives of the Doctrine

as a matter of historical theology examining later theologians.[8] More recently in the field of NT studies, there have been studies examining Luke-Acts' portrayal of the ascension.[9]

Hebrews does not give us a historical account[10] of the ascension of Jesus as, for example, does Luke-Acts. However, "[m]ore than any other book in the NT, Hebrews brings out the theological significance of the ascension."[11] It is more common in NT scholarship to focus on the exaltation of Christ in Hebrews, the concept of the heavenly tabernacle, or Jesus's session at the right hand (*cf.* Ps 110:1) as a major theme in Hebrews than to specifically refer to his ascension and entrance into heaven.[12]

As such, the ascension in Hebrews scholarship has largely been a neglected topic. This is surprising when one considers that in the milieu of the first century "ascent stories were popular in the thought of the time, particularly among the Jews. Half a dozen Old Testament pseudepigrapha credit their heroes with visits to the heavens."[13] What Andrew Purves writes regarding pastoral theology can easily be applied to scholarship in Hebrews: "We can hardly speak of the heavenly priesthood of Christ without dealing

---

of Christ's Ascension Part 4: The Exalted Jesus and God's Revelation," *BSac* 141 (1984): 112–19. Michael Horton, "Atonement and Ascension," in *Locating Atonement: Explorations in Constructive Dogmatics,* ed. Oliver D. Crisp and Fred Sanders (Zondervan, 2015): 226–250. A homiletical reflection on the ascension can be found in George C. Fuller, "The Life of Jesus, after the Ascension (Luke 24:50–53; Acts 1:9–11)," *WTJ* 56 (1994): 391–398. Fuller makes only a brief reference to Hebrews. Robert Peterson in *Salvation Accomplished by the Son: The Work of Christ* (Crossway, 2012) discusses the ascension in chapter 5 and Hebrews specifically (171–178).

8  William H. Marrevee, *The Ascension of Christ in the Works of St. Augustine* (University of Ottawa Press, 1967). Andrew Burgess, *The Ascension in Karl Barth* (Ashgate, 2004).

9  Arie W. Zwiep, *The Ascension of the Messiah in Lukan Christology* (Brill, 1997). David K. Bryan and David W. Pao, eds., *Ascent into Heaven in Luke-Acts: New Explorations of Luke's Narrative Hinge* (Fortress Press, 2016), see 253–262 for a thorough biography of writing on the ascent in Luke-Acts from 1995–2016. Eric Franklin, "The Ascension and the Eschatology of Luke-Acts," *SJT* 23 (1970): 191–200. Matthew Sleeman, *Geography and the Ascension Narrative in Acts* (Cambridge University Press, 2009). John F. Maile, "The Ascension in Luke-Acts," *TynBul* 37 (1986): 29–59. Ming Gao, "Heaven and Earth in Luke-Acts" (PhD diss., Trinity International University, May 2015). Mikeal Carl Parsons, "The Ascension Narratives in Luke-Acts" (PhD diss., Southern Baptist Theological Seminary, 1985). K. Giles, "Ascension," in *Dictionary of Jesus and the Gospels,* ed. Joel B. Green, Scot McKnight, and I. Howard Marshall (Intervarsity, 1992): 46–50.

10  Cortez introduces his study as "focused on the theology of ascension and not on its historicity or elucidation of its circumstances, because *Hebrews itself is not concerned with such matter* [referring to the latter elements]" (emphasis added; "Anchor of the Soul," 9).

11  W. J. Larkin Jr., "Ascension," in Dictionary of Later New Testaments and Its Development, ed. Ralph P. Martin and Peter H. Davids (Intervarsity, 1997), 98.

12  Similarly, Cortez ("Anchor of the Soul," 6) notes that Hebrews scholarship has focused on the sacrifice and seating of Christ at God's right hand more than the actual entrance of Jesus into heaven.

13  Morton Smith, "Two Ascended to Heaven: Jesus and the Author of 4Q491," in *Jesus and the Dead Sea Scrolls,* ed. James H. Charlesworth (Doubleday, 1992), 294.

with the ascension.... Yet today the doctrine [of the ascension] languishes unnoticed...."[14]

We will tentatively define ascension in Hebrews as the movement of the incarnate glorified Son 'upward' and 'inward' into the divine glory, where he sits at the right hand of the Father. Hebrews does not narrate an ascent journey from the earth, nor is the ascent of Jesus, the Son, a visionary experience. The ascension is the movement the Son into the heavenly throne room where he goes into the true tabernacle and then sits down at God's right hand. This is, of course, his exaltation. However, Hebrews does pay particular attention to the movement of the person. He goes inward into the true holy of holies that must be cleansed, and he goes upward to the divine throne. As we will see later in this study, this is consistent with various portraits in Second Temple Judaism.

For Hebrews and other Second Temple texts, heaven is a "place." Resurrected or glorified human beings can enter into this place and, subsequently, into the presence of God. Heaven is not incorporeal. For Hebrews, the Son entering God's presence is an ascension—a movement. The Son is perfected and glorified (his state) and then positioned by virtue of a movement to sit at God's right hand in this new human state. He is and remains truly human and incarnate, so we have chosen the term 'ascension' to highlight the reality and even physicality of the Son's going to the highest position over all creation. 'Exaltation' is the broader term referring to the Son's status but ascension is the more narrow term focusing on the movement of position, both position as a status and position as a place moving to the highest point over all creation. Thus, we have chosen the more precise term ascension as it allows us to focus on how Hebrews sees the movement as essential.

### Survey of Scholarship

The ascension remains an understudied element in the book of Hebrews. At the beginning of his 2008 dissertation, Felix Cortez states there is no major study of the ascension in the letter of Hebrews.[15] In what follows, we will survey some of the more recent literature in Hebrews that discusses the role of the ascension.

---

14 Andrew Purves, *Reconstructing Pastoral Theology: A Christological Foundation* (Westminster John Knox, 2004), 107. This statement may be a bit hyperbolic on Purves's part, but not by much.

15 Cortez, "Anchor of the Soul" 5. He does note Robert David Kaylor's "The Ascension Motif in Luke-Acts, the Epistle to the Hebrews, and the Fourth Gospel" (PhD diss., Duke University, 1964), 83–125. However even Kaylor's work does not focus exclusively on Hebrews.

First, in his 1960's book *Heavenly Sanctuary and Liturgy in the Epistle to the Hebrews,* Aelred Cody devotes chapter 4 of part 2 to a discussion of aspects of the ascension of Christ in Hebrews.[16] Christ's ascension into heaven is the fulfillment of the Day of Atonement.[17] "The heavenly liturgy of Our Lord in Hebrews, like the heavenly sanctuary in which it is performed, is an antitype of an institution of the Old, the perfect realization of that which was only foreshadowed under the Old Dispensation."[18] The death of Christ is the sacrifice. He "suffered and died in order that He might penetrate beyond the veil by His Resurrection and Ascension..."[19] This penetration beyond the veil "consummates the world of salvation in the presence of God."[20] The sacrifice on the cross "enables the celestial High Priest to enter the heavenly sacrifice, according to the Levitical type."[21] Christ's entrance into heaven allows the completion of redemption.[22] For Cody, the ascension is not the primary concern of Hebrews, but the means by which Hebrews is able to speak of the session of Christ (i.e., the seating of Christ at the right hand of the Father).[23] Christ's session is the fulfillment of his ministry and his saving humanity, the priesthood of Christ having been perfected.[24]

Christ's ascension then entails the perfection of Christ's priesthood, as Cody has discussed with the "celestial perfection of Christ's humanity." Christ's "exaltation to the right hand of God...inaugurated the plentitude of His power to reign over the destinies of the universe and to bring others salvation with Him in the heavenly city."[25] Thus, Cody concludes:

> [P]erfect salvation comes to us only through the glorified mediator who has passed from this world to the next, to achieve salvation for us in the heavenly sanctuary. The priesthood of Christ is perfected in the exaltation of the Ascension, that the liturgy of Christ may be perfected in the heavenly sanctuary, before the face of God.[26]

---

16 *Heavenly Sanctuary and Liturgy in the Epistle to the Hebrews: The Achievement of Salvation in the Epistle's Perspective* (Grail, 1960).
17 Ibid., 168–169.
18 Ibid., 169–170.
19 Ibid., 171.
20 Ibid.
21 Ibid., 174–175.
22 Ibid., 175.
23 Ibid., 175–176.
24 Ibid., 176.
25 Ibid. Cf. 86–116.
26 Ibid., 180.

Cody's work has several strengths. First, it emphasizes the role of Christ's glorified humanity. Cody makes no apologies for being rather traditional and creedal in his articulation of the natures of Christ even if some modern scholarship might criticize this approach as being anachronistic. Nevertheless, he sees the important role of a glorified humanity in completing the work of the Son in accomplishing salvation. Second, he highlights the unity of cross and ascension with respect to Hebrews' view of the accomplishment of redemption. Third, Cody makes use of the typological pattern between the Old and the New. The main weaknesses of Cody's work stem primarily from its datedness. For example, there is limited discussion of Second Temple background to ascension but does not take note of the similarities between Hebrews and apocalyptic traditions.[27]

Written in 2001, Timo Eskola's *Messiah and the Throne* explores the background of the exaltation Christology in the NT.[28] Examining the heavenly throne in Second Temple sources, he argues that merkabah mysticism "provides a model for the enthronement" in NT Christology.[29] With the use of Ps 110, early Christians portrayed Jesus as the exalted Davidic figure enthroned in heaven.[30] Building a careful case, Eskola gives attention to resurrection and enthronement passages throughout the NT.

When Eskola turns to the book of Hebrews, he writes, "Exaltation Christology appears to be the backbone of the theology of the writer. The description of Christology is quite clearly based on an ascent structure and such pattern has often been noted by scholarship."[31] Eskola begins examining Heb 1:3–4 with the Christology that follows in Heb 1.[32] Christ becomes the object of worship as only God was worshipped.[33] He also notes that there is an "obvious polarity between the angels and the divine Son."[34] But through the "metaphor of the throne the Son is identified as God himself."[35] Hebrews identifies

---

27 He discusses *T. Levi* 3.5–6,8 pp.51–55.; on apocalyptic similarities: 26–36, 80, 82, *et al.*
28 *Messiah and the Throne: Jewish Merkabah Mysticism and Early Christian Exaltation Discourse*, WUNT 2/124 (Mohr Siebeck, 2001).
29 Ibid., 156.
30 Ibid., 157, 168–177, et al.
31 Ibid., 202–203. He cites William Lane, *Hebrews 1–8* (Word, 1991) and L.D. Hurst, *The Epistle to Hebrews: Its Background and Thought*, SNTS 65 (Cambridge, 1990). Eskola notes that merkabah mysticism has not often been seen as a background to the ascent in Hebrews. Furthermore, while authors have paid attention to exaltation and the heavenly tabernacle in Hebrews, the ascent has not received the attention in Hebrews with regard to how it shapes the theology as a whole.
32 Eskola, *Messiah and the Throne*, 203–207
33 Ibid., 203–204.
34 Ibid., 205.
35 Ibid.

*Introduction to the Ascension* 7

the Sonship with kingship and the fulfillment of Davidic kingship.[36] The fulfilment of the Davidic passages portray Christ's exaltation, and this exaltation "resembles a heavenly journey that leads to the holy throne of Glory in the heavenly Temple."[37] On Heb 8:1 and 10:12, Eskola shows the linkage between the cultic and royal features in this ascension.[38]

Later in his work, Eskola discusses the heavenly throne in Hebrews and its relationship to atonement or cultic discourse.[39] While not limiting his discussion to Hebrews, Hebrews figures prominently in this portrayal. For Hebrews, "[t]emple symbolism is thus explicit" and "has been exploited for the needs of Christology."[40] "The resurrected Christ serves as high priest in heaven providing the true atonement."[41] For Eskola, the "throne is the place where atonement is obtained...The blood sacrifice must be taken on that throne which, through atonement, becomes the throne of grace."[42] Eskola demonstrates that exaltation and atonement are brought into a unified portrait. Based on the figure of Melchizedek in Hebrews, the Davidic heir is both king and priest having ascended into heaven before the heavenly throne of God.[43]

The strongest feature of Eskola's work is the relationship between merkabah mysticism and NT exaltation Christology linked through Ps 110. He rightly notes the importance of the feature of ascent, especially as a key feature of Hebrews. Eskola does not oversimplify the complex lines of evidence and features that helped give rise to early articulations of Christology. For Hebrews, he rightly argues "[t]he whole letter is relying on apocalyptic cosmology and enthronement discourse."[44] The ascent is not secondary, nor merely a metaphor that can be shed like a husk once the reader discerns a greater point. Instead, it is the ascent into heaven that reveals the glory of Christ. The Christology of Hebrews has a "scheme of humiliation and exaltation" that "produces a simple ascent structure in this Christology."[45]

Felix Cortez has offered a major and detailed treatment entirely on the ascension of Christ in the book of Hebrews in his 2008 dissertation.[46] His

---

36 Ibid., 206.
37 Ibid., 207.
38 Ibid.
39 Ibid., 251–269.
40 Ibid., 253.
41 Ibid.
42 Cf. ibid., 259–261.
43 Ibid., 261–263.
44 Ibid., 209.
45 Ibid., 210.
46 Cortez, "'Anchor of the Soul.'"

work is the only one of its kind that we have found in our research.[47] Given the detail and length of the thesis, we will only be able to highlight key aspects of it here. Cortez's main thesis is that the ascension of Jesus is (1) the enthronement of the Son where the promises of the Davidic covenant are inaugurated, (2) the appointment of the faithful high priest, and (3) the inauguration of the new covenant.[48] His intention is to highlight the fulfillment of Davidic themes in the ascension as primary, rather than the typical readings of the Day of Atonement imagery or Moses' covenant inauguration.[49] For Cortez, the Day of Atonement motif and the symbolism of Moses' covenant inauguration are only secondary, to be integrated into a larger picture of the Davidic figure in whom the Davidic covenant is fulfilled who then inaugurates the new covenant.[50]

In chapter 2, Cortez examines the background of the Davidic covenant as well as the portrayal of an ideal Davidic king in the Hebrew Bible and Second Temple Judaism. The purpose of this chapter is to survey the features of Davidic traditions in early Judaism. He begins by an examination of 2 Sam 7 and the institution of the Davidic covenant.[51] One of the more important features for his later argument is that the Davidic King is a Covenant Mediator who renews the Mosaic Covenant. For example, he writes "the Davidic king is designated God's 'son' and 'firstborn' (2 Sam 7:14; Pss 2:6–7; 89:27) embodying Israel, the covenant people, which is also called 'son' and 'firstborn' (Exod 4:22–23; cf. Jer 3:19; 31:9). In this way God legitimizes the Davidic king as Israel's proxy."[52] Thus, the Davidic covenant narrowed the role of Israel's covenant faithfulness to David's covenant faithfulness.[53] "God's election of the 'son' of David centralizes his relationship with Israel to the person of the king."[54] Cortez is thorough in his examination of the Davidic figure in the Deuteromistic history, Ezekiel 37, and Second Temple texts. He highlights specific ways in which the king is a figure of covenant renewal, which is significant for his conclusions.

In the third chapter of his dissertation, Cortez examines the six key explicit ascension passages in the letter to the Hebrews: Heb 1:6; 4:14–16; 6:19–20;

---

[47] Some of the other more recent works we note below either do not offer such in-depth analysis only discussing ascension as part of a broader thesis. Cortez specifically focuses on the ascension.

[48] Cortez, "Anchor of the Soul," 455–457.

[49] Ibid., 9–42.

[50] Ibid., 39–40.

[51] Ibid., 54–71

[52] Ibid., 63–64.

[53] Ibid., 65–67.

[54] Ibid., 76.

9:11–14, 24; and 10:19–25. Concerning 1:5–12 Cortez argues, as a whole "the catena describes the enthronement of the Son 'at the right hand of the majesty on high'"[55] and οἰκουμένη refers to the heavenly world that is the age to come.[56] Cortez concludes "Jesus *became* the Son at the ascension in terms of royal power, he *was already* Son in terms of his identity."[57]

Next, Cortez examines Heb 4:14–16 and places this passage within the argument of the letter as a whole. He concludes that Jesus, the Son of God, being the high priest who has passed through the heavens is "a summary of the main points of the exposition of chaps. 1–2."[58] The ascension itself explains why Jesus is a great high priest.[59]

The third ascension text Cortez examines is Heb 6:19–20.[60] The author of Hebrews "creates an analogy between Jesus's ascension and the entrance of the high priest into the holy of holies of the Israelite sanctuary."[61] Hope "is described as entering the holy of holies in the sense that it is anchored on God's throne itself in the heavenly sanctuary by means of the oath."[62] Jesus then is the forerunner, the fulfillment of Ps 8, and his ascension "confirms God's original purpose" for humanity and makes it possible for them to fulfill it.[63]

Fourth, Cortez turns his attention to Heb 9:11–14, 24 and 10:19–25 in order to explore the way the ascension inaugurates the New Covenant in Hebrews. He shows how Heb 9:1–10 explains the transition between the Old and New Covenants.[64] Cortez argues that Hebrews is unconcerned with dividing the tabernacle in heaven. Jesus's entrance into heaven and "the greater more perfect tabernacle" "inaugurates the greater realities of the new covenant that makes possible what the first covenant cult was not able to accomplish: provide forgiveness and access to God."[65] The ascension consummates the covenant. Turning to Heb 9:24–28, Cortez shows how the ascension brings access to God and the covenant inauguration is the dawning of the age to come. Sin is removed. Thus, the Day of Atonement serves as "the epitome of the Israelite cult, against which Jesus's sacrifice and ascension are compared and shown superior."[66] Highlighting the rhetorical strategy of Hebrews, Cortez

---

55  Ibid., 235.
56  Ibid., 222–223.
57  Ibid., 265. Emphasis original.
58  Ibid., 296.
59  Ibid., 300.
60  Ibid., 300–324.
61  Ibid., 303.
62  Ibid., 311–312.
63  Ibid., 314.
64  Ibid., 327–347.
65  Ibid., 354.
66  Ibid., 398.

shows how patterns from the Old Covenant build on similarities but also how Hebrews capitalizes on and emphasizes differences.[67]

Finally, Cortez highlights how the ascension is able to become a point of exhortation. Believers have come to the Heavenly Jerusalem (Heb 12:18–29). This passage brings to climax the motif of drawing into God's presence. God speaks from Mt. Zion, enthrones the Son, appoints him as high priest, and thus inaugurates the New Covenant.[68]

In his concluding chapter (ch. 4), Cortez surveys and reviews his argumentation. The ascension is Jesus's enthronement as king. It is his appointment as high priest. It is the inauguration of the New Covenant.[69] From these three main aspects, he draws three additional 'sub-aspects:' (1) the enthroned king "makes it possible for believers to enter into God's 'rest;'" (2) since Jesus mediates a new covenant he "implements a major reorganization of the cult;" and (3) "Jesus's sacrifice cleanses believers from the transgressions committed under the new covenant."[70] Finally the renewal of the covenant entails, in fulfillment of the OT motif, the consecration of the sanctuary, the better heavenly sanctuary.[71]

Cortez's thesis is compelling and deserves a wider readership.[72] He pays close attention to the text of Hebrews and surveys various interpretative options for every major point of debate in the passages he examines. He reaches his conclusion carefully and judiciously and successfully makes his connections between features of the Davidic covenant in the Hebrew Bible and the features related to the covenant inauguration in Hebrews.[73]

In his work on the resurrection and atonement in Hebrews, David Moffitt examines some aspects of the ascension in chapter 3.[74] Moffitt shows that the

---

[67] Ibid., 404–412.
[68] Ibid., 444.
[69] Ibid., 455–457.
[70] Ibid., 457–459.
[71] Ibid., 460–462.
[72] It has more recently been published as *Within the Veil: The Ascension of the Son in the Letter to the Hebrews* (Fontes, 2020).
[73] Two other dissertations written around this time: Catherine Anne Playoust, "Lifted Up from the Earth: The Ascension of Jesus and the Heavenly Ascents of Early Christians" (ThD diss., Harvard University, 2006) focuses primarily on the *Apocryphon of James,* the *Ascension of Isaiah,* and *The Gospel of John* and thus only devotes pages 70–76 to Hebrews. James M. Carlson's "A Great High Priest Who Has Passed Through the Heavens: In Quest of the Apocalyptic Roots of the Epistle to the Hebrews" (PhD diss., Marquette University, May 2008) work is devoted to the history of how apocalyptic texts have been used for as background for interpreting Hebrews. He classifies heavenly ascents into three types: (a) visions of God appearing in the temple; (b) visions from the Persian period to the Herodian period where figures ascend into heaven to encounter God; (c) first through third century AD encounters of a figure in heaven who is exalted, usually over angels. He places Hebrews in this category.
[74] *Atonement and the Logic of the Resurrection in the Epistle to the Hebrews* (Brill, 2011).

resurrection of the Son's humanity is crucial for his ascension into heaven to sit at God's right hand. It is with a human body that Christ ascends back into heaven and this human body has been "imbued with God's glory, all the glory that Adam lost, and with indestructible life."[75] The righteous human finally is enabled to dwell with God.[76] Moffitt begins by examining the background of Ps 8:5 interpreted as part of Moses' ascension.[77] He also examines accounts of human ascents during Second Temple Judaism since they "belong to a coherent subgenre of Jewish apocalyptic literature."[78] He includes especially 1 En. and 2 En. as accounts of bodily ascents. Enoch is the glorified figure who—as a glorified human—is fit to approach the divine throne.[79] Enoch as the glorified human is ontologically distinct from angels.[80] Thus, "it is virtually certain that the author is thinking in terms of *human* ascension into heaven in Heb 1–2."[81] For Moffitt, this analysis is part of a larger picture demonstrating that the resurrection is fundamentally important to Hebrews even if it receives little direct attention. Moffitt argues that because Christ ascends as resurrected,[82] this resurrected human ascension is the attainment of the eschatological destiny of humanity (Heb 2:5–9). It is as a resurrected human that Christ is able to go into heaven where the act of atonement is completed. Christ offers himself in resurrected body before the heavenly throne.

Moffitt's work has challenged scholarship to rethink the importance of the resurrection in Hebrews. His conception of the atonement as taking place in heaven has also created a bit of a stir along with critique. Nevertheless, Moffitt's overall thesis is compelling and well argued. His attention to Second Temple sources as well as the text of Hebrews exemplifies careful scholarship. Our own work will dovetail with points of his argument. We agree with Moffitt's articulation of Jesus ascending into heaven in a resurrected body, and we hope to draw attention to the role of the Son in ascending as the glorified eschatological man.

Another work that we should draw quick attention to is Jody Barnard's *The Mysticism of Hebrews*.[83] Barnard's work further advances study into the

---

75 Moffitt, *Logic of the Resurrection*, 146.
76 Ibid., 147.
77 Ibid., 150–162.
78 Ibid., 163.
79 Ibid., 178.
80 This distinctive is an important point to note particularly when we interact with Crispin Fletcher-Louis' various works.
81 Ibid., 180.
82 Moffitt's argument for the ascension of the resurrected one stands against scholars who would argue that for Hebrews there is only death followed by exaltation or some kind of spiritual ascent, a sort of 'going to heaven when you die.'
83 *The Mysticism of Hebrews: Exploring the Role of Jewish Apocalyptic Mysticism in the Epis-*

apocalyptic background of Hebrews, particularly the early mysticism that surrounds apocalyptic works. For our concern here, in chapter four, Barnard examines the apocalyptic background of the heavenly temple and how it shapes the use of Hebrews' heavenly tabernacle.[84] He rightly concludes "the cosmology of Hebrews belongs to the same Jewish apocalyptic and mystic context, and that the heavenly sanctuary is likewise imagined in terms of a multi-chambered structure."[85]

In chapter five, Barnard examines in more depth the heavenly high priesthood of the Son in Hebrews.[86] Again, Barnard surveys the possible backgrounds.[87] Against the Second Temple background, the heavenly ascent of the exalted figure entails a transformation. Barnard sees Heb 1:3–4 as indicative of the Son's priestly investiture. He then shows how 1:5–14 unpacks this investiture. There is a connection between son-hood and priesthood, which Barnard also notes is similar to T. Levi.[88] Barnard sees the appointment to heavenly priesthood as "the beginning of an intimate relationship with God, which is specifically characterized in terms of becoming a son to him."[89] After also examining the investiture of the Son in Heb 1:8–9, Barnard concludes that Hebrews "regards Jesus as a human who ascended into heaven and was transformed into a priest...it is over the heavenly (angelic) cult that Christ has become a high priest."[90]

In chapter six, Barnard discusses the heavenly enthronement of the Son, particularly his coming to reside on the throne of God in the divine glory. Barnard concludes that the Son, especially as creator (1:10–12) is one whose "identity aligns him with God himself."[91] The Son as sharing in the divine glory is unified with YHWH and is "the visible manifestation of God upon the throne in the celestial Holy of Holies, that is 'the Glory.'"[92] Barnard continues to keep in purview how this portrait intertwines with apocalyptic mysticism.

Barnard's work is insightful and ambitious in its scope. While most of his exegesis relates to Heb 1, he makes a compelling case.[93] While he is concerned

---

tle to the Hebrews, WUNT 2/331 (Mohr Siebeck, 2012).

84 Ibid., 85–118.

85 Ibid., 118. Here in our chapter 4, we disagree that Hebrews sees the heavenly sanctuary as multi-chambered.

86 Ibid., 119–143.

87 Ibid., 120–130.

88 Ibid., 137–138.

89 Ibid., 138.

90 Ibid., 142.

91 Ibid., 153.

92 Ibid., 156.

93 He returns again to Heb 1 in chapters 8–9 (pp. 221–275). It is beyond the scope of our survey to interact in detail with all of his work. We will, as opportunity allows, interact with

with more than heavenly ascents, following Barnard's argument leaves little doubt that the ascent tradition has an apocalyptic and mystical background. Other aspects of his thesis may be debatable, such as to what degree the believing community was involved in mystical experience to commune with the Son;[94] however, these aspects are beyond our concern here.

PROPOSAL

The scholarship surveyed has drawn attention to the *where* of the ascension (a heavenly tabernacle/throne), the *why* of Jesus's ascension (for priesthood, atonement, session, etc.), the *mode* of Jesus's ascension (in a resurrected body), and the *background* of Jewish eschatological expectations and apocalyptic thought behind the ascension in Hebrews. There remains, however, the need to discuss what, according to Hebrews, is the *grounds* for the ascension of the Son. Our thesis seeks to explore the connection between Sonship, obedience, and the ascension, and thereby establish the Son's earthly activity as the basis for his qualification to ascend to his eschatological destiny.

Sonship is vital to Hebrews. As Cortez notes, "In order to understand what the role of the ascension and the enthronement of the Son in the Letter is, it is first necessary to understand the meaning of the title 'Son' in the Letter. Both are inextricably connected."[95] While our survey of scholarship has highlighted some aspects of Sonship in relationship to the ascension, we believe there remains fruitful ground for further exploring this relationship. Sonship in Hebrews operates around two poles: namely divine Sonship and the Davidic-vocational aspects of sonship.[96] We will show that the author of

---

him in our exegesis of Heb 1 below. Suffice it to say, we find much in common with Barnard. His portrayal of the Son as the ascended human but also one radiating the divine glory in identity with YHWH is very similar to the understanding we will articulate below. If Barnard's work impacts Hebrews scholarship to the degree that we believe it should, it will be hard to ignore how the apocalyptic mystical background allows Hebrews to bring forth a high Christology. It will be hard to maintain a "low-but-exalted-figure" Christology that does not see Hebrews as displaying the Son as truly God and divine.

94 Barnard, "Mysticism of Hebrews," 171–212 (ch. 7).
95 Ibid., 248.
96 We put Davidic and vocational aspects together because as we will seek to show, the Davidic aspects of sonship entailed functional aspects of how the Davidic figure was supposed to act as YHWH's son. We are also not denying the aspects of priesthood as vital to Hebrews. Amy Peeler (*You Are My Son: The Family of God in the Epistle to the Hebrews*, LNTS 486 [T&T Clark, 2014], 106) sees the two predominant features as high priest and Sonship. See also Mikeal Parsons, "Son and High Priest: A Study of the Christology of Hebrews," *EvQ* 60 (1988): 195–216; Donald Hagner, "The Son of God as Unique High Priest: The Christology of the Epistle to the Hebrews," in *Contours of Christology in the New Testament*, ed. Richard N. Longenecker (Eerdmans, 2005), 248, 255–57. On Messiology in Hebrews see David Flusser, *Judaism and the Origins of Christianity* (Jerusalem: Magness Press, 1988), 246–279, entitled "Messianology and

Hebrews posits Jesus as a Son who shares in the divine identity of YHWH, but also central to the eschatology of the Son/Messiah's vocation is his ascension back into heaven as king and priest.

The ascension for Hebrews is the eschatological glorification of the promised Davidic King-priest. However, in order for this eschatological transition to be effected first upon the Messiah and then upon those in solidarity with him, the Messiah's earthly life must be characterized by Adamic-kingly obedience in the humble submission to God necessary to secure his glorified entrance into heaven as a forerunner for his people. In his humanity, Jesus is the Adamic-Davidic son. While previous Hebrews' scholarship has noted the Adamic hints in the background of Hebrews, we will advance this to show that these Adamic-king features are doing significant work in the text.[97] Thus, an Adamic-Davidic obedience qualifies him for ascension as the king-priest. But this obedience-to-ascension motif also reveals that Jesus's sonship is a divine, eternal, pre-existent Sonship. For the author of Hebrews, the obedience of Jesus as the Adamic-Davidic son serves as the grounds for Jesus's ascension into the heavenly tabernacle. Jesus's obedience that grounds ascension reveals that Jesus is the divine Son who has always shared in the divine glory. Thus, the ascension of the true eschatological human serves to reveal that the ascended one was more than an exalted man but God's eternal Son.

Focusing on NT theological issues in the book of Hebrews, and more narrowly on aspects of NT Christology in Hebrews, our goal is to advance the understanding of Sonship and ascension in Hebrews by showing how the author brings together aspects of his divine Christology with a Second Adam Christology. We seek to show that the ascension is crucial in this link. It is our goal to contribute to the study of Hebrews by showing that it is the human Adamic-kingly obedience of the Son that qualifies him for his ascension. Within this larger demonstration of his action to qualify for ascension, we show that the portrayal of the Son's cry to God for salvation (Heb 5:7) taps a theological motif that has richer background in the Psalms then previously explored. To ascend into glory as the true Messianic King, the Son displays true trust in fulfillment of the motif of the righteous sufferer in the Psalms.

## Argument

Our work is divided into five major chapters (chapters 2–6). In chapters two and three, we offer a careful exegesis of Heb 1, paying particular attention to

---

Christology in the Epistle to the Hebrews."

97 Thanks to David Moffitt for pointing out in an email that arguing that the Adamic features do significant work in the text advances the discussion beyond his own work and others.

the background of the texts quoted. Against some of the more recent models of Christ's Sonship in Heb 1, we argue that the Son is in fact eternally divine. At the same time, the Son's exaltation into heaven is the fulfillment of the Davidic promises. The Son's installment on the throne *via* ascent is his Davidic kingship, but also the revelation of his eternal glory. Hebrews sees the eschatological Davidic Messiah as ascending to the actual throne of YHWH himself.

In chapter four, we examine Heb 2, paying particular attention to how the role and function of sonship is also a fulfillment of humanity. We argue that this use of sonship in Heb 2 entails a 'Second-Adam Christology' where Christ is the fulfillment of the true destiny of humanity. The background comes from Ps 8 and Gen 1:26–28. To be human is to be YHWH's son. In his exaltation, being crowned with glory and honor, Christ realizes the eschatological end of humanity. He is thus in this Adamic identity a corporate head pioneering the way into heaven *via* his ascent. Finally, the priesthood themes introduced at the end of chapter two directly relate to this Second Adam Christology. In both the Hebrew Bible and Second Temple texts, the portrayal of priests ascending into the earthly tabernacle have an Adamic identity bringing humanity into God's presence. Both Christ's kingly reign and his installment as high priest are aspects of this Adamic sonship and point to the fulfillment of Ps 8. Thus, in Hebrews, sonship operates along two key points: divine and Adamic-Davidic.

In chapter five, we examine the ascension texts in Hebrews, specifically Heb 1; 4:14–16; 6:19–20; 7:26; 8:1–6; and 9:11–14, 23–26. Christ's ascension into heaven is part of his becoming high priest where he is able to be a greater mediator of a greater covenant. We explore the picture portrayed of the heavenly tabernacle. The Son's obedience qualifies him to enter heaven and mediate for the people. Christ cannot enter into heaven unless he himself is first the eschatological glorified figure.[98] Thus, the ascension has both royal and cultic features.

Finally, in chapter six, we examine the key concept of the obedience of the Son for the qualification to ascend into heaven. Here two key passages receive attention: Heb 5:7–10 and 10:5–14. The phrase καίπερ ὢν υἱός points to the divine Sonship of Jesus. This divine Sonship stands in contrast to the qualification the son undergoes as he learns suffering. The two aspects of sonship in Hebrews again return to purview. In 5:7, Jesus fulfills true trust and

---

98  For Hebrews, ascension is entrance into heaven as a human being. It is not a vision of heaven, a metaphor for encountering God, or an extra-bodily mystical ascents. It is movement into heaven by the Son in a new glorified humanity. For three general categories of ascents in apocalyptic literature see Carlson, "A Great High Priest," 113–115.

obedience to God in the face of death. We demonstrate that this trust and obedience fulfills a Davidic motif found especially in the Psalms of the LXX: David is delivered when he trusts in YHWH. This trust and obedience is a fulfillment of what it means to be truly human. Hebrews sees a typological recapitulation and fulfillment of this motif. The ultimate fulfillment of this trust is glorification and ascension to the divine throne. The motif of obedience leading to ascension is found in the argument of Heb 10:5–14. In fulfilling the Adamic and Davidic aspects of sonship, the Son qualifies himself for ascent into heaven and for the ascension of those who believe and obey him.

One final note with respect to style. Because of the aspects of divine Sonship as well as Davidic sonship found in the book of Hebrews, we alternate between capitalization "Son/Sonship" and lowercase "son/sonship," using capitals to highlight the eternal Sonship and divine identity of Jesus with YHWH. When the whole person of Jesus is in view, we also capitalize Son. Lowercase "son/sonship" is used when referring to the Davidic, Adamic, or vocational aspects of sonship.[99] This is only a pedagogical tool for our explanation; at times both aspects are in view or a distinction is artificial and cannot be easily made. Indeed, the final goal of Hebrews is to portray Jesus as the Son of God in all the fullness that this title entails, and to exhort readers to hold fast to this confession of the faith.

---

99 For example, "Jesus is the Davidic son," "Jesus's royal sonship," or "Jesus's obedience is an act of sonship."

## Chapter 2

# Sonship and the Deity of Christ in Hebrews 1, Part 1

### Introduction

THE FIRST CHAPTER OF Hebrews sets the tone and tenor for the Christology of the entire book. Within this chapter the basic framework of this Sonship and its relationship to the exaltation granted by the Father is laid out for us. From the beginning of the work one can see how Ps 110 read in conjunction with Ps 2 drives the argument and shapes the conception of Sonship for the author. In Hebrews chapter one, while Jesus is distinguished from God the Father, as Son he is portrayed as sharing in the identity of God but also as the one who is now exalted within and over all the creation. In this chapter, we will offer a detailed exegesis of Heb 1:1–5, the first four verses of which introduce the Son, setting up a high (divine) Christology and establishing the Son as the one exalted to God's right hand.

Our contention is that the Christology of Heb 1 fits into what is typically categorized as a high Christology, where the Son shares in the divine attributes reserved for God alone. There is a uniqueness to his Sonship. However, Hebrews displays this uniqueness in and through the fulfillment of Messianic Davidic royal categories. The Messiah is exalted in an ascension to YHWH's throne. It is the eschatological fulfillment of the OT paradigm, but as such the ascension is into heaven itself. Thus, the Son is not merely a royal son but the exaltation in his royalty reveals him to be the divine and eternal Son. The ascent of the Son plays a turning point in the revelation of the Son, and God himself.

## Heb 1:1–4

### The Son as the Climax of Revelation

The book of Hebrews is driven by eschatology.[1] Its theological articulation is rooted in a notion of apocalyptic eschatology that sees the purposes of God unfolding in a climax through the work of the Son, Jesus Christ. In the work of Jesus, the age to come—a concept rooted in the Hebrew Bible and developed in Second Temple Judaism[2]—has now been inaugurated, according to Hebrews.[3] For Hebrews, this inauguration of the age to come drives both the theology of the book and the ethical exhortations for the people of God.

In this framework of eschatology Hebrews begins its Christology: Πολυμερῶς καὶ πολυτρόπως πάλαι ὁ θεὸς λαλήσας τοῖς πατράσιν ἐν τοῖς προφήταις ἐπ' ἐσχάτου τῶν ἡμερῶν τούτων ἐλάλησεν ἡμῖν ἐν υἱῷ... (Heb 1:1). The verse contrasts the previous revelations of God with the climactic revelation where God speaks in his own Son—clearly identified as Jesus Christ. We have here the apex of God communicating to his people from heaven on high as he speaks to the Son inviting him upward.

While the author of Hebrews does not devalue the previous revelations of God through the prophets, it has now been surpassed by the eschatological revelation of the Son. The phrase ἐπ' ἐσχάτου τῶν ἡμερῶν τούτων (Heb 1:1) speaks of the dawning of the "age to come," which Hebrews sees as inaugurated in the work of Jesus Christ. The prepositional phrase ἐν υἱῷ (1:1) is likely acting as a dative of agency or means. God has spoken in the agency of

---

[1] See C.K. Barrett's classic essay "The Eschatology of the Epistle to the Hebrews," in *The Background of the New Testament*, ed. W.D. Davies (Cambridge University Press, 1964), 363–93; Charles Edwin Carlston, "Eschatology and Repentance in the Epistle to the Hebrews," *JBL* 78 (1959): 296–302; David DeSilva, "Entering God's Rest: Eschatology and the Socio-Rhetorical Strategy of Hebrews," *TJ* 21 (2000): 25–43; Scott D. Mackie, *Eschatology and Exhortation in the Epistle to the Hebrews*, WUNT 2/223 (Mohr Siebeck, 2007). See also Scott D. Mackie, "Early Christian Eschatological Experience in the Warnings and Exhortations of the Epistle to the Hebrews," *TynBul* 63.1 (2012): 93–114; M.O. Oyetade, "Eschatological Salvation in Hebrews 1:5–2:5," *Ilorin Journal of Religious Studies* 3.1 (2013): 69–82; William Robinson, "Eschatology of the Epistle to the Hebrews: A Study in the Christian Doctrine of Hope," *Encounter* 22 (1961): 37–51; Kenneth Schenck, *Cosmology and Eschatology in Hebrews*, SNTS 143 (Cambridge University Press, 2007), 78–111; Gert Steyn, "The Eschatology of Hebrews As Understood within a Cultic Setting," in *Eschatology of the New Testament and Some Related Documents*, ed. Jan G. Van Der Watt (Mohr Siebeck, 2011), 429–540; Alexander Stewart, "Cosmology, Eschatology, and Soteriology in Hebrews: A Synthetic Analysis," *BBR* 20.4 (2010): 545–560; G.K. Beale, "Eschatology," in *Dictionary of the Later New Testament and Its Developments*, ed. Ralph P. Martin & Peter H. Davids (Intervarsity, 1997), 334–335.

[2] For an overview of the age to come in Second Temple Literature see David Moffitt, *Atonement and the Logic of the Resurrection in the Epistle to the Hebrews* (Brill, 2011), 81–118.

[3] Heb 1:2; 2:5; 6:5; 9:11, 26; 10:1.

another person, like he had ἐν τοῖς προφήταις. Since these clauses offer contrasts, the use of ἐν would most naturally be read as denoting means in both. We may not entirely rule out a dative of sphere with the phrase ἐν υἱῷ since the content of the revelation is the Son himself: God spoke "in Son." What he has now revealed is the Son and the means of his speaking was in the exaltation of the Son.

This ἐν υἱῷ is the first of four anarthrous uses of the word 'son' in Hebrews.[4] The anarthrous uses function qualitatively, which does not translate well into English.[5] Ellingworth notes, "Hebrews' use of the absolute title 'Son' is distinctive" but he does not immediately elaborate except to say it differs from the

---

4 In Hebrews the noun υἱός occurs twenty-four times. Some of its uses do not concern our argument here. Four times it speaks of descendants of particular figures (7:3; 11:21, 22, 24). Four times it refers to the people of God or Christians (2:10; 12:5, 7, 8). Three times, coming as part of an argument that the audience of believers are sons, it refers to general principles related to how fathers treat sons (12:5, 6, 7). Once it is used in the enigmatic title ἢ υἱὸς ἀνθρώπου. Three times it is used with a possessive 'υἱός μου' (1:5; 5:5; 12:5 in vocative: υἱέ μου). Four times it appears in the title 'Son of God' (4:14; 6:6; 7:3; 10:29), clearly referring to Jesus Christ. Once it appears with the article in 1:8 τὸν υἱόν. Finally, υἱός is used four times without the article (1:2; 3:6; 5:5; 7:28).

5 See Daniel Wallace, *Greek Grammar Beyond the Basics* (Zondervan, 1996), 245; Cockerill, *Hebrews*, NICNT (Eerdmans, 2012), 90; Lane, *Hebrews 1–8,* WBC 47A (Word, 1991), 11; Ellingworth, *Hebrews,* NIGTC (Eerdmans, 1993), 93; Webster, "One Who is Son: Theological Reflections on the Exordium to the Epistle to the Hebrews," in *The Epistles to the Hebrews and Christian Theology,* eds. Richard Bauckham, Daniel R. Driver, Trevor A. Hart, and Nathan MacDonald (Eerdmans, 2009), 78. Westcott writes, "The absence of the article fixes attention upon the nature and not the personality of the Mediator of the new revelation. God spake to us in one who has this character that He is Son" (*Hebrews* [Macmillan, 1889], 7).

C.K. Barrett on ἐν υἱῷ provides the gloss 'in a Son' stating that this refers to "one who in his essential nature is a son and thus a member of the divine family" ("The Christology of Hebrews" in *Who Do You Say I Am? Essays on Christology* [Westminster John Knox, 1999], 114). On the anarthrous use, Geerhardus Vos writes that the sonship "does not refer to an office, but to His nature" (*The Teaching of the Epistle of Hebrews* [Eerdmans, 1956], 75). This is an important point which bears emphasis because royal sonship is, as we will show, an important category for Hebrews, particularly in understanding obedience and ascension. Nevertheless, the identity of Christ as Son in Hebrews extends deeper to what we might identify as an ontological sonship (Vos's language) of the Son's sharing in the divine identity (Bauckham's language). David MacLeod argues the lack of the article focuses "on the nature of the new revelation—Son-type of revelation as opposed to a prophet-type or servant type" ("The Finality of Christ: An Exposition of Hebrews 1:1–4," *BSac* 162 [2005], 214). However, we argue that Hebrews uses the contrasts of revelation types to point us to the great identity of the Son who is qualitatively identified with the Father. Sam Janse argues that the article is left out because it is a reference to a proper name, "in this text a very precisely qualified Son is intended, *the* Son of God" (*"You Are My Son" The Reception History of Psalm 2 in Early Judaism and the Early Church* [Peeters, 2009], 119). Highlighting the qualitative use, Victor Rhee writes, "This anarthrous usage emphasizes the quality, nature, or essence of the noun and draws attention to the essential character of the one who is Son" ("The Role of Chiasm for Understanding Christology in Hebrews 1:1–14," *JBL* 131.2 [2012]: 344–345).

phrase "Son of God."[6] Koester believes that the lack of the article "highlights the singularity of God's Son in contrast to the multitude of prophets."[7]

In the last days the revelation is the Son being given. Hebrews is giving us the identity—not an indefinite "a son [of God]" nor a title that an individual now bears "the son of god" but rather "in Son." The author of Hebrews would have the audience understand the identity of "Son" not merely as an office that Jesus bears but as the uniqueness of his identity. The qualitative use with a lack of the article ἐν υἱῷ is because Hebrews is concerned not only with contrasting two types of revelation but also with understanding the unique feature of the revelation. The one through whom God speaks is "Son." This identity is, as Hebrews will show, deeper than a vocation or office Jesus carries out. For Hebrews, his bearing and fulfilling the royal office of David is predicated on the reality of the Sonship relationship being an eternal relationship now manifest in creation as the Son is exalted within it.[8]

As "Son," Jesus shares in the divine identity[9] with the Father so that the qualities, activity, and identity attributed to YHWH in the OT is also attributed to the one who is "Son."[10] One cannot minimize the royal and Davidic aspects emphasized in the use of Ps 2:7 and 2 Sam 7:14. Yet, the one who is the climax of God's revelation and the fulfillment of God's plan to establish human vice-regency over creation is the very one who has existed in a filial relationship with God prior to the manifestation of this revelation in the last days.[11] Royal sonship coalesces with identifying Jesus as divine in the theme of enthronement.[12] Royal sonship is the vehicle by which the divine Sonship is revealed. Thus, the content of this last day revelation of God's speech is of

---

6 Ellingworth, *Hebrews*, 93–94.

7 Koester, *Hebrews: A New Translation with Introduction and Commentary*, AB 36 (Doubleday, 2001), 177.

8 Vos, *Teaching of the Epistle to the Hebrews*, 73–84; Amy Peeler, *You Are My Son*, LNTS 486 (T&T Clark, 2014), esp. 10–29, 61–63; John Webster, "One Who is Son," 78–83. Martin Hengel speaks of the 'beginning [pre-existence] being illuminated by the end [exaltation]' and an inner necessity to pre-existence (*The Cross of the Son of God* [SCM, 1986], 67–70, 84–85). See also Richard Bauckham, *Jesus and the God of Israel: God Crucified and Other Studies on the New Testament's Christology of Divine Identity* (Eerdmans, 2008), 20–31.

9 Richard Bauckham, *God Crucified: Monotheism and Christology in the New Testament* (Eerdmans, 1998) and *Jesus and the God of Israel*.

10 On the quality, activity, and identity see our argument below. See also Bauckham, *Jesus and the God of Israel*, 18–20, 50–57, 236–244.

11 On the filial relationship of the Son to the Father see Amy Peeler (*You Are My Son*, 11, cf. 10–29), who reads Hebrews 1:14 "through the lens of familial relationship." See also Webster, "One Who is Son," 75–78.

12 Timo Eskola, *Messiah and the Throne: Jewish Merkabah Mysticism and Early Christian Exaltation Discourse* (Mohr Siebeck, 2001), 160–175, 203–216, 326–331; Peeler, *You Are My Son*, 37–40, 61; and Aquila H. I. Lee, *From Messiah to Preexistent Son* (Wipf & Stock, 2005), 250–283, esp. 266–267, 271–277, and 279–283.

one who participates in the identity of God and is identified to as bearing the quality as 'Son' in relation to God.

Recently Appointed Heir but Active at the Creation

Further indicating that the text's primary concern is the identity of the Son, the author begins a series of relative clauses concerning the person and work of this one who has been identified as Son.[13] God's speech comes in the identity of the Son and what has happened to the Son at the turning point of the ages. Although C.K. Barrett expresses surprise that the reference to the final inheritance comes before the reference to creation,[14] with Christ as the apex of God's eschatological event, Hebrews argues from inheritance back to creation. The Son's current status as exalted in royal enthronement reveals who he was *before* he came to be exalted. Hebrews identifies Christ as superior to angels both in terms of his current exalted status and with respect to his preexistent identity.[15]

First, the Father has appointed or established the Son as the heir of all things. The exaltation of the Son serves as a driving theme. He is made heir, although he was qualitatively Son. This appointment,[16] in conjunction with his self-offering, ushers in the transition into the eschatological age to come (Heb 9:11–12, 23–26; 10:1, 11–13). The Father appoints (ἔθηκεν). Τίθημι is the same verb used in the LXX Ps 109:1 where the royal son has enemies put under him while he is invited to sit upon the throne. In this Psalm, YHWH establishes the authority of the Davidic son similar to God the Father establishing the heir. David's rule in the royal Psalm entails an establishment of sovereignty as David is put up over the inheritance and the enemies are put under David. In Ps 2:6, the LXX uses καθίστημι, synonym of τίθημι[17], for the son's establishment

---

13  There are four relative clauses that begin in 1:2b–4. They are: ὃν ἔθηκεν...δι' οὗ καί...ὃς ὢν...φέρων τε (Lane, *Hebrews 1–8*, 8). Bruce organizes this section around a sevenfold confirmation (*The Epistle to the Hebrews*, Rev. ed. NICNT [Eerdmans, 1990], 46–50).

14  "The Christology of Hebrews," in *Who Do You Say I Am? Essays on Christology* (Westminster John Knox, 1999), 115. Referencing final inheritance before referencing creation is not quite as surprising if we consider how the exaltation/ascension is the means by which our author sees always was/has been in terms of the identity of the Son.

15  Gert Steyn, "Hebrews' Angelology in Light of Early Jewish Apocalyptic Imagery," *Journal of Early Christian History* 1.1 (2011): 147–148, 151–152, 157–158. Also Gert Steyn, "Addressing an Angelomorphic Christological Myth in Hebrews?" *HvTSt* 59.4 (2003): 1119–1125.

16  There are other contexts in the NT were τίθημι can mean appoint (1 Tim 2:7; 2 Tim 1:11; 1 Pet 2:8). It is also used in the Messianic reference for God's establishment of a stumbling stone in Zion (Rom. 9:33; 1 Pet 2:8). See Harold Attridge, *The Epistle to the Hebrews*, Hermeneia (Fortress, 1989), 39n.62, and Schreiner, *Commentary on Hebrews* (B&H Publishing, 2015), 55n.4.

17  The cognate of καθίστημι is ἵστημι but our point is that καθίστημι and τίθημι are can be used to describe the same concept, royal appointment.

on the throne in Zion.[18] Hebrews's word choice (ἔθηκεν) may be influenced by the LXX itself.

One text where Harold Attridge identifies the use of τίθημι for installation to a status is LXX Ps 88:28[19] κἀγὼ πρωτότοκον θήσομαι αὐτόν, ὑψηλὸν παρὰ τοῖς βασιλεῦσιν τῆς γῆς. This verse is generally acknowledged by commentators to be the text that serves in the background when Hebrews identifies Jesus as the πρωτότοκος in 1:6,[20] but allusions to Ps 89 [LXX 88] may be broader than just one verse. Τίθημι is also used in LXX 88:26 καὶ θήσομαι ἐν θαλάσσῃ χεῖρα αὐτοῦ καὶ ἐν ποταμοῖς δεξιὰν αὐτοῦ, where the royal David king is established to rule over creation and again in LXX 88:30 where the seed of the royal son is established.[21]

For Hebrews, Christ is not only established or set as king, but the scope of his appointment is over all creation (ὃν ἔθηκεν κληρονόμον πάντων). Commentators again point to a background in the LXX at Ps 2:8 αἴτησαι παρ' ἐμοῦ, καὶ δώσω σοι ἔθνη τὴν κληρονομίαν σου καὶ τὴν κατάσχεσίν σου τὰ πέρατα τῆς γῆς.[22] There is a rich OT background to the concept of Israel's inheritance that flows from the Abrahamic promises. Specifically, in Gen. 17:5,[23] there is the regular

---

18  LXX Ps 2:6 Ἐγὼ δὲ κατεστάθην βασιλεὺς ὑπ' αὐτοῦἐπὶ Σιων ὄρος τὸ ἅγιον αὐτοῦ.

19  Attridge, *Hebrews*, 39n.62.

20  Attridge, *Hebrews*, 56n.70; Bruce, *Hebrews*, 56; Cockerill, *Hebrews*, 105; Ellingworth, *Hebrews*, 118; Koester, *Hebrews*, 192; Lane, *Hebrews 1–8*, 26; Schreiner, *Hebrews*, 67; *etc.* Schreiner points to Exod 4:22 as the background (*Hebrews*, 67; cf. Koester, *Hebrews*, 193). This background is also correct. The outworking of royal sonship of the Davidic kingship is a furthering and a narrowing of Israel's sonship/kingship. In fact, the king in the OT stands as a representative head of the people, in corporate solidarity with them.

21  LXX 88:30 καὶ θήσομαι εἰς τὸν αἰῶνα τοῦ αἰῶνος τὸ σπέρμα αὐτοῦ καὶ τὸν θρόνον αὐτοῦ ὡς τὰς ἡμέρας τοῦ οὐρανοῦ. Some recent studies have highlighted the importance of the theme of solidarity between Jesus and God's people in Hebrews. Peeler highlights this concept with a view towards familial theme (*You are a Son*, 71–102, 109–114). Ole Jakob Filtvedt sees Jesus a prototype, drawing on the exodus motif, Christ having gone on before his people as their ideal representative, thus there is solidarity, intimacy, and representation (*The Identity of God's People and the Paradox of Hebrews*, WUNT 2/400 [Mohr Siebeck, 2015], 58–82). See also Kevin McCruden, *Beneficent Christology in the Epistle of Hebrews* (de Gruyter, 2008), 113–21. In light of these recent studies that have highlighted the solidarity of Jesus with the people of God as an important theme in Hebrews, the theology in LXX Ps 88 (MT/Eng. 89) may be more important that we often recognize. YHWH says of the Davidic King ὕψωσα ἐκλεκτὸν ἐκ τοῦ λαοῦ μου ("I exalted a chosen from my people" LXX 88:20/MT 89:20). In the name of YHWH ὑψωθήσεται τὸ κέρας αὐτοῦ ("his horn shall be exalted"). In obedient reliance upon YHWH, he cries for deliverance (LXX 88:27/MT 89:27) and as a result is established as firstborn. All are repeated motifs in Hebrews. In chapter 6 below, we discuss more fully the Son crying out for deliverance in obedience. In chapter 4, we discuss Heb 2 and the motif of solidarity and representation.

22  Attridge, *Hebrews*, 40; Bruce, *Hebrews*, 46; Cockerill, *Hebrews*, 92–93; Ellingworth, *Hebrews*, 95; Lane, *Hebrews 1–8*, 12; Schreiner, *Hebrews*, 55; *etc*.

23  Lane, *Hebrews 1–8*, 12, cites H. Langkammer, "'Den er sum Erben von alley eingesetz hat' (Hebr 1,2)," *Biblische Zeitschrift* 10 (1966): 273–280, as the earliest source of argumentation. See also Ellingsworth, *Hebrews*, 94. Bruce notes that the inheritance is an extension of the

conception of Israel's heritage in the land of Canaan, and in the Davidic royal ideology it is the king who is the true ruler and inheritor as the land/world is subjected to him. Because Davidic royal ideology is the seed which germinates messianic expectations, that "the appointment of a royal or other 'messianic' figure to an inheritance is a common motif is not surprising, cf. Isa 53:12; Dan 7:14; Pss. Sol. 17:23; 1 Macc 2:57."[24]

Hebrews, as well, shares in this motif that the messiah is the royal heir, albeit the inheritance is expanded to encompass all creation. "Inheritance is the logical extension and fruition of sonship."[25] Nevertheless, the author of Hebrews is not content to focus merely on the current status of the Son. This Son is also the one through whom God both makes 'the ages' and brings them to a climax.[26] All that has its existence in the created realms can be attributed to the work of the Son. This concept is no small feature of ancient Jewish monotheism.[27]

The Father used the agency of the Son to create: δι' οὗ καὶ ἐποίησεν τοὺς αἰῶνας (Heb 1:2). Other passages in the NT describe this same sort of agency to the Jesus (John 1:3; Col 1:16). Attridge notes that the use of τοὺς αἰῶνας is "unique in early Christian texts that affirm Christ's protological role."[28] The Son is not merely the one who arrives to usher the transition from this age to the age to come,[29] but he had existed and was the one by whom God made these ages. The concept of God making both this age and the age to come is illustrated in 4 Ezra 6:7, "I answered and said, "What will be the dividing of the times? Or when will be the end of the first age and the beginning of the age that follows?"[30] 4 Ezra 7:113 "But the day of judgment will be the end of this

---

Abrahamic promise but does not mention Gen 17:5 (*Hebrews*, 48n.15). Schreiner makes use of the OT background in Israel's inheritance without specifically mentioning Abraham (*Hebrews*, 55). Notice also the use of τίθημι in LXX Gen. 17:5 "...ὅτι πατέρα πολλῶν ἐθνῶν τέθεικά σε," which may suggest a further allusion or at least conceptual overlap. As Lane puts it, "the investiture of Abram as heir marks the beginning of redemptive history" (*Hebrews 1–8*, 12). Hebrews will return again to the inheritance theme and seed of Abraham in ch. 2.

24  Attridge, *Hebrews*, 40n.65.

25  Cockerill, *Hebrews*, 92. This point can be further justified by noting that in the OT, Israel is God's son (Exod 4:22); the Davidic king is God's royal son with an inheritance; and in Pauline theology Christ's is God's Son, and Christians are adopted as God's sons both sharing in the inheritance.

26  Heb 1:2 δι' οὗ καὶ ἐποίησεν τοὺς αἰῶνας. Heb 9:26 νυνὶ δὲ ἅπαξ ἐπὶ συντελείᾳ τῶν αἰώνων εἰς ἀθέτησιν [τῆς] ἁμαρτίας.

27  Bauckham, *Jesus and the God of Israel*, 86–87, 154–156; N.T. Wright, *The New Testament and the People of God* (Fortress, 1992), 248–250.

28  Attridge, *Hebrews*, 41.

29  E.g., Heb 9:26b νυνὶ δὲ ἅπαξ ἐπὶ συντελείᾳ τῶν αἰώνων εἰς ἀθέτησιν [τῆς] ἁμαρτίας διὰ τῆς θυσίας αὐτοῦ πεφανέρωται.

30  Cf. 4 Ezra 7:50, where "the Most High has made not one world but two." This reference most likely has in view the two-age structure of the universe as both spatial and temporal

age and the beginning of the immortal age to come, in which corruption has passed away." Jewish monotheism was rather strict in its belief that YHWH made the heavens and the earth.[31]

What is truly key to monotheism is God's unique relationship to creation with his distinction as before it, over it, and above it. Even when there are exalted mediatory figures in a divine heavenly council, they do not impinge upon the true uniqueness of God alone as above *all* his creation.[32] Furthermore, in our passage while the Son is distinct and he is the means through which the Father acts to create, the Son is related to the creation in the exact same manner as the Father.[33] Thus, on the distinction between Creator and creation, the Son is identified with the Creator; while an agent of the Father, he is nevertheless designated as partaking in the divine identity.

## The Son as ΑΠΑΥΓΑΣΜΑ and ΧΑΡΑΚΤΗΡ

In advancing the identity of the Son, Hebrews describes the Son as ὃς ὢν ἀπαύγασμα τῆς δόξης καὶ χαρακτὴρ τῆς ὑποστάσεως αὐτοῦ (Heb 1:3). The Son is identified in a unique relationship to the Father. The Father, who has spoken in his Son, did so because of the Son's identity in sharing in the divine glory and being the impress of the Father's nature.

The first difficulty encountered in these words is whether ἀπαύγασμα is active or passive. An active meaning would identify the Son as radiating the

---

(Bruce Longenecker, *Eschatology and the Covenant: A Comparison of 4 Ezra and Romans 1–11* [Bloomsbury, 2015], 81). "4 Ezra's world was designed as an *agon* (4 Ezra 7:127–128)" (Jason Zurawski, "The Two Worlds and Adam's Sin: The Problem of *4 Ezra* 7:10–14," in *Interpreting 4 Ezra and 2 Baruch: International Studies*, ed. Gabriele Boccaccini and Jason M. Zurawski [T&T Clark, 2014], 106). Thus, God has made the world and Adam (7:50), but also after the judgment, there is a coming world. The righteous have "treasures laid up to be shown in the last time" (7:77), while the wicked have torment in store for the last days (7:84).

31  N.T. Wright, *The New Testament and the People of God*, 248–50; Richard Bauckham, "Divinity of Jesus Christ in the Epistle to the Hebrews," in *The Epistles to the Hebrews and Christian Theology* (Eerdmans, 2009), 16. See also the discussion below of God and the Son making 'all things.'

32  Larry Hurtado, *One God, One Lord: Early Christian Devotion and Ancient Jewish Monotheism*, 2nd ed. (T&T Clark, 1998), 25–27, 83–85, 90–92; Bauckham, *Jesus and the God of Israel*, 14–16; Paul Rainbow, "Monotheism and Christology in I Corinthians 8. 4–6," (DPhil. diss., University of Oxford, 1987), 52–56. Rainbow writes, "The comparison formula 'Who is like God?' found so frequently throughout the literature implies that there is an absolute qualitative difference between the God of Israel and all others" (55). The transcendence of God means that references to god were "beings superior to man in power but incapable of comparison with God in kind" (56).

33  This thought and wording was spurred by Bauckham's remark concerning the Son's relationship to angels; he writes: "Thus in three key respects—creation, sovereignty and worship—*the Son is related to angels precisely as God is*" ("Divinity of Jesus Christ," 21, emphasis mine).

divine glory while a passive meaning would suggest that the Son merely reflects the divine glory. Both the active and passive senses are known in other contemporary sources, so scholars are divided over the issue.[34]

The active uses of ἀπαύγασμα include Philo *Spec. Leg.* iv.123 ἅτε τῆς μακαρίας καὶ τρισμακαρίας φύσεως ἀπαύγασμα, which describes how God breathed into the soul of man. This usage is clearly active since reason is breathed into man like a ray of light from God's nature (ἅτε τῆς μακαρίας καὶ τρισμακαρίας φύσεως ἀπαύγασμα). *De Plantatione* 50 likewise delves into Philo's anthropology with respect to God's creation of man. Mankind is likened to the sanctuary of God,[35] or even the inheritance, even though Philo is firm on God's independence and lack of any need of human beings. The inner self of human beings is likened to a sanctuary that mimics the archtype (μίμημα ἀρχετύπου)[36] of heaven's sanctuary and thus the holy radiate splendor (ἁγίων ἀπαύγασμα). Paradise trees (the rational in man), modeled after an archetype, probably suggest active radiance of the rationality found originally in God as uncreated since God has imparted/planted this upon the true image of man.[37] In *Opif.* 146, man is described as composed of the same elements as the world but has an impression (ἐκμαγεῖον), a fragment (ἀπόσπασμα) and radiance (ἀπαύγασμα) of the nature of God (τῆς μακαρίας φύσεως) specifically, the divine reason imparted to him (λόγῳ θείῳ). Here there is less certainty that ἀπαύγασμα is active because ἐκμαγεῖον may suggest passive. But all three:

---

34  For example, BDAG prefers the active sense for Wis 7:26; Philo *Spec. Leg.* iv.123; *Opif.* 146; *Plant.* 50. However *EDNT* (1:118) identifies only Philo *Spec. Leg.* iv.123 as active while taking Wis 7:26; Philo *Opif.* 146; and *Plant.* 50 as passive. *TDNT* cites Wis 7:26; Philo *Spec. Leg.* iv.123; and *Opif.* 146 as in the active sense of effulgence and Philo *Plant.* 50 as passive in a manner synonymous to εἰκών. See also Scott Mackie, "Confession of the Son of God in the Exordium of Hebrews," *JSNT* 30.4 (2008): 441–442.

35  As part of the context, Philo distinguishes between man made in God's image, stamped with the spirit (χαραχθεὶς πνεύματι, *Plant.* 44), who is like the tree of life, bearing immortality and glory, from the man created of the clay. Man must cultivate the rational and choose the tree of life, and it is implanted within him. He then, is likened to a sanctuary and garden. This is part of Philo's concept that Paradise must be allegorized so that which is described as planted in Paradise is really that which is planted in the rational soul (*Plant.* 36–37). Man alone has the rational virtues (*Plant.* 41). Philo distinguishes between man, the body, and the true man, which is the mind, and the mind is synonymous with Paradise.

36  Cf. also *Plant.* 20 ἀκόλουθον οὖν ἦν τῆς ἀνθρώπου ψυχῆς κατὰ τὸν ἀρχέτυπον τοῦ αἰτίου λόγον ἀπεικονισθείσης.

37  Obviously, Philo's concept of glory, immortality, and rationality differs from concepts in the Hebrew scriptures and other sources in Second Temple Judaism. Philo is allegorizing and has been influenced by philosophical concepts and Platonic thought. The earthly vs. heavenly with concept of archtypes differs from Hebrews. In Philo, a conception of rationality is driving how he conceives heavenly. This difference is seen even in how he distinguishes the man made in clay from the aspect of man that was truly made in God's image, the rational, (*Plant.* 44). For how the archtype of heavenly functions and then is stamped on the earthly see *Ebr.* 133 where we note Philo's contrasting between invisible/immaterial and visible/material.

ἐκμαγεῖον, ἀπόσπασμα, and ἀπαύγασμα are used synonymously to describe how Philo understands humanity as God's image, which bears an intellectual sense. Like God, man radiates divine reason being gifted it by God, which may in the end tip the favor towards ἀπαύγασμα as active.

The usage of ἀπαύγασμα in Wis 7:26 is probably best viewed as passive because of the parallel with mirror (ἔσοπτρον)[38] and also as the image of God's goodness (εἰκὼν τῆς ἀγαθότητος αὐτοῦ). The grammar is not definitive. More importantly, wisdom is personified as an attribute of God and not a distinct entity. Wisdom 7:25 may in fact argue for aspects of an active sense because wisdom is more identified with God as a manifestation of his activity ἀπόρροια τῆς τοῦ παντοκράτορος δόξης εἰλικρινής, NETS: "an emanation of the pure glory of the Almighty."

Unlike Wisdom in LXX Prov 8:22ff which is created as one begotten (γεννᾷ με, 8:25) before creation is fashioned (8:25–26), the one identified as Son is uncreated sharing in the creation of all things. The Son is not founded in the beginning before the present age (πρὸ τοῦ αἰῶνος ἐθεμελίωσέν με ἐν ἀρχῇ, 8:23) but the means by which the ages were created. The focus for Hebrews is the category of glory, not just wisdom. As Amy Peeler states, "To say that Hebrews uses language employed elsewhere for Wisdom and Word does not prove that it uses that language in the same way."[39]

The argument that the writer of Hebrews understands ἀπαύγασμα as passive, a mere reflection of the glory God, is difficult to sustain. First, unlike in Philo, the Son is not created to radiate, nor is this radiance the rational inner-self. Rather the nature of his existence prior to exaltation is radiating. Second, the concept seems to be that of Shekinah glory not Adamic-image

---

38 *EDNT*, 1.118; Schenck, "Keeping His Appointment: Creation and Enthronement in Hebrews," *JSNT* 66 (1997): 106n.37. Scott Mackie sees a vacillation between active and passive ("Confession of the Son of God in the Exordium," 442).

39 *You are My Son*, 26. Jody Barnard reaches the same conclusion (*Mysticism of Hebrews*, WUNT 2/331 [Mohr Siebeck, 2012], 153). See also Marie Isaacs, *Sacred Space: An Approach to the Theology of the Epistle to the Hebrews*, JSNTS 73 (Sheffield Academic Press, 1992), 186–204, for a discussion of the use of Word and Wisdom. Isaacs finds any notion of the son pre-existing to be "unconvincing" (204) yet finds the idea of pre-existence through an appropriation of Wisdom categories, following a line similar to James Dunn's *Christology in the Making*. For an argument against Wisdom in Heb 1:1–4 see Daniel J. Ebert IV. "Wisdom in New Testament Christology with Special Reference to Hebrews 1:1–4" (PhD. diss., Trinity Evangelical Divinity School, 1998); and *Wisdom Christology: How Jesus Becomes God's Wisdom for Us* (Presbyterian and Reformed, 2011), 145–171. His point is that while there may be Wisdom strands incorporated into the earliest Christology, Hebrews 1:1–4 goes beyond and contains "elements that are foreign to the Jewish Wisdom figure" so that any Wisdom backgrounds have lost "independent significance" (170). Aquila Lee (*From Messiah*, 42–77) discusses Wisdom and *Logos* in Jewish texts exploring the possibility of its background for pre-existence. He concludes "personified divine attributes have never led to the development of divine hypostases separate from God" (84).

bearing function,[40] nor is the radiance, for Hebrews, something that comes to dwell in the Son as wisdom dwells in the holy ones (Wis 7:27–28), empowers the king (Wis 9:1–5), or mirrors the divine in personified mediation.

In ἀπαύγασμα τῆς δόξης, the Son is identified as sharing in the divine glory prior to his exaltation.[41] This radiance is not merely that of a mediatory figure entering in the presence of God, nor is it like Moses coming down from Mount Sinai reflecting the glory. Hebrews distinguishes the pre-temporal glory of the Son from that of angels (who enter God's presence and mediate the law) and Moses who served in God's house (Heb 3:1–6). Jody Barnard states the most salient feature in the various uses is "the affirmation of an essential unity between two objects";[42] in the case of Hebrews: YHWH and Son. The Son has a "unique unity with the divine Glory."[43] Barnard concludes "by describing the son as the ἀπαύγασμα τῆς δόξης, the author connects him with the incandescent manifestation of Deity enthroned."[44] The Son radiates divine glory as the Father would, and yet as the representation of the divine nature distinct from the Father.

While monotheism in Second Temple Judaism was to varying degrees comfortable with intermediary and mediatorial figures entering God's presence,[45] representing God, even making his glory or a revelation of God known,[46] there remains in this Jewish monotheism a stark contrast between

---

40 Hughes, *A Commentary on the Epistle to the Hebrews* (Eerdmans, 1977), 42. On the Rabbinic notion of Adam having a luminous body see David Aaron, "Shedding Light on God's Body in Rabbinic Midrashim: Reflections on the Theory of a Luminous Adam," *HTR* 90.3 (1997): 299–314. Alexander Golitzin, "Recovering the 'Glory of Adam': 'Divine Light' Traditions in the Dead Sea Scrolls and the Christian Ascetical Literature of Fourth-Century Syro-Mesopotamia,'" in *The Dead Sea Scrolls as Background to Postbiblical Judaism and Early Christianity: Papers from an International Conference at St. Andrews in 2001*, ed. James R. Davila, STDJ 46 (Brill, 2003), 275–308.

41 For a similar identification see John 17:5, 24.

42 Jody Barnard, *The Mysticism of Hebrews*, 151. Similarly, Mackie also sees ἀπαύγασμα as a multivalent term with both active and passive ("Confession of the Son of God in the Exordium," 444).

43 Barnard, *The Mysticism of Hebrews*, 151.

44 Ibid., 152.

45 2 Bar. 21:6; 48:10; 51:11; 1 En. 14:18–24; 39:12; 40:1ff; 47:1–3; 60:2; 4 Ezra 8:21–22. In 2 En. 14:2 [J] four hundred angels carry the Lord's crown. T. Levi 4:5 archangels are mediators in the presence of God and in 3:7 other angels go back and forth carrying messages to and from the angels of the Lord's presence.

46 In 4 Ezra, the angel Uriel is Ezra's guide. In 1 En. 17–36 the angel gives Enoch a tour of all creation and reveals mysteries to him. Cf. T. Levi 5:1–2. In 2 En. the angels take Enoch up on his ascent through the seven heavens. In Jub. 1:25–2:1, the angel of the presence writes the tablets and brings them. Cf. *Apoc. of Ab.* 12:10; 14:1–5; 15. For more detail on the angelology in Jewish Apocalypses see Harold Kuhn, "The Angelology of the Non-Canonical Jewish Apocalypses," *JBL* 67 (1948): 217–232; Randall Gleason, "Angels and the Eschatology of Heb 1–2," *NTS* 49 (2003): 101–107.

angels or mediatorial figures and YHWH, who alone is creator and ruler of all.⁴⁷ Gert Steyn has pointed out that while angels may enter the glory and shine like flames of fire there is a clear difference between the angels and the Son. "The angels are merely *transformed* (ποιῶν) into flames of fire and *reflect* the glory of God, whereas the Son is 'the exact imprint of *God's very being*' (χαρακτὴρ τῆς ὑποστάσεως αὐτοῦ) and radiates God's light himself in Hebrews 1:3."⁴⁸ Similar to the monotheism in Isaiah,⁴⁹ the mediators did not receive worship. They did not participate in the glory of God in a manner identifying them with God.⁵⁰ God did not share his glory; his identity was unique (Isa 42:8; 48:11).

---

47  1 En. 9:1–5 (note especially how the angels worship God and declare he made everything in v. 5). In 14:20–21 the angels cannot look directly upon God. There is a limit to how close they can get to throne. Cf. 1 En. 84:2–3; Apoc. Ab. 8:1–9:4; 10:4–15; Bauckham, *Jesus and the God of Israel*, 152–164; Hurtado, *One God, One Lord*, 82–92. Peter R. Carrell, *Jesus and the Angels: Angelology and the Christology of the Apocalypse of John* (Cambridge University Press, 1997), 53–76, examines angelology in the first century. His conclusions largely support Hurdado's conclusions. Carrell writes, "principal angels before the end of the first century CE were known to occupy roles as representative of God, and even as (junior) partner to God. But it is probably only beyond this period that an angel was recognized (by some) as a second power alongside God in heaven" (73). "Thus there is no reason to think that one angelic figure was the subject of widespread speculation about sharing in divine status or standing alongside God as an equal" (75). Cf. Paul Rainbow, "Monotheism and Christology," 52–59, 74–78.

48  Gert Steyn, "Hebrews' Angelology in Light of Early Jewish Apocalyptic Imagery," 150, emphasis original. L. Timothy Swinson shows how the use of LXX Ps 103 portrays angels as subordinate to the Son while the Son is equal in status and glory to the Father ("Wind and Fire in Hebrews 1:7: A Reflection upon the Use of Psalm 104 [103]," *TJ* 28.2 [2007]: 216–219, 221).

49  It is beyond the scope of our argument to discuss historical critical scholarship's view of multiple authorship of Isaiah, nor can we enter into the debate of how early monotheism existed. Even NT scholarship debates how much intermediary figures participated in divine glory. The general line of arguments by Hurtado and Bauckham is more convincing than the challengers. On some of the issues of monotheism see Bauckham, "Biblical Theology and Monotheism," in *Out of Egypt: Biblical Theology and Biblical Interpretation*, ed. Craig Bartholomew, et al. (Zondervan, 2004), 187–232, reprinted in *Jesus and the God of Israel*, 60–106; L.W. Hurtado, "First-Century Jewish Monotheism," *JSNT* 71 (1998): 3–26, reprinted in *How on Earth Did Jesus Become God? Historical Questions about Earliest Devotion to Jesus* (Eerdmans, 2005), 111–133; L.W. Hurtado, "Monotheism, Principal Angels, and the Background of Christology," in *The Oxford Handbook of the Dead Sea Scrolls*, ed. John J. Collins and Timothy H. Lim (Oxford, 2010), 547–565; L.W. Hurtado, *Lord Jesus Christ: Devotion to Jesus in Earliest Christianity* (Eerdmans, 2003), 27–53; L.W. Hurtado, "What Do We Mean by 'First-Century Jewish Monotheism'?" in *SBL 1993 Seminar Papers*, ed. David Lull (Scholars, 1993), 348–368; James D.G. Dunn, "Was Christianity a Monotheistic Faith from the Beginning?" *SJT* 35 (1982): 303–336; William Horbury, "Jewish and Christian Monotheism in the Herodian Age," in *Early Jewish and Christian Monotheism*, ed. Loren T. Stuckenbruck and Wendy E.S. North (T&T Clark, 2004), 16–44. Aquila H.I. Lee, *From Messiah to Preexistent Son*, also finds a blending between God and intermediary angels to be "unconvincing" (99); cf. discussion of textual evidence (85–89) and discussion of first century Jewish monotheism (21–25); Paul Rainbow, "Monotheism and Christology," 45–124.

50  See, for example, Larry Hurtado's now classic study *One God, One Lord*. Hurtado demonstrates that even though exalted figures could actively administrate God's work and function as an agent of the divine will, they never became objects of cultic devotion or wor-

However, according to Hebrews, the Son participates in the divine glory—and not merely by virtue of human exaltation. He participates as χαρακτὴρ τῆς ὑποστάσεως αὐτοῦ (Heb 1:3). Χαρακτήρ can be used to speak of coinage where impresses were made of the king or Caesar.[51] It can, in other literature, have some overlap with the concept of εἰκών.[52] Philo calls the human soul the τύπον τινὰ καὶ χαρακτῆρα θείας δυνάμεως.[53] In Apoc. Sedr.[54] 7.4 the comparison is given between Adam with the glory he radiates and the sun: ὁ δὲ ἥλιος καὶ Ἀδὰμ μίαν χαρακτῆρα ἦσαν. The latter denotes not so much an impress but an identity, whereas Philo is offering his interpretation of man's creation in the image of God. In 4 Macc 15:4 the impress is between parents and children. Parents impress the wonderful χαρακτῆρα of the soul and form upon their children.[55]

In Hebrews, the phrase ὑποστάσεως αὐτοῦ speaks of God's nature or the essence of God. As Helmut Köster identifies, "Here ὑπόστασις is parallel to δόξα. Both words are obviously describing God's essence."[56] "'Glory' (δόξα) is a designation of the divine reality or of the heavenly state and its usage is commonplace in the OT, post-biblical Judaism, and early Christianity."[57] Our text identifies the Son's participation in the realities of divinity.[58]

---

ship. On the principal agent often associated with administering God's will and work, Hurtado writes, "The principal agent figure is not the reflection of some sort of splitting off of the glory of God or the divine occupant of the throne pictured in Ezek 1:26–28" (89).

51 BDAG, 1077; *TDNT*, 9:419; *EDNT*, 3:456; Steven Muir, "The Anti-Imperial Rhetoric of Hebrews 1.3: χαρακτήρ as a 'Double-Edge Sword,'" in *A Cloud of Witnesses: The Theology of Hebrews in its Ancient Contexts*, ed. Richard Bauckham (T&T Clark, 2008), 174–186; Michael P. Theophilus, "The Numismatic Background of ΧΑΡΑΚΤΗΡ in Hebrews 1:3," *Australian Biblical Review* 64 (2016): 69–80. Theophilus emphasizes the aspects of authentication; it in no way implies "any deficiency or diminished nature" (79).

52 In Wis 7:26 ἀπαύγασμα and εἰκών are used as wisdom is a 'radiation/reflection of eternal life...and an image of his goodness ἀπαύγασμα γάρ ἐστιν φωτὸς ἀϊδίου ...καὶ εἰκὼν τῆς ἀγαθότητος αὐτοῦ. Philo at times uses it in relationship to man's creation in God's image.

53 Philo *Det.* 83; similarly: *Plant.* 44 κατὰ τὴν εἰκόνα θεοῦ χαραχθεὶς πνεύματι; *Leg.* 1:100 where the soul is like wax that can be impressed. The image of God on the rational soul is like that of a coin σημειωθὲν καὶ τυπωθὲν σφραγῖδι θεοῦ, ἧς ὁ χαρακτήρ ἐστιν ὁ ἀΐδιος λόγος (*Plant.* 18).

54 The Apocalypse of Sedrach dates anywhere from A.D. 150 to 500 although its final redacted form is from the Byzantine era according to S. Agourides in *The Pseudepigrapha*, ed. James H. Charlesworth (Doubleday, 1983), 1:606.

55 4 Macc 15:4b "On the tender nature of the child we impress a wonderful likeness [χαρακτῆρα θαυμάσιον] of soul and form, and especially mothers, who are more affectionate in their own feelings toward their children than fathers" (*The Pseudepigrapha*, ed. James Charlesworth [Doubleday, 1985], 2:560).

56 *TDNT*, 8:584.

57 Attridge, *Hebrews*, 43. He cites Gerhard von Rad, "כבוד in the OT," *TDNT*, 2:238–242; Gerhard Kittel, "The NT use of δόξα II," *TDNT*, 2:247–251; 2 Macc 2:8; Wis 9:10; Luke 2:9; 9:31; John 1:14; 2:11; 12:41–43; 17:1; Rom 6:4; 2 Cor 4:6; 1 Tim 3:16; 1 Pet 1:11, 21; 4:11; Eph 1:17; Rev 21:23. See also *EDNT*, 1:344–348.

58 Mackie writes "since the Son bears the 'impression' of his Father, he accurately rep-

There is distinction between the Father and the Son, and yet there is identity between them. The Son is more than a mere representative of the Father. His identity goes beyond that of the exalted mediatorial figures in Second Temple Judaism. His participation in the divine glory and imprint of the divine reality is greater than even humanity's image-bearing role. "By describing the Son in this way [ἀπαύγασμα τῆς δόξης and χαρακτὴρ τῆς ὑποστάσεως αὐτοῦ], the author expresses Christ's unity with YHWH and identifies him as the visible manifestation of God upon the throne in the celestial Holy of Holies, that is, 'the Glory.'"[59] Hebrews is giving us definitional language to formulate a concept of what Sonship actually entails. The Son participates in the reality of God.

## Upholding All By His Powerful Word

In making the case that the activity of the Son is also the activity of God, Hebrews points to the Son's role in creation and his providential sustaining of the creation. In the OT and subsequent Second Temple Judaism, YHWH creates. The Creator continues to uphold and sustain the creation. Hebrews ascribes this to the Son.

The Son is φέρων τε τὰ πάντα (Heb 1:3). Φέρων is used here to identify the Son's sustaining or upholding.[60] The other uses of φέρω in Hebrews (6:1; 9:16; 12:20; 13:13) are no real help in our understanding here. BDAG cites LXX Num 11:14 and Deut 1:9 where φέρω has the sense of sustaining and upholding, although it refers to Moses not God.[61] Hebrews focusing Son's sustaining of the entire creation not the merely the people of God.

In Heb 1:3, φέρω has the concept of bearing something forward and moving it to its end goal in his sustaining activity. As F.F. Bruce beautifully illustrates the conceptual nuance, "He upholds the universe not like Atlas supporting a dead weight on his shoulders, but as one who carries all things forward on their appointed course."[62] The Son, as God does in the OT, guides and governs all things by his Word.[63] He bears up all of creation precisely

---

resents his very being. The Father's impress of his being upon the Son is also determinative of his own identity, as Jesus' Father." He describes this as a "mutuality that is ultimately determinative for both their identities" ("Confession of the Son of God in the Exordium," 444).

59  Barnard, *Mysticism of Hebrews*, 156.

60  BDAG, 1051–1052. This description may be, in a conceptual sense, similar to Col 1:17b "καὶ τὰ πάντα ἐν αὐτῷ συνέστηκεν," but as we will note below goes further with the idea of moving it towards the appointed end.

61  BDAG, 1052. Given the context of the passages with Israel in her journey, the word usage may also convey Moses' inability to move her forward as well.

62  Bruce, *Hebrews*, 49.

63  Koester, *Hebrews*, 181, where he also cites Philo *Her.* 7. In Philo *Decal.* 155, God guides or

because, according to Hebrews, he himself is not a created being but one who participates in the reality of God.

The Son is not a product of the divine creative Word[64] but himself exercises the creative and sustaining Word. This exercise is not by delegation. The Son's word is of his [the Son's] power. In Wis 18:15, the all-powerful Word descends from heaven, the royal throne, ὁ παντοδύναμός σου λόγος ἀπ' οὐρανῶν ἐκ θρόνων βασιλείων.[65] This passage may bolster the case below that the address to the Son with "your throne O God is forever and ever" is understood by Hebrews as more than just Davidic language (1:8a). There is an eternal rule and an eternal sustaining of creation by the Son's word even prior to his exaltation as one within creation.[66] Unlike the warrior angel in Wis 18:16, who carries the sword of God's τὴν ἀνυπόκριτον ἐπιταγήν (a circumlocution for God's Word), the Son bears the word of his power as being one within the Godhead. God the Father has spoken (ἐλάλησεν) and revealed himself through the Son or simply ἐν υἱῷ who in himself bears the authority of the divine Word.[67]

Τὰ πάντα refers to all creation and perhaps both time and space.[68] Τὰ πάντα includes the full scope of all created which was encapsulated in 1:2 with τοὺς αἰῶνας.[69] The Son is sustaining all the creation, upholding it together. It is the same τὰ πάντα over which he has recently, in the course of events, been appointed heir by the Father (ὃν ἔθηκεν κληρονόμον πάντων, Heb 1:2). There may be some subtle parallels to Wisdom here when she is described as one who τὰ πάντα καινίζει, renews all things (Wis 7:27), and διοικεῖ τὰ πάντα

---

rules by the Logos (Ellingworth, *Hebrews*, 100).

64  Cf. Gen 1 for the power of God's creative Word.

65  By the Word of God from the throne, the angel, a 'stern warrior,' descends bearing God's authentic command (Wis 18:15b–16). Here the context is the judgment of God with coming destruction.

66  This is not, as G.B. Caird would criticize, to minimize the actual historical outworking of exaltation in the person of Jesus. G.B. Caird, "Son by Appointment," in *The New Testament Age: Essays in Honor of Bo Reinke* (Mercer University Press, 1984), esp. 1:76–77.

67  There may be an element of *logos* doctrine here, but we are inclined to think not. The point is not so much that the Son is the Logos, but that he actually bears all the divine authority so that his speech is not just a vassal for God's speech, but his speech is the same as YHWH's speech.

68  Cf. also Col 1:16, 17; Eph 1:10, where τὰ πάντα refers to the totality of the universe, including heaven, earth, and created angelic beings (James Dunn, *The Epistle to the Colossians and Philemon* [Eerdmans 1996], 90). In Eph 1:11 it refers to space and time, including events. On Eph 1:11, Harold Hoehner writes "The τὰ πάντα refers to all of God's providence and must not be restricted to God's redemptive plan. This coincides with verse 10 where "all things are described 'as those things in heaven and those things in earth'" (*Ephesians: An Exegetical Commentary* [Baker, 2002], 229). In Wis 7:27, she renews all things which may contain the idea of sustenance. She also orders all things.

69  Daniel J. Ebert, IV, "Wisdom in New Testament Christology with Special Reference to Hebrews 1:1–4" (PhD. diss., Trinity Evangelical Divinity School, 1998), 89n.161.

χρηστῶς, orders all things well (8:1).[70] Given that Hebrews is identifying a personal being 'the Son,' we should look beyond an identification of wisdom—which is arguably a personification of a divine attribute. Richard Bauckham has shown that "all things" is used in various texts to distinguish God's identity from the creation which God continues to rule over.[71] There is "an absolute distinction between God and all other reality,"[72] a distinction that Hebrews applies now between the Son and all reality.[73] The Son creates and sustains all creation. In the logic of the passage, the Son's work in sustaining the creation is not *per se* the work in his role of as kingly and eschatological exalted heir, but rather his work that has been and continues to be carried out as the ὢν ἀπαύγασμα τῆς δόξης καὶ χαρακτὴρ τῆς ὑποστάσεως αὐτοῦ (Heb 1:3). He did these things prior to exaltation.

The point is not to parse out actions in his activity and create a sort of schizophrenic approach to understanding S/sonship in Hebrews. Instead, even with Hebrews describing the Son "becoming" in his exaltation and appointment, the author peers back before that and gives us an identity for the Son that has been. On the one hand, the Son, in the event of his ascension, has been recently appointed heir of all (Heb 1:2), yet the one recently appointed as heir exercised care and power over creation prior to this activity of the Father exalting him. He was the agent of the Father serving as a means of creation because of his identity in being, ὤν, the radiance of glory and imprint of God's nature. Equally the one who now is heir of all has been bearing this creation, φέρων τε τὰ πάντα (Heb 1:3).

The Son's relationship to creation is being marked at points through this passage. As the argument unfolds, first he is the κληρονόμον πάντων, but then we find out he ἐποίησεν τοὺς αἰῶνας, and finally that he is actually sustaining it by φέρων τε τὰ πάντα τῷ ῥήματι τῆς δυνάμεως αὐτοῦ. Hebrews also uses the aorists ἔθηκεν and ἐποίησεν which denote here punctiliar action (considering the action as a whole) and events which are rightly translated into past tenses

---

[70] In the latter, "all things" is parallel to ἀπὸ πέρατος ἐπὶ πέρας εὐρώστως, "from one end of the earth to the other."

[71] Bauckham cites Isa 44:24; Jer 10:16; 51:19; Sir 43:33; Wis 9:6; 12:13; Add Esth 13:9, 10; Bel 5; 2 Macc 1:24; 3 Macc 2:3; 1 En. 9:5; 84:3; 2 En. 66:4; Jub. 12:19; Apoc. Ab. 7:10; Jos. Asen. 12:1; Josephus J.W. 5.218; 1QapGenar 20:13: 4QDb 18:5–9; Sib. Or. 3:20–23; Sib. Or. frg. 1:17; frg. 1:35; Ps-Sophocles; T. Job 2:4; Pr. Man. 2–3 (*Jesus and the God of Israel*, 154 nn. 6–7). We might also add 1 Chron 29:12, 14, 16; LXX Esth 14:19; 16:18, 21; Ps 119:91; LXX Amos 5:8; 2 Macc 7:23; 3 Macc 2:21; 5:28; Wis 1:14; 9:1. In John 1:3, the Logos creates all things with God. Of course, the rule over "all things" of creation may be given to a vice-regent/Adam, as in Ps 8:6 and Wis 10:1–2. Elsewhere all things are given to the Son: Matt 11:27//Luke 10:22; John 3:35; 13:3.

[72] Bauckham, *Jesus and the God of Israel*, 154.

[73] Cf. also below on Hebrews's use of Ps 102.

in English.⁷⁴ But this passage is contrasted with the ongoing sense that the present tense gives with the use of ὤν and φέρων.⁷⁵

One possible way to understand this grammatically is that he is only the radiance and exact imprint following his appointment where he is crowned with glory and honor. He is the one who is sustaining the creation only now that he is appointed heir. This would entail some kind of deification,⁷⁶ so that as human he bears divine qualities. There are Second Temple Jewish sources that suggest an exalted figure becoming *elohim*.⁷⁷ Crispin Fletcher-Louis has argued the importance for this type of glory-exaltation model for understanding the development of early Christology, especially in light of Adamic figures in Second Temple Judaism.⁷⁸ This position would seemingly fit with the argument in Heb 2 especially with the use of Ps 8. Indeed, now as exalted Son all is subject to him and not outside his rule (Heb 2:8b).

While this understanding of the passage is possible, we contend that it is not what Hebrews intends. Rather the author is pointing to the ongoing identity of the Son that is and even has been, irrespective of the point when

---

74 Wallace, *Greek Grammar*, 555–557; BDF §332.

75 Wallace, *Greek Grammar*, 518; BDF §319.

76 We say "some kind" because there are various forms and interpretations of what this deification could look like. It could entail representation in vice-regency so that God's qualities are exercises through the exalted one or it could entail on advancement of an ontological level.

77 Ps 82:1; 4Q491c frag. 1 col.6; 11 QMelchizedek; possibly also Jub. 40:7 and Jos. Asen. 22:3, 8, however these latter ones are more comparative and relative. See Crispin Fletcher-Louis, "On angels, men and priests (Ben Sira, the Qumran Sabbath Songs and the Yom Kippur Avodah)," Paper given at Conference in Zurich: "Gottesdienst und Engel" in January 2015, www.academia.edu/13408562/On_angels_men_and_priests_Ben_Sira_the_Qumran_Sabbath_Songs_and_the_Yom_Kippur_Avodah_ pp.1–2. For the description of Moses as *theos* see M. David Litwa, "The Deification of Moses in Philo of Alexandria," *The Studia Philonica Annual* 26 (2014): 1–27; Loren Struckenbruck, "'Angels' and 'God': Exploring the Limits of Early Jewish Monotheism," in *Early Jewish and Christian Monotheism*, ed. Loren T. Stuckenbruck and Wendy E.S. North (T&T Clark, 2004), 45–70.

78 Crispin Fletcher-Louis, *Christological Origins: The Emerging Consensus and Beyond*, vol. 1 of *Jesus Monotheism* (Cascade, 2015), 230–316. Crispin Fletcher-Louis anticipates developing this thesis further in the forthcoming volumes 2 and 3 of this series. See also Crispin Fletcher-Louis, "Some Reflections on Angelomorphic Humanity Texts Among the Dead Sea Scrolls," *Dead Sea Discoveries* 7 (Brill, 2000): 292–312; "The Worship of Divine Humanity as God's Image and the Worship of Jesus," in *The Jewish Roots of Christological Monotheism: Papers from the St. Andrews Conference on the Historical Origins of the Worship of Jesus* (Brill, 1999), 112–128, esp. 116–118, on the presence of Wisdom on the priest Simon ben Onias in Sir. 50 for his glorification and identification with YHWH. See also his thorough monograph on the DSS: *All the Glory of Adam: Liturgical Anthropology in the Dead Sea Scrolls* (Brill, 2002). Andrew Chester likewise includes discussion of Adam as an angelmorphic figure, as he argues that NT Christology forms out of the background of Second Temple Judaism's view of human transformation (*Messiah and Exaltation*, WUNT 207 [Mohr Siebeck, 2007], 45–121). See also J.R. Daniel Kirk, *A Man Attested By God: The Human Jesus of the Synoptic Gospels* (Eerdmans, 2016), 44–176, for a discussion of idealized human figures in the Hebrew Bible and Second Temple Judaism.

he was appointed heir. First, as Wescott points out, there is the use of the conjunctive τε, which "indicates the new relation of the statement which it introduces."[79] Thus in this clause his bearing the creation is precisely because of the identity of his being. Again Wescott notes, "The providential action of the Son is a special manifestation of His Nature and is not described in a coordinate statement: what He does flows from what He is."[80] Ellingworth suggests that here "In the present verse, τε may function as a link between ὢν and φέρων, at a higher syntactical level than the preceding καί."[81] Although we might quibble over the precise nuance of τε, Wescott's point stands that the activity of bearing up the creation is because of the identity of his being. In sustaining creation, the Son is acting not as an appointed vice-regent, a role the OT attributes to Adam and to the Davidic son, the latter especially in the royal psalms. The Davidic figure may govern and rule creation, but he is not described as sustaining it as deity would. In contrast, the Son is carrying out activity reserved for God.

Montefiore expresses the distinction well, "What is here being ascribed to the Son is the providential government of the universe, which is the function of God himself."[82] Even in Hebrews, God brought the world into being through his Word. For example, we read Heb 11:3 κατηρτίσθαι τοὺς αἰῶνας ῥήματι θεοῦ. This universe created by the Word of God continues to be actively sustained and carried forth by the τῷ ῥήματι τῆς δυνάμεως αὐτοῦ (Heb 1:3). The Son has not merely been delegated power to govern,[83] nor has the Son recently come to this power through appointment, both of which might further allude to post-exaltation activity and royal activity delegated to the Davidic heir. Rather, the Son creates and sustains creation by his powerful word. The Son is not merely the embodiment of the Logos or Wisdom; he is the one who utters the divine Word that sustains creation. N.T. Wright identifies the activity of creation and providential care for the creation two of the three main aspects of Jewish monotheism.[84] As Luke Timothy Johnson said if

---

79 Wescott, *Hebrews*, 13.
80 Ibid.
81 Ellingworth, *Hebrews*, 100.
82 Montefiore, *A Commentary on the Epistle to the Hebrews*, HNTC (Harper & Row, 1964), 35; quoted also in D.J. Ebert, "Wisdom," 89.
83 An example of this delegated power is that angelic beings were given ability to govern various aspects of creation, particularly various nations (T. Levi 5:3–7; 1 En. 56:5–6; Jub. 15.31–2). See also L.T. Stuckenbruck, "Angels of the Nations," in *Dictionary of New Testament Background*, ed. Craig A. Evans and Stanley Porter (Intervarsity, 2000): 29–31; Gleason, "Angels and the Eschatology of Heb 1–2," 99–101; Kuhn, "The Angelology," 226–30; Marie Isaacs, *Sacred Space*, 177.
84 *The New Testament and the People of God*, 248–251.

God's powerful word "belongs to the *Son*, Hebrews is once more dramatically asserting his [the Son's] identity as divine."[85]

### HEB 1:5—SONSHIP AND THE USE OF PS 2:7 AND 2 SAM 7:14

In order to show that the Son is unique and distinct from the angels, Hebrews begins its series of Scripture citations with identifying the unique address that the Son has from the Father. In the OT, both in the MT and in the LXX, angels can be identified as sons of God. Sometimes the LXX will translate בְּנֵי הָאֱלֹהִים as οἱ ἄγγελοι τοῦ θεοῦ (Job 1:6 & 2:1); other times it will have some variation of the more literal οἱ υἱοὶ τοῦ θεοῦ.[86] The identification of angels as sons of God, however, is distinct from the sonship role of Israel, and the Davidic King. Even more, the angels are never directly addressed as sons by name, nor does the Father single out a personal address to any particular angel.[87] Hebrews uses the Psalm to further identify the Son. Amy Peeler has argued that the introduction given to the quotations of Ps 2 and 2 Sam 7:14 serve as further identification of the Father and Son:

> [E]ven if the content said nothing about God, the citations would still disclose something about the character, or *ethos,* of God *simply because God is speaking them.* In the ancient world, there was a widespread understanding that speech disclosed character. By introducing these verses as God's speech, the author sets up the citations as a conversation between two persons. As such, the dual emphasis upon both the address and the addressor provides evidence of the *relationship* between God and the one to whom God is speaking.[88]

Psalm 2 concerns the exaltation of the Davidic King. The King is installed as on the throne in Jerusalem/Zion, and the nations are subjected under him. This installation makes the Davidic King YHWH's royal vice-regent and places him in a filial relationship with God, the high king of heaven (e.g. LXX 2:4 ὁ κατοικῶν ἐν οὐρανοῖς). The king is exalted. Craig Keener even suggests that

---

85 *Hebrews: A Commentary* (Westminster John Knox Press, 2006), 70.

86 Possibly Gen 6:2, 4. Second Temple Judaism understood these 'sons of God' to be angels. In Gen. 6:2, 4 the LXX retains οἱ υἱοὶ τοῦ θεοῦ. Other texts include Deut. 32:43 (LXX υἱοὶ θεοῦ); MT. Ps 29:1//LXX 28:1 (υἱοὶ θεοῦ); 89:6//LXX 88:7 (ἐν υἱοῖς θεοῦ); Ode 2:43 (ἐν υἱοῖς θεοῦ); Wis. 5:5 (ἐν υἱοῖς θεοῦ). Cf. Jody Barnard, *The Mysticism of Hebrews,* 160–161.

87 Koester, *Hebrews,* 191. Koester also writes, "'sons of God' is only used for angels collectively; in the Scriptures no one angel is called God's "son" in a singular sense." Cf. Amy Peeler, *You Are My Son,* 47–48.

88 Amy Peeler, *You Are My Son,* 31. Emphasis original.

"[p]robably the cultic acclamation of Davidic rule in Israel's royal psalms provided the earliest commentary on the promise of 2 Sam 7."[89]

Psalm 2 is used messianically in the Second Temple texts of 4QFlor and Pss. Sol. 17. As we note below, 4QFlor refers to a coming Davidic Messiah and uses Ps 2:1 in conjunction with 2 Sam 7. Psalm of Solomon does not make reference to the sonship aspects of Ps 2 but does use Ps 2:9, referencing the messiah's rod of iron to defeat the nations. Thus, the application of the Psalm, "did not involve a radical break with Jewish exegetical tradition, but rather a natural continuity…"[90] Hebrews focuses on exaltation, whereas 4QFlor references the defeat of the sons of Belial, and Pss. Sol. 17 references the subduing of nations.[91]

Hebrews applies the text to the Son as the one exalted to the ultimate Zion, heaven itself.[92] Son is both identified and installed in a royal office as he is invited into heaven. The idea of begetting is based on Ps 2, that is a royal installation in Zion. In the OT context, this was seen as an adoption of sorts of the Davidic king.[93] However, given that Hebrews identifies the Son within the identity of the Godhead, the author may see the phrase υἱός μου εἶ σύ not as a statement of what happens at exaltation but as an identification of who the Son has always been. YHWH is installing his Son on the throne in Zion, and for Hebrews, if YHWH has a Son, the Sonship must precede the installation, just as the glory of the Son precedes the revelation of this glory at coronation. This movement should not surprise because it is the same way YHWH

---

89 Craig Keener, *Acts: An Exegetical Commentary Volume 2: 3:1–14:28* (Baker, 2013), 2070.

90 Ellingworth, *Hebrews,* 112. For a full treatment of the background of the Psalm in Early Judaism and Christianity see Sam Janse, *"You Are My Son" The Reception History of Psalm 2 in Early Judaism and the Early Church*.

91 Heb 2:14–15 references the defeat of death and the devil, just not in the immediate context of quoting Ps 2.

92 Zion is only used once in Hebrews (12:22) but a clear contrast is set between Zion and Mt. Sinai. A Zion motif in Ps 2:6 probably impacts the way the author sees Zion, as well as being the heavenly rest the Son enters into. For a fuller discussion see Kiwoong Son, *Zion Symbolism in Hebrews: Hebrews 12:18–24 as a Hermeneutical Key to the Epistle* (Paternoster, 2005). He shows that Zion imagery is closely associated with the temple imagery and Ps. 110:1 (169–197). It is also associated with the New Covenant. See also Michael Kibbe, *Godly Fear or Ungodly Failure? Hebrews 12 and the Sinai Theophany* (de Gruyter, 2016). Kibbe regards 12:22–24 as "a summation of the whole letter itself: a heavenly setting, a city, angelic celebration, perfected saints, Jesus the mediator, sprinkled blood, and so on" (138).

93 Shirley Lucass, *The Conception of Messiah in the Scripture of Judaism and Christianity* (T&T Clark, 2011), 69; Deborah Rooke, "Kingship as Priesthood: The Relationship Between the High Priesthood and the Monarchy," in *King and Messiah in Israel and the Ancient Near East: Proceedings of the Oxford Seminar,* ed. John Day (T&T Clark, 2013), 193; John Day, "The Canaanite Inheritance of the Israelite Monarchy," in *King and Messiah in Israel and the Ancient Near East,* 81–85; Adela Yarbro Collins and John J. Collins, *King and Messiah as Son of God: Divine, Human, and Angelic Messianic Figures in Biblical and Related Literature* (Eerdmans, 2008), 13–14.

identifies and reveals himself in the OT: on the one hand, he is king in majesty and glory; on the other hand, he manifests and brings near in revelation his kingship, majesty, and glory.

Three things then we see with the use of Ps 2: (1) the Son receives the intimate and filial address from the Father; (2) the begetting of the Son pertains to his installation on the throne, which for Hebrews, is his ascension into the heavenly Zion; and (3) the hermeneutic of Hebrews leads the author to read Ps 2 Christologically and eschatologically. The Son does not become Son at the moment of his ascension; rather, he is the Son already (1:2–3a), but the exercise of sonship enters a new phase that entails royal exaltation over the creation and on behalf of the people of God.

The 'begetting' of the Son (ἐγὼ σήμερον γεγέννηκά σε) is not his birth, nor is it, strictly speaking, his adoption rather it is his royal installation.[94] This installation is a new phase of sonship as the Son has entered heaven as a king-priest on behalf of the people of God. The Father has identified his Son (1:5), who was eternal (1:2–3a, 10–12), and installed him on the throne in royal appointment so that he sits at the Father's own right hand (1:3b, 13). The Son received a heavenly calling to ascend as kingly and priestly appointment (3:1–2) because of his faithfulness to the Father (3:1–2). Psalm 2 is seen as the identification of the Son for two main reasons: (1) because of who the Son already was and has been and (2) because the Son carried out faithful obedience to the Father while on earth, now being worthy of receiving this heavenly Davidic installation.

Immediately after quoting Ps 2, Hebrews links it (καὶ πάλιν) with 2 Sam. 7:14 ἐγὼ ἔσομαι αὐτῷ εἰς πατέρα, καὶ αὐτὸς ἔσται μοι εἰς υἱόν (Heb 1:5b).[95] The latter was a "prominent *locus classicus* for the expectation of a promised future Davidic messiah during early Judaism."[96] The two passages are brought together in an example of *gezerah shawah* Jewish hermeneutical technique where two passages are linked because of the same word; in this case the

---

94 We do not find convincing Matthew Bates' argument that because the Psalm conveys reported speech it must originally be spoken at a time prior to the incarnation, a 'time before time' and thereby a defense of Christ's pre-existence. While Hebrews and the early church believed Christ had an eternal sonship, the key to the Psalm's use is the realization of redemptive history. Bates does not sufficiently explain why the category of "reported speech" must necessarily be before time and not in the mind of Hebrews's prophetic speech (from 'in time') now fulfilled. *The Birth of the Trinity: Jesus, God, and Spirit in the New Testament and Early Christian Interpretations of the Old Testament* (Oxford University Press, 2015).

95 Hebrews is not unique here. Sam Janse notes "in the learned tradition of Judaism and the Early Church these texts are closely linked" especially 4QFlor (*"You Are My Son" The Reception History of Psalm 2*, 120, 82–86).

96 Gert Steyn, *A Quest for the Assumed LXX Vorlage of the Explicit Quotations in Hebrews* (Vandenhoeck & Ruprecht, 2011), 49.

word is "son."[97] The phrase καὶ πάλιν was a well-known formula used in the NT (John 19:37; Rom 15:10–12; 1 Cor 3:20), haggadic Midrash, and Philo of Alexandria.[98] For Hebrews, it connects another address of the identification of the filial relationship between God and the Messiah. What was given as part of the Davidic covenant now finds its ultimate referent in the identification of the relationship between God and the Messiah.

2 Sam 7:14 comes from the Davidic covenant and promises a special relationship between David's descendant and YHWH. In 7:12, YHWH promises to raise up David's seed. This king will build a temple-house for YHWH's name and YHWH will establish his throne forever (2 Sam 17:13b). YHWH promises to establish a filial relationship between himself and David's heir. 4QFlor also uses 2 Sam 7 to show how YHWH will establish his own reign through a future David. With regard to a future David, it quotes 2 Sam 7:11,12–14; Amos 9:11 and then Ps 2:1. 4QFlor, similarly to Hebrews, interprets these deeds as YHWH's activities of the last days when YHWH will raise up and establish Zion with a Messiah and an Interperter of the law (4QFlor 1:11–12). Thus, Hebrews is not unique in linking Ps 2 and 2 Sam 7:14 which "were already joined to serve as messianic proof texts at Qumran."[99]

Hebrews identifies Jesus as the fulfillment of these verses as the Messiah. God promises to act as Father and be a Father. Likewise, the Messiah will be a son to God. In light of its linking with Ps 2:7, Hebrews may well have in view that the Messiah is the one who is now had his throne established forever (2 Sam 7:13, 16). But the Messiah's sonship announced in ascension reveals a deeper eternal Sonship in Hebrews' logic. Hebrews will later draw attention to the appointment of Jesus as a high priest who, as exalted above the heavens (7:26), holds this office permanently because he himself, in resurrection life (7:16 κατὰ δύναμιν ζωῆς ἀκαταλύτου),[100] continues forever (7:22). This possible connection to the eternal kingship is heightened when we note that his 'priesthood forever' is linked to Melchizedek, who is a type of the ultimate Son of God and is a king-priest (7:1–3; 15–16).

For Hebrews, the use of Ps 2:7 and 2 Sam 7:14 shows the royal exaltation of the true Davidic heir in fulfillment of the OT promises. The relationship

---

97 Richard Longenecker, *Biblical Exegesis in the Apostolic Period*, 2nd ed. (Eerdmans, 1999), 158; Herbert W. Bateman, IV, *Early Jewish Hermeneutics and Hebrews 1:5–13: The Impact of Jewish Exegesis on the Interpretation of a Significant New Testament Passage* (Peter Lang, 1997), 220.

98 Simon Kistemaker, *Psalm Citations in the Epistle to the Hebrews* (van Soest, 1961; repr. Wipf & Stock, 2010), 20. See also Gert Steyn, *A Quest for the Assumed LXX Vorlage*, 52. Attridge (*Hebrews*, 53n.40) also notes that Philo uses πάλιν to link Scripture citations in *Her.* 2, 122; *Conf.* 167; *Somn.* 1.166; 2.19; *Leg.* 3:4; *Sobr.* 8; *Plant.* 171. He adds 1 Clem 10:4, 6; 14:5; 15:3; Barn 6:2, 4.

99 Attridge, *Hebrews*, 53. See also Herbert W. Bateman, IV, "Two First-Century Messianic Uses of the OT: Heb 1:5–13 and 4QFlor. 1.1–19," *JETS* 38.1 (1995): 11–27.

100 Moffitt, *Logic of Resurrection*, 203.

between God and the Messiah is that of Father and Son. Although Second Temple literature is familiar with the exaltation of angels, the exaltation of the Son in his ascension to the throne is unique because the Son receives the royal address from the Father. He is announced and declared Son in being placed upon the throne, which is the eschatological culmination of Ps 2:7. Jesus being installed on the throne in heaven at the Father's own right hand has assured the fulfillment of the Davidic covenant, yet it has also heightened that fulfillment from the earthly exaltations of prior Davidic kings to the ultimate heavenly fulfillment. For Hebrews, eschatological fulfillment has both a horizontal and a vertical dimension,[101] as what comes at the end of the age surpasses the shadows that have come before.

## Functional Sonship as Revelatory of the Son's Ontology

The tendency of modern NT scholarship is to read Hebrews at this point as only concerned with functional sonship. There can be no doubt that Hebrews see the Son as κρείττων γενόμενος (Heb 1:4), in exaltation with regard to his role within creation. He has inherited the name Son as royal title ὅσῳ διαφορώτερον παρ' αὐτοὺς κεκληρονόμηκεν ὄνομα (Heb 1:4), which is superior to any angelic address. However, the Sonship that concerns Hebrews is not merely the sonship of his exaltation. It speaks to his identity.

Hebrews is not unconcerned with ontology,[102] although Hebrews does not discuss 'ontology' in the categories that we might, or even as later church

---

101 By "horizontal" we mean the transition from "this age" to "the age to come" on the plain of history. By "vertical" we mean an apocalyptic type approach where revelation from God comes down and the Son ascends "upward" into heaven itself. G.K. Beale writes, "One striking feature of the eschatology of Hebrews, though also a trait of NT eschatology elsewhere, is its two-dimensional nature: it is characterized by vertical and horizontal planes, or spatial and temporal elements" (*A New Testament Biblical Theology* [Baker, 2011], 143–144). K. Son discusses the interrelation of spatial and temporal images as it relates to Hebrews' eschatology, cosmology, and Zion as a heavenly temple (*Zion Symbolism*, 172–176). See also Gert Steyn, "The Eschatology of Hebrews," 431–442. It is not too much a stretch to say that the ascension of the Son allows us to tie together the horizontal and vertical aspects of Hebrews' eschatology.

102 *Contra* G.B. Caird, "Son by Appointment," 81. While Caird is right to point out that pre-existence can be an abstract concept, he is wrong sharply to dichotomize Hebraic vs. Greek modes of thought. Caird's essay is important, indeed seminal, despite a few weaknesses like this that more recent scholarship has not followed. He is right in what he affirms (the role of Ps 8, the exalted humanity, and the necessity of Christ being perfect) but wrong in what he denies (any place for ontology and pre-existence). Hurst, "The Christology of Hebrews 1 and 2" also rejects categories of pre-existence in Heb 1 (*The Glory of Christ in the New Testament: Studies in Christology in Memory of George Bradford Caird*, ed. L.D. Hurst and N.T. Wright [Clarendon, 1987], 151–164). On Ps 8's influence on Heb 1, see G.B. Caird, "The Exegetical Method of the Epistle of Hebrews," *Canadian Journal of Theology* 5 (1959): 44–51; Jared Compton, *Psalm 110 and the Logic of Hebrews*, LNTS 537 (T&T Clark, 2015), 19–38. For a more complete study of pre-existence and wisdom in the NT, see R.G. Hamerton-Kelly, *Pre-Existence, Wisdom, and the*

fathers would. One cannot simply state there is no ontology if it is not how later theologians would discuss ontology. If Hebrews is concerned to speak of God's revelation and activity, the onus is on scholars to prove why this concern for God's identity in his activity is not a form of 'ontology.' In fact, ontological concepts must be in view since it is not the appointment that makes the Son the Son.

The one who was Son and who bore all the quality and attributes of Sonship is taken and appointed the heir by God the Father. The name Son is superior, and in the ushering in of the last days the one who was Son, inherits sonship in a royal announcement for all creation to see. Thus, while the ἐγὼ σήμερον γεγέννηκά σε refers to the installation on the throne and the public pronouncement of Sonship at the exaltation, the phrase υἱός μου εἶ σύ identifies the relationship between God and Jesus. Hebrews sees the relationship as extending into eternity past. Then ἐν υἱῷ God reveals/speaks to usher in the last days of the age to come even though the Son also created the ages. Note as well ἐλάλησεν ἡμῖν ἐν υἱῷ (1:2) is not precisely the same as when God spoke to the Son in the royal address: υἱός μου εἶ σύ, ἐγὼ σήμερον γεγέννηκά σε (1:5). The Son will later be shown to manifest obedience, coming with the intent of obeying the Father (5:8; 10:5). Even more, prior to the coming of the Son, he is identified as sharing in the divine activity of God in relation to creating all things and sustaining the universe.

As Hebrews will say later with respect to the new priesthood, God's word of oath appoints/installs [καθίστησιν] υἱὸν εἰς τὸν αἰῶνα τετελειωμένον. He is not one who becomes a son in his being eschatologically perfected but rather one who is/has been Son and now in light of his obedience and suffering experience is exalted up in eschatological perfection.[103] The same is true with respect to the office of the king.[104] For Hebrews, the Son of God is one who has no beginning of days nor end of life (cf. 7:3, 28).[105]

---

*Son of Man* (Cambridge University Press, 1973; repr. Wipf & Stock, 2000). On Heb 1, he writes that it "is a good example of how the assumption that Jesus is pre-existent, like Wisdom, reflects on the exegetical tradition and transforms what were initially testimonies to his resurrection and exaltation into testimonies to his protological pre-existence" (246–247). See also Douglas McCready, *He Came Down From Heaven: The Preexistence of Christ and the Christian Faith* (Intervarsity, 2005). Victor Rhee discusses preexistence in "Christology in Hebrews 1:5–14: The Three Stages of Christ's Existence," *JETS* 59.4 (2016): 723–727.

103 We discuss the precise meaning of perfection later.

104 Our warrant in applying this to both kingship and priesthood can be found in the way that Ps. 2:7 is applied to both the appointment of the Son as royal king and heir (Heb 1:5) and to the office of priesthood (Heb 5:5).

105 Hebrews 7:3 is notoriously difficult. Hebrews main point though seems to be that Melchizedek is a type of Christ and his appearance in the OT text without any genealogy, or seeming being or end, is something that is a similar resemblance (ἀφωμοιωμένος) to the reality

We propose then that Hebrews is creating a new category for sonship that extends beyond just messianic. This is not to say there is no evidence of Messianic sonship in Hebrews and other NT documents. Hebrews, however, does not limit its concept of sonship to royal but uses the Messianic-royal to expand our vista of S/sonship and speak of a pre-temporal/eternal Sonship where the Son shares in the divine identity of God. Something "new" is imparted so much as the true Son is revealed. As Heb 1:5 uses Ps 2:7 and 2 Sam 7:14 it is not merely addressing royal sonship, but the author sees God addressing the one who is and has been Son. The acknowledgement of the Son, his exaltation to the throne, and receiving the inheritance of the age to come is not the son's adoption but rather the public affirmation of his identity. Hebrews sees sonship as expansive beyond just royal identity. Sonship is not conferred at exaltation but confirmed and proclaimed. Ascension is revelatory of the identity of God as having an eternal Son.[106] The Christology of Sonship in Hebrews is not one merely of what the Son (or son) becomes but also who the Son is. Messianic sonship revealed in his ascension is the gateway for expounding divine Sonship.

## Conclusion

The purpose of this chapter has been to examine Heb 1:1–5 in how it identifies the Son as divine. Hebrews 1 contains a high Christology in aspects of 1:3–4, but Hebrews also shows the Son as the one who has been installed on the Messianic throne as the fulfillment of Davidic Kingship. This installation presupposes an ascension, as the Son has been invited to sit at God's right hand following his offering of himself for the purification of sins.

It will be important for our thesis as a whole to show that the two aspects of sonship in the book of Hebrews are related to the ascension. In this respect, the 'begetting' of the Son in Heb 1:5 (with the use of Ps 2:7) is his royal installation. Hebrews draws together the functional aspect of sonship (as Christ is installed) but also sees the work of God as revelatory of the one who was Son from all eternity past. In the next chapter, we examine the eternal divine aspects of Sonship in Heb 1:6–14.

---

of who Jesus is as Son of God. Sonship is kingship but more. For Hebrews, S/sonship concerns ontology and pre-existence.

106 Jody Barnard, *The Mysticism of Hebrews*, 151–160, 237; Mackie, *Eschatology*, 213–215, 218. Often in apocalyptic literature the ascender is given specific revelation in their ascent (David Bryan, "A Revised Cosmic Hierarchy Revealed: Apocalyptic Literature and Jesus' Ascent in Luke's Gospel," in *Ascent into Heaven in Luke-Acts: New Explorations of Luke's Narrative Hinge*, ed. David K. Bryan and David W. Pao [Fortress, 2016], 72). Consider also the significance of revelation in Heb 2:1–4.

# Chapter 3

# Sonship and the Deity of Christ in Hebrews 1, Part 2

### Introduction

In this chapter, we will continue our examination of Hebrews 1 with special attention given to the deity of Christ. In many ways, this is a continuation of the last chapter as Heb 1 functions as a unit. There are three aspects we will highlight in this chapter. First, we will give attention to the Son being both the firstborn and the one who is worshipped by angels. Second, with the use of Ps 45, Hebrews addresses the Son with the vocative "God." Third, with the use of Ps 102, the Son is identified with YHWH as the Creator distinct from his creation. While Heb 1:6 and 1:8–9 highlight Messianic and kingship aspects (royal sonship), the text we will survey below show that Heb 1 identifies Jesus as Son who shares in the divine attributes. We conclude that Heb 1 identifies the Son as eternal who shares participates in the Godhead with the Father.

### Heb 1:6—The Son as Firstborn and Object of Worship

In Hebrews 1:6, the Son is identified as τὸν πρωτότοκον. Firstborn can refer to the birth order of children as in 'the one who was born first' (cf. eg. Luke 2:7; LXX Gen 48:18).[1] However, it can be associated with rank as the one who inherits. Reuben, Jacob's firstborn, is identified as preeminent in power, strength, and majesty (Gen 49:3; cf. also Deut 21:17 where the firstborn is the רֵאשִׁית אֹנוֹ "firstfruits of his strength"). While in ancient society preeminence was often associated with the child who was born first, it was not necessarily the case. For example, in Gen 25:31, Esau sells his right of firstborn to his younger

---
[1] BDAG, 894.

brother Jacob. In Jub. 19:29 Isaac blesses Jacob saying, "and may the LORD God be for you and for the people a father always and may you be a firstborn son. Go, my son in peace." Even in Gen 48:12–20, although Manasseh is 'firstborn,' Jacob/Israel gives the great inheritance blessing of being firstborn to Ephraim. In Jeremiah MT 31:9 LXX 38:9, Ephraim's descendants are collectively identified as God's firstborn. Thus, firstborn identifies a position of exalted status, particularly where the inheritance is passed on to the individual.

There are two important OT backgrounds for the identification of the firstborn here in Hebrews. Both refer to the exalted status of the group or individual. The first is the identification of Israel as the special chosen heir of God. She is the firstborn son of God. In Exod 4:22 we read: σὺ δὲ ἐρεῖς τῷ Φαραω Τάδε λέγει κύριος Υἱὸς πρωτότοκός μου Ισραηλ.[2] The passage identifies her unique relationship to God over other nations. She is chosen as special heir, and God has a unique covenant relationship with her. As Wilhelm Michealis states, "this designation as firstborn, which is almost a title in Exod 4:22 (it is applied to Ephraim in Ἰερ. 38:9 [LXX Jer 38:9]), expresses the particularly close relation in which God stands to Israel."[3] Set part from other nations, Israel is his chosen portion reserved for him in special relationship (Deut 32:8–9). MT Deut 32:8 says the nation's boundaries are fixed לְמִסְפַּר בְּנֵי יִשְׂרָאֵל; LXX ἀγγέλων θεοῦ; DSS 4QDeut^j: בני אלהים; 4QDt^q [ ] בני אל.[4] Israel's being the Lord's portion is consistent with the special firstborn status she has as a nation before him. This status is because God has chosen to exalt her above all nations in his covenant with her. In 4 Ezra 6:58, we find that although the other nations are descended from Adam (6:56), they are not special to the Lord but Israel is "your people, whom you have called your firstborn, only begotten...and most dear..." In Pss. Sol. 13:9, firstborn is the privileged position of a beloved son, and the discipline and admonishment the righteous receive is special as reserved for the cherished firstborn beloved son. Later, in Pss. Sol. 18:4, Israel receives discipline from the Lord as for "a

---

2 Similarly in Wis 18:13, going back to the Exodus tradition, when the firstborn sons in Egypt were destroyed ὡμολόγησαν θεοῦ υἱὸν λαὸν εἶναι, they lost their firstborn/sons so that they would acknowledge God's firstborn/son.

3 *TDNT*, 6:873. In *4QDibHama* (4Q504) III,4–7, Israel is called by God בני בכורי ("my son, my firstborn") (Florentino García Martínez and Eibert J.C. Tigchelaar, eds., *The Dead Sea Scrolls* [Eerdmans, 1998], 2:1014–1015). See also Brandon D. Crowe, *The Obedient Son: Deuteronomy and Christology in the Gospel of Matthew* (de Gruyter, 2012), 137–138.

4 Our main concern here is not the text critical issues. The DSS reading may be original. This would be the best way to explain LXX and be most consistent with the theology of Israel's special exalted status over and above all the nations. On the text critical issues in Deut 32:8 see Michael Heiser, "Deuteronomy 32:8 and the Sons of God," *BSac* 158 (2001), 52–74. See also Crowe, *The Obedient Son*, 138, for links between sonship and the Qumran texts of Deut, especially 4QDeutj and 4QDeutq.

firstborn son, an only child" in order to prepare her for the day the Messiah will reign (18:5).

The second important background is the references to the Davidic King as God's firstborn. "'Firstborn' is a royal term."[5] In Ps 89 MT (LXX 88), the descendent of David shall be exalted and called the firstborn.[6] In v. 21 the hand of YHWH will establish and strengthen him. In perhaps an echo of Ps 2:9, the LORD promises to crush his foes and strike down his enemies (89:24; Eng. 23). God's faithfulness and covenant love (חַסְדִּי) will be upon him (89:25; Eng. 24) so that in the name of YHWH the Lord exalts the horn of the anointed one. He is set up over the seas and rivers (89:26; Eng. 25). Most notably the Father/son relationship of the Davidic covenant in 2 Sam 7 applies to this Davidic son. The Davidic king enjoys a special filial relationship which enables him to cry out for deliverance with the intimate address to God as his father:

MT Ps 89: 27 (Eng. v.26) : הוּא יִקְרָאֵנִי אָבִי אָתָּה אֵלִי וְצוּר יְשׁוּעָתִי
LXX Ps 88:27 αὐτὸς ἐπικαλέσεταί με Πατήρ μου εἶ σύ, θεός μου καὶ ἀντιλήμπτωρ τῆς σωτηρίας μου·

The establishment of the Davidic heir's throne brings him into an exalted position over creation but also an intimate position with the YHWH. Establishing this filial intimacy, YHWH declares:

MT Ps 89:28 (Eng. v.27) : אַף־אָנִי בְּכוֹר אֶתְּנֵהוּ עֶלְיוֹן לְמַלְכֵי־אָרֶץ
LXX Ps 88:28 κἀγὼ πρωτότοκον θήσομαι αὐτόν, ὑψηλὸν παρὰ τοῖς βασιλεῦσιν τῆς γῆς.

There is here in Ps 89 the declaration of covenant grant between God and the future Davidic King, just as there was in 2 Sam 7. "The content of the covenant declaration is, on the one hand, inspired by the so-called formula of adoption from Ps 2:7; on the other hand the covenant formula of 2 Sam 7:14 is its background."[7] The Davidic king bears the title firstborn found in the ancient Near Eastern ideology of the king but also the "title of honor for Israel."[8] Just

---

5 L.D. Hurst, "The Christology of Hebrews 1 and 2," in *The Glory of Christ in the New Testament: Studies in Christology in Memory of George Bradford Caird*, ed. L.D. Hurst and N.T. Wright. (Clarendon, 1987), 159. Hurst notes that by the time of the Rabbis "firstborn" had also been given Messianic import.

6 Cf. John P. Meier, who writes, "The *prōtokos* theme is apparently continuing the Davidic-enthronement motif of the first two citations" ("Symmetry and Theology in the Citations of Heb 1,5–14," *Biblica* 66 [1985]: 510).

7 Frank-Lothar Hossfeld and Erich Zenger, *Psalms 2* (Fortress, 2005), 410.

8 Ibid.

as Israel was that nation highest above the nations in Deut 26:19; 28:1, so now that Davidic king is highest above all the kings.[9] The Davidic king is the true Israelite, and while the Davidic covenant will not be removed from David's heirs,[10] the king and his sons are obligated to walk in covenant faithfulness of obedience to God's law (Ps 89:31–35).[11] Thus, firstborn is a position of status and relationship granted to the Davidic king marking his unique position and role.

Heb 1:6 continues the thought that Jesus is Son in a most exalted position and bears a unique relationship to the Father. The concept of firstborn serves to designate a collective (e.g., Israel) or an individual "solely as an object of the special love of his father."[12] It is a statement of the filial relationship that Hebrews will begin to contrast with angels. The use of πρωτότοκος is 'sonship language' denoting status and special relationship but without containing any notion of literal birth or begetting.[13]

The next issue in the text is when did the Father bring his firstborn into the world (εἰσαγάγῃ τὸν πρωτότοκον εἰς τὴν οἰκουμένην, Heb 1:6)? What εἰς τὴν οἰκουμένην refers to is a matter of debate among scholars, although in recent years a consensus seems to be forming that this phrase refers to the Son's exaltation into heaven. The three main interpretive options are that it refers to the incarnation, the parousia, or the exaltation.[14]

In the past, the majority of interpreters have identified εἰσαγάγῃ τὸν πρωτότοκον εἰς τὴν οἰκουμένην with the incarnation of the Son.[15] In Luke's

---

9 Ibid., 411; John Goldingay, *Psalms Volume 2: Psalms 42–89* (Baker, 2007), 680. This theme of kingship extends from Adam, to Israel, and then to David. As Brandon D. Crowe writes "The Adamic-filial precedent of Genesis also makes sense of the identification of the nation of Israel as son of God (Exod 4:22–23; Deut 1:31; 8:5; 14:1–2; 32:4–6, 18–20, 43; Isa 1:2; Jer. 3–4, and others), and it provides the foundation for the sonship of the king (2 Sam 7:14; Ps 2:7, and others). Just as Israel as son was a royal nation since God was Israel's great King, so the Davidic king as the representative of the nation is identified as God's royal son," (*The Last Adam: A Theology of the Obedient Life of Jesus in the Gospels* [Baker, 2017], 29).

10 Ps 89:37–38 with its reference to the sun and moon has an interesting intertextual link to Jer. 33:25. God's covenant with the sun/day and moon/night witnesses the permanence and certainty of the Davidic covenant. Jeremiah also connects the New Covenant with the fulfillment of the Davidic covenant, a theme that Hebrews picks up on: God's exaltation of the Davidic heir marks the ushering in of the New Covenant.

11 Brandon D. Crowe has traced out this theme of obedience and covenant faithfulness as it is manifest in the Gospels' portraits earthly ministry of Jesus, see *The Last Adam*, esp. 172–182.

12 *TDNT*, 6:874.

13 Ibid.

14 One other option: Herbert Bateman, IV, argues it refers to Jesus' baptism (*Early Jewish Hermeneutics and Hebrews 1:5–13: The Impact of Jewish Exegesis on the Interpretation of a Significant New Testament Passage* [Peter Lang, 1997], 222). We find this unconvincing since there is no mention of angel worship at the baptism.

15 William Lane, *Hebrews 1–8*, WBC 47A (Word, 1991), 27.

gospel, angels do celebrate the coming of Jesus at his birth (Luke 2:8–14) although they give glory to God, not worship to Christ.[16] The phrase εἰσαγάγῃ... εἰς τὴν οἰκουμένην itself could echo the common Hebrew idiom הביא לעולם for giving birth, according to Harold Attridge who follows Michel and Spicq.[17] However, we concur with the rebuttal by Jody Barnard, "Attridge cites no examples of this so-called Hebrew idiom, however, and the examples provided by Michel and Spicq are in fact the same example of the second-century CE Rabbi Eleazar ben Azariah."[18]

Οἰκουμένην can mean the world and is used in places to designate the known world (Acts 11:28, *Mart. Pol.* 5:1), the whole earth (Matt 24:14; Rom 10:18), or a significant region (such as referring to the Roman Empire as the world in Acts 24:5 or the people of the empire in Luke 2:1). It can also refer to the inhabitants of the earth (Acts 17:31; Rev 12:9).[19] BDAG notes that when it refers to the earth it is to the exclusion of the heavenly world.[20] A good example of this kind of usage is Satan showing Jesus πάσας τὰς βασιλείας τῆς οἰκουμένης in Luke 4:5, which excludes anything in the heavenly realm.

G.B. Caird argues that the use of Ps 8 in 2:6–8 is the interpretative key to understanding 1:5–14, although he still believes that 1:6 refers to the incarnation.[21] He feels that Heb 10:5 lends support to this interpretation where it reads διὸ εἰσερχόμενος εἰς τὸν κόσμον.[22] However, this argument assumes that Hebrews uses οἰκουμένη and κόσμος synonymously. Caird also does not deal

---

16 Harold Attridge who takes the interpretation that the phrase refers to the incarnation writes in a footnote, "There is no need to posit any allusion to Luke 2:13, where, in any case, the angels do not worship the Son" *Hebrews*, Hermeneia (Fortress, 1989), 56n.67. See also Kenneth Schenck ("A Celebration of the Enthroned Son: The Catena of Hebrews 1," *JBL* 120 [2001]: 478) who also points out that Luke 2:13–14 shows the angels giving glory to God, not worshipping Jesus.

17 Attridge, *Hebrews*, 56n.67. Attridge cites Otto Michel, *Der Brief an die Hebräer*, 6th ed., KEK 13 (Vandenhoeck & Ruprecht, 1966), 113, and Ceslas Spicq, *L'Épître aux Hébreux* (Gabalda, 1953), 2:17.

18 Barnard, *The Mysticism of Hebrews: Exploring the Role of Jewish Apocalyptic Mysticism in the Epistle to the Hebrews* (Mohr Siebeck, 2012), 240.

19 Gareth Cockerill, *Hebrews*, NICNT (Eerdmans, 2012), 105, writes, "It often refers to the 'inhabited world'...."

20 BDAG, 699, s.v. "οἰκουμένη."

21 G.B. Caird, "Son by Appointment," in *The New Testament Age: Essays in Honor of Bo Reinke Volume 1*, ed. William C. Weinrich (Mercer University Press, 1984), 73–81. See also his earlier "Exegetical Method of the Epistle to the Hebrews," *Canadian Journal of Theology* 5 (1959): 44–51.

22 Ibid., 75–76. This impacts Caird's understanding of sonship. "Christ's appointment to sonship and thus to 'the highest place that heaven affords' rests on an eternal decree, reiterated (πάλιν) by God when Christ appeared on earth, even though the full implications of his status would be realized only when he had qualified for it by his earthly career" (76). Hebrews does not use the decree of the Father speaking to the Son to reference his coming into the world but his coming into the age to come in ascension/exaltation.

with the phrase τὴν οἰκουμένην τὴν μέλλουσαν in 2:5 which is the only other use of οἰκουμένη in Hebrews.[23] Failing to identify a connection between οἰκουμένη in 1:6 and τὴν οἰκουμένην τὴν μέλλουσαν in 2:5 is a significant weakness in any assertion that 1:6 refers to the incarnation. Furthermore, undermining this argument is the fact that 1:6 concerns Christ's superiority of the angels,[24] while 2:6–8 emphasizes humility in his incarnation where he has been made lower than the angels for a time.[25] Only in the exaltation does Christ, at least in his humanity, become superior to the angels (1:4).

After the church fathers Jerome and Gregory of Nyssa,[26] Wescott was one of the earliest modern scholars to argue that the Son being brought into the world refers to the parousia. Käsemann also follows this position.[27] One of Wescott's main lines of evidence is his insistence that the construction ὅταν with the aorist subjunctive describes either "a series of events reaching into an indefinite future, each occurrence being seen in its completeness" or "it may describe the indefiniteness of a single event in the future seen also in its completeness." He then concludes rather forcefully, "In other words ὅταν... εἰσαγάγῃ must look forward to an event (or events) in the future regarded as fulfilled at a time (or times) as yet undermined."[28] Therefore "at the Return He will enter it once more with sovereign triumph."[29]

Nevertheless, the grammatical evidence is not as absolute as Wescott argues. F.F. Bruce has pointed to 1 Cor. 15:27 where the phrase ὅταν δὲ εἴπῃ introduces a Scripture quotation and cannot be taken as a future address to be fulfilled between God and Christ.[30] There are other examples as well: in Matt. 13:32, the mustard seed's growth ὅταν δὲ αὐξηθῇ μεῖζον τῶν λαχάνων ἐστίν is future to its state when it is the smallest seed ὃ μικρότερον μέν ἐστιν πάντων τῶν

---

23 Ardel B. Caneday, "The Eschatological World Already Subjected to the Son: The Οἰκουμένη of Hebrews 1.6 and the Son's Enthronement," in *A Cloud of Witnesses: The Theology of Hebrews in its Ancient Contexts,* eds. Richard Bauckham, et al. (T&T Clark, 2008), 31. John Meier also writes, "It can hardly be the nativity of Christ on earth given the meaning of *oikoumenē* in Hebrews" ("Symmetry and Theology," 508).

24 We will discuss below whether Christ is worshipped because of his exaltation or because of his deity. Even if, as we hold, 1:6 refers to the exaltation, is the worship merely subsequent to the exaltation or is the ground of the worship the exaltation?

25 Kenneth Schenck, "A Celebration of the Enthroned Son," 478; Ardel B. Caneday, "The Eschatological World," 31.

26 B.F. Wescott (*Hebrews* [Macmillian, 1889], 22) cites Gregory of Nyssa's *Contra Eunomium* iv. Philip Edgcumbe Hughes (*A Commentary on the Epistle to the Hebrews* [Eerdmans, 1977], 58) notes that both Jerome and Gregory of Nyssa held this view while Chrysostom and Alcuin believed the verse referred to the incarnation.

27 Ernst Käsemann, *The Wandering People of God,* trans. Roy A. Harrisville and Irving L. Sandberg (Augsburg, 1984), 112.

28 Wescott, *Hebrews,* 22.

29 Ibid.

30 F.F. Bruce, *Hebrews,* rev. ed., NICNT (Eerdmans, 1990), 58n.78.

σπερμάτων; however, because it is accounting a general state of affairs, the actions are not necessarily future to the speaker. The same is true for Mark 4:15, 16, 29, 31, 32; Luke 21:30; John 2:10; 5:7; 16:21. All that is required in Heb 1:6 is that upon bringing the firstborn into the world, he will then speak. It is not necessarily a future event relative to the author and his audience. In fact, Ellingworth suggests: "If εἰσαγάγῃ does refer to a particular time" it may be "future for the speaker in the OT text, but past for the author of Hebrews."[31] Bruce mentions the same point that it may simply be future with "respect to time when Deut 32:43 was uttered."[32]

One remaining difficulty with Wescott's interpretation is that, like Caird, he assumes that οἰκουμένη refers to the present earth. His reasoning is that since Christ is not present on the earth now, the future event of his return must be the focus of the reference. Again, however, if οἰκουμένη refers to what 2:5 calls τὴν οἰκουμένην τὴν μέλλουσαν, then the events do not have to be future to the audience of Hebrews.

The final view, and the most plausible, is that Heb 1:6 addresses the exaltation of the Son at his ascension. First, the event in discussion is connected with 1:5. The speech of God in 1:6 is the same event as the speech of God in Heb 1:5. The superiority of the Son and the subjugation of the angels under him are both addressed. Even if the author had chosen not to connect the verses with πάλιν this connection would be clear; however, the use of πάλιν heightens the clarity.[33] Royal sonship and the Son's exaltation to this continues to be the theme of 1:5–6 and fits with the "inner logic of the catena."[34] Second, this view makes for a coherent argument back through 1:3–4 where he has become superior to the angels τοσούτῳ κρείττων γενόμενος τῶν ἀγγέλων.[35] As William Lane summarizes, "The context requires that οἰκουμένην be understood as the heavenly world of eschatological salvation into which the Son entered as his ascension."[36] Third, the use of οἰκουμένη in Hebrews points to the reality of the age to come inaugurated at Christ's ascent. Οἰκουμένη occurs in Hebrews only in 1:6 and 2:5 and in the latter passage it appears in the phrase τὴν οἰκουμένην τὴν μέλλουσαν, as we have already pointed out. Fourth,

---

31 Paul Ellingsworth, *Hebrews*, NIGTC (Eerdmans, 1993), 117.
32 Bruce, *Hebrews*, 58n.78.
33 Kenneth Schenck, "A Celebration of the Enthroned Son: The Catena of Hebrews 1," *JBL* 120.3 (2001): 478–479; Ardel Caneday, "The Eschatological World," 32–33; Bruce, *Hebrews*, 56; Craig Koester, *Hebrews: A New Translation with Introduction and Commentary*, AB 36 (Doubleday, 2001), 192.
34 Schenck, "A Celebration," 479.
35 Caneday, "The Eschatological World," 33.
36 Lane, *Hebrews 1–8*, 27.

when Hebrews refers to the present world it uses κόσμος as in 4:4; 9:26; 10:5; 11:7, 38.[37]

Finally, as both Kenneth Schenck and Ardel Caneday have pointed out, understanding the content to refer to the heavenly world to which the Son is exalted in ascension fits better with the larger theology of the book and its vision for eschatology. Schenck argues that it coheres with Hebrews' "use of imagery that points toward the heavenly realm as the true homeland of God's people."[38] Caneday has shown that this understanding fits with the authors argument in chapter 2 especially that the Son has ascended into eschatological glory to bring the glorification of God's "many sons,"[39] and that it coheres with the author's larger presentation of eschatology in the epistle, eschatology that functions around two eras of salvation history (this age and the age to come) and two realms (earthly and heavenly).[40]

The author of Hebrews is using the OT to identify the exaltation of the Son as a point where the angels are specifically called to worship him. The citation is from the Song of Moses, which can be found in Deut 32 and the book of Odes in LXX.[41] Scholars debate which form of the text the author has quoted. The difficulty arises when we compare MT with LXX. MT reads as follows:

Deut 32:43 הַרְנִינוּ גוֹיִם֙ עַמּ֔וֹ כִּ֥י דַם־עֲבָדָ֖יו יִקּ֑וֹם וְנָקָ֤ם יָשִׁיב֙ לְצָרָ֔יו וְכִפֶּ֥ר אַדְמָת֖וֹ עַמּֽוֹ׃

In MT, the call is for the nations to rejoice הַרְנִינוּ גוֹיִם֙ עַמּ֔וֹ. This phrase is different from the longer version in LXX, but the obvious difficulty is the origin of the phrase καὶ προσκυνησάτωσαν αὐτῷ πάντες υἱοὶ θεοῦ (LXX Deut 32:43).

---

37 Felix Cortez, "The Anchor of the Soul that Enters the Veil': the Ascension of the 'Son' in the Letter to the Hebrews" (PhD diss., Andrews University, 2008), 222.

38 Schenck, "A Celebration," 478; also Caneday, "The Eschatological World," 35.

39 Caneday, "The Eschatological World," 35–36.

40 Ibid., 36–38. For further discussion of Heb 1:6 and discussion of these interpretive option see Matthew Easter, *Faith and the Faithfulness of Jesus in Hebrews*, SNTSMS 160 (Cambridge University Press, 2014), 114–117; David Moffitt, *Atonement and the Logic of the Resurrection in the Epistle to the Hebrews*, NovTSup 141 (Brill, 2011), 69–118. Moffitt convincingly argues that the eschatological is in view with the use of οἰκουμένην. He concludes that 'we need not posit a spiritual/material dualism' with the use of the term (118).

41 This book is not to be confused with the Odes of Solomon. The earliest we find the book of Odes in LXX is Codex Alexandrinus (4/5th cent. C.E.). Other manuscripts that contain it include Codex Veronensis (RLXX from 6th cent. C.E; which only contains the Odes Exod 15:1–21; Deut 32:1–44; 1 Sam 2.1–10; Isa 5:1–9; Jon. 2:3–10; Hab. 3:1–10; Mary's Magnificat; and Dan 3:52–90); Codex Turicensis (TLXX from 7th cent. C.E. which only contains 1 Sam 2:6–10, Mary's Magnificat, Isa 38:10–20; the Prayer of Manasseh; Dan iii:26–45, 52–56, 57–90; *Benedictus*; *Nunc Dimittis*; *Morning Hymn*) and minuscule 55 (10th cent. C.E. which is only lacking Isa 5:1–9). See Gert Steyn, *A Quest for the Assumed LXX Vorlage of the Explicit Quotations in Hebrews*, FRLANT 235 (Vandenhoeck & Ruprecht, 2011), 65n.50.

## Sonship and the Deity of Christ in Hebrews 1, Part 2

The discovery of the DSS shed light on textual variants that are closer to LXX's use of υἱοὶ θεοῦ in Deut 32:43. It "provided evidence for the first time of Hebrew textual authority for the OT quotation for Heb 1:6."[42] Thus, "the Masoretic tradition has not preserved the portion in Dt. 32:43 quoted in Hebrews, but the Hebrew text of the Qumran 4QDeutq did."[43] 4QDeutq 32:43 reads similar to the opening lines:

4QDeutq 32:43   הרנינו שמים עמו והשתחוו לו כל אלהים

The phrase כל אלהים in the Hebrew of 4QDeutq 32:43 could more easily explain how LXX arrived at the translation υἱοὶ θεοῦ in Deut 32:43 or οἱ ἄγγελοι θεοῦ in Odes 2:43.[44] Other places where the translators of LXX change to אלהים include Ps 8:6, which Hebrews also quotes in chapter two, and Ps 97:7 [LXX 96:7]. The Hebrew of Ps 8:6 וַתְּחַסְּרֵהוּ מְּעַט מֵאֱלֹהִים becomes, in LXX ἠλάττωσας αὐτὸν βραχύ τι παρ' ἀγγέλους. Elsewhere LXX at times translates בני אלהים as ἄγγελος τοῦ θεοῦ,[45] but not always.[46]

The citation in Heb 1:6 is better identified as coming from LXX, especially because it bears close resemblance to the version of the Song of Moses found in the Odes:

Heb 1:6 προσκυνησάτωσαν αὐτῷ πάντες ἄγγελοι θεοῦ
LXX Deut 32:43...καὶ προσκυνησάτωσαν αὐτῷ πάντες υἱοὶ θεοῦ·...
Odes 2:43 ...καὶ προσκυνησάτωσαν αὐτῷ πάντες οἱ ἄγγελοι θεοῦ·...

Concerning whether or not the author of Hebrews was familiar with Odes, Ellingworth points out that the evidence that we have for Odes is only from the fifth century Codex Alexandrinus.[47] Radu Gheorghita also cautions about the availability of Odes,[48] although Lane finds Odes as the likely source.[49]

---

42 Gert Steyn, *A Quest for the Assumed LXX Vorlage*, 63.
43 Radu Gheorghita, *The Role of the Septuagint in Hebrews: An Investigation of its Influence with Special Consideration of the Use of Hab 2:3–4 in Heb 10:37–38*, WUNT 2/160 (Mohr Siebeck, 2003), 42.
44 On the issues and the possibility of the Divine Council behind the original text see Michael Heiser, "Deuteronomy 32:8 and the Sons of God," 52–74. He concludes that LXX and the DSS reading are more original than MT (59).
45 cf. Job 1:6; 2:1; 38:7 πάντες ἄγγελοί μου; compare also 4QDeutq 32:8 with LXX.
46 Deut 32:43 (LXX υἱοὶ θεοῦ); MT. Ps 29:1//LXX 28:1 (υἱοὶ θεοῦ); 89:6//LXX 88:7 (ἐν υἱοῖς θεοῦ); Odes 2:43 (ἐν υἱοῖς θεοῦ); Wis 5:5 (ἐν υἱοῖς θεοῦ).
47 *Hebrews*, 118–119.
48 Radu Gheorghita, *The Role of the Septuagint*, 42.
49 Lane, *Hebrews 1–8*, 28.

There are two possible texts in Second Temple Judaism where human individuals are the object of worship or veneration. First, in 1 En. 48:5 the Son of Man receives worship from all who dwell upon the earth.[50] In the context, the Son of Man is described as being given a name in the presence of the Lord of Spirits (48:2) as well as before the creation of the sun, moon, and stars (48:3). "He will become a staff for the righteous ones in order that they might lean on him and not fall" (48:4). In an allusion to Isa. 42:6 and 49:6, he is a light to the Gentiles, and in perhaps another messianic allusion to Ezek 34:4,16 he will be the hope of the sick. Then in 1 En. 48:5, "All those who dwell upon the earth shall fall and worship before him; they shall glorify, bless, and sing the name of the Lord of the Spirits."

The Son of Man is exalted over the earth as the eschatological judge.[51] He delivers the elect and righteous while vanquishing the unrighteous. He stands before the Lord of the Spirits and "his glory is forever and ever and his power is unto all generations" (49:2). The Elect One "shall sit on my throne, and from the conscience of his mouth shall come out all the secrets of wisdom" because the Lord of Spirits has "glorified him" (51:3). "He sits on the throne of glory and judges Azaz'el and all his company, and his army, in the name of the Lord of Spirits" (55:4). In 61:8, he is on the throne to judge.

These references are not necessarily to worship of the Son of Man as fully divine, or as equated with YHWH. There remains a subordination of the Son of Man. He may represent YHWH but he is not YHWH. As Adela Yarbro Collins and John J. Collins write, "The verse [1 En. 48:5] continues to say that they will glorify and sing hymns to the name of the Lord of Spirits. It is not implied that the Son of Man is worshipped as the supreme God, but rather that people perform *proskynesis* before him in recognition of his authority."[52]

The other possible parallel is found in the Life of Adam and Eve. In this text, which is a Midrash of the creation story in Genesis, upon Adam's creation, the angels are called to worship Adam. In contrast to Heb 2, humanity is not made "a little lower than the angels" but rather when the divine breath

---

50  In 1 En. 52:4, when he is executing his authority and orders in the judging of the earth, the passage states he will be "praised upon the earth" which suggests his exalted status but may not reflect worship as the divine is worshiped.

51  Adela Yarbro Collins and John J. Collins, *King and Messiah as Son of God: Divine, Human, and Angelic Messianic Figures in Biblical and Related Literature* (Eerdmans, 2008), 206. See also 11Q13 (11QMelch) where Melchizedek exercises the judgment of God (Elohim) especially exercising judgment over Belial and the evil spirits. Melchizedek carries out God's judgment (11Q13 Col. II.13), freeing the sons of light from Belial and all the spirits (cf. Heb 2:14). Part of what 11Q13 is doing is offering an interpretation Ps 82 and reading it in light of the eschatological end and redemption of the sons of light.

52  *King and Messiah as Son of God*, 207.

of life is breathed upon Adam, the angels are made to worship Adam in LAE 13:3–14:3:

> When God blew into you the breath of life and your countenance and likeness were made in the image of God, Michael brought you and made (us) worship you in the sight of God, and the Lord God said, "Behold Adam! I have made you in our image and likeness.' And Michael went out and called all the angels, saying "Worship the image of the Lord God, as the Lord God has instructed." And Michael himself worshipped first, and called me and said "Worship the image of God, Yahweh." And I [the devil] answered, "I do not worship Adam" And Michael kept forcing me to worship, I said to him, "Why do you compel me? I will not worship one inferior and subsequent to me. I am prior to him in creation; before he was made, I was already made. He ought to worship me.[53]

In the text the devil's rationale for not worshipping Adam is Adam's inferiority and being created subsequent to himself. However, the argument in Hebrews runs the opposite direction. The Son is presented as superior to the angels first by virtue of radiating the glory of God and being the χαρακτὴρ τῆς ὑποστάσεως αὐτοῦ (Heb 1:3). Second, the Son is portrayed as having an eternal existence prior to all creation, indeed creating all things with the Father. Gert Steyn has suggested the possibility that "the author of Hebrews was familiar with a similar tradition, transferring it from the first Adam to the last."[54] Even if Hebrews is aware of an angelic worship of Adam, the force of chapter one remains to set the Son as superior to the angels based not primarily upon a Second Adam category but upon a superior divine identity. There certainly are Second Adam conceptions in Hebrews' use of Ps 8 in Heb 2:6–8 but it is uncertain that this has influenced the thought of angels worshipping Jesus.

The theological point behind Hebrews' citation is that the Father calls the angels of heaven to worship the Son upon his installation. Using the citation to display God the Father as calling the angels to worship Christ, the author of Hebrews "indicated that God himself acknowledged the divinity of Christ."[55] Angels gathering around the throne is a familiar scene in Biblical and Second Temple texts,[56] but the distinction here is that the Son is now the object of worship. For the Son to be given worship again distinguishes the Son

---

[53] Translation from M.D. Johnson, *The Pseudepigrapha*, ed. J.H. Charlesworth (Doubleday, 1985), 2:262.
[54] Steyn, *A Quest for the Assumed LXX Vorlage*, 71. See also Bruce, *Hebrews*, 57.
[55] Steyn, *A Quest for the Assumed LXX Vorlage*, 68.
[56] Job 1:6; Isa 6:2–3; 2 Bar. 21:6; 48:10; 51:11; 1 En. 14:18–24; 39:12; 40:1ff; 47:1–3; 60:2; *et al.*

as superior to the angels since again angels are regularly seen in Biblical and Second Temple texts as refusing to receive worship.[57]

Angels may enter in and out of the heavenly throne room and the presence of God but Hebrews' point is that they never share in the divine glory and sit at the right hand of the throne of God (Heb 1:13: πρὸς τίνα δὲ τῶν ἀγγέλων εἴρηκέν ποτε…). For example, in the T. Levi 3:4, angels (the Holy Ones) dwell in the heaven right below God, with archangels serving in God's presence. There are angelic ministers in God's presence, and throne below, but an angel is seated at or on God's throne. In T. Levi, as in Heb 1:7, 14, the angels serve those who have salvation. T. Levi differs from Hebrews in that it sees archangels continuing to offer sacrifices, where in Hebrews Christ offers the final sacrifice into the Holy of Holies. In T. Levi. other angels continue to carry messages in and out of God's presence. In Hebrews, however, the Son having offered himself and entered the Holy of Holies in his ascension now sits down (9:23–26; 10:12).

In this light, Hebrews gives us a picture of just how high the exaltation of Jesus really is. It is entering into a privileged position reserved for God alone. Neither angels ministering in the realms of glory nor the Adamic exaltation passages mentioned above portray this level of equality with the divine glory. The Son sits at the right hand of the throne of God and shares in the royal sovereignty of God.

As Richard Bauckham articulates, the catena in Hebrews 1 displays Christ's superiority "imaged as spatial height (1:3–4) and expounded as qualitative difference."[58] Angels are servants or ministering spirits with ongoing activity, whereas Christ occupies the divine throne having finished his work.[59] The work of the Son is finished. He is crowned in regal authority in the throne room sitting beside God within the divine glory that he shares with the Father. Angels continue to worship and minister as created beings, made as winds and flames of fire. The contrast could not be more stark.

In 4 Ezra 8:20–24, in a prayer put on the lips of Ezra, we have a contrast between God's dwelling in eternity, on an eternal throne uttering forth an unchanging word, in contrast to the angels which can be commanded to change in wind and fire:

---

57 Rev 19:10; 22:8–9; Ascen. Isa. 7:21; 8:5; Tob 12:16–22; Apoc. Zeph. 6:11–15; Jos. Asen. 15:11–12. Cf. Richard Bauckham, *Climax of Prophecy* (T&T Clark, 1993), 120–32.

58 Richard Bauckham, *God Crucified: Monotheism and Christology in the New Testament* (Eerdmans, 1998), 33.

59 Ibid. Bauckham points out only the spatial difference "The angels, argues the passage, are no more than servants of God, whereas Christ, who occupies the divine throne itself, participates in God's own sovereignty and is therefore served by the angels (1:7–9, 13–14)."

> O Lord who inhabits eternity, whose eyes are exalted and whose upper chambers are in the air, whose throne is beyond measure and whose glory is beyond comprehension, before whom the hosts of angels stand trembling and at whose command are changed to wind and fire, whose word is sure and whose utterances are certain, whose ordinance is strong and whose command is terrible whose look dries up the depths and whose indignation makes the mountains melt away, and whose truth is established forever.[60]

Here we note several things concerning this text. First, the Lord is the one who dwells on high on his throne where nothing can compare to it. He inhabits eternity and in this way is above all. Second, created things change and perish because of the Lord's word. By implication, the Lord himself does not change because his word issues these commands and can undo creation. This point is important to remember in considering Hebrews' use of LXX Ps 101 below. There is a Creator-creature contrast. Additionally, angels fall into the side of the created. They change, specifically into wind and fire (cf. also Heb 1:7). Lastly, there is a notable difference between angels standing versus the Son being invited to sit in Heb 1.[61] This prayer reflects the royal throne room scene of God in contrast to angels around him.

For Hebrews, the worship of the Son along with his ascension into heaven entails him partaking of the exalted status at the height of heaven that is reserved for God alone. "The Son has been exalted to the most honorable position in the apocalyptic throne room of God. He sits as King and Judge on God's throne while the angels are serving them in cultic worship in the heavenly sanctuary."[62] The Son is superior and shares in divinity.

### Heb 1:8–9—Sonship and the Use of Ps 45:6–7

In Heb 1:8, the author uses Ps 45:6–7 [LXX 44:7–8] to identify another address given to the Son. He introduces the quote with πρὸς δὲ τὸν υἱόν which contrasts to the way in which Deut 32:43 has been introduced in 1:7 with καὶ πρὸς μὲν τοὺς ἀγγέλους λέγει. The quote allows the author to return again to

---

60 Translation from Bruce Metzger, *The Pseudepigrapha*, ed. J.H. Charlesworth (Doubleday, 1983), 1:542–543.
61 In 2 Bar. 21:6–7, the Lord reigns over the powers and angels who are "flame and fire". They are created and stand around the throne. In Jubilees 2:2, listing the spirits that "minister before him [the Lord]," we have "the angels of the spirit of fire, the angels of the spirit of the winds," along with other angelic spirits manifest as aspects of creation.
62 Gert Steyn, "Hebrews' Angelology in the Light of Early Jewish Apocalyptic Imagery," *Journal of Early Christian History* 1.1 (2011): 152.

the theme of the Son's reign and to draw attention specifically to the throne of the Son, a movement which will culminate with the use of Ps 110[109]:1 where the Son is placed to sit at the Father's right hand in the divine glory. The angels are made to be ministering spirits (ὁ ποιῶν τοὺς ἀγγέλους αὐτοῦ πνεύματα, Heb 1:7), at best they work and serve in the presence of the throne (cf. Isa 6:2–3; Jub. 2:2).[63] The Son, however, dwells on the throne and rules.

Psalm 45 is widely acknowledged as a royal wedding psalm.[64] Eaton suggests that, in light of ancient marriage rites, the Davidic king's wedding came "to be associated with the rites of enthronement."[65] In the psalm, the king is addressed with the vocative אֱלֹהִים.[66] While this psalm does not explicitly state that the king is YHWH's son, it does identify the uniqueness of the relationship between YHWH and the king.[67] The king is God's vice-regent[68] who stands on behalf of and acts for God. He is so exalted above the people that to see him in his royal splendor is like seeing a god.[69] While there is royal

---

[63] On the role of angels as divine agents of God see Larry Hurtado, *One God, One Lord*, 71–92.

[64] Hurst, "The Christology of Hebrews 1 and 2," 159; Goldingay, *Psalms Volume 2: Psalms 42–89*, 54; Peter Craigie, *Psalms 1–50*, WBC 19 (Thomas Nelson, 2004), 337; Christoph Schroeder, "'A Love Song': Psalm 45 in Light of Ancient Near Eastern Marriage Texts," *CBQ* 58 (1996): 417–432.

[65] John Eaton, *Kingship and the Psalms* (SCM, 1975), 119; Hans-Joachim Kraus, *Psalms 1–59*, trans. Hilton Oswald (Fortress, 1988), 456. Hebrews may read the 'anointing' of the Son as the placement upon the throne, the crowning with glory and honor. We are suggesting that Ps 45 is read as enthronement with Ps 2 and 8. The ascended Jesus who has heretofore been obedient is granted by the speaking of YHWH which identifies his eternal Sonship and confers an exalted state.

[66] *Contra* Wescott, *Hebrews*, 26. For a discussion of the vocative, see Murray Harris "The Translation of *Elohim* in Psalm 45:7–8," *TynBul* 35 (1984): esp. 77–88; C.F. Whitley "Textual and Exegetical Observations on Ps 45,4–7," *ZAW* 98.2 (1986): 281–282.

[67] YHWH is not identified by name in the psalm but only as אלהים (MT 45:3,8; Eng. v.2,7). We will assume that as part of Israelite religion, the Psalmist is referring to YHWH. If the psalm is a psalm of the sons of Korah, they elsewhere refer to YHWH as the great king, the true God, e.g., Ps 46:1, 7, 10–11; 47:2, 5–8. This God reigns over creation and over the nations.

[68] It is perhaps noteworthy both in terms of royal ideology in Israel and the Ancient Near East (ANE) and with respect of Hebrews' usage of the OT that in Ps 45:4 [MT v.4; LXX 44:4] the son as the royal King has splendor and majesty, הוֹדְךָ וַהֲדָרֶךָ [LXX: τῇ ὡραιότητί σου καὶ τῷ κάλλει σου], which is exactly the splendor of YHWH the uncreated one in Ps 104:1 הוֹד וְהָדָר לָבָשְׁתָּ. We should consider the references to garments in splendor on YHWH Ps 104:1 and Ps 102:25–27, where creation is a garment that wears out. These verbal and conceptual linking of words in the contexts of passages Hebrews cites may further suggest the author's linking of texts is hardly arbitrary proof-texting. While caution is warranted, if true, it may suggest the author of Hebrews is aware of more than just LXX, since the verbal parallels in between YHWH and the king in Ps 45/44:4 and Ps 103/104:1 are not clear in LXX.

[69] Note the similarities between YHWH and the king in the Psalm. First, the king has been blessed by God with physical beauty and appearance. Because of this the king is also described in the vocative a mighty one (גִּבּוֹר). Mighty is an attribute of God in the OT, one which has now become a descriptor to YHWH's earthly king (Deut 10:17; Neh 9:32; Isa 10:21; Jer 31:18). In the blessing of God, the human king is crowned in splendor and majesty (הוֹדְךָ וַהֲדָרֶךָ)

ideology, the ancient Israelite king was never deified in that way that surrounding cultures deified their kings.[70] In the passage, the king is not only addressed in the vocative אֱלֹהִים, he shares in the divine capacity in God's governance. The attributes of his reign are in line with the character of God. The king himself is under the authority of God as God has anointed him to this position (LXX 44:8; MT 45:8; Eng. 45:7).[71] These aspects, of course, leave the passage ripe for later Messianic interpretations.[72] However, unlike the original context of Ps 45, the author of Hebrews sees the Son sharing in the divine identity of the nature of God. The Son's glory and royal splendor is in fact YHWH's glory. God has spoken "in Son," who is the radiance of divine glory, and by speaking to the Son, God exalted him in ascension to the divine throne where the glory of YHWH alone resides. Hebrews takes up this messianic interpretation of the text but specifies that the text is God addressing his Son in his ascension to God's throne. The Son's ascent granted by the Father manifests the Son's sharing in eternal divine glory.

First, the author of Hebrews sees the Psalm as identifying the divinity of the Son, ὁ θρόνος σου ὁ θεὸς εἰς τὸν αἰῶνα τοῦ αἰῶνος. There are three options for translation of this phrase: (a) ὁ θεός as nominative and the subject "God is your throne"; (b) ὁ θεός as nominative and the predicate "your throne is God"; (c) ὁ θεός as vocative. Murray J. Harris notes that between options (a) and (b) "almost all proponents of the view that ὁ θεός is nominative prefer the former

---

just as YHWH is crowned in splendor and majesty. Here it is similar to Ps 21:15 "His [the king's] glory is great through your [YHWH's] salvation; splendor and majesty you [YHWH] bestow on him [the king]. Ps 96:6 describes YHWH: "Splendor and majesty are before him; strength and beauty are in his sanctuary." Like the divine king, the human king in Ps 45 has both splendor and majesty *and* strength and beauty. The king is the image of the divine. Like YHWH, the king rides out in victory for the cause of truth, meekness/humility, and righteousness (45:4; MT 5). He is the warrior who conquerors his enemies. In this he brings the foreign people under submission to him. Note how these themes link to Ps 2 and Ps 8. For similar arguments on the reflection between the Davidic monarch and YHWH's glory and splendor, see Herbert Bateman IV, "Psalm 45:6–7 and Its Christological Contributions to Hebrews," *TJ* 22.1 (2001): 10, 12–13; Murray Harris, "The Translation of *Elohim* in Psalm 45:7–8," 86–87.

70 Murray Harris, "The Translation of *Elohim* in Psalm 45:7–8," 83. Thomas Schreiner writes "In identifying the king as 'God' (Ps 45:6), the psalmist is not literally identifying the king as divine" (*Hebrews* [B&H, 2015], 71).

71 This anointing is a type of exaltation in itself. C.F. Whitley writes, "The act of anointing too effects a fundamental change in the character and outlook of man…Anointing was also a feature of the coronation of a king (I Reg 1,34–35; II Reg 11,12). This [the anointing], in addition to the belief that the king was divinely chosen (I Sam 10,24), invested him with a certain sanctity whereby he was regarded as the anointed of Yahweh (I Sam 12,3; 24,10; 26,11; II Sam 1,14)" ("Textual and Exegetical Observations on Ps 45,4–7," 282).

72 Attridge (*Hebrews*, 58n.93) notes *Gen Rab. 99*. John Goldingay notes that "in the post-monarchial period it came to be interpreted allegorically of the Messiah and his bride, the people of God" (*Psalms Volume 2: Psalms 42–89*, 54). Cf. Craigie, *Psalms 1–50*, 340–341.

translation [ὁ θεός is the subject]."⁷³ Although C.F.D. Moule says it is "conceivably a true nominative, construed as to mean 'Thy throne is God.'"⁷⁴

While in classical Greek the vocative would be θεέ, it is common in LXX⁷⁵ and NT to use the nominative as vocative.⁷⁶ In a less disputable example, Heb 10:7 also uses the nominative as vocative: τοῦ ποιῆσαι ὁ θεός τὸ θέλημά σου. Contextually the vocative makes the best sense. First, v. 8 ὁ θεός is parallel to the next address of the Father to the Son in v. 10 κύριε. Both passages are πρὸς δὲ τὸν υἱόν where the implied λέγει is understood from verse 7. There are also several places in LXX where ὁ θεός is used vocatively with the κύριε.⁷⁷ Ps 68:30 provides a clear grammatical example of another case with two nouns (although one is feminine and the other is masculine) preceded by the arti-

---

73   Murray J. Harris, *Jesus as God The New Testament Use of Theos in Reference to Jesus* (Baker, 1992), 212. He notes that only two commentators make the translation "thy throne is God": F.J.A. Hort, "Hebrews 1.8" (1894, unpublished manuscript in the R.L. Bensly Collection, Cambridge University Library), 3–5; A. Nairn, *The Epistle to the Hebrews* (Cambridge University Press, 1917), 31, 33–34; and Nairn, *The Epistle of the Priesthood*, 2nd ed. (T&T Clark, 1915), 306. We are aware of no commentators since the publication of Harris' work that have taken this position. According to Daniel Wallace if there are two nouns both with the article, the first in the order is the subject: "Hence, ὁ θρόνος σου would be the subject rather than ὁ θεός (*contra* most NT scholars who opt for either of these views)" (*Greek Grammar Beyond the Basics* [Zondervan 1996], 59n.81). Wallace, himself, argues that ὁ θεός is vocative, but he is merely pointing out taking ὁ θεός as predicate nominative would be a grammatically inaccurate view if it was a nominative not vocative. Commenting on LXX, Murray Harris makes this same point "'Your throne is God' is implausible in light of the articular θεός: an anarthrous θεός would have been expected in the predicate" (Harris, "The Translation of *Elohim* in Psalm 45:7–8," 89). Harris makes a similar point about word order as Wallace: if ὁ θεός were the subject, "one might have expected the word order ὁ θεός ὁ θρόνος σου κτλ. to avoid any ambiguity of subject" (*Jesus as God,* 215). See also Murray J. Harris "The Translation and Significance of 'Ο ΘΕΟΣ in Hebrews 1:8–9," *TynBul* 36 (1985): 129–162.

74   C.F.D. Moule, *An Idiom Book of New Testament Greek* (Cambridge University Press, 1959), 32. Also qtd. in Steyn, *A Quest for the Assumed LXX Vorlage,* 89n.63.

75   Examples in LXX where ὁ θεός is vocative include: Num 12:13; 1 Chr 16:35; Neh 5:19; 6:14; 13:14, 22, 29; Esth 14:19; Jdt 9:14; Tob 8:5, 15; 11:14; Pss 5:11; 16:6; 24:22; 26:9; 35:8; 41:2; 42:1, 2, 4; 43:2; 44:7; 47:10, 11; 50:3; 50:12; 50:16; 53:3, 4; 54:2; 54:24; 55:8, 13; 56:2, 6; 8; 58:2, 10,18; 59:3, 12; 60:2, 6; 61:8; 62:2; 63:2; 64:2, 6; 65:10; 66:4, 6; 67:8, 10, 11, 25, 29; 68:2, 6, 7, 14, 20; 69:2; 69:6; 70:1, 12, 18, 19, 22; 71:1; 73:1; 73:10; 73:22; 74:2; 75:7; 76:14, 17; 78:1,9; 79:4, 8, 15; 81:8; 82:2; 83:9, 10; 84:5, 7; 85:14; 98:8; 107:2, 6, 12; 108:1; 138:17, 19, 23; 143:23; Pss. Sol. 2:10, 15, 25; 5:4, 8, 11; 7:1, 2; 8:25, 27; 9:2, 3, 6, 8; 15:1, 2; 16:5, 6, 7; 17:1, 7, 8, 21; Hos. 8:2; Isa 26:9; 45:15. Some are clearer than others, for example in the prayers of Nehemiah and Jud. 9:14, as well as many in the psalms are undisputed vocatives. An electronic search for θεέ in Rahlfs LXX yielded only the following: 2 Sam 7:25; 3 Macc. 6:2; 4 Macc. 6:27; Odes Sol. 14:12; Sir. 23:4; Ezek 4:14; and Wis 9:1. Jody Barnard, *Mysticism,* 257, agrees with our conclusion that both LXX and NT commonly use ὁ θεός in the vocative.

76   See Wallace, *Greek Grammar Beyond the Basics,* 56–59. See our note above, as well as Attridge, *Hebrews,* 58n.91. Cf. F. Blass/A. Debrunner, *A Greek Grammar of the New Testament and Other Early Christian Literature,* trans. R. W. Funk (University of Chicago Press, 1961), 82.

77   See Ps 5:11; 54:24; 68:7 (although here 'ὁ θεὸς τοῦ Ισραηλ' could be descriptive 'the God of Israel' reflecting a common designation rather than vocative, but contextually the shift from μὴ ἐντραπείησαν ἐπ' ἐμοὶ οἱ ζητοῦντές σε makes the vocative much more probable); 68:14; 69:2, 6; 78:9; 83:9; 98:8; Pss. Sol. 5:11; 9:3; 17:1, 21.

cle: καὶ ἡ σωτηρία τοῦ προσώπου σου ὁ θεός, where the latter nominative ὁ θεός is a vocative.[78] Second, while figurative language is possible, the translation of a nominative "Your throne is God" or "God is your throne" would put it at odds with emphasis that the Son sits at God's right hand (Heb 1:3).[79] Hebrews consistently portrays God himself as sitting on the throne and the Son sitting next to him (1:3, 14; 8:1; 10:12; 12:2).[80] In fact, Hebrews is rather precise when it comes to the heavenly imagery. In the OT and Second Temple literature God is enthroned in heaven, and now in Hebrews and NT the Son is always delineated at God's right hand. It keeps the distinction between the Son and the Father while identifying the Son as one entering into the divine glory. Third, we should understand the translation to be the vocative in following MT[81] and LXX.[82]

The author of Hebrews takes the verse from Ps 45 and puts it on the lips of the Father as an address to the Son. Now it is something that is said of the Son, although this is not far from the original context where it was said to the Davidic King. It is the Father speaking to the Davidic son in identifying him. It reinforces the way that the Son is addressed by the Father in a way that the angels are not, or never can be. Addressing the Son as God in the vocative is

---

78  LXX Ps 76:14 ὁ θεός ἐν τῷ ἁγίῳ ἡ ὁδός σου and 78:9 ὁ θεός ὁ σωτὴρ ἡμῶν have a similar construction but the clause ὁ θεός precedes the other nominative. Again, though, ὁ θεός is vocative.

79  Cf. Cockerill, *Hebrews*, 109n.53. At best, the figure of speech could be identifying the God's sovereignty with the reign of the Son, which while in line with Hebrew's theology is not the best rendering of our immediate text. As Meier puts it, "God (the Father) has a throne in heaven, *at the right of which* the Son sits. Granted this key image, it is difficult to understand what it would mean to our author to say that God (the Father) *is* the eternal throne *on which* the Son sits" ("Symmetry and Theology," 514). Wescott's interpretive gloss, "'Thy kingdom is founded upon God, the immovable Rock'" (*Hebrews*, 25–26) is really no help. Certainly, the Davidic and Messianic kingdom is by God's establishment *via* covenant grant. It still imposes something upon the context. While Wescott cites examples of God identify as a hiding place, a rock, a fortress, and a dwelling place, nowhere else in Scripture is God identified as a throne, instead it is preferable to see God as a ruler who is upon the throne. The hope of the Davidic king is that he will be established upon the Lord's throne (1 Chr 29:23; 2 Chr 9:8; cf. also *4QDibHama* [=4Q504] IV 7–8 יושב על כסא ישראל לפניך כול "and he [David] would sit in front of you [the LORD] on the throne of Israel forever"), not upon the Lord as his throne. The Davidic Son is set upon the throne of David which is at God's right hand but is not identified with God. Barnard prefers the vocative but does not see any theological difficulty in taking ὁ θεός as the subject if we were to take the description as a "more metaphorical understanding of God as the Son's throne in terms of an impression of the intimacy that exists between God and his bosom-dwelling Son" (*Mysticism*, 258; cf. John 1:18; *Sefer Yetzirah* 6:4).

80  Again Cockerill, *Hebrews*, 109n.53; Meier, "Symmetry and Theology," 514.

81  Harris, "The Translation of *Elohim* in Psalm 45:7–8," 129–162; *Jesus as God*, 187–204.

82  The vocative δυνατέ is already used in LXX Ps 44:4, 6, which is slightly different from MT which has גִּבּוֹר in v. 4 but not in v. 6 (cf. Harris, *Jesus as God*, 215). Attridge also points to the Aquila's revision of LXX where θεέ is used (*Hebrews*, 58 cf. also Wescott, *Hebrews*, 25). Cockerill notes the same in Theodotion (*Hebrews*, 109n.53).

"not very startling after the statements about creation, eternal preexistence, and conservation of creation in 1,2b–3b."[83]

The Son's throne is as God's εἰς τὸν αἰῶνα τοῦ αἰῶνος. First, we should consider that this could be a reference to the Davidic aspect of the throne. It is possible that this quality of reigning forever is the future aspect now that he has been appointed to the throne, in much the same way that he is a priest forever now that he is appointed (cf. Ps 110:4; Heb 5:5–6).[84] For example, in Dan 7:18 when the saints are given the kingdom of the Most High, it is καθέξουσι τὴν βασιλείαν ἕως τοῦ αἰῶνος καὶ ἕως τοῦ αἰῶνος τῶν αἰώνων.[85]

The Son could be bearing the name God as a function of vice-regency due to his appointment, rather than pointing to eternal identity in the Godhead, ontological statements, or pre-existence.[86] Certainly, Hebrews sees the

---

[83] Meier, "Symmetry and Theology," 514. Also, Schreiner, "Furthermore, the deity of the Son fits with the Son's role as Creator (1:2,10), his divine nature (1:3,11–12), his preservation of the world (1:3), and his being worshipped by angels (1:6)" (*Hebrews*, 71). Timo Eskola writes, "Therefore the reader cannot avoid the impression that, in this passage, Jesus as the Son is identified as God" (*Messiah and the Throne: Jewish Merkabah Mysticism and Early Christian Exaltation Discourse*, WUNT 2/124 (Mohr Siebeck, 2001), 206).

[84] If we follow Hebrews' argument concerning the priesthood of Jesus, it certainly does not extend into eternity past. We are raising the possibility that the reign does not either.

[85] MT: וְיַחְסְנוּן מַלְכוּתָא עַד־עָלְמָא וְעַד עָלַם עָלְמַיָּא

[86] G.B. Caird, "Son by Appointment," 74–75. It is possible that in this way the Son bears the name of God only in his appointment. It would mean that the Son is not sharing in the identity of YHWH in Hebrews but only bearing the identity and name as an appointed vice-regent. For example, in 11Q13 2.9 (11QMelch) Melchizedek [there is debate whether he is angelic or Davidic/Messianic in this text] bears the name of YHWH so that Isa 61:2 "year of the YHWH's favor" becomes "the year of favor of Melchizedek" (לשנת הרצון למלכי צדק). He carries out YHWH's judgments and brings in the reign of God 2.13,17–20. Thus, it is written of his work of YHWH's behalf: "Your God reigns" (2.23 [במשפט] [י]עליו כתוב כאשר אל[ לצי אומר[ מלך ון אלוהיך). See J.D. Kirk, *A Man Attested by God: The Human Jesus of the Synoptic Gospels* (Grand Rapids: Eerdmans, 2016) 121–124. Melchizedek takes his seat in the heavenly council and judges over divine beings. 2:10 ישפוט אלוהים בקורב אל[ בעד]ת [נ]צב אלוהים. In 2:11, Melchizedek in fulfillment of Scripture takes (returns to? שובה) his seat in the highest to judge: למרום שובה אל ידין עמים. The assembly gather around him as the effector of judgment as they would YHWH (e.g., Ps 7:7–8). On the identity of Melchizedek see Anders Aschim, "Melchizedek and Jesus: 11QMelchizedek and the Epistle to the Hebrews," in *The Jewish Roots of Christological Monotheism: Papers from the St. Andrews Conference on the Historical Origins of the Worship of Jesus*, ed. Carey Newman, James Davila, and Gladys Lewis (Brill: 1999), 132–135. Aschim follows the 'mainstream reading' that Melchizedek is an angel. Similarly, De Jonge, M. and Van Der Woude, A.S. "11Q Melchizedek and the New Testament," *NTS* 12.4 (1966): 301–326; Gareth Lee Cockerill, "Melchizedek or 'King of Righteousness'," *EvQ* 63.4 (1991): 305–312; Eric Mason, '*You Are a Priest Forever' Second Temple Jewish Messianism and the Priestly Christology of the Epistle to the Hebrews*, STDJ 74 (Brill, 2008), 168–190. Mason concludes Melchizedek is a heavenly angelic figure (185–186). See also Fletcher-Louis, *All the Glory of Adam: Liturgical Anthropology in the Dead Sea Scrolls* (Brill, 2002), 216–218; Israel Knohl, "Melchizedek: A Model For The Union Of Kingship And Priesthood In The Hebrew Bible, 11 QMelchizedek, And The Epistle To The Hebrews," in *Text, Thought, and Practice in Qumran and Early Christianity*, ed. Ruth A. Clements and Daniel R. Schwartz (Brill, 2009), 255–266. Fitzmyer calls Melchizedek in this

Son reigning as Messiah now (e.g, 2:5–8). In the OT, the throne of David was expected to last forever.[87] The OT expectation focused more on a lasting dynasty. In this sense, David's throne (and that of his seed) would be established forever.[88] Later, it becomes then an expectation that the Messiah would reign forever.

In the OT, it is YHWH who founds this throne. YHWH's throne is the ultimate one which is eternal and forever.[89] David's throne is forever from the time of anointing, but this is founded upon YHWH's throne extending into eternity past as well as future. In the Hebrew of Ps 102:13 (LXX 101:13; Eng. 102:12) it is YHWH's enthronement which is forever: וְאַתָּה יְהוָה לְעוֹלָם תֵּשֵׁב, which LXX translates as the eternality of YHWH himself: σὺ δέ, κύριε, εἰς τὸν αἰῶνα μένεις. In Ps 93:2, YHWH's throne is established from old as he is everlasting.[90] Unlike in some Second Temple texts where exalted figures dwell and exercise authority under the heavenly throne in distinction from it,[91] He-

---

text a "heavenly redemptive figure" ("Further Light on Melchizedek from Qumran Cave 11," *JBL* 86 (1967): 25–41). Paul Rainbow ("Melchizedek as a Messiah at Qumran," *BBR* 7 (1997): 179–194) argues the figure is a royal messianic Melchizedek who is God's agent. He states, "For in certain ceremonial contexts the human king of Israel too could be called "God" (Ps 45:7 MT; cf. Isa 9:5) by virtue of his official exaltation to share in unique prerogatives of Yahweh (Ps 110:1; 1 Chr 28:5; 29:23)" (182). It is clear in NT that glorified aspects of Christ's humanity are what qualify him to judge (Acts 17:31; 1 Cor. 15:23–25; Heb 2:5–9), yet, Hebrews sees the OT texts as revelatory in their identification of the Son who shares in the divine being and eternality of God. Bauckham briefly discusses the difference between 11QMelch and Heb 1:8 in "Monotheism and the Christology of Hebrews 1," *Early Jewish and Christian Monotheism*, ed. Loren T. Stuckenbruck and Wendy E.S. North (T&T Clark, 2004), 182. He notes that Melchizedek does not participate in divine identity, "what makes it [Heb 1:8] of special significance is that this text (Ps 45[44].6) speaks of the eternal divine throne as 'your throne, O God'. Sitting on the divine throne was the most powerful symbol Jewish monotheism had for the inclusion of a figure in the exercise of the unique divine sovereignty over all things. Standing in the divine council, as Melchizedek does, does not carry the meaning which sitting on the divine throne carries" (182). See also Murray Harris, "The Translation and Significance of 'Ο ΘΕΟΣ in Hebrews 1:8–9," 154n.78.

87 2 Sam 7:13, 16; 1 Kgs 2:45; 9:5; 1 Chr 17:12, 14, 27; 22:10; Ps 89, esp. vv. 4, 29, 36; Ps 132:11–12. See also Wis 6:21, the king who honors wisdom will reign forever (in light of 8:13 and 9:8, this probably alludes to a Davidic/Solomonic dynasty).

88 2 Sam 7:13, 16; 1 Kgs 2:45; 9:5; 10:9; 1 Chr 17:12, 14; 22:20; Ps 89:4, 29, 36; 132:12.

89 Pss 9:7; 102:12; 145:13 Lam 5:19.

90 In Ps 93:1, YHWH establishes the world, and it is never moved, but his throne is from old. In LXX (92:2), it would seem to imply that YHWH's throne (i.e., his rule) started at creation: ἕτοιμος ὁ θρόνος σου ἀπὸ τότε; yet YHWH is eternal: ἀπὸ τοῦ αἰῶνος σὺ εἶ. In MT Ps 90:2 YHWH is God from everlasting to everlasting, before the mountains were brought forth and the earth was formed.

91 Rev 4:4; T. Levi 3:3–9; 1 En. 19–21 (esp. 21 where Uriel is the chief angel and then governs sun, moon, and stars); 61:10 (all the hosts under the Lord); 71:1; 75:1–3; 79:6; 82:7; 2 En. 29:4–5. David Bryan ("A Revised Cosmic Hierarchy Revealed: Apocalyptic Literature and Jesus' Ascent in Luke's Gospel," in *Ascent into Heaven in Luke-Acts: New Explorations of Luke's Narrative Hinge*, ed. David K. Bryan and David W. Pao [Fortress, 2016], 68–69) writes "Authority is ascribed to various celestial entities (typically for a specific duration), but it cannot be forgotten that the presentation of the hierarchy begins with 'the Lord of all the creation of the world' who 'or-

brews is bringing Christ's throne into identification with YHWH's throne as he has ascended to God's right hand.[92] "Through the metaphor of the throne the Son is identified as God himself."[93]

Our contention is that Hebrews goes beyond just identifying Christ's vice-regency as an exalted agent for judgment to say that the one who is exalted shares in God's being not merely by virtue of exaltation but in fact prior to exaltation. Indeed, God has spoken in the Son by the acts carried out by the Son, *but the Son has always been Son* even now being manifested as Son. While in the OT David's throne was described as YHWH's throne—a metaphor for YHWH's establishment of it—Hebrews sees the eschatological Davidic Messiah as ascending to the actual throne of YHWH himself. He does not merely function now as designated potentate but is in fact sharing in the divine glory as one who has done so from eternity past. Thus, as Meier puts it, "Once we understand *ho theos* as an address to the Son, the reference to the eternal throne must be taken in the widest sense: it symbolizes not just the exaltation after Christ's death, but rather the eternal rule which the preexistent divine Son has exercised from all eternity."[94] It is not the divination of the human king now an *elohim* for Hebrews, it is the revelation of the Son who was *elohim/YHWH* forever and ever into the past. The revelation of the Son in his ascension/exaltation is also a revelation of aspects that he bore forever albeit now are crowned upon him in Davidic/Adamic humanity.

Hebrews sees the activity of the Son as the basis for the distinction of Son over and above other humans. The Son's behavior has been noble and righteous ἠγάπησας δικαιοσύνην καὶ ἐμίσησας ἀνομίαν (Heb 1:9a). First, this echoes what was expected of kings and rulers in the OT. Second, it identifies the king as one who images the character of God. His entire reign is characterized as that of uprightness: καὶ ἡ ῥάβδος τῆς εὐθύτητος ῥάβδος τῆς βασιλείας σου (Heb 1:8b).

It is the behavior of the Son that leads to his anointing. He has loved

---

dered' Uriel (1 En. 82:7), who is the 'leader' (79:6) over the 'host of heaven' (82:7), which consists of a myriad of levels of 'leaders,' 'captains,' and 'divisions' (82:11–20). The specific levels of the heavenly hierarchy are important, but the fundamental point of these heavenly descriptions is to remind the hearer that God is the ultimate authority of the cosmos as well as the source and foundation of all other authority structures." Bryan also points to the hierarchy amongst the angels in 1 En. 20:1–7; 2 En. 19:3–5; T. Levi 3:5; T. Ab. 1:4; 13:10; 3 Bar. 11:4, 6–8[G]; T. Sol. 2:4–7; 7:7; LAE 3:2; 13:2 (Bryan, "A Revised Cosmic Hierarchy," 67). Cf. also Kuhn, "The Angelology of the Non-Canonical Jewish Apocalypses," *JBL* 67 (1948): 221–30; "In general, the schemes of rank [among angels] are based upon considerations of relative power or authority" (224).

92 Cf. also Bruce, "Messiah's throne, in fact, *is* God's throne" (*Hebrews*, 60n.91).
93 Eskola, *Messiah and the Throne*, 205.
94 Meier, "Symmetry," 514–515. See also Gert Steyn, "The *Vorlage* of Psalm 45:6–7 (44:7–8) in Hebrews 1:8–9," *HvTSt* 60.3 (2004): 1093–1094.

righteousness and hated wickedness (ἠγάπησας δικαιοσύνην καὶ ἐμίσησας ἀνομίαν, 1:9a).[95] The phrase is ἡ ῥάβδος τῆς εὐθύτητος for a 'just rule.'[96] As vice-regent, the Davidic king was to reflect the character of YHWH. The same way that YHWH reigns is the same way that the king is to reign.[97] His anointing is based upon this character he has demonstrated in obedience to God. Διὰ τοῦτο identifies the reason the Son is anointed. Like David before him, the Son has demonstrated a dependance upon God in obedience to him. The filial relationship between them is demonstrated in the way the Son behaves. God is his God (ὁ θεὸς ὁ θεός σου, 1:9b) and the Son has displayed that in reflecting the Father's character.

More clearly than previously in Hebrews, we can see how for our author sonship functions in two clear ways. First, addressed as God and bearing the attributes of God, our author sees the Son as God yet distinct from the Father. The Son does not bear these attributes merely by virtue of exaltation or as language figurative of his vice-regency. The author of Hebrews stretches the origins of the OT language of the king's representation of the divine as

---

95 The practice of righteousness in the rule of the Messiah is an important theme. This goes back to the Davidic Kingship. David administers justice and righteousness to the people (2 Sam 8:15: מִשְׁפָּט וּצְדָקָה; LXX κρίμα καὶ δικαιοσύνην). In 1 Kgs 10:9, Solomon is to execute the same (מִשְׁפָּט וּצְדָקָה; κρίμα ἐν δικαιοσύνῃ). The Queen of Sheba acknowledges this righteousness and justice in 2 Chr 9:8 and 1 Kgs 10:9. In Ps 72:1–2, as the royal son/king (לְבֶן־מֶלֶךְ?) Solomon asks YHWH to have YHWH's justice and righteousness that he might judge in righteousness and justice. In Isa 9:7 and 16:5 the throne of the seed of David is established on justice and righteousness. Jer 23:5 and 33:15, the seed of David executes justice and righteousness in the land. The hope of salvation is that YHWH will fill Zion with justice and righteousness and this flows from the exalted YHWH (Isa 33:5), although David or his heir is not mentioned. In Pss. Sol. 17:19–20 no one in Jerusalem is fit because no one among them "practiced righteousness or justice; from their leader to the commonest of the people…the king was a criminal and the judge disobedient; (and) the people sinners." In v. 22 David is given strength to "destroy the unrighteous rulers" driving them out "in wisdom and righteousness." In vv. 26–27 the Davidic King leads in righteousness and does not tolerate unrighteousness. The Messiah is a righteous king, and in his days there shall be no unrighteousness among the people, v. 32. He is anointed in his righteousness (v. 32) and empowered as one dependent upon the Lord (v. 34). The consistent theme is righteousness characterizes the kingdom of the Messiah; there is no toleration of sin, unrighteousness, or wickedness. He knows who are 'the children of their God' (v. 27) and leads a sanctified people (v. 43). An interesting contrast between Pss. Sol. 17 and the portrait of the Messiah in Hebrews is the theme of weakness. For Pss. Sol. the Messiah "will not weaken in his days (relying) upon his God…the blessing of the Lord will be with him in strength, and he will not weaken" (17:37–38). But for Hebrews, Jesus has weakness and in it he relies on God only later to receive exaltation to glory.

96 Ellingworth, *Hebrews*, 123. Wis 10:11 uses σκῆπτρα βασιλείας to describe the righteous man who is lifted up out of the dungeon and made to run, almost certainly an echo to Joseph (cf. 10:15–20, esp. v. 18 which mentions the Red Sea).

97 YHWH rules in truth and righteousness in his judgments. Job 37:32; Pss 89:14 (righteousness and justice are the foundation of his throne); 96:13; 97:2; 98:9; 103:6; Isa 5:16; Jer 9:24; Tob 3:2.

adopted son to indicate to his readers the great fulfillment of the promises of God have come as God has spoken in 'a Son.' He is qualitatively a Son and has been from all eternity past. In the distinction between YHWH and creation—the Son is part of the being of YHWH, identified with all the attributes that only YHWH bears. It is insufficient to our author's language to argue that the exaltation somehow bridges the distinction our author wishes to maintain. Exaltation is not deification. God the Father has spoken 'in Son' revealing the true nature of God as Father and Son.

### Heb 1:10–12—The Unchanging One: Sonship and the Use Ps 102:25–27

The use of Ps 102:25–27 [LXX 101:26–28[98]] is connected as another quotation from God the Father spoken to the Son with a simple καί. One noticeable difference between LXX and Hebrews is ἀλλάξεις[99] in LXX becomes ἑλίξεις[100] followed with the addition of ὡς ἱμάτιον[101] in Hebrews. In MT, we read כִּלְבוּשׁ תַּחֲלִיפֵם וְיַחֲלֹפוּ and the Hiphael of חָלַף has the sense of to change or substitute. The LXX translation ὡσεὶ περιβόλαιον ἀλλάξεις αὐτούς (LXX Ps 101:27b) follows closely MT כִּלְבוּשׁ תַּחֲלִיפֵם (Ps 102:27) but neither have the added ὡς ἱμάτιον as Hebrews does (1:12). Ἀλλάσσω means to change or exchange and can be used of property, wages, and phsyical objects like garments.[102] Hebrews use of ἑλίξεις αὐτούς, ὡς ἱμάτιον (1:12) does not refer to changing them but their wearing out so that they are rolled up as if to be put away. Either Hebrews is

---

98 There is some difficulty with respect to variants among LXX manuscripts as well. We do not wish to simply ignore them, but these difficulties are beyond the scope of our concerns here. On these difficulties, see Steyn, *Quest for the Assumed LXX Vorlage*, 105–108.

99 This reading itself is not cut and dried, as there are several textual variants here in LXX. Steyn notes the variant "which reads ἑλίξεις by B' R (*ellixis*) L" (He εἰληξης) A" (1219 ἱλιξις, 55 εἰλειξεις). The witnesses that support the variant reading all belong to the Lower Egyptian text tradition" (*Quest for the Assumed LXX Vorlage*, 106).

100 There are some textual variants here in Hebrews but ἑλίξεις is found in P46, ℵ2, A, B, D2, *et al;* while ἀλλάξεις is found in ℵ*, D*, a few early translations, and Athanasius. The textual variant is hardly a major problem, and it is best to assume that ἑλίξεις is original to Hebrews while some manuscripts change it back to ἀλλάξεις in order to conform Hebrews to LXX it was quoting.

101 Again there is a textual variant here in the manuscripts; P46, ℵ2, A, B, D (which omits καί), and 1739 all favor this reading, while D2, Ψ, *Byz* K L P, and a large number of unicials favor the ommision of ὡς ἱμάτιον. Again, it is more likely that ὡς ἱμάτιον, is original, having a slightly earlier manuscript to support it and other manuscripts may have dropped ὡς ἱμάτιον to conform to LXX.

102 "ἀλλάσσω," BDAG, 45. Cf. for example LXX Gen 31:7; 35:2; 41:14; Exod 13:13; Lev 27:10, 27, 33; 2 Sam 12:20; 1 Kgs 5:28; 21:25; 2 Kgs 5:5, 23; Ezra 6:11, 12 [where it is used to describe changing one's word]; Neh 9:26; 1 Macc 1:49; 3 Macc 1:29; Pss 101:27; 105:20; Wis 4:11; 12:10; Sir 7:18; 33:21; Isa 24:5; 40:31; 41:1; Jer 2:11; 13:23; 52:33. In this list the word can be used for changing God's law (e.g., Isa 24:5) or changing the glory of God for idols (e.g., Ps 105:20; Jer 2:11).

following a textual variant,[103] or perhaps he is purposefully using ἑλίσσω to allude to the eschatological end of the heavens and earth.[104] For example, Isa 34:4 καὶ ἑλιγήσεται ὁ οὐρανὸς ὡς βιβλίον, καὶ πάντα τὰ ἄστρα πεσεῖται ὡς φύλλα ἐξ ἀμπέλου καὶ ὡς πίπτει φύλλα ἀπὸ συκῆς,[105] or as later in Rev 6:14 καὶ ὁ οὐρανὸς ἀπεχωρίσθη ὡς βιβλίον ἑλισσόμενον καὶ πᾶν ὄρος καὶ νῆσος ἐκ τῶν τόπων αὐτῶν ἐκινήθησαν.[106]

This use of ἑλίσσω would be more in line with Hebrews' later discussion of the heavens being shaken and coming to an end in 12:26–27.[107] The strong contrast that Hebrews draws attention to is between the changeable, that which can be shaken, and that which is unchangeable. The future kingdom, which is the saints' heritage, cannot be shaken. This is grounded in God's unchanging, unshakeable character. This takes us back to Hebrews 1:10–12 where our author is contrasting the created, which is perishable, changeable, and expires, with God's nature, which is indestructible, unchangeable, and unending. God is entirely unlike his creation. There is no aging, becoming weary,[108] growing old, wearing out, or changing of his nature in God.

Since Hebrews uses the text of the Psalm as something the Father says to the Son so that the Son is addressed as κύριε, it is important to note a key difference between MT and LXX. MT v. 26 has no vocative 'Lord' (either יהוה or אדני), whereas LXX has an addition of the vocative address κύριε.[109] MT in v. 25 (Eng. v. 24) does have a vocative as an appeal to God: אֵלִי. It is also clear throughout the context of the Psalm that the speaker is addressing YHWH. It is our contention that there is no major theological difference between the absence or presence of the vocative. The Psalm is talking about יהוה/κύριος. As we follow down through the immediate context of the Psalm, the Psalmist expects a future people to come and worship the LORD (וְעַם נִבְרָא יְהַלֶּל־יָהּ).[110] YHWH is the one who dwells in heaven and from on high he looks down hearing the cries of his people (vv.20–21; Eng. 19–20):

---

103 See footnotes above and Steyn, *Quest for the Assumed LXX Vorlage*, 106.

104 Kenneth Schenck however writes, "we cannot conclude definitively that the author used it with special significance" (*Cosmology and Eschatology in Hebrews*, SNTSMS 143 (Cambridge University Press, 2007), 124).

105 ἑλίσσω is found only in Job 18:8 and Isa 34:4 in LXX; ἐξελίσσω is used in 3 Kingdoms 7:45.

106 Heb 1:12 and Rev 6:14 are the only places ἑλίσσω is found in NT.

107 Cf. Ellingworth, *Hebrews*, 126, "This quotation [Ps 101/102] and the quotation in Hg. 2:6 in Heb 12:26 help to explain one another."

108 Isa 40:28b,c "The LORD is the everlasting God, the Creator of the ends of the earth. He does not faint or grow weary;" this is contrasted with youth in v.30. In Ps 121:4, he does not slumber or sleep, which indicates he does not become tired or weary.

109 Ellingworth, *Hebrews*, 126, notes that κύριε is omitted in LXX א.

110 The Hebrew יָהּ is a shortened form of יהוה; LXX: λαὸς ὁ κτιζόμενος αἰνέσει τὸν κύριον. One cannot help but speculate that perhaps the author of Hebrews is reading this Psalm es-

כִּי־הִשְׁקִיף מִמְּרוֹם קָדְשׁוֹ יְהוָה מִשָּׁמַיִם ׀ אֶל־אֶרֶץ הִבִּיט׃
לִשְׁמֹעַ אֶנְקַת אָסִיר לְפַתֵּחַ בְּנֵי תְמוּתָה׃

ὅτι ἐξέκυψεν ἐξ ὕψους ἁγίου αὐτοῦ, κύριος ἐξ οὐρανοῦ ἐπὶ τὴν γῆν ἐπέβλεψεν τοῦ ἀκοῦσαι τὸν στεναγμὸν τῶν πεπεδημένων, τοῦ λῦσαι τοὺς υἱοὺς τῶν τεθανατωμένων,

By the time the text goes on to speak of the creator (יָסַדְתָּ), the second person and 'your hands' (יָדֶיךָ) refers to the activity of YHWH. MT is clear it is YHWH who laid the foundation of the earth (MT 102:26 לְפָנִים הָאָרֶץ יָסַדְתָּ וּמַעֲשֵׂה יָדֶיךָ שָׁמָיִם), and the vocative κύριε in LXX reinforces this. The OT commonly describes YHWH as the one who has founded the creation, earth, or heaven and earth.[111] On the basis of the Biblical text, it is not too strong to say that YHWH alone founds these things.[112] As Herbert Bateman points out, "the original focus of Ps 102:25–27 was upon Yahweh's immutability and permanent rule over the affairs of earth; even during the second temple period, whenever Ps 102 is quoted, it maintains direct reference to Yahweh (cf. 11QPsa and *Lad. Jac.* 7:35)."[113] Hebrews attributes this divine activity to the Son.[114]

---

chatologically. Now in the Son, YHWH has indeed created a new people as the Son is crowned with glory and is bring many sons to glory. While it is impossible to be certain, it would follow the general pattern in the use of the OT in the NT that NT writers were not oblivious to the context as they quoted and indeed often took it into consideration as motivation for the quotations. Consider MT/LXX vv. 20–21 that the LORD looked down from heaven and saw his people in captivity and those sons of death (בְּנֵי תְמוּתָה; τοῦ λῦσαι τοὺς υἱοὺς τῶν τεθανατωμένων). This sounds strikingly like Hebrews 2:15b καὶ ἀπαλλάξῃ τούτους, ὅσοι φόβῳ θανάτου διὰ παντὸς τοῦ ζῆν ἔνοχοι ἦσαν δουλείας.

111 Cf. MT and LXX Job 38:4; Ps 89:11 [LXX 88:12]; 104:5 [LXX 103:5]; Isa 48:13; 51:13, 16; Zech 12:1. In Amos 9:6 (MT) YHWH builds the upper chambers of heaven, founds his vault on the earth, and pours the seas (LXX reads slightly different). It is noteworthy that Ps 8 says the same thing about YHWH/God: LXX 8:4 ὅτι ὄψομαι τοὺς οὐρανούς, ἔργα τῶν δακτύλων σου, σελήνην καὶ ἀστέρας, ἃ σὺ ἐθεμελίωσας. NETS translates the emphatic σὺ ἐθεμελίωσας as "you alone founded." MT 8:4 (Eng. 8:3): כִּי־אֶרְאֶה שָׁמֶיךָ מַעֲשֵׂי אֶצְבְּעֹתֶיךָ יָרֵחַ וְכוֹכָבִים אֲשֶׁר כּוֹנָנְתָּה Ps 8 goes on to describe the uniqueness and exalted status of humanity under God's creation. The Psalm sees YHWH as the unique creator even with humanity's being exalted in a crowning of glory and honor. There remains a Creator/creature distinction.

112 Cf. Isa 37:16, where the Lord alone is enthroned above the cherubim because he [alone?] made the heavens and earth; 44:24 לְבַדִּי to referring to creation cf. also 42:5; 45:12.

113 Bateman, "Psalm 45:6–7 and Its Christological Contributions to Hebrews," 9. The evidence continues to support Bauckham's judgment that in Hebrews 1 the Son shares in the divine identity of YHWH; cf. Richard Bauckham "Monotheism and the Christology of Hebrews 1," 167–185. James Thompson highlights the changeableness of angels verses the unchangeable Son who "does not belong to the created order" ("Structure and Purpose of the Catena in Heb 1:5–13," *CBQ* 38.3 (1976): 358 [cf. context 357–359]).

114 Harold Attridge writes, "In construing the addressee of the psalm as the Son, Hebrews relocates the affirmations once made about Yahweh's majesty" ("The Psalms in Hebrews," in *The Psalms in the New Testament*, ed. Steve Moyise and Maarten J.J. Menken [T&T Clark, 2004], 202).

The creation may perish, but YHWH remains. The Creator-creature distinction is in stark contrast here.[115] So while LXX adds the vocative κύριε, it is entirely consistent with the context. κύριε refers to YHWH and not a messianic or Davidic 'lord.' "[T]he author, since he has identified Jesus as divine, feels free to cite a psalm about Yahweh and apply it to Jesus Christ as well."[116] In the use of Ps 102 [LXX 101] in Hebrews, the author maintains the Creator-creature distinction and applies it to distinguish the Son from the angels.[117] "This quote also works to highlight the enduring nature of the Son.... With this address to the Son, God makes clear that his Son possess an eternal nature."[118]

When LXX says that ἀπεκρίθη αὐτῷ ἐν ὁδῷ ἰσχύος αὐτοῦ (LXX 101:24), the human speaker answers that he will listen to YHWH tell of the fewness of his days,[119] but it shifts back that unlike the human speaker YHWH does not have this fewness or a cutting short of days. Indeed, ἐν γενεᾷ γενεῶν τὰ ἔτη σου (LXX

---

115 This is true in both MT and LXX. Some have suggested that Ps 102 was read Messianically, and there is the possibility of two figures being identified. This does not seem to be evident in the text itself.
116 Schreiner, *Hebrews*, 74.
117 Crispin Fletcher-Louis has taken issue with the notion of a Creator-creation distinction (*Christological Origins: The Emerging Consensus and Beyond*, vol. 1 of *Jesus Monotheism* [Cascade Books, 2015], 293–316). Andrew Chester agues "the boundary between angels on the one hand, and what may obviously seem to be personifications or representations of God, on the other hand, appears fluid in places at least; so too does the boundary between heaven and earth, the divine realm and the human realm" (*Messiah and Exaltation*, WUNT 207 [Mohr Siebeck, 2007], 51). He suggests "there is further evidence of at least some overlap between divine attributes and angelic figures" (58). However, whether or not Hebrews is aware of these traditions and other Second Temple Jewish texts, Hebrews does maintain a strong Creator-creature distinction and is arguing against any kind of conflation, overlap, or sliding scale in share of divine and creaturely attributes. Paul Rainbow defends the concept with careful documentation concluding, "the strong Jewish emphasis on the creatorship of God, even with respect to the gods, affirms his qualitative uniqueness and absolute transcendence. The Jewish God is the sole member belonging to the class of deity in the strict sense" ("Monotheism and Christology," 58). He states similar things regarding the Creator and creation distinction in Paul Rainbow, "Jewish Monotheism as the Matrix for New Testament Christology: A Review Article," *NovT* 33.1 (1991), 83–84. "Jewish writers were careful to maintain the conceptual gulf between God and the world" (86).
118 Amy Peeler, *You Are My Son: The Family of God in the Epistle to the Hebrews*, LNTS 486 (Bloomsbury T&T Clark, 2014), 57.
119 Radu Gheorghita argues that the pronoun αὐτῷ is "neither the psalmist, nor God." It "can be, however, the κύριος of vv. 13–22, the Davidic king who shall build up Zion and appear in glory" (*The Role of the Seputuagint in Hebrews*, 61). Gheorghita is following Stephen Moyter "The Psalm Quotations of Hebrews 1: A Hermeneutic-Free Zone?" *TynBul* 50.1 (1999): 19–21. The trouble with this view is that Gheorghita and Moyter do not give any evidence for why we should understand LXX Ps 101:26ff to refer to a Davidic king. What evidence in LXX or elsewhere do we have that the Davidic king founded the earth and his hands established the heavens? Appeals to the overlap between YHWH's and David's ruler are spurious. Referring to the divine qualities and adoption of the Davidic king are stretched. They are certainly true elsewhere but nowhere is David co-equal or even vicreroy at creation.

101:25) and τὰ ἔτη σου οὐκ ἐκλείψουσιν (LXX 101:27).[120] This is because YHWH establishes the creation while he, himself, is eternal (LXX 101:26–28).[121] The contrast maintained in LXX, and echoed by Hebrews, is between the perishable creation and the imperishable God.[122] The creation will change and come to ruinous destruction but YHWH remains (LXX Ps101:27a σὺ δὲ διαμένεις) and he is the same (LXX Ps 101:28a σὺ δὲ ὁ αὐτὸς εἶ). Hebrews also ascribes the act of creation and the quality of imperishability to the Son. Hebrews takes those things which are properly described only in reference to YHWH and distinguish him from everything else and identifies the Son as having this same capacity. The identity of YHWH is revealed as Father and Son.

It is possible that Hebrews reads Ps 102:23–24 (MT vv.24–25; LXX 101:23–24) messianically so that it became a prophecy of crucifixion.[123] But if it was

---

120  Ellingworth suggests a possible reference to Christ's enthronement in LXX 101:14 with σὺ ἀναστὰς (*Hebrews*, 125). This is certainly possible that Hebrews read LXX in this way—or at least saw the verse as fulfilled Christologically. If true, it would further strengthen the possibility of Hebrews understanding divine attributes/identity as something that Christ possess. We should notice that the "you" of v. 14 is clearly "YHWH/κυριος" in v. 13: σὺ δέ, κύριε, εἰς τὸν αἰῶνα μένεις, καὶ τὸ μνημόσυνόν σου εἰς γενεὰν καὶ γενεάν. This verse is similar to the eternality of the Lord in LXX 101:25 ἐν γενεᾷ γενεῶν τὰ ἔτη σου. There is also a possible parallel between Hebrews 13:8 Ἰησοῦς Χριστὸς ἐχθὲς καὶ σήμερον ὁ αὐτὸς καὶ εἰς τοὺς αἰῶνας and Ps 101:28 [LXX] σὺ δὲ ὁ αὐτὸς εἶ, καὶ τὰ ἔτη σου οὐκ ἐκλείψουσιν.

121  Bauckham (rightly in our estimation) notes that when it comes to creation YHWH is consistently portrayed as the sole Creator (*Jesus and the God of Israel: God Crucified and Other Studies on the New Testament's Christology of Divine Identity* (Eerdmans, 2008), 9–10, 154–159). While God's Wisdom and Word can be portrayed as participating in creating "None of the principal angels or exalted patriarchs is portrayed as participating in the work of creation, and it has hardly ever been suggested that they are" (*Jesus and the God of Israel*, 159). Bauckham lists the following texts in defense of YHWH as the sole Creator: Isa 40:26, 28; 42:5; 44:24; 45:12, 18; 48:13; 51:16; Neh 9:6; Hos 13:4 LXX; 2 Macc 1:24; Sir 43:33; Bel 5; Jub 12:3–5; Sib. Or. 3:20–35; 8:375–376; Sib. Or. frg. 1:5–6; frg. 3; frg. 5; 2 En. 47:3–4; 66:4; Apoc. Ab. 7:10; Ps-Sophocles; Jos. Asen. 12:1–2; T. Job 2:4 (*Jesus and the God of Israel*, 9n.8). See also N.T. Wright's summation of Jewish monotheism, especially YHWH as sole creator and distinct from creation *New Testament and the People of God* (Fortress, 1992), 248–259, esp. 248–250, 254. Rainbow "Monotheism and Christology" 57–58.

122  Cf. Steyn: "He [the Son] was present and active as an agent at the creation and his nature is stable, immutable and permanent, whilst the angels are transitory and the whole of creation temporary" (*Quest for the Assumed LXX Vorlage*, 102). On the Creator-creature distinction in Judaism and NT, see also Bauckham *Jesus and the God of Israel*, 154–155. With respect to 1:7–12 Victor (Sung Yul) Rhee, writes "the entire passage speaks of the unchangeable nature of the Son in a literal sense, which includes his preexistent stage ("Christology in Hebrews 1:5–14: The Three Stages of Christ's Existence," *JETS* 59.4 [2016]: 723).

123  The Hebrew vocative אֵלִי highlights the cry to God but is lacking in LXX. It is a plea for deliverance—it seems to be deliverance from death and being cut off. LXX simply has μὴ ἀναγάγῃς με ἐν ἡμίσει ἡμερῶν μου. Attridge cites B.W. Bacon, "Heb 1,10–12 and the Septuagint Rendering of Ps 102,23," *ZNW* 3 [1902] 280–285 as seeing a Messianic reference in LXX but Attridge dismisses this as "unlikely" (*Hebrews*, 60n.122). Also, Bruce, *Hebrews*, 62n.102. C.F.D. Moule argues for a Messianic understanding (*The Birth of the New Testament* [London, 1962], 78–79). L.D. Hurst follows this Messianic reading ("The Christology of Hebrews 1 and 2," 160–

read as a prophecy of the crucifixion, it would be reading the text as the Messiah speaking to God. The Messiah would return to address YHWH as the unchanging one in v. 26ff. We believe, however, this interpretation would go too far and there is little in the background and history of interpretation to support it.[124] It is these latter verses that Hebrews places now in the context of an address from God to the Son, thereby identifying the Son as YHWH and unchanging.[125] If our author is reading the text messianically, it would seem that he sees v.25b as beginning the address of the Father to the Son/Messiah, as Robert Hall has argued.[126] He proposes that the beginning of the Psalm would have been read as a cry of Jesus' affliction. Then the shift to the second person in LXX 101:25b (ἐν γενεᾷ γενεῶν τὰ ἔτη σου) begins the degree where God sings a response to Jesus.[127]

Hall sees this as "God answering him [the Messiah] by decreeing him Creator whose years do not fail. God by fiat as naturally [sic] invests Jesus with the creative activity, eternity, and godhead of the Son as he enthrones him at his right hand or appoints him a priest forever."[128] But this misses the point precisely: it is not that Jesus is now invested with these attributes in contrast to creation, it is that Jesus has always had these attributes. The Son was there in the beginning already and laid the foundation. His years have no end—not by virtue of resurrection but by virtue of who he is and was. Perhaps instead of getting muddled in "pre-existence" terminology, we should focus on the personal categories of the Son. He is described as a personal being, 'the Son,' with existence before creation and with this existence being on par

---

161). Radu Gheorghita, *The Role of the Seputuagint in Hebrews,* 61–62; Moyter, "The Psalm Quotations of Hebrews 1," 19–21.

124 *Contra* Lane, *Hebrews 1–8,* 30. Ellingworth notes that the psalm does not seem to have been interpreted Messianically in rabbinic circles (*Hebrews,* 126).

125 James Thompson, "it is probably that the author has selected this particular text because he found there what he wanted to accent: the contrast between changeable creation and immutable creator" ("Catena in Heb 1:5–13," 359–360). See also Matthew Bates' discussion *The Birth of the Trinity Jesus, God, and Spirit in the New Testament and Early Christian Interpretations of the Old Testament* (Oxford University Press, 2015), where he discusses prosopological exegesis and the address between the Father and the Son. While we do not agree with Bates at every point, he is right to highlight the address of the Father to the Son. This certainly identifies a "personal agency" on the part of the Son (172). The speaker of the Psalm is seen to be God who addresses the Son directly (172–173). Bates is correct: "contra, the much later Arius, he [the Son] is not a creature" (174).

126 Robert G. Hall, "Pre-existence, Naming, and Investiture in the *Similitudes of Enoch* and in Hebrews," *Religion and Theology* 18 (2011): 329. We also find Compton's argument for a messianic exegesis of the Psalm unconvincing for the same reasons (*Psalm 110 and the Logic of Hebrews,* JSNTS 537 (T&T Clark, 2015), 31–36).

127 Hall, "Pre-existence," 330.

128 Ibid.

with all the descriptions of YHWH. Hebrews clearly is identifying that YHWH (God) is Father and Son in persons.

Rather than overestimating how often the writer of Hebrews sees a Messianic voice or Father-Messiah interaction in the text, it probably remains best to keep to a minimalist reading that highlights the contrast between the Creator who remains eternal and the human being whose life can be cut dreadfully short. The Son is thus identified on the Creator side of the Creator-creature distinction present in Jewish monotheism.[129] But in Hebrews' use of Ps 102[101] Christ does not take up the human half of the divine-human interaction but the divine role of one who lasts forever. Hebrews does not appeal to the Psalm to see the Son as the voice of the one crying out for deliverance (a theme that reoccurs later, Heb 5:7) but instead as the Lord the unchanging one. Even if Hebrews was influenced by the early verses of the Psalm, the actual verses used of the Father speaking to the Son have the Father calling out to the Son as an address of one sharing in all the divine attributes.

The OT describes humans as those who waste away like a garment (Job 13:28; Isa. 50:9). In Sir 14:17 flesh becomes old like a garment, and references the curse of death of the Old Covenant (LXX πᾶσα σὰρξ ὡς ἱμάτιον παλαιοῦται· ἡ γὰρ διαθήκη ἀπ' αἰῶνος Θανάτῳ ἀποθανῇ). In Isaiah it is the creation that will wear out like a garment (Isa. 51:6, 8). In fact, in Ps 103 creation is like YHWH's garment (LXX Ps 103:1–2, 6).[130] Hebrews has already quoted LXX Ps 103:4 in verse 7, quoting Ps 101 LXX further connects these two passages via the theme of the garment. Indeed it may be, in part, the verbal link from the context that leads Hebrews to place the two verses in his argument.

Heb 1:8–12 takes the contrast beyond angels as ministers and the Son as exalted and identifies angels as created, that which is changing and temporary, while the Son is unchanging.[131] He is eternal not merely by virtue of exaltation to the Davidic throne that lasts forever into the future.[132] He is eternal by virtue of being distinct from and prior to all creation, including the angels.

---

129 John P. Meier, "Symmetry and Theology," 518. The focus of the quotation is protology and the Son's timelessness. The sweep of creation's history in contrast to the Son's eternality is the focus rather than "concern with apocalyptic events of the end-time" (Meier, "Symmetry and Theology," 519).

130 See also Isa 40:22.

131 Peeler writes, "Because the angels are associated with creation, this verse sharply contrasts him [the Son] with their temporality" *You Are My Son*, 57. Kiwoong Son, *Zion Symbolism in Hebrews: Hebrews 12:18–24 as a Hermeneutical Key to the Epistle* (Paternoster, 2005), 120–123.

132 In 2 Bar. 21:4–11, angels are around the divine throne but there is a clear distinction in authority but also angels as created vs. YHWH as the creator. He is the true Immortal One. Even within a so-called 'heavenly council' there is a Creator-creature distinction. The "Mighty One" (YHWH) has created all creation and has "established the fountain of light with yourself" (2 Bar. 54:13), wisdom is under this divine throne.

G.B. Caird and L.D. Hurst have resisted the notion of pre-existence in this passage.[133] While the concern is valid that "pre-existence" is often referenced but is an ill-defined concept, we would contend that Hebrews shows the Son not simply to be pre-existent but rather to have all the eternal qualities that YHWH himself has that sets him apart from the creation that wears out.[134]

The use of κύριος in Heb 1:10 follows the pattern of the early Christian interpretation, where texts in the OT that refer to YHWH in MT and are translated as κύριος in LXX are taken to apply to Christ. This use of κύριος in the NT shows that while the early church saw Jesus as the Messiah and therefore a king or Davidic lord and perhaps by implication (in some limited sense) a counter-imperial claim,[135] these did not exhaust the scope of what they meant in referring to Jesus the Messiah's Lordship. When they identify Christ as Lord, they see this an identification with YHWH of the OT, albeit now with a distinction of Father-God-Lord and the Son-Lord. The Son is identified as more than a mere agent of YHWH in creating but is identified as YHWH the one who created. The Son being identified as κύριος/YHWH is more than him being the authority of another or acting on behalf of YHWH as a vice-regent would.

The revelation of the Messiah who ushers in or inaugurated the

---

133 Caird, "Son by Appointment," and Hurst "The Christology of Hebrews 1 and 2."

134 We believe this is the strength then of Bauckham's proposal for the terminology of "divine identity." So, for example, in Deutero-Isaiah, part of the polemic against the gods is that YHWH alone creates and declares the end from the beginning. Or for example in 2 Bar. 21 where the angles are in the heavenly council (vv. 4–6), we find with respect to God "For you alone this exists so that you may create at once all that you want" (v. 7). In 1 En. 83:3, God alone created all things.

135 Jörg Rüpke suggests that Clement of Rome made an association between Jesus' title of high priest and the role of the Roman emperor ("Starting Sacrifice: Flavian Inovations in the Concept of Priesthood and Their Reflections in the Treatise 'To The Hebrews,'" in *Hebrews in Contexts*, ed. Gabriella Gelardini and Harold W. Attridge [Brill, 2016], 125). Jason Whitlark has recently argued that Hebrews was written to a primarily Gentile audience to encourage them to resist imperial Rome and its recent triumph in Emperor Flavian (*Resisting Empire: Rethinking the Purpose of the Letter to 'the Hebrews'* [T&T Clark, 2014]). He also offers an interesting proposal on how Hebrews 13:20–21 would have been heard in a Roman Imperial context: Jason Whitlark, "The God of Peace and His Victorious King: Hebrews 13:20–21 in Its Roman Imperial Context," in *Hebrews in Contexts*, ed. by Gabriella Gelardini and Harold W. Attridge (Brill, 2016), 155–178. On an anti-imperial use of χαρακτήρ in Heb 1:3 see Steven Muir, "The Anti-Imperial Rhetoric of Hebrews 1.3: χαρακτήρ as a 'Double-Edge Sword,'" in *A Cloud of Witnesses: The Theology of Hebrews in its Ancient Contexts*, ed. by Richard Bauckham, Daniel Driver, Trevor Hart, and Nathan MacDonald (T&T Clark, 2008), 170–186. For implications on how "We have no lasting city" in Hebrews 13:14 might have been understood against a Roman background see Harry O. Maier "'For Here We Have No Lasting City" (Heb 13:14a): Flavian Iconography, Roman Imperial Sacrificial Iconography, and the Epistle to the Hebrews," in *Hebrews in Contexts*, ed. Gabriella Gelardini and Harold W. Attridge (Brill, 2016), 133–154. See also some representative comments in Koester, *Hebrews*, 78–79, 185, 187, 239, 292–293 particularly for contrasts between Christ in Hebrews and Caesar Augustus.

eschatological promises of God is also a revelation of YHWH himself. He has enacted his great promises. He has spoken 'in Son' who is like him in all ways (eternal, radiating divine glory, possessing divine attributes, etc.).[136] This revelation goes beyond a mere appropriation of Second Temple wisdom or Logos categories.[137] These could be personified and even agents of YHWH in his acts of creation and providence.[138] The very category of sonship is being reshaped, now defined by God's revelation and the ascension of the Son himself into heaven. The ascension of the Son is the enthronement of YHWH himself as Father installs eternal Son.

While we cannot minimize the eschatological conception of Christ's role in Hebrews and its significance, Heb 1 sees Christ's superior Sonship as more encompassing than just eschatological. "It is clear that Christ's superiority to the angels is not simply an eschatological matter. Christ, the creator of earth and heaven, is the creator of the angelic realm."[139] YHWH will change the heavens and earth,[140] but YHWH is immutable, he does not change, fade, or wear down with the passage of time. As Kenneth Schenck puts it "Hebrews does not seem to know of any time when Christ cannot be considered a son (or even *the* Son) in some sense."[141]

---

[136] In 1 En. 62:15–16 with the exaltation and glory of the Son of Man the righteous elect ones "shall wear garments of glory. These garments of yours shall become the garments of life from the Lord of the Spirits. Neither shall your garments wear out, nor your glory come to an end before the Lord of the Spirits." This is a glorification of the saints grounded on the Son of Man's ascent to the throne. While in Heb 2 the Son is 'crowned with glory and honor', part of the focus on Heb 1 is that the exalted one has possessed and shared this glory prior to the exaltation (even into eternity past) while it is now visibly manifest now in ascension.

[137] Peeler, *You Are My Son*, 26; Barnard, *Mysticism*, 152–154

[138] Hurtado, *One God, One Lord: Early Christian Devotion and Ancient Jewish Monotheism*, Second Edition. (T&T Clark, 1998), 41–50; Bauckham, *Jesus and the God of Israel*, 16–17.

[139] Attridge, *Hebrews*, 60. Cf. Meier, "'Symmetry and Theology," 517–518." Steyn comments, "Both [Ps 45 (44):7–8 and Ps 102 (101):26–28] deal with the theme of the *eternal reign* of the Son who is addressed as '*God*' (if θεός is taken as a vocative in this instance), thereby contributing to the author's argument that the Son is superior to the angels. In contrast to the transitory nature of the angels, stands the eternal throne and the never-ending kingdom of the Son" (emphasis original. *Quest for the Assumed LXX Vorlage*, 82–83).

[140] See later in Hebrews where the writer picks up this motif in Hebrews 12:26–8, although Hag 2:21 (Eng. 2:6) is the immediate verse quoted. We should consider the possibility that this motif serves as book ends. YHWH, who is eternal, brings the eschatological kingdom which cannot be shaken. Of course, those who enter into the glory of the Son via transformation into the new glorified humanity ('sons of glory') themselves will not be shaken. But it is YHWH himself who is the true everlasting one. Anything that enables his people to endure and not pass away is the product of the gracious gift effected by the work of the Son to bring in (achieve/accomplish; indeed, merit might not be too strong a word) the eschatological kingdom. Recently, Philip Church has shown how Heb 1:10–12 with the use of Ps 102 [LXX101] connects to the theme and motif of the renewal of creation ("Hebrews 1:10–12 and the Renewal of the Cosmos," *TynBul* 64.1 [2013]: esp. 280–286). See also Bates, *Birth of the Trinity*, 171–174.

[141] Kenneth Schenck, "Keeping His Appointment: Creation and Enthronement in He-

## Conclusion

The purpose of this chapter has been to give a detailed exegesis of Heb 1:6–14, in order to explore the conception of S/sonship in Hebrews. There is no doubt that in Hebrews 1 the Son is the exalted one. He is the Davidic Messiah who has been exalted to the right hand of God. This entails entering into the divine glory of YHWH.

Nevertheless, this announcement of the royal Son in exaltation/ascension is also a revelation of God himself. God has spoken 'in Son.' Previously, we argued that this Son radiated the glory of God prior to exaltation. He was involved in creation itself and continues to uphold creation. Hebrews displays the Son as pre-existent prior to the fulfillment of his Messianic vocation. In fact, with the use of Ps 102, Hebrews places the Son on the 'divine' side of the Creator-creature distinction. He is worshipped as God and declared "God" with the use of Ps 45.

This eternal Sonship sets the Son apart from exalted angels. His glory is not angelomorphic nor is there a scale of being upon which the Son and angels share attributes but perhaps with differing intensity. The Son is Son, which angels are not. The Son is uncreated, which angels are not. The Son is worshipped, while angels are not. These features unique to the Son are neither angelic nor Adamic-human. In this respect, we have borrowed Bauckham's characterization of 'divine identity'.

We have consistently shown that Heb 1 demonstrates a "high Christology." While the use of 2 Sam 7:14; Pss 2; 45; 110:1 conveys Messianic themes, these themes do not detract from a Christology where the Son is truly God, albeit a Son distinguished from his Father. In this respect, Hebrews is not unconcerned with making statements that clearly have certain ontological implications. Thus, the Son is not angelic, nor is he merely Messianic or human. Rather the Son is a revelation of God and who God is. It is worth noting that the primary defense of God speaking 'in Son' are examples of God speaking *to* the Son. He spoke to his Son at the installation of the Son's heavenly enthronement. This revelation of who God is has been made known in the working of the Son and an eschatological climax where the Son is installed on the throne of God in heaven through a royal exaltation, ascension into heaven itself. God is identified as Father *and* Son, as one person speaks to another, and they speak revelation into creation. Thus, it is the fulfillment of the royal Messianic features through ascension into heaven that God declares the

---

brews," *JSNT* 66 (1997): 95.

eschatological Davidic son is in fact his unique eternal Son. He is the Messianic son who in his ascension is revealed as the true Son of God the Father.

As we will see in the next chapter, the author of Hebrews does not have any problem seeing Jesus in terms of humanity and as one bearing the human vocation in order to become the eschatological man. However, in the same way, he does not see Jesus, the Son, as merely an exalted figure. The exaltation of the Son, confessed by the early church, has radical implications for the identity of God himself and thus their worship. The high Christology comes to be known through the activity of God revealing himself. This revelation occurs when the Father calls to the Son as Son and ushers him up into the divine glory and installs him on the very throne of the Most High God.

## Chapter 4

# The Adamic Vocation of Sonship in Hebrews 2

### Introduction

Having looked at Hebrews 1 and the Christology therein, we turn our attention to Hebrews 2. As our thesis unfolds, we will demonstrate that the Epistle to the Hebrews contains an implicit Second Adam Christology that serves to advance its argumentation concerning the work of Christ to bring humanity to eschatological glory. The flow of the argument in Hebrews 1 and 2 goes beyond a simple "Hebrews 1: Jesus is divine" and "Hebrews 2: Jesus is human." Both chapters are tied together with the thread of the exaltation of Christ, although this chapter focuses on the work of Christ that leads to his being crowned in kingly and human honor and glory. Jesus—the eternal Son—is both the Davidic son and a new Adam, the first of the eschatological 'new man' who will in turn bring many sons to glory through his work. In tracing this argument, our first task in this chapter will be to define a Second Adam Christology. Then, we will move into a more detailed exegesis on Hebrews 2 by first paying special attention to the use of Ps 8 with an eye towards the background behind it. This Second Adam Christology (a) illuminates Hebrews' conception of Christ as ἀρχηγός, (b) is the manner in which Hebrews understands Christ's representation for the σπέρματος Ἀβραάμ, and thus (c) undergirds the significance of the humanity and superiority of Christ in the epistle. Christ stands in solidarity with his people both in his earthly work but now too in his heavenly work on their behalf. Finally, we return to the theme of ascension and show how chapter two is not isolated from this important theme.

## Second Adam Christology: A Working Definition

Second Adam Christology is usually a designation used to refer to Paul's discussion in Rom 5 and 1 Cor 15, where he draws direct correlations and contrasts between the role of Adam and the role of Christ in their respective acts of disobedience and obedience or their roles as head of humanity and the new humanity. In our discussion of the text of Heb 2, we will use this same designation to show how Hebrews conceptualizes Christ in light of Ps 8 and Christ's relationship to the people of God. In using this designation, we are making no statements about the relationship between Paul and Hebrews but assume that both are drawing from the background of the role of Adam in Second Temple Judaism. In order to briefly establish a working definition, we shall turn to two NT scholars whose work in Christology has strongly influenced the direction of the study of Christology for this generation of NT scholarship.

In 1977, C.F.D. Moule, in his work *The Origin of Christology*, brought one of the early challenges to the notion that a 'high' Christology of later Christian writers must have evolved from an original low Christology.[1] His work sketched how Christ was conceived by the early church not only as an individual, but personal experience was attached to Christ so that early Christians considered the corporate implications of Christ. He seeks to go beyond Oscar Cullmann's Christology via titles to look at the corporate experience of Christ.[2] Of particular interest early in his work is his discussion on the relationship between the title Son of Man, its background in Dan 7, and the corporate dimension of this exalted figure.

Moule writes concerning the Danielic Son of Man:

> It is often pointed out that the Danielic vision constitutes a meditation on the supremacy of Adam over the rest of nature in the Genesis creation stories. Perhaps it is even more apposite to recall that Ps 8 expresses surprise and admiration that God has exalted frail man to this position of supremacy. All in all, then, the human figure of Dan. 7 is highly appropriate to the ministry of Jesus. On this showing, it is not a *title* for Jesus, but a symbol of vocation to be utterly loyal, even to death, in the confidence of ultimate vindication in the heavenly court. Jesus is alluding to 'the (well known, Danielic) Son of Man' in this vein. As Dr. Morna Hooker has shown, this

---

[1] C.F.D. Moule, *The Origin of Christology* (Cambridge University Press, 1977), 6.
[2] Ibid., 8. Cf. Oscar Cullmann, *The Christology of the New Testament*, trans. S.C. Guthrie and C.A.M Hall (SCM, 1959).

makes good sense of the Marcan sayings about the Son of Man's authority: it is the authority (whether in heaven or on earth) of true Israel, and so, of authentic Man, obedient through thick and thin, to God's design.[3]

Later in his work, building on this discussion, Moule remarks that contained in Hebrews 2 *"in nuce* is an Adam-Christology."[4] He marks this by the conception of vindication in glory and corporate representation of God's people. Jesus, after his temptation and agony, has now "by his flesh...made the transition from earth to heaven."[5] While Jesus is exalted in heaven, he has gone ahead to enable the believer to make such a transition to exaltation.[6] Jesus "is identified as the one who alone fulfilled the glorious destiny designed, according to Ps 8, for mankind as a whole."[7] His crowning is the crowning to which mankind was destined. His fulfillment guarantees a corporate fulfillment upon believers.

James D.G. Dunn's *Christology in the Making* has also been influential in the study of the Christology of the early church. He too suggests that Heb 2 contains something akin to a "Adam-Christology." He characterizes this concept as "[t]he divine program for man which broke down with Adam has been run through again in Jesus—this time successfully."[8] Similar to Moule, Dunn highlights the concepts of solidarity with humanity, recapitulation of Adam's task, and progenitor of a new humanity.[9] Dunn concludes, "The way in which Jesus becomes last Adam is by following the path taken by the first Adam."[10]

For both Moule and Dunn, what constitutes a Second Adam Christology is representation and recapitulation with fulfillment. Adam represented humanity and in a Second Adam Christology, Christ represents a new humanity. There is recapitulation but also eschatological advancement: humanity carried to glory and destiny. The Second Adam not only repeats but completes or fulfills the activity of the first Adam therefore setting things right. He is

---

3 Moule, *Origin*, 14. Emphasis original. Seyoon Kim reaches a similar conclusion: "With 'the Son of Man'" then Jesus intended to reveal himself to be the divine figure who was the inclusive representative (or the head) of the eschatological people of God, i.e. the Son of God who was the head of the sons of God...he intended to reveal his mission in terms of gathering or, as it were, creating, God's eschatological people who, represented or embodied in him as their head, would be elevated (or made) God's sons" (*The Son of Man as the Son of God* [Eerdmans, 1985], 36).
4 Moule, *Origin*, 101.
5 Ibid.
6 Ibid.
7 Ibid.
8 James D.G. Dunn, *Christology in the Making*, 2nd ed. (SCM, 1989) 110.
9 Ibid., 110–111.
10 Ibid., 113.

rewarded with dominion and regal sovereignty over creation in an Adamic-like capacity.[11]

Second Temple Judaism considered the fulfillment of the eschaton to be patterned after Adam and the Garden of Eden.[12] Thus, the restoration of the saints and their vindication entailed an endowment or crowning with the glory of Adam.[13] "Adam Christology" taps into the notion of God's destiny of glory for humanity and Davidic royal ideology. These are motifs of exalted sonship and vice-regency under YHWH. For Hebrews, the activity of Christ as an act of obedience leads to a crowning of his humanity with glory and honor. It is the movement from humiliation to exaltation. In Hebrews, this entails an ascent in resurrected state from earth to heaven. This is much like the movement of Second Temple Judaism where the righteous are lowly and suffering in this age but exalted in the age to come at the judgment.

Second Adam theology takes its cue from Second Temple Judaism's beliefs in the age to come that provided part of the seed bed for early Christian theology regarding the inaugurated eschaton and work of the Messiah. This flourishes in various ways in early Christianity, including Paul's articulation, early gospel writer's reflections on Jesus' Son of Man tradition, and early Christian inaugurated eschatology. It is our proposal that this 'Adam Christology' explains Hebrews' reflection on the work of Christ and his exaltation in Heb 2:5–18. We propose that Hebrews has a "Second Adam Christology" that explains in part how Hebrews conceptualizes not only the work of Christ as obedient to death followed by exaltation and appointment to high priesthood. Furthermore, It is the backdrop for the representative nature of Christ's humanity where he is the apex of true humanity who is also corporately connected to believers who will share in this true humanity of the eschaton.

## Ps 8 in the Argument of Heb 1 and 2

The argument of Heb 2:5–18 flows directly out of the argument of the

---

11 More recently, Kenneth Schenck has used narrative substructure analysis to reach the same conclusion on Heb 2. He shows that Hebrews' argument is dependent on the notion that God's original intent was to crown humanity with glory and honor and this original destiny has been fulfilled in Christ (*Cosmology and Eschatology in Hebrews* (Cambridge University Press, 2007), 51–59).

12 See discussion below in its relationship to understanding Heb 2. On Second Adam Christology and Second Temple Judaism see N.T. Wright, *The Climax of the Covenant* (Fortress, 1992), 20–23; *The New Testament and the People of God*, 262–268; David M. Moffitt, *Atonement and the Logic of Resurrection* (Brill 2011), 81–118, 133–142. Seyyoon Kim briefly discusses the evidence in *The Origins of Paul's Gospel* (Mohr Siebeck, 1981; Reprinted: Wipf and Stock, 2007), 186–193.

13 See discussion below.

exaltation and identity of the Son in Heb 1. Continuing with a mention of angels, the writer begins with a concern over the dominion and rulership of the eschatological age. Angels were not designated 'Son' to sit at God's right hand; however, more positively, angels did mediate the Law, which proved reliable in its promised condemnation for trespasses (Heb 2:2). Now, however, angels are not those who have dominion and authority over the age to come (Heb 2:5). Angels may have been mediators in the age that is passing away, but no longer in the coming age. The theme of inheritance and subjection harkens back to 1:5; when the Son is brought as τὸν πρωτότοκον εἰς τὴν οἰκουμένην, the angels are placed in subjection to him. They are under him, and they offer worship to the superior one (1:6).

The phrase τὴν οἰκουμένην τὴν μέλλουσαν (2:5) refers to the eschatological "age to come" (1:2 ἐπ' ἐσχάτου τῶν ἡμερῶν). It is rooted in the Second Temple distinction between the present age and the age to come,[14] which grounds the thought pattern of Hebrews. This inbreaking of the eschaton drives the argument of Hebrews in significant ways, as we have previously highlighted (Heb 1:2–3, 6; 2:5).[15]

Speculation on the rulership of angels over human realms and nations is quite common in Second Temple Judaism.[16] As Hebrews focuses on the glorification of the Son through his ascension, the Son is unlike angels both in his identity (chapter 1) and in his movement from humiliation to exaltation for redemption (chapter 2). The Son, while eternal, is in his presentation either lower (on earth) or higher than angels (glorified in heaven), but he is never on par with them. The Son, not angels, is a mediator and a priest.[17] The drama of redemption hinges below or above them but is not focused on them.

---

14  Some of the Second Temple references that divide history into two ages include 4 Ezra 7:50, 113, 8:1; 2 Bar. 15:7.

15  See C.K. Barrett's classic essay "The Eschatology of the Epistle to the Hebrews," in *Background of the New Testament*, ed. W.D. Davis (Westminster John Knox, 1964), 363–393; Scott Mackie, *Eschatology and Exhortation in the Epistle to the Hebrews* (Mohr Siebeck, 2007); Kenneth Schenck, *Cosmology and Eschatology in Hebrews*, 78–111; Moffitt, *Atonement and the Logic of Resurrection*, 45–144; Matthew Easter, *Faith and Faithfulness* (Cambridge University Press, 2014), 78–131.

16  We have discussed some aspects of this speculation concerning angels in the previous chapter. See J. Daryl Charles, "The Angels, Sonship and Birthright in the Letter to Hebrews," *JETS* 33/2 (1990): 171–178; Harold Kuhn, "The Angelology of the Non-Canonical Jewish Apocalypses," *JBL* 67 (1948): 217–232; Randall Gleason, "Angels and the Eschatology of Heb 1–2," *NTS* 49 (2003): 101–107; Gert Steyn, "Hebrews' Angelology in Light of Early Jewish Apocalyptic Imagery," *Journal of Early Christian History* 1.1 (2011): 143–164; L.T. Stuckenbruck, "Angels of the Nations," in *Dictionary of New Testament Background*, ed. Craig A. Evans and Stanley Porter (Intervarsity, 2000), 29–31; Marie Isaacs, *Sacred Space: An Approach to the Theology of the Epistle to the Hebrews* (Sheffield Academic, 1992), 177.

17  Contra Second Temple Jewish works like Apoc. Ab. 10:3–4; Songs of the Sabbath Sacrifice; T. Levi (esp. 5:7); Tob 12:15; etc.

The destiny of creation for redemption and the eschatological end of glory is largely unconcerned with angels and angelology. Hebrews is set within the broad features in apocalyptic literature in Second Temple Judaism; at the same time, the Son is exalted above the kinds of angelic exaltation we see in Second Temple texts. Ascension in Hebrews concerns human destiny drawing near into God's presence and it is not a movement from corporal earth into a non-corporeal realm either angelic realm or a Platonic conception.[18]

The author of Hebrews does not merely lay out that Christ is divine in chapter one, only to turn and pursue a different tact in chapter two that the son is human.[19] While these two aspects of deity and humanity of the Son summarize key points, the author of Hebrews is driven by the eschatology of his argument. Thus, chapters one and two serve a unified argument. Even in chapter one, there is the crucial movement of Christ in making purification for sins and sitting down at the right hand of the Father. The argument points to both the divinity of 'Son,'[20] his role as the Davidic Messiah crowned in

---

[18] Those more in favor of Philo's influence include: Lala Kalyan Kumar Dey, *The Intermediary World and Patterns of Perfection in Philo and Hebrews* (Scholars, 1975); James W. Thompson, *The Beginnings of Christian Philosophy: The Epistle to the Hebrews* (Catholic Bible Association of America, 1982). A more mediating position is taken by Ronald Williamson, *Philo and the Epistle to the Hebrews* (Brill, 1970), who was at least against direct influence not necessarily denying similarities. Later Robert Williamson ("The Background of the Epistle to the Hebrews," *ExpTim* 87 (1976): 232–237) sees the possibility of Merkavah mysticism serving as a background. Cf. Kenneth Schenck, "Philo and the Epistle to the Hebrews: Ronald Williamson's Study after Thirty Years," *The Studia Philonica Annual* 14 (2002): 112–135. L.D. Hurst is more critical of the Platonic background: *The Epistle to the Hebrews: Its Background and Thought* (Cambridge, 1990), 7–42. Robert Thurston ("Philo and the Epistle to the Hebrews" *EvQ* 58.2 (Apr.–June 1986): 133–143) sees Philonic elements correlating to aspects of the Christology of Hebrews. Jody Barnard (*The Mysticism of Hebrews: Exploring the Role of Jewish Apocalyptic Mysticism in the Epistle to the Hebrews*, WUNT 2/331 (Mohr Siebeck, 2012, 11–17, 95–104) argues against a Philonic background in favor of Jewish mysticism and apocalyptic. Kiwoong Son (*Zion Symbolism in Hebrews: Hebrews 12:18–24 as a Hermeneutical Key to the Epistle* [Paternoster, 2005], 74, 177–184) argues, because of the spatial and temporal elements, Sinai and Zion symbolism fits within Jewish apocalyptic speculation on Zion not Platonic metaphysical dualism. On Philo's cosmology, see Robert McIver, "Cosmology as a Key to the Thought-World of Philo of Alexandria," *Andrews University Seminary Studies* 26.3 (1988): 267–279. On Hebrews' cosmology, see also Edward Adams, "The Cosmology of Hebrews," in *The Epistle to the Hebrews and Christian Theology*, ed. by Richard Bauckham, et al. (Eerdmans, 2009), 122–139; Jon Laansma, "Hidden Stories in Hebrews: Cosmology and Theology," in *A Cloud of Witnesses: The Theology of Hebrews in its Ancient Contexts*, ed. by Richard Bauckham, et al. (T&T Clark, 2008), 9–18; "The Cosmology of Hebrews," in *Cosmology and New Testament Theology*, ed. by Jonathan Pennington and Sean M. McDonough (T&T Clark, 2008), 123–143.

[19] Moffitt, *Atonement and the Logic of Resurrection*, 52n.9, 58.

[20] Contra Caird "Son by Appointment," in *The New Testament Age: Essays in Honor of Bo Reicke Volume 1* (Mercer University Press, 1984); Hurst "The Christology of Hebrews 1 and 2," in *The Glory of Christ in the New Testament: Studies in Christology in Memory of George Bradford Caird*, ed. L.D. Hurst and N.T. Wright (Clarendon, 1987); Compton, *Psalm 110 and the Logic of Hebrews* (T&T Clark, 2015) who argues features like Ps 8, exaltation, and the Son's humanity

Messianic reign, and the representational role he has for humanity.[21]

The theme that runs through Heb 1–2 is the exaltation of the Son as he ascends into heaven and is invited to sit at the Father's right hand (LXX Ps 109:1 in Heb 1:13). Hebrews, like other writers in the early church, sees Pss 2, 8, and 110 as fulfilled by Jesus as he is resurrected and ascends into heaven. He is the Messiah given dominion over all things, installed in Zion/heaven, and sitting within the divine glory of God. The Son, in his work and in his own embodiment, ushers the creation through the eschatological transition by himself going from being one lower than the angels in humanity to becoming the heir via ascension into exaltation. Having established in chapter one that Jesus is called 'Son' and 'begotten' as an installment and public proclamation of accession to the throne (1:5), we see Jesus the Son invited to sit at God's own right hand (1:13), which has never happened to angels. He is the heir, τὸν πρωτότοκον (1:6), given a royal installation which makes him the first of the new creation. It is in this humanity (Ps 8; Heb 2:5–8) that the Son is invited into the presence of God. It is this taking on humanity and becoming the first of the new creation that is important to the argument of Heb 2.

Part of our larger argument in this thesis is that sonship operates on two "levels," or with two key "poles," even within the one series of events of death, resurrection, and ascension. The Son is on the one hand divine, radiating the divine glory from before exaltation-ascension, but on the other hand radiates this glory outward as the true Messiah and ultimate fulfillment of humanity's destiny. This latter aspect (being crowned and endowed with glory and honor) is something that the Son does for those he represents as the head of the new humanity. The reigning Son serves as YHWH's viceregent installed on the throne with glory and honor, but also as representative of the people of God. This concept is indebted to the notion of Davidic king where the king is representational of God's people, which is itself reminiscent of the king being raised up as the ideal man, both the leader of God's people and also the true inheritor of the divine reign of God.

## Hebrews 2:6–8

Having laid out the context up to Heb 2:6, we turn to quotation of Ps 8:5–7 (Eng. 4–6) from LXX in Heb 2:6–8.[22] In the psalm, the 'royal human' is identified

---

as reasons not finding any elements of divine Christology in Heb 1, esp. in the use of Ps 102.
  21 Michael Kibbe offers similar thoughts to the relationship of Hebrews 1–2 (*Godly Fear or Ungodly Failure? Hebrews 12 and the Sinai Theophany* [de Gruyter, 2016], 152–156).
  22 For a discussion of LXX, see Wenceslaus Mkeni Urassa, *Psalm 8 and Its Christological Re-Interpretations in the New Testament Context: An Inter-Contextual Study in Biblical Herme-*

as reigning over that which God has made. A key difference is between the Hebrew מֵאֱלֹהִים and LXX παρ' ἀγγέλους.[23] While the writer of Hebrews uses LXX more regularly in his quotation of the Hebrew Scriptures, LXX serves the argument of Hebrews in two ways. First, Hebrews is concerned with showing the superiority of the Son over the angels. While Jewish angelology often placed angels over man and as governor of the nations,[24] Hebrews needs to make clear that in the eschaton man will rule over angels and so Jesus as Son and king of the age to come now rules over the angels. While the angels may have played an important mediating role in the Old Covenant (Heb 2:2, cf. also Acts 7:53; Gal. 3:19), this role is surpassed by the exaltation of Jesus, the Son. Humanity is that which inherits the eschatological glory which is fulfillment of Adam's destiny.[25]

Second, the argument capitalizes on the temporal aspect of the phrase βραχύ τι παρ' ἀγγέλους (Heb 2:7; LXX Ps 8:6). In the Greek βραχύ has a decidedly temporal point while the Hebrew מְעַט has no temporality.[26] The author highlights this in 2:9a τὸν δὲ βραχύ τι παρ' ἀγγέλους ἠλαττωμένον βλέπομεν Ἰησοῦν. Hebrews exploits that βραχύς can have a temporal and a quantitative sense. Without minimizing the quantitative sense of being lower than the angels in rank, he capitalizes on the temporal aspect as well, that this lower station was only for a time. His double meaning, combining both temporal and quantitative senses in his interpretation, is a point that can be made from his use of LXX but not the Hebrew. Hebrews focuses on the Son becoming a little

---

neutics (Peter Lang, 1998), 67–72.

23 Simon Kistemaker notes that Aquila, Symmachus, and Theodotian have θεόν (*Psalm Citations in the Epistle to the Hebrews* [Wipf and Stock, 2010], 30).

24 LXX Deut 32:8–9. Harold Kuhn "The Angelology of the Non-Canonical Jewish Apocalypses," *JBL* 67 (1948): 217–232; Stuckenbruck, "Angels of the Nations," 29–31.

25 The glorification of humanity in some Second Temple texts is "angelomorphic," but Hebrews goes to great pains to avoid such a conclusion concerning the Son's glorification. For a basic overview of the evidence, see Andrew Chester, *Messiah and Exaltation* (Mohr Siebeck, 2007), 58–80, 363–381 (although Chester does not follow Fletcher-Louis on some of the latter's larger points about Adamic worship, 62); Crispin Fletcher-Louis, "Some Reflections on Angelomorphic Humanity Texts among the Dead Sea Scrolls," *Dead Sea Discoveries* 7.3 (Brill, 2000): 292–312; *All the Glory of Adam: Liturgical Anthropology in the Dead Sea Scrolls* (Brill, 2002), 88–251; Steyn, "Addressing an Angelomorphic Christological Myth in Hebrews?" *HvTSt* 59.4 (2003): 1107–1128; and "Hebrews' Angelology in Light of Early Jewish Apocalyptic Imagery," 143–164. Himmelfarb notes that one common feature of apocalyptic literature and heavenly ascents is that "ascent often means displacement of angels, for with surprising frequency human beings come to stand closer than the angels to God" (*Ascent to Heaven in Jewish and Christian Apocalypses* [Oxford University Press, 1993], 68). Himmelfarb discusses human transformation in ascents in terms of investiture (36–46), and then in terms of the transformation of the righteous dead (47–71). One conclusion of Himmelfarb is that "the boundaries between human beings and angles are not very clear" (70). Unlike in the Second Temple Texts surveyed by Himmelfarb, this is not true for Hebrews.

26 BDAG, 147. For a temporal use of βραχύ τι see LXX Isa 57:17.

lower than angels for a period of time so that in his exaltation, when the declaration of Son is announced in his ascension, he also in humanity is being crowned with glory.

Third, the psalm describes 'man' as being crowned with glory and honor δόξῃ καὶ τιμῇ ἐστεφάνωσας αὐτόν (LXX 8:6; Heb 2:7). In the psalm, "verses 4–6 proclaim the glory of humankind as the apex of God's creation."[27] Hebrews takes Ps 8 as eschatologically fulfilled when Jesus is glorified and granted the inheritance. Thus, the psalm is read not as something concerning the original creation of man *per se*, but that which has now happened in the 'subjection of the world to come' (2:5).[28] Angels, for all their authority, glory, and gathering under the divine throne, are not the apex of God's creation and are not the true reigning beings in the age to come. Thus, Hebrews sees the destiny of the creation brought to climax as the Son dies and then is granted exaltation to reign over all things.

The Son in his humanity becomes the exalted man who is crowned with glory and ushered up into heaven to receive the eschatological inheritance. He has been raised up and appointed Messianic King (1:5), he has been anointed because of his righteous behavior (1:9 ἔχρισέν σε ὁ θεὸς ὁ θεός σου, clearly Messianic connotations), and he has been seated at the right hand of God (1:13). This is the language of royal installment. Now, Jesus is seen as having glory and honor as a result of what has occurred to him (cf. 1:3b–4), not merely as the result of the aspects of his eternality (1:3a). Just as in Adam, humanity was appointed over all the creation, the Son is the one who God ἔθηκεν κληρονόμον πάντων (1:2b).

Hebrews has already been concerned to articulate the exaltation of the Son and his inheritance of all things. Amy Peeler has pointed out, however, that being heir and having all things under his feet has already been alluded to in Hebrews, specifically we see the concepts in 1:2 with κληρονόμον πάντων and Heb 1:13's use of LXX Ps 109:1 ὑποπόδιον τῶν ποδῶν σου.[29] The sovereignty of humanity over all things "precisely describes the inheritance God grants to his Son," to which we might add Hebrews also shows the inheritance being granted to all the "sons of glory" the Son also redeems.[30] Reading Pss 8 and 109:1 (MT 110:1) together is common in the evidence we have from the early

---

27  Leonard Maré, "The Messianic Interpretation of Psalm 8:4–6 in Hebrews 2:6–9: Part 1," in *Psalms and Hebrews Studies in Reception*, ed. Dirk J. Human and Gert Jacobus Steyn (T&T Clark, 2010), 102.

28  Rabbinic literature would later take the questions of Ps 8:4 "what is man that you are mindful of him…?" as something which the angels asked the Lord. See the discussion below.

29  Peeler, *You Are My Son: The Family of God in the Epistle to the Hebrews*, 69. See her helpful chart.

30  Ibid.

church. Schenck argues this "suggests that early Christianity always understood Ps 8 to apply to Christ as the Last Adam, the one who fulfills the true destiny of humanity, a destiny they were never able to fulfill on their own. Once the psalm is applied to Christ in this way, it can be related to Ps 110:1 of Christ's exalted state."[31] Ps 8 is read and applied concerning the eschatological destiny of humanity, which has now been entered into by Christ as the ἀρχηγός. Thus, for several reasons, in Hebrews' use of Ps 8, the concept of a Second Adam is at work in the mind of the writer.[32]

First, the background of Ps 8 references the role of humanity in creation and reflects the theology of Gen 1:26–28.[33] The psalm reflects the concept of vice-regency common to the ANE where humanity is installed under the high King but in exaltation over all the creation. The vice-sovereign or viceroy exercises dominion on God's behalf over everything that God has made. While Ps 8:7a [Eng. v. 6] does not use the same words for dominion as in Gen 1:26–28, it uses the hiphil form of מָשַׁל, which means not only to give someone dominion but also to make them a ruler or lord.[34] In Ps 8:7b [Eng. v. 6], the notion of God putting all under man's feet is the idea that God has set, ordered, or determined that this man should have dominion. It entails imagery

---

31 Kenneth Schenck, *Cosmology and Eschatology in Hebrews*, 58.

32 Moffitt, *Atonement and Logic of the Resurrection*, 133–144; Peterson, *Hebrews and Perfection An Examination of the Concept of Perfection in the 'Epistle to the Hebrews'* (Cambridge: Cambridge University Press, 1982), 52, 56–57, 63; Urassa, *Psalm 8*, 203; Bruce, *Hebrews*, 72; Dunn, *Christology*, 110; Schenck, *Cosmology and Eschatology*, 58; Frank J. Matera, *New Testament Christology* (Westminster John Knox, 1999), 192; Hubert James Keener, *A Canonical Exegesis of the Eighth Psalm: YHWH's Maintenance of the Created Order through Divine Reversal* (Eisenbrauns, 2013), 181; R.G. Hamerton-Kelly, *Pre-Existence, Wisdom, and the Son of Man* (Wipf and Stock, 2000), 247–248; etc. See also for backgrounds on Adam and Second Adam: J.R. Levison, *Portraits of Adam in Early Judaism: From Sirach to 2 Baruch* (Sheffield Academic, 1988); Felipe de Jesús Legarreta-Castillo, *The Figure of Adam in Romans 5 and 1 Corinthians 15: The New Creation and Its Ethical and Social Reconfiguration* (Fortress, 2014), 33–117.

33 See for example Edward Mason Curtis, "Man as the Image of God in Genesis in Light of Ancient Near Eastern Parallels" (PhD diss., University of Pennsylvania, 1984), 332. "Ps 8 does not use the term 'image of God,' but it is generally recognized that there is a relationship between Gen 1 and Ps 8. There is clearly a thematic relationship between the texts in that both emphasize man's pre-eminent position in creation and describe man's dominion as if man were a king." Curtis however does not see any direct literary dependence. Aage Bentzen (*King and Messiah*, ed. G.W. Anderson [Basil Blackwell, 1970], 41–44) links kingship to the 'first man' via Gen 1 and Ps 8.

34 *CHALOT*, 219. See also Daniel 11:39 "He shall deal with the strongest fortresses with the help of a foreign god. Those who acknowledge him he shall load with honor. He shall make them rulers over many and shall divide the land for a price." Kenneth Matthews (*Genesis 1–11:26*, 169) draws connections between Gen 1:26 and Ps 8. Ian Hart ("Genesis 1:1–2:3," 320) notes, "This psalm does not mention the image of God; but it does confirm that Israel applied royal ideology to mankind in general: an important plank in the argument for a functional interpretation of the image." He quotes P. Humpert that the psalm is "an actual commentary on Genesis 1:26ff."

of a vice regency receiving his installment to royalty and sovereignty by the authority of the high sovereign.[35]

On Gen 1:26–28, it is readily acknowledged by most Bible scholars today that the concept of man's creation in the image of God establishes his functional sonship, which entails regal imagery as a vice-regent under God but over God's created world.[36] Humanity is established in kingship, albeit a delegated kingship, vice-regency, under the authority of the highest King.[37] In this, the early chapters of Genesis fit strongly within an ANE setting.[38] In Second Temple Judaism, Adam could be recognized as a highly exalted ruling figure, even a viceroy.[39] Philo brings this out in *On the Creation*, 148:

---

35  It would be interesting to explore the implication for the notion of a covenant and suzerain-vassal treaties, but this is beyond our scope. It may be possible to suggest that covenant is not far from the author's thought in Ps 8, given the ordering and setting of a viceroy in place.

36  Stephen Herring, *Divine Substitution: Humanity as the Manifestation of Deity in the Hebrew Bible and the Ancient Near East* (Vandenhoeck & Ruprecht, 2013), esp. 108–127. "The king's image in ancient Mesopotamia...functioned as an extension of presence much like a son" (22). Catherine Leigh Beckerleg, "The 'Image of God in Eden: the Creation of Mankind in Genesis 2:5–3:24 in Light of *mīs pî pīt pî* and *wpt-r* Rituals of Mesopotamia and Ancient Egypt" (Ph.D. diss, Harvard University, 2009), 161–193; Edward Mason Curtis, "Man as the Image of God in Genesis in Light of Ancient Near Eastern Parallels," 330–358; D.J.A. Clines, "The Image of God," *TynBul* 19 (1968): 53–103; Phylliss A. Bird, "'Male and Female He Created Them': Gen 1:27b in the Context of the Priestly Account of Creation," *HTR* 74.2 (1981): 129–159; Kenneth A. Matthews, *Genesis 1–11:26* (B&H, 1996), 170; J. Richard Middleton, *The Liberating Image: the Imago Dei in Genesis 1* (Brazos, 2005); Dexter Callender, Jr., *Adam in Myth and History: Ancient Israelite Perspectives on the Primal Human* (Eisenbrauns, 2000), 21–38; Sigmund Mowinckel, *The Psalms in Israel's Worship*, trans. D.R. Ap-Thomas (Eerdmans, 2004), 50–61; Ian Hart, "Genesis 1:1–2:3 As Prologue to the Book of Genesis," *TynBul* 46.2 (1995): 317–324; Peter Gentry and Stephen Wellum, *Kingdom Through Covenant: A Biblical-Theological Understanding of the Covenant* (Crossway, 2012), 184–202, esp. 200: "The relationship between humans and God is best captures by the term sonship." G.K. Beale, *Temple and the Church's Mission: A Biblical Theology of the Dwelling Place of God* (Intervarsity, 2004), 81–96; *A New Testament Biblical Theology* (Baker, 2011), 29–58, 401–406; Gerhard von Rad, *Old Testament Theology* (Prince, 1965), 1:144–147; J.D. Kirk, *A Man Attested by God: The Human Jesus in the Synoptic Gospels* (Eerdmans, 2016), 48–59; Meredith Kline, *Kingdom Prologue: Genesis Foundations for a Covenantal Worldview* (Two Age, 2000), 42–46.

37  C. Wynand Retieff ("A Messianic Reading of Psalm 8," *OTE* 27.3 [2014]: 992–1008), also draws out this vice-regency and representative aspects in Ps 8 against the background of royal ideology. Cf. John Goldingay, *Old Testament Theology Volume 1: Israel's Gospel* (Intervarsity, 2003), 110–114; Stephen Dempster, *Dominion and Dynasty: A Theology of the Hebrew Bible* (Intervarsity, 2003), 57–62.

38  J. Richard Middleton, *The Liberating Image*, 93–145; Clines, "Image of God," 80–85; Hart, "Genesis 1:1–2:3," 318–319. See also J.R. Levison, *Portraits of Adam*.

39  Darrell Bock, *Blasphemy and Exaltation in Judaism: The Charge Against Jesus in Mark 14:53–65* (Baker, 1998), 115–119. See also Alexander Toepel, "Adamic Traditions on Early Christian and Rabbinic Literature," in *New Perspectives on 2 Enoch: No Longer Slavonic Only*, ed. Andrei A. Orlov and Gabriele Boccaccini (Brill, 2012), 323. In some cases, Adam is seen as exalted and the faithful ones who keep the Law will find exaltation and glory like him. In other cases, Adam is the transgressor of the Law *par excellence* and therefore the faithful Israel is not to be like him since he lost his glorious inheritance. In this respect, there is not a single "theology of

And with great beauty Moses has attributed the giving of names to the different animals to the first created man, for it is a work of wisdom and indicative of royal authority, and man was full of intuitive wisdom and self-taught, having been created by the grace of God, and, moreover, was a king. And it is proper for a ruler to give names to each of his subjects. And, as was very natural, the power of domination was excessive in that first-created man (ὑπερβάλλουσα δ' ὡς εἰκὸς δύναμις ἀρχῆς ἦν περὶ τὸν πρῶτον ἐκεῖνον ἄνθρωπον), whom God formed with great care and thought worthy of the second rank in the creation, making him his own viceroy (ὁ θεὸς ἠξίου δευτερείων, ὕπαρχον μὲν αὐτοῦ) and the ruler of all other creatures.[40]

From the Hebrew Bible, the instructions to the first humans are to subdue the earth and rule it is kingship language. Likewise, in the original context of Ps 8, YHWH has created and established אֱנוֹשׁ / בֶּן־אָדָם to rule and have dominion with all creation under humanity (MT Ps 8:7). This dominion includes sheep, oxen, beasts of the field, the birds of heaven, fish, and things in the sea (MT Ps 8:8–9), just as in Gen 1:26–27.

The first two key words in the Gen 1:26–28 are image (צֶלֶם) and likeness (דְמוּת). The two terms should be seen as near synonyms not as describing two different aspects of humanity.[41] The word צֶלֶם is often used to denote a statue or an idol (1 Sam 6:5; Num 33:52; 2 Kgs 11:18). Idols would stand as proxies for the divine being they represented. In the ANE, kings were considered to be 'sons' of the gods so that they were considered visible manifestations of the rule of the God.[42] Earthly kings themselves would erect images of their regal power in lands they had conquered as extensions of their power and to solidify claims to their dominion.[43]

---

Adam." Writers of various texts can employ the figure of Adam in a very utilitarian fashion to make the point they need.

40 *The Works of Philo: Complete and Unabridged New Updated Version*, trans. by C.D. Yonge (Henderickson, 1993), 21; *Philo, Works of: Greek Text with Morphology* (The Norwegian Philo Concordance Project); also cited in Darrell Bock, *Blasphemy and Exaltation*, 115.

41 It is beyond our scope to review the long history of interpretation. Suffice it to say, in earlier centuries it was frequent to assign different aspects to humanity based on the different words. The use of image and likeness in Gen 5:1, 3; 9:6 leads most scholars to assume they are near synonyms. See for example Hart, "Genesis 1:1–2:3," 321; Eugene Merrill, "Covenant and Kingdom: Genesis 1–3 as Foundation for Biblical Theology," *Criswell Theological Review* 1.2 (1987): 299. Bruce Waltke (*Genesis: A Commentary*, [Zondervan, 2001], 66n.51) disagrees that image and likeness are synonymous.

42 Gordon Wenham, *Genesis 1–15* (Word, 1997), 30; Phyllis Bird, "Male and Female He Created Them," 137–144; J. Richard Middleton, *The Liberating Image*, 93–145; Tryggve N.D. Mettinger, *King and Messiah: The Civil and Sacral Legitimation of the Israelite King* (Gleerup, 1976), 259–268.

43 Gerhard Von Rad, *Genesis*, trans. John H. Marks (Westminster, 1961), 60. In discussing

The fact that man's function is royal becomes even more clear when we recognize that man is to *subdue* (כבשׁ) the earth and have *dominion* (רדה) over creation. These are regal words that are reminiscent of what conquering nations or kings would do over enemy territories. For example, Leviticus gives instructions on how a slave should be ruled over (רדה; Lev 25:46, 53; 26:17). רדה can also describe the dominion of a king (1 Kgs 5:4), or of a nation over a region (Isa 14:6). In language that surely echoes a creation mandate, when Israel enters the promise land, she is given the charge to subdue it (Num 32:22, 29; Josh 18:1). This charge will entail not only bringing nature under the Israelites' realm, but also the nations presently occupying the land.[44] The point for us is that humanity is given this charge in its creation as part of a regal function. As Dempster states, "humanity is functioning as a type of priest-king, mediating God to the world and the world to God."[45] This representation as image and likeness is a kind of sonship.

Psalm 8 not only uses the hiphil form of מָשַׁל, the terms "crowned" (עטר), "glory" (כבוד), "honor" (הדר), and the phrase "place under his feet" (שַׁתָּה תַחַת־רַגְלָיו) are royal images.[46] Humanity manifests the rulership of YHWH in a position under his authority but over all else so that the "human's authority is bounded by God's sovereignty."[47] Mark Kinzer states that both in Jewish interpretive circles around the turn of the Common Era and in modern

---

the use of Ps 8:6 with Ps 110 in 1 Cor 15, Adela Yarbro Collins and John J. Collins note that the first chapter of Genesis' use of image and likeness "draws upon royal ideology" (*King and Messiah as Son of God: Divine, Human, and Angelic Messianic Figures in Biblical and Related Literature* [Eerdmans, 2008], 110). For a discussion on the relationship between image and rule see Middleton, *The Liberating Image*, 50–60.

44 We might note the interesting typology here. The promised land of Israel functions as a type or a shadow of the future eschatological inheritance. Second Temple literature described the eschatological destiny of humanity as a new Eden, where humanity is in a new inheritance. Also, the motif of "rest" in Hebrews draws together both the days of creation and the promise of inheritance and views it in light of Christ's entrance into heaven.

45 Stephen Dempster, *Dominion and Dynasty*, 62.

46 Gentry and Wellum, *Kingdom Through Covenant*, 196. On "place under his feet" they cite Egyptian poem texts like Poem of Thutmoses III, Assyrian Royal texts, and the Phoenician inscription Karatepe A.i.16. Marvin Tate ("An Exposition of Psalm 8" *Perspectives in Religious Studies 28* [2001]: 355), shows the association of humanity's royal qualities and God's.

47 Leonard P. Maré, "The Messianic Interpretation of Psalm 8:4–6," 110. We disagree with Maré who states, "The privileged position of humankind as portrayed in this psalm should never be understood as the glorification of humankind" (although on p. 112 he points out the "glory of humankind" is not proclaimed in "isolation from the glory of God," which is more accurate). It is precisely this appointment to rulership that is in fact a delegated glory. Various Second Temple writers, especially in the DSS recognized this. See also Marvin Tate's remark: "The 'glory and splendor' of humanity is derivative and bounded by the majestic name of God" ("Exposition of Psalm 8," 359).

exegetical discussions "the relationship between the psalm and the creation texts in Genesis is recognized."[48]

In Pseudo-Philo's LAB 13:9–10, it is revealed through Moses that if God's people keep the Law, they will receive the Adamic blessing. As Hayward summarizes, "God's ways are now available to men in the commands given to Moses, particularly those relating to the cult."[49] At the place of creation the first man was taught, "If you do not transgress what I have commanded you, all things will be subject to you" (v. 9), which echoes both Gen 1:26–28 and Ps 8. In this revelation, Moses is also shown Paradise as what "men have lost by not walking in them" (God's commands). Then in v. 10 as the Law is given to Moses "regarding the salvation of the salvation of the souls of the people," Moses is told, "If they will walk in my ways, I will not abandon them but will have mercy on them always and bless their seed; and the earth will quickly yield its fruit, and there will be rains for their advantage, and it will not be barren." This links Adam's destiny, with Abrahamic promises 'to their seed,' and blessings of keeping Torah (cf. Lev 26:4; Deut 28:4,11,12).

With the prominence of this concept of vice-regency in the psalm, Doug Green reaches the conclusion that Ps 8 is first about the royal identity of David.[50] It is the Davidic King who comes to be regarded as the 'image of God.'[51] Green discusses the use of Ps 8 to refer to all humanity, the so-called "democratic" interpretation.[52] His argument, similar to the argument by N.T. Wright, is that in the unfolding redemptive history of the OT, Israel becomes a new Adam and Israelite royal ideology portrays King David as a Second Adam.[53] In

---

48 Mark Stephen Kinzer, "'All Things Under His Feet': Psalm 8 in the New Testament and in Other Jewish Literature of Late Antiquity" (PhD diss., University of Michigan, 1995), 94.

49 C.T.R. Hayward, "The Figure of Adam in Pseudo-Philo's Biblical Antiquities," *JSJ* 23.1 (1992): 6. For another discussion of Adam in Pseudo-Philo's LAB, see Kinzer, "All Things Under His Feet," 192–205.

50 Douglas Green, "Psalm 8: What is Israel's King that You Remember Him?" http://www.academia.edu/7222228/Psalm_8_What_Is_Israels_King_That_You_Remember_Him.

51 Mettinger, *King and Messiah*, 291. Similarly, Aage Bentzen (*King and Messiah*, 41–44) sees a linking between Israelite kingship, the king's sonship, and the "First Man" of Ps 8 and Gen 1.

52 Green, "Psalm 8," 1–2.

53 Ibid., 3; N.T. Wright, *The Climax of the Covenant*, 20–23; *The New Testament and the People of God*, 262–268. For a discussion of royal ideology in Israel's king as God's son see also Adela Yarbro Collins and John J. Collins, *King and Messiah*, 1–47. Commenting on Ps 2 and 110, they remark: "As God's surrogate, he [the Davidic King] is sovereign of the whole world by right" (22). However, they do not link these psalms to Ps 8. See also Moule, *The Origin of Christology*, 152 and Middleton, *The Liberating Image*, 24–28. While not discussing Ps 8, Crispin Fletcher-Louis ("King Solomon, Bearer of the Image of God, Incorporative Representative of God's People [1 Kings 3–4]," paper presented at the St. Andrews "Son of God" Conference, June 6–8, 2016) shows how in 1 Kings 3–4 Solomon is an Adamic figure. The larger purpose of his paper is to vindicate N.T. Wright's thesis of Adamic figure and incorporative representation of

this vein, J. Richard Middleton goes so far as to state that Ps 8 has a clearer royal ideology than Gen 1.[54] Brandon Crowe writes, "the language in Psalm 8 not only is spoken of humankind in general, echoing language of Genesis 1 but can preeminently be applied to a royal representative who embodies the kingly role given to Adam."[55] Likewise, Hubert Keener has identified royal imagery in Ps 8.[56] Keener, however, suggests that when Ps 8 is read within its editorial position in the Psalms, it "tempers the Davidic hope," since "just as the ideal Davidic king is a function as YHWH's vice-regent through wisdom and Torah piety, so also is corporate humanity to function as YHWH's vice-regent through wisdom and Torah piety."[57] This view, however, reads Davidic vice-regency in distinction from corporate humanity. Instead, Davidic vice-regency is the further fulfillment of Adamic-human vice-regency so that Davidic figures are corporate of the new humanity God is created to undo the fall.[58] Its position in the Psalter enhances rather than tempers Davidic and royal ideology. So as Green further argues, there is a link between Adam and Davidic ideology since originally Adam had a royal identity:

> There is a stream of theological reflection in the Old Testament... that speaks of Israel and her kings using what may be called second-Adam imagery: the godlike (or near-divine) human, the son of Man crowned with divine splendor, who rules over the animal kingdom, and by extension

---

the Messiah from a particular OT passage.

54  *Liberating Image*, 57.

55  *The Last Adam: A Theology of the Obedient Life of Jesus in the Gospels* (Baker, 2017), 39. He continues, "Thus, what is true of Adam in the garden (being made in the royal image of God) is later seen with particular clarity in the anointed king who models the royal image of God representatively (cf. Ps 21:5)…it must be emphasized, the institution of the monarchy has a precedent in the royal role of humanity that is present already in the creation of Adam and Eve. Thus the kingship dovetails with the royal realities that have been part of humankind having been made in the image of God from the beginning" (39–40). Crowe also stresses the representative features of this kingship in the OT as we are as well in Hebrews 2. His discussion also explores the Daniel 7 figure as a representative Adamic-figure, which does not directly concern our argument.

56  Hubert James Keener, *A Canonical Exegesis of the Eighth Psalm*, 66–73.

57  H.J. Keener, *A Canonical Exegesis*, 88. Here the reading is defended by discussing the role of Ps 1–2 in the opening of the psalm as well as the similarities between Ps 8 and 144. On the importance of Davidic identity in shaping the Psalter, and the relationship between the king and Torah piety with respect to the king being an exemplar, see Jamie A. Grant, *The King as Exemplar: The Function of Deuteronomy's Kingship Law in the Shaping of the Book of Psalms* (Society of Biblical Literature, 2004). He also discusses how the king is an idealized figure and a democratized figure within the community (282–289).

58  N.T. Wright, *Climax of the Covenant*, 20–23; *The New Testament and the People of God*, 262–268; Crispin Fletcher-Louis, "King Solomon, Bearer of the Image of God." As Collins and Collins (*King and Messiah*, 15, 22–24) point out in ancient backgrounds and Israel (cf. Ps 45:6; Isa 9) the king could be called an *elohim*, which is precisely the identification in Ps 8.

the animalized humanity of the Gentile kingdoms. Psalm 8 floats in this stream. Read in context of the Psalter, and read in the context of Israel's story, Psalm 8 is less interested in the dignity and worth of humanity in general, and more concerned with the dignity and worth, the glory and honor, of the true humanity, Israel, and the true human, David (and his descendants).[59]

If the psalm is solely about the creation of humanity in a reflection of Gen 1–2, the question should be raised: how or why would the psalmist speak of the Lord establishing strength because of his foes (MT 8:3 יִסַּ֥דְתָּ֗ עֹ֑ז לְמַ֥עַן צֹורְרֶ֑יךָ לְהַשְׁבִּ֥ית אֹ֝ויֵ֗ב וּמִתְנַקֵּֽם׃), or in LXX the Lord creating praise for the sake of enemies, to put them down (LXX 8:3 κατηρτίσω αἶνον ἕνεκα τῶν ἐχθρῶν σου τοῦ καταλῦσαι ἐχθρὸν καὶ ἐκδικητήν)? It would seem then the "putting all things under your feet" implies a subduing of these enemies even with the original context of the psalm.[60] Both MT and LXX have a striking parallel to the Davidic royal ideology in Ps 2:5–9.

It is no surprise, then, that Ps 8 becomes in Heb 2 an identification of Christ and his crowning with glory and honor in his exaltation. In fact, for Hebrews it is a false dilemma to ask whether Ps 8 is intended to be understood as anthropological or Messianic within the unfolding argument of chapter two.[61] The psalm is a reflection of the vice regency of humanity in its ANE setting, but it is also read now amongst the early Christians as Davidic and Messianic. Jesus in his humanity and Messianic function takes on that regal capacity as the true human. In using Ps 8, as Chris L. De Wet notes, "The author of Hebrews makes Jesus the representative human being."[62] He is the true climax of the eschatological vision for humanity. Describing the usage of Ps 8, Marie Isaac writes, "the ascension and exaltation are seen as the fulfillment of God's intention for the whole of humankind."[63] When Jesus becomes the installed king over all creation at his exaltation, he is designated Second Adam or Last Adam precisely because the original Adam had a royal function. Georg Gäbel argues Hebrews connects this Adam Christology to Christ's humiliation, exaltation, and the receiving of humanity's dominion:

---

59 Green, "Psalm 8," 7. See also Brandon Crowe, *The Last Adam*, 38–43.

60 One possible answer is a conception of *Chaoskampf* in triumph over evil forces at creation. This is certainly possible as creation of land is set against the תֹּ֫הוּ (Gen 1:2). However, this would only serve to highlight even more the kingly features of Ps 8. These concepts are not mutually exclusive. For example, Ps 72:8–17 links dominion over the earth, the nations subdued, and prosperity in the land.

61 Ellingworth, *The Epistle to the Hebrews* (Eerdmans, 1993), 151–152; Moffitt, *Atonement and the Logic of Resurrection*, 128; Peeler, *You Are My Son*, 73–74.

62 "The Messianic Interpretation of Psalm 8:4–6 in Hebrews 2:6–9: Part II," 122.

63 *Sacred Space*, 174.

> Hebr nimmt damit frühchristliche Adam-Christologie auf und deutet mit ihrer Hilfe die Erniedrigung und Erhöhung Christi. Als ἄνθρωπος und υἱὸς ἀνθρώπου ist Christus der Mensch schlechthin. In ihm wird der Ungehorsam Adams mit seinen Folgen aufgehoben; dem Menschen wird die Herrlichkeit und Herrscherstellung über alle Engeln zuteil.[64]

So, in its original context, the psalm explains the royal identity upon humanity, and within the context of the Psalter is probably used to identify the Davidic King as a sort of primordial man, or second Adam—a royal figure who rules and subdues YHWH's enemies on behalf of YHWH. The writer of Hebrews specifically seeks to show not only the fulfillment of this passage, but specifically its eschatological movement from lowliness to exaltation. The age to come is subjected to the man of Ps 8, a human, not angels. Nothing is left in rebellion against the Son (2:8 οὐδὲν ἀφῆκεν αὐτῷ ἀνυπότακτον). This "subjection of all under his feet" is true even if in the experience of their trials the believers do not seem to see it as a reality (2:8b Νῦν δὲ οὔπω ὁρῶμεν αὐτῷ τὰ πάντα ὑποτεταγμένα). It is likely that with 2:8–9, Hebrews sees the eschatological fulfillment of the Ps 8 unfolding within the categories of 'already'/'not yet' common to the NT. Believers see that Christ has suffered and is now this exalted one (2:9).

Fulfilling Ps 8, Jesus is the human man 'being remembered' by God (μιμνήσκῃ αὐτοῦ) and 'cared for' (ἐπισκέπτῃ αὐτόν) is the Son (Heb 2:6). This may actually be God remembering him because of his obedience to the vocation of sonship. As we will discuss in a later chapter, the Father hears the Son's cry to him because of the Son's godly reverence (Heb 5:7). The Son was obedient in the body prepared for him (Heb 10:5–7). This would be the state where the Son enters the world, which Hebrews continually characterizes as a state of weakness, albeit without sin. The Son becomes weak, lower than angels, yet the Father remembers him and cares for him. This remembering and caring may even connote God taking paternal notice of this figure in affliction—much as Israel in Exodus is heard in her affliction, or David is raised up out of his despair in various psalms. The Son, who has a unique Sonship, is sent by the Father into creation, made like his brothers in every respect, so that he could be crowned by the Father and lead the others to glory. This crowning entails an exaltation to priesthood which includes an ascension up

---

64 "Hebr[ews] takes up early Christian Adam-christology and uses it to interpret the humiliation and exaltation of Christ. As ἄνθρωπος and υἱὸς ἀνθρώπου, Christ is man *par excellence*. In him, Adam's disobedience and its consequences are abolished; man is bestowed with glory and dominion over all angels." Georg Gäbel, *Die Kulttheologie des Hebräerbriefes: Eine exegetisch-religionsgeschichtliche Studie* (Mohr Siebeck, 2006), 143–144.

into heaven. Moving up into heaven is the culmination of this crowning as the king-priest sits in the heavenly throne.

For Hebrews, then, the crowning with glory and honor is something that happened subsequent to Christ's coming into the world. Hebrews sees the effects of the fall as causing humanity to lack glory. This view is consistent with the teaching of the early church regarding sin, especially Paul, and also certain Second Temple texts that see Adam or humanity as lacking glory as a result of the fall. Glory, specifically the glory of Adam, is what awaits humanity at the end of the age. Kinzer summarizes the view of Adam and glory:

> The basic eschatological interpretation of Ps 8 is that which is seen in the Adam Books, Pseudo-Philo, and the Qumran literature: אנוש and בן-אדם both refer to renewed humanity, and thus to Israel, which is Adam's legitimate heir. In the age to come Israel will be exalted among the angels and will reign over the new creation; in this way Ps 8 will find its true fulfillment.[65]

But for Hebrews the transition of the Son from shame or weakness to glory is the inauguration of the eschaton and the representative of the new humanity moving from lowliness to exaltation. This representational feature, as we have argued above, is characteristic of what can be labelled "Second Adam Christology." With the nature of humanity and a representative human, Hebrews partakes of such staple features of "Second Adam" thought even though there is no direct mention of Adam. In this respect, driven by his hermeneutical methods, the author of Hebrews brings together both the anthropological aspects of Ps 8 with the fulfillment aspects in the exaltation-ascension of Jesus the Messiah.[66]

Second, there is also good reason to believe the reference to crowning and glory evokes Adamic imagery even if Ps 8 had not been explicitly cited. In Second Temple Judaism, there is a motif that the righteous sufferer is destined to inherit the glory of Adam. C. Marvin Pate has shown that the connection between Paul's conception of suffering and glory in the righteous saints has its "impetus" in Jewish apocalypticism. "These intertwined motifs are rooted in the belief, so prevalent in the Judaism of this period, that Adam's lost glory will be restored through righteous suffering."[67] For Second Temple

---

65 Kinzer, "All Things Under His Feet," 148.
66 Gert Steyn, "An Overview of the Extent and Diversity of Methods Utilised by the Author of Hebrews When Using the Old Testament," *Neot* 42.2 (2008): 336; Ellingworth, *Hebrews*, 152–153; Schenck, *Cosmology and Eschatology*, 56
67 C. Marvin Pate, *The Glory of Adam and the Afflictions of the Righteous: Pauline Suffering*

Judaism "suffering was a prerequisite for inheriting Adam's glory."[68]

Pate cites three texts from the DSS in defense of his thesis: 1 QS 4:22,23; CD 3:20 and 1 QHa 4:15.[69] These texts describe the future people of God inheriting the glory of Adam (כבוד אדם) as a reward over and against the wicked being punished. The glory of Adam restored is a reward for those who inherit the age to come.[70]

In 1 QS 3:18, mankind was created to rule the world. Later in 1 QS 4, the righteous are those who inherit an everlasting covenant (4:22 לברית עולמים [71]) with God. and he has sorted the righteous from the unrighteous. In this life, the righteous offer service "as a legacy to the sons of man so they might know good [and evil]," clearly an echo of Gen 2, but in the final state, the righteous inherit the כבוד אדם "glory of Adam" (4:23). This inheritance of glory includes various gifts such as "fruitful offspring with all everlasting blessings, eternal enjoyment with endless life, and *a crown of glory* with majestic raiment in eternal light" (4:7–8, emphasis added). "The 'crown of glory' recalls Ps 8:6."[72] It is a new or renewed humanity with Adamic blessing and glories.

Similarly, CD 3:20 describes man as inheriting the glory of Adam. In the context, various people starting with the sons of Noah are described as going astray from God. God has established a covenant with Israel for the faithful who are steadfast in God's precepts. Given that sons of Jacob and Israelites are described as going astray, it is quite possible that these faithful are seen as the true Israel. The faithful do the will (or commandments) of God, "which man must do in order to live by them" (3:15–16). They will receive a safe home in Israel. It is the steadfast who acquire eternal life, and "all the glory of Adam is for them" (3:20). When Adam sinned, his glory was lost, but the Qumran

---

in Context (Mellen Biblical, 1993), 67. See also Moffitt, *Atonement and Logic of the Resurrection*, 81–116. He focusses more of the 'age to come' in Second Temple literature but highlights the role of suffering in the Second Temple texts to bring the coming age and the glory of Adam (cf. esp. 84–88, 90, 112).

68 Pate, *Glory of Adam*, 67. He may overstate this a bit. It is perhaps better to say that some of the Judaism of the first century taught this.

69 Pate (*The Glory of Adam*, 67) and N.T. Wright (*New Testament and the People of God*, 265n.86) follow the older designation 1 QH 17:15; we have chosen to follow the structure of the scrolls proposed by Emile Peuch, "Quelques aspect de la restauration du Rouleau des Hymns (1 QH)," *JJS* 39 (1988): 38–55. This designation is also found in Florentinie García Martínez and Eibert J.C. Tigchelaar, *The Dead Sea Scrolls: Study Edition*, 2 vols. (Eerdmans, 1997). All English quotations and references are from this study edition.

70 N.T. Wright, *The New Testament and the People of God*, 265.

71 Interestingly, Heb 13:20 also contains the phrase διαθήκης αἰωνίου.

72 Kinzer, "All Things Under His Feet," 106. He goes on "...and while the word for crown here is (כליל) and the verb used in the psalm (עטר) are different roots, the two terms were interchangeable in the Hebrew of the period."

community as the people of God can live forever in Adam's original glory if they hold fast to Torah.[73]

Finally from the DSS, 1 QHa 4:14–15 promises that the faithful to God has "raised an [eternal] name...giving them as a legacy all the glory of Adam [and] abundant days (כבוד אדמ ו רוב ימים)." It is the eschatological end after atonement has been made and the dead are judged. The faithful inherit the glory of Adam which was lost in the fall. In 1 QHa 5:20–26, we have an expectation of glory for the servant who understands the way of the Lord. On the one hand, the one born of the woman (ומה ילוד אשה)—i.e., a human—is lowly dust mixed with water (מבנה עפר ומגבל מים) destined for punishment if he is wicked. However, if he is justified by the goodness and compassion of the Lord, he is destined to be glorified and to rule in delight (5:23b בהדרך תפארנו ותמשילנו ב[רוב עדנים) with everlasting peace (עם שלום עולם) and long life (ואורך ימים). The servant thanks the Lord because of the spirit in him his word does not depart from him (v. 25). The righteous experience this crowning of glory. This latter expectation may have echoes of royal ideology and especially humanity's royal role upon receiving glory.

Crispin Fletcher-Louis argues: "the Qumran community thinks of itself as the true Israel and true Adam, which is created to bear God's Glory."[74] He illustrates this from their liturgy:

> For the Dead Sea Scroll community, however, we can be sure that an angelo-morphic view of (the pre-lapsarian) *Urmensch* was related to a more exalted view of Adam as one created to bear God's Glory. In the first day's prayer for the weekly liturgy of the Words of the Heavenly Lights (4Q504, 506) there is a remarkable retelling of the creation story according to which Gen 1:26, the creation of Adam "according to the likeness (כדמות)" of God, is fused with Ezek 1:28, where the anthropomorphic form of God occupying the throne to Ezekiel's vision is described as (מראה דבות כבוד יהוה). The result is a prayer of thanksgiving to God that he has created "[Adam our fa]ther, in the likeness of [your] Glory ([אדם א[בינו] [יצרתה כרמות כבוד[כה])" (Q504 8 recto 4). In another part of this liturgy it is Israel who recapitulates the true Adam as the bearer of God's Glory (frags 1–2 iii2–4: "you have created us for your Glory [לכבודכה בדתנו]"), over against the nations who are nothing but a manifestation of the *tohu* (*wabohu*) of the pre-creation chaos.[75]

---

73 Kinzer, "All Things Under His Feet," 108.
74 Crispin Fletcher-Louis, "Some Reflections on Angelomorphic Humanity Texts among the Dead Sea Scrolls," 297.
75 Ibid. See also Crispin Fletcher-Louis, *All the Glory of Adam*.

In Jewish apocalyptic literature there is association with the glory of the age to come and the glory of Adam.[76] Those obedient to God receive glory. For example, in the day of judgment at the end of the age, "glory and honor shall be given back to the holy ones" (1 En. 50:1).[77] This glory comes with the elect on sitting on the throne (1 En. 51:3–5). The portion of the elect and righteous is glorious; they will reign in splendor, echoing the imagery of Dan. 12:1–3 (1 En. 58:1–2). The righteous elect wear garments of glory (1 En. 62:15). The seed of the righteous is preserved "for kingship and glory" (1 En. 65:12).

The glory bestowed on the righteous is found in more detail in 2 Bar. For example, in 2 Bar. 14:18–19, "a man is made guardian over your works." The world was created for him, not the reverse. This leads to the world equally being destined for the righteous (14:19). After suffering and tribulation in this fallen world, the righteous will receive "a crown with great glory" (15:8).[78] In fact, Adam was offered Paradise before his sin but now this glory awaits the righteous (2 Bar. 4). Baruch is, of course, privileged to see it like Abraham and Moses. Thus, this glory that awaits man is an Adamic glory of the age to come.[79] This world is a struggle of hardship for the righteous (2 Bar. 15:8). The world to come is also coming on their account, and with it comes "a crown with great glory" (15:7–8). After suffering (51:2), they shall be exalted and glorified (51:5). This glorification entails having the splendor of angels (51:5) but "the excellence of their righteousness will then be greater than that of the angels" (51:12). This is a restoration to glory and an exaltation over creation. Thus, the righteous are to prepare their souls for what is to come by suffering well (52:5–7). 2 Bar. rejects that Adam is the cause of a person's sin, instead "each of us has become our own Adam" (2 Bar. 54:19). The unrighteous will be punished and the faithful ones glorified because of their faith (2 Bar. 5:21).

4 Ezra sees a glory that awaits the righteous. This inheritance is like that which was given to Adam. While all are descended from Adam, it is God's people that are destined to possess the inheritance. They are the 'new Adam.' In 4 Ezra 6:54, "over these [cattle, beasts, and creeping things] you placed Adam as ruler over all the works which you had made; and from him we have all come, the people from whom you have chosen." The other nations come from Adam but are nothing, not being called by God to inherit (4 Ezra 6:56).

---

76 C. Marvin Pate, *The Glory of Adam*, 72–74.

77 All citations from *The Old Testament Pseudiphigrapha: Apocalyptic Literature & Testaments*, ed. James H. Charlesworth (Doubleday, 1983).

78 Moffitt (*Atonement and the Logic of Resurrection*, 112), rightly in our estimation, sees a possible allusion to Ps 8 here.

79 N.T. Wright (*Climax of the Covenant*, 24) states "The later writings of 4 Ezra and 2 Baruch witness the same theological position: Israel will be given the rights of Adam's true heir." He cites 4 Ezra 3:4–36; 6:53–59; 9:17ff.; 2 Bar. 14:17–19.

Why? Because Israel was created to inherit the created world: "You have said that it was for us that you created the world" (4 Ezra 6:55). Again in 4 Ezra 6:58, "But we your people, whom you have called your first-born, only begotten, zealous for you, and most dear, have been given into your hands." The chapter ends with a plea that since the world was created for Israel, how long will it be until the Lord grants it?

In chapter 7, we find again that the world was made for Israel's sake, but judgment was necessary because of Adam's transgression. Now, however, the righteous can expect to enter the greater world to come if they suffer well in trials in this world:

> But the entrances of the greater world are broad and safe, and really yield the fruit of immortality. Therefore unless the living pass through the difficult and vain experiences, they can never receive these things that have been reserved for them...Then I answered and said, "O sovereign Lord, behold, you have ordained in your Law that the righteous shall inherit these things, but the ungodly shall perish. The righteous therefore endure difficult circumstances while hoping for easier ones. (4 Ezra 7:13–14, 17–18a)

The eschatological end of glory waits for those who labor through hardship in following the Lord and his Law. "During the time that they lived in it [their mortal body], they laboriously served the Most High, and withstood danger every hour, that they might keep the Law of the Lawgiver perfectly" (4 Ezra 7:89). Thus, "they shall see with great joy the glory of him who receives them, for they shall have rest in seven orders" (4 Ezra 7:91). This includes orders of rest, glory, and immorality all because they have striven to obey and not yield to evil (4 Ezra 7:92–98). The climax is: "They hasten to behold the face of him whom they served in life and from whom they are to receive their reward when glorified" (4 Ezra 7:98). Like Hebrews, 4 Ezra sees some connection between Adam, inheritance, the eschatological glory, and the rest of God's people. Both are refracting themes from the OT and relating them to the eschatological end. The righteous suffering, obedient to the Lord, achieves the end of eschatological glory.

With regard then to Ps 8, what Mark Kinzer summarizes as the view of Qumran regarding the glory of Adam finds similar reflection in the other Second Temple texts surveyed above:

> For the Qumran community, as for many other Jews at the turn of common era, Gen 1 and Ps 8 were not read as descriptions of the present hu-

man position before God and the created order. Both texts were read in light of Ezek 28, which presents the Man in Eden as a divine or angelic being who fell from his exalted position. They were read protologically and eschatologically. Ps 8 was thus seen to promise heavenly wisdom, glory, and immortality for those who were cleansed from the polluting sin of Adam and his descendants.[80]

If our reading of Heb 2 and the use of Ps 8 is correct, we can bypass a precise answer to whether or not the use of 'son of man' in the passage refers to Jesus' title. On the one hand, it is quite possible that the early community was aware of the title, and that the title is in the background of what Hebrews is articulating.[81] On the other hand, 'Son of Man' was not a title the church used actively for Jesus after his resurrection and accession. Regardless of the interpretation that one takes on this issue,[82] the point of human representation and fulfillment of Adamic vocation stands.[83] Hebrews uses Ps 8 to show that Christ is the fulfillment of true humanity.[84] Remember Moule has remarked that Dan 7 contains "a symbol of vocation to be utterly loyal, even to death in the confidence of ultimate vindication in the heavenly court."[85] More clearly,

---

80  Kinzer, "All Things Under His Feet," 110. Since Hebrews does not seem to have any allusion to Ezek 28, it is beyond our scope to offer a treatment of this text. However, on the matter of Ezek 28 and the primal man described there being priestly in function see Dexter Callendar, Jr., *Adam in Myth and History: Ancient Israelite Perspectives on the Primal Human* (Eisenbrauns, 2000), 87–135.

81  Bruce, *Hebrews*, 73; George Guthrie and Russell Quinn, "A Discourse Analysis of the Use of Psalm 8:4–6 in Hebrews 2:5–9," *JETS* 49.2 (2006): 243. R.T. France ("The Writer of Hebrews as Biblical Expositor," *TynBul* 47 [1996]: 262) writes, "It is hard to imagine that any Christian, particularly a Greek-speaking Christian after the middle of the first century could have heard the phrase υἱὸς ἀνθρώπου without thinking of Jesus" (also quoted in Guthrie and Quinn, "A Discourse Analysis," 243). We disagree with Oscar Cullmann's statement (*The Christology of the New Testament*, 188) that the author of Hebrews "had quite precise information about the Son of Man doctrine." We agree with much of Cullmann's discussion of a Second Adam approach, yet it does not seem that 'Son of Man' is a technical title in Hebrews. We should see a Second Adam approach in the totality of what Hebrews is arguing but we must not hang the weight on the 'Son of Man' being a *terminus technicus* in Heb 2.

82  We favor the latter precisely because 'Son of Man' is not used as a title for Jesus outside of the gospels. We also set aside the NT scholarship debates of whether or not Jesus uses the phrase 'Son of Man' in the gospel primarily as merely self-referential or if he has the Dan 7 background in mind—on this the secondary literature is massive.

83  Regardless of one's position on the issue, Heb 2 unifies the anthropological and Christological reading of Ps 8.

84  Similarly Geoffrey Grogan ("Christ and His People: An Exegetical and Theological Study of Hebrews 2:5–18," *Vox Evangelica* 6 [1969]: 69) suggests that with the 'Son of Man' theme "in the section of the passage controlled by Psalm 8, for His dominion is an everlasting dominion, ... there is perhaps a suggestion that He is the Last Adam, the Head of the new humanity." Our argument is that it is more than a mere suggestion but governs the argument as a whole.

85  See above. Moule, *Origin*, 14.

this is precisely the motif that Hebrews sees fulfilled in the person and work of Jesus, even without a possible contested reference to Dan 7 with the phrase 'son of man.'[86] The declaration of Pss 2:7 and 110:1 is a vindication in the heavenly court as the Son having been faithful on earth in suffering is exalted up over creation. Read within the context of Hebrews' theological concern for the exaltation, Ps 8 is both anthropological and Christological because Christ is a second Adam fulfilling Adamic vocation and receiving Adamic glory in exaltation.[87] The Adamic role is fulfilled with the Son of David exalted to the throne.

There is one other possibility that may influence Hebrews' use of Ps 8. There is a Rabbinic tradition of reading Ps 8 as referencing Moses' ascension to receive the Law. It is found particularly in *Talmud Babli b. Shabbath 88b–89a*, where the angels complain that Moses should ascend into heaven. In 88b, the question of Ps 8:5 is put on their lips:

> R. Joshua b. Levi also said: When Moses ascended on high, the ministering angels spake before the Holy One, blessed be He, 'Sovereign of the Universe! What business has one born of woman amongst us?' 'He has come to receive the Torah,' answered He to them. Said they to Him, 'That secret treasure, which has been hidden by Thee for nine hundred and seventy-four generations before the world was created. Thou desirest to give to flesh and blood! What is man, that thou art mindful of him, And the son of man, that thou visitest him? O Lord our God, How excellent is thy name in all the earth! Who hast set thy glory [the Torah] upon the Heavens!'[88]

In *b. Rosh Hash* 21b and *b. Ned.* 38a, Moses is identified with Ps 8:6.

> Rab and Samuel [gave different interpretations of a certain text]. One said: Fifty gates of understanding were created in the world, and all were given to Moses save one, as it says, Yet thou hast made him but little lower than a God. (*b. Rosh Hash* 21b)[89]

---

86 It is our opinion that Dan 7 is not in view in Heb 2 but that the same motif is at work.

87 David Moffitt, *Atonement and the Logic of Resurrection*, 135–143, esp. 142–143. F.F. Bruce (*The Epistle to the Hebrews*, 72–73) sees a second/last Adam theology in the use of Ps 8. On the other hand, Harold Attridge (*The Epistle to the Hebrews* [Fortress, 1989], 75) argues a Second Adam Christology is not used. He believes that the Abrahamic lineage is more important, yet if N.T. Wright's understanding of Adamic Christology is to be preferred—and we believe it is—the mention of 'seed of Abraham' is precisely part of what an Adamic Christology would entail. First Israel and finally the Messiah has an Adamic vocation. The seed of Abraham is the new Adam. (Cf. Kinzer, "All Things Under His Feet," 262–263).

88 *The Babylonian Talmud: Seder Mo'ed*, ed. Isidore Epstein, trans. H. Freedman (London: Soncino, 1938), 1:421–422.

89 *The Babylonian Talmud: Seder Mo'ed*, ed. Isidore Epstein, trans. H. Freedman (London:

Wise: for Rab and Samuel both said, Fifty gates of understanding were created in the world, and all but one were given to Moses, for it is said, For thou hast made him [sc. Moses] a little lower than God. Meek, for it is written, Now the man Moses was very meek. (*b. Ned.* 38a)[90]

As Moffitt points out, *Talmud Babli* is late, most likely between the fifth and seven century CE, although the tradition could perhaps be pushed back to during the first half of the third century.[91] However Kinzer, following Wayne Meeks, has argued that "Moses as a Second Adam figure is prevalent in Jewish and Samaritan literature at the turn of the common era."[92] Furthermore, Moses is seen as a figure ascending into heaven where he receives the Law, especially in *Pseudo-Philo's* LAB and Ezekiel the Tragedian's *Exagōgē*.[93] This tradition is also represented in Rabbinic sources.[94] Thus, it is quite possible that the tradition of Ps 8 with Moses was circulating in the first century CE.[95]

Several elements then are suggestive for Hebrews. First, the contrast between angels and the Son set out in Heb 1 continues into Heb 2. The use of Ps 8 is read in conjunction with Ps 110 as an ascension into heaven and crowning with royal eschatological glory. Second, the introduction of Moses in Heb 3 is not a switch in the subject but a continuation of the theme. Moses received the Law via angels (Heb 2:1–4). This was an ascent of sorts, possibly Hebrews being aware of traditions to see Moses in Ps 8 and most certainly aware of ascent traditions of Moses or reading the crowning of Moses with glory of Torah. Third, Hebrews is concerned with demonstrating that Christ is enthroned as the new humanity, the eschatological end. As Wayne Meeks writes of the Rabbinic and non-Rabbinic traditions, "Moses' elevation at Sinai was treated not only as a heavenly enthronement, but also as a restoration of the glory lost by Adam. Moses, crowned with both God's name and his image, became in some sense a 'second Adam,' the prototype of a new humanity."[96]

---

Soncino, 1938), 3:90.

90  *The Babylonian Talmud: Nashim*, ed. Isidore Epstein, trans. H. Freedman (London: Soncino, 1936), 3:119.

91  Moffitt, *Atonement and the Logic of the Resurrection*, 151.

92  Mark Stephen Kinzer, "'All Things Under His Feet,'" 97; cf. Wayne Meeks, *The Prophet-King: Moses Traditions and Johannine Christology* (Brill, 1967), 222–223, 232–233.

93  See further discussion in chapter 5.

94  W. Hall Harris III, *The Descent of Christ: Ephesians 4:7–11 and Traditional Hebrew Imagery* (Baker, 1996) 64–122.

95  Moffitt, *Atonement and the Logic of the Resurrection*, 160; Kinzer, "All Things Under His Feet," 206–208.

96  Wayne Meeks, "Moses as God and King," in *Religions in Antiquity*, ed. J. Neuser (Leiden: Brill, 1968), 364–365. Also qtd. in Kinzer, "All Things Under His Feet," 168n.32. In Philo and some of the apocryphal and pseudiphigraphal writings, Moses is a king (Meeks, *The Prophet-King*, 107–117, 147–154).

## Heb 2:8b–10—Seeing Jesus Made Perfect Through Suffering.

The author of Hebrews sees the fulfillment of the psalm realized as all things are put under the feet of Christ (2:8 ἐν τῷ γὰρ ὑποτάξαι [αὐτῷ] τὰ πάντα). The author also recognizes that he and his audience do not yet see all things as under Christ's feet (2:8 Νῦν δὲ οὔπω ὁρῶμεν αὐτῷ τὰ πάντα ὑποτεταγμένα). This dichotomy capitalizes on the eschatological tension of the overlap of the ages. The age to come has begun, in that the Son has been appointed Messiah on the throne. He presently controls all things (2:8 οὐδὲν ἀφῆκεν αὐτῷ ἀνυπότακτον), yet the author also admits that Christians do not yet see all things under the control of Christ. It is as if the reign of Christ has to work its way out within the present creation even though the King has been installed on the throne. The present experience of the believers in their suffering is a reminder that while Christ is seated on the throne, and thus has all under his authority. It is not as if Christ is not authoritative over these things. Instead, the reality of suffering remains present in the community as they are awaiting the glory which the Son has already entered. It is also not as if God forgot to put some element of creation under the control of the Son when he crowned him with glory and honor. Indeed, the Father left nothing independent or unsubjected (ἀνυπότακτος) from Christ.

The subjection of all things to the Son and the οὐδὲν ἀφῆκεν αὐτῷ ἀνυπότακτον (2:8) is different from his role in the act of creation and upholding creation in 1:2–3 (δι' οὗ καὶ ἐποίησεν τοὺς αἰῶνας and φέρων τε τὰ πάντα τῷ ῥήματι τῆς δυνάμεως αὐτοῦ). As we have seen, these are aspects of the work of the Son in his divine identity, doing that which God alone does. However, with Ps 8 and here in 2:9, what Hebrews has in view is the appointment of the Son (1:2 ὃν ἔθηκεν κληρονόμον πάντων). Just as Adam was appointed heir, now the Son is heir of the creation with the expectation of ushering in the new creation. However, there remains at present an overlap of the ages in which the Son is exercising rulership as heir but has not fully ushered the sons of glory to their inheritance and unshakable kingdom.

What the believers have witnessed is the work of Jesus, the Son, in his humiliation on the cross. By faith, they recognize and "see" that Jesus has been crowned with glory and honor. This is part of the Christian confession, specifically that Jesus Christ is Lord. This confession arose very quickly in the life of the early Church as the resurrection and ascension of Jesus was interpreted as a Messianic crowning (Acts 2:24–36, especially v. 36).

The means by which Jesus receives this crowning in royal eschatological glory is through suffering. So, Jesus is the Son who enters creation by taking on flesh and blood (2:14a), being made like those who will be his brothers (2:17a). In this state he is τὸν δὲ βραχύ τι παρ' ἀγγέλους ἠλαττωμένον (2:9a). He does not enter as the ruling eschatological man. He does not come crowned in the glory of the last Adam. This is important for Hebrews because to usher in the eschatological state, Jesus will be the one who himself embodies the transition from 'this age' to the 'age to come.' For Hebrews, God does not just bring the eschatological with the coming of the Messiah; it is the Messiah through whom God actualizes the transition of the ages, just as the Messiah also effects the transition from Old Covenant to New Covenant. The Son is the first to enter into the 'age to come.' He first suffers as part of 'this age,' then he is crowned in glory and ascends into heaven. This ascension predicated on suffering first is the fulcrum upon which the two ages turn. Thus, he is the righteous sufferer *par excellence* who by this suffering not only effects the transition but representatively initiates it for all who will believe and obey him (5:9).

It is because of his suffering death (2:9 διὰ τὸ πάθημα τοῦ θανάτου) that he is crowned with eschatological glory (δόξῃ καὶ τιμῇ ἐστεφανωμένον). God makes the founder of his people's salvation (2:10 τὸν ἀρχηγὸν τῆς σωτηρίας αὐτῶν) perfect through suffering (διὰ παθημάτων τελειῶσαι). This enables others to enjoy the eschatological glory of inheriting as sons would. The Son brings in other sons to glory (2:10 πολλοὺς υἱοὺς εἰς δόξαν ἀγαγόντα) by the means of how he achieved the glory. "The dominion of man over creation which is celebrated in Psalm 8, is seen by the author of the epistle to be secured in one Man, Jesus. Through His death this may be realized in others who, by grace, receive His title because they enter his inheritance...and are so called 'sons' of God."[97]

Twice Hebrews uses the διά followed πάθημα. First, there is διὰ τὸ πάθημα τοῦ θανάτου (2:9) where διά plus the accusative τὸ πάθημα denotes cause.[98] The crowning with eschatological glory is because of the suffering unto death that Jesus experienced. Second, there is διὰ παθημάτων (2:10). Διά with the genitive παθημάτων denotes means.[99] Through suffering, the Son becomes the eschatological man. He starts as lower than the angels in his earthly life, and by means of his suffering, he is able to be crowned and raised in royal ascension as the first of the new creation, ruling the age to come. The inheritance

---

97 Geoffrey Grogan, "Christ and His People," 67–68.
98 "διά," BDAG, 225.
99 Ibid., 224. Although BDAG notes that "At times διά w. Gen seems to have causal mng" citing Rom. 8:3 and 2 Cor 9:13 (BDAG, 225), this is not a common usage, and it is best to see suffering as the means or instrumentality by which the Son is perfected. This would align with the fuller explanation Hebrews gives on the role of suffering in bringing in the eschatological in 5:7–8.

is achieved because of his suffering. There is no transition of the ages without Jesus going through a suffering death to effect the transition. The grounds for the perfecting of the Son that leads to his ascension is the suffering of Christ, as we will unpack below.

This raises the question: why is suffering necessary for the achievement of the age to come? In fact, Hebrews sees it as fitting (2:10 ἔπρεπεν) that God should accomplish it this way in order to save the people of God. Hebrews has already pointed to the eternal glory that the Son had (1:2–3), yet the word ἔπρεπεν denotes a rightness, fittingness, or suitableness[100] that this is the path that the Son should walk according to the Father. The reference to the Father creating may also highlight that it was the Father who established the order of man over his creation.[101]

First, to answer this question, it is fairly standard in Second Temple Jewish texts that the glory of the eschaton awaited the righteous sufferers of Israel. The expectation was that at the end of the age Gentiles and unfaithful Israelites would be judged and punished, but those who remained pious Jews would receive the eschatological rewards. Commenting on *Pesher to Habakkuk* (1QpHab), David Moffitt characterizes what could be more generally true of suffering and its relationship to the eschatological age in Second Temple Texts: "this last age appears to be a final era of reward and vindication that will come after the period of suffering and humiliation inflicted on the community."[102] Of course, not all Second Temple texts are as sectarian as Qumran, but the same general principle applies for the righteous sufferers among God's people. The pious sufferer who does not yield is part of the true people of God. The pious sufferers are then eschatologically rewarded with glory akin to Adam's glory.[103] We noted above the theme of suffering and its relationship to the crown of glory in 2 Baruch. The outcome of endurance in suffering will be participation in the future glory, "For when you endure and persevere in his fear and do not forget his Law, the time again will take a turn for the better for you. And they will participate in the consolation of Zion" (2 Bar. 44:7). The righteous "endure much labor" in this life and will receive "great light in that world which has no end" (2 Bar. 48:50). Present suffering is for the preparation of one's soul for inheriting the eternal glory (2 Bar. 52:4–7).

---

100 BDAG, 699.

101 The phrase αὐτῷ, δι' ὃν τὰ πάντα καὶ δι' οὗ τὰ πάντα is clearly a reference to God. For Hebrews, the Son does not exalt himself or ascend on his own authority. Rather God the Father crowns him with glory and honor. He speaks to his Son *a la* the royal degree of Ps 2:6 and Ps 110:1. In 5:5 we read that Christ does not glorify himself (Οὕτως καὶ ὁ Χριστὸς οὐχ ἑαυτὸν ἐδόξασεν). Therefore 2:10a must be referring to the work of the Father upon the Son.

102 *Atonement and the Logic of Resurrection*, 84.

103 See the discussion of Adam's glory above.

This is summarized by 2 Bar. 15:8 "For this world is to them [the righteous] a struggle and an effort with much trouble. And accordingly which will come, a crown with great glory."

4 Ezra also sees the outcome of the suffering of the righteous is the reception of their eternal inheritance. For example, 4 Ezra 7:14: "Therefore unless the living pass through the difficult and vain experiences, they can never receive those things that have been reserved for them." The Lord has ordained that the righteous shall inherit the world in the age to come (4 Ezra 7:17), so "the righteous therefore can endure difficult circumstances while hoping for easier ones." In the fourth vision of 4 Ezra 9–10, the motif of the weeping woman and its interpretation is important for the restoration of Zion. The woman is Zion (10:44) and her son is the city of Jerusalem (10:46). Even in 4 Ezra, the humiliation of Zion and the desecration of her sanctuary will give way to the future inheritance and eternal glory (10:20–24). The mourning of the righteous over Zion will give way to "the brightness of her glory" (10:50; cf. also 12:46–51). Zion is to bear her troubles and find restoration in returning to God's Law. 4 Ezra 10:15–16: "Now, therefore, keep your sorrow to yourself, and bear bravely the troubles that have come upon you. For if you acknowledge the decree of God to be just, you will receive your son back in due time." 4 Ezra 10:24: "Therefore shake off your great sadness and lay aside many sorrows, that the Mighty One may be merciful to you again, and the Most High may give you rest, a relief from your troubles." Ezra is given hope in seeing the future glory that will come upon the righteous even though they suffer now. The coming Messiah will deliver these righteous in the judgment (12:32–35). God's people are exhorted to take courage because "the Mighty One has not forgotten you in your struggle (12:47). The righteous endure and seek mercy (12:46–48).

In these works, the glory, crown, and inheritance—all motifs connected to the age to come—will be given to the righteous who keep the Law, seek God's mercy, and endure suffering. Part of the purpose of these apocalypses is to reveal to the righteous what awaits them despite the sufferings of the present experiences of the community.[104] The present suffering and destruction will eventually give way to the eternal destiny of God's people if they endure in the present. Marvin Pate concludes, "Once again, in *4 Ezra*, like in *2 Bar.*, the idea that the lost glory of Adam will be restored to the righteous who suffer, seems clear."[105]

---

104 Both Apocalypses were most likely written after the Fall of Jerusalem in 70 AD. Cf. John J. Collins, *The Apocalyptic Imagination: An Introduction to Jewish Apocalyptic Literature*, 2nd ed. (Eerdmans, 1998), 195–196, 212–213; George Nickelsburg, *Jewish Literature Between the Bible and the Mishnah*, 2nd ed. (Fortress, 2005), 270–285.

105 *The Glory of Adam*, 74.

Second, suffering is an important theme in Hebrews because of the redemptive role of the suffering of the Son. He has already established a chronological relationship between making purification for sin followed by sitting at the right hand of the Father (Heb 1:3b). Later, Hebrews will describe Christ as both the high priest and the sacrifice. He will more fully develop his atonement theology.[106] Hebrews sees death as the curse of the covenant that must be removed (Heb 9:15b ὅπως θανάτου γενομένου εἰς ἀπολύτρωσιν τῶν ἐπὶ τῇ πρώτῃ διαθήκῃ παραβάσεων τὴν ἐπαγγελίαν λάβωσιν οἱ κεκλημένοι τῆς αἰωνίου κληρονομίας). Death is the curse resulting from the fall and compounded by transgressions of the Old Covenant. Thus, the work of the Son is vicarious for the people of God so that they might receive the inheritance. The solidarity of the Son with his people, entails a substitutionary nature to his death. In fact, he tastes death for everyone (Heb 2:9 ὅπως χάριτι θεοῦ ὑπὲρ παντὸς γεύσηται θανάτου). He goes through the eschatological curse of death so that they can receive the eschatological inheritance of glory (which is paralleled to promise land, rest, and Mt. Zion). Like the Exodus generation brought out of slavery, Christ's suffering unto death redeems his people from slavery (Heb 2:15 καὶ ἀπαλλάξῃ τούτους, ὅσοι φόβῳ θανάτου διὰ παντὸς τοῦ ζῆν ἔνοχοι ἦσαν δουλείας). By means of his death, he destroys the slave master who wields the power of death (Heb 2:14 διὰ τοῦ θανάτου καταργήσῃ τὸν τὸ κράτος ἔχοντα τοῦ θανάτου, τοῦτ' ἔστιν τὸν διάβολον). Kenneth Schenck has used Greimas's system of plot analysis to show how this fits a larger story for Hebrews:[107] "For humanity, a tension exists between their inevitable death and their intended crowning with glory and honour. Whereas for Christ, his victorious death *entails* being crowned with glory."[108] The nature of Christ's sacrifice in his own victory over death and as the climax of the sacrificial system as one on behalf of God's people, then assures those in solidarity to Christ will have the final outcome destined for humanity.

The verb τελειόω is in Heb 2:10; 5:9; 7:19; 7:28; 9:9; 10:1, 14; 11:40; and 12:23. Christ himself is perfected into the glorification of the eschatological state (Heb 2:10 διὰ παθημάτων τελειῶσαι). Heb 12:2 uses τελειωτής calling the Christians to look to Jesus: ἀφορῶντες εἰς τὸν τῆς πίστεως ἀρχηγὸν καὶ τελειωτὴν Ἰησοῦν. As Silva points out, "Any interpretation of τελειωτής in 12:2 that is not

---

106 Simon J. Kistemaker, "Atonement in Hebrews" in *The Glory of the Atonement: Biblical, Theological, and Practical Perspectives: Essay in Honor of Roger Nicole*, ed. Charles E. Hill and Frank A. James III (Intervarsity, 2004), 163–175.

107 Kenneth Schenck, *Cosmology and Eschatology*, 51–77. Matthew C. Easter (*Faith and the Faithfulness of Jesus*, 35–48) also discusses Ps 8 and Heb 2 with respect to the 'pessimistic story of humanity.'

108 Schenck, *Cosmology and Eschatology*, 59.

consonant with τελειοῦν, in 2:10 and 5:9 stands self-condemned."[109] Heb 5:14 and 6:1 use τέλειος and τελειότης, respectively. In these latter two verses, the references are to maturity of believers, those who have left behind elementary doctrines and moved on to solid food.

Lane notes, "In ceremonial texts of the Pentateuch the verb is used to signify the act of consecrating a priest to his office (Exod 29:9, 29, 33, 35; Lev 4:5; 8:33; 16:32; 21:10; Num 3:3)."[110] Both Lane and Attridge observe its use in τελειοῦν τὰς χείρας translating the idiom "to fill the hands" (מלא יד) with reference to installation of Levitical priests.[111] Citing Exod 29:22, 26, 27, 31, 34; Lev 7:27; 8:21, 25, 28, 31, 33, Attridge notes that "the noun τελείωσις (מלאים), especially in the phrase 'the ram of consecration,' can refer to Levitical consecration."[112] John Walters outlines the contrast between the Levitical consecration and the fulfillment in the order of Melchizedek:[113] "the author is operating within an eschatological time frame...the levitical system was a pointer to a greater and more perfect ministry performed by Jesus which is truly eschatological."[114] However, while the cultic usage may serve as a distant background for Hebrews, it is not what is primarily in view.[115] Gerhald Delling writes more broadly of the usage in Hebrews:

> The use of τελειόω in Hb. for the most part follows a special use of the verb in the LXX. Here, too, τελειόω τινά means "to put someone in the position in which he can come, or stand, before God" (Hb. 7:19; 10:1), whether in the narrower sense as a priest who may perform his cultic functions before God or in the broader sense as a non-priest, 10:14. Here again the τετελειωμένος (7:28) is χριστός (as in Lv. 4:5 LXX; 21:10), the high-priest. Naturally in Hb., both here and elsewhere, cultic terminology is used to clarify the very different mode of operation in the new order of salvation: οὐδὲν ... ἐτελείωσεν ὁ νόμος (7:19) or in acknowledgment of the cultic law of the OT which foreshadows the definitive order: It could not permanently

---

109 Moises Silva, "Perfection and Eschatology in Hebrews," *WTJ* 39 (1976): 65.
110 *Hebrews 1–8*, WBC 47A (Word, 1991); 57; cf. also Cockerill, *Epistle to the Hebrews* (Eerdmans, 2012), 139n.67; Gerhald Delling, "τελειόω," *TDNT*, 8:80–84.
111 Lane, *Hebrews 1–8*, 57; Attridge, *Hebrews*, 85. See also Peterson, *Perfection*, 26–30, and Albert Vanhoye, *The Letter to the Hebrews: A New Commentary* (Paulist, 2015), 105, for use in LXX.
112 Attridge, *Hebrews*, 85.
113 John R. Walters, *Perfection in New Testament Theology: Ethics and Eschatology in Relational Dynamics* (Mellen Biblical, 1995), 85–98.
114 Ibid., 94.
115 Attridge, *Hebrews*, 85; Lane, *Hebrews 1–8*, 57; cf. also Cockerill, *Hebrews*, 139n.67, who notes "alone it was not a technical term for this act," citing Peterson, *Perfection*, 29–30.

"qualify" the priest "for cultic ministry" (10:1); the offerings prescribed by it were unable κατὰ συνείδησιν τελειῶσαι (9:9).[116]

Delling is correct that there is an aspect here in Hebrews' usage of the importance of being qualified for priestly ministry. While God has qualified Jesus, the υἱός (5:8f.; 7:28), "to come before him" in priestly action,"[117] τελειόω cannot be narrowed simply to priestly categorization. First, as we noted in 2:10 τελειῶσαι is parallel to δόξῃ καὶ τιμῇ ἐστεφανωμένον. Second, in 7:19 we read οὐδὲν γὰρ ἐτελείωσεν ὁ νόμος which is hardly descriptive of priestly consecration. Third, in 7:28 the word of oath appoints υἱὸν εἰς τὸν αἰῶνα τετελειωμένον could refer to priestly consecration, this reference does not satisfy the contrast on the old order of priesthood where ὁ νόμος γὰρ ἀνθρώπους καθίστησιν ἀρχιερεῖς ἔχοντας ἀσθένειαν. Here the contrast is against the old covenant order of high-priesthood, under which the priests were consecrated or appointed as those ἔχοντας ἀσθένειαν, in distinction from God's oath appointing a priest εἰς τὸν αἰῶνα τετελειωμένον. The contrast is between two states, where τετελειωμένον is not the consecration itself but the resultant state of the one God set apart as the true and final high priest. As Cullmann writes, "the cultic interpretation alone is too narrow and represents an abridgement."[118]

A second view of 'perfection' in the book of Hebrews can be labeled the moral or ethical view. This view does not necessarily have to believe that Jesus was sinful and moved to moral perfection[119] but merely that there is a development and growth in the humanity of Christ in his suffering and through his obedience. Wescott states, "The conception of τελειῶσαι is that of bringing Christ to the full moral perfection of his humanity (cf. Luke xiii. 32)."[120] In his recent commentary, Vanhoye summarizes this view as the transformation of the human nature in the person of Christ.[121] While Christ took on a sinless perfect nature, it was nevertheless imperfect in the sense that

---

116 Gerhald Delling, "τελειόω," *TDNT*, 8:82.

117 Ibid., 8:83.

118 Oscar Cullmann, *The Christology of the New Testament*, 92–93.

119 Cullmann states, "the author of Hebrews is bound to be particularly interested in the sinlessness of Jesus..." (*Christology*, 93). Cf. Wescott, *Hebrews*, 128; Walters, *Perfection in New Testament Theology*, 146.

120 Wescott, *Hebrews*, 49. Commenting on Christ's learning obedience in 5:8 he writes, "The Lord's manhood was (negatively) sinless and (positively) perfect, that is perfect relatively at every stage; and therefore He truly advanced by 'learning' (Luke ii. 52...) while the powers of His human Nature grew step by step in a perfect union with the divine in His one Person" (128). Thus, in Hebrews, his "perfection was seen on the one side in the complete fulfillment of man's destiny by Christ through absolute self-sacrifice, and on the other in His exaltation to the right hand of God" (129).

121 Albert Vanhoye, *Hebrews*, 75–77, 104–106.

it embodied weakness.[122] It could suffer and die, thus is was not "an already perfect nature." It took on sin and death and therefore could be transformed. "This transformation was effected by God himself and perfectly accepted of Jesus for the good of all humankind. God made the humanity of Jesus perfect through suffering."[123] Vanhoye sees this as the glorification of humanity so that "mankind's calling has therefore found its fulfillment."[124] Hoekema takes this view, writing, "To be truly human means to develop."[125] He concludes "Our Savior was made perfect through suffering and through learning obedience in an actual process of development. His was not a life of shadow-boxing, but of real struggle."[126] Similarly, Hughes writes, "What was essential was that starting, like Adam, with a pure human nature, he should succeed where Adam failed."[127] Hughes sees Christ's perfection as "progressively achieved as he moved toward the cross."[128] So Christ retains his integrity, and the manner in which he faces suffering is "the establishment of his integrity."[129] Cullmann emphasizes the susceptibility to temptation as part of the 'weakness.'[130] Thus, Christ's 'learning obedience' in Heb 5:8 "presupposes an inner human development."[131]

A third view of the use of τελειόω is what is called the vocational or experiential model. The 'perfection' then is the "testing and proving of Christ" in a way that reflects his development or gaining of "educational experience."[132] Seth M. Simisi traces the earliest articulation of this view to a 1935 article by Otto Michel.[133] Peterson argues that we are not allowed to interpret the idea

---

122 Vanhoye, *Hebrews*, 76. Vanhoye describes it as a "frail and mortal nature" in *A Different Priest: The Epistle to the Hebrews* (Convivium, 2001), 111.

123 Vanhoye, *Hebrews*, 76.

124 Vanhoye, *A Different Priest*, 110; see also *Hebrews*, 74: "He made it [the way he faced his suffering death] the occasion of a perfect offering, of filial obedience to God and fraternal solidarity with humankind." This 'filial obedience' is what we seek to identify as an Adamic obedience, fulfilling the role of the Adamic-Davidic Son-king who stands representatively over the people of God.

125 Anthony Hoekema, "The Perfection of Christ in Hebrews," *Calvin Theological Journal* 9 (1974): 36.

126 Ibid., 37.

127 Hughes, *Hebrews*, 188.

128 Ibid., 187.

129 Ibid., 188.

130 Cullmann, *Christology*, 94–95.

131 Ibid., 97. Cullmann (Ibid., 100) suggests a possible analogy to Rom. 5:12ff with the relation between Adam and sinful humanity paralleled to Jesus and those he sanctifies. He does not follow through though and connect this more fully as one can *via* the use of Ps 8 in Heb 2.

132 Seth M. Simisi, "An Investigation into the Teleios ('Perfection') Motif in the Letter to the Hebrews and Its Contribution to the Argument of the Book" (Ph.D. diss., Dallas Theological Seminary, 2012), 41.

133 Simisi, "An Investigation into the Teleios ('Perfection') Motif," 41n.99. He cites Otto Michel's "Die Lehre von der Christlichen Vollkommenheit nach der Anschauung des Hebräer-

"in terms of the profane notion of 'educational correction.'"[134] The point is not that the Son had imperfections such that he had to move from imperfection to perfection by means of suffering. Lane seems to conclude in favor of this, without denying the eschatological view:

> The "perfection" of Jesus in this context (cf. 5:8–9; 7:28) has functional implications. The emphasis falls on the notion that he was fully equipped for his office. God qualified Jesus to come before him in priestly action. He perfected him as a priest of his people through his sufferings, which permitted him to accomplish his redemptive mission.[135]

Lane is correct that the phrase 'perfected through sufferings' "anticipates the full development of the paragraph, which moves from the champion motif of vv. 10–16 to the presentation of Jesus as high priest in vv. 17–18."[136] Notably, however, this perfection motif flows from him being the true human, the fulfillment of Ps 8, who is crowned with glory and honor. This development says as much about being the ideal human as it does about being the priest of his people. As several scholars note, Jesus' humanity and perfection as high priest allows the author to develop his notion of Christ's solidarity with his people in Heb 2. F.F. Bruce puts it: "Man, created by God for his glory, was prevented by sin from attaining that glory until the Son of Man came and opened up by his death a new way by which humanity might reach the goal for which it was made...the perfect Son of God has become his people's perfect Savior opening up their way to God."[137] There is a sense in which he is fitted for this task by virtue of his experience of suffering. Bruce will later describe "he was made perfect" as "fully qualified to be the Savior and High Priest of His people."[138]

G.B. Caird has a similar variation of this model.[139] Christ's perfection comes in his obedience that leads to his ascension whereby he stands as the representative for God's people. For Caird, Heb 2 concerns "Jesus as the fulfillment of human destiny."[140] Thus, in order to become the Savior, he "had to share to the utmost all the conditions of human life. He must leave no human

---

briefes," *Theologische Studien und Kritiken* 106 (1935): 139.

134 Peterson, *Perfection*, 93.
135 Lane, *Hebrews 1–8*, 57–58.
136 Ibid., 58.
137 Bruce, *Hebrews*, 80.
138 Ibid., 132.
139 Simisi ("An Investigation," 42n.103) cites Caird as "one of the earliest...for this interpretive approach."
140 G.B. Caird, "Just Men Made Perfect," *The London Quarterly and Holborn Review* 191 (1966): 91.

experience unexplored, and in particular he must fathom the very depths of temptation."[141] P.J. Du Plessis states, "By unflagging perseverance under circumstances entirely equivalent to all the exigencies of human nature He [Jesus] crowned redemptive history."[142]

The most notable proponent of the so-called vocational or experiential model is David Peterson, whose work *Hebrews and Perfection* is well-argued and documented, remaining a standard in the field. There is little doubt that one cannot understand the notion of Christ's perfection without seeing its relation to his vocation particularly his appointment to being a high priest. Christ was made perfect forever and thus became a high priest (in 7:28 note the use of the perfect tense: εἰς τὸν αἰῶνα τετελειωμένον). While Peterson does not rule out aspects of Christ's exaltation in perfection, the focus remains on Christ's preparation for his office. "In 5:9, as in 2:10, Christ is 'qualified' in his capacity as Savior of his people. The description of his function in this case is 'source of eternal salvation.'"[143] Peterson has argued that there is an Adam Christology undergirding the use of Ps 8 through which we "catch a glimpse of how Christ 'realized to the uttermost the absolute dependence of humanity upon God.'" Nevertheless, Peterson recognizes that the focus on the notion of Christ's perfection is how the death of Christ is "the means by which the salvation of men is achieved."[144] Even here, though, Peterson maintains that Christ's glorification over all things is, as per Ps 8, presented primarily in terms of the functional element of dominion over all things.[145] Peterson summarizes "perfecting involved a whole sequence of events: his proving in suffering, his redemptive death to fulfil the divine requirements for the perfect expiation of sins and his exaltation to glory and honour."[146] One of the strengths of the vocational model, as Simisi summarizes, is that it "puts more emphasis on the Christ event as a whole."[147]

One of the particular strengths of Peterson's view is the role of the suffering of Christ in achieving the perfection of Christ. McCruden states, "Christ's suffering [is seen] not simply as the preliminary ground for subsequent heavenly glorification but as in some sense constitutive of Christ's perfection itself."[148] Although we should not narrow Hebrews' concept of perfection to

---

141 Ibid., 91–92.
142 *ΤΕΛΕΙΟΣ: The Idea of Perfection in the New Testament* (Kampen: J. H. Kok, 1959), 232.
143 *Hebrews and Perfection*, 97.
144 Ibid., 101.
145 Ibid., 52–54, and esp. 121.
146 Ibid., 73.
147 Simisi, "An Investigation," 45.
148 Kevin McCruden, *Solidarity Perfected: Beneficent Christology in the Epistle to the Hebrews* (de Gruyter, 2008), 11. In part, McCruden is using Peterson to argue that the 'perfection

"exaltation" or "glorification" itself, while we cannot deny overlapping semantic fields. Peterson draws strong attention to the role of suffering in 2:9–10 in relationship to 'perfecting' Christ:

> [I]t is misleading to place the emphasis on Christ's exaltation to the heavenly sphere *per se* as the means by which he is essentially qualified or perfected. The statement that he was perfected διὰ παθημάτων suggests that suffering was *part of the process by which he was perfected*, not merely a preliminary to it or the ground of it. The διὰ παθημάτων of 2:10 is not simply synonymous with the expression διὰ τὸ πάθημα τοῦ θανάτου of 2:9. The use of διά with the accusative in verse 9 stresses that the suffering death was the *ground* of Christ's exaltation, whereas the genitive with the preposition in verse 10 stresses that suffering was something *through* which Christ had to pass.[149]

As we will develop the argument with relation to the ascension of Christ, Christ's suffering is an act of obedience. He displays true human trust and obedience to God in the midst of suffering. His role as leader of the people makes his actions that of a second Adam, a true David entrusting himself to God. This suffering obedience qualifies him for perfection, and he achieves glory and honor of the eschatological state by means of obedience. As this obedient and now perfected one, he can progress back up into heaven, fitted to be the Savior for his people.[150] He is the true and glorified man ascending into God's presence. G.B. Caird stresses the humanity of Christ in this entire movement. If he was going to be like his brothers in all things, then he could not "rely on powers on which they cannot draw."[151] Instead, he offers obedience, prayer, and the life of faithful trust to God.[152]

More recently, Kevin McCruden has proposed a model he calls "Divine Attestation" for how one should understand the use of τελειόω.[153] Based upon

---

as glorification model' is too narrow an understanding.

149 Peterson, *Hebrews and Perfection*, 68.

150 Note how Peterson (*Hebrews and Perfection*, 124) handles this: "The transfer to heavenly glory, which leads to his 'appearance' in the heavenly tabernacle and his heavenly session, may well imply such a concept, but this is not the essential meaning of the perfecting of Christ." Here we have to be careful to distinguish between words and concepts. 'Perfection' does not mean his ascension but his 'being made perfect' does lead to his ascension. It includes his resurrected-glorified state but unique to Christ's perfection is that he is fitted for his role as the leader of God's people.

151 G.B. Caird, "Just Men Made Perfect," 92.

152 We discuss this more fully in chapter 5, while examining Heb 5:7–10.

153 Kevin McCruden, *Solidarity Perfected*. See also "Christ's Perfection in Hebrews: Divine Beneficence as an Exegetical Key to Hebrews 2:10," *Biblical Research* 47 (2002): 40–62; "The

# The Adamic Vocation of Sonship in Hebrews 2

extensive investigation of the term in available non-literary papyri, he argues τελειόω has a technical sense.[154] In a number of cases it refers to the notarization or execution of a legal document.[155] This execution is formal, official, public, and definitive.[156] McCruden argues that this feature can be found in Hebrews with God speaking definitively in the Son (1:1–2) and is confirmed by the similar usage of βεβαιόω and its cognates in Heb 2:2–3; 3:14; 6:6, 9; 9:17; and 13:9.[157] In both Hebrews and the papyri, "there exists an abiding concern to display or reveal something in a very clear, definitive, official and public sense… in Hebrews the application of τελειοῦν to Christ functions to reveal a theological content concerning the person of Christ."[158] McCruden goes on to connect this attestation primarily to a demonstration of Christ's *philanthropia*:[159]

> What is specifically disclosed or attested about Christ is his solidarity and intimacy with the faithful…the language of perfection as applied to Christ in 2:10 functions to display, attest, and fundamentally make manifest the character to Christ, namely, the beneficent Son marked by divine *philanthropia* for the faithful.[160]

There are several commendable aspects to McCruden's study, particularly his attention to non-literary papyri, his attention to the suffering of Christ, and his connection to God's speaking in the Son as divine attestation. The study, however, has several weaknesses. First, it focusses on non-literary papyri almost to the exclusion of other background material, particularly literary material, which presents a methodological weakness.[161] How certain can we be that the primary background or the primary referent is the very narrow technical terminology of non-literary papyri particularly since in these contexts there is an absence of a discussion of suffering and of any notion of the age to come which certainly shapes how we understand τελειόω in Hebrews?[162]

---

Concept of Perfection in the Epistle to the Hebrews," in *Reading the Epistle to the Hebrews: A Resource for Students*, ed. Eric F. Mason and Kevin B. McCruden (Society of Biblical Literature, 2011), 209–229.
154 *Solidarity Perfected*, 26–37.
155 Ibid., 27–31.
156 Ibid., 31.
157 Ibid., 38–39.
158 Ibid., 41.
159 Ibid., 67–69.
160 Ibid., 69.
161 Although he does discuss the cultic background of LXX: Ibid., 12–15.
162 Our point is that the attention to non-literary papyri is important and an addition to the field of study concerning τελειόω, but in drawing conclusions for Hebrews one cannot use non-literary papyri to the exclusion of other evidence. This is particularly true since non-liter-

Second, if it is indeed divine attestation—why not more strongly connect it to eschatology and the presentation of the Son?[163] In fact, this connection is what we see in Heb 1:5 and 5:5 respectively with the use of Ps 2:7. Jesus is presented and definitively attested as Son by the Father. Indeed, only through the revelation of Jesus' suffering can the Son be raised up in this divine attestation closely linked to exaltation and ascension. This attestation could be even further connected to the theme of God's oath in Hebrews being executed in the exaltation and ascension of the Son (Heb 6:17–20). Finally, McCruden does little to connect this divine attestation to the experience of believers in the sense that they too can look forward to this τελειόω (10:1, 14).[164] While he argues there is divine communion now that the community of believers experiences, he does not show how 'divine attestation' as a technical term would apply to believers.[165] Whatever one makes of τελειόω, one must show a parallel experience between what happens to Christ in his perfection and the subsequent perfection believers come to experience.

---

ary papyri is in a sense its own genre. Technical terms in them, for example in bills of sale or legally executed documents, do not necessarily mandate that the same words are used as technical terms in other contexts, particularly literary usage.

163 McCruden (*Solidarity Perfected*, 11) finds the eschatological/glorification model's "principal weakness to be that it tends to subordinate—and to that degree diminish—the role of suffering in the perfecting of Christ in order to emphasize his glorification." He follows Peterson (*Hebrews and Perfection*, 68), suggesting that suffering in this view is preliminary grounds for heavenly glorification not "constitutive of Christ's perfection itself." This argument is a false disjunction. Whatever one's view of 'perfection,' the experience of 'perfection' by Christ is not the same condition as his experience of weakness and suffering.

164 Simisi ("An Investigation," 51) may have this line of thought in view when he remarks, "following the definitive model does not help the reader appreciate the content and message of Hebrews," but this criticism is vague, especially since McCruden (*Solidarity Perfected*, 122–139) seeks to work his model into the social setting and literary character of Hebrews. Although McCruden does not entirely avoid aspects of 'content and message' in relationship to the original readers, one may find it a bit wanting at this point since it misses aspects of the presentation of Christ via Pss 2:7 or 110:1.

165 McCruden does note how the believer finds sanctification in the body of Christ, and comments on a "reciprocal movement of Christ's highly personal approach to the faithful and the approach of faithful [sic] to God is beautifully expressed in the hortatory section of 10:19–22" (*Solidarity Perfected*, 120). He points to the believers' "renewed relationship" that Christ enables, allowing "for an analogous relationship of intimacy between God and the faithful" (117). Our concern is more specific: if Christ's 'perfection' is divine attestation, what is the believer's 'perfection'? Perhaps McCruden would argue it is the attestation to believers sharing in the salvation of the Savior. If one were to adopt this argument, it would result in a reductionist use of τελειόω, as if to say "believers are perfected" is simply to say "believers are saved." It is insufficient to say "believers have God's attestation." Elsewhere, McCruden ("The Concept of Perfection," 225) does say, "In the broadest sense believers experience perfection in the age to come when they inherit a kingdom that transcends all manner of corporeal existence (12:26–27; 13:14) and enter into the glory of God's transcendent presence. Perfection for others refers ultimately, then, to the completion of the divine plan of salvation when God endows humanity with honor and glory."

A final view of the use of τελειόω in Hebrews has been called the "eschatological view." It sees the perfection of Christ primarily as his glorification and/or exaltation. In this view 'perfection' is "best understood in terms of 'the world to come.'"[166] In light of Hebrews' usage of the dawning of the 'age to come' in the person of Christ and the use of Ps 8 to show Christ to be the true human heir, Christ's perfection is understood principally as his being fitted to be a partaker in the age to come—the pioneer who leads God's people into it. In this view, the aspect of Christ's perfection as his being fitted to be a Savior is not excluded, rather this specific function of Christ is subordinate to the larger eschatological concerns of Hebrews.[167] He can be the Savior because he, himself, is delivered from death and fitted as the first of the age to come. Furthermore, this view does not deny that an aspect of Christ's being 'made perfect' is the access to God that now the people of God can share in.[168] Moises Silva, looking at LXX background with the cultic sense of τελειόω, concludes that "the Epistle of Hebrews does support this view by bringing together the idea of *perfection* with that of *sanctification* (2:10–11); 10:14) and with the broader notion of our approach to God (7:19)."[169] Here Peterson is certainly correct: "The Son's eschatological inheritance could not be secured nor his Sonship decisively manifested for the salvation of his people until he had carried out the earthly ministry designed for him as Messiah."[170] Silva, quoting Ridderbos, makes connections to Paul's theology with its strong eschatological bent.[171] More specifically on Hebrews, he continues, "therefore, the perfecting of human conscience (9:9; 10:1, 14) is not a reference to forgiveness or fitness to approach God which OT saints did experience (cf. Ps 32 and Rom. 4), but to the enjoyment of the time of the fulfillment, the new epoch introduced by the Messiah through his exaltation."[172] "It is likely,

---

166 Simisi, "An Investigation," 58. Simisi's work as a whole argues for the eschatological view.

167 For example, one of the strengths of John Walters' work (*Perfection in New Testament Theology*) is his sensitivity to eschatology in Hebrews without ruling out the ethical implications this brings upon the believer, 150–152.

168 Peterson, in *Hebrews and Perfection*, notes of this eschatological perspective in Hebrews. It is not as if in his understanding he intentionally minimizes or disregards it.

169 Moises Silva, "Perfection and Eschatology," *WTJ* 39 (1976): 61–62.

170 *Hebrews and Perfection*, 125.

171 "Perfection and Eschatology," 67. Allen Wikgren ("Patterns of Perfection in the Epistle to the Hebrews," *NTS* 6 (1960): 164) makes some of the same connections with respect to the title πρωτότοκος.

172 "Perfection and Eschatology," 68. We would adopt a more nuanced understanding of the OT with regard to how Hebrews views its ineffectiveness. However, the point remains, the ineffectiveness that Hebrews sees is precisely that of eschatological categories. For example, the failure of the Levitical priesthood is both a moral failure of the priests themselves and a structural inability to usher in the age to come. A 'shadow' at best can only ever remain a

therefore, that the audience will hear 'perfection' after sufferings as a parallel expression for his exaltation after death."[173] Although 'perfection' is linked to the subsequent exaltation we should remain clear that perfection, in itself as used by Hebrews, does not necessarily entail ascension or spatial movement into the heavenly realm.[174]

In his perfected state, Christ *becomes* the source of eternal salvation (5:9 ἐγένετο...αἴτιος σωτηρίας αἰωνίου) just as he becomes exalted (e.g., 1:4 κρείττων γενόμενος) and becomes high priest (5:5 γενηθῆναι ἀρχιερέα; 6:20 ἀρχιερεὺς γενόμενος εἰς τὸν αἰῶνα). This 'being made perfect' where he also becomes a high priest is described by our author as a glorification: Οὕτως καὶ ὁ Χριστὸς οὐχ ἑαυτὸν ἐδόξασεν γενηθῆναι ἀρχιερέα (5:5). All high priests must be called by God to this honor; they do not appoint themselves to it, οὐχ ἑαυτῷ τις λαμβάνει τὴν τιμὴν ἀλλὰ καλούμενος ὑπὸ τοῦ θεοῦ (5:4). Also in chapter 2, being crowned with glory and honor in verse 9 is parallel to being perfect in 2:10:

Ιησοῦν διὰ τὸ πάθημα τοῦ θανάτου δόξῃ καὶ τιμῇ ἐστεφανωμένον
τὸν ἀρχηγὸν τῆς σωτηρίας αὐτῶν διὰ παθημάτων τελειῶσαι

Christ being the ἀρχηγός, discussed more fully below, suggests that while Christ is fitted for a vocation, there are aspects of his 'being made perfect' that must then be coming to all humanity. Fulfilling Ps 8, as heir now 'perfected' he is granted the inheritance and is leading humanity to the final eschatological destiny. "Presenting Christ's superiority as the one who fulfills the eschatological divine destiny for humanity, the author points first to the τελείωσις of Christ (2:10) as the "pioneer" or "chief leader" of the believers' eternal salvation."[175] In Heb 12:2, Jesus is τῆς πίστεως ἀρχηγὸν καὶ τελειωτήν. In this respect, Christ's fulfillment of human destiny is conceptually what we are labeling 'Second Adam,' and like the Adamic-David kingly sons of the OT. Being this Adamic figure entails corporate representation of God's people.[176] This Adamic role gives us not only a sense of the connection between

---

shadow. Silva's point could be nuanced *a la* Hebrews 11 that heroes of the faith in the OT still experienced "salvation" as they looked to the greater coming age which Hebrews now sees as having dawned.

173  David deSilva, *Perseverance in Gratitude: A Socio-Rhetorical Commentary on the Epistle "to the Hebrews,"* (Eerdmans, 2000), 197; cf. also Silva, "Perfection and Eschatology" 66; J.M. Scholer, *Proleptic Priests: Priesthood and the Epistle to the Hebrews* (JSOT, 1991), 195–196.

174  Schenck, *Cosmology and Eschatology*, 69–71.

175  Simisi, "An Investigation," 174.

176  See for example N.T. Wright, *The Climax of the Covenant*, 21–26, 46–47: "It is endemic in the understanding of kingship, in many societies and certainly ancient Israel, that the king and the people are bound together in such a way that what is true in the one is true in principle of the other" (*Climax*, 46). G.W. Grogan, "The Old Testament Concept of Solidarity in Hebrews,"

ἀρχηγός and 'perfection' terminology but also a sense of the how fundamental these terms are to Hebrews' entire argument. "The perfection of Jesus may be equated with his glorification in the Heavenly Sanctuary, thus outfitting him as the ἀρχηγός and τελειωτής of those who confidently follow him into the heavenly holy place."[177] It is as if the whole force of what he is previously said is the weight behind 12:2. Finally, in 12:23 we read that in the assembly of the firstborn there are πνεύμασιν δικαίων τετελειωμένων. "This final occurrence of τελειο- indicates that humanity has now fully attained the promise for which it was created, and proleptically indicates the goal of humanity."[178]

Harold Attridge and James Thompson have pointed to 4 Macc 7:13–15 and the martyrdom tradition for a background use of τελειόω.[179] This background is convincing for several reasons. First, as in Hebrews, the martyr is perfected through suffering. Second, he despised the torments of his death, like Christ in Heb 12:2. Third, the piety of the martyr facing death and the manner of his facing death is vital for the outcome and what qualifies the suffering as acceptable, similar again to Heb 5:7–8. Fourth, the martyr is perfected because he governed his passions through "devout reason," ὁ εὐσεβὴς λογισμός (4 Macc 7:16). He stands in contrast to the one who cannot govern his passions because of διὰ τὸν ἀσθενῆ λογισμόν (4 Macc 7:20). Note the distinction here between godly pious reason leading to perfection or completion against weak reason. The pious "endure every pain for the sake of virtue" (4 Macc 7:22).[180] The godly ones, like the patriarchs, believe that to God they do not die but live (7:19), again similarly the heroes of the faith in Heb 11. With this context

---

TynBul 49.1 (1998): 159–173, esp. 163: "King and nation can have a common identification (Nu. 20:14–21; 22:5)." On Adam, Adam-like figures in Israel and Israel's king see also G.K. Beale *A New Testament Biblical Theology*, 29–116. For a short introduction see Graeme Goldsworthy, *The Son of God and the New Creation* (Crossway, 2015), 59–82, which is his chapter "Adam the Son of God." Crispin Fletcher-Louis takes the Kingship-Image Bearer and Incorporative Representation thesis as a means of understanding 1 Kings 3–4. He sees the theme as broader in the OT than just this passage but shows how this passage illuminates our understanding of the motif: Fletcher-Louis, "King Solomon, Bearer of the Image of God"; Seth D. Postell, *Adam as Israel: Genesis 1–3 as the Introduction to the Torah and Tanakh* (Pickwick, 2011), esp. 129–167. Joshua Jipp (*Christ is King: Paul's Royal Ideology* [Fortress, 2015], 149–165) discusses how the King both share in God's reign and represents God's people: "the entire nation is wrapped up with the life and destiny of their Davidic king" (161). For Hebrews, Jesus is the royal Adamic-Davidic figure who suffers with true obedience and faith thereby securing human destiny for 'sons of glory,' the seed of Abraham.

177  Mackie, *Eschatology and Exhortation*, 196.
178  Joshua Jipp, "The Son's Entrance into the Heavenly Word: The Soteriological Necessity of the Scriptural Catena in Hebrews 1.5–14," *NTS* 56 (2010): 568.
179  Harold Attridge, *Hebrews*, 86; James Thompson, *Hebrews* (Baker, 2008), 66; cf. also Wilfred Knox, "The 'Divine Hero' Christology in the New Testament," *HTR* 41.4 (1948): 245.
180  One can obviously see here the influence of Stoicism, which developed the idea of the "ideal sage, perfect through the possession of all virtue" (Attridge, *Hebrews*, 84).

in view, in 4 Macc 7:15, we find that by loyalty to the law they are perfected in death: ᾧ μακαρίου γήρως καὶ σεμνῆς πολιᾶς καὶ βίου νομίμου, ὃν πιστὴ θανάτου σφραγὶς ἐτελείωσε.

The elderly man is said to have "despised torments unto death on account of his piety," τῶν μέχρι θανάτου βασάνων περιεφρόνησεν δι' εὐσέβειαν (4 Macc 7:16). While Hebrews does not place the emphasis on governing passions in suffering as 4 Macc does and it also does not use εὐσέβεια but εὐλάβεια in 5:7, there remain core similarities and overlapping concepts.[181] There is a sense that obedience, even in suffering, leads to perfection. Simisi states, "It is best to understand Eleazar not perfected in death, but in his zeal to the law."[182] Perfection has a sense of completion and living to/with God, most likely alluding to the eschatological resurrection life that awaits faithful martyrs. As 17:15 states "Piety won the victory and crowned her contestants," θεοσέβεια δὲ ἐνίκα, τοὺς ἑαυτῆς ἀθλητὰς στεφανοῦσα with 17:18 "on account of which [reference 'their endurance] they now stand beside the divine throne and live the life of the age of blessing," δι' ἣν καὶ τῷ θείῳ νῦν παρεστήκασιν θρόνῳ, καὶ τὸν μακάριον βιοῦσιν αἰῶνα. The enduring believer goes before the throne in the blessing that is above.

The role of Jesus in Heb 2 is to bring about Adamic glory of the age to come through his own suffering (2:9).[183] The Second Adam undoes the fall. When Christ fulfills the human/Adamic vocation and conquers death, he opens the path for others to come to glory with him and through his representative work. The purpose of God is to πολλοὺς υἱοὺς εἰς δόξαν ἀγαγόντα (Heb 2:10). Here the context is the work of the Father: the Son is the author of his (God's) salvation. So, if the Father is going to bring sons to glory, there must be τὸν ἀρχηγὸν τῆς σωτηρίας αὐτῶν (Heb 2:10). There must be a pioneer and originator who can accomplish what the people of God need. If the people of God need perfection and glorification, then the ἀρχηγός must experience it first.

Like many places in Hebrews, this motif draws on the OT. Lane suggests, "The motif of God's leading many sons is familiar from the OT, particularly in connection with the Exodus from Egypt, where the divine initiative is frequently stressed (e.g., Exod 3:8, 17; 6:6–7; 7:4–5)."[184] "The title ἀρχηγός belongs to the imagery of redemption from bondage, exodus, and journey to

---

181 Matthew C. Easter (*Faith and the Faithfulness*, 160–163) concludes, "Therefore, this possible parallel to the Maccabean virtue of piety (εὐσέβεια) as the noble character to a martyr strengthens our reading of εὐλάβεια in Heb 5:7 as a posture of faithful reverence rather than fear" (162).

182 "An Investigation," 78.

183 See C. Marvin Pate, *The Glory of Adam*, 66–75, where he shows that righteous suffering was believed to be rewarded in Second Temple Judaism with Adamic glory.

184 Lane, *Hebrews 1–8*, 56.

the promised rest."¹⁸⁵ Attridge suggests that there may be David messianism involved in the background on the usage¹⁸⁶ even though it is not used directly of David in LXX.

While ἀρχηγός can mean leader, ruler, or prince,¹⁸⁷ here in Hebrews it certainly connotes someone who begins something as originator or founder.¹⁸⁸ Paul Ellingworth and William Lane, in their respective commentaries, suggest a more Hellenistic background of the champion or pioneer who blazes a path for followers.¹⁸⁹ This interpretation has a degree of validity based on the context: (1) the notion of the Son being necessary to bring other sons to glory, (2) the description of Jesus as a forerunner πρόδρομος in 6:20, and (3) the exhortation Heb 12:1 gives that we are to run with endurance because Jesus τῆς πίστεως ἀρχηγὸν καὶ τελειωτήν has already suffered and received exalted glory.

None of this negates our proposal of a Second Adam Christology, in fact, it enhances it. Christ's act of obedient suffering accomplishes the redemption of the people of God and achieves their eschatological glory. While Delling does not connect the use of the idea to Ps 8, he does write "Yet Jesus is also ἀρχηγὸς τῆς πίστεως in the sense that as the first man He gave an example of faith in God, that by His death He 'fulfilled' this faith in God's unconditional love and its overcoming of the barrier of sin, and that He thereby gave this love concrete and once-for-all actualisation in the history of salvation."¹⁹⁰ The community of believers is exhorted to faithful suffering in order to receive their eschatological glory precisely because Jesus' Second-Adam-obedience has opened and cleared the way. As Thompson writes, "The language allows the author to exploit both the solidarity of the Son with his people and the Son as the one who opens the way."¹⁹¹ If there is not a new man inaugurating a new age, there is no inheritance for God's people.

## Heb 2:11–13—Jesus' Solidarity with His People

The solidarity between Christ and his people begins with ὅ τε γὰρ ἁγιάζων καὶ

---

185 Peterson, *Hebrews and Perfection*, 69.
186 Attridge, *Hebrews*, 87–88.
187 BAGD, 112. Cf. Acts 5:31
188 Ibid. Used only here and in 12:2. Gerhard Delling ("ἀρχηγός," *TDNT*, 1:487) notes that Philo considered Adam and Noah to be ἀρχηγέτης while also confirming the Hellenistic background of the concept of "hero."
189 Lane, *Hebrews 1–8*, 56–57, and Ellingworth, *Hebrews*, 161. Many scholars note the background and usage in reference to Hercules: Delling, "ἀρχηγός," *TDNT*, 1:487; Knox, "Divine Hero Christology," 247–248; McCruden, *Solidarity Perfected*, 50–59; Thompson, *Hebrews*, 63.
190 Delling, "ἀρχηγός," *TDNT*, 1:488.
191 Thompson, *Hebrews*, 63.

οἱ ἁγιαζόμενοι (Heb 2:11). Christ is the one who sanctifies them. The work of Christ sanctifies God's people. This concept is similarly stated in 10:14 with 'perfection' terminology: μιᾷ γὰρ προσφορᾷ τετελείωκεν εἰς τὸ διηνεκὲς τοὺς ἁγιαζομένους. The blood of Christ sanctifies believers as he is their offering, ἐν ᾧ ἡγιάσθη where the referent is τὸ αἷμα τῆς διαθήκης (10:29). Christ suffered in order to sanctify his own people ἁγιάσῃ διὰ τοῦ ἰδίου αἵματος τὸν λαόν (13:12). While ὁ ἁγιάζων often refers to YHWH in LXX (e.g., Exod 31:13; Lev 20:8; 21:15; 22:9, 16, 32),[192] in this case it clearly refers to Christ. While it is tempting to suggest a larger Christological point to Jesus being YHWH, this seems to be beyond the scope of Hebrews' consideration here. Certainly, Christ acts for his people but this activity in solidarity stresses their unity so that the Father can act on both the Son and the people. The Father (2:10 Ἔπρεπεν γὰρ αὐτῷ) brings sons to glory by perfecting τὸν ἀρχηγὸν τῆς σωτηρίας αὐτῶν διὰ παθημάτων. The pioneer, Christ, by virtue of a suffering that leads to perfection in crowning glory, is also ὁ ἁγιάζων. Ellingworth notes the relationship between sanctify and perfection: "Ἁγιάζω thus reflects the cultic and ethical aspects of τελειόω in v. 10."[193] The Father has sanctified/perfected him as corporate head and thus, he in turn sanctifies his people. We also get the first hints of the high priest theme with which the chapter ends.

Interpreters have long debated how to understand ἐξ ἑνὸς πάντες (2:11). It points to an obvious unified origin between Jesus and his people and reflects the argument of solidarity between Christ and his people that the author has been building. A common understanding is to see it referring to God or the Father.[194] That it refers to God or the Father is plausible because the role of the Father starts the statement in verse 10 (Ἔπρεπεν γὰρ αὐτῷ). The Father is able to glorify the sons since the Father has made perfect the Son through his suffering. The sons share in the reward achieved by the Son. In this respect, the eschatological realities are given to Christ and God's people from God as they are (or will be) crowned with glory. Other interpretations suggest that a person is in view, typically Adam or Abraham. Since σπέρματος Ἀβραάμ is mentioned in 2:16 it could be possible that Abraham is in view. However, this theory seems unlikely because Hebrews nowhere focuses on Christ being of the line of Abraham. In fact, such a view might undercut Hebrews' later argument that Christ's priesthood is superior to the Levitical priesthood because Abraham paid tithes to Melchizedek (7:1–11). In light of the demonstrated 'Second Adam Christology,' it is tempting to see ἐξ ἑνὸς πάντες as a reference

---

192 Lane, *Hebrews 1–8*, 58.
193 Ellingworth, *Hebrews*, 164.
194 Ellingworth (*Hebrews*, 164) lists Chrysostom, Cyril of Alexandria, Thomas Aquinas, Bleek, Westcott, Windisch, Moffatt, Spicq, F.F. Bruce, Montefiore, Braun, Attridge, and Lane.

to Adam. However, Hebrews' use of Ps 8 is not to Adam as an historical figure but rather the destiny of humanity that has come first upon the Son.

In the context, ἐξ ἑνὸς πάντες should simply be translated "all are from one" or "all our from one source." It does not directly refer to the Father although it may be a subtle allusion, since the Father is involved in glorifying the Son and the sons. They certainly share in a common humanity as the Son became like children sharing in their flesh and blood (2:14) so that ἐξ ἑνός probably has in view the common humanity. However, the immediate focus is on the redemption and transformation to glory—both have a common source: the work of the Father in and through the suffering of the Son. For this reason, we should not see ἐξ ἑνός as a direct reference to the Father since part of the means by which the Father perfects the Son is through the Son's obedience suffering. This act of the Son becomes a representative act that effects both his glorification and the glorification of the children he became like. "Thus, although Hebrews stresses the unique supremacy of Jesus, he does not do so at the expense of his solidarity with the rest of humanity."[195]

Seemingly then that ἐξ ἑνός as 'one source' or some variant has in view both the shared humanity of Christ and his people as well as the shared eschatological end that the Father gives to the Son and the sons, since the work of Christ entails solidaric representation. "Christ and his people are members of the same family, for they have one origin.... Certainly He is the 'firstborn' (πρωτότοκος) (1.6) and their sonship is by grace (2.9f), but it is a real membership of the same great family of God."[196] Jesus "is the originator of the distinct faith-trust that he maintained to its fulfillment in his being raised from the dead by God, and in this distinctive faith-trust lies the salvation (σωτηρία) of those who call themselves Christians."[197] James Swetnam goes a bit further on this point, arguing that ἐξ ἑνός includes the faith-trust of Abraham's seed before the coming of Christ and after in light of Christ's perfecting.[198] He proposes that it is two faith-trusts that function as one.[199] We think understanding it as a double faith-trust goes too far.[200] On the one hand, we agree

---

[195] Marie Isaacs, *Sacred Space*, 174. Isaacs rejects the argument that there is a concept of Second/Last Adam theology in Hebrews (168).
[196] Geoffrey Grogan, "Christ and His People," 68. Though Grogan does not specifically mention the point, it is worth highlighting again 'πρωτότοκος' is an eschatological title or role for Jesus.
[197] James Swetnam "The Crux at Hebrews 2,9 and Its Context," *Biblica* 91.1 (2010): 108–109.
[198] Swetnam, "Εξ ἑνός in Hebrews 2,11," *Biblica* 88 (2007): 521.
[199] Ibid., 522.
[200] This is not to deny the NT teaches that believers experience salvation through faith and trust in Christ or as Heb 5:9 speaks of this 'faith-trust' as obeying Christ. It is simply to say one cannot read too much into ἐξ ἑνός.

with Swetnam when he states, "Jesus has had his faith-trust vindicated and wishes to celebrate this vindication so that his brothers can be strengthen in the face of death (Heb 2,14–15).".[201] However, we should not narrow ἐξ ἑνός to mean faith-trust. Rather it speaks of the common origin where both the Son and the sons, in their common humanity, are glorified by the working of the Father through the suffering of the Son which was marked by his obedient faith. His obedient faith-trust certainly warranted his glorification and accomplished the glorification of those in solidarity with him, a point which returns us to the motif of the 'Second Adam.'

The Son can join with the sons in the heavenly assembly precisely because he put his trust in God for himself and on behalf of the seed of Abraham. The corporate relationship between Christ and the sons of glory is so close that Heb 2:11 tells us that he calls them brothers. Then, Heb 2:12 quotes Ps 22:22 [MT: 22:23; LXX: 21:23].

Aside from the minor textual difference (LXX: διηγήσομαι; Heb 2:12: ἀπαγγελῶ), which corresponds better with MT, the wording is the same. Hebrews sees Christ as representative of "brothers" in the great congregation leading them in singing worship. What is noteworthy is that Ps 22 is well-known in the gospel traditions, used to refer to Christ's suffering. Hebrews, however, seems to choose a verse from later in the psalm in order to emphasize the solidarity between Christ and his people.[202] In the psalm, the sufferer is raised up before the Lord after his deep humiliation. Narratively, this is the same movement that Heb 2 has in mind. The quotation of the psalm is likely more than a mere coincidence on the narrow reading of just one verse.[203] Hebrews takes the passage and reads it in light of the eschatology that has now been fulfilled in Jesus Christ. As C.H. Dodd writes in his classic study, "The conclusion is that Jesus is Messiah, or Son of Man, in the sense that He has passed from death to glory and universal sovereignty as representative Head of a redeemed mankind."[204] Jesus as the exalted one leads the heavenly assembly in praise to the Lord, a theme Hebrews returns to in 12:22–23.

Finally, in Heb 2:13, Jesus becomes the representative 'truster' of God with the use of Isa 8:17–18. The quotation portrays Jesus as the culmination and typological fulfillment of Isaiah's trust.[205] Gert Steyn has pointed to

---

201 Ibid., 523.

202 McCruden, *Solidarity Perfected*, 63; Ellingsworth, *Hebrews*, 167–168; Attridge, "The Psalms in Hebrews," in *The Psalms in the New Testament*, ed. Steve Moyise and Maarten J.J. Menken (T&T Clark, 2004), 208.

203 Simon Kistemaker, *The Psalm Citations*, 84; Ellingworth, *Hebrews*, 167.

204 C.H. Dodd, *According to the Scriptures* (Fontana Books, 1965), 20.

205 Christopher Richardson, *Pioneer and Perfecter of Faith* (Mohr Siebeck, 2012), 23–24. He helpfully discusses the background to Isaiah's trust (21–22). Cf. Brian Pate, "Who Is Speak-

*The Adamic Vocation of Sonship in Hebrews 2*

original context as a backdrop for Hebrews' use: "Isaiah trusted the Lord because he knew that he and his children were signs and symbols (σημεῖα καὶ τέρατα, Isa 8:18; cf. σημείοις τε καὶ τέρασιν, Heb 2:4) of God's reign on Mount Zion (Isa 8:18)."[206] Similarly the Son's trusting in God and handing his life over to God is ultimately that which brings him to Mt. Zion and qualifies him for his ascension.

The role of humanity has always been to live in obedience under God and his command.[207] As the prophet stood with the remnant and trusted God along with those who were left, so Jesus trusts God along with the family that belongs to him.[208] Thus, having trusted God through suffering in offering himself in obedience, he is fit to lead the people of God in their trust of God. Christ is not the object of trust but the one who trusts in faith.[209] So "as the new representative of humanity (2.5–9), Jesus is presented as *the* exemplary, faithful witness, whom God's people must consider and imitate..."[210] He is *the* man of faith offering up *the* human obedience in solidarity and representation. His "brothers" must follow and imitate him, but this imitation is effective only so far as his act of obedience was representational. Lane concludes that there is here both representation and solidarity what we have labels under the rubric of 'Adam Christology':

> Jesus is now the representative head of a new humanity which is being led to glory through suffering...Although the concept of the people of God as τὰ παιδία, "the children," of the exalted Son is not found elsewhere in the NT, the image of family suggests an intimacy of relationship and a tenderness that broadens the concept of solidarity.[211]

The completion of the Adamic vocation for Christ through obedient suffering makes Jesus the perfect exalted king and high priest as the Father has exalted him, per Ps 110. Thus, having been the forerunner into eschatological

---

ing? The Use of Isaiah 8:17–18 in Hebrews 2:13 as a Case Study for Applying the Speech of Key OT Figures to Christ," *JETS* 59.4 (2016): 732, 738–741.

206 Steyn, *Quest for the Assumed LXX Vorlage*, 159. See also 167–168 for a discussion of elements that may bring LXX Ps 21 and Isa 8:17–18 into closer context containing the some of the same ideas such as the sufferer trusting God and the theme of the remnant. We concur with Steyn's conclusion "The Son thus identifies himself closely with humankind" (168).

207 Adam received the command in the garden; Israel received commands in the Law. On the relationship between Adam and Israel, see especially Seth D. Postell, *Adam as Israel*, esp. 114–118.

208 Lane, *Hebrews 1–8*, 60.

209 Easter, *Faith and the Faithfulness*, 155.

210 Richardson, *Pioneer and Perfecter*, 25, emphasis original.

211 Lane, *Hebrews 1–8*, 60.

glory, he can also serve as priestly representative. In his office, Jesus is superior to the angels, but he is also a superior representative of the people having walked through weakness to the eschatological glory. In short, he succeeded where Adam failed. While Heb 1:3 makes clear that Christ is superior as the ἀπαύγασμα τῆς δόξης and the χαρακτὴρ τῆς ὑποστάσεως αὐτοῦ, Heb 2 demonstrates his fitness for the vocation of ruling over creation as the representative man. Thus, in the last days God has spoken ἐν υἱῷ. Jesus' taking on Adamic sonship was necessary to enact the transition of the ages. In both the divine and Adamic aspects of Sonship, Christ is superior to angels and to other human beings, including Moses and the patriarchs.

### Heb 2:14–18—Made Like His Brothers to Become a High Priest

Heb 2 goes on to detail what the incarnation of the Son entails, exploring the depths of what incarnation must mean. If he is going to represent his brothers, he has to become like his brothers in all ways (2:17). Incarnation is necessary for the representation and solidarity he has with them.

The author describes the state of humanity and specifically the "children" whom Christ is representing as "partaking in flesh and blood" (2:14a Ἐπεὶ οὖν τὰ παιδία κεκοινώνηκεν αἵματος καὶ σαρκός). Their condition is later described as a state of weakness (4:15, cf. possible allusions in 5:2 and 7:28). The children are in slavery to death; they are subject to it. In their lives, they face struggles and temptations (4:15), so—in order to be their ἀρχηγός—he has to start where they start, in the sub-eschatological state of being 'a little lower than angels.' Thus, αἵματος καὶ σαρκός highlights not just humanity but a weakness disassociated from the end for which God created man. The lowly human estate is one of utmost vulnerability because it can age, wither, and perish. The lowly condition is far inferior to the resurrected, glorified, imperishable state of the new creation destiny of humanity (cf. 1 Cor 15:50). Hebrews argues that because those Jesus is going to save were flesh and blood, then καὶ αὐτὸς παραπλησίως μετέσχεν τῶν αὐτῶν he partakes of all that they are, without sin (2:14). He must enter creation with ability to die for the precise reason that he will effectively destroy death's power by his own death: ἵνα διὰ τοῦ θανάτου καταργήσῃ τὸν τὸ κράτος ἔχοντα τοῦ θανάτου (2:14). He will be the priest who fights the devil and destroys him,[212] but in a "surprise" reversal, death is defeated by one who yields to death and trusts God

---

212 Cf. for example 1QM xv. Here the High Priest takes up the fight against Belial. In xvi.11–16 the priests join the fight with the High Priest. The High Priests fights with his brothers and they remove Belial. This magnifies God and brings glory to Zion as God keeps his covenant.

for deliverance. In a sense, he fights by not fighting but by "giving up his soul." Yet, this is not a mere succumbing but a perfect trust in his Father for victory. "In the background of 2:5–10 and 2:14–15, we may see the picture of Gen 1–3 and the teaching of the Prophetic and Apocalyptic writers about the restoration of paradise in the End-time, the victory over death and sin and Satan."[213] Christ does not enter creation as the eschatological man but rather as a man in all human weaknesses yet without sin (4:15) so that in his act of obedience that culminates in the suffering death of the cross—a death of the eschatological judgment—he then can pioneer into the glorious eschatological end of humanity. He becomes the eschatological man in an act of representative Adamic-like obedient trust in God.

Thus, he does not help angels but σπέρματος Ἀβραάμ (Heb 2:16). The redemption, the age to come, and the triumph over the devil is not for angels to share in.[214] At first glance this reference may seem curious, but it is precisely as representative man, a last Adam, that the Son helps his brothers, the people of God. This reference to σπέρματος Ἀβραάμ suggests further that redemptive historical categories from Genesis are in view for our author. The future lies through the seed of Abraham.[215] The seed will possess the promises, the inheritance, and the eschatological glory.[216] As the seed, Israel failed to obey YHWH thus she was unable to be the means of bringing this age and defeating Satan. God narrows 'the seed' by installing a royal son-king, one who is put forth as Second Adam.[217] Put another way, Israel fails at sonship, so the king is set forth by YHWH as his son and as a representative of the sons, the 'seed of Abraham.' Or even using another metaphor in Hebrews, the "house" (i.e., God's people) is constituted under the representative man who stands for them and acts upon their behalf (cf. 3:1–6). In the OT and in subsequent

---

213 David Peterson, *Hebrews and Perfection*, 62.

214 In 1QM angels join the fight with the High Priest against Belial. In some Second Temple texts, humanity is glorified to essentially be on par with angels in the heavenly glory.

215 T.D. Alexander, *From Paradise to Promised Land: Introduction to the Pentateuch*, 2nd ed. (Baker 2002), 127. Gary Smith ("Structure and Purpose in Genesis 1–11," *JETS* 20 [1977]: 318) writes "the blessing given to Adam and Noah is essentially the same as that given to Abram." On Adam's commission passed through Noah and Abraham, see Beale, *Temple*, 94–96.

216 Alexander, *From Paradise to Promised Land*, 103–111, discuss the conception of seed as a royal lineage and how it shapes the narrative in Genesis.

217 N.T. Wright (*People of God*, 263) writes: "the narrative [of Genesis] quietly insists that Abraham and his progeny inherit the role of Adam and Even." Again, "Abraham is to restore what Adam has done" (266) citing *Genesis Rabbah* 14.6. See also 4 Ezra 6:54–59. Beale (*New Testament Biblical Theology*, 47) writes, "God then gave the essence of the commission of Gen 1:28 to Abraham (Gen 12:2; 17:2, 6, 8, 16; 22:18), Isaac (Gen 26:3–4, 24), Jacob (Gen 28:3–4, 14; 35:11–12; 48:3, 15–16) and Israel (see Deut 7:13 and Gen 47:27; Exod 1:7; Ps 107:38; Isa 51:2, the latter four of which state the beginning fulfillment of the promise to Abraham in Israel)" (see also 48–52 for even more textual support). See also Kinzer, "All Things Under His Feet," 262–263.

Second Temple Literature, Israel, or 'the seed of Abraham,' as God's people, take up the Adamic vice-regency and have the promise of Adamic glory awaiting them. Per Second Temple Judaism, only the seed of Abraham is destined for the glory of Adam. In 1QHa 4:14–15 for those who loyally served the Lord, their seed (זרעם) receives the glory of Adam and their inheritance (ולהנחילם בכול כבוד אדם). As N.T. Wright puts it, "Abraham's children are God's true humanity, and their homeland is the new Eden."[218] Glory and crowning thus comes first upon the royal Second Adam son, the true human fulfilling Ps 8, and then upon the seed of Abraham,[219] who have been destined for this glory. "The fulfillment of God's promises to Abraham is nothing less than the inheritance of all the glory of Adam…the hope the writer holds out appears to be the hope of the restoration of the human being to a position and status before the fall."[220]

In order to advance our defense of the conception of a Second Adam Christology undergirding Heb 2, we note the way that the work of Christ functions as a corporate representation in Heb 2:10–18. As stated above, an Adam Christology will entail representation of the people of God just like Adam represented humanity. There was an absolute necessity for Jesus to become like his brothers in order to stand as their representative. As Heb 2:17 states, ὅθεν ὤφειλεν κατὰ πάντα τοῖς ἀδελφοῖς ὁμοιωθῆναι. This obligation (ὀφείλω) is in part because the High Priest must be called from among the people (5:1–4; esp. v. 1 Πᾶς γὰρ ἀρχιερεὺς ἐξ ἀνθρώπων λαμβανόμενος). Hebrews uses the purpose clause: ἵνα ἐλεήμων γένηται καὶ πιστὸς ἀρχιερεὺς τὰ πρὸς τὸν θεόν (2:17). While the earthly ministry of Christ is in offering himself as a sacrifice, his 'becoming' a high priest has in view his glorification (cf. 5:5–6).[221] Christ's

---

218 Wright, *Climax of the Covenant*, 23.

219 Hebrews, like other NT passages, sees Christians as this seed. 'Seed' is not used to talk about physical lineage as it was in the original contexts, but the concept is applied to all who believe in Jesus, cf. Schreiner, *Hebrews*, 106–107.

220 Moffitt, *Atonement and the Logic of Resurrection*, 137; cf. also 142–143, where he writes that Jesus' ascension into heaven is "the entry of *the* representative of God's people into the eternal promised land." Thus, "when God crowned him with glory and honor, he became the first human being to regain all that Adam lost. The Son is a kind of Second Adam to whom all things are subjected."

221 This is a larger exegetical issue in Hebrews that often conflicts with issues of historical and systematic theology. Vos ("The Priesthood of Christ in Hebrews," in *Redemptive History and Biblical Interpretation* [P&R, 1980], esp. 148–160) takes up this argument and relates it to Christ's entrance into heaven. See also Richard Gaffin, Jr., "The Priesthood of Christ: A Servant in the Sanctuary," in *The Perfect Savior: Key Themes in Hebrews*, ed. Jonathan Griffiths (Intervarsity, 2012), 49–68; Michael Kibbe, "Is It Finished? When Did it Start? Hebrews, Priesthood, and Atonement in Biblical, Systematic, and Historical Perspective," *JTS* 65.1 (2014): 25–61. Suffice it to say, the focus in Hebrews on Christ becoming a priest is on the eschatological nature of his priesthood and is subsequent to his being perfected and raised up so that he can ascend into heaven.

becoming a high priest is grounded in his having been made perfect, for in 7:28, we see, "His being made perfect precedes his appointment, as the verbal tense sequencing clarifies: appoints (καθίστησιν) is in present tense; having been made perfect (τετελειωμένον) is in the perfect participle."[222]

The priestly function in the Hebrew Bible and in later literature was to be crowned with Adam's glory and represent God's people before the presence of God via the atonement-making process. Once the sacrifice had been made on the altar, the priest would enter the sanctuary and the Holy of Holies for the Day of Atonement with his robes and vestments on. The robes represented the wearing of the glory of God and the twelve stones on them represented the tribes. Thus, the priests would bring the seed of Abraham into the glory of the tabernacle. In the high priest's representation, the 'seed of Abraham' is represented before God and mediation takes place.

The robes and priestly vestments were seen to be symbolic of Adamic-human glory. They are his honor and glory: Exod 28:2 καὶ ποιήσεις στολὴν ἁγίαν Ααρων τῷ ἀδελφῷ σου εἰς τιμὴν καὶ δόξαν contains the same language of Ps 8 that Hebrews has applied to the current glorified status of Christ. Again, this 'honor' and 'glory' language returns in 5:4–5. In 2:7, 9 δόξῃ καὶ τιμῇ "recalls the investiture of Aaron to the high priesthood, when God bestowed upon him "glory and splendor" (Exod 28:2, 40 LXX). It may be proper to find in the state that Jesus was crowned with glory and splendor another anticipation of his high priesthood (cf. 1:3)."[223] In Zech 6:11 and Sir 45:12, the investiture of the high priest is a crowning of sorts.[224]

The fact that the priests mediated God's presence through the tabernacle/tent complex is itself a reminder to the temple-mediating function that Adam played in the garden. Adam's two main roles are to work and keep the garden. G.K. Beale has successfully argued that the garden of Eden is a temple.[225] Adam's commission to 'cultivate' (עבד) and 'keep' (שמר) uses verbs that typically refer to the priestly role of serving or guarding in the tabernacle.[226]

---

222 Jared Calaway, *The Sabbath and the Sanctuary* (Mohr Siebeck, 2013), 147.
223 Lane, *Hebrews 1–8*, 49.
224 Sebastian Fuhrmann, "The Son, the Angels and the Odd: Psalm 8 in Hebrews 1 and 2," in *Psalms and Hebrews: Studies in Reception*, ed. Dirk J. Human and Gert Jacobus Steyn (Bloomsbury T&T Clark, 2010), 96.
225 *Temple and the Church's Mission*. See also Moshe Weinfeld "Sabbath, Temple and the Enthronement of the Lord: The Problem of the Sitz im Leben of Genesis 1:1–2:3," in *Mélanges bibliques et orientaux en l'honneur de M. Henrie Cazelles*, ed. A. Caquot and M. Delcour (Butzon and Bercker, 1981), 501–512; Gordon J. Wenham, "Santuary Symbolism in the Garden of Eden Story," in *I Studied Inscriptions from Before the Flood: Ancient Near Eastern, Literary, and Linguistic Approaches to Genesis 1–11*, ed. Richard S. Hess and David Toshio Tasumura (Eisenbrauns, 1994), 399–404.
226 Beale, *Temple*, 67. What we do not explore here is that in the ANE it was a royal func-

The imagery of a temple enhances the royal ideology of God since "sitting in the temple is an expression of his sovereign rest or reign."²²⁷ The conclusion for Adam's role could not be clearer:

> Thus, the implication may be that God places Adam into a royal temple to begin to reign as his priestly vice-regent. In fact, Adam should always best be referred to as a 'priest-king', since it is only after the 'fall' that priesthood is separated from kingship though Israel's eschatological expectation is of a messiah priest-king (e.g., see Zech. 6:12–13).²²⁸

In short, God in his sovereignty actively creates and then sits down in Sabbath rest. Adam is established (more literally 'rested,'²²⁹) in a human vice-regency that offers priestly service to God over the creation while offering an eschatological Sabbath rest once the eschatological is ushered in.²³⁰ Adam being allowed to eat of trees in the garden suggests echoes to the priest who were later allowed to partake of the sacrifice offered in the temple. Even in Jub. 3:27, as Adam is expelled from the garden, he "offered a sweet-smelling sacrifice—frankincense, galbanum, stacte, and spices," which suggests a priest leaving the temple.²³¹ Crispin Fletcher-Louis, after examining the OT in more detail, concludes there is a correlation between Adam as God's image/idol and the high priest as God's image/idol. Thus, "the high priest was also believed to be the true or second Adam. This idea is probably present already in Ezek 28:12–16 and is otherwise clearly attested in Sir 49:16–50:1 (Hebrew text)."²³² Fletcher-Louis has argued in more detail that the glorification of

---

tion to keep gardens. Kings in their opulence could afford the luxury of building and maintaining massive gardens as a sign and exercise of their stately power and regality. Consider as example the hanging gardens of Babylon. On the temple function of 'serve' and 'keep/guard' see also Herring, *Divine Substitution*, 118n.180; Hart, "Genesis 1:1–2:3," 332–333.

227  Beale, *Temple*, 63. Meredith Kline (*Kingdom Prologue*, 87–90) also emphasizes the priestly role of man in the garden arguing: "Priesthood is man's primary office. It was with the priestly experience of beholding the Glory of the Creator in his Edenic sanctuary that human existence began" (87).

228  Beale, *Temple*, 70.

229  Gen 2:15, וַיַּנִּחֵהוּ. Beale, *Temple*, 69–70.

230  The work of Meredith Kline explores such themes of eschatology and Sabbath rest. In particular, see *Kingdom Prologue*, 34–38. He stresses the enthronement aspects of Sabbath rest. See also Moshe Weinfeld, "Sabbath, Temple and the Enthronement of the Lord," 501–512.

231  Beale, *Temple*, 77–78. Jared Calaway (*The Sabbath and the Sanctuary*, 174) points out that "pleasing odor" or "soothing odor" is "ubiquitous in the priestly instructions for the sacrificial cult with the smoke of burnt animal offering (e.g., Gen 8:21; Lev 1:9, 13, 17; Num 15:3, 13, 14, 24; 28:2), cereal offerings (e.g., Lev 2:2, 9, 12), and even libations (e.g., Num 15:10; 28:8)." He also points to Jubilees 21:9. Felip de Jesús Legarreta-Castillo (*The Figure of Adam*, 70) also notes this priestly portrait here in Jubilees. Callender (*Adam in Myth and History*) points out that Jubilees sees Eden as a prototype of the temple, citing also J.R. Levison, *Portraits of Adam*, 93.

232  Crispin Fletcher-Louis, "God's Image, His Cosmic Temple and the High Priest," in

Simon in Ben Sira in the Hebrew of Sir 50 leads to the brothers and fellow priests being glorified "the whole scene fulfilling the vision of Ps 8:4–8."[233] For example, "the high priest's garments are those of the pre-lapsarian Adam."[234] So also, "in Sirach 50:12–13 the true Adam receives sacrificial offerings at the LORD's own table, the altar."[235]

> And in the nation's liturgy her liturgy [sic] there is a memorial (להזכיר) to the Most High (v. 16); a memorial, that is, of humanity as we were originally created to be. But the clearest allusion to Psalm 8 comes in vv. 11–13 where Simon, wearing the garments of Glory (כבוד) gives honour (יהדר) to the court of the sanctuary as he ascends the altar and is surrounded by his fellow priests—his crown (עטרת)—in their glory (בכבודם). When he has mounted the altar the Hebrew says that there "he stood over the arranged pieces (i.e. the sacrificial offerings)". The language is odd, and the Greek has, understandably, changed it to "he was standing by the hearth of the altar". The oddity is explained if the language is deliberately chosen so that the scene fulfills Ps 8:7: here we see the true Adam ruling over all God's works, with all things under his feet; all sheep, oxen and beasts of the field.[236]

Again, Simon the priest being glorified with fellow priests suggests the priestly-Adam leading many sons to glory motif. As N.T. Wright succinctly states, "the high priest ruling over Israel is like Adam ruling over all creation…"[237]

---

*Heaven on Earth: The Temple in Biblical Theology*, ed. T. Desmond Alexander and Simon Gathercole (Paternoster, 2004), 96. On the primal and Adamic figure being priestly in Ezek 28:11–19 see Dexter Callender, Jr., *Adam in Myth and History*, 87–135, 206–212. On Ben Sira, Fletcher-Louis ("On angels, men and priests [Ben Sira, the Qumran Sabbath Songs and the Yom Kippur Avodah]" (paper presented at the "Gottesdienst und Engel" Conference in Zurich, January 2015], 19) writes: "the priesthood in the temple fulfills the identity that God intended for Adam on the sixth day of Creation. He is the one crowned with glory and honour, standing over the sacrificial portions just as Adam was created to have dominion over the sheep, oxen and the rest of creation (Psalm 8). Ben Sira is simply a faithful interpreter of Exod 25–40 where Aaron is dressed as the true image-idol that Adam was created to be; with garments of glory and beauty like those that would adorn the statue (the *tselem*) of a deity."

233 Crispin Fletcher-Louis, "2 Enoch and the New Perspective on Apocalyptic," in *New Perspectives on 2 Enoch: No Longer Slavonic Only*, ed. Andrei Orlov, Gabriele Boccaccini, Jason Zurawski (Brill, 2012), 133–134; see also "The Temple Cosmology of P and the Theological Anthropology in the Wisdom of Jesus ben Sira," in *Of Scribes and Sages: Early Jewish Interpretation and Transmission of Scripture*, ed. Craig A. Evans (Sheffield Academic, 2004), 69–113; *Collected Works. Volume 1: The Image-Idol of God, the Priesthood, Apocalyptic and Jewish Mysticism* (Wipf & Stock/Whymanity, forthcoming), 1–57.

234 Fletcher-Louis, "The Temple Cosmology of P," 47.
235 Ibid., 48.
236 Ibid., 49.
237 *People of God*, 265.

Michael Morales has summarized the relationship between tabernacle, priesthood, and Adam:

> Taken together, the tabernacle and priesthood constituted something of a celestial globe, as it were, within Israel's midst, a renewed dwelling with God in a consecrated cosmos. Within this sphere the Adamic identity of the high priest in particular is fundamental to the Pentateuch's cultic theology—he functioned as a true or second Adam within the restored Eden of the tabernacle. As such the high priest, exalted above his brothers as the one 'upon whose head the anointing oil was poured and who was consecrated to wear the garments' (Lev 21:10), is the one dubbed 'messiah' in the Pentateuch, *hakōhēn hammāšîaḥ* (Lev 4:3,5,16; 6:22)…The Day of Atonement was an *entrance rite*, and the messiah's office—his labor and mission was defined by that entry.[238]

In this respect, as a priest bearing Adamic-glory, the priests "ascended" into the presence of God annually on the Day of Atonement. As a whole, Michael Morales has shown how the movement of the priests into the Holy of Holies is an ascension into the presence of God. It recapitulates Adam in the garden. Adam's expulsion is reversed on the Day of Atonement.[239] It also connects to the mountain symbolism and ascending into God's presence in Mt. Sinai and Zion.[240] "The one able to ascend is the Adam-like high-priest, with blood, on the Day of Atonement. *This* is the way YHWH has opened for humanity to dwell in his Presence."[241] It is this ascension that Hebrews now sees fulfilled in Christ. In his act of suffering, he is the sacrifice and then in his glorified state where he is as the eschatological man who pioneers the way into heaven. He is the true Second Adam, a greater high priest, going into the true sanctuary, heaven itself. The Adamic role is priestly and kingly. Or we might say, as much as the king in the OT bears the imagery of a second Adam figure, so also does the priest. For example, in T. Levi 17:3 we see the anointed high priest ἔσται ἡ ἱερωσύνη αὐτοῦ τιμία, καὶ παρὰ πᾶσι δοξασθήσεται, which is similar language that we have in Heb 2:6 δόξῃ καὶ τιμῇ ἐστεφάνωσας αὐτόν and the priestly

---

238 L. Michael Morales, *Who Shall Ascend the Mountain of the Lord? A Biblical Theology of the Book of Leviticus* (InterVaristy, 2015), 175. He also writes, "Anointed to the office of high priest, Aaron will place the role of the new Adam of this new creation within the drama of the tabernacle system of worship" (118). On the garden and tabernacle/temple parallels, see Beale, *Temple*, 66–80.

239 *Who Shall Ascend*, 176–177.

240 On Sinai and Zion, see also Jon D. Levenson, *Sinai and Zion: An Entry into the Jewish Bible* (Harper Collins, 1985), 126–134; he shows Zion is an Edenic Temple.

241 Morales, *Who Shall Ascend*, 177, emphasis original.

installment language of 5:4, 5 καὶ οὐχ ἑαυτῷ τις λαμβάνει τὴν τιμήν...Οὕτως καὶ ὁ Χριστὸς οὐχ ἑαυτὸν ἐδόξασεν.

Thus, Christ is the human vice-regent. As the kingly-son and also the high priest, he fulfills both aspects of Adamic figures.[242] Christ is the king and high-priest, a Second Adam, which entails bringing humanity to the perfection of glory. As Peterson summarizes of 2:5–18, "It is specifically an Adam Christology that merges into the picture of Christ as the perfect representative of his people in a priestly ministry, making atonement for their sins before God."[243]

## CONCLUSION

The purpose of this chapter has been to argue that Heb 2 contains a Second Adam Christology. We began by laying out a basic definition of this Adam Christology, specifically looking at the early work of C.F.D. Moule and James D.G. Dunn. After briefly explaining the connection between Heb 1 and 2, we turned our attention to a more specific exegesis of Heb 2.

Our exegesis understands Ps 8 not only against its ANE background and the role of kingship, but also in light of Second Temple and post-Second Temple use of the psalm. Our intent is to show how that psalm both contains aspects of the purpose of humanity and how it can also be read in a kingly and then Messianic/eschatological way. Our contention is that Hebrews does just this. One should not force a wedge between the anthropological and the Christological understanding of the psalm in its usage in Hebrews. It is precisely because the Son in his Messianic office is the ideal eschatological man, the true king, that we find Ps 8 being deployed. It gives further hope for the Christian because he stands in solidarity with those he represents.

The suffering of Christ leads to his glorification, which is sharing in the glory of Adam. Christ is the leader of God's people into the eschatological destiny that awaits humanity. This is to be read against the background of Second Temple texts, which despite their varied contexts and important differences, echo aspects of these themes as we have shown. Christ's suffering leads to his being perfected, which is primarily a reference to him entering the eschatological state of humanity. Here he serves as a representative and high priest of God's people.

This priestly representation entails Adamic aspects. He is the one who was faithful and therefore exalted. He now leads the people of God into the presence of God as he is their faithful and merciful high priest. Having laid

---

242 Beale, *Temple*, 299.
243 *Hebrews and Perfection*, 63.

this foundation of the Second-Adam role of the Son, we can in the next chapter turn our attention more specifically to the ascension texts in Hebrews. Here we will further see how Christ is the eschatological fulfillment by ascending into the true heavenly temple.

To this point, we have focused on how Hebrews sees Jesus as 'the Son.' He is Son in terms of sharing in the divine identity of God. He has an eternal existence as Son which is manifest in and through his Messianic office (as we have seen from Heb 1). Furthermore, he who had glory from the beginning has now ascended into glory as the Father declares the Son to be His Son. This fulfills Pss 2 and 110.

Yet Hebrews capitalizes on the vocational aspect of the Son. The Son is son in his humanity. He is the Adamic-Davidic son *par excellence.* Thus, there is a linking between Pss 2, 8, and 110 and a cohesion between Heb 1 and 2. In and through the vocation of suffering where he exhibits perfect trust, the Son becomes the first heir of the eschaton. He is the true 'firstborn' who has been qualified for the reception of the gifts of the 'age to come.' Because of this, he can stand in solidaric representation of God's people. He has ascended as the first from among the new people of God having become the new creation, triumphant Second Adam. Having, in his earthly activity, fulfilled the role of the true human, he has won the prize of the perfection, whereby he enters up into the presence of God. He is the true man who merits the eschaton for those who will obey him, a theme which we will return to in chapter six.[244]

---

[244] My conclusions in chapters 2-4 on S/sonship and the Christology in the book of Hebrews are, in many ways, similar to the conclusions of R.B. Jamieson in *The Paradox of Sonship: Christology in the Epistle to the Hebrews* (InterVarsity, 2021). We had communicated a bit about Hebrews while I was originally writing my dissertation but had already arrived at our conclusions independent of each other. The most obvious major point of agreement between Dr. Jamieson's work and my own is that there are two aspects of Sonship, both the divine Sonship and the Davidic Messianic sonship at work. Jamieson intentionally reads Hebrews with the "toolkit" of some of the language of Classical Christology (23–48) to help unpack what Hebrews is doing whereas I have sought to engage more directly in historical-grammatical exegesis as my methodology. This is not to say he does not support his project with exegesis. I find myself agreeing with his exegetical conclusions (compare my work above with *Paradox* 49–69 and 76–93). One major conclusion where we both align is: Hebrews presents both an eternal divine Sonship and a sense in which the Son becomes Son in exaltation. Both of us agree this resolves the complexities and apparent paradoxes in Hebrews. One difference is I have sought to intentionally develop the Adamic-human aspects as foundational to the Davidic Messianic sonship. I see the latter as a capstone to the former. Hebrews brings them into unison within the author's understanding of redemptive-history being fulfilled in the person of the Son. In the language of Biblical Theology, David was a type of Second-Adam figure. Of course, my project moves forward to engage the issues of the ascension and how the Son qualifies himself for ascension. Jamieson agrees that "Messianic anointing [Ps 45:6–7 and Heb 1:8–9 in exaltation to God's throne] is a response to and a ratification of the Son's obedient life" (129). We both agree that the exaltation of the Son in his Davidic Messianic capacity is revelatory of the eternal Sonship (137), as I said at the end of chapter two the functional sonship is revelatory of the ontol-

Before we can discuss the role of obedience with respect to the ascension, we must turn our attention in the next chapter to the actual ascension texts in Hebrews. In these texts, we find that the Son ascends into heaven as the high priest of the age to come. We have already made the case that the language of priesthood and new humanity crowning in glory and honor are intertwined and that this is Second Adam language. The ascension of the Son as a royal priest, a Second Adam, signals the dawning of the age to come.

---

ogy of the Son. Unfortunately, due to the timing of edits and publication, I did not have time to interact with Jamieson's work in the revision of this thesis for publication. I believe my own project here, while different in a number of ways, dovetails with aspects of his work and that the different projects bolster some of the key conclusions of the other with specific regards to Christology in the book of Hebrews.

## Chapter 5

## The Son Ascends into the Heavenly Tabernacle

### Introduction

THIS CHAPTER TRACES THE way Hebrews portrays the ascension of the Son through the entire book. In the last three chapters, we have already begun to examine the portrait of Jesus Christ as S/son both in terms of a divine identity, where he shares in the identity of YHWH, and in terms of a Second Adam Christology, where his being crowned in glory takes humanity to its eschatological destiny. Working through the ascension passages allows us to examine the relationship in Hebrews between Sonship and the king-priest role that the Son takes on. It is as the crowned royal priest, the Second Adam, the eschatological man, that the Son goes into heaven, which is the true tabernacle, the true Zion.

It should be remembered that Hebrews conceives the work of the Son as eschatological. God has spoken and accomplished the eschatological end which he has planned. The activity of the Son ushers in this transition from the old age into the age to come. But in the climax of the age, the activity of redemption moves from earthly to that which is accomplished in heaven, the archetype. This transition from earthly to heavenly is not just Platonic categories, as older scholars suggested. Instead, we see the climax of eschatology, an eschatology which contains both temporal elements (old/new) and vertical elements (earthly/heavenly). This correlation between earthly and heavenly is well attested in Second Temple Judaism.

The climax of redemption is God's revelation in the Son, and the work of the Son will move the destiny of humanity upward to the heavenly, fulfilling the 'age to come.' Thus, a royal son installed on the throne is not installed in an earthly Zion but is installed where the earthly Zion pointed: a heavenly Zion. The earthly throne of David's coronation is surpassed by the heavenly throne upon which the Messiah sits, the very throne of God. In the same way, the earthly tabernacle which the OT Levitical high priest enters is surpassed by that which it was created to image, namely a heavenly archetype. Thus, the eschatological high priest would not go into the earthly tent but ascends into heaven itself. He will take the pattern of sacrifice from that which is repeated under the Old Covenant and transition it to the final and eschatological where the Son finishes the offering and sits down. All of this is dependent upon the motif that God created heaven for himself where he sits on a throne. It combines the motifs of mountain/Zion with kingly throne and priestly-tabernacle/temple. Coronated in his offices, the Son ascended upward to fulfill these offices, thereby giving to God's people, the future sons of glory, the eschatological perfection.

### Cosmology: A Throne in a Heavenly Tabernacle

It is generally recognized in Second Temple Jewish literature, especially apocalyptic literature, that God dwells on a throne in heaven and this throne is within a heavenly temple. As Cody states, "the theme of the heavenly sanctuary corresponding to the earthly sanctuary was a commonplace in Judaism, and the theme as it is presented by Hebrews shows more in common with the Rabbinic and Jewish-apocalyptic literature, and above all with the OT itself, on which the later Jewish literature was built, than it does with Philo."[1] Despite a diversity in ascension accounts, the portrait of the heavenly sanctuary is a common feature of the various ascents recorded in apocalyptic literature. Jody Barnard writes, "in the apocalyptic visions of God enthroned, the heavenly throne of Glory is characteristically located in the celestial Holy of Holies (e.g., 1 En. 14:18–20; 47;1–4; 71:5–7; 4Q403 1 ii 10–16; 4Q405 20 ii–21–22 1–11; T. Levi 3:4; 5:1; Rev 4–5; cf. Isa 6:1–6)."[2] The common feature does not mean all Second Temple texts are exactly the same in their description. In some texts, heaven itself is a temple; in others, the true temple is in heaven.[3]

---

[1] Aelred Cody, *Heavenly Sanctuary and Liturgy in the Epistle to the Hebrews: The Achievement of Salvation in the Epistle's Perspective* (Grail, 1960), 35.

[2] *The Mysticism of Hebrews: Exploring the Role of Jewish Apocalyptic Mysticism in the Epistle to the Hebrews* (Mohr Siebeck, 2012), 144.

[3] Eric Mason, "'Sit at My Right Hand': Enthronement and the Heavenly Sanctuary in Hebrews," in *A Teacher For All Generations: Essays in Honor of James C. Vanderkam*, ed. Eric Mason (Brill, 2012), 902; George MacRae, "Heavenly Temple and Eschatology in the Letter to the Hebrews," *Semeia* 12 (1978): 182–185; Craig Koester, *The Dwelling of God: The Tabernacle in the Old Testament, Intertestamental Jewish Literature, and the New Testament* (Catholic Biblical Association of America, 1989), 58–75; Beale, *Temple and the Church's Mission: A Biblical Theol-*

The tradition of YHWH dwelling in a heavenly temple goes back to the Hebrew Bible. It is common in ANE literature to see temples on earth as representative structures where the worshippers have access to God through the liturgy. The earthly temple is a gateway to heaven. For the ancient Israelite, the ark of the covenant was YHWH's footstool (1 Chr 28:2; Pss 99:5; 132:7; Lam 2:1;[4] Ezek 43:7), as if entering the Holy of Holies was entering into YHWH's throne room itself. God's glory fell out of heaven into the Holy of Holies. This is most likely what is reflected in Isa 6:1. As Isaiah sees a vision of God, the glory of God flows down into the Holy of Holies like a royal robe. The smoke and thresholds of the temple shaking is much like God's appearing on Mt. Sinai (e.g., Exod 19:18). For Isaiah, seeing a vision of YHWH in the temple is akin to catching a glimpse of that which radiates out of heaven, or like the cosmic mountain of Sinai where Moses ascended up to God's presence.[5]

But the tabernacle/temple was only symbolic of the greater temple in heaven. Heaven is the throne of YHWH (Pss 11:4; 103:19; Isa 66:1). Heaven is his true temple (Ps 11:4; possibly Ps 18:6; Mic 1:2; Hab 2:20).[6] YHWH sits in the heavens (Ps 2:4). Thus, the Lord sits above the circle of the earth (הַיֹּשֵׁב עַל־חוּג הָאָרֶץ) and stretches out the heavens like a curtain and spreads them like a tent to dwell in (הַנּוֹטֶה כַדֹּק שָׁמַיִם וַיִּמְתָּחֵם כָּאֹהֶל לָשָׁבֶת), Isa 40:22.[7]

In Wis 9:8, we find Solomon building a temple that is an image of the one in heaven: εἶπας οἰκοδομῆσαι ναὸν ἐν ὄρει ἁγίῳ σου καὶ ἐν πόλει κατασκηνώσεώς σου θυσιαστήριον, μίμημα σκηνῆς ἁγίας, ἣν προητοίμασας ἀπ' ἀρχῆς. Then in 9:10, wisdom is sent to Solomon from heaven, from the glorious throne of the Lord (ἐξ ἁγίων οὐρανῶν καὶ ἀπὸ θρόνου δόξης σου πέμψον αὐτήν). Heaven is the dwelling place of God, his sanctuary where his throne resides.[8]

---

*ogy of the Dwelling Place of God* (Intervarsity, 2004), 29–80, esp. 48–50; Jon Levenson, "The Temple and the World," *The Journal of Religion* 64.3 (1984): 282–297. Levenson also discusses the relationship between Sabbath, Temple, and YHWH's enthronement (289–291). Hebrews links Christ's ascension into glory with the fulfillment of Land/Sabbath rest (Heb 3–4). The enthronement of the Son is how YHWH manifests his own kingship with the Son coming to the promised Tabernacle/Sabbath rest in the heavenly Tabernacle.

4 Here the footstool is probably a metonymy for the whole temple that has been destroyed.

5 In the next chapter, we discuss the view in Second Temple Judaism that Moses' ascent up Sinai was into heaven itself.

6 For a discussion of all the texts in the Hebrew Bible that possibly convey a heavenly temple, see Elias Brasil de Souza, "The Heavenly Sanctuary/Temple Motif in the Hebrews Bible: Function and Relationship to the Earthly Counterparts" (PhD diss., Andrews University, 2005). He finds that already early in the Hebrew Bible there is a structural correspondence between the earthly model of the tabernacle/temple and a heavenly tabernacle/temple (cf. esp. 493–495). Beale comes to similar conclusion (Beale, *Temple*, 48–60).

7 LXX ὁ κατέχων τὸν γῦρον τῆς γῆς, καὶ οἱ ἐνοικοῦντες ἐν αὐτῇ ὡς ἀκρίδες, ὁ στήσας ὡς καμάραν τὸν οὐρανὸν καὶ διατείνας ὡς σκηνὴν κατοικεῖν,

8 For a more detailed discussion of Wis. 9:8, see Cody, *The Heavenly Sanctuary*, 17–21. He

1 Enoch entails several descriptions of heaven, the throne room, and perhaps multiple layers within heaven itself. In 1 En. 14, Enoch ascends up into heaven in a vision. As Enoch ascends he sees a house (14:10) and a second house (14:15) where the latter is greater than the former. In the vision, he enters a house (14:13) built with tongues of fire (14:16). Inside is a throne (14:18), and upon this throne the "Great Glory" sits with a gown that radiates downward (14:20). Enoch is borrowing from Biblical imagery such as Isa 6 and Ezek 1.[9] It is difficult for Enoch to look up into the glory; not even the angels can go near the throne but are pictured as under it (1 En. 14:21–25). All of this suggests heaven is like a great Temple with a Holy Place and a Holy of Holies where the throne is.[10] Himmelfarb points out that 14:9 contains a reference to the outer chamber, making the parallel even more precise.[11] Finally, it seems then that Enoch is invited to go up near the gate but never truly into the heavenly throne room itself (1 En. 14:25).

1 Enoch 18 may suggest multiple layers to heaven. The four winds are between heaven and earth (18:2–3). They "turn heaven" and cause the star and sun to set (v. 4). The mountains are described as pressing into heaven itself, like the throne of God (v. 8). Later, this throne is described as resembling the throne on which the Lord "will sit when he descends to visit earth with his goodness" (25:3). It will be the throne of judgment (25:4).

In the *Similitudes of Enoch*, we have imagery of multiple dwelling places in heaven for the holy ones (angels), 39:3–5. The righteous ones (saints) will dwell under the wings of the Lord of the Spirits (39:7–8). Later in the book, the Elect One, the Son of Man, will sit upon the throne of the Lord to judge (51:3; 55:4; 61:8–9; 62:6; 71:29). In 1 En. 71, Enoch ascends with the angel into the heavens. Here he sees the rivers of fire and the reservoirs of the stars and luminaries, and then he is carried off into the heaven of heavens. Here he sees crystal and living fire, which echoes Ezek 1 and imagery of the divine throne (71:5–6). The angels are there encircling the throne of glory (71:7–8). Again, this suggests temple imagery. As Barnard notes "the 'house' in the *Similitudes* corresponds to the second house of Enoch's vision (14:15–23) i.e., the inner sanctuary and most holy place."[12]

In T. Levi, after falling asleep, Levi is given a vision of the "high mountain" (2:5). He enters up into the first heaven (2:7) from where he sees a luminous

even goes so far as to suggest "Wis. 9:8 affords the best background for an understanding of the notion of the heavenly sanctuary in the Epistle to the Hebrews" (20).

9 George MacRae ("Heavenly Temple and Eschatology," 183) concurs.
10 Cf. also Barnard, *Mysticism of Hebrews*, 58.
11 Martha Himmelfarb, *Ascent to Heaven in Jewish and Christian Apocalypses* (Oxford University Press, 1993) 14.
12 Barnard, *Mysticism of Hebrews*, 58.

second heaven (2:8–9). Then he is told by an angel he will "see another heaven more lustrous and beyond compare" (2:9). He is told he will ascend to this third heaven where he will "stand near the Lord" (2:20). In chapter three, we are given further descriptions of these three levels. The lowest is the realm of fire, snow, and ice (3:2). This lowest level is right above the earth, and from it spirits are dispatched for punishment of men's sins (3:2). The second heaven is where the armies of angels await to come in judgment (3:3). The third heaven is the "uppermost heaven" where the Great Glory in the Holy of Holies dwells (3:4). Again, the heavens have a temple like structure with an outer court, an area like the holy place where the angels dwell waiting, then a Holy of Holies with the throne room of God. In the Holy of Holies, the archangels serve before the throne and offer "propitiatory sacrifices" (3:4). When heaven finally opens for Levi, he sees "the Holy Most High sitting on the throne" (5:1). Levi is given the priesthood until the LORD comes to dwell with Israel (5:3). The vision then repeats in chapter eight where seven men in white clothing (angelic figures?) put the vestments of priesthood on Levi. As Eskola concludes, "the apocalyptic idea of the temple in heaven may be clearly seen in the structure of the heavenly realm."[13]

In 2 Bar. 4:3–6, we have the Lord promising to reveal another building which may be a reference to the heavenly city of Jerusalem (4:1–2 references the city) or specifically to the heavenly temple in heaven that will come with a new Jerusalem. The phrase "It is not this building that is in your midst now; it is that which will be revealed, with me" (4:3) is probably referring to a heavenly temple to be revealed when the new Jerusalem is revealed. This "building" was prepared before the paradise in Eden[14] and shown to Adam before his sinning (4:3). When he sinned, it was taken away (4:3). It was shown to Abraham in the covenant ratification events of Gen 15, as God passed between the animals (4:4). Finally, Moses saw it on Mt. Sinai, "when I showed him the likeness of the tabernacle and all its vessels" (4:5). This taking up of Moses is again referenced in 59:3–4. Not only is Moses given the Law, but he is shown "the likeness of Zion with its measurements which was to be made after the likeness of the present sanctuary" (59:4). Like Enoch, Moses is given

---

13 Eskola, *Messiah and the Throne: Jewish Merkabah Mysticism and Early Christian Exaltation Discourse* (Mohr Siebeck, 2001), 79. On other possible parallels between T. Levi and Hebrews, see James M. Carlson, "A Great High Priest Who Has Passed Through the Heavens: In Quest of the Apocalyptic Roots of the Epistle to the Hebrews" (PhD diss., Marquette University, 2008), 137–147.

14 In Wis 9:8, when Solomon builds the temple, it is a copy of that which God had prepared from the beginning μίμημα σκηνῆς ἁγίας, ἣν προητοίμασας ἀπ' ἀρχῆς. The language suggests heavenly temple imagery is behind 2 Bar. 4.

a tour of the scope of creation from the depths of the Abyss to the greatness of Paradise (59:5–12).

From Qumran, we should briefly highlight the *Songs of the Sabbath Sacrifice*. Philip Alexander writes, "no other early Jewish text, either at Qumran or elsewhere, describes the heavenly temple in such detail as Sabbath Songs, or correlates it so closely with the earthly tabernacle."[15] In the *Songs of the Sabbath*, there is a spatial correspondence between the worship on earth and the heavenly worship. For example, God has established angels, the holy ones, to be like priests in heaven (4Q400 frag. 1, col. i–ii). The angelic beings become mighty and stand in the heavenly council of the holy of holies (4Q400 frag. 1, i.9–13). The council consists of "the utterly holy ones (קדושי קדושים) [... di]vi[ne] godlike beings, priests of the highest heaven (... אלים [ ] ל [...]) "(כוהני מרומי רום ה[קר]בים...)(4Q400 frag. 1, 1.19–20). The priests are not the earthly Levitical priests but heavenly angelic beings who enter into the presence of God. The divine beings are those called to the highest heights (Masik 1:9–12). Thus, God dwells in the highest heavens which is likened unto the Holy of Holies. He is exalted above all, and the angelic godlike beings regularly give him praise and exalt him further (cf. for example 4Q403 frag. 1 col. 1). 4Q405 (frags. 14–15) further indicates the correspondence between the earthly and the heavenly, highlighting how the angels (i.e., living gods) are ingrained on the vestibules and in the inner holy of holies.

The inner shrine, the heavenly holy of holies, we have the royal throne of God where the angels do not sit (4Q405 frags. 20(col. ii)–22, l. 2 ]-- מושב ככסא מלכותו ב[ד]בירי כבודו. לוא ישבו). The cherubs fall down before the throne, blessing the image of the throne-chariot (ll. 7–8). The angels are beneath the shining vault, under the seat of glory. Here one can certainly detect imagery similar to Ezekiel, perhaps mixing with the throne room scene of Isa 6.[16] Perhaps, it is this angelic imagery under the throne of God that Hebrews has in mind in Heb 1:13a πρὸς τίνα δὲ τῶν ἀγγέλων εἴρηκέν ποτε· κάθου ἐκ δεξιῶν μου. There is a clear separation between the angels and God the King on the throne in *The Songs of the Sabbath Sacrifice*. These songs "offer a vision of the celestial temple, which is clearly modeled upon Israel's earthly sanctuaries."[17]

Philo and Josephus portray a different picture of the universe, so that the entire universe is structured like the temple, not merely heaven. In Philo, the temple was a copy of universal archetypes (*Mos.* 2.74–76) and in Josephus,

---

15 Philip Alexander, *The Mystical Texts: Songs of the Sabbath Sacrifice and Related Manuscripts* (T&T Clark, 2006), 55, qtd. in Barnard, *Mysticism*, 102.

16 Barnard, *Mysticism*, 102, argues that Songs VII–XII "display considerable dependence upon Exodus 25–40, 1 Kings 6–8, 1 Chronicles 28–29, 2 Chronicles 2–7 and Ezekiel 40–48."

17 Ibid.

*Ant.* 3.123, it represented the whole of nature τῆς τῶν ὅλων φύσεως (i.e., the universe). In 3.122–134, we have a description of the tabernacle and the objects in the tabernacle. The tabernacle is an "imitation of the system of the world," μίμησιν τῆς τῶν ὅλων φύσεως (3.123) The Holy of Holies is for God alone. It is the innermost sanctum of "Heaven devoted to God" τὸ μὲν γὰρ τρίτον αὐτῆς μέρος τὸ ἐντὸς τῶν τεσσάρων κιόνων, ὃ τοῖς ἱερεῦσιν ἦν ἄβατον, ὡς οὐρανὸς ἀνεῖτο τῷ θεῷ (3.123). However, the outer court and the holy place is for the priests. These places symbolize the sea and earth respectively, i.e., the entire world. Similarly in 3.180–181, we see that the temple represents the whole of the world (3.180 εἰς ἀπομίμησιν καὶ διατύπωσιν τῶν ὅλων). The outer court is the sea and the Holy Place symbolizes the land, which man has access to, but the Holy of Holies, the third division, is set apart because man cannot access heaven (3.181 τὴν δὲ τρίτην μοῖραν μόνῳ περιέγραψε τῷ θεῷ διὰ τὸ καὶ τὸν οὐρανὸν ἀνεπίβατον εἶναι ἀνθρώποις).[18] The cosmic symbolism in Philo and Josephus continues portraying the seven lamps of the lampstand as the seven planets (Josephus, *Ant.* 3.145; *J.W.* 5.217; Philo, *Her.* 221–225 [227 portrays it as heaven]; *Mos.* 2.102–105; *QE* 2.73–81).[19]

Generally, with his Platonic ideals, Philo distinguishes the outer courts and the Holy Place as the realm of sense and sight, symbolized by the land, earth and sea (*Mos.* 2.81–83; *QE* 2.83; *Ebr.* 134), from the Holy of Holies as the realm of non-corporeal and intellect (*Mos.* 2.80; *Ebr.* 135–136.) As MacRae summarizes of Philo: "In most of the relevant passages, the court and the outer shrine together represent the sense-perceptible (αἰσθητός) world, including the heavens, while the holy place represents the intelligible (νοητός) world, the unchanging world of ideas is the proper dwelling of God (see especially *QE* 2.91–96)."[20] Koester, however, points out that Philo is not consistent in the cosmic symbolism in the temple/tabernacle.[21] In fact, "only in *Questions on Exodus* does Philo consistently divide the tabernacle into Platonic regions with the holy of holies as the intelligible realm, the forecourt as the supralunar region of the perceptible realm, and the outer court as the sublunar region (*Q.E.* 2.69, 83, 94)."[22]

---

18 George MacRae, "Heavenly Temple and Eschatology," 184; Beale, *Temple*, 45–48.
19 Beale, *Temple*, 46. Koester, *The Dwelling of God*, 60, has a useful chart comparing the symbolism of the tabernacle in Philo and Josephus.
20 MacRae, "Heavenly Temple and Eschatology," 185.
21 Koester, *The Dwelling of God*, 62. See page 61 also where he states that "Philo does not Platonize the tradition…consistently."
22 Ibid., 62; cf. also Barnard, *Mysticism*, 99, "it is only in his *Questions on Exodus* that Philo consistently divides the tabernacle into *Platonic* regions." Barnard (*Mysticism*, 95–104) outlines some key differences between Philo and Hebrews. For example, in *QE* 2.91 heaven "is without transient events and is unchanging" in contrast to Jesus' heavenly ascent which entails inaugu-

While we need to be careful against minimizing the different authors and their unique contexts, we can make the general conclusion that in Judaism and Second Temple Judaism, heaven was recognized as the true temple with the throne of God dwelling in it. In the later apocalyptic thinking of the Second Temple period, God reigns from the throne. His judgment will be manifest from the throne, and on some occasions an exalted figure will ascend into the divine presence like the movement into the inner Holy of Holies. This ascension can be to receive revelation, or to be granted exalted status to judge the earth.

## Ascension Texts in Hebrews

### Heb 1

While we have already discussed Heb 1 in detail, here we wish to highlight briefly how the opening chapter is shaped with a view towards the ascension of Christ. The opening chapter focuses on the identity of the Son, but the movement of the chapter draws attention to the climactic exaltation of the Son. The Son is called up to ascend to the right hand of the Father in heaven. He comes into the divine throne room and sits next to God within the divine glory. Eskola writes, "Christ's exaltation resembles a heavenly journey that leads to the holy throne of Glory in the heavenly Temple," as the Son is the Davidic "priest-king who make purification for sins before his entering upon the throne."[23] His taking a seat in heaven, in the very presence of the throne of glory, assumes an ascending upward into heaven.

First, in 1:3 we have the reference to the Son sitting down next to the Majesty in heaven. The language reflects Hebrews' understanding of the fulfillment of Ps 110:1 [LXX 109:1]. The Son having completed his work of purification progresses to sit at God's right hand. This is clearly the referent of τῆς μεγαλωσύνης ἐν ὑψηλοῖς. The LORD is one who dwells on his throne in heaven (e.g., 1 Kgs 22:19//2 Chr 18:18; Pss 2:4; 11:4; 103:19; Isa 66:1; 1 En. 14:16–25; T. Levi 5:1; etc.). An ascent is not described in 1:3, but it is presupposed. Somehow the Son had to move upward into the very presence of God to take his seat beside the throne of God.

Second, the first OT verse that the author brings to our attention is Ps 2:7 which concerns the royal exaltation of the Davidic king. The author is probably aware of the context of the Psalm, especially in 2:6 Ἐγὼ δὲ κατεστάθην

---

ration of the new covenant (97).

23  Eskola, *Messiah and the Throne*, 207.

βασιλεὺς ὑπ' αὐτοῦ ἐπὶ Σιων ὄρος τὸ ἅγιον αὐτοῦ. Zion is seen as God's holy mountain and the Davidic king, the royal son of God, is portrayed as established up on Zion. Heb 12:22–23 sees Jesus, the "firstborn," established in Zion. In Second Temple Judaism, Zion is seen as the heavenly Jerusalem or the place of the heavenly temple.[24] The use of Ps 2:7 may be associated with an allusion to the ascension, which is the announcement of the royal and divine Son.

Lastly, Heb 1:13 quotes LXX Ps 109:1. The call to sit at God's right hand is the climax of the chapter, and has already been brought to our attention by 1:3. The Son has come to sit down at the right hand of God. This assumes entrance into the divine glory through ascending upward. We see similar sitting on the throne of God in 1 En. 51:3; 55:4; 61:8–9; 62:2, 6.[25] While 1 En. does not seem to directly reference Ps 110:1, Hengel has argued that an assimilation of Dan 7 and Ps 110:1 is behind these texts.[26] The use of Ps 110:1 [LXX 109:1] is to defend the enthronement of the Son. The text presupposes ascending upward into the divine glory, since the Father calls the Son to "sit at my right hand." While a heavenly journey is not detailed for the reader, ascension is the backdrop to this exaltation where the Son rules with all the power and authority of the Father himself. The royal exaltation in Ps 2:7 and Ps 110:1 as used by Hebrews will serve as a backdrop for the author's later discussion of the Son's ascension into heaven as the high priest, as he will specifically draw connection between verses 1 and 4 of Ps 110 [LXX 109].

Heb 4:14–16

The author of Hebrews returns again to the theme of a high priest who has passed through the heavens (4:14). The high priest (ἀρχιερεύς) was already mentioned in 2:17 and 3:1, but now Hebrews for the first time combines the concept of Jesus as ἀρχιερεύς with his passing through the heavens, echoing the theme introduced in 1:3. Attridge writes, "Christ's entry into the presence of God has not been described precisely as a 'passage through the heavens' (διεληλυθότα τοὺς οὐρανούς), although the notion is implicit in earlier

---

24 Kiwoong Son, *Zion Symbolism in Hebrews: Hebrews 12:18–24 as a Hermeneutical Key to the Epistle* (Paternoster, 2005), 51–163; Levenson, *Zion and Sinai: An Entry into the Jewish Bible* (Harper Collins, 1985), 111–142.

25 Aquila Lee (*From Messiah to Preexistent Son* [Wipf & Stock, 2005], 24) has argued "only Wisdom [9:4, 10] and the Enochic Son of Man can be said therefore to provide real—but limited—precedents for the Christian claim that the exalted Jesus shares in the heavenly throne of God."

26 Hengel, *Studies in Early Christology* (T&T Clark, 1995), 186–190.

references," citing 1:3, 13; 2:9–10.[27] In 3:1 though, the argument that the believers have a heavenly calling (κλήσεως ἐπουρανίου) presumes that Jesus has ascended into heaven. Jesus is confessed as apostle and high priest (3:1). The Father has called the Son to heaven in his declaration to sit at his right hand. He has been made the high priest of our confession, having cleared the way to heaven by his own path of suffering which leads to glory (2:9–10, 14–15). It is the believers' destiny of glory and sanctification that is their heavenly calling. The Son demonstrated faithfulness to God and God rewarded him with his appointment (Heb 3:2 πιστὸν ὄντα τῷ ποιήσαντι αὐτόν).[28] So also, as the believers consider the faithfulness of the Son, they are being exhorted to remain faithful. The kingdom awaits them if they stand fast. Since Jesus has already been introduced as a merciful and faithful high priest (Heb 2:17), here the believers are exhorted to turn to him rather than away from him being assured that they will find help and grace. Hebrews will develop the priesthood theme in 5:1–10, where as a priest he was appointed from among men. As one from among men, he is not unfamiliar with weakness, defined as crying out for help. After being faithful through weakness, he is perfected. Because of his appointment to perfection, the believer can seek him.

Although οἱ οἰούρανοί is previously only mentioned in reference to the Son's creating them (1:10), it would have been common to the audience to understand that God sits enthroned in heaven (or above the heavens),[29] and thus the Son sitting at the Father's right hand would necessitate his ascension into heaven. Nevertheless, this is the first explicit mention that the Son's glorification and session at God's right hand is because he has passed through the heavens. Hebrews connects the movement to the role of Christ's priesthood, since heaven itself is the true tabernacle, made by God. Hebrews is exhorting the listeners that they have not merely a high priest, but one who has passed through the heavens. The Son's priesthood is distinct and superior, having achieved perfection and glory that the Old Covenant priesthood did not (7:19, 27–28; 8:7; 9:9; 10:2). Just as Christ has ceased from his suffering, so believers will one day cease from their suffering if they hold fast to the confession (6:18; 10:23; 12:1–23).

---

27 Attridge, *The Epistle to the Hebrews* (Fortress, 1989), 139.

28 Ποιέω in 3:1 does not mean that the son is created. This notion would fly in the face of all the author has said in Heb 1. Rather it refers to his appointment. This is akin to the language of Acts 2:36 κύριον αὐτὸν καὶ χριστὸν ἐποίησεν ὁ θεός where ποιέω refers to appointment and installation to office in exaltation.

29 Ps 110 is prominent from the formation of Christianity. Cf. David M. Hay, *Glory at the Right Hand: Psalm 110 in Early Christianity*, SBLMS 18 (Abingdon, 1973); Hengel, *Studies*, 133–163; Aquila Lee, *From Messiah*, 210–239.

Hebrews prefers to the use the plural 'heavens' (1:10; 4:14; 7:26; 8:1; 9:23; 12:23, 25), although it does on occasion use the singular 'heaven' (9:24; 11:12[30];12:26[31]). Unlike some ascent structures in apocalyptic and mystic texts, Hebrews does not focus on the journey through the heavens and the revelation of these heavens,[32] rather Hebrews focuses on the reality of an ascension by the Son of God (4:14 τὸν υἱὸν τοῦ θεοῦ).[33] Our author focuses on the identity of the one who ascends into heaven, the Son of God, and the office of this Son is the great high priest (4:14 ἀρχιερέα μέγαν). It is the Son, who shares in the divine identity, who is exalted into glory by ascending up through the heavens (Heb 1), but he also does so as a high priest, going up into the heavenly temple just as an OT high priest might enter up into the presence of God by entering the Tabernacle and the holy of holies.[34] He has been made like us in every respect, and then after his suffering death is glorified up into heaven in a bodily ascent.[35]

The reality of the ascension of the Son of God allows the author to press home two exhortations upon his audience: (1) hold fast to the confession (4:14 κρατῶμεν τῆς ὁμολογίας); (2) draw near to the throne of grace with confidence (4:16 προσερχώμεθα οὖν μετὰ παρρησίας τῷ θρόνῳ τῆς χάριτος). In the mind of the author, neither of these exhortations would be possible apart from the ascension of Jesus. As Eskola writes, *"The kingdom of YHWH was seen to be*

---

30 In 11:12, the reference is to the τὰ ἄστρα τοῦ οὐρανοῦ, which is not necessarily 'heaven' or 'the heavenlies' as modern readers think of it. Nevertheless, in the ancient worldview, stars in the sky/heaven were above the earth but below the actual dwelling place of angels and God, if we were to stack the realms into levels.

31 Here the author is quoting the OT and follows the singular of LXX. NETS translates τὸν οὐρανὸν as 'the sky.' Compare LXX Hag 2:6 (ἐγὼ σείσω τὸν οὐρανὸν καὶ τὴν γῆν καὶ τὴν θάλασσαν καὶ τὴν ξηράν) with MT Hag 2:6: אֲנִי מַרְעִישׁ אֶת־הַשָּׁמַיִם וְאֶת־הָאָרֶץ וְאֶת־הַיָּם וְאֶת־הֶחָרָבָה.

32 Jody Barnard (*Mysticism*, 116) writes, "although Hebrews does not express Christ's otherworldly journey in narrative form, a narrative of ascent is clearly presupposed."

33 Felix Cortez ("'The Anchor of the Soul that Enters the Veil': the Ascension of the 'Son' in the Letter to the Hebrews," [PhD diss., Andrews University, January 2008], 279), in contrasting Hebrews with heavenly journeys and tours, concludes Hebrews' "interest lies, instead, in the result of the process (i.e., that Jesus has been exalted), rather than the process itself (cf. 7:26)." Timo Eskola (*Messiah and the Throne*, 351) writes, "Jesus' enthronement is described as an ascent story where the messianic figure, in his resurrection, approaches the throne of Glory. In an act of installation he is enthroned at the right hand of God, and becomes the Lord of the whole universe." Eskola goes on to show that this grounds the concept of 'Son of God' (366).

34 Amy Peeler, *You Are My Son: The Family of God in the Epistle to the Hebrews* (T&T Clark, 2014), 12–13, 42, 45, 51–52; Scott Mackie, *Eschatology and Exhortation in the Epistle to the Hebrews* (Mohr Siebeck, 2007), 174; Eskola, *Messiah and the Throne*, 202–207; Jody Barnard, *The Mysticism of Hebrews*, 149–156. However, Barnard seems to read ὃς ὢν ἀπαύγασμα τῆς δόξης καὶ χαρακτὴρ τῆς ὑποστάσεως αὐτοῦ as reference to the Son as enthroned Son.

35 Heb 2:9–10; 2:14–15; 5:5. We follow Moffitt (*Atonement and the Logic of the Resurrection in the Epistle to the Hebrews* [Brill, 2011], esp. 144–148), that this glorification also entails the resurrection of Jesus.

*realized and fulfilled in the Lordship of Christ who sits on the throne of Glory.* Obedience to God was now primarily obedience of faith to Christ..."[36] Thus, the community of faith cannot abandon the confession of Christ without abandoning YHWH as a whole. Once the 'age to come' has been inaugurated, one cannot merely slip backward into the practices and liturgy of the old age.

First, in this context, the confession is that Jesus is the Son of God. Jesus passing through the heavens as high priest is connected in the mind of the author to the confession that Jesus is the Son of God.[37] The nature and type of S/sonship that Jesus enjoys has been unpacked in Hebrews 1–2.[38] The work that the Son has done in passing through the heaven is the reason for the readers to hold fast to their confession, and is the ground or basis for not abandoning what they have believed and confessed. One cannot abandon the way God has spoken 'in Son' at the climax of redemptive history.

Second, it is the high priest's, Jesus', suffering, being tempted like us, and his ability to sympathize with us that brings the believer confidence to approach the throne of grace. It is Christ's earthly pre-resurrection and pre-ascension experiences that relate to the believers' ability to come before God. As the high priest has passed through the heaven (4:14 διεληλυθότα τοὺς οὐρανούς), so the believers, in holding fast to their confession, and in their need to hold fast in the midst of trials and sufferings, are exhorted to come to the throne of God with confidence (4:16 προσερχώμεθα οὖν μετὰ παρρησίας τῷ θρόνῳ τῆς χάριτος). The Son, as an Adamic figure, crowned in glory and appointed high priest, has realized the hope. They go in prayer to where the Son as priest is already.

Because of the nature of the high priest and his experiences that prepared him for his ascension, namely temptation and suffering, the high priest is able to sympathize with the believer. This nature is expressed by the double negative: we do not have one who is unable to sympathize (4:15). The audience might be tempted to think that since Jesus is the Son of God, per their confession and the articulation especially in Heb 1, this Son, who radiates the glory of God, is the χαρακτὴρ τῆς ὑποστάσεως αὐτοῦ, and is exalted to God's hand, is so unlike them that he would be unable to help, understand, or have true merciful compassion in their need.[39] Consider further that with

---

36 *Messiah and the Throne*, 368, italics original.

37 Scott Mackie, "Confession of the Son of God in Hebrews," *NTS* 53 (2007): 114–117; "Heavenly Sanctuary Mysticism," *JTS* 62 (2011): 84; *Eschatology and Exhortation*, 216–230; James Kurianal, *Jesus Our High Priest: Ps 110,4 As the Substructure of Heb 5,1–7,28* (Peter Lang, 1999), 154–155.

38 Attridge, *Hebrews*, 139; Ellingworth, *The Epistle to the Hebrews* (Eerdmans, 1993), 267. Johnson (*Hebrews: A Commentary* [Westminster John Knox, 2006], 139) also notes that this is the first time 'Son of God' as a title has been used.

39 Lane (*Hebrews 1–8* [Word, 1991], 114) writes similarly, "A possible objection that Jesus'

Heb 1 using Ps 102 to refer to the Son, the author has labored to stress that the Son is like the Lord and unlike creation, in that he does not wear out and remains for years without end. Thus, the author now needs to connect Christ with the suffering of believers—it was indeed a true suffering that the Son experienced. So, the author points to the commonality between the believers' current situations, whatever they might be, and the earthly experience of Christ: weakness. The Son has been tempted by all kinds of experiences (4:15 πεπειρασμένον δὲ κατὰ πάντα). To emphasize that these experiences are the same kinds of experiences the believers share, Hebrews includes καθ' ὁμοιότητα, (4:15)[40] but maintains that Christ did not sin (χωρὶς ἁμαρτίας, 4:15 cf. also 7:26[41]). This lack of sin did not preclude him from having genuine human weakness and the need to cry out to God for help. Thus, the high priest can sympathize because he shared in real human experience.

Hebrews has already drawn attention to the human state of Jesus in 2:17–18, where the author identifies the Son as one who was κατὰ πάντα τοῖς ἀδελφοῖς ὁμοιωθῆναι (2:17).[42] This was necessary (ὤφειλεν) so that the Son could become a high priest ἵνα ἐλεήμων γένηται καὶ πιστὸς ἀρχιερεὺς τὰ πρὸς τὸν θεόν (2:17). As the author remarks later in 5:1, the high priest must come from among men. The Son suffered when tempted (2:18 πέπονθεν αὐτὸς πειρασθείς), and thus is able to help those being tempted (2:18 δύναται τοῖς πειραζομένοις βοηθῆσαι). The high priest may now be in heaven, but he has been fitted to help the suffering precisely because he experienced every sort of suffering and temptation in the weakness of humanity in his earthly life. The presence of Christ in heaven does not make him too distant to help but assures the reader that he has been perfectly fitted to help. In short, he has (1) experienced earthly weakness and (2) passed through to the Father's right hand where he is now perfectly fitted to help. It is in this eschatological perfection at his seat at the throne of grace that assures the listener that the Son is a sure and true help who will not turn a deaf ear or a blind eye. He is both able to help and seemingly willing to help. Consider the repetitive phrasing from

---

exalted status as high priest in heaven implied his aloofness from the weariness and discouragement of the Church in a hostile world is anticipated in v 15."

40  The temptations are of the same quality or kind. There is a 'likeness' or similarity between them. The ὁμοιότης is used in Gen 1:11, 12 to describe how seeds produce plants of the same kind from which they came (καθ' ὁμοιότητα). Interestingly, 4 Macc. 15:4 describes mothers as more sympathetic to their children than fathers, even though all parents love their children, because mothers pass on likeness of soul and form to them (ψυχῆς τε καὶ μορφῆς ὁμοιότητα εἰς μικρὸν παιδὸς χαρακτῆρα θαυμάσιον ἐναποσφραγίζομεν).

41  This concept, that Christ had no sin, is used by other NT authors: 1 Peter 2:22; 1 John 3:5.

42  The use of ὁμοιωθῆναι in 2:17 and καθ' ὁμοιότητα in 4:14 shows that in the latter the writer is returning to things already introduced. He will now develop this further into chapter 5.

2:18 δύναται τοῖς πειραζομένοις βοηθῆσαι and 4:16 εὕρωμεν εἰς εὔκαιρον βοήθειαν. [43]

Once again, Hebrews sees the path of the Son to glory (exaltation and ascension) to be one that leads first through suffering. He expects a path of suffering for the believer because it was the path for Jesus. In his logic, the author works backwards from the ascension of the Son through the heavens to view the Son's suffering as qualifying him for the glory and honor. Since the Son who suffered has now ascended, believers in their own suffering can approach the throne of grace where the Son sits, knowing they will find one who is sympathetic. The knowledge of Christ's ascension gives assurance of the reality answers to their crying for help. The Son had cried for help and was heard by God in heaven who enabled him to ascend into heaven. Believers in their suffering can cry to heaven for help and be heard through a high priest who has gone there on their behalf. The ascension of the Son because of his faithfulness in suffering becomes both the pattern that awaits the believer, and the grounds of assurance for believers in their present experiences.

In verse 4:16, we have the second of four uses of θρόνος in Hebrews (1:8; 4:16; 8:1; 12:2). The first in 1:8 refers to the Son's throne as God's throne lasting forever, as previously discussed. In 8:1, it refers to Christ sitting at the right hand of God's throne: ὃς ἐκάθισεν ἐν δεξιᾷ τοῦ θρόνου τῆς μεγαλωσύνης ἐν τοῖς οὐρανοῖς. Instead of referencing God directly, the phrase τοῦ θρόνου τῆς μεγαλωσύνης is a circumlocution.[44] Finally, in 12:2 it is a reference to Christ sitting at God's right hand: ἐν δεξιᾷ τε τοῦ θρόνου τοῦ θεοῦ κεκάθικεν.

The throne is God's throne in 4:16. In the Hebrew Bible, that God has set himself up as a ruler and heaven is likened to a great temple,[45] and in it he has established his throne.[46] This is even more common in Second Temple

---

[43] It is speculation, but one may wonder if at least some of the audience, because of their experiences, questioned the ability of the Son of God to help. Such questioning could be just a normal human psychological response to trauma and trials, or it could be theologically motivated by not having an active temple sacrificial ritual to participate in (either because Christian community has parted ways with the Old Covenant or possibly because the temple has been destroyed by the time of writing).

[44] Hebrews of course does directly state that the Son is at God the Father's right hand in 10:12.

[45] References where the Lord is described in heaven as a holy temple include Ps 11:4; Mic 1:2; Hab 2:20. The latter two describe a holy temple in contrast to earth, which probably reflects not the Jerusalem temple but most likely the heavenly temple, especially when the post-exilic date is considered. In Ps 18:6, David cries to the Lord who is in his holy temple. Heaven is most likely in view (not the Jerusalem temple or tabernacle, depending on how one dates the Psalm and if one agrees with the inscription that David wrote it) (1) because of the contrast with Sheol in v. 5 and earth v. 7 and (2) because YHWH comes down from heaven v. 9 and from there he utters his voice v. 13.

[46] 1 Kgs 22:19//2 Chr 18:18; Ps 103:19; Isa 66:1.

Judaism,[47] but here it is specifically designated as a τῷ θρόνῳ τῆς χάριτος where the genitive is adjectival, describing the character of the one reign on the throne. The designation, ὁ θρόνος τῆς χάριτος, "occurs nowhere else in the NT, the LXX, or the Apostolic Fathers."[48] Normally when figures are given visions of the throne of God, they bow and express their own unworthiness (Isa 6). Nevertheless, Hebrews exhorts the believers to approach the throne of grace confidently because they will find help. This contrast between the unapproachable and the approachable is made in 12:20–24. One could not approach Mt. Sinai when Moses ascended to the mountain, and it was so terrifying even Moses trembled with fear (12:21), but now, the believer can approach the new and better Mt. Zion.

First, we should note that this throne was unapproachable under the terms of the Old Covenant, based on Leviticus.[49] Even as the high priest went into the tabernacle with the ark of the covenant symbolizing the footstool of God's throne, incense spread through the Holy of Holies clouding the visibility of God's presence. As we will see below, the throne of God is likened to the mercy seat of the ark of the covenant—the true ark/throne is in heaven.

Second, it is a throne of grace because of the work of the Son to offer a secure atonement. By ascending bodily into heaven on the basis of his sacrifice, he has provided atonement. Christ is the forerunner of humanity into heaven so that believers can approach, but also being a minister of the New Covenant, Christ's work assures the believers that the throne is now the place of grace being ministered to them by their high priest. Unlike the Law (10:1), Christ and his work can perfect the worshipper so that they can draw near to God (10:19–22).

It is specifically the completion of the work of Christ, in contrast to the ongoing and provisional nature of the Old Covenant, that allows the author to call the throne a τῷ θρόνῳ τῆς χάριτος. Later the believers are exhorted not to turn away from God, lest his flaming wrath come upon them in judgment (10:26–31), the exhortation is to not turn away in their struggles but find help precisely because God, via the merciful and graceful high priest, dwells on a throne of grace.[50] While for Hebrews, the throne is not one of grace apart from the mediation of Jesus Christ—and Hebrews has stern warnings for the

---

47 See our discussion above. e.g., 1 En. 14:18–20; 47:1–4; 71:5–7; 4Q403 f1.ii.10–16; 4Q405 f20. ii.21–22 1–11; T. Levi 3:4; 5:1; see also Timo Eskola, *Messiah and the Throne*, 65–120.

48 Cockerill, *The Epistle to the Hebrews* (Eerdmans, 2012), 227n.25.

49 Ibid., 227; Lane, *Hebrews 1–8*, 115.

50 Barry Joslin ("Christ Bore the Sins of Many: Substitution and the Atonement in Hebrews," *SBJT* 11.2 [2007]: 91–95) has discussed the concept of wrath in Hebrews and its relationship to substitution and atonement.

community—it is God's throne that the believers are approaching. Thus, it is not as if the Son is merciful and gracious, but the Father is wrathful.[51] Nevertheless, the author sees the fulfillment of redemptive history where the believer is now able to approach God because a glorified human-son, who is also revealed to be an eternal divine Son, has representatively ascended up into the presence of God and taken his seat within the divine Glory. The Son's ascension, as the climax of redemptive history, is the apex of the community's confession and serves as a basis for receiving help from God.

## Heb 6:19–20

Keeping with the notion of Christ ascending into heaven, the author describes the Christian as the one who has a hope εἰσερχομένην εἰς τὸ ἐσώτερον τοῦ καταπετάσματος (Heb 6:19). Jesus has entered into heaven, which is a true tabernacle/temple. Just as the earthly tabernacle had a veil dividing the outer holy place from the inner tent (Holy of Holies), so Jesus enters into the very throne room of God behind the curtain. This entry becomes the foundation of the Christian hope. It also indicates the union of the Son's offices of king and priest. The ascension is both an ascension of the king to be installed on the throne as well as an ascension of the eschatological high priest into the true temple/throne room of God.[52]

The grammar is debated in vv. 18–20. Specifically, what is the referent of εἰσερχομένην? With respect to its syntax, the phrase εἰσερχομένην εἰς τὸ ἐσώτερον τοῦ καταπετάσματος does not explicitly refer to Jesus. However, Jesus is forerunner: ὅπου πρόδρομος ὑπὲρ ἡμῶν εἰσῆλθεν (6:20). The argument assumes that Jesus has gone εἰς τὸ ἐσώτερον τοῦ καταπετάσματος (6:19). Ὅπου is used here as a conjunctive with a designation of space.[53] The aorist εἰσῆλθεν denotes punctiliar action, and in this instant refers to the past event of Christ's ascension. He has gone as a forerunner (πρόδρομος) to the same place where the believer's hope is now located, namely εἰς τὸ ἐσώτερον τοῦ καταπετάσματος. Before

---

51 While Hebrews does not mention Exod 34 directly, mercy and graciousness are key covenant attributes of YHWH in his revelation to Israel. MT וַיִּקְרָ֨א יְהוָ֥ה ׀ יְהוָ֖ה אֵ֣ל רַח֥וּם וְחַנּ֛וּן אֶ֥רֶךְ אַפַּ֖יִם וְרַב־חֶ֥סֶד וֶאֱמֶֽת. LXX καὶ παρῆλθεν κύριος πρὸ προσώπου αὐτοῦ καὶ ἐκάλεσεν Κύριος ὁ θεὸς οἰκτίρμων καὶ ἐλεήμων, μακρόθυμος καὶ πολυέλεος καὶ ἀληθινός. In other places LXX most often translates חֶסֶד as ἔλεος when it is refering to the divine attribute. In Wis 3:9 and 4:15, mercy and grace are upon God's chosen ones because he watches over them.

52 In Hebrews, the themes of God's eschatological rest, temple/tabernacle, Mt. Zion, promised land/inheritance are all intertwined. The eschatological is both horizontal as a climax of salvation history and vertical as a movement toward heaven. Eskola (*Messiah and the Throne*, 207) notes, "His ascension has both cultic and royal features." Cf. Barnard, *Mysticism*, 148.

53 "ὅπου," BDAG, 717.

answering the question of grammar, let us examine the function of Christ's role in these verses.

Forerunner, πρόδρομος, is found only here in the NT, and in LXX it is used only in Num 13:20 πρόδρομοι σταφυλῆς, "forerunner of grapes," and Isa 28:4 ὡς πρόδρομος σύκου, "like early figs." Outside of the Hebrew canon it is used in Wis. 12:8 where wasps of the forerunner of the coming armies προδρόμους τοῦ στρατοπέδου. This motif of an advanced guard, or an announcement that precedes the full coming, is found in some of the secular Greek literature. In Eur. *Iph. Aul.* 424, we have a messenger that comes before the return of Agememnon's daughter to prepare him: ἐγὼ δὲ πρόδρομος σῆς παρασκευῆς χάριν. In Heroditus, *Hist.* 1.60.4, we have a reference to heralds running before the woman Phya as part of plan to bring back Pisistratus. These heralds were προδρόμους κήρυκας προπέμψαντες. It is more commonly used of troops who are advance guards of the rest of the advancing army, for example Heroditus, *Hist.* 7.203.1; 9.14.2; and Polybius, *Hist.* 12.20.7.[54] This warrior analogy may fit together then with Hebrews' conception of Jesus as ἀρχηγός in Heb 2:10 and 12:2.[55] Attridge correctly draws out the soteriological connection: "it evokes the image of movement on the path to heavenly glory that Christians are called upon to tread in Christ's footsteps. Whether as a military or athletic metaphor, the title suggests the basic soteriological pattern."[56] Christ's ascension paves the way for the salvation and perfection of the people of God. Thus, as a number of commentators note, the usage of πρόδρομος is similar to Christ described as an ἀρχηγός (cf. 2:10; 12:2).[57]

Particularly with the analogy to the harvest in LXX (Num 13:20; Isa 28:4), Hebrews may have in mind something analogous to Paul's metaphor of the firstfruits, ἀπαρχή.[58] It is not merely that Jesus 'runs ahead,' but as E.K. Simpson writes, "this Forerunner embraces far wider ends than that of preparation. It proclaims an accomplished work of redemption and signalizes the first fruits of a mighty aftercrop. Precursor is a relative term implying a sequence."[59] There is clearly a strong connection in our author's mind between

---

54 *TDNT*, 8.235; see also *EDNT* 3.154; Attridge, *Hebrews*, 185n.92, for other examples. Attridge also notes that LXX usage is paralleled by Theophrastus, *Hist. plant.* 5.1.5.

55 *TDNT*, 8.235; see also *EDNT* 3.154.

56 Attridge, *Hebrews*, 185.

57 Ibid.; cf. Cockerill, *Hebrews*, 291; Johnson, *Hebrews*, 173; Craig Koester, *Hebrews: A New Translation with Introduction and Commentary* (Doubleday, 2001), 330; Lane, *Hebrews 1–8*, 154; James Moffatt, *The Epistle to the Hebrews* (T&T Clark, 1979), 90; Thomas Schreiner, *Commentary on Hebrews* (B&H, 2015), 204.

58 *TDNT*, 8.235.

59 E.K. Simpson, "The Vocabulary of the Epistle of Hebrews, Part 2," *EQ* 18 (1946): 187, qtd. in F.F. Bruce, *The Epistle to the Hebrews* (Eerdmans, 1990), 155. Lane (*Hebrews 1–8*, 154) also notes that the usage implies sequence.

Christ's entering heaven into God's presence in a glorified state, which is the believer's firm present hope and predicates the exhortation that we enter God's presence in 4:16, and believers having entered it already in some sense in 12:22. The heavenly destiny of the Savior and his transition from suffering to glory is the destiny of the believer in Christ (2:9–10; 3:1 κλήσεως ἐπουρανίου μέτοχοι; 3:14; 12:2, 10). As the eschatological man (a Second Adam and true/final King), Jesus moves from suffering to glory which culminates in his being crowned with glory and honor on Mt. Zion in the heavenly throne room (cf. Pss 2:6, 7; 8:5, 6; 110:1; Heb 1:3d, 5a, 8–9, 13; 2:5–10). This is an ascension into the heavenly throne/tabernacle.

Thus, if we follow the logic of Hebrew's argument, while the grammatical referent of εἰσερχομένην εἰς τὸ ἐσώτερον τοῦ καταπετάσματος (6:19) is not Jesus, nevertheless the connection is made precisely because Jesus has gone in first via ascension. Returning again to the question of the precise referent of εἰσερχομένην, there are two options: its referent is (1) ἣν ὡς ἄγκυραν (6:19); or (2) ἐλπίδος (6:18). If the grammatical referent is to ἣν ὡς ἄγκυραν, the structure would essentially be as follows:

ἣν ὡς ἄγκυραν ἔχομεν τῆς ψυχῆς
```
         | ἀσφαλῆ
  τε καὶ | βεβαίαν
     καὶ | εἰσερχομένην εἰς τὸ ἐσώτερον τοῦ καταπετάσματος,
```

In this construction, ἀσφαλῆ, βεβαίαν, and εἰσερχομένην εἰς τὸ ἐσώτερον τοῦ καταπετάσματος are descriptors that modify the phrase of the anchor of our soul (ἄγκυραν... τῆς ψυχῆς). It is the anchor that goes behind the curtain. While not impossible, it would be a mixing of metaphors. Two difficulties arise here. The first difficulty is that the construction is a bit abnormal for this reading. We have adjective—adjective—participial clause all in parallel. We also have the adjectives linked with τε καὶ while the the participial clause is linked with καί. This actually suggests then that they are not three parallel modifiers of ἄγκυραν.

Instead, it is better to see the grammatical construction as follows:

τῆς προκειμένης ἐλπίδος
```
     | ἣν ὡς ἄγκυραν ἔχομεν τῆς ψυχῆς
     |          | ἀσφαλῆ
     |   τε καὶ | βεβαίαν
 καὶ | εἰσερχομένην εἰς τὸ ἐσώτερον τοῦ καταπετάσματος
```

*The Son Ascends into the Heavenly Tabernacle* 151

In this way in Heb 6:19, ἄγκυραν is described as ἀσφαλῆ τε καὶ βεβαίαν, but both ἄγκυραν ἔχομεν τῆς ψυχῆς and εἰσερχομένην εἰς τὸ ἐσώτερον τοῦ καταπετάσματος describe the nature of the hope the believer has. It is our hope that is like an anchor, and that hope goes behind the veil precisely because the object of it is Jesus Christ whom the believers are being exhorted to hold fast to throughout the whole epistle. On a grammatical level, the referent of the phrase εἰσερχομένην εἰς τὸ ἐσώτερον τοῦ καταπετάσματος is τῆς προκειμένης ἐλπίδος because the person to which this hope refers to is Jesus, the high priest ὅπου πρόδρομος ὑπὲρ ἡμῶν εἰσῆλθεν Ἰησοῦς (6:20). Jesus is behind the veil in the heavenly tabernacle *as the forerunner of his people*, therefore the hope is certain and steadfast.

ESV makes this connection to 'hope' clear: "(v. 18) we who have fled for refuge might have strong encouragement to hold fast to the hope set before us. (v. 19) We have this as a sure and steadfast anchor of the soul, a hope that enters into the inner place behind the curtain."[60] The hope enters behind the inner curtain precisely because Christ enters behind the curtain: ὅπου πρόδρομος ὑπὲρ ἡμῶν εἰσῆλθεν Ἰησοῦς (6:20). The argument comes full circle because God has made an oath and effected it in Jesus' ascension.

It is tempting to see the hope set before the believer (6:18 τῆς προκειμένης ἐλπίδος) as heaven (or specifically the inheritance), or Christ in heaven.[61] If one holds to this view, it is clear for Hebrews that the reason for such a vivid and certain hope is because of Christ's ascension into heaven as forerunner, and the believers themselves are assuredly called there because Christ their High Priest and Savior is there.[62] However, we propose that Hebrews is perhaps more vivid than this.

We propose that the way Hebrews envisions the hope coming to be set before us is in the ascension itself. The ascension is the presentation of the Son in eschatological glory. Πρόκειμαι can mean something placed before or

---

60 NRSV is similar here: "We have this hope, a sure and steadfast anchor of the soul, a hope that enters the inner shrine behind the curtain" (v19). NASB differs, reading: "take hold of the hope set before us. 19 This hope we have as an anchor of the soul, a hope both sure and steadfast and one which enters within the veil, (18b–19)" but sees "sure and steadfast" as modifying ἐλπίδος not ἄγκυραν.

61 Attridge (*Hebrews*, 182–183) sees hope as synonymous with promise; Cockerill (*Hebrews*, 289) remarks that "entrance [into heaven] is the goal 'laid before' them by God through the high-priestly work of Christ"; Johnson (*Hebrews*, 173) sees the hope as Christ going into heaven and believers also inherit this promise; Lane (*Hebrews 1–8*, 153) says the hope is "present and future salvation"; cf. Moffatt, *Hebrews*, 88–89; Hughes, *A Commentary on the Epistle to Hebrews* (Eerdmans, 1997), 234.

62 Attridge (*Hebrews*, 182) writes, "The object of 'flight,' like the object of 'participation,' is a reality that is heavenly because the ground of hope, Christ, has a heavenly status 'within the veil.'"; cf. Cockerill, *Hebrews*, 291.

exposed in public view, such as in Jude 7 where Sodom and Gomorrah are set before us as examples of judgment by fire: πρόκεινται δεῖγμα πυρὸς αἰωνίου δίκην ὑπέχουσαι.[63] But in Hebrews the presentation is not a mere setting into public view or setting up an example. Even more, the use is slightly different from what we see later in Hebrews. In Heb 12:1–2, it is first the pathway of a race that is set before believers, τρέχωμεν τὸν προκείμενον ἡμῖν ἀγῶνα (v. 1), and then (v. 2) this pathway parallels the journey through the suffering cross Christ endured for the final joy set before him, ἀντὶ τῆς προκειμένης αὐτῷ χαρᾶς ὑπέμεινεν σταυρόν.

In LXX, πρόκειμαι can refer to the presentation table and elements in the Tabernacle set before the Lord (Exod 38:9; 39:17; Lev 24:7; Num 4:7). This use of tabernacle imagery of presentation should give pause. Hebrews has more in mind than the temporal goal to be realized.[64] The presentation of the believer's future heavenly hope is the Son being set before us as one who has gone through suffering into heaven in ascension.[65] The hope is grounded in the Son set up and installed as the king/priest at God's right hand. Just like an anchor is set, so the hope is προκειμένης. The hope is before believers like a strong steadfast anchor and is behind the veil because that is ὅπου πρόδρομος ὑπὲρ ἡμῶν εἰσῆλθεν Ἰησοῦς (6:20). Christ having gone behind the veil makes certain that believers have a high priest of a particular kind, an eschatological perfection. In Heb 8:1 the author returns state that our eschatological high priest is at God's right hand τοιοῦτον ἔχομεν ἀρχιερέα ὃς ἐκάθισεν ἐν δεξιᾷ τοῦ θρόνου τῆς μεγαλωσύνης ἐν τοῖς οὐρανοῖς, which our author identifies as the point he is driving towards with Κεφάλαιον δὲ ἐπὶ τοῖς λεγομένοις (8:1). Just like the elements in the temple are presented before the Lord and placed in the tabernacle, the Son is presented before His Father and placed to sit at the right hand of the Divine Throne.

Jesus comes before God, drawing near for us. The Son's ascending is his presentation in a royal installment, "You are my Son, today I have begotten

---

63 "πρόκειμαι," BDAG, 871.

64 Cf. BDAG πρόκειμαι "3 to be subsequent to some point of time as prospect, of a goal or destination," which typically has a dative of persons.

65 Commentators do pick up on the fact that Christ's ascension into heaven is the basis for hope (Attridge, *Hebrews*, 182–184; Cockerill, *Hebrews*, 290–291; Johnson, *Hebrews*, 172–173; Lane, *Hebrews 1–8*, 153). Schreiner (*Hebrews*, 204) also rightly brings in aspects of the atonement here which is related to Christ's priestly role. However, we are seeking to be more specific. At the ascension, the Father declares to the Son: "you are my Son." This declaration also becomes affirmation to believers to likewise make such a confession. The Son, as Second-Adam, ascends into heaven. His procession up into heaven in that ascension is the 'set before them hope.' The act of the Son ascending at the behest of the Father is the act of the Father setting hope before the community of believers. We are seeking to draw out what the act of ascension presents before the believers.

you"; "I will be to him a father, and he shall be to me a son"; "Sit at my right hand until I make your enemies a footstool for your feet" (Heb 1:5, 13; Pss 2, 8, 110), so that the believers specifically 'see' the one "who for a little while was made lower than the angels, namely Jesus, crowned with glory and honor because of the suffering of death" (Heb 2:9). The presenting of the heavenly hope is grounded upon the Father's presenting of the Son himself into the heavenly tabernacle/throne in the Son's own ascension.[66] It is a τῆς προκειμένης ἐλπίδος (6:18) because the Son has been set as an anchor.

The ascension being the hope set before believers fits with the portrait that believers in wilderness/exile pursue Christ even in the midst of suffering. Our point is that while heaven is certainly the future presented to the believer it is precisely because in the ascension of Jesus the royal eschatological man is presented as one over the age to come/heavenly kingdom. The goal to which Christians flee is set before them because Christ ascended has been set before them.

While believers are fleeing exiles, the hope is presented, or set before believers, in God's appointment of the Son in an act of exaltation marked by his ascension: in 5:5–6 Christ γενηθῆναι ἀρχιερέα[67] ἀλλ' ὁ λαλήσας πρὸς αὐτόν· υἱός μου εἶ σύ, ἐγὼ σήμερον γεγέννηκά σε· καθὼς καὶ ἐν ἑτέρῳ λέγει σὺ ἱερεὺς εἰς τὸν αἰῶνα κατὰ τὴν τάξιν Μελχισέδεκ. The ὁ λαλήσας πρὸς αὐτόν is like the ancient royal exaltation ceremonies where the presentation is for the benefit of the witnesses, a king's subjects and even enemies. The vice-regent is installed, bearing his status from the higher regent in the suzerain-vassal treaties, in an act of enthronement. The speaking of God to the Son is the Son's glorification/exaltation in an ascension into heaven, whereby the Father in an oath makes the Son the eschatological high priest/king. The ascension of the Son is not a private event but a royal installment over all creation in the pattern of the Adamic/Davidic king/priest. For our author, the reality of Jesus' ascension sets immovable hope before the believer. As Feliz Cortez concludes, "Therefore, Jesus' ascension *confirms* God's original purpose of 'glory and honor' for human beings not only in the sense that it brings that purpose into realization in the person of Jesus but, more importantly, in the sense that it makes possible its fulfillment for them."[68]

---

66 James Kurianal (*Jesus Our High Priest*, 209) shows how God the Father speaking the words that Jesus is the high priest effects the declaration. This, of course, happens at the ascension.

67 Notice that aspect of Christ *being* made something by the pronouncement of the Father, referencing Ps 2:7 which is the royal installation of the Davidic son on Mt. Zion (2:6–7).

68 "Anchor of the Soul," 314. See also Moffitt, *Atonement and the Logic of Resurrection*, 142–143.

Thus, the oath to the heirs of the promise (6:17, cf. 7:17) is LXX Ps 109:4 ὤμοσεν κύριος καὶ οὐ μεταμεληθήσεται Σὺ εἶ ἱερεὺς εἰς τὸν αἰῶνα κατὰ τὴν τάξιν Μελχισεδεκ. To be this priest and have this oath fulfilled, the priest of Melchizedek must have indestructible eschatological life[69] and go into the true heavenly tabernacle (7:16–17, 20–22; 8:1–2). These two realities fulfilled makes the hope for believers superior and certain (7:19 κρείττονος ἐλπίδος δι' ἧς ἐγγίζομεν τῷ θεῷ). This serves Hebrews' larger purpose of exhorting believers not to waiver from their confession of this faith since now eschatological realities have been effected, eschatological realities that the Old Covenant could not effect but only looked forward towards as a shadow points to the true reality.

God had made an oath, ἐμεσίτευσεν ὅρκῳ (6:17), to Abraham (6:13–14) and the heirs of the promise (6:17). This oath is fulfilled in the fulfillment of Ps 110:4 in Jesus' exaltation/ascension: as Jesus goes into heaven as the high priestly forerunner, he ἀρχιερεὺς γενόμενος εἰς τὸν αἰῶνα (6:20). Just as the original Melchizedek blesses Abraham (7:6–7), which makes Melchizedek's priesthood superior to Levi's priesthood because Abraham is superior to Levi by virtue of being his forefather,[70] so also now the heir of the Melchizedek priesthood blesses the heirs of the promise of Abraham by going into heaven on their behalf as a forerunner for them.

Melchizedek and the priesthood of Melchizedek connects God's oath of Ps 110:4 to the fulfillment of Jesus. In this way, he effects the promise of God to Abraham: "Surely I will bless you and multiply you" (6:14; cf. 7:1, 6).[71] The final

---

69 In 7:16, "indestructible life" ζωῆς ἀκαταλύτου is not a reference to eternal Sonship but rather a reference to the resurrection life Christ receives: Moffitt, *Atonement and the Logic of Resurrection*, 146–148, 198–208; Bruce, *Hebrews*, 169; Johnson, *Hebrews*, 188; Lane, *Hebrews 1–8*, 184; Schreiner, *Hebrews*, 223; contra Cockerill, *Hebrews*, 323. This is made clear with the contrast to the Levitical priests dying διὰ τὸ θανάτῳ κωλύεσθαι παραμένειν (v. 23), whereas Christ has the oath σὺ ἱερεὺς εἰς τὸν αἰῶνα where the 'forever' is not into the eternal past but a future forever having been installed. Furthermore, it is grounded on the Son's *having been made* perfect forever, υἱὸν εἰς τὸν αἰῶνα τετελειωμένον (v. 28). Finally, Christ cannot be a priest into eternity past because the high priest, according to Hebrews' own logic, must come from among men (5:1), which does not happen until the incarnation (2:14, 17). The priest must experience God's act of exaltation (5:5), which is his being 'perfected' into the glorified eschatological man evidenced in ascension.

70 The logic here is the superior person blesses the inferior person, 7:7. So if Melchizedek blesses Abraham, and Abraham is superior to Levi being his forefather, then Melchizedek (and his priesthood) is superior to Levi (and his priesthood). Even more Hebrews draws the analogy that Levi was still ἔτι γὰρ ἐν τῇ ὀσφύϊ τοῦ πατρὸς ἦν ὅτε συνήντησεν αὐτῷ Μελχισέδεκ. Abraham's reception of blessing then implies that Levi also is a recipient of the blessing Melchizedek gave Abraham. While the Levitical priesthood received tithes under the Torah, Levi being ἐν τῇ ὀσφύϊ of Abraham pays tithes to a superior priesthood of Melchizedek.

71 God promises to bless Abraham (6:14), and in 7:1 attention is drawn to the fact that Melchizedek blesses Abraham as a priestly intermediary for the Most High God.

blessing of inheritance and eschatological human perfection, humanity's glorification, is realized through God's promise and the fulfillment in the greater Melchizedek who helps Abraham's offspring (2:16). Attuned to the unfolding climax of redemptive history, the eschatological perfection was not reached through the Levitical priesthood (7:11). Therefore, the present hope of the believer is a better hope, κρείττονος ἐλπίδος (7:11). It is the means by which we draw near to God, δι' ἧς ἐγγίζομεν τῷ θεῷ (7:19), which explains the present tense of 6:19 as our hope εἰσερχομένην εἰς τὸ ἐσώτερον τοῦ καταπετάσματος.[72]

In LXX, the phrase τὸ ἐσώτερον τοῦ καταπετάσματος is used twice to denote going behind the inner curtain that separated the Holy Place from the Holy of Holies where the ark of the covenant was located. In Exod 26:33 the ark of the covenant is brought in and placed behind the ἐσώτερον τοῦ καταπετάσματος. This inner veil διοριεῖ τὸ καταπέτασμα ὑμῖν ἀνὰ μέσον τοῦ ἁγίου καὶ ἀνὰ μέσον τοῦ ἁγίου τῶν ἁγίων (Exod 26:33b). The second use of phrase is specifically on the Day of Atonement in Lev 16:2. Aaron is given instruction that he is not to go into the Holy of Holies any time he wishes. The sanctuary behind the veil is the place that symbolizes the throne room of God where God dwells over the ark of the covenant, the place of propitiation ἐν γὰρ νεφέλῃ ὀφθήσομαι ἐπὶ τοῦ ἱλαστηρίου (16:2). The ark of the covenant is like the throne of God or the footstool of God who dwells in heaven (1 Chr 28:2; Ps 132:7). God's presence is manifest from above the ark (Exod 25:22 ἄνωθεν τοῦ ἱλαστηρίου; MT מֵעַל הַכַּפֹּרֶת).

For Hebrews the phrase εἰς τὸ ἐσώτερον τοῦ καταπετάσματος (6:19) represents Jesus' ascension into heaven itself. Hebrews typically is not specific about the layout of heaven.[73] For example, the author uses the plural 'the holy places' to refer to the heavenly sanctuary, which as Cortez has pointed out is used in LXX to speak of both tents of the Holy Place and the Holy of Holies together.[74] Hebrews does refer to heaven τῆς σκηνῆς τῆς ἀληθινῆς (8:2). 'The tent (τὴν σκηνήν)' (8:5; cf. Exod 25:40; 26:1) probably refers to the tent/tabernacle as a whole with its two internal rooms of the Holy Place and Holy of Holies. The intention of Hebrews is not to parse out division within heaven,

---

72 Just as Jesus has ascended as forerunner into the heavenly tabernacle/Mt. Zion, so also the believer is exhorted to draw near to God, and in a sense is described as doing just that via Christ's representation. In 12:22, The perfect προσεληλύθατε denotes a past action with present results. The believer "has come/drawn near," but is regularly coming/drawing near. In Hebrews 'drawing near' (προσέρχομαι) is an exhortation in 4:16 and 10:1, but also a reality for the believer accomplished by Jesus' mediation and priesthood 7:19, 7:25, 10:1.

73 Cortez ('Anchor of the Soul,' 347) writes, "Hebrews does not show interest in a division in the heavenly sanctuary"; cf. Ellingworth, *Hebrews*, 446–447; Hughes, *Hebrews*, 289; Koester, *Hebrews*, 409.

74 Cortez, "Anchor of the Soul," 341–346.

but to make the analogy connect to the work of the high priest. Just as the high priest in the First Covenant goes εἰς τὸ ἐσώτερον τοῦ καταπετάσματος, the Melchizedekian high priest of the New Covenant goes into the heavenly throne room of God where we have the true manifestation of God. What was once done each year in the earthly tent of the shadow is now done climactically and finally with Jesus' ascension into heaven itself. We are assured of the finality of it both in terms of the redemption of God's people and mankind reaching the eschatological state in the forerunner's entering in and becoming a high priest forever (6:20).

## Heb 7:26

In this section, the focus of the author is on the contrast between the Levitical priesthood and Christ's priesthood of the order of Melchizedek. The section begins in 7:11 by highlighting the inability of the Levitical priesthood to attain the perfection of the eschatological state for humanity as the indicator of the need for another priest after a different order, namely Melchizedek.[75] The author constructs an "if...then" argument: Εἰ μὲν οὖν τελείωσις διὰ τῆς Λευιτικῆς ἱερωσύνης ἦν...τίς ἔτι χρεία κατὰ τὴν τάξιν Μελχισέδεκ ἕτερον ἀνίστασθαι ἱερέα (Heb 7:11).[76] A new order of priesthood is needed because the Levitical priesthood as part of the Law (7:11 ὁ λαὸς γὰρ ἐπ' αὐτῆς νενομοθέτηται)[77] could not bring this perfection needed by God's people.[78]

The priesthood of Christ is not on the basis of physical descent, but rather on the qualification of indestructible life (v. 16).[79] David Moffitt has con-

---

[75] This 'indestructible life' is the quality of the 'age to come.' cf. 2 En. 65:10[J] "But they [the righteous] will have a great light, a great indestructible light, and paradise, great and incorruptible. For everything corruptible will pass away, and the incorruptible will come into being, and will be the shelter of the eternal residences."

[76] David Moffitt (*Atonement and the Logic of Resurrection*, 203) argues, rightly in our view, that ἀνίστασθαι is a double entendre. It references the resurrection of Jesus, which is a central qualification of his priesthood of a new order.

[77] The Law and Levitical priesthood are seen as one complex belonging to the old order, not of the age to come. Both the Law and Levitical priesthood, as one united system, are unable to effect the transition from 'this age' to 'the age to come' or 'the world to come τὴν οἰκουμένην τὴν μέλλουσαν.' This is echoed in 7:19 οὐδὲν γὰρ ἐτελείωσεν ὁ νόμος.

[78] See the previous discussion of 'perfection,' which denotes eschatological glory. For the people of God, this includes being free from sin, but also more than that. In the case of Jesus, the author sees Jesus as both free from sin in his earthly life and still needing the state of eschatological humanity.

[79] Joshua Jipp ("The Son's Entrance into the Heavenly World: The Soteriological Necessity of the Scriptural Catena in Hebrews 1.5–14," *NTS* 56 [2010]: 572) writes, "it is precisely the key attribute of the Melchizedekian priest of 'the power of indestructible life' (7.16) which is parallel to God's act of perfecting the Son...and it is this quality of the Son's eternality which qualifies him to be the Mechizedekian priest."

vincingly demonstrated that ζωῆς ἀκαταλύτου is not a reference to divine nature or eternal sonship but to the resurrection of Jesus Christ.[80] This resurrection life is the glory and honor that Christ has been crowned with (2:5–10). The two-age contrast of Hebrews is central to the contrast between the Levitical priesthood, which belongs to the Law Covenant, and the Melchizedek priesthood, which belongs to the New Covenant. The former is marked by weakness, death, a failure to move beyond perpetual succession, and therefore is transitory.[81] While the latter Covenant, as characteristic of the inbreaking of the age to come, accomplishes the perfection of eschatological life, which includes the removal of sins, the enabling of the worshipper to draw near to God, and perfection for believers, and is therefore eternally forever.[82] Thus, the nature of the two priesthoods as an eschatological divide is distinguished as follows:

| Levitical (this age) | Melchizedek (age to come) |
|---|---|
| v. 11 unable τελείωσις...ἦν | v. 16 ζωῆς ἀκαταλύτου |
| v. 16 σαρκίνης | v. 17 σὺ ἱερεὺς εἰς τὸν αἰῶνα |
| v. 18 ἀθέτησις | v. 19 κρείττονος ἐλπίδος |
| v. 18 ἀσθενὲς καὶ ἀνωφελές | v. 22 κρείττονος διαθήκης |
| v. 19 οὐδὲν γὰρ ἐτελείωσεν ὁ νόμος | v. 21 σὺ ἱερεὺς εἰς τὸν αἰῶνα. |
| v. 23 διὰ τὸ θανάτῳ κωλύεσθαι παραμένειν | v. 24 ὁ δὲ διὰ τὸ μένειν αὐτὸν εἰς τὸν αἰῶνα |
| v. 28 ἀσθένειαν, | v. 24 ἀπαράβατον |
| | v. 25 πάντοτε ζῶν |
| | v. 28 εἰς τὸν αἰῶνα τετελειωμένον |

Figure 5.1 The Levitical and Melchizedekian Preisthoods

We have included σαρκίνης as descriptive of the Levitical priesthood; it probably denotes more than just the physical lineage to the Levitical priest as σάρξ can be descriptive of the state of humanity under the present evil age, in contrast to the age to come/resurrection/Holy Spirit—especially in Pauline theology.[83] In Heb 2:14 αἵματος καὶ σαρκός is the state of weakness subject to

---

80  Moffitt, *Atonement and the Logic of Resurrection*, 198–208.

81  Jipp ("The Son's Entrance," 572) writes, "The emphasis on life and eternity in opposition to death and temporality is the primary trait of the Melchizedekian priesthood and is confirmed throughout ch. 7."

82  Notice the important repetition of the phrase 'εἰς τὸν αἰῶνα' in vv. 17, 21, 24, and 28. It is the nature of the indestructible life the new Melchizedekian priest has. It is the absence of death (v. 23), weakness (v. 18, 28), and uselessness (v. 18), but in fact, it guarantees an effective office that is able to save and bring people to God and into eschatological perfection of the age to come since he is πάντοτε ζῶν εἰς τὸ ἐντυγχάνειν ὑπὲρ αὐτῶν (v. 25), this later phrase being explanatory of ζωῆς ἀκαταλύτου.

83  Hebrews also seems to be contrasting the Law with (resurrection) power: ὃς οὐ κατὰ νόμον ἐντολῆς σαρκίνης γέγονεν ἀλλὰ κατὰ δύναμιν ζωῆς ἀκαταλύτου. This would highlight the

death that Christ enters into in his incarnation. The Levitical priesthood as σαρκίνης never had the ability to defeat death but was subject to it. It could not effect the transition to τελείωσις. Thus, Levitical priests being appointed κατὰ νόμον ἐντολῆς σαρκίνης (Heb 7:16) is conceptually equivalent with them ἔχοντας ἀσθένειαν (Heb 7:28).[84] This points us to the theme of sin in the earthly Levitical high priests.

Under the Levitical priesthood the sacrifices need to be offered by the priest daily πρότερον ὑπὲρ τῶν ἰδίων ἁμαρτιῶν θυσίας ἀναφέρειν (Heb 7:27). The sharpest possible contrast between the Levitical priesthood and the Melchizedekian priesthood of Christ is thus set forth. The Levitical high priest had his own sins to regularly and consistently deal with even before he could minister for the people (7:27 ἔπειτα τῶν τοῦ λαοῦ). The Son is different. He is ὅσιος ἄκακος ἀμίαντος, κεχωρισμένος ἀπὸ τῶν ἁμαρτωλῶν (7:26), even in his taking on humanity's flesh and blood (2:14) and succumbing to death. It is clear then when 2:17 describes the Son as ὅθεν ὤφειλεν κατὰ πάντα τοῖς ἀδελφοῖς ὁμοιωθῆναι, it excludes sin or unholiness (see also 4:15 χωρὶς ἁμαρτίας). Hebrews portrays the Son as a righteous sufferer. One who, like God, loved perfect righteousness and hated wickedness. As 'flesh and blood' like us, he was subject to temptation but without sin, his obedience and death as the righteous sufferer effected the eschatological transition. In effecting this transition, he is made a priest forever—a priest of the eschatological life—where his one act is sufficient for all time as the eschatological sacrifice that is able to save those who draw near to God.

In his commentary on Hebrews, Gareth Cockerill has proposed that in 7:26 ὅσιος be translated as 'covenant keeping' rather than 'holy.' In LXX, ὅσιος is used to speak of one who is devout before God in behavior and practice, not cultic holiness.[85] In LXX Psalms, it is a common rendering for the Hebrew חָסִיד.[86] In 1 Macc. 7:17, it describes the faithful who have been slaughtered. In 1 Macc. 12:45, it is used as a near synonym with εὐσεβής (12:45 ὁσία καὶ εὐσεβὴς ἡ ἐπίνοια). In Isa 55:3, referencing the eternal covenant God made

---

sub-eschatological character of the Old Covenant. It is removed or nullified because of its weakness and uselessness (7:18), obvious antonyms of 'power.'

84 See also Attridge, *Hebrews*, 202: "The adjective 'indestructible' (ἀκατάλυτος) paraphrases the descriptions of the eternality of the new priesthood and offers a marked contrast to the notion of corruptibility inherent in 'fleshly.'"

85 Similarly, Barnabas Lindars (*The Theology of the Letter to the Hebrews* [Cambridge University Press, 1991], 79) writes, "[A]s will be shown in 10:1–10, the holiness of Jesus is not a matter of ceremonial purity but of moral purity, which is demonstrated in his complete offering of himself."

86 LXX Pss 4:4[3]; 11:2[12:1]; 15[16]:10; 17[18]:26; 29[30]:5; 30[31]:24; 31[32]:6; 36[37]:28; 42[43]:1; 49[50]:5; 51[52]:11; 78[79]:2; 84[85]:9; 85[86]:2; 96[97]:10; 115:6[116:15]; 131[132]:16; 144[145]:10, 13, 17; 148:14; 149:1, 5, 9.

with David (διαθήκην αἰώνιον; בְּרִית עוֹלָם), LXX translates the Hebrew חַסְדֵי דָוִד הַנֶּאֱמָנִים as τὰ ὅσια Δαυιδ τὰ πιστά.[87] It is used again to translate the root חסד in a context that highlights the theme of covenant faithfulness, this time from YHWH and his promise to David. Thus, Cockerill defends his translation of ὅσιος:

> The LXX uses this term in the plural, usually followed by the "of God," to designate the community of Israel (Pss 149:1–2; 79:1–2; 139:9, 16) and especially those in Israel who maintained their covenant relationship with God and others (Pss 12:1; 18:26; 32:6). Thus this word does not describe some speculative, preincarnate holiness but the faithfulness of the incarnate Son in his relationship to the Father as he learned what it meant to be an obedient human being.[88]

We would further the argument that ὅσιος in 7:26 entails covenant keeping by noting that in several cases in the Psalms, the context of the holy one (or covenant keeping one) who finds himself in dire suffering and his only recourse is to cry out for YHWH's deliverance. This is especially prominent in LXX Pss 4:4 [MT 4:3]; 11[12]:2; 42[43]:1; and 85[86]:2. Hebrews' thought here then works in conjunction with what he has said in 5:7. The Son is the obedient covenant keeper fulfilling the pattern of Davidic righteousness. He is a devout one who cries to God in despair and is heard because of εὐλαβείας.[89] His being ὅσιος is not abstraction. His being handed over to death before exaltation has manifested godliness. Ὅσιος is also in LXX Ps 15[16]:10 to describe the one who the Lord will not abandon to Sheol, which became a known Messianic psalm in the early gospel preaching of Acts. Christ was seen as the covenant keeping pious one, who although crucified was not abandoned by God His Father. As Cockerill writes, "The exalted Son has lived an obedient human life and so can be declared 'untouched by evil.'"[90] As we will show further in the next chapter, it is this obedient human life that is the grounds for his exaltation/ascension. Like the elements of ascent in apocalyptic texts, we have one who is righteous on earth qualified to be transformed and ascend (Gen 5:24;

---

87 An English rendering would be something like 'the sacred/hallowed things of David are trustworthy/faithful'; NETS: "the sacred things of Dauid that are sure" or as the also propose in a marginal note "the sacred things of Dauid that are sure."

88 Cockerill, *Hebrews*, 339–340.

89 We will return to this theme in our next chapter to show how Christ's obedience of sonship is the condition for his exaltation/ascension into heaven. See also Jipp, "The Son's Entrance," 572, where he comments on connections between ch. 7 and 5:7–10.

90 Cockerill, *Hebrews*, 340.

1 En. 1:1–8; 15:1; 62:15–16;[91] 71:1, 5, 14–16; 2 En. 67:1–3;[92] 2 Bar. 51:7–12[93]; T. Levi 3:1–10 and 4:2;[94] T. Ab. 20:11–14;[95] T. Isaac 4:46–47[96]).[97]

In Heb 7:27, Jesus offered himself up: τοῦτο γὰρ ἐποίησεν ἐφάπαξ ἑαυτὸν ἀνενέγκας. Τοῦτο refers more narrowly to offering himself for the people, since Hebrews is clear that Jesus has no need to offer himself for his own sin, of which he had none. The clause ὃς οὐκ ἔχει καθ' ἡμέραν ἀνάγκην (7:27a) has the focus on the high priest's daily work as the main emphasis in contrast to the Son's ἐφάπαξ (7:27b). Yet as the daily work of the high priest is mentioned, we note it is first ὑπὲρ τῶν ἰδίων ἁμαρτιῶν, so this is a second contrast in the author's purview.

It is this high priest who has now been exalted above the heavens (7:26 ὑψηλότερος τῶν οὐρανῶν γενόμενος).[98] That the Son has received indestructible life of the age to come[99] establishes that the Son has also now ascended into heaven. He has become exalted above the heavens. Hebrews frequently uses the participle γενόμενος to indicate change in the experience of the Son in the exercise of his offices.[100] In 1:4, Christ in his exaltation becomes

---

91 Although here it is the Son of Man sitting on glory (62:5) and the elect and righteous receiving eschatological deliverance.

92 2 En. 66:7[J]: "How happy are the righteous who shall escape the LORD's great judgment; for they shall be made to shine seven times brighter than the sun." This proclamation is followed by Enoch's ascension where he is made to stand in the face of God for eternity. Previously in 66:1–5, Enoch is exhorting the people to walk in righteousness. There is a clear connection between walking in righteousness and ascension.

93 What awaits the righteous is living in the heights [of heaven] with the stars; the excellence of the righteous becomes greater than the angels. Also in 2 Bar. 54:21, the faithful ones are glorified.

94 Particularly notice that in 4:2, "The Most High has given heed to your prayer that you be delivered from wrongdoing, that you should become a son to him, as a minister and priest in his presence." Also notice the fulfillment of the Abrahamic promise upon Levi in 4:6 "Because those who bless him shall be blessed, and those who curse him shall be destroyed."

95 This is an ascent into heaven at death. Abraham is taken into Paradise where "there are the tends of my righteous ones and where the mansions of my holy ones, Isaac and Jacob, are in his bosom…" The point remains, the reason Abraham ascends into heaven at death is because he is righteous.

96 Isaac approaches the altar in 4:39. In 4:42, after being told the priesthood is not easy, they are exhorted to persevere in piety "in order that each one may petition the Lord successfully." When men are removed from the earth they will be presented before the Lord (4:46), and "For their earthly conduct will be reflected in heaven and the angels will be their friends because of their perfect faith and purity" (4:47).

97 On the righteous being raptured/ascending into heaven see Barnard, *Mysticism*, 63–68; Zwiep, *The Ascension of the Messiah in Lukan Christology* (Brill, 1997), 36–79.

98 Like T. Levi 3–4, there is a connection between ascension and investiture with the priesthood.

99 Jipp ("The Son's Entrance," 572) is correct that this is equivalent to God's perfecting of the Son.

100 One parallel to Christ would be the author's account of Noah's experience where he then becomes an heir: καὶ τῆς κατὰ πίστιν δικαιοσύνης ἐγένετο κληρονόμος.

superior to angels.¹⁰¹ In 2:17, the Son has become a merciful and faithful high priest. In 5:5, we are told Christ οὐχ ἑαυτὸν ἐδόξασεν γενηθῆναι ἀρχιερέα where the Father speaking to the Son in Ps 2:7 is the Father's exalting the Son, and by extension his becoming a high priest. In 5:9, the Son τελειωθεὶς ἐγένετο. In 6:20, the Son has become high priest after the order of Melchizedek κατὰ τὴν τάξιν Μελχισέδεκ ἀρχιερεὺς γενόμενος εἰς τὸν αἰῶνα. In 7:16, Christ has become a priest on the basis of indestructible life.¹⁰² In 7:22, Christ has become the guarantee of a greater covenant.

Hebrews thus describes the Melchizedekian priest not just as an exalted figure but as the exalted figure *par excellence.* He is ὑψηλότερος τῶν οὐρανῶν γενόμενος (Heb 7:26)—where the genitive τῶν οὐρανῶν is partitive. It is similar to τοσούτῳ κρείττων γενόμενος τῶν ἀγγέλων, in that the Son is exalted above all aspects of the created realm. The use of γινόμαι in 7:26 is also reminiscent of 1:4 (and perhaps 2:17; 5:5, 9, 6:20; 7:16). Hebrews does not give us a conception of tiered realms in the heavens themselves,¹⁰³ but simply places the Son as now above the heavens. His exaltation is not only a transition into the eschatological man with indestructible life, but it entails an ascension into heaven. He is sitting at God's right hand next to the throne of divine glory. He occupies this place of honor precisely because he both bears eternally the divine glory (1:3) and because now he has perfected humanity crowned in glory and honor (2:6–10). Thus, there is a linking of the Sonship theme with his joint offices of kingship and priesthood with the ascension as the Son as he has been εἰς τὸν αἰῶνα τετελειωμένον (7:28).

While the reference to "becoming high above the heavens" in 7:26 is a relatively minor clause in the whole argument of chapter seven, it nevertheless shows the concern that Hebrews has between Sonship and ascension. Ascension into heaven is interrelated to the eschatological transition that has been enacted upon Christ as he becomes the glorified high priest (5:5).¹⁰⁴ The tran-

---

101 For the relationship between ascension and cosmic hierarchies, see David Bryan, "A Revised Cosmic Hierarchy Revealed," in *Ascent into Heaven in Luke-Acts: New Explorations of Luke's Narrative Hinge*, ed. David K. Bryan and David W. Pao. (Fortress, 2016), 64–74.

102 In 7:20, it is used to speak of the Levitical priests becoming priest not by an oath, in contrast to Christ being made a priest with an oath.

103 In contrast to some Second Temple speculation and possibly Paul in 2 Cor 12:2 (although the precise meaning of Paul is debated).

104 Kurianal (*Jesus Our High Priest*, 211) argues the pronouncement of priesthood is "proclaimed to the Son *having-been-made-perfect*."; Pss 2:7 and 110:4 are not proclaimed in the same "moment" but that Ps 110:4 follows the proclamation of Ps 2:7. There does seem to be a consistent logical order to the usage of Pss 2 and 110 in Heb 1 and 5:5–6. Kurianal is correct that "the author is aware of the tension between the *pre-existence* of the Son and his *having-been-made-perfect* and *becoming* High Priest." Sonship, both royal and divine, is announced at the ascension (cf. Heb 1), but the Son cannot serve as the eschatological high priest unless he has been

sition from this age to the age to come is enacted in the drama of the exaltation and ascension of the Son. This transition is the moment in God's divine drama that he enacts the pronouncements of Ps 2:7 and Ps 110:1—"You are my Son, today I have begotten you;" and "Sit at my right hand." In this pronouncement, the Son is identified as a new priest forever (5:6; 7:11, 16–17, 21, 24) in a new place—above the heavens themselves.

## Heb 8:1–6

If there is any doubt that Hebrews has been addressing the priesthood and exaltation of Christ into heaven, at this point the author directly tells the audience in vv. 1–2 in summation of his argument thus far. He points out not only that the Christian has a high priest, but he also identifies the kind of high priest (v. 1 τοιοῦτον) in differentiation to the high priest of the Old Covenant. The clause τοιοῦτον ἔχομεν ἀρχιερέα looks forward to the clause: ὃς ἐκάθισεν ἐν δεξιᾷ τοῦ θρόνου τῆς μεγαλωσύνης ἐν τοῖς οὐρανοῖς (Heb 8:1).

This is a slight variation of wording from what he has said in Hebrews 1:3d:

1:3d ἐκάθισεν ἐν δεξιᾷ τῆς μεγαλωσύνης ἐν ὑψηλοῖς,
8:1b ὃς ἐκάθισεν ἐν δεξιᾷ τοῦ θρόνου τῆς μεγαλωσύνης ἐν τοῖς οὐρανοῖς,

Our author is still working with his usage of Ps 110:1. Τῆς μεγαλωσύνης is a circumlocution for God, common among Jewish writers. The key differences between 1:3d and 8:1b are the addition of τοῦ θρόνου and changing ἐν ὑψηλοῖς to ἐν τοῖς οὐρανοῖς. The author is pulling together themes he has been hinting at. As Cockerill puts it, "At this crucial point in his argument (8:1) he expands this description..."[105] The Son takes his seat at the right hand of the throne which places him within the divine glory of YHWH. The act is an exaltation into heaven itself. Just as in the tabernacle the Levitical priest ascends inward into the Holy of Holies, so Christ, as king and priest, ascends upward into the heavenly throne room of God and is seated there.

The author will begin to develop his distinction between the Old Covenant, which is inferior, and the New Covenant. The New Covenant is superior in terms of redemptive history because in the climax of the eschaton, the heavenly is revealed. Every aspect of previous revelation is but a shadow of the true, ultimate, and eschatological. The climax of God's plan is fulfilled in the work of the Son but is also fulfilled in heaven itself. The earthly

---

crowned with the glory and honor that are 'τελειωθείς.'
105  Cockerill, *Hebrews*, 351.

*The Son Ascends into the Heavenly Tabernacle* 163

tabernacle, which was symbolic for approaching God and the throne room of God is now replaced by the ascent of the Son into the true throne of God, heaven itself. This contrast between the Old Covenant and the New is found in 8:1–6 before the author moves into his use of Jeremiah in 8:7–12. The current high priest under the New Covenant is one who is seated in heaven. In 8:2, heaven is the true tent in part because it has been built by the Lord and not man.[106] In the phrase τῶν ἁγίων λειτουργὸς καὶ τῆς σκηνῆς τῆς ἀληθινῆς, the clause καὶ τῆς σκηνῆς τῆς ἀληθινῆς is epexegetical and does not imply two parts of the heavenly tent.[107] If heaven is the true tent, in heaven is the true throne. Because the true tent not built with human hands it is not of this creation (9:11 τοῦτ' ἔστιν οὐ ταύτης τῆς κτίσεως).[108] It is the model on which the Old Covenant tabernacle has been based (8:5). The heavenly tent is original, true, and therefore superior with a superior ministry done in it as Christ ascends into it. The tent of the Old Covenant is inferior, a copy, made by man, and of this creation. The redemption that ushers in the age to come cannot be effected within the Old Covenant tent.

Christ must be a priest who ascends into heaven since there are already priests who offer gifts on earth according to the Law (8:4). First, this puts Law or the Old Covenant on the level of being inferior because it is earthly. It is part of the shadow and the transient. It has been unable to usher in the eschatological perfection and allow all worshippers to enter the presence of God. Second, 8:4 may speak of both the institutions of Tabernacle and Temple as they served as functions of the Law. Indeed notably, neither Tabernacle or Temple is mentioned by name here, although we can presume that is what is of the earth. Even so referring to that which is on earth, Hebrews is most likely referring to the entire sacrificial complex of the Law Covenant. If the Son served on earth (i.e., in that tabernacle), he could not be a priest by the Law because we already have those priests appointed. The Law cannot appoint other priests outside of the Levitical priesthood. It cannot enact a new priesthood of the order of Melchizedek. Third, the present tense in ὄντων τῶν προσφερόντων κατὰ νόμον τὰ δῶρα (8:4) may or may not suggest that the author is writing before the destruction of Jerusalem in AD 70. It is not definitive that this mandates Hebrews be dated pre-70 AD. In fact, the present could be a

---

106 ὁ κύριος is used here to refer to God the Father, not the Son in his ascended role.

107 Ellingworth, "Jesus and the Universe in Hebrews," *EvQ* 58 (1986): 344; *Hebrews*, 404; Koester, *Hebrews*, 376. Cockerill (*Hebrews*, 354) says they "refer to the same reality"; he rightly points out that contemporary examples of a two-part heavenly temple "show little connection with Hebrews"; *contra* Addridge, *Hebrews*, 218; Benjamin Ribbens, *Levitical Sacrifice and Heavenly Cult in Hebrews*, BZNW 222 (de Gruyter, 2016), 105.

108 Being 'not of this world' means that it is part of τὴν οἰκουμένην τὴν μέλλουσαν.

historical present, indicating that we 'have had that,' namely earthly priests in an earthly sanctuary, which has not worked (7:11, 8:7). His point in 8:4 is not that the Son cannot be a priest of Levi because no priest has come from the line of Judah as he says in 7:14. Nor does he specifically mention the failure of the Levitical priesthood to attain perfection as in 7:11. Rather, the argument is that Christ cannot be priest on earth because we already have that.

The Law sets up the Levitical priesthood as priests who serve on earth. The phrase κατὰ νόμον (8:4) speaks of what has been established by the institution of the Law Covenant that Moses inaugurated. Similar language has already been used in 7:5 (κατὰ τὸν νόμον) to speak of the instructions to take tithes and in 7:16, noting that Christ is not a high priest κατὰ νόμον. In 7:12, a change in the priesthood requires a change in the Law. And, in 7:28, ὁ νόμος speaks of the actions of the Law in appointing priests in weakness, almost as if to personify the activity of Law by stating "the Law appoints..." It already appoints priests, specifically weak, inferior, non-eschatological ones. Thus, the institution is settled with its requirements, there is no place for the Son/Messiah to be a priest within this institution. There is no place for the eschatological man, a priest of indestructible life. The main point of the contrast is between heaven and earth. Because a priesthood in the latter realm is/has been, Christ must be a priest who ascends into heaven.

This reassertion of the heavenly priesthood in 8:1–2 allows the author to point to the superiority of the New Covenant over the Old Covenant. He writes, νυν[ὶ] δὲ διαφορωτέρας τέτυχεν λειτουργίας. The νῦν is an eschatological contrast. In Christ's being gloried and appointed Melchizedekian priest (e.g., 5:5) of the New Covenant, his ministry is better. It is of a superior quality with a sacrifice of himself that is both definitive and effective without need of repetition. The location of the priesthood in heaven and Christ's ascension into heaven grounds part of Hebrews' argument for the superiority of the ministry of the Son.

Heb 9:11–14

At this point in the text, our author is intertwining his conception of heaven with the work of Christ ascending into heaven. The Son, having offered himself on the cross as a blood sacrifice on earth and now in a resurrected state, ascends through heaven to the Father's right hand. For Hebrews, this movement parallels the high priest in the Old Covenant offering the sacrifice on the altar and then progressing inward into the Holy of Holies. The earthly high priest went through the earthly tent and stood before the earthly footstool of YHWH's throne. The yearly repetition and the earthly activity signals activity that is of 'this age,' incomplete, and imperfect. However, the nature of the work of the Son as the heavenly high priest who ascends into heaven and before God's true throne marks an ushering in the age to come. This act is, therefore, complete, unrepeatable, and eschatologically perfect or climactic as *the* work of redemption.

At the climax of the ages, Christ ascends into the true tent/tabernacle in heaven. The appearing of Christ (9:11 Χριστὸς δὲ παραγενόμενος ἀρχιερεὺς τῶν γενομένων ἀγαθῶν) may refer to the incarnation, but it most likely refers to the work of Christ being presented as high priest to ascend into heaven. His 'appearing' is not intended to indicate that he had not been seen previously but rather, refers to his being set forth as king-priest in royal exaltation. The author may include in his conception the presentation of the Son as the sacrifice on earth followed up with the exaltation or he may have in mind simply the presentation in exaltation and ascension. We favor the latter interpretation just slightly because the priest is τῶν γενομένων ἀγαθῶν, and it is Christ who has transitioned into the eschatological man in resurrection that then ascends upward into heaven. Just as the high priest would offer a sacrifice on the altar and then present himself after his own sacrifice for his sins as one ready to ascend into the earthly tabernacle, the Son is identified as one, who upon death and resurrection, is presented in heaven to finish the work by ascending into heaven. God the Father presents the Son by calling the Son to ascend through the tent so that he appears by going through the heavenly tabernacle (9:11 παραγενόμενος...διὰ τῆς μείζονος καὶ τελειοτέρας σκηνῆς).

Scholarship has debated what Hebrews means when stating that the Son ascends διὰ τῆς...σκηνῆς (9:11). There are several interpretations of the preposition διά in the phrase διὰ τῆς μείζονος καὶ τελειοτέρας σκηνῆς. A preliminary question is whether the preposition is that of means or locative. Διά may denote 'by means of' or 'through' in an instrumental sense.[109] Lindars offers the interpretive gloss, "by means of a heavenly as opposed to an earthly sanctuary."[110] On the one hand, the other uses of διά denote means (9:12 οὐδὲ δι᾽ αἵματος τράγων καὶ μόσχων διὰ δὲ τοῦ ἰδίου αἵματος); on the other hand, it could be locative in parallel with entering heaven (9:12 εἰσῆλθεν ἐφάπαξ εἰς τὰ ἅγια).[111] Seemingly, τὰ ἅγια and τῆς...σκηνῆς function as parallel descriptors of the same place, namely heaven itself.

---

109 Cody, *Heavenly Sanctuary*, 159; Cortez, "Anchor for the Soul," 351; Koester, *Hebrews*, 408–409; Lindars, *The Theology of the Letter to the Hebrews*, 94; Vanhoye, *A Different Priest: The Epistle to the Hebrews* (Convivium, 2001), 271, 273.

110 Lindars, *Theology*, 94.

111 Taking it to be locative: Attridge, *Hebrews*, 245; Ellingworth, *Hebrews*, 450; Lane, *He-*

However, not all agree that τῆς μείζονος καὶ τελειοτέρας σκηνῆς is, in fact, the heavenly throne room. Two other prominent interpretations of what the 'tent' refers to include: (1) Christ's body;[112] and (2) the outer heavens that exclude the sanctuary throne room of God.[113] Those who see it as referring to the body of Christ find a parallel between the phrase διὰ τῆς μείζονος καὶ τελειοτέρας σκηνῆς and διὰ τοῦ ἰδίου αἵματος.[114] In this interpretation, his body would need to be a resurrected state because of the phrase τοῦτ' ἔστιν οὐ ταύτης τῆς κτίσεως.[115] The strongest parallel commending this interpretation comes in 10:20 where Christ's flesh is called the veil.[116]

With respect to the wider implications for understanding Hebrews' cosmology, William Lane believes that διὰ τῆς...σκηνῆς indicates that there is a heavenly outer tent which Jesus passed through in order to enter the heavenly Holy of Holies. He writes, "The syntax of vv 11–12 demands that a distinction be made between the σκηνή, "front compartment," through which Christ passed and τὰ ἅγια, "the sanctuary," into which he entered."[117] If the earthly counterpart has an outer tent (the Holy Place) that the priest passed through then the heavenly must have two 'tents' that Jesus passes through.[118] This argument is certainly plausible. And it has a compelling logic to it. It coheres to a tight representation between the earthly sanctuary and the heavenly sanctuary. Furthermore, G.K. Beale has shown that the Holy Place in the tabernacle/temple was symbolic of the visible heavens while the Holy of Holies was symbolic of the divine throne room.[119]

As Lane himself notes, passing through the heavens as an outer court could not be a reference to passing through visible heavens. He writes, "the qualifying phrase οὐ χειροποιήτου τοῦτ' ἔστιν οὐ ταύτης τῆς κτίσεως... indicates the reference is not to a passage through visible heavens but to heaven as the dwelling place of God and the angels."[120] However, it would be uncharacteristic

---

brews 9–13, 236; Schreiner, *Hebrews*, 267n.426.
112 Including Chrysostom, John Calvin, Aelred Cody, and Albert Vanhoye.
113 Lane, *Hebrews 9–13*, 238.
114 Cody, *Heavenly Sanctuary*, 163; Vanhoye, *A Different Priest*, 277.
115 Albert Vanhoye, *A Different Priest*, 276–279. He notes that the resurrection of Christ was the "first act of the new creation" (279). Although, Cody (*Heavenly Sanctuary*, 161–165) does not state this specifically, he seems more of the cross in view with respect to Christ's work in his humanity, "The sacrifice of Christ has pride of place" (165).
116 Outside of Hebrews, one could cite John 1:14 Καὶ ὁ λόγος σὰρξ ἐγένετο καὶ ἐσκήνωσεν ἐν ἡμῖν, where his incarnation is him 'tabernacling' among us.
117 Lane, *Hebrews 9–13*, 238.
118 See also Cody, *Heavenly Sanctuary*, 149.
119 G.K. Beale, *The Temple*, 34–35, 54. He also cites early Judaism's view that the Holy Place symbolized the heavens (45–47), especially Philo, *Her.* 227.
120 Lane, *Hebrews 9–13*, 238.

of Hebrews to use the adjective μείζονος καὶ τελειοτέρας to speak of something earthly, of this age, or that is subject to passing away.[121]

We would respond further to Lane by noting that if τῆς μείζονος καὶ τελειοτέρας σκηνῆς refers to outer aspects of the heavenly sanctuary, it becomes irrelevant to the argument of Hebrews, which nowhere focuses on the symbolism of the holy place.[122] Second, as Cockerill notes, Heb 9:12 indicates what the location is with the clause εἰσῆλθεν ἐφάπαξ εἰς τὰ ἅγια.[123] Going through the tent and entering εἰς τὰ ἅγια are synonymous. "Hebrews does not seem to be interested in any distinction between two sections in the heavenly sanctuary."[124] Christ enters into heaven or passes through in his progress to sit at the right hand of the divine throne. Hebrews is not speculating on how the universe is structured like all the aspects of the earthly tabernacle. Rather, the earthly most holy place where God's footstool resided is surpassed by the heavenly throne room itself, and Jesus passed through/into it. For Hebrews, the outer section with the veil is not part of the heavenly but a parable for the earthly Old Covenant.

More recently, Kenneth Schenck has argued that Christ's passing through the heavens is in fact passing from the earth, which entails passing through the created heavens, into the highest heaven. He sees a distinction between the singular οὐρανός in 9:24, and the plural οὐρανοί in 4:14 and 7:26.[125] The plural would be the created heaven while the singular would be the unshakeable heaven above creation where God dwells. Schenck's argument is different from Lane's because he argues that there are not rooms in the heavenly tent in Hebrews (an outer heavens and an inner heaven).[126] He agrees that the outer room represents the imperfection of the Old Covenant which did not allow access to God.[127]

Jody Barnard also argues that the heavenly tent in Hebrews has an outer tent consisting of the heavens and the inner tent being 'heaven,' specifically the throne room of God. Barnard sees τῆς μείζονος καὶ τελειοτέρας σκηνῆς referring to the inner tent, rightly, because it has to be something not of this

---

121 For Hebrews, aspects of the heavens are part of the 'transitory' cf. 1:10–11; 12:26.
122 Cortez, "The Anchor of the Soul," 350.
123 Cockerill, *Hebrews*, 390.
124 Cortez, "The Anchor of the Soul," 350, cf. also 347.
125 Kenneth Schenck, "An Archaeology of Hebrews' Tabernacle Imagery," in *Hebrews in Contexts*, ed. Garbiella Gelardini and Harold W. Attridge (Leiden, 2016), 247. However, we should note that in 9:23 the phrase "τῶν ἐν τοῖς οὐρανοῖς τούτοις" which is referring to the things in heaven not of this creation.
126 Ibid., 249–250.
127 Ibid., 248. He also is clear that "Hebrews knows nothing of an outer chamber to the heavenly tabernacle" (*Cosmology and Eschatology in Hebrews* [Cambridge University Press, 2007], 180).

creation, τοῦτ' ἔστιν οὐ ταύτης τῆς κτίσεως,[128] but then he sees the plurality of heavens (4:14; 7:26; 9:23) speaking of an outer tent. Thus, he tries to distinguish between an outer σκηνή and τὰ ἅγια (the inner sanctuary).[129] Σκηνή is used in Heb 8:2, 5; 9:2, 3, 6, 8, 11, 21; 11:9; 13:10. Heb 11:9 refers to Abraham living in tents. Heb 13:10 probably refers to priests serving in the tabernacle, in contrast to the altar "we [believers] have," likely the altar in heaven. Σκηνή in 8:2 refers to the heavenly tabernacle without reference to the outer tent specifically.[130] In 8:5, σκηνή refers to the Old Testament tabernacle as a whole. In 9:2, it refers to the earthly tabernacle where a first section is distinguished from the second (vv. 2–3). Σκηνή, in 9:3, refers specifically to the second tent, the Holy of Holies. In 9:6, 8 σκηνή refers to the outer tent on the earthly tabernacle. In 9:11, it refers to the heavenly tent 'not of this creation.' In 9:21, σκηνή is the tabernacle (most likely as a whole) which is cleansed by the sprinkling of blood which becomes an analogy for Christ's work in heaven.

Thus, we find that σκηνή is never explicitly linked to an outer heavens (τοί οὐρανοί). Hebrews does not articulate a progression through outer aspects of the tent.[131] For Hebrews, there is not an outer and inner tent in heaven. First, Hebrews never explicitly distinguishes an inner and outer tent in heaven. In fact, Hebrews' use of 'heavens' in 1:10–11 and 12:26 refers to that which is of the creation. It is unlikely that these uses refer to an outer portion of the tent. For Hebrews, here the 'tent' is eschatological and 'new creation.' Likewise, for Hebrews the outer tent in the Old Covenant symbolized the 'present age' that passes away. Accordingly, there is an eschatological logic to Hebrews' not believing that heaven has an inner and outer tent.

Returning to 9:11, the tent refers to heaven itself. It is the same referent as 9:12 εἰσῆλθεν ἐφάπαξ εἰς τὰ ἅγια. The phrase διὰ τῆς μείζονος καὶ τελειοτέρας σκηνῆς is also the same referent as in 8:2 τῶν ἁγίων λειτουργὸς καὶ τῆς σκηνῆς τῆς ἀληθινῆς.[132] The same parallel concepts appear in passages referencing the making of the tent, for example, 8:2 ἣν ἔπηξεν ὁ κύριος, οὐκ ἄνθρωπος and 9:11 οὐ χειροποιήτου.[133] The same tent, and the same activity of God's making it

---

128 *Mysticism*, 113.

129 Cf. ibid., 115–116.

130 First, there is no explicit mention of an outer tent here. Second, our larger argument seeks to demonstrate Hebrews does not believe the heavenly tabernacle has an inner and outer tent.

131 Schenck, *Cosmology and Eschatology*, 180.

132 Koester, *Hebrews*, 409. Recognizing the parallel between 8:2 and 9:11, 12 resolves the objection that 9:11's use of σκηνῆς and 9:12's use of τὰ ἅγια could not refer to the same thing since that would be redundant. In fact, we already have this so-called redundancy in 8:2 where the phrase 'τῆς σκηνῆς τῆς ἀληθινῆς' is epexegetical, defining τῶν ἁγίων.

133 Cf. Acts 7:48–49 and 17:24. The former reference includes a quotation of Isa 66:1.

*The Son Ascends into the Heavenly Tabernacle* 169

is in view in both passages. Koester concludes, "Since perfection cannot be found outside the presence of God, 'the more perfect tent' must be the place where God is present."[134]

These passages continue to evidence that Hebrews does not see Christ the high priest entering through a symbolic Holy Place and then into the Most Holy Place. For our author, the Holy Place is symbolic of what is of 'this age.' The Son ascends one time into the 'age to come' tent which is heaven itself. It is a tent οὐ χειροποιήτου, τοῦτ' ἔστιν οὐ ταύτης τῆς κτίσεως (9:11). Heaven is the tabernacle that is of the age to come. The Son ascending into heaven is the climax of redemption and consummates humanity's access to God while at the same time revealing the Son's glory.

The author of Hebrews uses the contrast between the two tabernacles, the earthly shadow and the heavenly reality, to heighten the contrast between salvation history epochs:[135]

| Old Covenant | New Covenant |
| --- | --- |
| earth | heaven |
| present age | age to come |
| passing away | eternal |
| shadow tent | true tent, εἰκών |
| repetitious sacrifices | once for all sacrifices |
| various priests, Levitical | eternal priest, Melchizedekian |

The heavenly tabernacle does not need an inner and outer sanctuary, or inner and outer tents, precisely because built into the very structure of the Old Covenant tabernacle is the representation of the epochal ages and the distinction between the Old Covenant and the New Covenant. In the Old Covenant, according to Hebrews, the outer and inner tents were actually symbolic. There is in the Old Covenant age of the shadow (the outer), which is the earthly, and the true reality (the inner), which is heaven itself. The Old Covenant pattern set up with the two tents of daily (outer) and yearly (inner) is replaced and superseded by the New Covenant. Under the New Covenant, the shadow of the Old Covenant is the "outer" tent of the earthly tabernacle, whereas what was the inner tent is superseded by heaven and the Son/High Priest's ascent into heaven. In other words, the New Covenant shapes how one views the original two tents of the Old Covenant. The New Covenant revealed shows

---

134 Koester, *Hebrews*, 409.
135 Cf. Koester, *Hebrews*, 404–405, for two similar charts.

that the two tents in the Old Covenant were symbolic of the two ages as a whole. There is no outer tent to heaven because the outer tent of the earthly tabernacle was itself symbolic of the whole 'this age' to be surpassed by the 'age to come.' Consider the structure of the tabernacle which Hebrews itself sees as a parable for the two-age structure:[136]

| Old Covenant Tent: | |
|---|---|
| Outer tent<br>First<br>Daily sacrifices | Inner tent<br>Second<br>Once a year |
| This age | Age to come |
| Earth/Old (First) Covenant | Heaven/New (Second) Covenant |

Figure 5.2 The Tent as Two Ages

Therefore, for Hebrews, when under the Old Covenant, there exists a standing outer tent, and the worshipper is supposed to understand that the true way to God is not yet opened (9:8 τοῦτο δηλοῦντος τοῦ πνεύματος τοῦ ἁγίου, μήπω πεφανερῶσθαι τὴν τῶν ἁγίων ὁδὸν ἔτι τῆς πρώτης σκηνῆς ἐχούσης στάσιν). Now, with the revelation of the eschatological, there is no first tent anymore because it has been surpassed once the true way into the holy has been revealed. The first tent is a parable or symbolic of the 'present age,' but once the age to come has been revealed and inaugurated, the Old Age with its Old Covenant passes away. Therefore, 9:9 ἥτις παραβολὴ εἰς τὸν καιρόν where the ἥτις refers back to τῆς πρώτης σκηνῆς in 9:8. The first section of the tent under the Old Covenant was for regular ongoing services (9:6 τὰς λατρείας ἐπιτελοῦντες), just as the Old Covenant worship could not perfect the conscious (9:9 καθ' ἣν δῶρά τε καὶ θυσίαι προσφέρονται μὴ δυνάμεναι κατὰ συνείδησιν τελειῶσαι τὸν λατρεύοντα) but now in the New Covenant the true sacrifice does (9:14). Schenck sees the outer room of 9:8

---

136 Steve Stanley ("Hebrews 9:6–10: The 'Parable' of the Tabernacle," *NovT* 38.4 [1995]: 398) reaches a similar conclusion drawing a somewhat similar chart for the representations in 9:8 and 9:9, 10 respectively. We have emphasized in our diagram the two-age construct. We also set out the relationship between daily sacrifice and the Day of Atonement followed by the Levitical Day of Atonement in contrast to Christ's sacrifice in a second diagram below. Lane (*Hebrews 9–13*, 224) also regards the front compartment of the tabernacle as a spatial metaphor for the first covenant and the second compartment (the Holy of Holies) as a part of the spatial metaphor for the second covenant. Norman Young ("The Gospel According to Hebrews 9," *NTS* 27 [1981]: 202) writes that the "language of 'first tent' has a clear eschatological purpose: it means the old covenant order now in the process of dissolution." Schenck (*Cosmology and Eschatology*, 98) writes, "the first and second tent of the tabernacle is in fact an eschatological parable of the two epochs of salvation history."

as allegorized "in terms of imperfection and hindrance to God's presence." Calaway picks up on the symbolism that Hebrews finds in the Old Covenant with its two tents. He writes, "the two tents, therefore are at the literal level, the holy place and the most holy place, but, figuratively speaking, they signify the current and future ages."[137]

Thus, for Hebrews, a change to the eschaton entails a shifting of the sacrificial patterns. The daily repeated sacrifices become paradigmatic of the yearly repeated Day of Atonement. Where the once yearly Day of Atonement becomes paradigmatic of the eschatological atonement that was 'once for all time.'[138] It is the eschatological shift so that yearly and repetitious falls away, just as the old age and the Old Covenant are falling away (8:13).

| Tabernacle: | Daily Repeated (Symbol of this age) | Yearly Day of Atonement (Symbol of age to come) |
|---|---|---|
| Two Ages: | Yearly Day of Atonement (Reality of the Old Age) Earthly Tabernacle Old (First) Covenant | Once for all Atonement (Age to Come Realized) Heavenly Tabernacle New (Second) Covenant |

Figure 5.3 Atonement and the Two Ages

All this is accomplished by the true high priest, the Second Adam in glory and honor, ascending into heaven itself. Keeping in mind our discussion of Heb 2, the vestments the high priest wore were seen as symbolic of Adamic glory restored. The high priest going into the Holy of Holies was likened to Adam going into Eden, Paradise, and/or heaven itself. Hebrews sees all this fully realized in the ascension of the Son.

For Hebrews, when there is one earthly tabernacle under the Old Covenant, the two tents are needed in order to point towards and teach the future coming of the New Covenant with its 'once for all sacrifice.' The entering of the Adam-priest to the inner sanctuary with the blood of propitiation to cleanse the ark is symbolic of the true presentation of propitiation before God's throne in heaven. The outer daily ceremonies become symbolic of regular yearly atonement ritual of the Old Covenant. While the inner yearly becomes symbolic of the 'once for all.' But when the age to come arrives, all that is needed in the true tent/sanctuary is the final room, God's throne. Only the

---

137 Jared Calaway, *The Sabbath and the Sanctuary* (Mohr Siebeck, 2013), 112.
138 Schenck (*Cosmology and Eshatology*, 149–150) writes similarly, "The first tent becomes a parable of this present age, which involves multiplicity and imperfection (and, in fact, the whole earthly tent), while the 'one-time' nature of the new age is also implied by the second, inner sanctuary."

final room is needed because the Old Covenant is passing away and is paradigmatic of the present age.

The outer tent does not belong to the 'age to come' and is not needed in the greater, more perfect tent. An ongoing ministry of continually standing to present sacrifices is not needed because the Son has entered heaven and sits, so an outer tent in heaven is not only unnecessary but would detract from the full realization of the Son's heavenly ministry. Just as the Old Covenant has fallen away, giving way to the perfect, so also the true and perfect tent has no distinctive inner and outer tents. Calaway writes, "The buffer of the first tent between the worships and the second tent represents the present age, literally a 'parable' for the current season. This current season contrasts with the age to come (6:5; cf. 2:5)."[139] The climax of the Old Covenant system was the high priests once a year entry into the Holy of Holies, but this ritual has now been superseded by the reality to which it pointed as the 'shadow.' "The age to come, moreover, is characterized by access to the second tent, the final set of correspondences being between the first earthly tent [the whole Old Covenant tabernacle] and the second more perfect tent that is heaven itself."[140] For Hebrews, the true throne room entered had no outer tent to it. Again, the outer tent was symbolic of the present age that passed away. The Son's ascension is an entering into the true and ultimate tent thereby effecting the eschatological climax by which a true and final redemption is accomplished.

Not everyone agrees that εἰς τὸν καιρὸν τὸν ἐνεστηκότα (9:9) is referencing eschatological ages. Thomas Schreiner thinks that this clause should be translated as "for the present time" and "designates the era of the new covenant."[141] More likely, however, τὸν ἐνεστηκότα refers not to current time (Rom. 8:38; 1 Cor. 3:22, 7:26) but "the present age" in a similar way as Gal. 1:4 (ἐκ τοῦ αἰῶνος τοῦ ἐνεστῶτος πονηροῦ).[142] Another reason that we recognize that εἰς τὸν καιρὸν τὸν ἐνεστηκότα refers to Old Covenant non-eschatological age is because of the sacrifices described. As we noted above, the ongoing rituals of the outer tent in 9:6 become symbolic of the entire Old Covenant sacrificial system. In 9:9, the Old Covenant gifts and sacrifices cannot perfect the conscience and in 9:10 are only bodily and ritual. The language καθ' ἥν refers to that which is of the present age, the sacrificial system of the present age (the Old Covenant). We have, then, in parallel:

---

139 Calaway, *Sabbath and Sanctuary*, 112.
140 Ibid., 113.
141 *Hebrews*, 263.
142 Admittedly Galatians has the clear descriptor "evil."

9:9 δῶρά τε καὶ θυσίαι προσφέρονται μὴ δυνάμεναι κατὰ συνείδησιν τελειῶσαι τὸν λατρεύοντα

9:10 μόνον ἐπὶ βρώμασιν καὶ πόμασιν καὶ διαφόροις βαπτισμοῖς, δικαιώματα σαρκός

This parallels the presentation of the Old and New Covenants in 9:13–14, where Old Covenant sacrifices are ἁγιάζει πρὸς τὴν τῆς σαρκὸς καθαρότητα (9:13), but the New Covenant sacrifice purifies the conscience, καθαριεῖ τὴν συνείδησιν ἡμῶν ἀπὸ νεκρῶν ἔργων (9:14). Lastly, notice that 9:9 begins with the temporal reference of the present age and 9:10 ends with the reference to the age to come with μέχρι καιροῦ διορθώσεως ἐπικείμενα. The first section of the tabernacle is symbolic or a parable for the present age. The whole Old Covenant had repeated sacrifices (9:9–10, 13) just as the outer tent did (9:6). However, this covenant is in place *until* (μέχρι) the time of the new order is effected. Christ's sacrifice and his ascension into the true and greater tabernacle effects the eschatological age to come. He is the ἀρχιερεὺς τῶν γενομένων ἀγαθῶν (9:11), not the non-eschatological priests of the present age. Thus, as C.K. Barrett notes, "The heavenly tabernacle and its ministrations are from one point of view eternal archetypes, from another, they are eschatological events."[143]

Keeping in mind the eschatological structure of the Old Covenant tabernacle, its symbolism of the two ages, and the distinctions between the Old Covenant and New Covenant will help the modern-day interpreter navigate the complex and often confusing use of "first" and "second" with reference to the 'tents.' On the one hand, "first" and "second" tent refers to the divisions with the original tent of the Old Covenant.[144] The entrance of the Old Covenant priests entails a movement through the first into the second. On the other hand, the "first tent" becomes an indicator of the whole Old Covenant Tabernacle (regardless of its own subdivision into two distinct tents), while the "second" tent becomes a referent to the true eschatological final tent. The author of Hebrews uses 'first' and 'second' referents with multiple referents:

> In Hebrews 9:2–3 the numbers 'first' and 'second' refer to the outer and inner tents respectively, and a reader encountering verse 8 for the first time would infer that the existence of the first (outer) tent was a figurative

---

[143] C.K. Barrett, "The Eschatology of the Epistle to the Hebrews," in *The Background of the New Testament*, ed. W.D. Davies (Cambridge University Press, 1964), 385.

[144] Norman Young ("The Gospel According to Hebrews 9," 199): "The first and second tent are respectively the Holy Place and the Holy of Holies, as Hebrews itself asserts in verses 2 and 3."

explanation that the way 'into the holy of holies' (in the tabernacle, τὰ ἅγια) had not yet been disclosed. But the alert reader would notice that the only previous occurrence of τὰ ἅγια (definite, neuter plural) was in 8:2 where it referred to the heavenly temple. This reader would then infer that 'the first tent' (ἡ πρώτη σκηνή) might also refer to the entire wilderness tabernacle, or perhaps the temple as in 8:5. Hebrews 9 uses πρoτῶς and δεύτερος both temporally and spatially, and ἅγιας and σκηνή for the earthly and heavenly sanctuaries, both as a whole and also as various parts. Thus, there is a *double entendre* with reference to both outer tent and entire sanctuary, and the earthly and heavenly temples."[145]

Under the Old Covenant the first tent of the tabernacle structure never passes away. However, in light of the New Covenant, the Old Covenant is passing away so Hebrews can speak temporarily of the 'first tent still standing' (9:8 ἔτι τῆς πρώτης σκηνῆς ἐχούσης στάσιν). The content of "first tent" and "second tent" has a dual referent. Just as the first covenant passes away so the first, i.e., earthly, tent/sanctuary passes away since the new/second covenant is superior (8:7-8, 13) in the same way heaven's tabernacle is superior. The rhetorical shift does not necessitate that the author see "heaven" and "heavenlies" as two tents. "'The greater more perfect tent' contrasts with the total structure mentioned in 9.1; there is no distinction of parts implied. We are not, therefore, to understand Christ making any passage through some preliminary physical (or other) means of access."[146] For the author, heaven itself is the true ultimate second tent. The first tent is passing away as part of the Old Covenant. The spatial referents serve the eschatological.[147]

---

[145] Philip Church, "The Temple in the Apocalypse of Weeks and in Hebrews," *TynBul* 64.1 (2013): 121–122. Paul Ellingworth ("Jesus and the Universe in Hebrews," 344) also notes this use of 'first' and 'second' as both temporal and spatial; these "assymmetrical features are all the more remarkable in a passage in which formal features are closely parallel" (345). We maintain that "remarkable" is a matter of perspective. When one weighs in the driving temporal contrast of old (first) vs. new (second) covenant and the major emphasis on eschatology, not just vertical cosmology, it is, though brilliant in its usage of the OT and cosmology, a complete and tightly argued construction—one might almost say a foregone conclusion to the OT imagery the author has been weaving together.

[146] "The Gospel According to Hebrews 9," 203–204.

[147] George MacRae ("Heavenly Temple and Eschatology," 188) has highlighted this eschatological feature in Hebrews: "There is for Hebrews an additional dimension of the temple imagery which is not commonly found in the Jewish types of imagery, though it is not excluded from them. That is the eschatological dimension, which mingles a time framework with the spatial images." However, more recently, Phillip Church ("Temple in the Apocalypse of Weeks," 109–128) has highlighted how Solomon's temple in the Apocalypse of Weeks anticipates the eschatological temple.

The earthly tabernacle was built based upon the pattern of the heavenly tabernacle. God's true dwelling place, his true temple/throne/tabernacle, is heaven itself. MacLeod disagrees that the true tabernacle in heaven existed in Moses' day because it belongs to the New Covenant and because "Exodus 25 does not say that Moses saw a heavenly sanctuary."[148] However, Hebrews does see the pattern (8:6 τύπος) as something real and true so that the earthly is a copy (ὑπόδειγμα) of the heavenly. The difference is not only eschatological (old vs. new) but also apocalyptic (earthly vs. heavenly). It is based on the OT concept, also prominent in Second Temple texts, that heaven is the throne room of God.[149] In the Exodus narrative, God has the tabernacle built so he can descend from his house-throne in heaven and have a portable sanctuary to dwell in the midst of God's people. But with the climax of eschatology the drama of redemption takes place not in the copies, but in the real and true to which they pointed.[150]

Thus, for Hebrews, the structure of the earthly teaches one about the structure of the ages. Christ's ascension into heaven is not a movement through two tents but a movement from earth to heaven. He fulfills the eschatological Day of Atonement by a movement into heaven itself. This movement effects the transition from the Old Covenant age into the New Covenant which is of the age to come. Going from 'weakness' into a glorified body having been 'perfected,' he brings human resurrected flesh into the 'age to come.' The "first/outer tent" is nothing now the eschatological perfected man has ascended into the presence of the divine throne.

---

148 David J. MacLeod, "The Cleansing of the True Tabernacle," *BibSac* 152 (1995): 63n.9. He goes on to argue what was seen was not an "original" or "archetypal" currently existing but prophetic to what was to come, paralleling it to Ezekiel's vision of the temple. This point fails in two ways: (1) it is not consistent with what Hebrews actually argues: indeed, the earthly is based on a heavenly archetype; and (2) there is no hint in Hebrews that a new tabernacle is built in heaven for Jesus' ministry. Rather the conception is that Jesus' work is superior because it is completed in the true dwelling place of God. Additionally, for MacLeod to be right one has to ignore OT and Second Temple connotations that God's true dwelling was always in heaven so that what was on earth pointed to what was greater. God is a king who has sat down in heaven having established his dominion over all the created realm. The tabernacle/temple theology of the OT was that it was the connection point to YHWH himself, a gateway from earth to heaven itself. From heaven, where God sat, his royal robes and glory trailed into the holy of holies where the ark of the covenant was like his footstool.

149 However, as we have noted, Second Temple texts often saw various levels of heaven, with outer heavens and an inner throne room of God. Or they saw the outer tent as symbolic of the sky-stars 'heavens. There was a tiered structure to the universe. In some case the whole temple/tabernacle complex was symbolic of all creation. See sources we have previously documented.

150 MacLeod, "The Cleansing of the True Tabernacle," 63n.9, following T.F. Torrence, sees the tabernacle as only pointing ahead. This perspective misses the interplay between eschatology and the heaven/earthly distinction.

If we are correct then, the ascension in 9:11 and 12 are syntactically parallel, not a progression through outer heavenly tents into inner ones. As Norman Young writes, it is "beyond question that the parallel to εἰς δὲ τὴν δευτέραν (Heb 9:7) is in Heb 9. 12, 25 εἰς τὰ ἅγια. There is no question that ἡ δεθτέρα in Heb 9. 7 means the Holy of Holies, and thus we must give the same meaning to τὰ ἅγια in Heb 9. 12, 25 and no less certainly also in Heb 9. 8 and 24."[151] Syntactically, Christ's going διὰ τῆς μείζονος καὶ τελειοτέρας σκηνῆς (9:11) is the same as εἰσῆλθεν ἐφάπαξ εἰς τὰ ἅγια (9:12). This parallel means that διὰ τῆς μείζονος καὶ τελειοτέρας σκηνῆς is most likely locative[152] whereas the following διά clauses, δι' αἵματος τράγων καὶ μόσχων (9:12) and διὰ δὲ τοῦ ἰδίου αἵματος (9:12), indicate the means.[153] Switching the use of διά to means is easily identifiable when we recognize that Hebrews is contrasting the effectiveness of sacrifices especially in 9:13–14.[154] What is repetitious takes place in the outer tent, hence there is no outer tent 'in heaven' passed through. "The fact that Heb 7.27 can speak of this [entire earthly] high-priestly activity as a daily event should warn us against dismissing too readily the idea of the fore-tent being a symbol of the whole older order."[155] When it comes to the heavenly tabernacle in Hebrews, "We are not, therefore, to understand Christ making any passage through some preliminary physical (or other) means of access."[156]

Before moving on, an observation must be made concerning the variations between singular 'holy' and plural 'holies' when referring to the tabernacle. In 9:1, the author of Hebrews can speak of the entire earthly tent in the singular τὸ ἅγιον κοσμικόν. This earthly singular 'tent' contrasts to the heavenly tent, τῆς μείζονος καὶ τελειοτέρας σκηνῆς (9:11). Just as there is a first covenant (the Old, 8:7, 13; 9:15, 18; 10:9) and a second covenant (the New, 8:7; 10:9) so there is the old/original/earthly tent which was temporarily 'first' and the true 'second' tent. The true heavenly tent is second in terms of the climax of revelation, temporally it is revealed after the first. But it is original in an eternal sense because Moses was instructed to build the 'first/earthly' Tabernacle after the pattern he was shown in heaven. Hebrews does not give any

---

151 "The Gospel According to Hebrews 9," 199.

152 Attridge, *Hebrews*, 245–246; Lane, *Hebrews 9–13*, 236–238; Ellingworth, *Hebrews*, 450–451; Mackie, *Eschatology and Exhortation*, 178–179.

153 *Contra* Cortez ("Anchor of the Soul," 351), who argues that all three uses of διά are instrumental, although we agree that the "greater and more perfect tabernacle" "denotes the heavenly sanctuary as a whole" (354). Young ("The Gospel According to Hebrews 9," 203–204) also takes all three as instrumental, arguing that the local interpretation of διὰ τῆς μείζονος καὶ τελειοτέρας σκηνῆς takes the clauses as referring to some kind of fore-tent in heaven.

154 Young (ibid., 204) sees the uses of διά as expressions of the superiority of the new order of the age to come. Also Schenck, *Cosmology and Eschatology*, 164.

155 Young, "The Gospel According to Hebrews 9," 201.

156 Ibid., 204.

indication that the pattern in heaven was a two-stage tent[157] but the pattern in heaven was the throne room. The two stages built in the earthly as a parable to display what was truly necessary to enter God's presence.

We find, in 9:8, the use of the plural τὴν τῶν ἁγίων ὁδόν. The use of the plural genitive here though could perhaps refer in correspondence to the Holy *of Holies* in 9:4 (Ἅγια Ἁγίων). In 9:25, the plural refers to the Holy of Holies entered only once a year (εἰσέρχεται εἰς τὰ ἅγια κατ' ἐνιαυτόν). So that the contrast in 9:24 is between Christ not entering holy places, i.e., the earthly holy of holies, made by hands (οὐ γὰρ εἰς χειροποίητα εἰσῆλθεν ἅγια) but heaven (εἰς αὐτὸν τὸν οὐρανόν). The plural 'holies' here in 9:24 and 25 does not describe two tents but the inner tent of the earthly and that to which it corresponds, namely heaven.

Hebrews can also alternate between the singular and the plural as it does in 8:2 where the author speaks of the plural τῶν ἁγίων and the singular τῆς σκηνῆς τῆς ἀληθινῆς. Nothing in the author's use of "the holy places" to refer to heavenly necessarily entails that the heavenly tabernacle is divided into two tents. The argument for two tents in heaven pushes Hebrews' analogy too far, by reading other Second Temple Jewish texts' cosmology[158] into the text rather than Hebrews more apparently eschatological contrast.[159] Furthermore, for Hebrews to take up this concept would undermine the eschatological contrast the author constructs where the "true tent" of heaven is preceded by the temporal "first tent" not a spatial outer tent in the heavens.

---

157 Contra Barnard, *Mysticism*, 115–116; Ribbens, *Levitical Sacrifice*, 105–106.

158 For example, 1 En. 14:1–20; T. Levi 3. For a discussion of these texts see L.D. Hurst, *The Epistle to Hebrews: Its Background and Thought* (Cambridge, 1990), 24–33; cf. C.K. Barrett, "The Eschatology of the Epistle to the Hebrews," 386–389; April D. De Conick, "Heavenly Temple Traditions and Valentinian Worship: A Case for First-Century Christology in the Second Century," in *The Jewish Roots of Christological Monotheism: Papers from the St. Andrews Conference on the Historical Origins of the Worship of Jesus*, ed. Carey Newman, James Davila, and Gladys Lewis (Brill: 1999), esp. 310–317.

159 We are not saying that Hebrews is unconcerned with cosmology nor arguing Hebrews has nothing to say about it. Ascension is at the same time both a cosmological event ('going up' from earth to heaven) and an eschatological event—the climax of the OT Day of Atonement. Now the true high priest enters *once for all time* (eschatological) in the true tabernacle of the throne room of God (cosmological). Here it is worth referencing Geerhardus Vos, *The Teaching of the Epistle to the Hebrews* (Eerdmans, 1956), especially chapter three "The Epistle's Philosophy of Revelation and Redemption" (49–87). His diagrams on pages 56 and 57 are correct so far as they represent the eschatological and the true *eikōn* being revealed in contrast to the OT. However, one might wish that the diagram could also accurately represent the role of Christ's ascension ('going up') and in bringing ('down'[metaphorically]) this genuine revelation (the heavenly reality being manifest in the 'age to come'). Vos remains correct that the New Testament/Covenant revelation "is the substance of the Heavenly Reality" (57, etc.). Cf. C.K. Barrett, "The Eschatology of the Epistle to the Hebrews," 385, who compares the relationship between "eternal archtypes and eschatological events."

One reason why the author of Hebrews, unlike some Jewish apocalyptic writers in his time, is largely unconcerned with a detailed, tiered structure of ascent is because Hebrews' largest concern is the eschatological shift from this age to the age to come, which entails the shift from earthly to the heavenly. As Jody Barnard writes, "although Hebrews does not express Christ's otherworldly journey in narrative form, a narrative of ascent is clearly presupposed, a narrative which aligns closely to the movement envisaged in certain ascent texts (e.g., *1 En.* 14:8–23; *2 En.* 3–22; *Apoc. Ab.* 15–20; *ALD* 4:4–6; *T. Levi* 2–5)."[160] Certainly, Hebrews shares in the apocalyptic structure of the universe and echoes the ascent structure we see in the literature. Yet the lack of a more explicit articulation of a journey or process of ascent is striking.

The lack of detailed ascent structure leaves Hebrews to describe the ascension of the Son as simply διὰ τῆς μείζονος καὶ τελειοτέρας σκηνῆς (9:11). The path of the Son to the throne of God is through the heavenly tent. It is not the tent that is κοσμικόν "worldly" (9:1), which is pejorative.[161] The worldly would have been built by human hands (8:5b; 9:2 κατεσκευάσθη[162]). Instead, this tent is built by God himself and is not of this creation (τοῦτ' ἔστιν οὐ ταύτης τῆς κτίσεως), i.e., not the worldly of 'this age.' Thus, the Son has offered a greater sacrifice, inaugurated a greater covenant, become the greater eschatological priest, and ascended into the greater tent. The capstone of this movement is the Son's ascension, which secures redemption and makes it possible for the sons of God to draw near to God, joining the heavenly assembly. The lack of speculation of levels in heaven spatial hierarchy and angelic hierarchies in each level serves to further highlight the superiority of the Son in his ascension. His superiority is one of redemptive history: he is the new priest of the greater order going to the greater tabernacle. His superiority is one of vocation: he is the true human crowned with glory and honor. His superiority is one of identity: he is God's eternal Son sitting down on God's eternal throne. All this is revealed in his ascent to the Father's right hand.

Because Christ has sat down at the right hand of God in heaven, the Old Covenant sacrifices are no longer necessary. In fact, Christ did not enter heaven by means of the blood of goats and calves (9:12 οὐδὲ δι' αἵματος τράγων

---

160 Barnard, *The Mysticism of Hebrews*, 116–117.
161 Attridge, *Hebrews*, 232.
162 Κατεσκευάσθη is not a divine passive here. Just like in LXX Exod 40:17, we have the passive to describe Moses' work: "ἐστάθη ἡ σκηνή" (40:18 καὶ ἔστησεν Μωυσῆς τὴν σκηνήν). Κατασκευάζω is not used anywhere in LXX to describe the construction of the tabernacle, however that is certainly what Hebrews 9:2 has in view. In Exod 25:1–31:11 we have YHWH giving instructions on how to prepare the tabernacle and in 35:30–39:43 Bezalel is identified as skilled and then goes on to construct it. However, Moses, following YHWH's command, is the one who erects it and consecrates it (Exod 40:1–33). Cf. Attridge, *Hebrews*, 232.

καὶ μόσχων) but through his own blood (9:12 διὰ δὲ τοῦ ἰδίου αἵματος). A blood sacrifice is the instrumentality or the means[163] by which priests were granted access to God. For all the contrasts that Hebrews draws between Old Covenant and New Covenant, and between earth and heaven, there is at this point a commonality. There is a connection between the need for blood sacrifices. While the repeated sacrifices in the Old Covenant are ineffective and imperfect and in the New Covenant the sacrifice is effective and perfect (9:12b αἰωνίαν λύτρωσιν εὑράμενος). The sacrifice is perfect in both the sense of its ability to accomplish what was intended and in the sense of being the climactic eschatological sacrifice. "Jesus' entrance into the 'greater and more perfect tabernacle' inaugurates the greater realities of the new covenant that make possible what the first covenant cult was not able to accomplish: provide forgiveness and access to God."[164] Likewise, as the high priest went into the tabernacle as an Adamic figure covered in a vest of glory symbolizing Israel, so the true high priest enters crowned in greater honor and glory, a Second Adam to bring many sons to glory. Ascension connects to sonship.

Importantly, with respect to the Day of Atonement, Hebrews does not stretch the parallels into a full-blown allegory. In other words, the author focuses on the sacrifice, contrasting the blood of goats and bulls with the blood of Christ, and he also focuses on the ascension of Christ into the heavenly temple. These points allow him to contrast the effectiveness and the accomplishment of the New Covenant work with the incomplete and ongoing works under the Old Covenant. Priests in the Old Covenant had to stand and continue to minster in the earthly sanctuary, but Christ sat down in the heavenly sanctuary indicating his work is finished. Thus, as Schenck writes, "Christ's heavenly priesthood is at root a metaphor built on the efficacy of his atoning death coupled with his ascension to the highest heaven—the heaven's Holy of Holies."[165]

For Hebrews, Christ's sacrifice inaugurates the New Covenant just as there was a necessary sacrifice to inaugurate the Old Covenant (9:18–21). Here again, Hebrews is able to switch the metaphor of sacrifice quickly from the Day of Atonement motif (9:12–14) to the sacrifice Moses makes in Exod 24. Hebrews' focus on Christ's sacrifice remains but the author moves on to compare Christ's sacrifice to a different OT motif, covenant inauguration. The logic is that the Old Covenant failed to take away sins with finality. Furthermore, God's people were transgressors of this covenant (9:15; cf. esp. Jer 31:32). The

---

163 Note the use of διά plus genitives.
164 Cortez, "Anchor of the Soul," 354.
165 Kenneth Schenck, "A Celebration of the Enthroned Son," 479.

death of Christ redeemed God's people from their transgressions of the Law.¹⁶⁶ Moses inaugurated the first covenant by sprinkling the people and the articles of the tabernacle with blood. In the same way, for the New Covenant, there must be a death to inaugurate the covenant and purify the true tabernacle in heaven.

Heb 9:23–26

Verses 23–26 return to the theme of ascension and its relationship to the covenant sacrifice of Christ for the establishment of the New Covenant. The author draws parallels again between the Old and New Covenant showing that it was necessary (9:23 ἀνάγκη) also for the true heavenly tabernacle to be cleansed. This cleansing is required because the Old Covenant tent is the "shadow" while the New Covenant tent is the real, the image, the true and greater tent. If the shadow, earthly, had to be cleansed to inaugurate the first covenant, the argument is essentially how much more must the final, eschatological one also be cleansed. The cleansing is absolutely necessary. The earthly implements were copies (9:23 τὰ μὲν ὑποδείγματα) of the heavenly things (9:23 τῶν ἐν τοῖς οὐρανοῖς τούτοις). Hebrews is not distinguishing between heavenlies and heaven in any form of precise technical nomenclature. He simply has in view the heaven/earth dualism that is divided both spatially and eschatologically. This eschatology is at work with the notion of a greater (κρείττοσιν; cf. 1:4; 6:9; 7:7, 22; 8:6; 10:34; 11:16, 35, 40; 12:24) sacrifice being needed for the true heavenly tent to be cleansed.

Christ has entered heaven itself (9:24 ἀλλ᾽ εἰς αὐτὸν τὸν οὐρανόν). Thus, not only is Christ the better sacrifice but he provides the better ministry in the true tent which is heaven itself. Hebrews does not think here of a true and greater tent being in heaven but rather of the tent/tabernacle that is the true throne room of God in heaven itself. Thus, Christ cannot minister in the earthly tabernacle. He is a different kind of priest. He has been granted the eschatological perfection of glory, and therefore, he must ascend into the true place where the true and final atonement sacrifice is presented before God's very presence (9:24 νῦν ἐμφανισθῆναι τῷ προσώπῳ τοῦ θεοῦ ὑπὲρ ἡμῶν). Once again, appearing in heaven is contrasted with the Old Covenant priest appearing in a sanctuary made by human hands (cf. 9:11). In 9:11, the point is stated in the positive: he enters into the greater more perfect tent *not* made with human hands (9:11 διὰ τῆς μείζονος καὶ τελειοτέρας σκηνῆς οὐ χειροποιήτου) whereas in

---

166 For a discussion of death, sacrifice, and substitution see Barry Joslin, "Christ Bore the Sins of Many," 81–91.

9:24 the wording is slightly different that he does not enter into the holy place made with human hands (οὐ γὰρ εἰς χειροποίητα εἰσῆλθεν ἅγια Χριστός). The contrasts being drawn, however, convey the same lines of thought regarding the superiority of the heavenly tent and the entrance of Christ into it for his priestly ministry.

That which is made by human hands and served its function on earth is the ἀντίτυπα τῶν ἀληθινῶν (9:24). It is the copy, the symbol. This concept is clearly connected to the thought the author introduced as early as 8:5 οἵτινες ὑποδείγματι καὶ σκιᾷ λατρεύουσιν τῶν ἐπουρανίων. As the author will later put it, these things are a shadow of the good things that are to come (10:1 Σκιὰν γὰρ ἔχων ὁ νόμος τῶν μελλόντων ἀγαθῶν). The pattern is in heaven, that made by human hands is merely a copy of the pattern (8:5b citing Exod 25:40). Thus, the true and greater is revealed at the eschatological climax with Christ's ascent into heaven itself. The work of Christ is greater in two ways: there is a "vertical" contrast from what is done on earth to what is done in heaven and there is the eschatological contrast, a "horizontal" contrast, between what was done in the past in a repeated fashion versus what the Son has done once for all time.[167] In a manner reminiscent of apocalyptic literature, we have the climax in heaven of the great eschatological activity of one ascending into the throne room of God's presence.

Christ has entered into heaven (9:24 ἀλλ' εἰς αὐτὸν τὸν οὐρανόν), and heaven is the parallel to ἅγια in 24a. Thus, these verses should put to rest the debate over whether heaven is a realm of an outer tent passed through or whether heaven is the sanctuary itself. Hebrews is clear that the sanctuary is heaven itself. The varying, well-meaning interpretations, discussed above, have at their core an overzealous pressing of the language of Hebrews into a literalism beyond the author's intent. His goal is not to recount speculation in heavenly journeys or to pass through various stages of a complex heaven. His goal is the typology: Christ's ascent into heaven itself is the climax of the OT repetitious actions displayed on earth.

Along these lines, typology is probably at work when Hebrews speaks of the heavenly tabernacle needing to be cleansed to inaugurate the New Covenant (9:23 Ἀνάγκη οὖν τὰ μὲν ὑποδείγματα τῶν ἐν τοῖς οὐρανοῖς τούτοις καθαρίζεσθαι).[168] David MacLeod has outlined at least nine interpretations of

---

[167] See Vos, *Teaching of the Epistle to the Hebrews*, esp. 55–68; Scott Mackie, *Eschatology and Exhortation*, esp. ch. 5.

[168] David J. MacLeod, "The Cleansing of the True Tabernacle," *BibSac 152* (1995): 63. R.B. Jamieson ("Hebrews 9.23: Cult Inauguration, Yom Kippur and the Cleansing of the Heavenly Tabernacle," *NTS* [2016]: 582) notes, "the logic undergirding his inference seems to be that the earthly tabernacle needs to be cleansed precisely because the heavenly one would one day be

the cleansing of heaven's tabernacle.[169] There is a connection of the sacrifice, both to the high priest taking the sacrifice of atonement into the tabernacle (Lev 16) as a propitiation and also to Moses' sacrifice to cleanse and prepare the worship in the tabernacle. In a concept similar to inauguration, Ellingworth sees it as dedication.[170] However, Schreiner points out that an inauguration of the heavenly sanctuary is not convincing "for he speaks of purification dealing with forgiveness rather than the establishment of the heavenly sanctuary."[171] As we have labored to show, the author of Hebrews sees the heavenly sanctuary as something that preexists and is the pattern for the earthly so it does not come into existence or inauguration at the sacrifice-ascension. Schreiner further remarks, "The heavenly things don't refer to the people of God or to the conscience. Nor is there any notion here that the heavenly places are defiled and literally need cleansing."[172]

The two most compelling proposals are (1) the 'inauguration of the heavenly tabernacle;' and, (2) 'the cleansing of the sphere of communion.' R. B. Jamieson rightly argues that while entrance of Christ into heaven entails covenant inauguration as part of Hebrews' broader argument in chapter nine, "there is...no sense in which 'cleansed' in 9.23 is a cipher for 'inaugurated.'"[173] The language of Hebrews should not be stretched to a precise literalism. Jesus Christ poured out his blood on earth as a sacrifice, and we have no indication that Hebrews or any other author thought that a sacrifice was made in heaven or that Jesus literally and physically sprinkled his blood in heaven itself. However, a sacrifice and cleansing of sin for the remission of sins was necessary to approach God. Christ having done this for the sins of the people, accomplished redemption, and on this basis he enters heaven to minister. The path is cleared, and in this way, cleansed as people are enabled to approach God through Christ the high priest and sacrifice. We conclude, then, in the concept of "cleansing" the typological pattern is repeated.[174] The throne of God is a throne of grace because of the sacrifice and the ascension of the sacrificed one. MacLeod argues that "the author's language should not, of course, be

---

cleansed by Christ." This point is that because the Law is a 'shadow' of the good things to come. Jamieson also notes some Second Temple texts that state or imply that the heavenly temple could be defiled, particularly by the Watchers and sinning angels (581–582) citing 4Q400 f1.i.14; 1 En. 7:1; 9:8; 10:11; 12:4; and 15:3–4.

169  David J. MacLeod, "Cleansing of the True Tabernacle," 60–71.
170  Ellingworth, *Hebrews*, 477.
171  Schreiner, *Hebrews*, 283.
172  Ibid. For the former view see Bruce, *Hebrews*, 281–19; Attridge, *Hebrews*, 262. For the latter, see Lane, *Hebrews 9–13*, 247.
173  R.B. Jamieson, "Hebrews 9.23," 578. MacLeod ("Cleansing of the True Temple," 69) notes that as "attractive as this proposal is, it does not solve the problem."
174  Schreiner, *Hebrews*, 283; Cockerill, *Hebrews*, 416.

## The Son Ascends into the Heavenly Tabernacle 183

pressed to mean that the heavenly sanctuary is literally defiled. He was not thinking so much of a place as he was of relationships."[175] However, the bodily ascension of a resurrected human being who has been sacrificed for the people serves as a cleansing trailblazer. The cleansing referenced here is probably not indicating that heaven was corrupted by sin and defiled, but rather that the way for humanity is achieved by the ascension of the Son. In order for God's people to experience grace and God's presence by access, purification must be effected in the place where they will come. Heaven needs to be cleansed, not because of impurity, but to prepare the way of access.[176] The issue being addressed through cleansing is not heaven's defilement, but rather its need to be prepared for the presence of humanity. Cockerill expands on this to show the connection is in the typological pattern:

> Christ's sacrifice cleanses the heavenly Sanctuary by analogy with the way in which animal sacrifices cleanse the "pattern." Furthermore, since cleansing was prerequisite to entering the Mosaic Tent, the cleansing of the heavenly appears to have been accomplished by the "once-for-all" sacrifice of Christ which procured his high priestly entrance...it was the sins of the people and not the earthly character that polluted the Mosaic sanctuary. Their sins formed a barrier that prevented them from coming into God's presence and exposed them to his wrath. If sin erected a barrier forbidding entrance into the sanctuary that was a "pattern," how much more did it bar the way into the "true" Sanctuary in which God dwells... Thus by cleansing the heavenly Sanctuary Christ removed this otherwise impregnable barrier and the accompany threat of judgment.[177]

Christ enters in a glorified perfected state, but it is his sacrifice and now glorified self that makes entry possible for God's people. His ascension as Son is the advance guard purifying the temple so that others can follow and find God's grace. The parallel to the Day of Atonement is that since the sacrifice has entered God's presence, heaven is prepared/cleansed for God's people to enter and draw near to God. Jesus being present before God in heaven assures the believers that they have communion with God, and dwell in the company of the saints, because Christ's sacrifice is absolutely effective.

Two aspects of the Day of Atonement are not paralleled in Hebrews. First, once cleansing in God's presence takes place, the high priest comes

---

175 MacLeod, "Cleansing of the True Temple," 70.
176 We see this point as slightly different than Attridge's view that the reference is to consciences being cleansed.
177 Cockerill, *Hebrews*, 416.

back to cleanse the altar. This action in the Old Covenant was probably symbolic of the outward working of purification from God's presence into God's people and perhaps the cosmos itself. Second, Hebrews does not make use of the Azazel goat which departs, separating Israel's sins from her.

Christ's appearing before God applies the sacrifice effecting it for the people of God. Thus, while the sacrifice secures redemption and pays the penalty for the transgression, the high priest must also take the sacrifice into the presence of God. There is a necessity for the sacrifice to enter the presence of God. In 9:25, Christ's not offering himself repeatedly is parallel to the high priest who did just that in taking blood into the holy of holies: οὐδ' ἵνα πολλάκις προσφέρῃ ἑαυτόν, ὥσπερ ὁ ἀρχιερεὺς εἰσέρχεται εἰς τὰ ἅγια κατ' ἐνιαυτὸν ἐν αἵματι ἀλλοτρίῳ. In this respect, Christ offering himself once for all time is his ascending into the heavenly temple.[178]

A better sacrifice was needed (9:23 κρείττοσιν θυσίαις), and there is a putting away of sin in his sacrifice (9:26b εἰς ἀθέτησιν [τῆς] ἁμαρτίας διὰ τῆς θυσίας αὐτοῦ). But this sacrifice needed to be brought into God's presence (9:24b νῦν ἐμφανισθῆναι τῷ προσώπῳ τοῦ θεοῦ ὑπὲρ ἡμῶν). Christ was not going to offer himself repeatedly (9:25a οὐδ' ἵνα πολλάκις προσφέρῃ ἑαυτόν) as the high priests did in regularly entering the tabernacle (9:25b). If Christ was going to offer himself repeatedly there would need to be repeated and regular suffering sacrifice of himself (9:26a ἐπεὶ ἔδει αὐτὸν πολλάκις παθεῖν ἀπὸ καταβολῆς

---

178 At this point David Moffitt's thesis is highly contested. Jared Compton, review of *Atonement and the Logic of Resurrection in the Epistle to the Hebrews* by David M. Moffitt, *TrinJ* 36 (2015): 133–135; Joshua Jipp, review of *Atonement and the Logic of Resurrection in the Epistle to the Hebrews* by David M. Moffitt, *BBR* 22.2 (2012): 298–299; Michael Kibbe, "Is It Finished? When Did It Start? Hebrews, Priesthood, and Atonement in Biblical, Systematic, and Historical Perspective," *JTS* 65.1 (2014): 25–61; review of *Atonement and the Logic of Resurrection in the Epistle to the Hebrews* by David M. Moffitt, *Themelios* 37.1 (2012): 69–70; Nicholas J. Moore, review of *Atonement and the Logic of Resurrection in the Epistle to the Hebrews* by David M. Moffitt, *JTS* 64 (2013): 675; David Schrock, "Resurrection and Priesthood: Christological Soundings from the Book of Hebrews," *SBJT* 18 (2014): 89–114. A century before Moffitt, Geerhardus Vos ("Priesthood of Christ, 155) noted in a manner similar to Moffitt: "making purification of sin is undoubtedly a priestly act and it precedes here [1:3] the sitting down at the right hand of God. This does not necessarily prove, however, that is also precedes the entrance into heaven, or that the author identifies it with the death upon the cross. It is quite possible that the writer in connection with the phrase thought of the entrance itself of Christ into heaven, of His appearing before God, of His cleansing, as it elsewhere is expressed, of the heavenly tabernacle (cf. 9:23–28)." Discussing 5:1, Vos (156) writes, "The identification between the προσφορά and the crucifixion is not a necessary one and in each case requires demonstration. For the προσφέρειν can also include and even mean exclusively the self-presentation of Christ in heaven, or the application of His blood to the heavenly things, or however this act may be called." Vos argues that in 8:3 the use of προσφέρειν is exclusively a heavenly act. Vos argues that προσφέρειν in 9:25–28 includes death and entrance into heaven. Ribbens ("Ascension and Atonement," 18) writes "Christians throughout all generations have concluded that Hebrews depicts Jesus's post-ascension presentation of himself in heaven as part of his atoning sacrifice.

κόσμου). If there was this repetitious offering, it would mean Christ's work was not complete and did not actually accomplish the perfection. One must conclude, there is here a connection between sacrifice of the cross and ascension into heaven just as there is connection between the annual offering on the altar and progression into the Tabernacle's Holy of Holies at the Day of Atonement. Christ's suffering and his ascending into heaven are unified in one grand event. If he had not suffered and shed his blood on behalf of sin, there could be no glorious ascension. If there is no ascension, Christ has not truly offered himself and secured access to God for God's people. The Son must represent sons on the cross and in heaven.

The work of Christ brings the perfect sacrifice and ushers in the eschatological Day of Atonement. History is transformed from 'this age' to 'the age to come.' Note 9:26b νυνὶ δὲ ἅπαξ ἐπὶ συντελείᾳ τῶν αἰώνων εἰς ἀθέτησιν [τῆς] ἁμαρτίας διὰ τῆς θυσίας αὐτοῦ πεφανέρωται. The appearing at the end of the age is both in sacrifice and his going into the presence of God into heaven's throne room (cf. 9:24 νῦν ἐμφανισθῆναι τῷ προσώπῳ τοῦ θεοῦ ὑπὲρ ἡμῶν). Both verses use νῦν eschatologically while ἐμφανισθῆναι and πεφανέρωται are synonymous. But his ascension is grounded on his sacrifice (9:26 διὰ τῆς θυσίας αὐτοῦ) just as the earthly high priest entered by means of the blood of another ἐν αἵματι ἀλλοτρίῳ (9:25).

Having come from among the people (5:1), Christ enters heaven as the high priest. As king and priest entering heaven, he is the glorified Second Adam. He has been perfected through suffering (2:10) but representatively going into heaven for his people, he still calls them brothers (2:11). We completely concur with Moffitt's assessment that Christ must ascend into heaven in a resurrected body. In order to be the inheritor of the age to come, he must have become the glorified man. Jesus is the Son entering the Divine glory, a glory which he had before creation, but he is also the royal Davidic king, the true Adam, inheriting the glory for which man was destined. In the Son, these two offices king and priest come together and are eschatologicly fulfilled. Our author has used Pss 2, 8, and 110 to bring these elements together seeing them climax in the activity of the Son ascending into heaven.

The cross is the eschatological day of judgment in advance upon Christ—the Day of Atonement sacrifice, and the ascension is the eschatological progression into God's presence that was symbolized by the High Priest going into the Tabernacle. Christ's sacrifice for his people enables him to enter God's presence on behalf of His people taking the cleansing effectiveness into God's presence. As Cortez writes, "In summary, we should identify the entrance of Christ into the heavenly sanctuary in v. 24 with his manifestation at the end of the age in v. 26 because the first (v. 24) presupposes his sacrifice; and the second (v. 26), the heavenly nature of that sacrifice."[179] There is an interplay between the once for all time sacrifice of Christ on the cross and the priestly working of Christ to sanctify his people as he is in the presence of God: μιᾷ γὰρ προσφορᾷ τετελείωκεν εἰς τὸ διηνεκὲς τοὺς ἁγιαζομένους (10:14). Christ's bearing the sins of many is an allusion to Isa 53 and the type of death Christ died:

Heb 9:26 εἰς τὸ πολλῶν ἀνενεγκεῖν ἁμαρτίας
Isa 53:12 καὶ αὐτὸς ἁμαρτίας πολλῶν ἀνήνεγκεν

Christ's offering of himself is his death because there is a parallel between Christ's one time offering and the general principle that man can die only once:

| 9:27 καὶ καθ' ὅσον ἀπόκειται τοῖς ἀνθρώποις ἅπαξ ἀποθανεῖν, | => | μετὰ δὲ τοῦτο κρίσις |
| 9:28 οὕτως καὶ ὁ Χριστὸς ἅπαξ προσενεχθεὶς | => | ἐκ δευτέρου χωρὶς ἁμαρτίας ὀφθήσεται εἰς τὸ πολλῶν ἀνενεγκεῖν ἁμαρτίας |

The author may have in view Christ's second coming as the execution of judgment[180] that delivers God's people which would make the parallel even more precise, or it may be that only the first clauses are parallel. The latter view is preferred because Christ's going through death has effectively dealt with the judgement and the transgressions of sin (2:9b, 14; 9:15b). The death redeems, as it bears the sins. Kenneth Schenk argues for this same parallel writing, "human death is parallel to Christ's offering, just as human judgment is parallel to Christ's return without sin."[181] Christ dies ἅπαξ and passes through judgment ἅπαξ. "Christ thus partakes in the same sequence of 'first death and then judgment' common to all humanity."[182] Yet Christ's vindication and being crowned with glory in resurrection assures the effectiveness and finality of the sacrifice (2:9, 14; 7:24–25). His ascension and exaltation to God's right

---

179 Cortez, "Anchor for the Soul," 393.
180 Either way there are similarities between Christ's return to deliver when he comes again and Christ's sitting "until his enemies should be made a footstool for his feet" in 10:13b.
181 Kenneth Schenck, "Archaeology of Hebrews' Tabernacle," 245.
182 Richard Nelson, "'He Offered Himself' Sacrifice in Hebrews," *Interpretation* 57.3 (2003), 254.

hand is God's satisfaction in Christ. He is perfected; he receives the proclamation of Pss 2:7//110:1 as described in Heb 5:5–6; he receives the oath of God in order to become the eschatological perfected high priest (Ps 110:4//Heb 7:21–22) of the New Covenant precisely because the death effected the transition to the New Covenant by dying for the sins committed under the Old and clearing the way into God's presence.

The shed blood of Christ enables his entrance into the throne room on behalf of those he represents (9:24 νῦν ἐμφανισθῆναι τῷ προσώπῳ τοῦ θεοῦ ὑπὲρ ἡμῶν). Christ's work on the cross is followed by his resurrection to indestructible life and his entrance into the sanctuary, which is an appearing before the face of God even as the OT high priest would enter into the earthly representation of God's throne and presence. As Nelson puts it, "Hebrews thus unites Christ's resurrection and exaltation/ascension into a single concept (13:20)."[183] But in this resurrection-exaltation/ascension complex we see Christ is declared as Son. He is made the priestly son in order to represent sons of glory. As the true man, he pioneers the way into heaven. Our contention is that any interpretation that does not see a linkage between sonship and ascension in the book of Hebrews will entertain a deficient view of what Hebrews sees as the climax of redemption. God's people manifesting sonship in God's presence is the great hope of the OT, and what Hebrews sees as the climax of redemption is carried out by the one who is Son—both in eternal divine glory, and in human perfection.

## Conclusion

The purpose of this chapter has been to examine the ascension texts in the book of Hebrews. We have sought to set the ascension against the background of apocalyptic Judaism which portrays heaven as a temple where the throne of God resides. After briefly reviewing Heb 1, we considered Heb 4:14–16 where Christ is the high priest who has ascended through the heavens. The high priest has ascended, but he is able to sympathize with the weaknesses of believers because in his earthly life he experienced weakness. Upon his ascension, he sits at God's right hand in exalted glory, and thereby enables believers to approach the throne of grace. The high priest in God's presence is the true man, crowned in glory interceding for God's people so that they have access. In this respect, Christ's glorified human sonship is integral for God's people to approach God.

---

183 Richard D. Nelson, "He Offered Himself," 255.

Second, we examined Heb 6:19–20. The key motif here is that Christ is the forerunner. The Son's presence in heaven in the glorified state is the surety and guarantee of the hope that believers have. The Son has moved from suffering into the glorious state of the eschatological man which is the same destiny that awaits the believer who perseveres in their confession. In this respect, Christ is the true Son who ascends into the heavenly Zion assuring that other sons will come to glory, giving them hope in their present experiences. The royal installment on the Son in heaven through ascension is the hope of the believer. In his progression into heaven and onto the throne we are assured that the eternal Son has also become a high priest forever. Hebrews concludes that the one who is eternal Son is installed as the Davidic son-king and serves as an eternal high priest who has experienced the consummation of humanity's eschatological glory. He now mediates for believers.

Third, continuing to examine the ascension and the priesthood of Christ, we discussed Heb 7:26 locating it in the context which contrasted the order of the Levitical priesthood with the order of Melchizedek. We argued that the former is sub-eschatological, while the latter is eschatological. The former belongs to 'this present age,' while the latter is the climax that is 'the age to come.' Here again, we see the themes of weakness and temporary appointments contrasted with the finality, eternality, and perfection to the true priest. Because the priest of Melchizedek's order is the true eschatological man, crowned in glory and honor, he ascends into the true tabernacle. The Son qualifies himself to enter this eschatological state by his obedience and covenant keeping. He is the true man who is then rewarded with the eschatological destiny of glory. Thus, the priest now appointed to the true throne in the true and greater tabernacle is the one who is Son and has been made perfect forever. "Son" refers to the identity of Christ in his uniqueness and divine Sonship while 'made perfect forever' describes his having inherited the glory and honor that was human destiny. He is Son, but he is also the eschatological man, the Adamic-Davidic son, who is king and priest.

Fourth, we looked at 8:1–6 to show how these themes continued in Hebrews' argument. The true High Priest, Jesus the Son, must ascend into heaven. The finality of redemption demands that it be completed not in the earthly tabernacle, which is a shadow, but in the true and eschatological tabernacle, heaven itself.

Finally, we examined Heb 9:11–14, 23–26. We showed that Hebrews does not conceive the tabernacle in heaven to have two rooms but rather views heaven as a single tent, as the eschatological fulfillment. For Hebrews, the Old Covenant Tabernacle had two rooms because the outer room was ultimate symbolic of the 'present age' which had to pass away when the true and final ascension into the throne room was fulfilled in the New Covenant. Two points are very clear: first Hebrews is contrasting earthly and heavenly as part of the larger contrast between Old Covenant and New Covenant which is primarily an eschatological contrast; and second, this earthly/heavenly contrast with its eschatological flavor puts Hebrews squarely into the context of apocalyptic thinking and bears some of the features of Second Temple ascents into heaven. Of course, Hebrews has unique aspects in that it is concerned with showing a permanent exaltation of the Son, not merely a journey through heaven. Nevertheless, the Son ascending to the throne is a revelation. It is an inauguration of the New Covenant and an eschatological fulfillment of the Day of Atonement. The Son's ascension applies the sacrifice made on the cross. The ascension effects the age to come, bringing the transition of the ages. Ascension brings the Son to sit down on the divine throne crowned in all the royal glory that was human destiny, and, at the same time reveals the glory the Son had before the creation of all things. There is an interplay here: if Christ has ascended into heaven, he is the final true sacrifice. If Christ is the final true sacrifice of atonement, then he must ascend into heaven, the true tabernacle. If Christ is the true sacrifice and truly in God's presence, believers cannot be abandoned the confession of faith. If the Christians to whom Hebrews writes fall away, there is no longer a sacrifice for sins because the drama of redemption has reached its eschatological consummation. This consummation is in the Son, Jesus. Therefore, one cannot abandon a confession of Sonship and Lordship. The Son is at the right hand of the Father having completed his mission of redemption. He now lives to intercede, and the audience must continue to make use of this permanent, eternal, 'age to come' intercession he offers.

Thus, we concur with others like Timo Eskola: "Exaltation Christology is not a minor aspect in the letter, but the main foundation on which the whole train of thought has been constructed. For the writer, the key event of eschatology is Christ's enthronement. His ascension has both cultic and royal features."[184] These cultic and royal features can be traced back to the OT where the priests enter the tabernacle and the kings rule from Zion. Both are linked to Adamic features. Kings are the new vice-regent and the true Israelite *par excellence* (or at least that is the expectation). Priests are the cultic Adams going into the new Eden with the glory of God on them and in corporate solidarity with God's people. In both cases the Adams ascend: kings to Mt. Zion and priests into the throne room that is the inner Holy of Holies. "Christ's

---

184  Eskola, *Messiah and the Throne*, 207.

entry into 'heaven itself' is a key Christological moment for the writer."[185] It is the culmination of kingship and priesthood all in the one who is Son.

We will now turn to examine how the Son is qualified for this ministry. Specifically, his earthly life of human obedience qualifies him to become this eschatological man. The Son did not just come as the glorified-crowned eschatological man. Through living true human devotion, and manifesting sonlike qualities expected in the Adamic-Davidic figure, the Son merited for himself and his people the status of the eschatological man. Put another way, the Son walks the human path of obedient trust-fidelity in the midst of suffering, so that he can be the first of the new humanity ushered into eschatological glory. We will make this case in our penultimate chapter.

---

185 Edward Adams, "The Cosmology of Hebrews," in *The Epistle to the Hebrews and Christian Theology*, ed. Richard Bauckham, et al. (Eerdmans, 2009), 134–135.

## Chapter 6

# The Son's Adamic Obedience Leads to Ascension

### Introduction

UP TO THIS POINT, we have examined the designation of Jesus as Son in Hebrews 1, we have examined the Son's glorification as fulfillment of Adamic-Davidic kingship in Hebrews 2 and then turned our attention to the use of the ascension in the book of Hebrews. This chapter will draw together the previous discussion and focus specifically on two passages: Heb 5:7–10 and 10:5–14. We will argue that Christ's self-sacrifice is an act of active obedience, in which he becomes the righteous sufferer *par excellence*. Just as David in the Psalms often appeals to his righteousness or godliness so that God would answer his prayers, so Jesus is heard in his suffering because of godly piety. This piety can only be a function of the Son's humanity. Hebrews sees Christ as the eternal Son who takes on the Adamic-Davidic role so that by his righteous suffering he achieves the eschatological glory on behalf of his people. It is here where we see the interplay between eternal Sonship and sonship/kingship. It is out of this true human obedience that he is qualified to become the eschatological man, a king and high priest, who ascends into the true tabernacle. It is this explication of the grounds of the ascension in its relationship to the Adamic-Davidic sonship that we seek to advance the discussion of the ascension in Hebrews beyond the work of scholars like Cortez and Moffitt. In Hebrews' treatment of the ascension, the author returns full circle to his "philosophy of revelation."[1] Thus we find: the fulfillment of the typology pattern of sonship in Adam or David reveals to all that he is the true Son. His sonship is in full identity with humanity due to his acts on their behalf and in obedience to the Father, and his Sonship is also in full identity

---
1 Geerhardus Vos, *Teaching of the Epistle of Hebrews* (Eerdmans, 1956), 49.

with the Father. The Adamic-Davidic son ascending to the throne and into divine glory reveals that this son is truly Son.

## Heb 5:8a καιπερ ων υιος

For Hebrews, the state of being Son is a condition applied prior to both the suffering of Christ and the exaltation of Christ. Christ's ascension and exaltation is a declaring, announcing, and revealing of the Sonship of Jesus, but our author sees Sonship also as a unique pre-existent designator of the one who came. The Son is Son prior to his ascension and being crowned with glory. Hebrews does not use the category of Sonship to speak referentially back to one who was not previously son. An example of a referential identification would be if an individual might say, "Queen Elizabeth II was born April 21, 1926." Strictly speaking, she was not Queen at the time of her birth, but rather became Queen later. The speaker used the title of her later status to refer to her at a time before she bore the status of Queen. If one applied this referential concept to Jesus as a lens for understanding Hebrews' conception, it could be suggested that although Jesus became S/son at his ascension, this designation as Son is only referential and any pre-exalted reference to the Son as Son does not describe a state, condition, or identity prior to exaltation. Such an argument, however, is not what the author of Hebrews is conveying. As we have already shown in Heb 1, while the exaltation of Christ is in view, Hebrews sees the Son as pre-existent and sharing in the glory, attributes, eternality, and identity of godhood. All that is ascribed to YHWH in the OT is ascribed to the Son of the Father in both the Son's exaltation but especially also in His pre-exalted state.

Here we must return again to consider the three other anarthrous uses of υἱός in Hebrew before discussing καίπερ ὢν υἱός in 5:8.[2]

1:2a—ἐπ' ἐσχάτου τῶν ἡμερῶν τούτων ἐλάλησεν ἡμῖν ἐν υἱῷ

3:6a—Χριστὸς δὲ ὡς υἱὸς ἐπὶ τὸν οἶκον αὐτοῦ

7:28—ὁ λόγος δὲ τῆς ὁρκωμοσίας τῆς μετὰ τὸν νόμον υἱὸν εἰς τὸν αἰῶνα τετελειωμένον

The first reference in 1:2, which we have discussed above, concerns the identity of the Son in the revelation of God. The glory of the Son is equal to the

---

2 We do not discuss occasions where there a possessive pronoun instead of an article, such as 1:5 υἱός μου εἶ σύ or ἔσται μοι εἰς υἱόν. Here the possessive pronoun serves a similar function to the definite article, while also identifying the Father-Son relationship between God and Jesus.

glory of God. God has spoken in a qualitatively superior revelation to that of the prophets—he has spoken not simply by means of the Son, but it is in the fullness of the revelation of the Son that God has revealed. This revelation entails, from Heb 1:3, the one who has been dwelling in the divine glory as ὢν ἀπαύγασμα τῆς δόξης, being the χαρακτὴρ τῆς ὑποστάσεως αὐτοῦ, who was the co-Creator (δι' οὗ καὶ ἐποίησεν τοὺς αἰῶνας) and upholds the universe (φέρων τε τὰ πάντα τῷ ῥήματι τῆς δυνάμεως αὐτοῦ). His ὢν υἱός in 5:8 is the equivalent of his ὢν ἀπαύγασμα τῆς δόξης καὶ χαρακτὴρ τῆς ὑποστάσεως αὐτοῦ in 1:3. In 1:2 the qualitative of υἱός describes Jesus not just as one who becomes Son or is exalted into the role of sonship. Although it is only in the "last days that God has spoken in Son," the Son existed as Son prior to his work and prior to his roles. The revelation of the Son is a revelation of God, specifically the means by which the Father makes himself known. A parallel idea is found in John's gospel, where the Logos tabernacles in our midst (ἐσκήνωσεν ἐν ἡμῖν), καὶ ἐθεασάμεθα τὴν δόξαν αὐτοῦ (Jn 1:14), so that to see the Son is to see the Father (Jn 14:8 ὁ ἑωρακὼς ἐμὲ ἑώρακεν τὸν πατέρα). This is not to say that Hebrews and John are identical in all points, but Hebrews does place the identity of the Son as being within the godhead along with the Father.

In Heb 3:6, the glory of the Son stands in contrast to the glory of Moses. In 3:1, the believers are to consider their heavenly calling, which is probably a reference to the ascension of Christ and the eternal inheritance of believers who now in Christ are 'sons of glory.' It is a mixing of the ascension theme with the theme of inheritance in typological fulfillment to Israel's entrance to her promised land inheritance. However, Jesus is greater than Moses. He is τὸν ἀπόστολον καὶ ἀρχιερέα τῆς ὁμολογίας ἡμῶν (3:1). He is high priest as one who ascended into heaven and apostle as the one who is sent as God's "self-revelation and authorized representative."[3] Attridge notes the function of this role as "the messenger of the divine name implicit in the psalm quotation of 2:12. It thus recalls the role assigned to various intermediaries between God and humanity, functions that Jesus fulfills in a pre-eminent way."[4]

The obedience of Jesus is brought into focus: He obeyed God who appointed him (3:1 πιστὸν ὄντα τῷ ποιήσαντι αὐτόν). Ποιήω does not mean here 'to make,' but speaks of the work of God designating or appointing him in his exaltation. The Son is not included in the 'all things' which are created (cf. 1:2 δι' οὗ καὶ ἐποίησεν τοὺς αἰῶνας; 1:3 φέρων τε τὰ πάντα; 1:10a σὺ κατ' ἀρχάς, κύριε, τὴν γῆν ἐθεμελίωσας; and 1:10b καὶ ἔργα τῶν χειρῶν σού εἰσιν οἱ οὐρανοί). Jesus is, for Hebrews, the uncreated one (1:10–12), similar to Acts 2:36 ὅτι καὶ κύριον

---

3 Cockerill, *The Epistle to the Hebrews* (Eerdmans, 2012), 159.
4 Attridge, *The Epistle to the Hebrews* (Fortress, 1989), 107.

αὐτὸν καὶ χριστὸν ἐποίησεν ὁ θεός, τοῦτον τὸν Ἰησοῦν ὃν ὑμεῖς ἐσταυρώσατε. Cockerill cites LXX 1 Sam 12:6 and Mark 3:14 as further examples.[5]

The faithfulness of Jesus and Moses is compared, but the glory to which they are appointed is contrasted. Moses is in the house (3:5 Μωϋσῆς μὲν πιστὸς ἐν ὅλῳ τῷ οἴκῳ), but Jesus is over the house as the builder. The comparative begins πλείονος γὰρ οὗτος δόξης παρὰ Μωϋσῆν ἠξίωται (3:3). The builder of the house has more honor than the servant in the house (3:3 καθ᾽ ὅσον πλείονα τιμὴν ἔχει τοῦ οἴκου ὁ κατασκευάσας αὐτόν). The comparative καθ᾽ ὅσον links not only the clauses but puts 'glory' and 'honor' into proximity of thought. Jesus' glory and honor refers to his exaltation (2:7, 9). The faithfulness of Jesus was his obedient suffering unto death, which resulted in being crowned with glory and honor. The activity of Christ in this death makes him considered worthy (3:3 ἀξιόω) of the heights of his exaltation in glory and honor. Being the obedient one *par excellence* is the condition through which he becomes the exalted one *par excellence*. It is because of his death (2:9b διὰ τὸ πάθημα τοῦ θανάτου δόξῃ καὶ τιμῇ ἐστεφανωμένον), and through it (2:10 διὰ παθημάτων τελειῶσαι), that he is crowned with glory and honor.

This is perhaps another reason to take ἀπαύγασμα in 1:3 as active with the Son ὢν ἀπαύγασμα τῆς δόξης. In the OT, Moses had radiated the glory of God, having come down form the mountain to which he had ascended. Moses' face would shine with the reflection of the glory of God (Exod 34:29, 35). Even more, the Lord would speak with Moses when Moses would enter the earthly tent (Exod 33:9), but Moses could not see God's face and live, even though he was speaking 'face to face' (Exod 33:11, 19–20)—he could not see the fullness of God's glory. Nonetheless, the Son's ascension has brought him before the face of God (9:24b νῦν ἐμφανισθῆναι τῷ προσώπῳ τοῦ θεοῦ ὑπὲρ ἡμῶν). The glory of the Son is greater than that of Moses, even while both were faithful to God the Father.

Concerning v. 4, Attridge remarks, "The 'greater honor' is most clearly evident in the case of God who is 'the fashioner' of the universe (ὁ δὲ πάντα κατασκευάσας). Here the author exploits the cosmic metaphorical value of the term 'house' in extending his analogy."[6] He goes on to state that there is no such identification between Christ and "the fashioner."[7] Before ruling out such identification the question should be asked: Why does the author of Hebrews extend the analogy to the cosmic level? It could be that the author is merely grounding the analogy. He is just pointing out that people build houses while in fact only God has truly fashioned all things into existence.

---

5 Cockerill, *Hebrews*, 162; cf. also Attridge, *Hebrews*, 108n.50.
6 Attridge, *Hebrews*, 110.
7 Attridge, *Hebrews*, 110.

Hebrews may be saying in effect, "I'm only contrasting relative glories of people living in the house vs. the builder of the house, but yes, we know God has made it all." Still, we should be careful here because Hebrews does not see three levels of glory in view as if Moses' glory is great, Jesus's glory is greater, but God's is the greatest.

While God is clearly the creator of all things, the Son has been shown to equally share in the creation of all things (again: 1:2, 3, 10a, 10b). There is a distinction here between the use of house referring to the people of God and the use of 'house' as referring to the universe as a whole. Hebrews clearly is not removing God from purview when referencing Jesus as the builder—yet he does bring Jesus and God into the closest possible proximity giving us greater clarity of what it means for Jesus to be Son. Sonship is not conditioned upon faithfulness or upon his act of building but is who he is. God has fashioned all, the Son participated in this fashioning as an eternal person sharing in the eternal divine glory, but now the Son who acted in faithfulness has built the house of the people of God.

Schreiner notes that while Christ is specifically titled as the builder of the house, an analogy is constructed: "God as the Creator of the universe deserves glory and honor, so too Christ as the Builder of the house is honored above Moses."[8] The authority that God has over creation is equal to the authority that the Son has over the people of God who are the new creation 'sons of glory.' The Son is not merely appointed in the house, but over the house. That appointment over the house is precisely because his suffering death results in the establishment or building of the house itself. The people of God only become such, and share as 'sons of glory,' because Christ is the true Son who accomplishes it.

Christ's suffering and exaltation into glory as the pioneer builds and establishes the people God. Christ's role in inaugurating the covenant is on par with God as the great covenant maker. He makes the house of God's people. On the one hand, he is the only source of salvation as only YHWH is the source of salvation according to the OT. On the other hand, it is his human obedience to the Father that achieves the inheritance of glory given to all sons. God comes and speaks 'in Son' revealing himself. In contrast, Moses is only the servant who testifies to the coming revelation (3:5 ὡς θεράπων εἰς μαρτύριον τῶν λαληθησομένων), but God has spoken in Son who reveals the glory of God. Christ's faithfulness as Son makes him the one over the house (3:6 Χριστὸς δὲ ὡς υἱὸς ἐπὶ τὸν οἶκον αὐτοῦ), but not *in the house* as Moses was. The servant-Son contrast is precisely the same as the house-builder contrast.

---

8 Thomas Schreiner, *Commentary on Hebrews* (B&H, 2015), 117.

Similarly, both Moses and Jesus are faithful and receive glory but, the degrees of glory are qualitatively (not just quantitatively) different and distinct.

3:3 πλείονος γὰρ οὗτος δόξης παρὰ Μωϋσῆν ἠξίωται
  καθ᾽ ὅσον πλείονα τιμὴν ἔχει τοῦ οἴκου ὁ κατασκευάσας αὐτόν...
3:5 Μωϋσῆς μὲν πιστὸς ἐν ὅλῳ τῷ οἴκῳ αὐτοῦ...
3:6 Χριστὸς δὲ ὡς υἱὸς ἐπὶ τὸν οἶκον αὐτοῦ

Christ's Sonship is his authority over the house. His work has accomplished and built the house, just as his work with God has built the cosmos. The identity of the Son is not then merely a functional role or a title as inheritor. For Hebrews, inheritance and building are brought into unison, just as in chapter one the Son's role of Creator and exalted firstborn function together in the one person. This use of the anarthrous υἱός is part of Jesus' very identity; Sonship highlights his uniqueness and his superiority.

As we have been arguing, it is not simply that the Son inherits that which belongs to the Father; instead, the Son is over God's house as builder and establisher of it. The Son is both the one who is the forerunner into the inheritance, and the one who is the fashioner of it. The Son may not be directly equated to God by explicit identification here. He is however described as carrying out and accomplishing that which is reserved for God alone. His superior glory is not merely by virtue of greater faithfulness than Moses or qualitative obedience, but a greater quality to the personage. God identifies Moses as "my servant" throughout the Pentateuch, but God identifies Jesus as Son.

Before returning to 5:8, let us look at the final anarthrous use of υἱός in Hebrews, namely 7:28. The context of the verse is a discussion of the nature of Christ's priesthood as one continuing forever (7:24). Because Christ lives to make intercession, he is able to help those who draw near (7:25). Unlike the priests of the Old Covenant, he does not have to offer a sacrifice for his own sins, since he has none (7:26–27). He has now been exalted above the heavens in this priesthood (7:26b). Then we have a parallel structure in v. 28.

| ὁ νόμος γὰρ | ἀνθρώπους καθίστησιν ἀρχιερεῖς | ἔχοντας | ἀσθένειαν |
| ὁ λόγος δὲ τῆς ὁρκωμοσίας ... | υἱόν | εἰς τὸν αἰῶνα | τετελειωμένον |

For the sake of clarity in identifying the parallel structuring we have omitted τῆς μετὰ τὸν νόμον, which highlights the chronological ordering between the

Law and the oath, just as there is an ordering between the first and second covenant. There is a difference between who is appointed, as well as a difference of the condition in which he is appointed. Sonship is no more titular than ἀνθρώπους is a title here. It is a statement of identity—the nature or makeup of the individual. As Gerhardus Vos puts it: "The law appoints to the office such as are men, the word of the oath a Son. This, it will be observed, implies a contrast between human nature and sonship: the Son as Son is not human, but divine."[9] The law appoints a man to be a high priest. The law appoints a man who is in a state of weakness at the time of his appointment. This weakness, on the one hand, is inclusive of his sinful state and need to make atoning sacrifices for himself; on the other hand, it speaks more broadly of the sub-eschatological state that is venerable and under slavery to death. In weakness man is subject to death. We will discuss this more below as we examine 5:1–4. Suffice it to say we have the identity of the 'who' along with the 'what' of the condition he is in.

In the same way, the 'word of the oath,' which refers to 7:21–22 and the oath of Ps 110:4, also appoints a priest. We have in 7:19–20 the contrast: οἱ μὲν...χωρὶς ὁρκωμοσίας with ὁ δὲ μετὰ ὁρκωμοσίας. Similar to how 3:6 omits the repetition of πιστός from 3:5 when it makes a μέν...δέ contrast between Moses and Christ, 7:20 omits the repetition of εἰσὶν...γεγονότες. Clearly, however, the contrast is in how Levites were made priests versus how the Son is made a priest. Hebrews will do the same thing in 7:28; first the Law: ὁ νόμος γὰρ ἀνθρώπους καθίστησιν ἀρχιερεῖς, but when referring to the Son, the reader needs to supply the καθίστησιν ἀρχιερεῖς. Hebrews is able to make the connection of comparing and contrasting all the stronger. Further in 7:28, he makes a difference between the present tense ἔχοντας describing the Levitical high priests as ἔχοντας ἀσθένειαν, and the perfect tense τετελειωμένον referring to the Son's experience. The weakness was always the present state of the man who were appointed priests.[10] However, the Son is τετελειωμένον, where the perfect participle denotes past action with results continuing to the present 'having been perfected.' Perfection, as we have regularly shown and will discuss again below, refers to the eschatological state where Jesus is crowned with glory and honor. It is something that the Son *becomes*. He becomes incarnate in weakness, but then he is raised up having been perfected into the eschatological humanity in appointment as king and priest. While Christ shared in the earthly life of weakness that is common to humanity, he was

---

9 Vos, "The Priesthood of Christ in Hebrews," in *Redemptive History and Biblical Interpretation* (P&R, 1980), 150.

10 The Levitical high priests have the weakness of sin and being sub-eschatological (subject to dying and death) throughout their entire ministry.

able to die and be subject to death. Now, he has moved on from this state into the new phase of humanity. Christ's priesthood is eschatological characterized by his 'having been made perfect.'

The identity of the perfected one here is 'Son.' 'Son' is not just something characterized by his eschatological state. He is not just 'Son' in appointment, any more than the priests were 'man' only after appointment. Certainly, in Heb 1:5 the exaltation of the Son is the royal announcement and declaration of Sonship. It is his Messianic appointment and accession to rulership. Yet there is a distinction here between υἱόν and εἰς τὸν αἰῶνα τετελειωμένον, just as there is a distinction between ἀνθρώπους and ἔχοντας ἀσθένειαν. Although weakness is what describes the man at the time of his appointment to priesthood, the man is not a man because he has weakness. In the same way, the Son is not a son because he has been perfected. Rather perfection describes the state in which a Son is appointed. Thus, the appointment to kingship-priesthood is not the condition by which he becomes a son—although this is true in a Messianic sense. Rather, Hebrews sees Sonship as something that resonates much deeper than the office of priesthood, just as humanity is a deeper category to the priests appointed in the Old Covenant.

Sonship, then, is not an office or a type of category for priest. It is not a functional sonship that Hebrews has in view here, but something that is definitional of the person or being appointed. While there is an appointing to the throne and a begetting of the son in exaltation and ascension, the one who ascends to take superiority already is and has been Son. Hebrews is consistent in its usages of the anarthrous υἱός to designate in a qualitative sense the existence or nature of the one appointed priest. So, while the Son moves from weakness to eschatological glory and is appointed king/son and high priest, for Hebrews Sonship is a much broader and deeper category than the office or eschatological existence of Jesus.

Now we return 5:8 καίπερ ὢν υἱός, ἔμαθεν ἀφ' ὧν ἔπαθεν τὴν ὑπακοήν. Καίπερ is used five times in the NT (Phil 3:4; Heb 5:8; 7:5; 12:17; 2 Pet 1:12). Each time it is concessive, being used when the author is speaking of a particular state of affairs in contrast to another state. It is used as a conjunctive "while there is statement X, also statement Y," although X and Y seem at least contrastive.

Let us illustrate:

| | Statement X | Statement Y |
|---|---|---|
| Phil 3:4–5 | οὐκ ἐν σαρκὶ πεποιθότε | καίπερ ἐγὼ ἔχων πεποίθησιν καὶ ἐν σαρκί |

|         |                                                      |                                                           |
|---------|------------------------------------------------------|-----------------------------------------------------------|
|         | Put no confidence in the flesh                       | although I have reason for confidence also in the flesh[11] |
| Heb 7:5 | οἱ μὲν ἐκ τῶν υἱῶν Λευὶ…                             | καίπερ ἐξεληλυθότας ἐκ τῆς ὀσφύος Ἀβραάμ                  |
|         | τὴν ἱερατείαν λαμβάνοντες                            | ἀποδεκατοῦν                                               |
|         | The sons of Levi receive the priesthood              | although coming from the descendant of Abraham … to take tithes |
| Heb 12:17 | μετανοίας γὰρ τόπον οὐχ εὗρεν                     | καίπερ μετὰ δακρύων ἐκζητήσας αὐτήν                       |
|         | he found no opportunity to repent                    | although he tearfully sought it.                          |
| 2 Pet 1:12 | Διὸ μελλήσω ἀεὶ ὑμᾶς ὑπομιμνῄσκειν περὶ τούτων    | καίπερ εἰδότας                                            |
|         | Therefore, I will remind you concerning this        | although you know                                         |

In Phil 3:4–5, Paul is commanding that we not boast in the flesh, although he himself has much in which he could boast. In Heb 7:5, the sons of Levi receive tithes from their brothers and in this sense are superior to all the rest of Israel although they are all descendants of Abraham. Although we would expect equality because all the tribes are descendants of Abraham, in actuality, Levi is appointed in the Law to receive tithes. In Heb 12:17, Esau has no opportunity to repent but not for lack of trying, in fact, even though not having the opportunity he actively sought it out. Finally, in 2 Pet 1:12, Peter is reminding his audience of these qualities (cf. 1:5–7) even though, in fact, they already do know them. We conclude that the similar construction in Heb 5:8 conveys similar meaning with one difference: our designated 'statement Y' precedes what we have labeled 'statement X.' Thus, in Heb 5:8, the phrase καίπερ ὢν υἱός is contrastive to the main clause ἔμαθεν ἀφ' ὧν ἔπαθεν τὴν ὑπακοήν.

'Being Son' is placed in contrast to learning because, as we have been arguing, sonship is more than a mere office in these anarthrous uses of υἱός. It is describing the being Jesus, who he is, not merely what he does. The present active participle signals that he exists as Son, this existence as son is clearly prior to exaltation/perfection. Furthermore, this sonship is unique and divine. In fact, if it were merely a Davidic sonship in view, the contrastive construction would not work.

Following the OT, we should expect the David sonship to learn obedience and even undergo discipline. Consider 2 Sam 7:14, "I will be to him a father, and he shall be to me a son. When he commits iniquity, I will discipline him

---

11 Paul is in effect saying, "If you want to boast, I have a lot I could boast about."

with the rod of men, with the stripes of the sons of men."[12] Or again, speaking of Davidic kings, we can examine Ps 89:30–33:

[30] If his children[13] forsake my law and do not walk according to my rules,
[31] if they violate my statutes and do not keep my commandments,
[32] then I will punish their transgression with the rod and their iniquity with stripes,
[33] but I will not remove from him my steadfast love or be false to my faithfulness.

Israel as YHWH's son was expected to be disciplined by the Lord: Deut 8:5, "Know then in your heart that, as a man disciplines his son, the LORD your God disciplines you."[14] We also see this in Second Temple literature:

Wis 11:9–10
ὅτε γὰρ ἐπειράσθησαν, καίπερ ἐν ἐλέει παιδευόμενοι, ἔγνωσαν πῶς μετ᾽ ὀργῆς κρινόμενοι ἀσεβεῖς ἐβασανίζοντο· τούτους μὲν γὰρ ὡς πατὴρ νουθετῶν ἐδοκίμασας, ἐκείνους δὲ ὡς ἀπότομος βασιλεὺς καταδικάζων ἐξήτασας.
For when they were tested, although they were being disciplined in mercy, they learned how the impious, being judged in anger, were tormented. For these you put to the test like a father giving a warning, but the others you examined like a stern king passing sentence.

Pss. Sol. 18:4
ἡ παιδεία σου ἐφ᾽ ἡμᾶς ὡς υἱὸν πρωτότοκον μονογενῆ ἀποστρέψαι ψυχὴν εὐήκοον ἀπὸ ἀμαθίας ἐν ἀγνοίᾳ.
Your discipline for us (is) as (for) a firstborn son, an only child, to divert the perceptive person from unintentional sins.

---

12 Cf. also 1 Kgs 2:4 "that the LORD may establish his word that he spoke concerning me, saying, 'If your sons pay close attention to their way, to walk before me in faithfulness with all their heart and with all their soul, you shall not lack a man on the throne of Israel.'"

13 MT: בָנָיו; LXX οἱ υἱοὶ αὐτοῦ.

14 Brandon Crowe (*The Last Adam: A Theology of the Obedient Life of Jesus in the Gospels* [Baker, 2017], 62) points out how the father-son relationship is "among the central features of the entire book (Deut 1:31; 8:5; 14:1–2; 32:1–20, 43). ... This father-son relationship is a relationship of covenantal *obligation*, so that as son of God, Israel must be obedient to their divine Father." On Deut 8:5–6, Crowe writes, "*because* God disciplines Israel as a son, *therefore* Israel is to keep God's commandments" (Ibid., emphasis original). This helps make the point that we are arguing: Hebrews does not see the result of sonship as discipline and (learning) obedience as one would expect from the OT narrative. The author sees something unique to Jesus' Sonship which would lead one to expect him to be exempt from suffering. It is this higher quality of Sonship that leads to a surprise that he should suffer. This is precisely because, as we have argued he takes on the Adamic-Davidic features of sonship. See also Crowe, *The Last Adam*, 56–67, where he links Israel and Adam's sonship.

Later Hebrews will make use of this same theme as we see it in Proverbs (Prov 3:11–12 and Heb 12:5–10). Two things should be the focus of our attention here. First, we note μαστιγοῖ δὲ πάντα υἱὸν ὃν παραδέχεται (Prov 3:12; Heb 12:6). God chastises, whips, or heavily disciplines those he receives as sons. If one is to be received as a son, it is perfectly normal that one should expect to and will experience the disciplining hand of the Lord. Hebrews so argues this point that in 12:8 if one has not received discipline then they are not a son but an illegitimate child. Second, all sons should expect discipline, using the rhetorical τίς γὰρ υἱὸς ὃν οὐ παιδεύει πατήρ; (12:7). The question uses the earthly example to reflect on the heavenly nature of God as a father to his sons. God's discipline is his act of treating his people as son εἰς παιδείαν ὑπομένετε, ὡς υἱοῖς ὑμῖν προσφέρεται ὁ θεός (12:7a). Discipline for the purpose of obedience or even for correction is part and parcel of the full rights and privileges as son.[15]

This brings us back to Heb 5:8. Why does Hebrews introduce Christ's Sonship with καίπερ ὢν υἱός and then a statement of learning obedience ἔμαθεν ἀφ' ὧν ἔπαθεν τὴν ὑπακοήν? It is important that we feel the full force of this concessive. Everything Hebrews says about sonship in chapter 12 would negate any use of a concessive if there was not something different about the sonship of Christ. The background material for Davidic sonship and Israelite sonship would lead one to expect not a concessive conjunction but an intensifier. If Heb 5:8 was arguing in accordance with this line of background material in 12:5–10, one would expect something like "because he was a son" or "especially since he was a son."[16] All true sons are supposed to go through discipline and learning, which may actually entail suffering, for correction or shaping.

David deSilva has proposed that καίπερ ὢν υἱός be read with what is previous in 5:7 rather than with what follows in v. 8. He proposes that "this reading would emphasize that it was Jesus' virtue (piety) rather than his filial connection with God that led to his resurrection."[17] Thus, the clause καίπερ ὢν υἱός is subordinate to what has followed. So deSilva provides the following translation to emphasize what he believes is the focus: "who learned obedience through what he suffered, offering prayers and petitions in the days of his flesh to the one who was able to rescue him out from death and being heard on account of his piety (although he was a son)."[18] One advantage of

---

15 Again, see Crowe, *The Last Adam*, 62–63, on the linking of sonship and covenantal obedience as a major feature in Deuteronomy.

16 Johnson, *Hebrews*, 147, has made a similar point.

17 David deSilva, *Perseverance in Gratitude: A Socio-Rhetorical Commentary on the Epistle "to the Hebrews"* (Eerdmans, 2000), 192.

18 Ibid., 193.

deSilva's interpretation is that it allows him to read 5:7 and 12:5–11 more in line with each other—the latter expanded to believers what the former has said of Jesus. DeSilva rejects that καίπερ ὢν υἱός points to and highlights the uniqueness of the Son here. Another advantage is that καίπερ often, though not necessarily, connects with what is previous (see above).

We, however, do not find deSilva's view convincing. The first reason is precisely because the Davidic background strongly connects piety to aspects of sonship. In other words, in the Davidic psalms, suffering and piety are equal to belonging to God's family. We are led by this background to expect sons to learn obedience and demonstrate filial relationship precisely because of obedience and trust. This is what a son, the Davidic king, does. He trusts God; based on the Deuteronomic kingship requirement he is the obeyer of the law *par excellence* and a model for the people. Furthermore, sons get disciplined by their fathers. To say we should read the passage as Jesus was "heard because his piety, although he was a son" makes little sense since the Davidic figure in his sonship is always heard because of piety, and that piety is a fundamental demonstration of the nature of sonship. One cannot contrast the two. Against the OT background, deliverance because of pious trust and sonship are fluid concepts, one leads to the other and *vice versa*.[19] There is nothing contrastive between filial relationship and vindication because of piety.

Thus, we return to the notion that Hebrews is pointing to a unique Sonship of Christ. Wescott highlights the uniqueness of Jesus' Sonship saying, "In one sense it is true that the idea of Sonship suggests that of obedience; but the nature of Christ's Sonship at first sight seems to exclude the thought that He should learn obedience through suffering."[20] Attridge has concluded, "the force of the remark is that Jesus is not an ordinary son, who might indeed be expected to learn from suffering (12:4–11), but the eternal Son."[21] Again we want to intensify the statement by adding: it would be *the most natural thing* to expect that a son in relationship to YHWH is not exempt but must expect discipline. Consider how often in the Psalms, David being son appeals most of all to his piety and righteousness to be heard (e.g., Pss 7:3–8; 18:20–24; 26:1–3; 45:7; etc.). Other times, David's piety is on display as, like an ideal Israelite, he

---

19 We could also note the same between Israel's relationship with YHWH as son and the promise of blessings for obedience. The graciousness of being 'adopted' as God's son as a nation was supposed to lead to covenant fidelity. Israel is to trust and rely on YHWH for vindications. As 'son,' Israel is to show fidelity. Or reversely, pious fidelity manifests the true sonship Israel has—Israel is to practice justice and righteousness (for example in treatment of orphans and widows), precisely because this is what YHWH does. Circularly, sonship leads to trust and trust leads to the vindication of the sons.

20 B.F. Westcott, *The Epistle to the Hebrews* (Macmillan, 1889), 130.

21 Attridge, *Hebrews*, 152.

*The Son's Adamic Obedience Leads to Ascension*

makes the Lord his refuge, which itself is an act of obedience and piety (Pss 5:11; 7:1; 11:1; 16:1; 18:2, 30; etc.).

'Son' means something beyond a Davidic category (or Adamic/Israelite category).[22] David Peterson similarly writes, "It is true that, in one sense, 'the idea of sonship suggests that of obedience,' but the Sonship of Jesus has been expounded in such a fashion in Heb 1 as to highlight the apparent incongruity of such words as 'he learned obedience through what he suffered' being applied to him."[23] "Auf jeden Fall ist mit καίπερ ὢν υἱός das ewige, präexistenent Wesen des Sohnes zum Ausdruck gebracht."[24] But with the portrayal of the Son in 1:1–14, how and why must the son be perfected? Is he not already a sharer in the divine identity? Cockerill sees it as an expression that "Christ's sonship did not cease while he was learning 'obedience.'"[25]

But it is not merely that Christ's Sonship did not cease during learning obedience. It is that the type and nature of Sonship that Hebrews sees as the Son's identity should have exempted him from suffering and learning obedience. The author of Hebrews sees Christ participating in a type of Sonship that is unique. It is a qualitatively different kind of Sonship that would excuse him from suffering. In this respect, it is not merely Davidic sonship, Adamic sonship, or sonship of the true and final Israelite. We will show below that this is in fact the nature of his obedience but the Sonship in view with the phrase καίπερ ὢν υἱός is an eternal and divine Sonship. It is a Sonship that so shares in the divine attributes of such a quality with the Father that we would expect him not to need nor desire to discipline this Son.

The nature of this Sonship should cause us to return to Heb 1 and read it more carefully. Hebrews operates with a deeper ontology[26] than merely divine wisdom now manifest as Davidic son, a mediating figure in creation, or an eternal Logos figure, especially with some kind of Philonic background. As we showed, the Son radiates the divine glory (1:3 ὢν ἀπαύγασμα τῆς δόξης) and is the χαρακτὴρ τῆς ὑποστάσεως αὐτοῦ (1:3). The Sonship is such an imprinting of the divine nature that Hebrews expects his readers to understand he should be exempt from suffering. Just as God in the OT is not dependent upon creation but is the master and sustainer of it, so the Son does not need creation or being shaped by experiences with it. His filial identity is so close

---

22 It certainly cannot mean 'son of God' in any angelic sense.
23 David Peterson, *Hebrews and Perfection: An Examination of the Concept of Perfection in the "Epistle to the Hebrews"* (Cambridge University Press, 1982), 93.
24 Egon Brandenburger, "Text und Vorlagen von Hebr. V,7–10," *NovT* 11 (1969): 201, "In any case, with καίπερ ὢν υἱός, the eternal, pre-existent essence of the Son is expressed."
25 Cockerill, *Hebrews*, 247.
26 In fact, we should find solutions that deny or eschew Hebrews having any type of ontology as both unsatisfactory and contrary to Hebrews' own argumentation.

to the Father that the attributes described of the Father can and are described of the Son in Heb 1. Since the Sonship is such that he is not of the changing nature of creation (see the discussion of 1:10–12), the author expects this unchanging nature of the Son means that we would not expect him to suffer or learn obedience.

It is not suffering and exaltation that makes the Son a son. In fact, it is prior to his suffering obedience and his perfection that he is Son. It is prior to his being "begotten" as installed Messianic kingship that he is Son. The grammar could not be clearer: καίπερ ὢν υἱός, ἔμαθεν ἀφ' ὧν ἔπαθεν τὴν ὑπακοήν (5:8). We have already discussed the use of καίπερ but now we note the usage of the present tense and aorist. First, we have the present active participle ὤν. Here it indicates the continuing state, while the aorist ἔπαθεν indicates a past (probably punctiliar) action. The Son existed in a state of Sonship before, during, and after he learned obedience. Even while 'being Son,' he learned, through a specific set of events, obedience. But it was not the learning of obedience that establishes his Sonship. Out of this obedience he καὶ τελειωθεὶς ἐγένετο (5:9). We will examine this more fully below, but for now this 'becoming perfect' is not becoming a Son. For Hebrews, Sonship is something that the Son already was.

We return to the motif of the Son being and becoming (see our discussion in Heb 1).[27] Certainly, for Hebrews, it is within creation as the fulfillment of Ps 8 that he τοσούτῳ κρείττων γενόμενος τῶν ἀγγέλων (1:4a) and inherits the name and Messianic designate on sonship (1:4b κεκληρονόμηκεν ὄνομα). There is exaltation and ascension, the royal proclamation being fulfilled as he ascends to the Father: υἱός μου εἶ σύ, ἐγὼ σήμερον γεγέννηκά σε (1:5), but the ascension is both an installment and also a proclamation of being. YHWH has put his king on the heavenly Mt. Zion, fulfilling the Psalm and the hope of Israel. The pronouncement is just as much a revelation of the glory of God. The Father has spoken to the Son, but in revealing himself he has also spoken ἐν υἱῷ. The category of Sonship is something revealed in and through Adamic and Davidic conceptions. Just as Israel was the firstborn destined for inheritance and a rest, so the Son has entered into and received the heavenly inheritance as the trailblazer for God's people—a greater Moses with a greater ascent. Yet, this ontological Sonship revealed in eschatological climax reveals a Son who was superior to all these categories of sonship. The Ps 8 transition

---

27 While we arrived at our conclusions separately from each other, R.B. Jamieson has likewise articulated the sense in which the Son becomes Son in Hebrews (*The Paradox of Sonship* [Intervarsity, 2021], 100–121, esp. 100–102, 105–106, 120) Jamieson and I are in large agreement of the two categories of usage for Son in Hebrews. Jamieson has helpful pointed to similar articulations in Athanasius and Cyril of Alexandria (113–116).

from lower than angels to crowned with glory and honor happens through suffering and because of pious obedient trust, but it happens to Jesus even though he has already always been Son. He brings the OT sonship to a climax precisely because he is, according to Hebrews, an eternal Son whose Sonship transcends these categories. Sonship is revealed in the eschatological climax, but the Son revealed is one who shares the divine identity with all the character and glory of God Himself.[28] Put succinctly, sonship (the functional) reveals Sonship (the divine).

## HEB 5:1–4 THE QUALIFICATION OF WEAKNESS FOR PRIESTHOOD

Heb 5:1–4 concerns the solidarity that a priest must have with those whom he represents. At this point the author of Hebrews will draw parallels between the priesthood of the Old Covenant and the priesthood of the Son, despite his ultimate goal of showing the superiority of the latter's priesthood. His larger point is to show the humility of the Son and his solidarity with human weakness followed by his subsequent glorification and exaltation that we see in his ascension (cf. 4:14–15 with the same movement from 5:1–6).

First, the author of Hebrews identifies the high priest as one who must be drawn from among men. He writes, Πᾶς γὰρ ἀρχιερεὺς ἐξ ἀνθρώπων λαμβανόμενος ὑπὲρ ἀνθρώπων καθίσταται τὰ πρὸς τὸν θεόν, ἵνα προσφέρῃ δῶρά τε καὶ θυσίας ὑπὲρ ἁμαρτιῶν (5:1). The high priest comes from man (ἐξ ἀνθρώπων) for the express purpose of being chosen to stand and represent them on their behalf (λαμβανόμενος ὑπὲρ ἀνθρώπων). Λαμβάνω has the notion of being appointed or being chosen or selected.[29] This returns the reader to the early arguments concerning the humanity of the Son: Ἐπεὶ οὖν τὰ παιδία κεκοινώνηκεν αἵματος καὶ σαρκός, καὶ αὐτὸς παραπλησίως μετέσχεν τῶν αὐτῶν (2:14a) and ὅθεν ὤφειλεν κατὰ πάντα τοῖς ἀδελφοῖς ὁμοιωθῆναι (2:17).

Earthly high priests, being from among men, can sympathize with the weaknesses of those they represent precisely because they themselves have weaknesses. The earthly high priest knows how to respond to the ignorant and the wanderer (5:2 μετριοπαθεῖν δυνάμενος τοῖς ἀγνοοῦσιν καὶ πλανωμένοις). The reason for or cause of (ἐπεί)[30] this ability is because the high priest himself has weakness (καὶ αὐτὸς περίκειται ἀσθένειαν). To drive home the point

---

28 R.B. Jamieson reaches the same conclusion as we do regarding the Son's "surprising" discipline and the relationship of Heb 5:8 to divine sonship (*The Paradox of Sonship*, 66–68).

29 "λαμβάνω," BDAG, 584, "The emphasis is not on gender but the human status of the chief priest in contrast to that of the unique Messiah vs. 5."

30 The two main uses of ἐπεί are for markers of time 'when/after' or a conjunction marking cause or reason. Clearly the latter is the function here ("ἐπεί," BDAG, 360).

that the high priest shares in the weaknesses, καί is used to intensify; it means "also." Περίκειμαι means to be surrounded by or beset with.[31] It can be used for "wearing/bearing" especially chains (Acts 28:20; 4Macc 12:3) or "hung" (Mark 9:42). Sib. Or. 5:228 describes being clothed (ἄστατε καὶ κακόβουλε, κακὰς περικείμενε κῆρας). Heb 12:1 uses it to denote surrounded when describing the great witnesses to the faith that have preceeded us. Here, Hebrews uses it more figuratively—the high priest is beset with weakness. There is a similar use in 2 Clem. 1:6, describing the darkness and blindness of a Christian pre-conversion ὃ περικείμεθα νέφος. For Hebrews, the high priest bears the same weakness of those whom he represents.

The evidence of sins in the high priest is simply that the high priest must offer a sacrifice for his own sins as well as the people he represents (5:3 καὶ δι' αὐτὴν ὀφείλει, καθὼς περὶ τοῦ λαοῦ, οὕτως καὶ περὶ αὐτοῦ προσφέρειν περὶ ἁμαρτιῶν). He has his own sins that he is obligated (ὀφείλει) to take care of. Twice more Hebrews will repeat this reminder that the priest must offer a sacrifice for himself when he offers it for the people. It is part of the inferiority of the Old Covenant system and the Levitical order of the priesthood. In 7:27 ὃς οὐκ ἔχει καθ' ἡμέραν ἀνάγκην, ὥσπερ οἱ ἀρχιερεῖς, πρότερον ὑπὲρ τῶν ἰδίων ἁμαρτιῶν θυσίας ἀναφέρειν ἔπειτα τῶν τοῦ λαοῦ. This is part of the inferiority of the Law (or first Covenant): it appointed priests who were weak, specifically beset with their own sin (7:28 ὁ νόμος γὰρ ἀνθρώπους καθίστησιν ἀρχιερεῖς ἔχοντας ἀσθένειαν). Here Hebrews capitalizes on the theme of weakness to contrast the failures of the pre-eschatological with the "perfection" aspects of the eschatological priesthood of the order of Melchizedek. When the Old Covenant priests of Levi were appointed, they had full failures and sin upon them. They were weak, whereas the "word of oath" of the New Covenant installs a priest who has been perfected, sharing now in the crowning and glory of the eschaton. Similarly in 9:7, the priest on the Day of Atonement entering the Most Holy Place must enter with blood for his sins and the unintentional sins of the people (ὃ προσφέρει ὑπὲρ ἑαυτοῦ καὶ τῶν τοῦ λαοῦ ἀγνοημάτων). He knows how to deal with these sins of ignorance because he himself is a weak sinner.

We find Hebrews is again contrasting the Old and New Covenants with their corresponding priesthoods.[32] The difference is that in the Old Covenant the priests had sins and had to offer sacrifices for themselves first as well as for the people. It is clear for Hebrews that Jesus has no sin in his earthly

---

[31] "περίκειμαι," BDAG, 801.

[32] On this comparison between priesthoods see Georg Gäbel, *Die Kulttheologie des Hebräerbriefes: Eine exegetisch-religionsgeschichtliche Studie* (Mohr Siebeck, 2006), 174–179, especially the helpful chart on 174.

life. He is perfectly obedient, even a fulfiller of the Law. Jesus is ὅσιος ἄκακος ἀμίαντος, κεχωρισμένος ἀπὸ τῶν ἁμαρτωλῶν (7:26). He did not offer a sacrifice for himself—he had no need of it (7:27 ὅσιος ἄκακος ἀμίαντος, κεχωρισμένος ἀπὸ τῶν ἁμαρτωλῶν). The moral purity of Jesus references his earthly life, not his resurrected or exalted state. It is not as if Jesus transitions from moral culpability and sinfulness into a state of moral perfection. It is precisely the point that if this is who he was, then he would have been like the high priests of old offering some sacrifice for themselves as well as the people. The Son only needed to offer something for the sins of the people, which he did once for all time (ἐφάπαξ). The Son did not experience sin or moral failure. He has been, as Heb 4:15, puts it χωρὶς ἁμαρτίας.

Yet, the similarity of the two priesthoods is that both participated in weakness. For the Old Covenant priests this weakness included sin, but for the Son it excluded sin. Nevertheless, the Son in his incarnation participated in the human condition, sinful activity excepted. He experienced the weakness of the human condition, the non-eschatological state which could be subjected to death (Heb 2:9–10). His status for a time was that of the pre-eschatological state where humanity was lower than angels and not crowned with glory and honor (2:9). He experiences real and genuine human conditions of suffering. He was tempted in every way that human beings face temptation (4:15 οὐ γὰρ ἔχομεν ἀρχιερέα μὴ δυνάμενον συμπαθῆσαι ταῖς ἀσθενείαις ἡμῶν, πεπειρασμένον δὲ κατὰ πάντα καθ᾽ ὁμοιότητα). He sympathizes with the weaknesses of those he represents just like the Old Covenant high priests (5:2). He has experienced the full human estate of weakness—including vulnerability, suffering, crying for help to God, and death itself—yet through that entire experience without succumbing to sinfulness in that ongoing estate of weakness (4:15; 7:26). He was flesh and blood with its entire vulnerability to death: 2:14 Ἐπεὶ οὖν τὰ παιδία κεκοινώνηκεν αἵματος καὶ σαρκός, καὶ αὐτὸς παραπλησίως μετέσχεν τῶν αὐτῶν. We should probably see this reference to flesh and blood not just to humanity but specifically the non-eschatological state of humanity. So, for example, Paul writes, ὅτι σὰρξ καὶ αἷμα βασιλείαν θεοῦ κληρονομῆσαι οὐ δύναται οὐδὲ ἡ φθορὰ τὴν ἀφθαρσίαν κληρονομεῖ (1 Cor. 15:50). Of course, Judaism and early Christianity believed in a bodily resurrection,[33] as does Hebrews,[34] but

---

[33] N.T. Wright, *The Resurrection of the Son of God* (Fortress, 2003), 85–200. For the argument that resurrection is progressively developed in Judaism reaching back into the Hebrew Bible itself, see Jon D. Levenson, *Resurrection and the Restoration of Israel: The Ultimate Victory of the God of Life* (Yale University Press, 2006). Levenson also illustrates the importance of the resurrection for Rabbinic Judaism.

[34] Moffitt, *Atonement and the Logic of Resurrection in the Epistle to the Hebrews* (Brill, 2011); Easter, *Faith and Faithfulness of Jesus in Hebrews* (Cambridge University Press, 2014), 82–83, 94–99, 118–124.

'flesh and blood' seems to refer to the state of vulnerability, subject to death, perishability. Thus, Hebrews sees his participation in flesh and blood with a purpose: ἵνα διὰ τοῦ θανάτου καταργήσῃ τὸν τὸ κράτος ἔχοντα τοῦ θανάτου, τοῦτ' ἔστιν τὸν διάβολον (2:14b). Being 'flesh and blood' is not merely being human, for Hebrews sees Christ's exalted estate as still human being crowned with glory and honor. Being flesh and blood is the weakness state, the sub-eschatological man with vulnerability to death. 'Flesh and blood' seems to be the human quality of destructible life. It is the state of humanity without the inheritance.[35] He suffered when tempted and thus can help those who are suffering (2:18 οὐ γὰρ ἔχομεν ἀρχιερέα μὴ δυνάμενον συμπαθῆσαι ταῖς ἀσθενείαις ἡμῶν, πεπειρασμένον δὲ κατὰ πάντα καθ' ὁμοιότητα).

## Heb 5:7–8b Suffering and Obedience

Having examined Christ's Sonship in 5:8 and the context of 5:1–4 with the requirement for the priesthood, we can now turn to 5:7–8b to examine the nature and role of the obedience that the Son offers. Certainly, Hebrews has already indicated the role of suffering in the perfection of the Son. We have seen this in 2:10b; God's intent is to save 'sons of glory' by τὸν ἀρχηγὸν τῆς σωτηρίας αὐτῶν διὰ παθημάτων τελειῶσαι. This suffering in true humanity has established the solidarity between Christ and those he represents. Hebrews uses Isa 8:17–18 to describe Jesus as the one who puts his trust in God (2:13 ἐγὼ ἔσομαι πεποιθὼς ἐπ' αὐτῷ).[36] Not only does the Son suffer when tempted,

---

35 *Contra* Moffitt, *Atonement and Logic of Resurrection*, 141. A point of clarification here: we certainly agree with Moffitt that Jesus' ascension into heaven is bodily ascension in true resurrection humanity. We are seeking a bit more specification as to the nature of the body now crowned in glory that Christ has. It is exalted humanity, which is slightly different than the concept of 'flesh and blood' as used in Hebrews. We agree that it is true humanity with 'indestructible life' (life of the new creation) in a resurrected state in which Christ ascends. In that respect, we certainly agree with Moffitt. 'Fleshly' in 5:7 and 9:10, 13 refers to something non/sub-eschatological. 10:20 may be the exception, if it is referring to ascending bodily. However, it may be focusing on the aspect of the sacrifice preparing the way. Because of the references to sacrifice, blood is more common in Hebrews (9:7, 12, 13, 14, 18, 19, 20, 21, 22, 25; 10:4, 19, 29; 11:28; 12:4, 24; 13:11, 12, 20). Nowhere does it unambiguously describe something in the eschatological state. The most common association is the sprinkling of blood association. In 12:4 it is clearly representative of death. Although 13:11–12 would be the strongest argument for blood being brought into the tabernacle as parallel to Christ's bodily (with blood) ascent. However, διὰ τοῦ ἰδίου αἵματος is most likely a description of means rather than a direct indicator that τοῦ ἰδίου αἵματος should be equated with his glorified body. In other words, it is likely more metaphorical as a reference to Christ's ascent: he shed his blood and because of it, (he ascends glorified into heaven to sanctify the people) rather than constitutive: it is through a body with blood that he ascends. Again, the ascent is bodily and in true humanity, we just do not think that this is how Hebrews is using 'flesh and blood.'

36 See the previous discussion.

but the Son offers perfect trust upon the Father, which brings him to exaltation and singing God's praises in the assembly of the righteous (Heb 2:12//Ps 22:22).

It is with this background in mind that we look at the suffering and cries of Jesus. Hebrews states ὃς ἐν ταῖς ἡμέραις τῆς σαρκὸς αὐτοῦ δεήσεις τε καὶ ἱκετηρίας πρὸς τὸν δυνάμενον σῴζειν αὐτὸν ἐκ θανάτου μετὰ κραυγῆς ἰσχυρᾶς καὶ δακρύων προσενέγκας καὶ εἰσακουσθεὶς ἀπὸ τῆς εὐλαβείας (5:7). In the days of his flesh,[37] describes the incarnation of the Son in his partaking of flesh and blood (2:14, 17a; 10:5a). It stands in contrast to the eschatological state of glorified perfection (Heb 2:6–9; 5:9). Flesh is the state of frailty and weakness which can be subject to death.[38]

First, this crying out to God echoes the language of the gospel describing both Jesus' experience in the garden of Gethsemane and on the cross.[39] For example, alluding to Ps 42:5–6, Jesus describes his soul as sorrowful unto death (Matt 26:38//Mk 14:34 περίλυπός ἐστιν ἡ ψυχή μου ἕως θανάτου), which suggests that the type of praying Jesus is going to do is crying out to the Lord in a manner after the Psalmist and the death-like experiences recounted in the Psalms. While there are not verbal parallels to Heb 5:7 here, Jesus is portrayed as praying with great sorrow, most likely with tears (given Ps 42:3 [LXX 41:4] ἐγενήθη μοι τὰ δάκρυά μου ἄρτος ἡμέρας καὶ νυκτός). His praying is a commitment to the Lord and a desire to do the will of the Lord even unto death (Matt 26:39, 42; Mark 14:36; Luke 22:42). Mark 14:36 even emphasizes the Father-Son relationship of the prayers: ἀββα ὁ πατήρ (cf. Sir 51:10 discussed below). Luke further emphasizes the human agony that Jesus experiences in these prayers: καὶ γενόμενος ἐν ἀγωνίᾳ ἐκτενέστερον προσηύχετο· καὶ ἐγένετο ὁ ἱδρὼς αὐτοῦ ὡσεὶ θρόμβοι αἵματος καταβαίνοντες ἐπὶ τὴν γῆν.[40] For our author, the prayers with cries and tears probably point not only to Gethsemane but experience of Jesus on the cross.[41] Richardson argues "the resemblance between κράζω (Matt 27.50) and κραυγή (Heb 5.7) is clear, while the terminology of ἀωαβοάω, βοάω,

---

37 Pss. Sol. 16:14–15 "When a person is tried by his mortality, your testing is in his flesh, and in difficulty of poverty. If the righteous endures all these things, he will receive mercy from the Lord." This sees the testing of the Lord as that which occurs in the flesh and the righteous endure and receive mercy.

38 Attridge, *Hebrews*, 149; Ellingworth, *The Epistle to the Hebrews* (Eerdmans, 1993), 287; Schreiner, *Hebrews*, 162.

39 Cockerill, *Hebrews*, 244; Hughes, *Hebrews* 182; Schreiner, *Hebrews*, 162–163.

40 Admittedly this verse is a textual variant, but there is a high degree of certainty that it is likely original to Luke both on internal evidence and external evidence.

41 Schreiner, *Hebrews*, 162–163; Cockerill, *Hebrews*, 244; Philip E. Hughes, *A Commentary on the Epistle to the Hebrews* (Eerdmans, 1977), 183. Bruce (*The Epistle to the Hebrews* [Eerdmans, 1990], 128) suggests not only Gethsemane but "the whole course of our Lord's humiliation and passion."

φωνέω, and φωνή μεγάλη provides supplementary evidence."[42]

Cockerill is correct though to see at some level the scope of Jesus' humanity in view even though it clearly culminates in Gethsemane and Golgotha. His entire earthly life was "characterized" by "the utter depend[ance] upon God."[43] Jesus Christ is the apex of the weakness of humanity crying out in humble dependence being the obedient Davidic-Adamic-son *par excellence*. Thus, he is granted the glory and honor of the eschatological humanity and called to ascend to the throne. Morales makes the connection to the obedience of Jesus, the Levitical ascension offering, and Adam's failure:

> This night of distress [in Gethsemane] and profound struggle opens a window into the innermost dynamic and spiritual reality symbolized and solicited by the ascension offering. As the quintessential offering—indeed, the altar's namesake—the ascension offering represented utter consecration to God, total self-surrender. Such a life is the life that must ascend as a pleasing aroma to the heavenly abode of God. Jesus' tormented night of prayer in the garden of Gethsemane, therefore, is not only the counter to Adam's self-willed failure in Eden's garden, but it stands for Jesus' fulfillment of the Levitical cultus.[44]

Second, this crying out to God for deliverance from death has a rich OT background.[45] Michael Easter has argued, "Cries or tears in the LXX are often used in prayers for deliverance in times of crises (as in Exod 3:7, 9; 2 Sam 22:7; 2 Kgs 20:5; Neh 9:9; Ps 18:6; Isa 30:19; 38:5; Jonah 2:2; 2 Macc 11:6; 3 Macc 1:16; 5:7; 5:25)."[46] Crying for deliverance from death is a particularly dominant motif in the Psalms.[47] William Lane writes, "In v 7 Jesus' passion is described

---

42 Richardson, *Pioneer and Perfecter of the Faith* (Mohr Siebeck, 2012), 77; see 76–77 for various charts on the similarities; see also 76n.246 for all the commentaries that link Heb 5:7 to Gethsemane and Golgotha.

43 Cockerill, *Hebrews*, 244; also qtd. in Schriener, *Hebrews*, 163.

44 L. Michael Morales, *Who Shall Ascend the Mountain of the Lord? A Biblical Theology of the Book of Leviticus* (Intervarsity, 2015), 269. Earlier he noted "At the heart and literary centre of the Pentateuch, as we have already seen, Adam's failure finds cultic fulfillment on the Day of Atonement, as the high priest ascents into the architectural garden of Eden with the blood atonement" (182). He goes on to link it to the mountain summit. We might then add it is the failure of both Adam *and* the Levitical cult (i.e., the Law covenant) the necessitates the work of the Son ascending into heaven. He is both the true Adam and the one ascending onto the true Mt. Zion, namely heaven itself, because his work brings the transition of the ages.

45 Attridge (*Hebrews*, 148–149) also points to the background on the Psalm and Hellenistic Jewish sources: "The language of the verse does, however, correspond quite closely to a traditional Jewish ideal of a righteous person's prayer, an ideal based on language in the Psalms and developed explicitly in Hellenistic Jewish sources."

46 Easter, *Faith and the Faithfulness*, 162; cf. also 121–122.

47 This would include deliverance from 'the deep,' Sheol, and 'the pit.'

in its entirety as priestly prayer, taking advantage of the expression of those psalms that were interpreted within the Christian communities in light of Jesus' passion."[48] It is the Davidic son now fulfilled who prays these prayers. His crying out connects to a theme in the Psalms themselves. In other words, we are not seeking to find one or two Psalms that Hebrews has in view, but a motif in numerous Davidic Psalms themselves. The Davidic king, as representative of true humanity, is portrayed in the Psalms as the righteous one who cries out to the God. He experiences great humiliating trials and is raised up out of them by God precisely because God hears the prayers of his adopted son-king. All he can do in his humiliating trials is trust God, exercise fidelity, and wait for God's deliverance. It is our contention then that Jesus' cries and supplications during his earthly life fulfill a perfect obedience in the pattern of Adamic-Davidic sonship.

Similarly, David Schrock puts it: "Facing death, he [Jesus] cried out for salvation, and like David in the Psalms, and because of his greater covenantal obedience under the old law, he was heard and raised from the dead."[49] Hebrews, however, does not put the emphasis on "obedience under the old law," but on trust, reverence, and piety. There is the covenantal filial relationship God-Israel and God-David (both a sonship) that entails trust and reliance—the true vocation of humanity. In fact, this obedience seems to stand in somewhat of a distinction from 'the old law' with respect to the requirement of sacrifice (10:5). Hebrews focus seems to be on Jesus fulfilling aspects that precede the Law and even supersede the Old Covenant Law, although certainly Jesus is not portrayed as a lawbreaker.

The perfect obedience and dependence of the Son fulfills the sonship role of true humanity in order to achieve the eschatological perfection. God is able to exalt and perfect the Son as the Davidic-Adamic king, representative of the true eschatological humanity, precisely because when suffering he offered full human obedience. John Walters summarizes it thus:

> Whatever else it might involve for Christ's perfecting, certainly this passage itemizes the following ingredients: δέησις, ἱκετηρία, εὐλάβεια, ὑπακοή, μάθησις, and πάθος; prayer, entreaty, devotion, obedience, (the process of) education, and experience (enduring or suffering). None of these ingredi-

---

48 Lane, *Hebrews 1–8*, WBC 47a (Word, 1991), 120. Jared Compton (*Psalm 110 and the Logic of Hebrews* [T&T Clark, 2015], 72) also believes that the loud cries and tears here are "probably recalling, once more (2.12), the lament tradition in the Psalter, perhaps Ps 21 LXX in particular" in conjunction with (a) the Jewish martyr tradition from 2 Macc and 3 Macc; and (b) the Jesus tradition, especially his Gethsemane prayer.

49 David Schrock, "Resurrection and Priesthood: Christological Soundings from the Book of Hebrews," *Southern Baptist Journal of Theology* 18 (2014): 99.

ents is specifically reserved for Christ alone as übermensch; they are part and parcel to what is expected of humanity by God.[50]

In line with how Hebrews views the OT Scriptures, the author of Hebrews views Jesus as the eschatological fulfillment bringing to climax the Davidic kings' trust in the Father that leads to his vindication/enthronement. Consider again the use of LXX Ps 44:7–8 in Heb 1:8–9, especially 1:9 where the anointing, which we take as the installation of the Son, is conditioned on his righteous behavior: ἠγάπησας δικαιοσύνην καὶ ἐμίσησας ἀνομίαν· διὰ τοῦτο ἔχρισέν σε ὁ θεὸς ὁ θεός σου ἔλαιον ἀγαλλιάσεως παρὰ τοὺς μετόχους σου (1:9). The reason the Son is worthy to be the exalted royal Davidic king-messiah is precisely because (διὰ τοῦτο) his character, and earthly obedience to God that loved righteousness and hated lawlessness. He is righteous and godly and therefore God raises him up in ascension. In this motif, being the true Davidic king is also fulfilling the Adamic destiny. "Until Christ had successfully stayed the course through every trial, he could not fulfill God's plan for humanity as outlined in Psalm 8."[51] Being the true Davidic-Adamic figure who exercises obedient trust through trials qualifies the eternal Son to fulfill humanity's destiny and ascend into heaven. To establish this, we will examine the role of God and his son's crying out to him.

Jesus is described as offering prayers and supplications μετὰ κραυγῆς ἰσχυρᾶς. It is perhaps significant that LXX uses κραυγή to describe Israel's cries to the Lord in her affliction prior to her deliverance from Egypt. Israel's slavery leads to her cries for deliverance as much as Jesus, the fulfiller to the Exodus-to-Rest/Inheritance paradigm, cries out for deliverance from death—in order to ultimately save those enslaved to sin and death (2:15 ἀπαλλάξῃ τούτους, ὅσοι φόβῳ θανάτου διὰ παντὸς τοῦ ζῆν ἔνοχοι ἦσαν δουλείας). Consider the following uses of κραυγή in LXX Exodus: τῆς κραυγῆς αὐτῶν ἀκήκοα (3:7); καὶ νῦν ἰδοὺ κραυγὴ τῶν υἱῶν Ισραηλ ἥκει πρός με (3:9).

The sons of Israel cry out in their affliction. The Lord their God hears them because of the father-son covenant relationship between him and his people. For God's people to be redeemed from slavery and to be taken to their inheritance, they first cry out to the Lord in great affliction. God helps the sons of Abraham (cf. Heb 2:16). But the Son is greater than Moses (3:1–6), even though he himself offers up the human-sonship cries of affliction.

As King, David cries out to the Lord who hears his prayers for deliverance in 2 Sam 22:7//LXX Ps 17:7.

---

50 John Walters, *Perfection in New Testament Theology: Ethics and Eschatology in Relational Dynamics* (Mellen Biblical, 1995), 110.

51 Ibid., 111.

## The Son's Adamic Obedience Leads to Ascension

2 Sam 22:7//LXX Ps 17:7
καὶ ἐν τῷ θλίβεσθαί με ἐπεκαλεσάμην τὸν κύριον καὶ πρὸς τὸν θεόν μου ἐκέκραξα· ἤκουσεν ἐκ ναοῦ ἁγίου αὐτοῦ φωνῆς μου, καὶ ἡ κραυγή μου ἐνώπιον αὐτοῦ εἰσελεύσεται εἰς τὰ ὦτα αὐτοῦ.
When I am afflicted I will call upon the Lord, and to my God I will shout, and from his shrine he shall heed my voice, and my cry shall be in his ears. (NETS)

Two things should be noted from the context of 2 Sam 22//LXX Ps 17 [Ps 18 in MT and Eng.][52] First, David undergoes a death-like ordeal. In 17:3, the Lord is the deliverer, refuge, and rescuer. The one who saves the king-son is YHWH. David will call upon Him and he will be saved by Him. Being saved from his enemies (17:4) is the equivalent of being lifted out of death:

LXX Ps 17:4–6
αἰνῶν ἐπικαλέσομαι κύριον καὶ ἐκ τῶν ἐχθρῶν μου σωθήσομαι.
περιέσχον με ὠδῖνες θανάτου, καὶ χείμαρροι ἀνομίας ἐξετάραξάν με
ὠδῖνες ᾅδου περιεκύκλωσάν με, προέφθασάν με παγίδες θανάτου.
When I praise, I will call upon the Lord, and from my enemies I shall be saved. Pangs of death encompassed me, and wadis of lawlessness alarmed me; pangs of Hades encircled me; snares of death outran me. (NETS)

The Psalm contains a general movement from crying out under oppression in humiliation to being delivered and exalted. This brings us to the second point we should note. David is heard in the Psalm because of his righteousness. While the exact phraseology of εἰσακουσθεὶς ἀπὸ τῆς εὐλαβείας (Heb 5:7) is not found, the same concept is contained in the Psalm. The king has obeyed God in piety. The king has exhibited trust in the Lord for deliverance and the Lord did not fail him. The Lord hears (17:7) because of the character of the king. The Lord's deliverance of the king is because of the king's righteousness and blamelessness before the Lord:

LXX Ps 17
21 καὶ ἀνταποδώσει μοι κύριος κατὰ τὴν δικαιοσύνην μου καὶ κατὰ τὴν καθαριότητα τῶν χειρῶν μου ἀνταποδώσει μοι,
22 ὅτι ἐφύλαξα τὰς ὁδοὺς κυρίου καὶ οὐκ ἠσέβησα ἀπὸ τοῦ θεοῦ μου,
25 καὶ ἀνταποδώσει μοι κύριος κατὰ τὴν δικαιοσύνην μου καὶ κατὰ τὴν καθαριότητα τῶν χειρῶν μου ἐνώπιον τῶν ὀφθαλμῶν αὐτοῦ.

---

[52] All references will be to LXX in the following discussion of this psalm.

> 21 And the Lord will reward me according to my righteousness, and according to the cleanness of my hands he will give back to me,
> 22 because I kept the ways of the Lord and did not impiously depart from my God,
> 25 And the Lord will reward me according to my righteousness and according to the cleanness of my hands before his eyes. (NETS)

This pattern or theme is repeated in a number of the early Davidic Psalms.[53] David is the ideal figure of one who trusts in the Lord and cries out to him for deliverance. He is heard because of his character, his righteousness, or his behavior in keeping the Law of God. He is the true obedient son, who learns obedience by displaying absolute trust by crying out during some sort of suffering ordeal. This pattern, for Hebrews, reaches its eschatological fulfillment in the earthly life of Christ who is the true human, the ultimate Adamic-Davidic 'son' who succeeds where humanity has failed. Because of his obedience, transgressions are borne for God's people and the New Covenant is inaugurated. This eschatological transition from Old to New hinges on the human-sonship obedience which qualifies Jesus for his glorification and ascension. This is the fulfillment of the Davidic psalms where David finds deliverance. The pattern reaches eschatological fulfillment in Christ's glorification/ascension.

In our argument, we will first examine more direct verbal parallels where the same terminology used in Heb 5:7 is described of Davidic prayers. Secondly, we will look at other Psalms where there is not the same verbiage but thematic parallels remain. Our argument is not that Hebrews has in mind a specific Psalm but rather that it is a motif that we find in the Psalms. The Lord hears the Davidic king because of his righteousness/godliness. With the eschatology of Hebrews, he sees this paradigm reaching eschatological climax in the true and final heir of David just as Pss 2, 8, 17[18], 21[22], 39[40], and 109[110] all find their climax-fulfillment in Jesus the true and greater Son.

Consider how Heb 2 has used LXX Ps 21 [Eng./MT Ps 22].[54] We know from the gospels' accounts that Ps 22 was seen as the paradigm for Jesus' suffering

---

53 By 'early' we simply mean in the order they are compiled in the book of Psalms. Shirley Lucass (*The Concept of the Messiah in the Scriptures of Judaism and Christianity* [Bloomsbury T&T Clark, 2011], 78–79) makes note of this in the kingship Psalms. She documents this extensively (78–79nn.76–94). It is beyond the scope of our argument to explore the *chaoskampf* theme. See also Mowinckel, *The Psalms in Israel's Worship*, trans. D.R. Ap-Thomas (Eerdmans, 2004), 42–80; he discusses the corporate representation in the 'Royal Psalms.'

54 As we look at the various Psalms below, it is beyond the scope of our argument to compare LXX with MT.

on the cross. As we noted above, Hebrews seems at least partially aware of either the gospels or perhaps early oral accounts of Christ's suffering.[55] Richardson, however, has correctly noted, "Rather than being dependent upon a single source, the author seems immersed in multiple sources that center on the themes of suffering and pious devotion to God."[56]

Consider how Heb 2:12 quotes LXX Ps 21.[57] One of the main purposes that this Psalm seeks to illustrate is that when David cried to the Lord, the Lord heard: Ps 21:25b καὶ ἐν τῷ κεκραγέναι με πρὸς αὐτὸν εἰσήκουσέν μου.[58] This is exactly what we see in Heb 5:7 δεήσεις τε καὶ ἱκετηρίας...μετὰ κραυγῆς ἰσχυρᾶς καὶ δακρύων προσενέγκας καὶ εἰσακουσθείς. David is commended in the great assembly παρὰ σοῦ ὁ ἔπαινός μου ἐν ἐκκλησίᾳ μεγάλῃ (LXX Ps 21:26) which may be echoed, at least thematically, in Heb 12:22–23 where God's people have come, at least spiritually, to the heavenly Mt. Zion precisely because Jesus Christ has bodily ascended into heaven, the great assembly, now called ἐκκλησίᾳ πρωτοτόκων ἀπογεγραμμένων ἐν οὐρανοῖς (Heb 12:23). Easter has concluded, "Heb 5:7–9 offers another clear connection in Hebrews between Jesus' faithfulness amid suffering and his resurrection."[59]

LXX Ps 21 is linked with Isa 8:17–18:

καὶ ἐρεῖ Μενῶ τὸν θεὸν τὸν ἀποστρέψαντα τὸ πρόσωπον αὐτοῦ ἀπὸ τοῦ οἴκου Ιακωβ καὶ πεποιθὼς ἔσομαι ἐπ᾽ αὐτῷ.
ἰδοὺ ἐγὼ καὶ τὰ παιδία, ἅ μοι ἔδωκεν ὁ θεός, καὶ ἔσται εἰς σημεῖα καὶ τέρατα ἐν τῷ οἴκῳ Ισραηλ παρὰ κυρίου σαβαωθ, ὃς κατοικεῖ ἐν τῷ ὄρει Σιων.
And one shall say, "I will wait for God, who has turned away his face from the house of Iakob, and I will trust in him.
Here am I and the children whom God has given me, and they shall become signs and portents in Israel from the Lord Sabaoth, who dwells on Mount Sion." (NETS)

It is Jesus who is the Messianic son displaying trust in the LORD who dwells

---

55 Patrick Gray, *Godly Fear: The Epistle to the Hebrews and Greco-Roman Critiques of Superstition* (Society of Biblical Literature, 2003), 196.
56 Christopher Richardson, *Pioneer and Perfecter*, 82.
57 Patrick Gray (*Godly Fear*, 197) also sees Pss 22 and 116 [LXX 21 and 114–115] as possible backgrounds to Heb 5:7. He writes "Nothing from either psalm appears in direct, unmistakable quotation in Hebrews. If the question is framed in terms of demonstrable familiarity or likely influence, the scales tip towards Ps 22. Not only does Hebrews quote this psalm (in 2:12); it is moreover the primary text read by the early church as a description of Jesus' passion" (198). Swetnam ( "The Crux of Hebrews 5,7–8," *Bib* 81 [2000]: 354) finds Ps 22 as a background more plausible than the agony of Gethsemane.
58 See also Bruce, *Hebrews*, 128; Easter, *Faith and the Faithfulness of Jesus*, 163.
59 Easter, *Faith and the Faithfulness of Jesus*, 163.

on Zion. This Son is then exalted up into the presence of God in Zion, the true temple where God dwells. The Son sets himself forward in true humanity on behalf of the future 'sons of glory' and becomes the forerunner into heaven precisely because of an unfailing human obedience-trust that fulfills the appointed role of humanity and warrants the eschatological perfection destined for humanity.

First, David in the Psalms is described as offering petitions (δέησις) to the Lord. Below, we will examine some of the Psalms and the context for David's petitions. He stands as righteous and obedient in contrast to the ungodly who forget the ways of the Lord. Thus, in dependence, he cries out to the Lord needing deliverance from death-like experiences. For example, in Ps 5:2–3, we have David crying out in petition to the Lord:

Ps 5:2–3
Τὰ ῥήματά μου ἐνώτισαι, κύριε, σύνες τῆς κραυγῆς μου·
πρόσχες τῇ φωνῇ τῆς δεήσεώς μου, ὁ βασιλεύς μου καὶ ὁ θεός μου. ὅτι πρὸς σὲ προσεύξομαι, κύριε·
To my words give ear, O Lord; take note of my cry.
Pay attention to the voice of my petition, my King and my God, because to you I will pray (NETS)

He appeals to the Lord for help against wicked enemies who are full of ungodliness (5:11 κατὰ τὸ πλῆθος τῶν ἀσεβειῶν αὐτῶν) because the Lord blesses the righteous (5:13). David anticipates entering the house of the Lord (Ps 5:8a ἐγὼ δὲ ἐν τῷ πλήθει τοῦ ἐλέους σου εἰσελεύσομαι εἰς τὸν οἶκόν σου).

In Ps 6, David cries out to the Lord's mercy with tears and anguish (6:7–9). Then in 6:10 we read, εἰσήκουσεν κύριος τῆς δεήσεώς μου, κύριος τὴν προσευχήν μου προσεδέξατο. David has great weakness and needs the Lord's mercy (LXX 6:3a ἐλέησόν με, κύριε, ὅτι ἀσθενής εἰμι). David needs deliverance since no one in death remembers or worships the Lord (LXX 6:6 ὅτι οὐκ ἔστιν ἐν τῷ θανάτῳ ὁ μνημονεύων σου· ἐν δὲ τῷ ᾅδῃ τίς ἐξομολογήσεταί σοι;).

Similarly in Ps 16, we have David crying to the Lord with petition. Appealing on account of his own righteous behavior, David asks for close attention because he has no deceit (16:1 Εἰσάκουσον, κύριε, τῆς δικαιοσύνης μου, πρόσχες τῇ δεήσει μου, ἐνώτισαι τῆς προσευχῆς μου οὐκ ἐν χείλεσιν δολίοις). David has no injustice in him and thus the Lord should hear him (LXX Ps 16:3–4). He appeals: ἐγὼ ἐκέκραξα, ὅτι ἐπήκουσάς μου, ὁ θεός· κλῖνον τὸ οὖς σου ἐμοὶ καὶ εἰσάκουσον τῶν ῥημάτων μου (16:6). Again in this Psalm, David's enemies are ungodly while he himself is righteous.

In LXX Ps 27, David cries to the Lord (Ps 27:1). Again, he makes petition to the Lord and is heard because he is righteous while his enemies are not.

LXX Ps 27
2 εἰσάκουσον τῆς φωνῆς τῆς δεήσεώς μου ἐν τῷ δέεσθαί με πρὸς σέ, ἐν τῷ με αἴρειν χεῖράς μου πρὸς ναὸν ἅγιόν σου.
6 εὐλογητὸς κύριος, ὅτι εἰσήκουσεν τῆς φωνῆς τῆς δεήσεώς μου.
2 Listen to the voice of my petition, as I petition you, as I lift up my hands toward your holy shrine.
6 Blessed be the Lord, because he listened to the voice of my petition.
(NETS)

The Lord revives the flesh of David (Ps 27:7) and delivers his anointed one (27:8b καὶ ὑπερασπιστὴς τῶν σωτηρίων τοῦ χριστοῦ αὐτοῦ ἐστιν). Even more with the themes we find in Hebrews, in this Psalm the deliverance of David is the deliverance and empowerment of God's people (27:8a). David appeals that the people of God will be lifted up forever just as he was (27:9).

In LXX Ps 30 [MT 31], David finds himself in dire need with the Lord being the only one who can deliver him. He was afflicted (v. 10), his eyes and soul troubled (10), his life failed in pain (11), his strength weak in impoverishment (11b ἠσθένησεν ἐν πτωχείᾳ ἡ ἰσχύς μου), his is like a dead person (13a ἠσθένησεν ἐν πτωχείᾳ ἡ ἰσχύς μου). In this utter despair, David cries out to the Lord against the ungodly, and his petition is heard. Ps 30:23 ἐγὼ δὲ εἶπα ἐν τῇ ἐκστάσει μου Ἀπέρριμμαι ἄρα ἀπὸ προσώπου τῶν ὀφθαλμῶν σου. διὰ τοῦτο εἰσήκουσας τῆς φωνῆς τῆς δεήσεώς μου ἐν τῷ κεκραγέναι με πρὸς σέ.

Another Psalm we might consider is LXX Ps 114 [MT 116:1–9].[60] In this Psalm, there is no opening identification of David being the author, but we see the same sort of crying out to the Lord during a death-like ordeal. "In his days" the author cries out to the Lord who will listen and hear his petition:

LXX Ps 114:1–4
Ἀλληλουια. Ἠγάπησα, ὅτι εἰσακούσεται κύριος τῆς φωνῆς τῆς δεήσεώς μου,
ὅτι ἔκλινεν τὸ οὖς αὐτοῦ ἐμοί, καὶ ἐν ταῖς ἡμέραις μου ἐπικαλέσομαι.
περιέσχον με ὠδῖνες θανάτου, κίνδυνοι ᾅδου εὕροσάν με· θλῖψιν καὶ ὀδύνην εὗρον.

---

60 August Strobel, "Die Psalmengrundlage der Gethsemane-Prallele Hebr 5:7ff.," ZNW 45 (1954): 255–257. "Es läßt sich nicht leugen, daß die bestehenden Gemeneinsamkeiten zwischen Ps 114/115 und der zentralen Hbr-Aussage überraschend sind und zwar nich nur der Gedankenfuhrung nach, sodern auch im Wortbestand ... daß es unumstößlich klar ist, daß der fragliche Hbr-Text zur Sprache der Psalmen in einemem unmittelbaren Verhältnis steht" (256).

καὶ τὸ ὄνομα κυρίου ἐπεκαλεσάμην Ὦ κύριε, ῥῦσαι τὴν ψυχήν μου.
Hallelouia. I loved, because the Lord will listen to the voice of my petition, because he inclined his ear to me, and in my days I will call.
Pangs of death encompassed me; hazards of Hades found me; affliction and grief I found.
And on the name of the Lord I called: "Ah Lord, rescue my soul!" (NETS)

The Psalmist is delivered from death in order to enter the rest of the Lord:

LXX Ps 114:6–8
φυλάσσων τὰ νήπια ὁ κύριος· ἐταπεινώθην, καὶ ἔσωσέν με.
ἐπίστρεψον, ἡ ψυχή μου, εἰς τὴν ἀνάπαυσίν σου, ὅτι κύριος εὐηργέτησέν σε,
ὅτι ἐξείλατο τὴν ψυχήν μου ἐκ θανάτου, τοὺς ὀφθαλμούς μου ἀπὸ δακρύων καὶ τοὺς πόδας μου ἀπὸ ὀλισθήματος.
The Lord is one who protects infants; I was brought low, and he saved me.
Return, O my soul, to your rest, because the Lord acted as your benefactor, because he delivered my soul from death, my eyes from tears, my feet from slipping. (NETS)

The Psalmist enters rest for his soul (114:7 εἰς τὴν ἀνάπαυσίν σου) in the country of the living where he is pleasing before the Lord (114:9 εὐαρεστήσω ἐναντίον κυρίου ἐν χώρᾳ ζώντων). Again, we find in the Psalms this motif of the Lord hearing the cries of the sufferer who calls out to him in a state of lowly humiliation.[61] The petition is heard and there is deliverance from death.

There are other Psalms in LXX where David or another Psalmist offers petitions to the Lord (33:16; 38:13; 39:2;[62] 54:2; 60:2; 65:19; 85:6; 87:3; 101:1, 18; 105:44; 114:1; 118:169; 129:2; 139:7; 140:1; 141:3, 7; 142:1; 144:19). Sometimes the themes we have highlighted form similar backgrounds, other times less so. Despite differences, the consistent pattern is the Lord lifts the life/soul of the godly ones. He hears their petitions, and part of their godliness is that when they are ground down in lowliness of suffering, they demonstrate absolute dependence upon God. They put their hope in him, they trust him, they rely on him, and he does not abandon them. The Lord values their life and raises them up.

---

61 In MT, Ps 116 corresponds to both LXX 114 and 115. Perhaps one should consider LXX Ps 115:4, 6 [MT 116:13, 15] as related to these themes. It is, however, beyond the scope of our argument to explore text critical issues and even differences between LXX and MT. Our focus remains on the broad overarching theme of a cry to the Lord in a death-like ordeal and deliverance because the Lord hears.

62 We will discuss this below since Heb 10:5–9 quotes LXX Ps 39 [MT/Eng. Ps 40].

We should stress that the possible background for Hebrews goes beyond merely looking for a few verbal parallels. Taking other selected Psalms (esp. 1–2; 18–21; and 118–119), Jamie Grant has further explored in the Psalms how the Davidic King is the model and prime exemplar of both dependence on YHWH and obedience to YHWH in the form of piety to the Torah.[63] It is an outworking of the Deuteronomic theology of kingship.[64] Similarly, pointing to the links between Pss 1 and 2, Mettinger argues the king at his coronation pledges to fulfill the Law, and the king's sonship is "a motivation for the king's commitment to the Law."[65] The king must rely solely on YHWH, and like the true Israelite he must obey.[66] It is outside the scope of our thesis to interact with Grant's entire thesis; nevertheless, it shows that these motifs we are identifying in Hebrews as important for human-Adam and Davidic sonship-kingship are woven into the very fabric of the Psalter. In part then, this reflects the relationship between YHWH and his king. God acts as a Father and the king as 'son' "enjoys divine protection and help,"[67] which these Psalms put on display as the Davidic figure cries out for help and deliverance. James L. Mays brings out this connection between David and the Psalter as a whole, not just between David and individual Psalms:

> [T]he Davidic connection directs the reader to think of each psalm and the entire Psalter as an expression of faith in the reign of the LORD as the sphere in which individual and corporate life is lived. It does so because it is quite impossible to separate David from his identity as king chosen to be the regent and agent on earth of God's reign over God's people and the nations of the world.[68]

---

[63] Jamie A. Grant, *The King as Exemplar: The Function of Deuteronomy's Kingship Law in the Shaping of the Book of Psalms* (Society of Biblical Literature, 2004). Other scholars have noted the linkage between Pss 1 and 2, for example see Robert Cole, "An Integrated Reading of Psalm 1 and 2," *JSOT* 98 (2002): 75–88. Jerome Creach ("Like a Tree Planted by the Temple Stream: The Portrait of the Righteous in Psalm 1:3," *CBQ* 61 [1999]: 34–46) has argued that the language of Ps 1:3 is temple, Zion, and Garden of Eden language. He connects the Psalm to post-exilic times and an early move for Torah replacing the temple. However, if the roots of Ps 1 are deeper in an earlier tradition, there could be further linking of Zion, kingship, Eden, and Adamic figures with righteous obedience. Cole ("Integrated Reading," 87) shows some connection between root words in 1:3b and 2:8, 10.

[64] Grant, *The King as Exemplar*, 65–69.

[65] Tryggve Mettinger, *King and Messiah: The Civil and Sacral Legitimation of the Israelite King* (Gleerup, 1976), 290.

[66] Grant does not draw this out, but this kingship obedience goes back to Adam of which Israel is established to echo/repeat/fulfill. See Seth D. Postell, *Adam as Israel: Genesis 1–3 as the Introduction to the Torah and Tanakh* (Pickwick, 2011), esp. 114–118.

[67] Mettinger, *King and Messiah*, 291.

[68] James Mays, *The Lord Reigns: A Theological Handbook to the Psalms* (Westminster John Knox, 1994), 98.

A note of caution at this point is warranted. We should be careful between too readily assuming that something recent OT scholarship has brought to our attention is necessarily something that the author of Hebrews understood. By comparison, the ancient writers did not have all the technical skills and historical critical tools available to modern scholars in their study of the text. First, however, ancient authors were familiar with the concept of corporate representation, solidaric identities, and the piety of kingship in obedience to the gods.[69] This is true throughout the ANE and Greco-Roman culture.[70] Second, the NT authors, following similar hermeneutical principles in their day, understand the Scriptures as having an eschatological end.[71] It is unsurprising that the author of Hebrews would see that Christ fulfills a regular motif in the OT.

The cry of the righteous sufferer is a sustained motif, not merely a verbal allusion or two. In the Psalms, often a Davidic kingly figure, and now thereby the Messiah, cries out to the Lord for deliverance so that he may be raised in triumph over enemies. Shirley Lucass documents numerous examples of the king going through some ritual trial leading to death or being encompasses by the waters, the deep, Sheol, the pit, or enemies. In the ordeal, the king cries out to YHWH who then delivers him because of his righteousness.[72] The king is delivered from the waters, the pit, enemies, death, Sheol, etc. Lucass

---

69 Joshua Jipp (*Christ is King: Paul's Royal Ideology* [Fortress, 2015], 54–60, 149–165) briefly discusses this background in OT Israel. Creach (*The Destiny of the Righteous in the Psalms* [Chalice, 2008], 73) notes that "there seems little doubt that David has become [in the Psalter] not only a symbol of the monarchy but a symbol for Israel." Cf. Mowinckel, *The Psalm in Israel's Worship*, 42–61, esp. 46 and 51, where he draws out how the people are incorporated into the king: "[T]his representative personality in the royal Temple in Jerusalem was the king himself." Not every point of Mowinckel larger thesis, particularly an enthronement festival in Israel, has been followed but such discussion would take us too far afield. The larger aspects of corporate representation remain recognized.

70 See, for example, Dale Launderville, *Piety and Politics: The Dynamics of Royal Authority in Homeric Greece, Biblical Israel, and Old Babylonian Mesopotamia* (Eerdmans, 2003), esp. 43–51, 99–145 (ch. 2), 317–331; also Jipp, *Christ is King*, 46–54, on Hellenistic Kingship discourse.

71 Richard Longenecker (*Biblical Exegesis in the Apostolic Period* [Eerdmans, 1999], 158–159) mentions the similarity between the Dead Sea community and early Christian writing, "On a principle of corporate solidarity, such passages regarding Israel's king and David's son would lend themselves to a fulfillment understanding by any group that believed itself to be culminating the hope of Israel." Cf. Simon Kistemaker, *The Psalm Citations in the Epistle to the Hebrews* (Wipf and Stock, 2010), 61–94. Susan Docherty (*The Use of the Old Testament in Hebrews*, WUNT 2/260 [Mohr Siebeck, 2009], 144–152) suggests "the author [of Hebrews] is more indebted to the hopes and expectations of 'traditional' Davidic messianism than some commentators allow" (150). Marie Isaacs, *Sacred Space: An Approach to the Theology of the Epistle to the Hebrews* (Sheffield Academic Press, 1992), 167: "our author's principal model for Jesus' sonship is the Davidic king, as taken up in current Jewish eschatological expectations" (cf. also 169–170, 172–178).

72 *The Concept of Messiah*, 76–79.

concludes "The king asks not only to be delivered but to be set on high, that is, raised up, 'resurrected.'"[73] This is precisely the motif that reaches fulfillment in Hebrews in the true Son who entrusts himself to YHWH who is able to save the king from death. In this salvation, Jesus the king is resurrected and installed via a royal enthronement that entails an ascent into heaven to sit on the divine throne.

Thus, we might return again to the example of the motif in LXX Ps 30 [MT 31], since we find 30:6 is recorded in Luke 23:46 as being uttered by Jesus at his death.[74] We have in LXX Ps 30:6 the ultimate act of trust εἰς χεῖράς σου παραθήσομαι τὸ πνεῦμά μου. Originally this is David crying to the Lord to take refuge in him now fulfilled by the true Davidic figure, the Messiah. In LXX 30:11, 13 we again have David in this near death or death-like experience of wasting away, being utterly weakened and downtrodden to the point of death. The ultimate vindication is being hidden in the secret place in the presence of God (κατακρύψεις αὐτοὺς ἐν ἀποκρύφῳ τοῦ προσώπου σου), and God is sheltering them in a tent (30:21 σκεπάσεις αὐτοὺς ἐν σκηνῇ). In terms of possibly more direct language, LXX Ps 30:23 is most significant: Ἀπέρριμμαι ἄρα ἀπὸ προσώπου τῶν ὀφθαλμῶν σου. διὰ τοῦτο εἰσήκουσας τῆς φωνῆς τῆς δεήσεώς μου ἐν τῷ κεκραγέναι με πρὸς σέ. While we have no direct indication that Hebrews is specifically influenced by this passage, it is possible that an early Christian reading of this text would have seen it ripe for eschatological interpretation of God delivering the true David, the Messiah, and bringing him up into the presence of God as in Pss 2 and 110. The point remains that it is another Psalm where David displays ultimate trust, cries out to God, and is vindicated up out of his death-like ordeal into God's presence. This larger motif in the Psalms is fulfilled in Hebrews by the obedience of the Son who cries out.

One final passage that may serve to solidify this cry of the righteous sufferer as a Davidic motif is LXX Ps 88:27–28 [MT 89]. In this Psalm that anticipates the rise of the new Davidic king in fulfillment of God's covenant with David, the king is portrayed as one who looks to YHWH as his Father to save him.

LXX Ps 88:27–28
αὐτὸς ἐπικαλέσεταί με Πατήρ μου εἶ σύ, θεός μου καὶ ἀντιλήμπτωρ τῆς σωτηρίας μου·
κἀγὼ πρωτότοκον θήσομαι αὐτόν, ὑψηλὸν παρὰ τοῖς βασιλεῦσιν τῆς γῆς.

---

73 Ibid., 79.
74 It may also serve as the motif behind Peter's exhortation to Christians in 1 Pet 4:19, since in 1 Pet 2:23 Christ is described as entrusting himself to God.

He shall call upon me, 'My Father you are, my God and supporter of my deliverance!'
And I will make him a firstborn, high among the kings of the earth. (NETS)

While there is no direct verbal parallel between Heb 5:7 and LXX Ps 88:27–28, they share the same themes of the Davidic king being the 'son' of YHWH and calling out to God as his father. He trusts God and asks God to save him. Out of this crying-trust, YHWH promises to make him firstborn—the highest of the kings of the earth. This promise becomes parallel to v. 30a where we find the appointment of his seed forever καὶ θήσομαι εἰς τὸν αἰῶνα τοῦ αἰῶνος τὸ σπέρμα αὐτοῦ. We have already argued that πρωτότοκος in Heb 1:6 is probably an allusion to Ps 88:28. While we should be careful about over-reading background passages into every element of the text of Hebrews, LXX Ps 88:27–28 does have the features of this motif that David (or David's heir) will be one who calls on God as his Father for salvation. This is what we see in Hebrews: the Messiah is the true son of YHWH, but also an eternal Son.[75] In establishing the 'seed of Abraham' he is raised up with an eternal reign whereby he will also bring 'sons to glory.' But this eternal Son in his incarnate humanity also is displayed as the true royal son exercises absolute trust in God. He is the true fulfillment of the Davidic-Adamic figure. Out of his trust, God has established him on the throne from where in his exalted humanity, he radiates the divine glory.

Our contention is then: Hebrews is theologically attuned to the Psalms particularly in the relationship between David as a corporate figure who represents the righteous acting as both a model and on behalf of the people of God. Not only is this demonstrated with the fulfillment of kingly Psalms such a Pss 2, 45, and 110, but also by Hebrews' attention to the corporate representation and human trust offered by the Son, which leads him to become the High Priest and head of the new humanity (Heb 2). Jerome Creach points out this theme in the Psalms is tied to historical situations of David:

> The Psalter identifies the righteous with Israel. It then focuses that corporate identity in a profound way by identifying David as the righteous who

---

[75] Here our argumentation is somewhat similar to James Swetnam's argument ("The Crux of Hebrews 5,7–8," 356). He reads καίπερ ὢν υἱός as including both divine sonship and in expansion 'son of Abraham' "or even 'son of man.'" We, however, see καίπερ ὢν υἱός specifically referring only to the divine sonship of Jesus. However, the vocation that Jesus engages in as he trusts the Father and cries out is precisely that of the true human. This is similar to Swetnam's larger argument. But we do not see this καίπερ ὢν υἱός as specifically "an adaptation of the pleas of Ps 22 [21]" rather the καίπερ ὢν υἱός only makes sense as contrastive because the vocation that Christ takes on is that of the Ps 22 (and Davidic) figure who fully trusts God.

suffers. David appears in twelve Psalms that present events in his life as contexts in which he prayed the words of those psalms (Pss. 3, 7, 18, 51, 52, 54, 56, 57, 59, 60, 62, 142). In almost every case David is presented as one who suffers, who pleads to God for mercy, and who expresses confidence that God will deliver him.[76]

In Sir 51:8–11, Jesus ben Sirach cries out to the Lord for his deliverance in order that he might not experience death. In 51:2, the Lord has redeemed his body from destruction (ἐλυτρώσω τὸ σῶμά μου ἐξ ἀπωλείας). The language is reminiscent of the OT where YHWH delivers from the chaotic depths/Deep (51:5a ἐκ βάθους κοιλίας ᾅδου) and from Sheol/Hades (51:6 ἤγγισεν ἕως θανάτου ἡ ψυχή μου, καὶ ἡ ζωή μου ἦν σύνεγγυς ᾅδου κάτω). Then Jesus ben Sirach remembers, very similarly to the Davidic figure in the Psalms, to cry out to the Lord (51:8–9). He asks to be delivered from death (5:9b καὶ ὑπὲρ θανάτου ῥύσεως ἐδεήθην). He cries to God as his Father in the midst of his affliction (51:10 ἐπεκαλεσάμην κύριον πατέρα κυρίου μου μή με ἐγκαταλιπεῖν ἐν ἡμέραις θλίψεως). The petition of Jesus ben Sirach was heard καὶ εἰσηκούσθη ἡ δέησίς μου, which leads to praising and blessing the name of the Lord (51:12). It is the cry of the righteous sufferer looking to YHWH for deliverance.

David deSilva notes the prayers with loud cries and tears are found in the faithful prayers of 2 and 3 Maccabees:[77]

2Macc 11:6
ὡς δὲ μετέλαβον οἱ περὶ τὸν Μακκαβαῖον πολιορκοῦντα αὐτὸν τὰ ὀχυρώματα, μετὰ ὀδυρμῶν καὶ δακρύων ἱκέτευον σὺν τοῖς ὄχλοις τὸν κύριον ἀγαθὸν ἄγγελον ἀποστεῖλαι πρὸς σωτηρίαν τῷ Ισραηλ.
When Makkabaios and his men heard that he was besieging the strongholds, they prayed to the Lord, together with the masses, with lamentations and tears, to send a good angel to save Israel. (NETS)

3Macc 1:16
Τῶν δὲ ἱερέων ἐν πάσαις ταῖς ἐσθήσεσιν προσπεσόντων, καὶ δεομένων τοῦ μεγίστου θεοῦ βοηθεῖν τοῖς ἐνεστῶσιν, καὶ τὴν ὁρμὴν τοῦ κακῶς ἐπιβαλλομένου μεταθεῖναι, κραυγῆς τε μετὰ δακρύων τὸ ἱερὸν ἐμπλησάντων,
Then the priests in all their vestments prostrated themselves and entreated Almighty God to help them in their present difficulty and make their

---

76 Jerome Creach, *The Destiny of the Righteous*, 8.
77 *Perseverance*, 190–191. Cf. also Attridge (*Hebrews*, 149n.155), who cites 2 Macc 8:29; 10:25; Sir 51:8. Also Compton (*Psalm 110*, 72) cites the same Maccabee texts.

assailant change his mind, and they filled the Temple with loud cries and tears. (NETS)

3Macc 5:7
τὸν παντοκράτορα Κύριον καὶ πάσης δυνάμεως δυναστεύοντα, ἐλεήμονα θεὸν αὐτῶν καὶ πατέρα, δυσκαταπαύστῳ βοῇ πάντες μετὰ δακρύων ἐπεκαλέσαντο, δεόμενοι
their Lord, the all-conquering who governs with all power, the merciful God and father, all of them beseeching him with unrestrained cries and tears. (NETS)

3Macc 5:25
οἱ δὲ Ἰουδαῖοι κατὰ τὸν ἀμερῆ ψυχουλκούμενοι χρόνον, πολύδακρυν ἱκετίαν ἐν μέλεσιν γοεροῖς τείνοντες τὰς χεῖρας εἰς τὸν οὐρανὸν ἐδέοντο τοῦ μεγίστου θεοῦ πάλιν αὐτοῖς βοηθῆσαι συντόμως.
But the Jews, drawing their last brief breath in tearful supplication and strains of lament, stretched out their hands to heaven and implored the Almighty God once more to help them speedily. (NETS)

These pleadings and prayers are cries of deep desperation. The only recourse here is to cry out to the Lord. The person praying is essentially powerless to act and needs the Almighty Lord to take action, as the only one who truly has the power and ability against such great persecution and oppression. It is very much the types of prayers we have witnessed in the Psalms. The types of prayer in 2 and 3 Macc "suggests that the author of Hebrews is drawing on cultural resonances with other depictions of fervent emotive prayers of the pious...His goal is to display Jesus' piety, an essential qualification for the high priesthood, which God confirmed through hearing Jesus' prayer."[78]

The question then arises "why is this such an essential qualification of high priesthood?" The answer, in part, is that it shows Jesus comes from among the people and is able to sympathize, which is necessary for the priesthood (5:1–4). But another part of Hebrews' showing he is qualified for the high priesthood is displaying his essential humanity. To be truly human is to depend upon God in one's entirety. Humans were created in this vassal-like

---

[78] deSilva, *Perseverance Through Gratitude*, 191. We omitted deSilva's "rather than making a specific reference to the Gethsemane tradition." We think that the Gethsemane tradition is also in the matrix of the backdrop. Hebrews is not making "specific reference" in terms of direct quotation or clear citation. However, it would seem to us that this 'praying in desperation' motif is a melting pot of a variety of backgrounds especially (1) the Psalms; (2) the martyr traditions; and (3) Jesus in Gethsemane and on Golgotha.

condition. Humanity was established to rule over creation, but under the great YHWH and trusting Him for all things. This is seen in David in the Psalms. It returns us to the theme of the Second Adam. Reaching the eschatological judgment, a suffering ordeal *par excellence*, and his moment of conquering the one holding the power of death (2:14–15), the son does not reach up with his own might and power to seize victory. He yields in perfect trust and subservient obedience. He pleads to the Father and entrusts himself to the Father. He fulfills his Second Adam vocation where Adam, and all subsequent 'second Adams' of Israel and the Davidic kings have been shown to have failed.[79]

It is through the experience of suffering that the Son learns obedience (5:8 ἔμαθεν ἀφ᾽ ὧν ἔπαθεν τὴν ὑπακοήν). He did not learn obedience as a step to result in Sonship or adoption to sonship. As discussed above, Hebrews sees Jesus as already a son prior to his coming into creation in the incarnation. Yet, this 'learning obedience' is by means of suffering (ἀφ᾽ ὧν ἔπαθεν). Commenting on ἔπαθεν and its relationship to v. 7, Franz Laub writes that ἔπαθεν "ist umfassende Formel für die Passion als Todesleiden."[80] The aspects of this learning are in his humanity—the suffering that takes place 'in the days of his flesh' (5:7 ὃς ἐν ταῖς ἡμέραις τῆς σαρκὸς αὐτοῦ). As Bruce McCormack states, "such 'learning' on the part of the eternal Son becomes comprehensible only where it is understood that the eternal Son does what he does *humanly*."[81] So while the Son has been described as one who does not wear out or perish (1:10–12 with Ps 102:25–27), this is precisely his earthly experience. He experiences weakness that leads to the exhaustion of his life in a sacrificial death. Through all of this he is the righteous Davidic-Adamic servant who relies wholly on God. He does not exalt himself but takes the Lord as his refuge. Thus, "[s]uffering taught the Son obedience, which was part of the process of 'being made perfect' that was the condition of him to become 'the source of eternal salvation' (5:8–9)."[82] His human obedience qualifies himself and the new humanity for the eschatological end, ascent into the presence of God.

---

79 Attridge ("Heard Because of His Reverence [Heb 5:7]," *JBL* 98 (1979):90–93) proposes a background of the prayers of Abraham and Moses in *Her.* 1–29. Both are figures who trust God and are delivered. He shows how both Abraham and Moses show reverence in their 'cries to God'. "Jesus, like Abraham, prayed with a loud shout, and like Moses, manifested genuine emotion" (93). Patrick Gray (*Godly Fear*, 199) argues against a connection.

80 Franz Laub, *Bekenntnis und Auslegung: Die paränetische Funktion der Christologie im Hebräerbrief* (Pustet, 1980), 130.

81 Bruce McCormick, "'With Loud Cries and Tears': The Humanity of the Son in the Epistle to the Hebrews," in *The Epistle to the Hebrews and Christian Theology*, ed. Richard Bauckham, et al. (Eerdmans, 2009), 66.

82 Richard D. Nelson, "He Offered Himself: Sacrifice in Hebrews," *Interpretation* 57.3 (2003): 253–254.

His 'partaking of flesh and blood' (2:14a Ἐπεὶ οὖν τὰ παιδία κεκοινώνηκεν αἵματος καὶ σαρκός, καὶ αὐτὸς παραπλησίως μετέσχεν τῶν αὐτῶν) entails the entire human vocation, including dependence upon God in times of trial. It was necessary for this ὅθεν ὤφειλεν κατὰ πάντα τοῖς ἀδελφοῖς ὁμοιωθῆναι (2:17). He is merciful and faithful because he has pled for mercy. He has undergone the full sum of human experience including the testing of temptation: ἐν ᾧ γὰρ πέπονθεν αὐτὸς πειρασθείς, δύναται τοῖς πειραζομένοις βοηθῆσαι (2:18). He was faithful to God who appointed him (3:2 πιστὸν ὄντα τῷ ποιήσαντι αὐτόν). The priest must come from among men and have human experience (5:1–4).

In this enduring through suffering, he will later in Hebrews be set forth as the exemplar to Christians (12:2–3). He succumbs to death (2:14) so that death might become the means of victory for God's people. Here we notice the ἵνα clause containing the genitival phrase διὰ τοῦ θανάτου. His cry is not then to be saved from death but 'out of death' (5:7 ἐκ θανάτου).[83] It is, to borrow the title from John Owen's historic work, *The Death of Death in the Death of Christ*.

His obedience is his active yielding himself to God's will whereby he exemplifies true human piety. Wescott succinctly summarizes: "Man's fall was due to disobedience: his restoration comes through obedience."[84] Jesus is the royal son who represents humanity. He is the ideal Adam who, by his obedience, achieves the age-to-come and the glory of awaiting humanity.[85] Thus, his being heard, see our discussion below, is his resurrection-ascension-installation, namely exaltation. His act of obedience makes the eschatological crowning with glory possible for both himself and his people.

The Son who cries loudly and with tears is then heard because of his godliness or piety (5:7 εἰσακουσθεὶς ἀπὸ τῆς εὐλαβείας).[86] The passage shows that God hears the Son because πρὸς τὸν δυνάμενον σῴζειν αὐτὸν ἐκ θανάτου (5:7) is a circumlocution for God. Referring to God as the one who hears and is able to save is consistent with the pattern we have highlighted from the Psalms

---

83 Joachim Jeremias, "Hbr 5,7–10," *ZNW* 44 (1952–1953): 109–111. Jeremias cites John 12:27 and Mark 14:36 as the tradition behind this understanding. Christ's being delivered from death was his being crowned with glory and honor. Jeremias pays particular attention to the participles arguing, "εἰσακουσθείς wird durch τελειωθείς erläutert: d.h. wir erfahren, daß bei diesem Erhörung in der Vollendung, der Krönung mit δόξα und τιμή (Hbr 2.7), bestand" (109).

84 B.F. Wescott, *The Epistle to the Hebrews* (Macmillan, 1889), 130. He cites Rom 5:19 as comparative.

85 See our discussion on Heb 2 and the relationship between the glory of Adam, eschatology, and the suffering of the righteous.

86 Neil Lightfoot ("The Saving of the Savior: Hebrews 5:7ff.," *Restoration Quarterly* 16 [1973]: 171) concludes that "the balance of weight" for the most likely meaning of *eulabeia* is piety, godliness, or godly fear." Cf. Gray, *Godly Fear*, 198–199, 205 (who also highlights the aspect of submission to the divine will); James Swetnam, "The Crux of Hebrews 5,7–8," *Bib* 81 (2000): 352.

where the Davidic king looks to the Lord God for refuge. Creach has argued that with the relationship between Pss 1 and 2 that "the placement of Ps 2.12d seems to indicate that righteousness was conceived largely as 'seeking refuge in Yahweh.'"[87] As Creach states regarding Ps 3 where David is cited in the historical titles, the Psalmist "makes David a 'literary vehicle' that exemplifies a piety of dependence on the Lord."[88] Or again regarding Book 1 of the Psalter, Creach writes that it seems plausible that it "should be read as an extended picture of true piety, seen in total reliance on Yahweh and exemplified by David."[89] This picture seen in total reliance is now fulfilled in the true Davidic king, the true and greater representative Adam, Jesus. Easter states, "Jesus participated fully in the human condition and realized humanity's divine intention [cf. Heb 2:5–8] by experiencing life after death...Jesus, as the faithful one *par excellence*, pioneers faith by exercising faith [in] the face of death, and he perfects faith by being raised from the dead."[90] This '*par excellence*'

---

87 Jerome F.D. Creach, *Yahweh as Refuge and the Editing of the Hebrew Psalter* (Sheffield Academic, 1996), 80.

88 Creach, *Destiny of the Righteous*, 60; Shirley Lucass, *The Concept of Messiah*, 79: "Yahweh rescues the king because of his righteousness." Gert Kwakkel (*According to My Righteousness: Upright Behavior as Grounds for Deliverance in Psalms 7, 17, 18, 26, and 44* [Brill, 2002]) has examined Pss 7, 17, 18, 26, and 44 noting the motif of the Psalmist asking for the Lord's deliverance because of his righteousness and faithfulness. With the exception of Ps 18, which is a royal psalm of thanksgiving, he rejects these as royal psalms (8–9, 61–62, 103–104, 133, 270–271). His point is there is not warrant for "the conclusion that a royal interpretation should be given to the numerous psalms which could also be read as having been recited by ordinary Israelites" (288). However, we think this misses the representative role of the king. The reason Israelites could appeal to God for deliverance and even hold up their own covenant fidelity as grounds for deliverance was because they were YHWH's sons (Exod 4:22–23, etc.), and the king was the son of God *par excellence* (cf. Mowinckel, *Psalms in Israel's Worship*, 47). While this is not the place to delve into a larger text, editing, and theology of the Psalms, our point is broader that the motif of the praying true son (whether Israelite or king) is taken up and fulfilled by Jesus. Mowinckel (*Psalms in Israel's Worship*, 46) points to 'corporate personality' where the king serves a representative of the people. On a broader approach to royal Psalms and the king seeking deliverance see Steven J.L. Croft, *The Identity of the Individual in the Psalms* (Sheffield Academic, 1987), 73–132, esp. 90–96, for the cries for vindication by the king. With regard to ceremonies Eaton (*Kingship and the Psalms* [SCM, 1975], 133) writes, "While the order of ceremonies and texts remains uncertain, the chief elements of royal suffering and exaltation are strongly attested, as is also the close relation to the assertion of Yahweh's kingship." This royal suffering, royal exaltation, and its close relation to the assertion of Yahweh's kingship are precisely the motifs we find in Hebrews.

89 *Yahweh as Refuge*, 80. Daniel Owens (*Portraits of the Righteous in the Psalms: An Exploration of the Ethics of Book I* [Pickwick, 2013], 190) comes to a similar conclusion: "the theme of YHWH as deliverer is at the center of the dialogue in Book I about character's outcome. The salvation of the king plays a central and explicit role in this section." Jamie Grant (*The King as Exemplar*, 65) rightly connects the idea that "the king, as Yahweh's co-regent, is completely reliant upon him" back to a "Deuteronomic worldview."

90 Easter, *Faith and the Faithfulness*, 164. Similarly, Reuben Omark ("The Saving of the Savior: Exegesis and Christology of Hebrews 5:7–10," *Interpretation* 12 [1958]: 47) writes "*obedience* is the condition for man's saving relation to God (3:18; 4:6, 11) and toward Christ (5:9). And

must be identified as a Second Adam category that Christ carries out as the eschatological man representative of God's people so they too can share in his glory. He is a corporate and representational head as the Adamic-Davidic son-king. For Hebrews, the true eternal Son acts out human kingly sonship depending solely upon God for deliverance.

Second, the cry is probably not so much a supplication for being spared from experiencing death, instead ἐκ θανάτου is a plea to be saved 'out of death.'[91] The Son is thus dependent upon an ultimate deliverance after experiencing death. The author of Hebrews considers the Son to have had this mindset when he states that Jesus ὃς ἀντὶ τῆς προκειμένης αὐτῷ χαρᾶς ὑπέμεινεν σταυρὸν αἰσχύνης καταφρονήσας ἐν δεξιᾷ τε τοῦ θρόνου τοῦ θεοῦ κεκάθικεν (12:2). The Son despises the shame of the cross but is willing to go through it, even unto death, for the joy of the glorious kingdom and eschatological resurrection and glorification that awaits him and the children he will bring to glory. Similarly, 4 Macc 14:1 speaks of the martyrs despising the suffering. The prize of the martyrs' victory for enduring "torments unto death" is "incorruption and long-lasting life," ἐν φθαρσίᾳ ἐν ζωῇ πολυχρονίῳ. 4 Ez. 2:36 calls God's people to "Flee from the shadow of this age, receive the joy of your glory." They are awaiting "everlasting rest" that comes at "the end of the age" (2:34). They are to "give thanks to him who called you to heavenly kingdoms." The prize is "glorious garments from the Lord."[92] In 2 Bar. 14:13 the righteous depart this world "without fear and are confident of the world which you have promised to them with an expectation full of joy." The expectation for this eschatological climax does not exempt one from suffering. Jesus' cry is not a failure but rather a recognition, like the Maccabean martyrs, he will be delivered out of death by God. To this end, Jesus entrusts himself to the Father.

The warrant or the basis for the Father hearing the cry of the Son does not rest on the eternal relationship between Father and Son (established in Heb 1), or the divine identity of the Son with the Father, but rather on the basis of the Son's εὐλάβεια. Ἀπό is used here to indicate the means or cause of the Father hearing the cries.[93] This usage is "abundant in the LXX."[94]

---

this response of *obedience* was the disposition of the Son, manifested in his 'godly fear,' which brought divine approval and answer to his prayer for deliverance from death, and likewise, meant for perfecting saviorhood" (emphasis original).

91 Attridge, *Hebrews*, 150; Bruce, *Hebrews*, 128; Cockerill, *Hebrews*, 243; Schreiner, *Hebrews*, 164; Westcott, *Hebrews*, 126; Gray, *Godly Fear*, 192–193; etc.

92 See also 4 Ezra 2:45 "He answered and said to me, "These those who have put off mortal clothing and put on the immortal and have confessed the name of God; now they are being crowned, and receive palms."

93 "ἀπό," BDAG, 106.

94 Lane, *Hebrews 1–8*, 109.

There are two main interpretations of εὐλάβεια in this passage. First, it can be translated as fear. In this interpretation the Son has a fear of death and his cries to God help him overcome his fear. Thus, he is heard specifically because of the great fear or anxiety he has. This would be similar to how εὐλάβεια is used in LXX. In LXX, it is found in only three places: Josh 22:24,[95] Prov 28:14, and Wis 17:8; in all three cases it means something like caution, discretion, or fear. Εὐλάβεια is used only one other time in Heb 12:28 to speak of how the Christian is to approach God in worship: μετὰ εὐλαβείας καὶ δέους. The participle is used in 11:7 εὐλαβηθείς. Given that the context there is Noah's act of faith, it seems unlikely that Noah was primarily motivated by fear but a reverence for the word God gave him.[96]

The verb εὐλαβέομαι is perhaps more helpful as a possible conceptual background. It is used much more in LXX.[97] Again, it can have a range of meaning such as 'cautious' (Job 13:25; Sir 18:27; Jer 15:17) or 'afraid' (1 Sam 18:15, 29; Isa 51:12; Jer 22:25). In several passages it speaks of reverence particularly as one looks to the Lord for deliverance, Prov 2:8,[98] 30:5; Nah 1:17; Mal 3:16. In this light, we agree with Ellingworth that "the meaning of the whole phrase εἰσακουσθεὶς ἀπὸ τῆς εὐλαβείας would then be that God heard Christ's prayer because it was offered to the end in a spirit of 'humble submission.'"[99]

Another area that probably has some influence on how Hebrews understands obedience is the theology of martyrdom in Second Temple Judaism. In martyrdom theology, godliness in and through suffering is rewarded with the eschatological life. The seven sons who are martyred in 4 Maccabees are promised the reward of the eschatological life in the age of blessing. Their suffering warrants their exaltation. This connection can be seen in 4 Macc 17. The mother of the martyrs is promised glory set in the heaven above the moon itself:

4 Macc 17:5

οὐχ οὕτω σελήνη κατ' οὐρανὸν σὺν ἄστροις σεμνὴ καθέστηκεν, ὡς σὺ τοὺς ἰσαστέρους ἑπτὰ παῖδας φωταγωγήσασα πρὸς τὴν εὐσέβειαν ἔντιμος

---

95 Ellingworth (*Hebrews*, 290) takes the use in Josh. 22:24 as "prudent respect for God"; NETS translates it as "caution."

96 Lane (*Hebrews 1–8*, 109) writes it "connotes attentiveness to the divine will or godly reverence."

97 Exod 3:6; Deut 2:4; 1 Sam 18:15, 29; 1 Esd 4:28; 1 Macc 3:30, 12:40; 2 Macc 8:16; 4 Macc 4:13; Prov 2:8, 30:5; Job 13:25, 19:29; Wis 12:11; Sir 7:6, 7:29, 18:27, 22:22, 23:18, 26:5, 29:7, 34:14, 41:3; Nah 1:7; Hab 2:20; Zeph 1:7, 3:12; Zech 2:17; Mal 3:16; Isa 51:12; 57:11; Jer 4:1, 5:22, 15:17, 22:25; Dan 4:5

98 The context begins back in 2:6: Prov 2:6–7 "Because the Lord gives wisdom, also from his presence come knowledge and understanding, and he stores up salvation for those who succeed; he will shield their journey" (NETS).

99 Ellingworth, *Hebrews*, 290.

καθέστηκας θεῷ, καὶ ἐστήρισαι ἐν οὐρανῷ σὺν αὐτοῖς.
Not so majestic stands the moon in heaven as you stand, lighting the way to piety for your seven starlike sons, honored by God and firmly set in the heaven.

An exaltation awaits on the basis of godliness (εὐσέβεια). The memorial to them in 4 Macc 17:10 is that "they vindicated their race looking unto God and enduring torments even unto death" (οἳ καὶ ἐξεδίκησαν τὸ γένος εἰς θεὸν ἀφορῶντες, καὶ μέχρι θανάτου τὰς βασάνους ὑπομείναντες). They vindicate not only themselves but their race (τὸ γένος), God's people, by their acts of dependency upon God even through their deaths. Their virtue or character and ability to endure was tested and rewarded with incorruptible life (4 Macc 17:12 τὸ νῖκος ἐν φθαρσίᾳ ἐν ζωῇ πολυχρονίῳ).

Character (ἀρετή[100]) of godliness is rewarded. The reward is the eschatological life. Elsewhere the reward is being in God's presence as the prize that results from the virtue displayed in suffering endurance (4 Macc 9:8). They were crowned as an athletic champion: θεοσέβεια δὲ ἐνίκα, τοὺς ἑαυτῆς ἀθλητὰς στεφανοῦσα, (4 Macc 17:15). This athletic motif is used similarly to encourage Christians to press on in Heb 12:1–2. As athletes are crowned for victory *because of* their endurance, the martyrs stand beside the divine throne with eternal life (4 Macc 17:18 δι' ἣν καὶ τῷ θείῳ νῦν παρεστήκασιν θρόνῳ, καὶ τὸν μακάριον βιοῦσιν αἰῶνα). Their death is a victory over enemies and a propitiation to God (4 Macc 17:19–22). Suffering through endurance with dependance upon God merits all the rewards, crownings, and exaltations that they experience. The point reinforces the relationship that Hebrews sees between Christ's act of obedience and reverence towards God and God's hearing their cry. However, his exaltation is not exaltation as one among many but exaltation *par excellence* to the very divine throne of God. Martin Hengel has cautioned that in reading the background of martyrs' exaltation, we must not miss the eschatological superiority of what Jesus is described to have experienced with the background of Ps 110:1:

> After his death the martyr and the suffering righteous one could be given a place of honour in paradise or even at the 'good' right side next to the throne of God, but he shares this place of honour with many other perfect righteous and pious ones who also 'throne' in proximity to God. A unique eschatological function or a granting of power was not associated with it.[101]

---

100 "ἀρετή," BDAG, 130, "a term denoting consummate 'excellence' or 'merit' within a social context...Exhibition of ἀρετή invites recognition, resulting in renown or glory."

101 Martin Hengel, *Studies in Christology* (T&T Clark, 1995), 217.

Importantly Christ's prayer, loud cries, and reverent fear are his acts where he learns obedience. In apocalyptic literature, a commonly held belief is that Adam's great sin was his failure to obey God.[102] In contrast to Adam, the righteous that suffer and maintain godliness will experience the resurrection and the rewards of the glorification in the eschaton.[103] The righteous persevere and trust God, obeying him.[104] The Davidic King and later Messianic expectation is that he will be one who submits to God's law, who is obedient, and who exercises reverent trust in God.[105] Hebrews is informed by these backgrounds. Hebrews shows us "a reverential Son, human like all other humans, who is submissive to God even to the point of severe suffering, and one thus qualified to be High Priest and leader of His people."[106] In his earthly sonship, however, the Son is not just like all humans, rather he is the fulfillment of humanity, greater than Adam and David because he fulfills the capacity of humanity by complete reverence and submission. His obedience in reverent trust is the grounds of his ascension into heaven. We propose that with this background from the Psalms now having reached their eschatological fulfillment in Christ's death and exaltation through resurrection and ascension, the questions are resolved concerning how/if Christ was heard. There is no need to posit the debated proposal that the text should be amended to read "not heard."[107] It is not a surprise to see the Messiah offer up the ultimate act of trust and go through the ultimate Psalmic humiliation-exaltation ordeal.

---

102  4 Ezra 4:30; 7:11, 46–48.

103  2 Bar. 15:7–8; 48:49–50; 51:1–2, 11–15; 52:6–7; 54:21; 4 Ezra 2:20–32, 34–41, 44–48; 7:88–98; T. Isaac 4:47; CD-A iii.12–20, those who are steadfast and follow God's precepts "will acquire eternal life, and all the glory of Adam is for them" (v. 20, *DSS: Study Edition*, 1:555). In 1QHa iv.14–15, "You [protect] the ones who serve you loyally, [so that] their posterity is before you all the days. You have raised an [eternal] name [forgiving] offence, casting away all their iniquities, giving them as a legacy all the glory of Adam [and] abundance of days" (*DSS: Study Edition*, 1:149).

104  In Pss. Sol. 14:1–5, the righteous endure discipline; they obey and live by his word forever; they are "the Lord's paradise, the trees of life." They are God's portion and inheritance, which probably has in view their eschatological glory and triumph.

105  Pss. Sol. 17:36–42 portrays the king as one who is righteous, wise, "His hope will be in the Lord" (v. 39), "mighty in his actions and strong in the fear of the Lord" (v. 40), faithful and righteous shepherd, and leading in holiness.

106  Lightfoot, "Saving of the Savior," 173.

107  See for example Brandenburger, "Text und Vorlagen," 191–199; Jeremias, "Hbr 5,7–10," 107–111; Laub, *Bekenntnis und Auslegung*, 130–134. Strobel ("Die Psalmengrundlage der Gethsemane-Prallele Hebr 5:7ff.," *ZNW* 45 [1954]: esp. 254–256) points to LXX Pss 114–115; see 259–264 for survey of German scholarship on "σῴζειν αὐτὸν ἐκ θανάτου" and "εἰσακουσθεὶς ἀπὸ τῆς εὐλαβείας"). We have argued that the thematic background is much broader.

## Heb 5:5–6, 9–10 Glorification, Perfection, and Ascension

In these verses, we see the relationship between Christ's obedience in godly trust and the resulting response of God. Christ has yielded himself in submission and absolute reliance on God in offering himself as sacrifice and entrusting himself to his Father. He has acted as the eschatological Adam, the true and final David, and he is raised up in the glory of exaltation ascending to the very throne of God. What David had experienced in accession to the throne in Jerusalem as YHWH's viceregent, Jesus Christ has received in being installed in the heavenly Zion at the divine throne at God's right hand. Again, Hebrews reads Pss 2, 8, and 110 and the Davidic destiny as fulfilled in the ascension of the Son and his session at God's right hand, i.e., his exaltation. In this event of this ascension, Hebrews is able to anchor his Sonship-Christology. He reveals Jesus as the divine Son but also as the Davidic King and priest of the order of Melchizedek. These later aspects are particularly dependent upon the ascension in that Christ would not have become installed King and heavenly priest if he did not first obey and then receive the right to ascend up into heaven.

In Heb 5:1–4, the author draws parallels between the weakness of the Levitical priest and the weakness of Christ. The Levitical priest never exalted himself to the office of priesthood but was installed by God which granted the rite for him to enter the earthly Holy of Holies on the Day of Atonement. He writes that οὐχ ἑαυτῷ τις λαμβάνει τὴν τιμήν (5:4a)—the priest did not appoint himself to the honor of priesthood. The priest was called by God: ἀλλὰ καλούμενος ὑπὸ τοῦ θεοῦ καθώσπερ καὶ Ἀαρών (5:4b). The reminder of Aaron here is that he was the first high priest appointed under the Old Covenant and is thus representational of all priests after him who were called by God to their office. Thus, by pointing to the first, Hebrews signals to the reader that the same is true of all the priests after Aaron who serve under the Old Covenant.

Hebrews goes on to compare the installation of Jesus into his priesthood with Aaron's installation. Once again, Hebrews uses a pattern of drawing comparisons and contrasts between the old order and the eschatological order. The fulfillment pattern of Hebrews' interpretation of the Scripture shows that, by God's design, things are repeated from the Old in the New while at the same time the New is always the superior, the climactic, and the eschatological. So, Hebrews highlights the comparison with Οὕτως καί, thus also, or perhaps in the same way also.[108] We expect then to see that Jesus did not exalt

---

108 Some other examples of "οὕτως καί" with specific comparison being drawn between the preceding and proceeding statements include Matt 17:12; 18:35; 23:28; 24:33; Mark 13:29; Luke 17:10; John 5:21; Rom 5:18–19, 21.

himself in the same way the Aaronic priest did not.

Hebrews highlights the Messianic role of the Son and his appointment with Οὕτως καὶ ὁ Χριστός. We have in 4:14 ἀρχιερέα μέγαν...Ἰησοῦν τὸν υἱὸν τοῦ θεοῦ followed by 5:1 Πᾶς γὰρ ἀρχιερεύς, with vv. 1–4 focusing on priesthood in general but when he returns to mention Jesus specifically, he uses the title "the Christ" or the Messiah. Therefore, we see the interplay between Sonship, Christ's humanity, and the offices of priesthood and kingship. The one who is the high priest is also the King-Messiah.

Jesus, the Christ, did not glorify himself (5:5 οὐχ ἑαυτὸν ἐδόξασεν). He did not install himself upon the throne nor make himself the high priest out of the exercise of his own power and prerogatives. His appointment to the high priesthood was not at his own behest but at God's (5:5 Οὕτως καὶ ὁ Χριστὸς οὐχ ἑαυτὸν ἐδόξασεν γενηθῆναι ἀρχιερέα). We should note the necessity of God's calling the priest (v. 4 καλούμενος ὑπὸ τοῦ θεοῦ) and compare it with the voice of God at the Son's exaltation (v. 5 καλούμενος ὑπὸ τοῦ θεοῦ). What the passage addresses is the calling and installation of the Son in his royal and priestly enthronement as it goes on to quote Pss 2 and 110.

Heb 5:4–5 alludes back to Son's crowning with glory and honor from Heb 2 where we saw Hebrews' use of Ps 8. Verse 4 describes the receiving of the priesthood as a receiving of honor, λαμβάνει τὴν τιμήν, and verse 5 describes it as a glorification ἐδόξασεν. This language is an echo of Ps 8 in Heb 2:7 δόξῃ καὶ τιμῇ ἐστεφάνωσας αὐτόν. The subject of ἐστεφάνωσας is God (cf. 2:4–5). God has subjected the world to Christ and installed him as the Messiah who is priest in fulfillment of true humanity. In Christ, humanity is crowned with glory and honor as the ideal man—the true Adamic figure representative of his people is raised up and ascends into heaven itself. The believer thus has seen Christ crowned with glory and honor through his death (2:9 βλέπομεν Ἰησοῦν διὰ τὸ πάθημα τοῦ θανάτου δόξῃ καὶ τιμῇ ἐστεφανωμένον).[109] Likewise, the Son offers up obedience that leads to his death. Even as he goes through death, he cries out in great trust, submission, and dependence to God. God hears his prayers because of the Son's godliness in his behavior as the representational Second Adam, and God crowns him as king-priest in ascension.

The active obedience of the Son in offering himself as sacrifice but also entrusting himself over to the Father, particularly in the culmination of the

---

109 Compare this with 2 Bar. 15:7–8 "And with regard to the righteous ones, those whom you said the world has come on their account, yes, also that which is coming is on their account. For this world is to them a struggle and an effort with much trouble. And that accordingly which will come, a crown with great glory." For Hebrews, the world to come is on account of *the* righteous one, the true David-Adam figure. The world is trouble and suffering for him, but on account of it and his response of godliness, he ushers in the eschatological perfection of humanity.

end of his life, warrants the Father raising up the Son. The Son has, like a greater and truer David, loved righteousness and trusted the Father in godly reverence. He is then crowned having displayed himself as qualified for it. The founder of salvation becomes perfect unto the eschatological state through suffering (2:10b τὸν ἀρχηγὸν τῆς σωτηρίας αὐτῶν διὰ παθημάτων τελειῶσαι). The mere fact of his suffering does not qualify him for exaltation. Rather, but the manner of his suffering which is in obedience, humble dependence, and absolute submission to God his Father qualifies him.

G.K. Beale describes Christ in his work as this true and greater Adam:

> [T]he portrayal of the ideal Adam's reign as "the Son of Man" from Ps 8, never completely realized in the OT period, is applied to Christ as the one who finally has started to "fill the shoes" of this exemplary human figure (Heb 2:6–9). Christ has done what the first Adam and Israel (the corporate Adam) failed to achieve. It is in this sense Christ's "fulfillment" of end-time prophecy that he is also to be understood as a "son" who was "made [eschatologically] complete" (not "perfected") and has begun to lead and will finish leading his people to their end-time completed salvation (see further 2:10; 5:8–9, 14; 6:1; 7:11, 19, 28; 9:9; 10:1, 14; 11:40; 12:2).[110]

Thus, the declaration of royal sonship upon Jesus is at his exaltation. His call to glorification is God's declaration of Ps 2:7 upon the Christ (Heb 5:5). Thus, ὁ Χριστὸς οὐχ ἑαυτὸν ἐδόξασεν, God glorified the Christ. The moment is when he becomes the high priest of the eschaton (γενηθῆναι ἀρχιερέα). What is spoken to the Christ, his call to be priest (5:5 ἀλλ' ὁ λαλήσας πρὸς αὐτόν), is the royal pronouncement of Ps 2:7 υἱός μου εἶ σύ, ἐγὼ σήμερον γεγέννηκά σε. The Father is granting the inheritance to the Son by installing him as the royal-Messianic king. The ἐγὼ σήμερον γεγέννηκά σε is not an eternal begetting[111] but the installing of the royal king on the throne. The Christ is the son in that now he has been granted the rule in the kingdom.

This is precisely how the Lord establishes his son in the heavenly Zion (Ps 2:6 Ἐγὼ δὲ κατεστάθην βασιλεὺς ὑπ' αὐτοῦ ἐπὶ Σιων ὄρος τὸ ἅγιον αὐτοῦ). In light of 5:8a, the Son is Son prior to suffering and prior to the declaration, but the sonship is proclaimed by the Father. When the Son is installed as the royal Davidic King, he also becomes the eschatological high priest. He is entering into the heavenly sanctuary on account of the sacrifice of himself. He also enters

---

110 G.K. Beale, *A New Testament Biblical Theology* (Baker, 2011), 142.

111 See our earlier discussion on Heb 1:5. *Contra* Bauckham, "The Divinity of Jesus Christ in the Epistle to the Hebrews," in *The Epistles to the Hebrews and Christian Theology*, ed. Richard Bauckham, et al. (Eerdmans, 2009), 34.

as one who has been fitted to be the priest in receiving his own eschatological perfection. Hence, the necessity of his own glorification through the impartation of resurrection or indestructible life. The priest who is appointed is 'Son,' but he has now been perfected and fitted to ascend (7:16–17, 21, 28). He is 'Son' who has been made royal-Messiah and priestly by virtue of God's proclamation. By this proclamation he bears all the aspects of Sonship both radiating divine glory and having glorified humanity of the completed eschatological man (1:5). Thus, Hebrews is able to link Ps 2:7 with Ps 110:1. Here in Heb 5:5, he follows the logic that if Ps 2:7 and Ps 110 are linked then the glorification of the Son is the moment he is also declared to be the high priest of the order of Melchizedek (5:6b σὺ ἱερεὺς εἰς τὸν αἰῶνα κατὰ τὴν τάξιν Μελχισέδεκ). The two passages are linked by what the Father says to the Son as he glorifies the latter calling him to ascend. Consider the linking: ὁ Χριστὸς οὐχ ἑαυτὸν ἐδόξασεν γενηθῆναι ἀρχιερέα ἀλλ᾽ ὁ λαλήσας πρὸς αὐτόν...καθὼς καὶ ἐν ἑτέρῳ λέγει. If he is a priest of the new order, he must also enter into the heavenly temple so that the declaration of Ps 110:1 "sit at my right hand" is an ascension of the king-priest.

The Father has declared the sonship, inviting the Son to come up and sit at his right hand. The Son enters the divine glory because he has satisfied the Father having made purification for sin,[112] completing his task in earthly obedience. Therefore, the Father directs the Son to come and sit (1:3c καθαρισμὸν τῶν ἁμαρτιῶν ποιησάμενος ἐκάθισεν ἐν δεξιᾷ τῆς μεγαλωσύνης ἐν ὑψηλοῖς). There is no exaltation without an ascent into heaven for Hebrews. The glorified man crowned in regality of 'honor and glory' enters God's presence and sits within the divine glory. This action is the destiny of Adam fulfilled in the one who was also ὃς ὢν ἀπαύγασμα τῆς δόξης καὶ χαρακτὴρ τῆς ὑποστάσεως αὐτοῦ (1:3a).

We notice then that Zion is not an isolated theme tacked on at the end of Hebrews. Instead, it is integral related to Davidic sonship, glory, the eschatological man, and the heavenly assembly (Heb 12:22–23). Declaring Zion is greater than Sinai is a repetition of themes of the entire book just stated in a new way. Jesus who ascended and was installed in Zion is greater than Moses

---

112 This would suggest that it is not as if the sacrifice is not in some sense part of his "priestly" work—as theologians talk about the three offices of Christ. However, Hebrews is focused on the eschatological installment of the priest. He regularly uses γίνομαι to speak of the Son 'becoming' a high priest at his resurrection-ascension (5:5; 6:20). Ellingworth (*Hebrews*, 281) writes, "Γίνομαι is regularly used in Hebrews of Christ's 'becoming' a high priest; cf. 2:17; 5:9; 6:20; cf. 7:22, 26; more generally 1:4 of his exaltation." Heb 2:17 speaks of the necessity of the incarnation in order to become a high priest but makes no statement of when the high priesthood begins only what must happen in order to be a high priest. Thus, incarnation is a necessary condition for becoming a high priest, but it is not a sufficient condition since he must become the eschatological man via resurrection if he is to be the eschatological priest. The basis for his priesthood is not his weakness or succumbing to death, that is the old order, but the oath is given upon his resurrection "you are a priest of the order of Melchizedek" (7:16–17).

who ascended Mt. Sinai. The covenant Jesus inaugurated is greater than the covenant Moses mediated via the angels (2:1–4). The priesthood of the Old Covenant is surpassed by the greater priest of the New Covenant. Jesus ascended into the heavenly Jerusalem and now calls us there. He drew near so the believer can draw near (10:19–22). He is appointed firstborn, the Davidic heir and true Adam, and given the inheritance of the age to come. None of these motifs work without the exaltation of Christ being an ascension into heaven itself.

Hebrews' scholarship often talks boldly about the exaltation of Jesus, the appointment of the Son, and the climax of eschatology. All these motifs, as important as they are, hinge on Hebrews' belief that after his death and resurrection the Son of God, Jesus, ascended into heaven. Ascension is not a metaphor in Hebrews but an eschatological act that God carries out upon the Son. Heaven is where God dwells on his throne, and through ascension the Son, in glorified humanity, enters heaven. God has installed his Son on the throne which is the true reality after which the earthly tabernacle was patterned. For the Second Temple Jew, heaven is not a metaphor but a very real "place" from which God reigns and dwells over all the creation—and for Hebrews, a resurrected human being has now progressed up into heaven through the divine temple to the apex of all creation where God establishes his kingly rule. Hebrews does not focus on a mythic journey of ascent or a visionary mystical quest; but it makes Christ's ascension the crucial climax of redemption.

God, in installing his Son, has seen the work of the Son for God's people and is satisfied. The obedience of the Son in true humanity and in vicarious suffering in solidarity with his people makes the Son worthy of his ascension. The Son, in Hebrews thinking, is an eternal Son who had the divine glory from all eternity past—but his earthly and human activity makes him entirely worthy of bearing the fulness of divine glory as the eschatological man. Thus, the children of God will be able to become 'sons of glory' and have access to God's very presence in the true tabernacle that is heaven.

Up to this point, we maintained a certain meaning to "being perfected" in Hebrews based on our early arguments (cf. above chapter 4) but we must now return our attention briefly to examine the soundness of that notion. In chapter four, we have already surveyed the options for the meaning of perfection, arguing that Christ's being perfected is his becoming the eschatological man. "Perfection" in Hebrews is fundamentally an eschatological concept. As we noted previously, McCruden argues for a view of divine attestation:

Hebrews' portrayal of Jesus' profound humanity functions to say something about the character of Christ. Although he is God's Son (Heb 5:5, 8) and a Priest forever (Heb 5:6), Christ is essentially defined by his intimacy with the human condition. Such intimacy in consonant with the portrayal we have seen thus far of Christ as merciful and sympathetic. Perfection therefore signifies the depth of Christ's beneficence. Perfection, in other words, comments upon the extent of Christ's participation in the human sphere.[113]

First, one can find this "intimacy with the human condition" or some variation of the concept in every view of 'perfection.' Wescott and Cullmann see intimacy with the human condition in their 'moral' or 'ethical' view. Wescott emphasizes the Son's obedience and self-surrender to the Father: "He realized to the uttermost the absolute dependence of humanity upon God in the personal communion with Him...He fulfilled in a true human life the destiny of man personally...He fulfilled in His life, as Head of the race, the destiny of humanity by redemption and consummation."[114] Cullmann also states, "In order to lead humanity to its completion, the High Priest must go through the various stages of human life...he lived under the very same human conditions as we."[115] "[T]he High Priest not only completely enters the realm of humanity, but within that realm must participate in everything that is human."[116] Likewise, Peterson sees the obedience of the Son that leads to perfection as identity with humanity and sharing in true humanity to be qualified for his vocation: "When Jesus is described as 'perfected for ever', then the picture is...one who proved himself in the events of his human experience 'devout, guileless, undefiled',"[117] G.B. Caird argues that Christ won the right to open up the way into heaven:

> He himself was made perfect because he experienced to the full all the conditions of human life, because by a faith and obedience, a dependence on God which is open to all men to share, he won the right to enter God's presence, and won it not for himself alone but for all who were prepared to let him call them brothers.[118]

---

113 McCruden, *Solidarity Perfected: Beneficent Christology in the Epistle to the Hebrews* (de Gruyter, 2008), 114.
114 Wescott, *Hebrews*, 65–66.
115 Cullmann, *The Christology of the New Testament*, trans. S.C. Guthrie and C.A.M Hall (SCM, 1959), 93.
116 Ibid., 94.
117 Peterson, *Hebrews and Perfection*, 118.
118 G.B. Caird, "Just Men Made Perfect," *The London Quarterly and Holborn Review* 191

Second, this solidarity with humanity is precisely the feature of offering an Adamic obedience. Christ is the representative and the pioneer. He is undoing the curse of Adam in his vicarious suffering, but he is also advancing humanity to its eschatological end by virtue of obeying as the true Son. The 'perfection' that Christ experiences is glorification, the transition to the eschaton. His priestly action brings in the age to come; but in his own person the transition is first realized. The Son suffers as climax of the curse. His suffering is in a manner where he fully gives himself into God's hands trusting God to deliver him from death. This act is an action of Adamic-Davidic trusting-obedience. The Son, then, is not only the lever that moves 'the present evil age' into the 'age to come,' he is the trailblazing pioneer that enters first so that he can representatively bring his brothers with him. We find in the Son Adamic representation for God's people just as in the Psalms the Davidic King is not only an Adamic figure—a true and ideal man—he often is the one who leads the people before the throne of God. God installs his Son on Mt. Zion and the rest of the people of God experience the blessing as they acquiesce to and obey the installed Son-King. We agree with McCruden who writes, "the personal offering of Christ allows for an analogous relationship of intimacy between God and the faithful."[119]

The obedience of the Son leads him to be perfected and appointed the high priest. This obedience becomes the ground for his ascension. He lives a life of humanity in full solidarity with his people and in representation for them. Having thus been qualified and given the eschatological state, he carries humanity to its eschatological destiny. Just as the priest in the OT wore the robes of glory, so the Son was fully human. As human, he acted in the fullness of the human condition with trust upon the Father. Now he has entered God's presence as the true human and in representation of the people of God, sons he is bringing to glory. Fulfilling the Adamic role and destiny of humanity is vital to his becoming the high priest, and it is the grounds of his ascension. The same is true of the kingly aspects of the Adamic sonship. The king is exalted up onto God's royal throne because of his character, loving righteousness and hating wickedness. The obedience of the Adamic Son leads to his ascension and God's people in God's presence.

This movement is presented in the flow of the passage. Jesus is the great high priest who passed through the heavens (4:14a). He is 'the Son of God,' a confession to which believers are to hold fast. Jesus knows how to help us in our weakness and grant us mercy and grace. We can draw near to the 'throne

---

(1966): 93.

119 McCruden, *Solidarity Perfected*, 117.

of grace,' which is implicitly grounded on the facts that Jesus was weak but now ascended into God's presence as mediating high priest. Then, in 5:1–4, high priests are weak but called by God to their office. So also, Jesus was called by God; he was declared Son and installed/begotten in royalty in his exaltation-glorification. But this would not have happened if he had not exercised trust in human weakness and trial (5:7–8). Thus, he learned obedience and was perfected, i.e., became the eschatological man. As a result, he is the source of our salvation, being designated the priest of a better order, Melchizedek's order. There is a sort of symmetrical flow to the passage highlighting the repeated movement of the climax of redemptive history: weakness/humility leads to perfection/glorification/exaltation. Earthly humanity gives way to the ascension of the Son in the glorified state.

### Heb 10:5–9 Obedience to Establish the Second Covenant

Hebrews 10 returns again to the theme of the sacrifice of Christ in contrast to the sacrifices that took place under the law. The Old Covenant of the Law was only a shadow of the coming things (10:1a Σκιὰν γὰρ ἔχων ὁ νόμος τῶν μελλόντων ἀγαθῶν). Here again, the Law with the Levitical priests and earthly sacrifice is not itself part of the age to come but only a prefigurement of it. True reality is the eschaton that has been brought in by the work of the Son. Thus, the things that the Son fulfills are the true realities to which the administration of the Law did not belong (10:1 οὐκ αὐτὴν τὴν εἰκόνα τῶν πραγμάτων). The New Covenant is superior, with a superior priest, a superior sacrifice, and superior revelation.

The problem with the sacrifices of the Law is that they must be repeated. They cannot make the worshipper perfect in his drawing near to God (10:1 κατ' ἐνιαυτὸν ταῖς αὐταῖς θυσίαις ἃς προσφέρουσιν εἰς τὸ διηνεκὲς οὐδέποτε δύναται τοὺς προσερχομένους τελειῶσαι). This statement echoes back to the contrast between the sacrificial effectiveness outlined in chapter 9 esp. 9:9–14. The 'perfection' that they cannot bring is that of the eschatological state. In fact, under that Law only the priest can enter the holy of holies and the ability of the congregation to draw near is limited to participation in the outer courts. Hebrews' logic is simple: if the sacrifices in the Law accomplished what they pointed to instead of just prefiguring it as the shadow, then the sacrifices could have (a) ceased being offered and (b) would have purified the conscience of sin[120] (10:2 ἐπεὶ οὐκ ἂν ἐπαύσαντο προσφερόμεναι διὰ τὸ μηδεμίαν

---

120 The phrase συνείδησιν ἁμαρτιῶν denotes the cleansing of the conscience from the outgoing stain of sins guilt and corruption. If the conscience had been purified, it would have

ἔχειν ἔτι συνείδησιν ἁμαρτιῶν τοὺς λατρεύοντας ἅπαξ κεκαθαρισμένους;). Instead, they are offered yearly (10:3), and the worshiper is reminded of the presence of their sins and their inability to truly draw near to God. There is not a final act of mercy and an expiation of sin, but a regular reminder of the sin and moral impurity upon the people of God. Thus, Hebrews concludes that the blood of goats and bulls did not take away sin (10:4 ἀδύνατον γὰρ αἷμα ταύρων καὶ τράγων ἀφαιρεῖν ἁμαρτίας.) In fact, the earthly sacrifices were unable to take away sins in finality. The earthly sacrifices were also unable to be the true and final revelation of God; indeed, as the 'shadow' were never intended to be the final revelation of redemption. Earthly sacrifices were like a signpost pointing to that which must come. They were conducted in an earthly tabernacle that was a pattern, an inferior mirror image, of the heavenly. Both sacrifice and tabernacle initiated in the Law were prefigurements in terms of temporal priority (in terms of the horizontal unfolding of redemption) and shadows in terms of heavenly-earthly distinction.

The "form of the real" (10:1 τὴν εἰκόνα τῶν πραγμάτων) is Christ himself and his work—specifically the obedient activity that he carries out for the Father which entails his self-sacrifice. Hebrews uses LXX Ps 39:7–9 [MT. Ps 40:7–9; Eng. vv. 6–8]. The Psalm is placed as something spoken by the Son. In its original context, it is a Psalm of David, possibly a "royal liturgy of supplication."[121] "This psalm as a type of royal psalm helps to account for the individual and collective elements,"[122] elements that we see in Heb 2 with respect to Christ's kingship and corporate representation of his people. Our author sees the Psalm as something that is fulfilled in the work of the Son in his incarnation. He is the true and eschatological David who conducts himself in fulfillment of the Davidic ideal. In fact, the superscription in LXX itself may have been what causes the author to read the Psalm in this light: Εἰς τὸ τέλος· τῷ Δαυιδ ψαλμός (39:1). The general context is, again, David making a petition to the Lord and waiting for the Lord to act. The Lord then raises him up from the pit of misery (LXX Ps 39:3 καὶ ἀνήγαγέν με ἐκ λάκκου ταλαιπωρίας). David then goes on to tell of God's righteousness in the great assembly (LXX Ps 39:10a εὐηγγελισάμην δικαιοσύνην ἐν ἐκκλησίᾳ μεγάλῃ), which thematically is what Hebrews has portrayed Jesus doing in the heavenly assembly with the use of Ps 22:22 [LXX Ps 21:23] in Heb 2:12. The delivered Davidic son speaks of YHWH's greatness in the assembly. The Psalm ends with a fresh appeal by

---

meant the worshippers was holy, blameless, and undefiled, thus able to enter God's presence.
121 August Konkel, "The Sacrifice of Obedience," Διδασκαλια 2 (1991): 4.
122 Ibid., 5.

David to the LORD that he might be delivered from the new situation of trouble. David continually looks to the Lord.

At the center of the Psalm is the proclamation of David's obedience to the Lord that goes beyond just mere participation in the sacrifices. Here, Hebrews takes advantage of the rendering from LXX that highlights the obedience of David in doing the will of the Father: τοῦ ποιῆσαι τὸ θέλημά σου, ὁ θεός μου (LXX Ps 39:9).

Before discussing the interpretation, we note there is a textual variant in LXX in Ps 39:7. Aquila, Symmachus, and Theodotian[123] follow the variant that aligns more closely with the Hebrew: אָזְנַיִם כָּרִיתָ לִּי which is rendered as ὠτία δὲ κατηρτίσω μοι. However, as Lane points out, "the great uncials of ℵ, B, and A all contain the rendering of σῶμα not ὠτία."[124] As Attridge puts it "Hebrews exploits the contrast of sacrifice and willing obedience, yet the interpretative translation in LXX of 'body' for 'ears' also serves the purpose of the argument."[125] Karen Jobes has proposed that the change in Hebrews' use of LXX Ps 39 can be attributed to the phenomenon of paronomasia.[126] This proposal leads her to suggest that the variant is original to Hebrews.[127] However, Jared Compton has examined Jobes' thesis and argues it is not the most plausible solution to the issues.[128] Steyn also argues that the differences should be attributed to textual variation in LXX rather than the hand of the NT author.[129]

Hebrews is able to take a passage concerning David's dependence upon God marked out by obedience, not just mere sacrifice, and change its setting to contrast the eschatological act of obedience offered by the Son in his incarnation against the habitual repeated sacrifices of the Old Covenant. In a 'body' the true and final Adamic-Davidic kingly figure offers up an act of supreme and final obedience to God. He fulfills the vocation of true humanity in order to usher in the eschatological. He accomplishes this act on behalf of

---

123  See also Attridge, *Hebrews*, 274n.70.

124  Lane, *Hebrews 9–13*, 255n.m; see also the textual apparatus in Alfred Rahlfs and Robert Hanhart, eds., *Septuaginta* (Deutsche Bibelgesellschaft, 2006), 2:41. Ronald H. van der Bergh (rightly) argues that LXX Ps 39:7 should be σῶμα and Rahlfs' text should be amended ("A Textual Comparison of Hebrews 10:5b–7 and LXX Psalm 39:7–9," *Neotestmentica* 42.2 [2008]: 379).

125  Attridge, *Hebrews*, 274.

126  Karen Jobes, "Rhetorical Achievement in the Hebrews 10 'Misquote' of Psalm 40," *Biblica* 72 (1991): 387–396; "The Function of Paronomasia in Hebrews 10:5–7," *TrinJ* 13 (1992): 181–191.

127  Jobes, "Rhetorical Achievement," 388.

128  Jaren Compton, "The Origin of ΣΩΜΑ in Heb 10:5 Another Look at a Recent Proposal," *TrinJ* 32 (2011): 19–29.

129  Steyn, *A Quest for the Assumed LXX Vorlage of the Explicit Quotations in Hebrews* (Vandenhoeck & Ruprecht, 2011), 292. He argues, in part, that a personal modification of the OT quote would be atypical for the author of Hebrews. For text critical issues see also Ronald H. van der Bergh, "A Textual Comparison of Hebrews 10:5b–7 and LXX Psalm 39:7–9," 353–382.

the people of God. This great climax of obedience serves to inaugurate the New Covenant and transition from Old to the eschatological New. In doing the will of God, Jesus does away with the first covenant in order to establish the second (10:9b ἀναιρεῖ τὸ πρῶτον ἵνα τὸ δεύτερον στήσῃ). Christopher Richardson reaches a similar conclusion, arguing "king David's example of steadfast obedience in suffering and persecution was climactically recapitulated by Jesus."[130]

First Hebrews introduces the quotation of the Psalm with διὸ εἰσερχόμενος εἰς τὸν κόσμον. This is a reference to his incarnation and coming into the earthly world. Hebrews uses κόσμος four times, and each one clearly refers not the eschatological world or the heavenly but to this world. In 4:3 and 9:26, we have the reference to creation with the phrase καταβολῆς κόσμου. In 11:7, Hebrews speaks of Noah and his building of the ark as the act through which his house is saved and δι' ἧς κατέκρινεν τὸν κόσμον. The statement is part of the theme that Hebrews is building in chapter 11 that the heroes of the faith had assurance of things unseen and greater promises than just the things of this world. For example, Abraham in 11:10 ἐξεδέχετο γὰρ τὴν τοὺς θεμελίους ἔχουσαν πόλιν ἧς τεχνίτης καὶ δημιουργὸς ὁ θεός. Κόσμος should be seen as that which will be shaken at the end of the age to give way to the unshakeable kingdom God's people are inheriting (12:26). Our point remains that διὸ εἰσερχόμενος εἰς τὸν κόσμον speaks of the coming of the Son into this world in the incarnation where he has flesh and blood like those he will save (2:14, 17).

LXX Ps 39, then, is used as a Psalm that the Son confesses to God the Father in his incarnation as an expression of his entire earthly vocation.[131] The Son takes up all the features of humanity and offers up human obedience in order that he might achieve the true destiny and eschatological end that awaited humanity. His act of obedience qualifies him for this role. As the Davidic figure *par excellence*, the Son now confesses David's psalm to his heavenly Father.

In the original context of the Psalm, 'not desiring sacrifices and offerings' (θυσίαν καὶ προσφορὰν οὐκ ἠθέλησας) may be reminiscent of the critiques that the prophets have against the vain and empty repetition of the sacrificial system. Jesus echoes the prophet's critique as well. The author may have been aware of this aspect of Jesus' ministry. In Hebrews' use of this Psalm, the author may have specifically in view that Christ did not need to offer sacrifices for himself as the high priests of the OT did (7:27, cf. also 5:3). Because he has no need of these sacrifices, he is fit to offer something different, obedience

---

[130] Richardson, *Pioneer and Perfecter*, 95.
[131] Steyn, *Quest for the Assumed LXX Vorlage*, 295.

## The Son's Adamic Obedience Leads to Ascension 243

that will bring about the eschaton. He can mediate a new and better covenant because he himself does not have to offer the sacrifices of the Old.

The Son, in confessing this Psalm to the Father, also recognizes the futility of the Old Covenant and so offers up something greater. Hebrews has already indicated that the Old Covenant was not faultless (8:7) in that it had been broken by God's people who had transgressed it (8:9, 9:15). God, no longer taking pleasure in the sacrifices (note the repetition in 10:8 θυσίας καὶ προσφορὰς καὶ ὁλοκαυτώματα καὶ περὶ ἁμαρτίας οὐκ ἠθέλησας οὐδὲ εὐδόκησας), makes the Old Covenant obsolete (8:11) in light of the new and greater obedience the Son offers to the Father. The Son came with a greater mission and task than offering up sacrifices of goats and bulls. He comes to obey the Father and offer up himself paying for transgression under the Old Covenant (9:15). The Son, doing the will of the Father in his sacrificial death, does away with the first covenant and establishes the second/new covenant (Heb 10:9 τότε εἴρηκεν· ἰδοὺ ἥκω τοῦ ποιῆσαι τὸ θέλημά σου. ἀναιρεῖ τὸ πρῶτον ἵνα τὸ δεύτερον στήσῃ).

Notably, in Exod 24 when the first covenant was established, it was established with the obedience of the people in view. Moses gives the words of the Lord to the people and they respond with one voice: "All the words that the LORD has spoken we will do" (Exod 24:3).[132] This pledge of obedience is repeated again by the people once the sacrifice is made and the people hear the words of the Book of the Covenant (סֵפֶר הַבְּרִית; τὸ βιβλίον τῆς διαθήκης) in 24:7—"All that the LORD has spoken we will do, and we will be obedient."[133] Israel "hears" the covenant and pledges to "do and hear" it, i.e., to keep it (נַעֲשֶׂה וְנִשְׁמָע; ποιήσομεν καὶ ἀκουσόμεθα). Yet, as Hebrews draws to our attention through the use of Jeremiah, Israel did not keep the covenant (8:8–12; Jer. 31:31–34). The first covenant's inauguration is followed by Moses, Aaron, and the seventy elders ascending the mountain of God—Mt. Sinai. They 'go up' and are given a vision of the divine throne itself. They see God and beautiful sapphire under his feet.[134]

---

132 MT: וַיֹּאמְרוּ כָּל־הַדְּבָרִים אֲשֶׁר־דִּבֶּר יְהוָה נַעֲשֶׂה; LXX λέγοντες Πάντας τοὺς λόγους, οὓς ἐλάλησεν κύριος, ποιήσομεν καὶ ἀκουσόμεθα.

133 MT: כֹּל אֲשֶׁר־דִּבֶּר יְהוָה נַעֲשֶׂה וְנִשְׁמָע; LXX Πάντα, ὅσα ἐλάλησεν κύριος, ποιήσομεν καὶ ἀκουσόμεθα.

134 We should point out that there are similarities between Exod 24:10 and Ezek 1. "Under his feet" in Exod 24:10 probably implies YHWH's sitting at a throne which we have in Ezek 1:26. We also have the sapphire mentioned in both verses. There is also similarity in that God is anthropomorphized with feet in Exod 24:10, and with human likeness in Ezek 1:26. Ezek 1:28 describes these things as being the glory of the Lord which is the same thing in focus in Exod 24:17. Again in Exod 24:17 and Ezek 1:27 we have the appearance of fire. The reason we point this out is that Ezekiel becomes a latter influence for Apocalyptic thought, Merkabah mysticism, heavenly visions, and heavenly ascents (Peter Schäfer, *The Origins of Jewish Mysticism* [Princeton University, 2009], 34–52, 56–61, 104–108, 128, 134–139; Eskola, *Messiah and the*

The use of חזה in Exod 24:10 "probably conveys the idea that Moses and the other representatives of Israel had a visionary experience of the heavenly sanctuary/temple."[135] Then Moses is invited up further in a sort of heavenly ascent (24:12-15). The glory of the Lord descends on Mt. Sinai as Moses is up in the presence of God (24:16-17). The Mountain is like a version of the temple where the priests are allowed to progress so far, but the high priest progresses even further upward toward the throne where the glory of God dwells.[136] Because the people have professed obedience and the covenant has been inaugurated by blood, Moses is able to representatively progress up the Mountain into the sanctuary of God. "The implication can be drawn that the Sinaitic covenant occurred in the context of a heavenly sanctuary/temple experience."[137] God will then build a portable sanctuary so God can go with his people (Exod 25:8-9).

Ezekiel the Tragedian, in his work the *Exagōgē*, which dates from around the first part of the second century B.C.E,[138] describes Moses' going up in a

---

*Throne*, 67-68; Martha Himmelfarb, *Ascent to Heaven in Jewish and Christian Apocalypses* (Oxford University Press, 1993), 10-13; Christopher Rowland, *The Open Heaven: A Study of Apocalyptic in Judaism and Early Christianity* [Wipf & Stock, 2002], 84-88). Recently work has shown that Merkabah mysticism influences Hebrews' portrayal of Christ's enthronement (Timo Eskola, *Messiah and the Throne: Jewish Merkabah Mysticism and Early Christian Exaltation Discourse* (Mohr Siebeck, 2001), 202-211, 251-269; Jody Barnard, *The Mysticism of Hebrews: Exploring the Role of Jewish Apocalyptic Mysticism in the Epistle to the Hebrews* (Mohr Siebeck, 2012), especially chs. 5-6). With the Exodus background and the Second Temple tradition of Moses' ascent, the argument that Hebrews drawing connections between covenant inauguration and heavenly ascent is not far-fetched. That ascension inaugurates the new covenant see especially Feliz Cortez, "'The Anchor of the Soul that Enters the Veil': the Ascension of the 'Son' in the Letter to the Hebrews" (Ph.D. Diss., Andrews University, January 2008), 386-413; Barnard, *Mysticism*, 91-93, 97, 187.

135 Elias Brasil de Souza, "The Heavenly Sanctuary/Temple Motif in the Hebrews Bible: Function and Relationship to the Earthly Counterparts" (PhD. diss., Andrews University, 2005), 163. See his discussion (154-173) of the ascent motif, the imagery of lapis lazuli, the covenant meal on the mountain, and being under YHWH's throne. All of these passages lend support to an ascension motif and an opening of heaven itself on the mountain.

136 Beale, *Temple and the Church's Mission: A Biblical Theology of the Dwelling Place of God* (Intervarsity, 2004), 105-106; Morales, *Who Shall Ascend*, 87-88, 95-100. Morales writes, "The purpose of the tabernacle, then, will be to perpetuate the Sinai experience of engagement with God — YHWH's dwelling in the midst of Israel being the very essence of the covenant" (96). He also points out just as the Law was given at the summit of Sinai, so the Law was kept in the Holy of Holies (97).

137 de Souza, "The Heavenly Sanctuary" 489.

138 R.G. Robertson, "Ezekiel the Tragedian: A New Translation and Introduction" in *The Old Testament Pseudepigrapha*, ed. James H. Charlesworth (Yale University Press, 1985), 2:804. Moffitt (*Atonement and the Logic of the Resurrection*, 157), following Pierlguigi Lanfranchi (*L'Exagoge d'Ezéchiel le Tragique: Introduction, Texte, Traduction et Commentaire* [Brill, 2006], 10), dates it more broadly between the third and first centuries BCE. W. Hall Harris III (*The Descent of Christ: Ephesians 4:7-11 and Traditional Hebrew Imagery* [Baker, 1996], 124) considers there to be an emerging consensus of a second-century BCE date.

*The Son's Adamic Obedience Leads to Ascension*     245

dream to Sinai in an ascent like fashion in 67–82. Moses sees the throne of God set on Sinai (68 ἔ[δο]ξ' ὄρους κατ' ἄκρα Σιν[αί]ου θρόνον) and touching the clouds of heaven (69) which is theophanic language but also suggest Sinai peaks into heaven itself as the cosmic Mountain of God's temple. "[I]n ancient Near Eastern imagery the heavenly dwelling of a god is often set on a high mountain."[139] God, like a man, is sitting upon this throne with a crown.[140] God hands Moses the scepter in a royal symbol of his installation, and Moses notes, God "bade me mount the throne, and gave me the crown," εἰς θρόνον μέγαν εἶπεν καθῆσθαι· βασιλικὸν δ' ἔδωκέ μοι (74–75). He is given view of the entire earth (77 ἐγὼ δ' ἐσεῖδον γῆν ἅπασαν ἔγκυκλον),[141] perhaps imagery of a king surveying his dominion, and the stars fall down before him (79–82).[142] Moses is becoming a vice-regent.[143] This ascent is more of a visionary experience ascent, but it describes a kind of investiture of Moses. While texts available to us of *Exagōgē* are fragmentary, it illustrates the interpretation of "a tradition of Moses ascending from Sinai into heaven and being offered dominion and reign on the heavenly throne."[144] The interpretation of the dream comes in 83–89, specifically in 85–86. Moses will cause a throne to rise and rule over men: ἆρα γε μέγαν τιν' ἐξαναστήσεις θρόνου καὶ αὐτὸς βραβεύσεις καὶ καθηγήσῃ βροτῶν (85–86). Moses himself may even take on prophetic or perhaps even divine like qualities seeing the present, past, and future (89 ὄψει τά τ' ὄντα τά τε πρὸ τοῦ τά ὕστερον). Thus, W. Hall Harris III concludes, "Based on the imagery involved (regardless of debate over the status of Moses' deification)[145] it seems clear that a tradition of Moses' heavenly ascent is reflected in the *Exagoge*."[146] His ascension is his enthronement and in enthronement he then brings the covenant down to the people of God. As Kinzer writes, "The

---

139 Mark Kinzer, "'All Things Under His Feet': Psalm 8 in the New Testament and in Other Jewish Literature of Late Antiquity" (PhD diss., University of Michigan, 1995), 171, cf. also 165–166.

140 Bock, *Blasphemy and Exaltation in Judaism: The Charge Against Jesus in Mark 14:53–65* (Baker, 1998), 142: "if one reads the beginning parallels to Dan 7 and Ezek 1 correctly, it is God who gives him the throne." Cf. also Hengel, *Studies in Early Christianity*, 190.

141 This may even be vice-regency type language since the Lord 'sits above the circle of the earth'; cf. Isa 40:22 ὁ κατέχων τὸν γῦρον τῆς γῆς.

142 There are clear echoes to Joseph's dream here.

143 Mark Kinzer, "All Things Under His Feet," 172.

144 Moffitt, *Atonement and the Logic of Resurrection*, 157. See Hurtado (*One God One Lord: Early Christian Devotion and Ancient Jewish Monotheism*, 2nd ed. [T&T Clark, 1998], 57–59) for a brief introduction to the issues and varying interpretations.

145 Hengel (*Studies in Early Christology*, 191) is probably right that deification "would have as a consequence the 'abdication of God.'"

146 Harris, *The Descent of Christ*, 127.

*Exagoge* of Ezekiel the Dramatist therefore witnesses to the existence of a Moses' ascent-enthronement tradition in the second-century B.C.E."[147]

There is a mention of Moses' ascending Mt Sinai in Pseudo-Philo's *LAB*, which leaves the impression that when Moses ascended on Mt. Sinai, he was going into heaven itself. In *LAB* 11:15 we read of Moses' going up onto the mountain. Moses goes up the mountain and draws near the cloud. On the mountain, he is shown the tree of life and the various elements of the tabernacle that he is to make. While there he 'cuts off a branch' from the tree of life, "[t]hus the author apparently intended to portray the tree of life as actually present, and this implies that Moses made the ascent to paradise (heaven)."[148] In 12:1, we get a hint that perhaps Moses has not just ascended onto the mountain but into heaven: "And Moses came down. And when he had been bathed with invisible light, he went down to the place where the light of the sun and the moon are; and the light of his face surpassed the splendor of the sun and the moon."[149] Since Moses comes down to the place of the sun and moon, it seems our author is interpreting the ascent onto Sinai as one into heaven itself.[150] Moffitt summarizes, "Thus the *L.A.B.* appears to conceive of Moses having left the realm of this world and having gone into heaven."[151] As we discussed in chapter four, according to *LAB* 32:8–10 part of the revelation to Moses on Mt. Sinai was that if God's people would walk in God's ways they would have open to them the blessings of Paradise and the promises to Adam would be fulfilled in them. In that context, obedience to the temple cult and the celebration of the sacred festival (*LAB* 13:2–7) was the means of achieving the promises and blessings.

2 Baruch 59:3 describes the shaking of the heavens, "the heaven which are under the throne of the Mighty One were severely shaken when he [God] took Moses with him."[152] This probably implies that Moses was taken up into heaven since God took Moses with him. He is given revelation of a great number of things, but especially "the likeness of Zion with its measurements"

---

147 Mark Kinzer, "All Things Under His Feet," 179.
148 Ibid., 131.
149 In *The Old Testament Pseudepigrapha*, 2:319.
150 On Matt Sinai being associated with the tabernacle so that ascension to the mountain parallels the priest's ascension into the holy of holies and the throne room of God see Morales, *Who Shall Ascend*, 86–103.
151 Moffitt, *Atonement and the Logic of the Resurrection*, 158.
152 *LAB* 32:7–8 also seems to imply an opening of heaven itself on Mount Sinai. There "the earth was shaken from its firmaments ... the clouds lifted up their floods against the flame of fire so that it [the earth] would not burn up. Then the abyss was aroused from its very springs, and all the waves of the sea gathered together. Then Paradise gave off the scent of its fruit." Not only do the lower regions of the earth tremble and quake, but the fire of the Lord's glory descends, and the upper realm of heaven opens so much that one can smell the fruit of Paradise. cf. Hebrews 12:26 with a reference to God's voice shaking the earth at this revelation.

(59:4) and "the greatness of Paradise" (59:8), which is presumably heaven, and the multitude of the angels which cannot be counted (59:11). While this could be visionary, it is more probable with the description of the heavens being shaken "that the author of 2 Baruch intended his readers to understand that Moses was taken up into the very presence of God himself."[153]

In several places, Philo seems to indicate that Moses' going up into Mt. Sinai was a heavenly ascent.[154] In *Mut.* 7, Moses is described as "the spectator of the invisible nature, the man who really saw God (for the sacred scriptures say that he entered 'into the darkness,' by which they mean figuratively to imitated the invisible essence)," ὁ τῆς ἀειδοῦς φύσεως θεατὴς καὶ θεόπτης εἰς γὰρ τὸν γνόφον φασὶν αὐτὸν οἱ θεῖοι χρησμοὶ εἰσελθεῖν, τὴν ἀόρατον καὶ ἀσώματον οὐσίαν.[155] In *QE* 2.40 on Sinai, Moses goes beyond heaven and abides with God.[156] In *Mos.* 1:158 Moses is identified as one called 'the god and king of the whole nation' described as entering communion with God having "entered into the darkness where God was (εἴς τε τὸν γνόφον, ἔνθα ἦν ὁ θεός); that is to say, into the invisible, and shapeless, and incorporeal world, the essence (εἰς τὴν ἀειδῆ καὶ ἀόρατον καὶ ἀσώματον τῶν ὄντων)"[157]

For Philo, Moses is a "regal-like figure, a king-prophet who is given broad authority by God."[158] "Moses is the one figure who is portrayed as having seen God directly in this life without having been translated or without the aid of a vision."[159] It seems that Philo is aware of the tradition that Moses ascended to heaven at Mt. Sinai, even if Philo's intent in these passages is broader and influenced by his own cosmology and worldview.

Thus, Moses' ascending to receive the Law was his being given a vision of God and seeing the eschatological outcome that awaited humanity at the end of the age. The later Rabbis had a much fuller tradition of Moses' ascension into heaven.[160] "Moses' ascent 'on high' is understood as his inauguration

---

153  Harris, *The Descent of Christ*, 139.

154  I am appreciative of Harris, *The Descent of Christ*, 128–129, and Bock, *Blasphemy and Exaltation*, 137–140, for pointing to these references.

155  *The Works of Philo*, trans. C.D. Yonge. For Greek Text: *Philo, Works of: Greek Text with Morphology* (The Norwegian Philo Concordance Project).

156  *Philo: Questions and Answers on Exodus*, trans. Ralph Marcus, Loeb 401 (Harvard University Press, 1953), 82–83; Harris, *The Descent of Christ*, 129; cf. also Bock, *Blasphemy and Exaltation*, 138n.72.

157  Both Harris (The *Descent of Christ*, 129) and Bock (*Blasphemy and Exaltation*, 138–139) show how the language of Moses' ascending Matt Sinai is also similar language to Moses' departure at death, especially in *Mos.* 2.288–291.

158  Bock, *Blasphemy and Exaltation*, 138. See also Meeks, *The Prophet-King: Moses Traditions and Johannine Christology* (Brill, 1967), 107–117.

159  Ibid., 139.

160  It is beyond the scope of our thesis to fully examine the development and traditions of Moses' ascent into heaven particularly in the later Rabbinical period. On this see Harris,

as King and Prophet of Israel."[161] Yet, as Hebrews continually holds before the reader: the Law could not bring the perfection (7:19). It does not bring God's people up to their eschatological destiny of glory, nor does it bring the eschaton down to them. What was needed was a greater covenant (2:1–4; 7:19, 22; 8:6) with a greater Moses (3:1–6) with a greater ascension into the true temple, the true heavenly Mt. Zion. The one who ascended was Son over God's house, not like Moses who was merely a servant.

Because of the Son's ascension, now the believer comes not to Moses and Mt. Sinai, but to Zion where Christ has ascended (12:18–24). Furthermore, obedience to sacrifices and burnt offerings will not bring the glory of Adam or make perfect those who draw near,[162] rather one must come into the world "to do God's will." What is needed is the obedience of the Second Adam whereby he becomes qualified to ascend. In this obedience to the Father where he offers himself on behalf of his people, the Son becomes qualified to ascend into heaven, having himself won the eschatological glory in true human obedience. Thus, his act of obedience establishes the new covenant and grounds the ascension into heaven. As Attridge summarizes on the use of Ps 40, "Crucial for the way in which Christ establishes a covenant community in this text is the fact that he functions as a model of the virtue of fidelity."[163]

## HEB 10:10–14 CHRIST'S SACRIFICE AND ASCENSION

The work of Christ then is that he offered up his body in obedience to God, in order to do God's will. The believer's own sanctification comes through the obedience of the Son to the will of God ἐν ᾧ θελήματι ἡγιασμένοι ἐσμέν (10:10). Jesus obeying the will of his Father culminated in his obedience unto death where he served as a sacrifice of atonement for the people of God. Thus, διὰ τῆς προσφορᾶς τοῦ σώματος Ἰησοῦ Χριστοῦ ἐφάπαξ (10:10). The τῆς προσφορᾶς τοῦ σώματος refers not to the ascension of Christ but rather his earthly coming

---

*The Descent of Christ*, 64–95. See also Mark Kinzer, "All Things Under His Feet," 41–66 for a discussion of the Rabbinic linking of Moses with Ps 8, the glory of Adam, and ascent at Sinai to receive the Law. See Meeks, *The Prophet-King*, 181–196. Meeks (205) notes that for the Rabbis, Moses' ascent onto Matt Sinai was "the principle mark of his great superiority to David."

161 Meeks, *The Prophet-King*, 295. Also: "Jewish haggada...described Moses' ascent of Sinai as a heavenly enthronement" (232). In *Memar Marqah*, Moses is crowned with light and vest with YHWH's name.

162 10:2 probably has in view the eschatological aspect of perfection. Participating in the temple cult will not bring one to the glory of Adam. A new and greater person had to accomplish this. Jesus is able to bring this glory in his active obedience as the Adam-Davidic royal king-son.

163 Attridge, "The Psalms in Hebrews," in *The Psalms in the New Testament*, ed. Steve Moyise and Maarten J.J. Menken (T&T Clark, 2004), 210–211.

and doing the will of God (10:5 τῆς προσφορᾶς τοῦ σώματος; 10:7 ἰδοὺ ἥκω...τοῦ ποιῆσαι ὁ θεὸς τὸ θέλημά σου). We also note there is another comparison and contrast between Christ coming to do the will of God versus burnt offerings and sacrifices. The burnt offerings and sacrifices are offered up according to the Law (10:8b κατὰ νόμον προσφέρονται). They are not the eschatological offering of representative obedience that Jesus gives to the Father.

The parallel is between the sacrifices and burnt offerings offered outside the tabernacle on the altar and Christ who is crucified outside of the heavenly temple. God did not send Christ to offer burnt offerings and sacrifices, but instead sent him to obey his will, culminating in crucifixion. The sacrifice of obedience and utter submission leads Jesus to ascend. "Jesus' whole life was that to which the ascension offering gestured, morning and evening; and the cross itself, being nothing less than his life writ large, was but the capstone upon that obedience."[164]

The contrast between the Levitical Old Covenant and the final high priest of the New Covenant is between the former's continuation of service versus the latter's finishing his service and sitting down at the right hand of the Father in heaven. The Levitical high priest stands daily Καὶ πᾶς μὲν ἱερεὺς ἕστηκεν καθ' ἡμέραν λειτουργῶν (Heb 10:11). Here the author does not have in view Yom Kippur, but the daily work of the high priest in the earthly tabernacle. As we have argued previously, this daily work in the Holy Place is symbolic to our author of the lack of finality in the yearly Day of Atonement. The point the author is making is that we know the sacrificial system never brings completion and redemption because the priests always have to stand in an ongoing offering of sacrifices and burnt offerings (10:11a Καὶ πᾶς μὲν ἱερεὺς ἕστηκεν καθ' ἡμέραν λειτουργῶν).

It is not this way with the eschatological high priest, Jesus. In fact, not only does he ascend into heaven, he sits down at the right hand of the Father (10:12 οὗτος δὲ μίαν ὑπὲρ ἁμαρτιῶν προσενέγκας θυσίαν εἰς τὸ διηνεκὲς ἐκάθισεν ἐν δεξιᾷ τοῦ θεοῦ). This has been in view since chapter 1 (e.g., 1:3 καθαρισμὸν τῶν ἁμαρτιῶν ποιησάμενος ἐκάθισεν ἐν δεξιᾷ τῆς μεγαλωσύνης ἐν ὑψηλοῖς). Since he has sat down in fulfillment of Ps 110:1 (cf. 1:13), we are assured that the purification has been truly and effectively accomplished. The new priest is not like the priests of the Old Covenant. He finished the work of sacrifice and then ascended into the Father's presence to sit down. In 10:12, the phrase εἰς τὸ διηνεκές is parallel to ἐφάπαξ in 10:10 (also 7:27; 9:12; cf. ἅπαξ in 9:26, 28) and contrasts πολλάκις in 10:11. The anarthrous singular θυσίαν 'a sacrifice' also

---

164 Morales (*Who Shall Ascend*, 270) describes the offering as "not merely about negation, the expiation of sin."

stands in contrast to the plural θυσίας in 10:11. Now the Son is described as waiting until all his enemies are under his feet. The author again connects Ps 110:1 with Ps 8. The priest is also the reigning Davidic King and the Second Adam figure. He has taken his place on God's throne at God's right hand. The creation is being subjected to him as an outworking of his exaltation.

Again, here, Hebrews has in view spatial features. The sitting down and being at God's right hand assumes what he has previously said about the Son's ascension into heaven. He will go on and connect it to the access that believers have to the presence of God, particularly via prayer (10:18–21). The act of obedience of Jesus, the Second Adam, is the ground upon which the promise of the New Covenant is established. "Christ by obedience fulfills the promise of the new covenant that the law will be written on our hearts, that we will be God's people...The fulfillment of this covenant makes possible forgiveness (Je 31:34b), and a new boldness in coming to God."[165] This covenant is the eschatological fulfillment, so that its scope is not merely fulfillment of the earthly tabernacle but is instead the fulfillment of the heavenly reality in a final once for all act. The Son comes to earth, offers obedience by dying as the sacrifice that is the true sacrifice of atonement. Having offered himself up in death, the Son is resurrected and ascends back into heaven. He ascends as one crowned with glory and honor. The Son having offered himself in obedience to the Father has earned the right to sit at the Father's own right hand. His work is complete, his obedience has secured a people to himself, made redemption by securing their perfection/sanctification, and established the New Covenant with the assurance of forgiveness of sins. The fact that the Son actually sits down displays that his work as sacrificial offering has accomplished its purpose, and as an act of obedience the Father is satisfied.

## Conclusion

In this chapter, we focused our attention primarily on understanding two passages in Hebrews, namely 5:7–10 and 10:5–14. Our intent has been to demonstrate the nature of Jesus' obedience and that this obedience establishes the grounds for his ascension into heaven. We began by examining the contrastive clause καίπερ ὢν υἱός. We demonstrated that this clause refers to the eternal divine Sonship that Jesus has always possessed, according to the author of Hebrews. So, the argument of Hebrews leads us to expect that this type of sonship is so identified with God's nature that one would expect for this Son to be able to forego suffering. This Sonship is in distinction from the

---

165 August Konkel, "The Sacrifice of Obedience," 6.

sonship aspects that are both human and Davidic. Yet Hebrews has both the 'high Christology' of Sonship and the so-called 'low-Christology' of humanity, albeit humanity that comes to be exalted. As Richard Nelson writes, "Hebrews simultaneously promotes a 'Christology from above,' in terms of the exalted Son and heavenly high priest, and a 'Christology from below,' portraying one who willingly and obediently suffered in flesh and body under circumstances of deepest shame."[166] While we largely concur with Nelson here, it is the divine aspects that are the "high Christology" and the high priest aspects are part of the "low Christology,"[167] although the figure who is lowly from among the people becomes the exalted high priest. Nevertheless, the heavenly high priesthood aspects of Christology are connected to Christ's humanity and role as an Adamic figure. In the true fulfillment of humanity, he ascends into heaven and sits at God's own right hand.

In order to fulfill this role of humanity, Christ exercises obedient trust in God, his Father, in the midst of suffering unto death. Not only does Christ suffer in deepest shame, but in the midst of suffering he embodied a perfect humanity, demonstrating a total dependence upon God the Father in obedience to his will. Not only is the Son morally perfect in his behavior by lacking transgressions, he shows true humbled dependence which is the mark of true humanity, he cries out in trust, and is marked on earth by faithfulness. This is the point of Heb 5:7 and 8b. He trusts the Father. He learns obedience with respect to the fulfillment of human destiny. As yet-to-be-crowned king, he demonstrates himself as bearing the same morals as God in heaven and thus he 'loves righteousness and hates wickedness' (Heb 1:9). It is the exercise of true humanity actively obeying God's will to the fullest and manifesting the character of the Father while depending upon the Father that qualifies him for his ascension to the Father's right hand. This brings sanctification and perfection to the believer. As Scott Mackie writes, "The Son's obedient endurance of all the pertains to 'human being-ness' not only demonstrated his divine Sonship (5:7–9), it has also imparted to his high priestly ministry an authentic ability to represent humanity before God."[168] This representation entails heavenly ascension into God's presence.

---

166 Nelson, "He Offered Himself," 258.

167 Here we could exchange "high Christology" for the phrase "divine Christology" or "divine Sonship" and the phrase "low Christology" for the phrase "human Christology" or "human sonship."

168 Mackie, *Eschatology and Exhortation in the Epistle to the Hebrews*, WUNT 2/223 (Mohr Siebeck, 2007), 174. The obedience within creation certainly demonstrates the filial relationship prior to all creation. However, we should note that it is primarily in the glorification/exaltation of the Son that we have a revelation of his divine Sonship. Thus, Ps 2, "you are my Son" refers not simply to the present enthronement but becomes a revelatory declaration of the Father to the Son of the glory that Son always had. See our argument from Heb 1.

The background for this figure who cries out to the Lord for deliverance is primarily found in the Psalms, especially the Davidic Psalms. It is because of this active obedience, this dependent trust in the midst of suffering, that the Son is qualified for his perfection. He is crowned with glory and honor in his humanity precisely because he completes the role of the true human: trusting God for vindication through the ordeal of trial. Because he completes the vocation of humanity, he is given the eschatological role of humanity: all things under his feet in the fulfillment of Ps 8 rulership. In this, having been made perfect, he ascends into heaven as the priest-king and sits at the right hand of the Father. In his humanity, he has been qualified to be there in corporate representation of the people of God who will follow him by trust and obedience.

Finally, we turned our attention to these same motifs in Heb 10:5–14. With the use of Ps 40 [LXX Ps 39], we established that Hebrews sees Christ as the true Davidic figure who does not merely obey Law through sacrifices, but in his body exercises obedient trust to God who is his Father. Hebrews distinguishes the act of offering sacrifices, a summation of the Old Covenant, from the true task of the vocation of 'son,' which is to trust God. This has always been the expectation YHWH has for his 'sons'. It is this act of obedient trust which leads to his shed blood and sacrificial death that inaugurates a greater covenant. Just as the Old Covenant was seen as being inaugurated by shed blood (9:18) and by a heavenly ascent of the servant Moses (8:5 and Second Temple texts discussed above), so Hebrews sees Jesus' act of greater covenant inauguration as accomplished through both a sacrifice of blood and an ascent into heaven. This ascension is the enthronement of the true Davidic son, the very Son of God. Redemption has been effectively accomplished; the eschatological end has been brought to completion. The Son of God, having exercised Davidic-Adamic obedience now sits down in heaven. He is the royal figure, the true high priest, and revealed to be the eternal Son of God. It is the active obedience in humanity that qualifies Christ to ascend. It is this ascension which is his installation and royal enthronement. As the Son ascends, the Father proclaims of him: "You are my Son, today I have begotten you." Thus, the people of God have set before them one who is a high priest to whom they can turn, but also they have set before them the eternal Son of God who is the ground and hope of their confession.

Christ's work is the true Adam offering up the true human obedience in total absolute dependence. He is set forth as the true and climactic man in his total reliance on and entrusting himself to the Father. This act is the fulcrum which leverages open the 'age to come.' Without Christ serving as the pioneer in this 'active obedience', the rest of humanity trusting in Christ cannot find its way into the new creation Christ himself has inaugurated. He is, as it were, the tip of a wedge, going through first and opening access for others. His earthly obedience grounds his ascension since his obedience secured eschatological perfection and the Father then glorified him in ascension with the royal announcement of Ps 2:7 and Ps 110:1.

We conclude that, in Hebrews, S/sonship and ascension are intertwined. The Son becomes human in his incarnation. As corporate head, he is an Adamic and Davidic figure. Because he is the Adamic-Davidic figure, all the responsibilities of trust and representation are placed upon him. He fulfills these roles. Because he fulfills these roles, he qualifies to ascend, and the Father glorifies his Son crowning him with glory and honor. The Son is the 'author and perfecter' of the faith. In this ascension, where he sits down as high priest, the eternal glory of the Son is revealed—a glory that he had with the Father before the world began. Hebrews would have us understand that the Son is both the one who shares in the divine identity and the one who is the fulfillment of the Adamic-Davidic identity. Just as God reveals his person and his glory in the OT through the acts of redemption, so also the Son is revealed in this great act of redemption, the dawning of the age to come, which is inaugurated in the ascension of the Son of God to the divine throne.

# Chapter 7

# Conclusion

THE GOAL OF THIS thesis has been to contribute specifically to the study of NT theological issues in the book of Hebrews. More narrowly, it is an exploration of the relationship between Sonship and ascension in the book of Hebrews. We have sought to contribute by showing how the ascension links aspects of the author's divine Christology and Second Adam Christology. Previous references to a Second Adam Christology have not gone far enough in showing how it influences the author's larger understanding of Christ's work, especially in relationship to his ascension. Our contention has been that through an active obedience of trust in the Father the Son qualifies himself to become the true eschatological man and thus ascend into heaven.

## Summary of the Argument

We have argued that, in Hebrews, Christ's S/sonship is portrayed around two key poles: the divinity of Jesus Christ as the eternal Son of the Father and as the Davidic-Adamic son who fulfills the vocation of true humanity. In this latter aspect, Jesus obeys God in his earthly-life, entrusting himself fully to the Father. In his fidelity, he is qualified because of godliness to become the eschatological man, raised up and glorified in perfection. Having been crowned with the glory and honor in true humanity, he ascends into heaven. Not only is this ascension achieved because of the aspects of Adamic obedience but also because the Father declares that Jesus is the true Son. The Son's ascent and exaltation into glory is the means by which the Father speaks 'in Son' and reveals that the Son has enjoyed an eternal filial relationship with God the Father. These two aspects of S/sonship are unified around the motif of the ascent of the Son into heaven. We have sought to establish our thesis through four main lines of argumentation.

First, in chapters two and three, we engaged in a close exegetical reading of Heb 1. We focused attention on the author's use of the OT to establish his case that the Son's ascension and seating at the right hand of the Father is both messianic and revelatory of his divine Sonship. The Son is one who had glory with the Father before the foundation of the world (Heb 1:2–3) and was active in the act of creation (Heb 1:10–12). In the portrayal of Heb 1:10–12, the Son is identified on the divine side of the Creator-creation distinction. The Son is also the royal Davidic figure who has been invited to ascend up Mount Zion and sits at the Father's right hand (Heb 1:4, 5, 13). He has been given the future world (Heb 1:6) and reigns from heaven because he loved righteousness and hated wickedness (Heb 1:8–9). As the enthroned Messiah, he is simultaneously identified as truly God and eternal in his reign. Thus, we argued that Hebrews has a "high Christology" where the Son is eternal and truly God.

Arguing that Hebrews has a high Christology is not new to NT scholarship.[1] However, recent studies in the Christology of Hebrews by G.B. Caird, L.D. Hurst, and Kenneth L. Schenck have challenged this once standard reading of Heb 1.[2] The tide has perhaps now turned towards this understanding of Heb 1 as concerned almost exclusively with the exaltation of the Son.[3] These studies raise the question afresh whether Hebrews (esp. Heb 1) portrays any conception of the Son as preexistent or possessing an eternal divine Sonship.[4] We endeavor to redirect attention back to the aspects the Son's divinity by pointing to his sharing in the divine identity, borrowing this language

---

[1] E.g., Harold Attridge, *The Epistle to the Hebrews* (Fortress, 1989), 43, 58; F.F. Bruce, *The Epistle to the Hebrews* (Eerdmans, 1990), 59–60, 63; Gareth Lee Cockerill, *The Epistle to the Hebrews* (Eerdmans, 2012), 99–100, 109–114; Paul Ellingworth, *The Epistle to the Hebrews* (Eerdmans, 1993), 119, 122–123; Lane, *Hebrews 1–8* (Word, 1991), 11, 13, 30; David Mealand, "The Christology of the Epistle to the Hebrews," *The Modern Churchman* 22.4 (1979): 180–187; C.K. Barrett, "The Christology of Hebrews," in *Who Do You Say I Am? Essays on Christology*, ed. by Mark Allan Powell and David R. Bauer (Westminster John Knox, 1999), 114–116; Donald Hagner, "The Son of God as Unique High Priest: The Christology of the Epistle to the Hebrews," in *Contours of Christology in the New Testament*, ed. Richard N. Longenecker (Eerdmans, 2005), 248–252; Philip Hughes, "The Christology of Hebrews," *Southwestern Journal of Theology* 28 (1985): 20–21; etc.

[2] G.B. Caird, "Son by Appointment," in *The New Testament Age: Essays in Honor of Bo Reicke Volume 1* (Mercer University Press, 1984), 73–81. L.D. Hurst "The Christology of Hebrews 1 and 2," in *The Glory of Christ in the New Testament: Studies in Christology in Memory of George Bradford Caird*. Edited by L.D. Hurst and N.T. Wright (Clarendon Press, 1987), 150–164; Kenneth Schenck, "Keeping His Appointment: Creation and Enthronement in Hebrews," *JSNT* 66 (1997): 91–117.

[3] For example, Jared Compton, *Psalm 110 and the Logic of Hebrews* (T&T Clark, 2015), 19–38.

[4] Two correctives to this trend are Amy Peeler, *You Are My Son: The Family of God in the Epistle to the Hebrews* (T&T Clark, 2014), esp. 10–63 and R.B Jamieson *The Paradox of Sonship: Christology in the Epistle to the Hebrews* (InterVarsity, 2021).

from Richard Bauckham.[5] While using the concept of divine identity, we also demonstrated that the functional aspects of sonship are for Hebrews revelatory of the eternal aspects of Sonship. Thus, one does not have to abandon all the insights of Caird, Hurst, and Schenck. Instead, the discussion can be pushed forward to show how the Son taking on the roles of the true man and messianic king become revelatory of who he has always been. Thus, we concluded that Hebrews' use of LXX Ps 44 (MT 45) and LXX Ps 101 (MT 102) does indeed identify the Son as divine in the midst of a larger argument concerning his exaltation.

Some recent NT scholarship has questioned whether there is a firm Creator-creature distinction in Second Temple Judaism.[6] The question is raised: is God and his glory absolutely distinct and unique or is there more of a sliding scale of being, where figures can be exalted into divine-like status. This issue is particularly raised when angels and glorified individuals are considered. Crispin Fletcher-Louis and Andrew Chester would see a more direct line from exalted figures and glorified Adam figures to aspects of worship and divinity. While we are not speaking for every text in the Second Temple era, it is clear for Heb 1 that there is a firm contrast between the Creator and the creature. Furthermore, it is our contention that the Son is fully identified as partaking eternally on the Creator side of this distinction. We have relied on the lines of thought with regard to the nature of Second Temple Jewish Monotheism represented in the works of Richard Bauckham, Larry Hurtado, N.T. Wright, and Paul Rainbow, seeking specifically to apply them to our understanding of Heb 1.[7] As Gareth Cockerill writes, "The attribution of creation directly to the Son goes beyond the agency of v. 2 and thus underscores the inclusion of the Son within the Godhead."[8] We have taken the monotheistic background and the Son's inclusion within God's uniqueness and shown how aspects of the

---

5 Esp. his "'Monotheism and the Christology of Hebrews 1," in *Early Jewish and Christian Monotheism*, ed. Loren T. Stuckenbruck and Wendy E.S. North (T&T Clark, 2004); "Divinity of Jesus Christ in the Epistle to the Hebrews," in *The Epistles to the Hebrews and Christian Theology*, ed. Richard Bauckham, Daniel R. Driver, Trevor A. Hart, and Nathan MacDonald (Eerdmans, 2009), 36; and *Jesus and the God of Israel: God Crucified and Other Studies on the New Testament's Christology of Divine Identity* (Eerdmans, 2008).

6 Crispin Fletcher-Louis, *Christological Origins: The Emerging Consensus and Beyond*, vol. 1 of *Jesus Monotheism* (Cascade Books, 2015), 293–316; Andrew Chester, *Messiah and Exaltation* (Mohr Siebeck, 2007), 45–80

7 Larry Hurtado, *One God, One Lord: Early Christian Devotion and Ancient Jewish Monotheism* (T&T Clark, 1998), 25–27, 83–85, 90–92; Bauckham, *Jesus and the God of Israel*, 14–16; N.T. Wright, *The New Testament and the People of God* (Fortress, 1992), 248–259; Paul Rainbow, "Monotheism and Christology in I Corinthians 8. 4–6" (D.Phil. thesis, University of Oxford, 1987), 52–56; Peter R. Carrell, *Jesus and the Angels: Angelology and the Christology of the Apocalypse of John* (Cambridge University Press, 1997), 53–76.

8 *Hebrews*, 112.

ascension, with the installation of the Son on the throne as Messianic King-son, is for Hebrews revelatory of an eternal Sonship.

Understanding Hebrews' Christology (and NT Christology more broadly) by appealing to Second Temple glorified figures will not by itself explain the portrayal we find in the texts. Entering glory and experiencing glorification does not make one equal with God to the extent demonstrated in Hebrews. ANE conception of vice-regency does not do justice to the Hebrew's usage of OT texts. Certainly, like some Second Temple figures, the Son is the one who enters glory as the exalted human, but he is also shown by our study to be one who had an eternal glory from the beginning. The purpose for our detailed tracing of this aspect of Heb 1 is to lay a solid foundation for our understanding of the phrase καίπερ ὢν υἱός in Heb 5:8. Appeal to sonship in Hebrews as a category limited to the exaltation does not sufficiently explain the concessive καίπερ ὢν υἱός.

Second, in chapter four, we gave careful attention to the exaltation of Christ as the true human being crowned in glory. He is the fulfillment of Ps 8 (Heb 2:5–9), as the exalted human-son the world to come has been subjected to him (Heb 2:5). Therefore, he is the fulfillment of a royal and Adamic Christology. We should not separate a messianic reading of Ps 8 from an anthropological one. The Messiah is the true eschatological man, and he has achieved this destiny through suffering to be crowned in eschatological glory. This background can be found in Second Temple texts. As the true Adam, Christ stands in solidarity with his people representing them. He has trusted the Father, and now he leads them in the heavenly assembly, fulfilling Isa 8 and Ps 22. This solidaric representation is a fulfillment of kingship-sonship and reaches its climax as Jesus is the first to ascend into heaven, a pioneer in advance of bringing the rest of the sons to glory. This representation has features of Adamic and Davidic kingship.

As the one who ascends into heaven, Christ is also the fulfillment of the high priesthood. We demonstrated that the role of the high priest was to bring the Adamic glory as representative of God's people into the presence of God. Of course, atonement had to be made as the blood of a sacrifice was carried into the presence of God and also sprinkled on the mercy seat. Christ's ascension into heaven is the completion of this. Heb 2, ending with a focus on the high priesthood of Christ, is a continuation of the Ps 8 Second Adam motif. The true and final high priest has been crowned with glory and now ascends into the true heavenly tabernacle to represent God's people in God's presence. In the incarnation, the Son became like humans in every respect, sharing in all temptation so that he would defeat death, and ascend into God's presence as the representative. His entrance secures the future entrance for God's people as the representative sonship continues with Christ the mediator in heaven. However, if the Son had not qualified himself in his true humanity by obedient suffering there would have been no perfecting of him in eschatological humanity. His obedience leading to eschatological perfection grounds the ascension in Hebrews.

Other studies before us have used similar language of 'Second Adam Christology' to describe the portrayal of Jesus in Heb 2.[9] Our own study has confirmed this. However, these studies have not followed the theme far enough and applied this concept to both the priesthood of the Son and his progression into the heavenly temple. David Moffitt has shown the connection of the ascension of the Son in a resurrection body to the importance of a heavenly offering.[10] Our study has progressed to focus more specifically on how the Adamic figure comes to ascend. We have sought to advance the discussion by demonstrating that the roles of Adam and priesthood are not separate motifs but interrelated. Adam (with his glory) had a priestly function and priests in the Hebrew Bible and Second Temple interpretation were considered bearers of the Adamic glory. We have applied the work of Crispin Fletcher-Louis on Adam and priestly-glory to specific texts in Hebrews.[11] This allows the reader of Hebrews to better understand why Hebrews would use Ps 8 and the motif of priesthood in such close proximity in Heb 2:6–18. He is not shifting to a new argument at the end of Heb 2 but further expanding his previous one. Even more, our understanding of Hebrews is advanced by recognizing the later themes in Hebrews of perfection, rest, priesthood, and entering the tabernacle remain rooted in his Adamic-Christology. This allows the interpreter of Hebrews to see the connection between the Adamic figure of Ps 8 and the later progression of the king-priest into the heavenly tabernacle. Just as priests are Adamic figures who enter the presence of YHWH in the tabernacle, so the true and final Adam has been glorified to ascend into

---

9 Dunn, *Christology in the Making* (SCM Press, 1989), 108–113; David Peterson, *Hebrews and Perfection: An Examination of the Concept of Perfection in the "Epistle to the Hebrews"* (Cambridge University Press, 1982), 51–63; Kenneth Schenck, *Cosmology and Eschatology in Hebrews* (Cambridge University Press, 2007), 51–59; Scott Mackie, *Eschatology and Exhortation in the Epistle to the Hebrews* (Mohr Siebeck, 2007), 48; Bruce, *Hebrews*, 72–77; Moffitt, *Atonement and the Logic of the Resurrection in the Epistle to the Hebrews* (Brill, 2011), 120–143.

10 *Atonement and the Logic of the Resurrection*.

11 E.g., *All the Glory of Adam: Liturgical Anthropology in the Dead Sea Scrolls* (Brill, 2002); "God's Image, His Cosmic Temple and the High Priest," in *Heaven on Earth: The Temple in Biblical Theology*, ed. T. Desmond Alexander and Simon Gathercole (Paternoster, 2004), 81–99; "The Temple Cosmology of P and the Theological Anthropology in the Wisdom of Jesus ben Sira," in *Of Scribes and Sages: Early Jewish Interpretation and Transmission of Scripture*, ed. Craig A. Evans (Sheffield Academic Press, 2004), 1–57.

the true heavenly tabernacle. Our conclusion is that the relationship between Adamic figure and the priest illustrates further the importance of ascension into the heaven tabernacle for the theology of Hebrews.

The author of Hebrews does not just use Ps 8 and an Adam Christology in Heb 2 and then toss it aside as he moves on to other issues, rather it is driving the force his argument of a priest and a glorified perfected person (cf. Heb 5 & 7), who has entered into the true and greater tabernacle not of this creation (Heb 8:1–6; 9). Our reaffirmation of the Second Adam Christology and our expansion of this portrait anchor our understanding of the obedience the Son learns (Heb 5:8). While scholars like Kenneth Schenck have proposed that Hebrews should be understood through the lens of the larger story of salvation history,[12] we have sought to advance this by demonstrating the ascension of Jesus is the ascension of the glorified Adam-priest into heaven. This moves us along to our conclusions concerning the grounds of or basis for the Son's ascension in Hebrews.

In chapter five, we examined the ascension texts in the book of Hebrews. We began first by surveying the background of a heavenly temple/tabernacle in the Hebrew Bible and Second Temple texts. In this background, heaven is the true throne of God where his glory dwells as he reigns over all. Thus, the Son's ascension into heaven is an ascent into the glorious throne room of God. Because Christ ascends to heaven as the faithful high priest, Hebrews can specifically identify the throne as a throne of grace (Heb 4:16). Believers are exhorted to remain faithful and hold fast to their confession that Jesus is the Son of God. In fulfillment of redemptive history, the Son sits at the Father's right hand having been crowned with glory and honor and mediates for believers because he remains human and can represent them in God's presence.

In Heb 6:19–20, Hebrews connects the hope that believers have with Jesus' ascension into the heavenly tabernacle. Since Christ has gone into heaven via the ascension, the believer's hope is secure, like an anchor. As the Son has been set in heaven before God, so a living hope has been set before the believer. As surely as Christ is in God's presence, because he is the forerunner, believers are assured of entering God's presence and having access to the heavenly throne room.

In Heb 7:26, Christ is the high priest who has been exalted into heaven. He is superior to the Levitical priesthood, which is sub-eschatological, weak, and unable to perfect the worshiper. Thus, a superior priest from the line of Melchizedek was needed. Melchizedek represents the king-priest. The Son

---

12 *Cosmology and Eschatology*, 51–59.

participating in the priesthood of Melchizedek represents the eschatological fulfillment of priesthood. This priest does not serve in the earthly tabernacle, where the Levites did, but ascends into heaven to serve as priest.

In Heb 8:1–6 this contrast continues. The Levitical priests served in the earthly tabernacle and offered various gifts and sacrifices. The true and final high priest serves in heaven. The earthly tabernacle was a copy of the original true heavenly one. Thus, the Old Covenant is eschatologically inferior to the New Covenant as was the mediation offered in the former. Christ mediates a better covenant as one who has ascended into heaven to sit at God's right hand.

The last ascension texts we examined are Heb 9:11–14 and 9:23–26. There, we saw that Christ brings about the fulfillment of the age to come by ascending into heaven after his sacrifice. He enters into heaven to cleanse the heavenly tabernacle and inaugurate the New Covenant. His ascension into heaven is the ascent into the true tent. Here, Hebrews combines the horizontal elements of eschatology ('this age'/'the age to come') with the vertical elements of earth and heaven. The original tabernacle had built into it the two tents of the two ages, just as the fulfillment now highlights the contrast between Levitical-earthly vs. Melchizedekian-heavenly contrasts. The eschatological atonement is fulfilled in the heavenly tabernacle as Christ's ascension into heaven is greater than the fulfillment of the Levitical priest's entrance into the earthly Holy of Holies. The final movement into heaven is 'once for all' with the final consummative sacrifice, that of Christ himself. The Son ascends to the throne through the true and greater heavenly tent. Through death/sacrifice, resurrection, and ascension the Son comes to represent believers in heaven itself. He suffered and died for them and ascends in resurrection as one of them to represent them as the true and final high priest who sits down at the Father's right hand. Once again, ascension cannot be considered in Hebrews without the dual aspects of S/sonship being in purview.

Finally, in chapter six we sought to draw these themes together through examining two key texts: Heb 5:7–10 and 10:5–14. We explained how the phrase καίπερ ὢν υἱός in Hebrews contrasts the eternal Sonship with the aspects of obedience as related to sonship. Since Jesus is eternal the Son of God one would almost expect to be exempt from suffering. Conversely, if only Davidic or messianic sonship were in view, we would not expect the concessive καίπερ ὢν υἱός.[13] This is especially true in light of informing texts like 2 Sam

---

13 For example, Compton's reference to this being "the one who is exalted son" is unsatisfactory (*Psalm 110*, 73). The "being a son" is contemporaneous with his learning suffering whereas exaltation is subsequent to suffering for Hebrews.

7:14b and Prov 3:11–12, cited in Heb 12:5–6. When the full force of the concessive is felt, we are compelled to reexamine the relationship between 'being Son' and 'learning obedience.' What we find, then, is the true Son learns obedience as the Adamic-Davidic figure even though he was always Son. He exemplifies true obedience to YHWH by trusting him. He is heard and vindicated because of his godliness.

While previous scholarship has explained the importance of Jesus' faithfulness especially in Heb 5:7–10,[14] we advanced the understanding by connecting specifically to his Adamic vocation from Heb 2. Similarly, scholars have noted that the gospel accounts of Gethsemane likely serve as a background to Heb 5:7[15] along with possible links to several Psalms.[16] We have drawn from this discussion but demonstrated that his trusting obedience has a deeper background in a much larger motif displayed in the Psalms, particularly the Davidic Psalms. This motif is the cry of trust in God in the midst of despair and death-like ordeals.

These Psalms display true piety as the Psalmist fulfills humanity's true vocation, namely trusting and obeying God with absolute reliance, foregoing self-reliance, and exemplifying total dependence upon God. This vocation is true for Adam, for Israel (God's firstborn son), and for David. We found this vocation of true humanity represented similarly in the Jewish martyrdom traditions. For Hebrews, what is described in 5:7 is rooted deeper into his understanding of redemptive history. We have used the label "active obedience" because it entails not just allowing oneself to suffer under God's design, resigned to God's plan, but rather fully relying on and crying out to God in obedient trust. As the Psalmist cries out to the Lord as his Rock and deliverance, so does the Lord Jesus Christ. The extensiveness of this motif and the fact that that it informs the background to Heb 5:7 has not been previously drawn out. Understanding Heb 5:7 in this light elucidates a key component of Jesus' work where the human-son vocation is brought to completion, an eschatological climax. Because of this completion of human destiny, Jesus is perfected and qualified to ascend into heaven as true eschatological man. No obedience would mean no qualification for being crowned in glory, and thus no grounds for ascending into heaven. The true Son who ascends has as Second Adam

---

[14] Michael Easter, *Faith and the Faithfulness of Jesus in Hebrews* (Cambridge University Press, 2014), 120–124, 157–164; Peterson, *Hebrews and Perfection*, 84–96; Christopher Richardson, *Pioneer and Perfecter of the Faith* (Mohr Siebeck, 2012), 15–107.

[15] Richardson, *Pioneer and Perfector*, 75–81; Compton, *Psalm 110*, 72.

[16] Richardson, *Pioneer and Perfecter*, 81–82; Easter, *Faith and Faithfulness*, 162–163; Compton, *Psalm 110*, 72; Lane, *Hebrews 1–8*, 120; August Strobel, "Die Psalmengrundlage der Gethsemane-Prallele Hebr 5:7ff.," *ZNW* 45 (1954): 255–257.

qualified himself to ascend as the true and final royal Davidic-Adamic figure. As the qualified one represents his people, so the obedient believer can come into the divine presence. The Son brought to glory brings many sons to glory.

This pattern repeats itself again in Heb 10:5–10. With the use of Ps 40 [LXX 39], Hebrews shows the Son as the true obedient Davidic son. His work in obedience establishes the New Covenant and supersedes the Old Covenant sacrifices and offerings. Jesus perfected obedience by becoming the sacrifice. This sacrifice of obedience leads to the ascension of the Son into heaven. The first covenant is done away with by the second covenant. Having offered the final sacrifice, the son, the true high priest, sits down once for all in heaven. He has "perfected for all time those who are being sanctified." Jesus is the eschatological sacrifice, and the eschatological high priest, and thus ascends into heaven, sitting down because his work is done. Jesus' obedient trust serves as the basis, qualification, and dare we say merit, for his ascension into heaven. He has secured his reign as the true king and true high priest because he exercised true human obedience. Thus, the Last Adam-David ascends into the true final Mt. Zion because he exercised the obedient trust that exemplifies the Davidic king. The Father calls his royal son up to heaven and appoints him king-priest (Pss. 2 and 110) because of the Son's faithful trusting obedience.

## Contribution to Scholarship

The goal of this thesis is to contribute to our understanding of a much-neglected theme in the book of Hebrews, namely, the ascension. As we noted in our introduction upon surveying scholarship of other studies have "drawn attention to the *where* of the ascension (a heavenly tabernacle/throne), the *why* of Jesus' ascension (for priesthood, atonement, session, etc.), the *mode* of Jesus' ascension (in a resurrected body), and the *background* of Jewish eschatological expectations and apocalyptic thought behind the ascension in Hebrews." Our focus has been to explore what Hebrews sees as "the *grounds* for the ascension of the Son."

First, we have sought to return attention to the aspect of divine Christology in Heb 1 and how the exaltation and ascension is revelatory of an eternal category of Sonship. We believe that this creates a more satisfactory understanding of the book and better explains the four anarthorous uses of υἱός in Hebrews 1:2; 3:6; 5:8; and 7:28, especially καίπερ ὢν υἱός in Heb 5:8. Our argument shows then a tightly knit connection where the Son is both divine Son and the one who obeys in his Adamic-Davidic vocation. Our argument seeks to resolve an apparent tension by demonstrating Hebrews' clear both/and approach to Christology with respect to Adamic-humanity and divinity. This becomes the key for unravelling the complexity of Heb 5:7–10. We arrive at a more thorough answer to questions concerning the use of the concessive καίπερ ὢν υἱός in Heb 5:8 and the nature of Jesus' learning of obedience. He is the divine Son but he learns and fulfills Adamic-Davidic obedience.

Second, we have sought to show that Second Adamic Christology is an important feature for understanding the book of Hebrews as a whole, specifically when it comes to Christ's priesthood, ascension into the true tabernacle, and his obedient trust in God the Father. As we noted above, we have sought to advance the previous understandings of Adamic-Christology. Our intent has been to demonstrate not merely that there is an Adamic background behind Hebrews, as other scholars have noted, but that these Adamic features do significant work in the text in relationship to Jesus' priesthood, kingship, and ascension. In fact, these three motifs can all be subsumed under an Adamic rubric. This points to Hebrews having a much deeper Biblical (OT) theology. Hebrews has intertwined royal themes of Adamic and Davidic figures. Kingship and priesthood are equally brought together, not just by Ps 110:4, but in the Adamic motif as a whole, with the ascension into the heavenly tabernacle to sit at God's right hand. There is a deeper structure to redemptive history at work for the author beyond just isolated choosing of messianic texts and New Covenant texts. Christ is the true eschatological man who having been crowned with glory ascends into the divine heavenly tabernacle of heaven. The whole of redemptive history has climaxed 'in these last days.'

Third, we have demonstrated that the grounds for Jesus' ascension resides in not only his suffering death but specifically in the godly character he displays in the midst of this suffering. Based on the author's use of the OT motif of the cry of trust, it was vital that Jesus yield himself to the Father and cry out in trust to the one able to save him from death. This act of godly piety is the basis on which God responds. Jesus' "being heard" is specifically his exaltation as he is made perfect in eschatological glory and invited to sit at the Father's right hand. He is called to ascend upward in fulfillment of Pss 2:7 and 110:1.

Previous scholarship in Hebrews has noticed how it is through the Son and his representation that God's people come to have access to God, but we have sought to expand this to demonstrate that the Son must first achieve his own access. Importantly, Hebrews does not make access to God dependent on Jesus' divine Sonship, but rather something that is predicated upon his fulfillment of the Adamic-Davidic sonship. The Second Adam must first accomplish what the true Adam-human should have always done: completely trust God and entrust himself to God. His work on the cross is not only redemptive, but it has been accomplished as a pioneer representing us in solidarity. As the true Adam, he must manifest the true character humanity is to have. In this way, Jesus qualifies himself for ascension by demonstrating true human obedient trust in the fashion of the Adamic-Davidic figure. Simply put, for Hebrews, there is no basis for bodily ascension as the messianic Davidic son if he does not first display the obedience of sonship as he trusts God in and through his death. Fulfilling this vocation brings his messianic ascension, which reveals the Sonship he had from all eternity past.

# Bibliography

Aaron, David. "Shedding Light on God's Body in Rabbinic Midrashim: Reflections on the Theory of a Luminous Adam." *HTR* 90.3 (1997): 299–314.

Adams, Edward. "The Cosmology of Hebrews." Pages 122–139 in *The Epistle to the Hebrews and Christian Theology*. Edited by Richard Bauckham, Daniel R. Driver, Trevor A. Hart, and Nathan MacDonald. Eerdmans, 2009.

Agourides, "Apocalypse of Sedrach: A New Translation and Introduction." Pages 605–613 in *The Old Testament Pseudepigrapha: Volume 1*. Edited by James H. Charlesworth. Doubleday, 1983.

Alexander, Philip. *The Mystical Texts: Songs of the Sabbath Sacrifice and Related Manuscripts*. T&T Clark, 2006.

Alexander, T.D. *From Paradise to Promised Land: Introduction to the Pentateuch*. 2nd ed. Baker 2002.

Anderson, H. "4 Maccabees: A New Translation and Introduction." Pages 531–564 in *The Old Testament Pseudepigrapha: Volume 2*. Edited by James H. Charlesworth. Doubleday, 1985.

Aschim, Anders. "Melchizedek and Jesus: 11QMelchizedek and the Epistle to the Hebrews." Pages 129–47 in *The Jewish Roots of Christological Monotheism: Papers from the St. Andrews Conference on the Historical Origins of the Worship of Jesus*. Edited by Carey Newman, James Davila, and Gladys Lewis. Brill: 1999.

Attridge, Harold W. *The Epistle to the Hebrews*. Hermeneia. Fortress, 1989.

Attridge, Harold W. "Heard Because of His Reverence (Heb. 5:7)." *JBL* 98 (1979) 90–93.

Attridge, Harold W. "The Psalms in Hebrews." Pages 197–212 in *The Psalms in the New Testament*. Edited by Steve Moyise and Maarten J.J. Menken. T&T Clark, 2004.

*Babylonian Talmud*. Edited by Isidore Epstein. Translated by H. Freedman. Soncino, 1935–1948.

Bacon, B.W. "Heb 1,10–12 and the Septuagint Rendering of Ps 102,23." *ZNW* 3 (1902) 280–285.

Barnard, Jody A. *The Mysticism of Hebrews: Exploring the Role of Jewish Apocalyptic Mysticism in the Epistle to the Hebrews*. WUNT 2/331. Mohr Siebeck, 2012.

Barrett, C.K. "The Christology of Hebrews." Pages 110–127 in *Who Do You Say I Am? Essays on Christology*. Edited by Mark Allan Powell and David R. Bauer. Westminster John Knox, 1999.

Barrett, C.K. "The Eschatology of the Epistle to the Hebrews." Pages 363–393 in *The Background of the New Testament*. Edited by W.D. Davies. Cambridge University Press, 1964.

Bateman, Herbert W., IV. *Early Jewish Hermeneutics and Hebrews 1:5–13: The Impact of Jewish Exegesis on the Interpretation of a Significant New Testament Passage*. Peter Lang, 1997.

Bateman, Herbert W., IV. "Psalm 45:6–7 and Its Christological Contributions to Hebrews." *TJ* 22.1 (2001): 3–21.

Bateman, Herbert W., IV. "Two First-Century Messianic Uses of the OT: Heb. 1:5–13 and 4QFlor. 1.1–19." *JETS* 38.1 (March 1995): 11–27.

Bates, Matthew. *The Birth of the Trinity: Jesus, God, and Spirit in the New Testament and Early Christian Interpretations of the Old Testament.* Oxford University Press, 2015.

Bauckham, Richard. "Biblical Theology and Monotheism." Pages 187–232 in *Out of Egypt: Biblical Theology and Interpretation.* Edited by Craig Bartholomew, Mary Healy, Karl Möller, and Robin Parry. Zondervan, 2004.

Bauckham, Richard. *Climax of Prophecy.* T&T Clark, 1993.

Bauckham, Richard. "Divinity of Jesus Christ in the Epistle to the Hebrews." Pages in 15–36 in *The Epistles to the Hebrews and Christian Theology.* Edited by Richard Bauckham, Daniel R. Driver, Trevor A. Hart, and Nathan MacDonald. Eerdmans, 2009.

Bauckham, Richard. *God Crucified: Monotheism and Christology in the New Testament.* Eerdmans, 1998.

Bauckham, Richard. *Jesus and the God of Israel: God Crucified and Other Studies on the New Testament's Christology of Divine Identity.* Eerdmans, 2008.

Bauckham, Richard. "Monotheism and the Christology of Hebrews 1." Pages 167–185 in *Early Jewish and Christian Monotheism.* Edited by Loren T. Stuckenbruck and Wendy E.S. North. T&T Clark, 2004.

Bauer, W., W. Danker, W.F. Arndt, and F.W. Gingrich. *Greek-English Lexicon of the New Testament and Other Early Christian Literature.* 3rd ed. Chicago, 1999.

Beale, G.K. "Eschatology." Pages 330–345 in *Dictionary of the Later New Testament and Its Developments.* Edited by Ralph P. Martin and Peter H. Davids. Intervarsity, 1997.

Beale, G.K. *A New Testament Biblical Theology.* Baker, 2011.

Beale, G.K. *Temple and the Church's Mission: A Biblical Theology of the Dwelling Place of God.* Intervarsity, 2004.

Beckerleg, Catherine Leigh. "The 'Image of God in Eden: the Creation of Mankind in Genesis 2:5–3:24 in Light of *mīs pî pīt pî* and *wpt-r* Rituals of Mesopotamia and Ancient Egypt." PhD diss., Harvard University, 2009.

Bentzen, Aage. *King and Messiah.* Edited by G.W. Anderson. Blackwell, 1970.

Bergh, Ronald H., van der. "A Textual Comparison of Hebrews 10:5b–7 and LXX Psalm 39:7–9." *Neot* 42 (2008): 353–381.

Bird, Phylliss A. "'Male and Female He Created Them': Gen. 1:27b in the Context of the Priestly Account of Creation." *HTR* 74.2 (1981): 129–159.

Blass, F., and A. Debrunner. *A Greek Grammar of the New Testament and Other Early Christian Literature.* Translated by R.W. Funk. University of Chicago Press, 1961.

Bock, Darrell. *Blasphemy and Exaltation in Judaism: The Charge Against Jesus in Mark 14:53–65.* Baker, 1998.

Brandenburger, Egon. "Text und Vorlagen von Hebr. V,7–10." *NovT* 11 (1969): 190–224.

Bruce, F.F. *The Epistle to the Hebrews.* Rev. ed. NICNT. Eerdmans, 1990.

Brueggemann, Walter. *Theology of the Old Testament: Testimony, Dispute, Advocacy.* Fortress, 1997.

Bryan, David K. "A Revised Cosmic Hierarchy Revealed: Apocalyptic Literature and Jesus' Ascent in Luke's Gospel." Pages 61–82 in *Ascent into Heaven in Luke-Acts:*

*New Explorations of Luke's Narrative Hinge*. Edited by David K. Bryan and David W. Pao. Fortress, 2016.

Bryan, David K., and David W. Pao, eds. *Ascent into Heaven in Luke-Acts: New Explorations of Luke's Narrative Hinge*. Fortress, 2016.

Burgess, Andrew. *The Ascension in Karl Barth*. Ashgate, 2004.

Caird, George B. "Exegetical Method of the Epistle to the Hebrews." *Canadian Journal of Theology* 5 (1959): 44–51.

Caird, George B. "Just Men Made Perfect." *The London Quarterly and Holborn Review* 191 (1966): 89–98.

Caird, George B. "Son by Appointment." Pages 73–81 in *The New Testament Age: Essays in Honor of Bo Reicke Volume 1*. Edited by William C. Weinrich. Mercer University Press, 1984.

Calaway, Jared C. *The Sabbath and the Sanctuary*. WUNT 2/349. Mohr Siebeck, 2013.

Callender, Dexter, Jr. *Adam in Myth and History: Ancient Israelite Perspectives on the Primal Human*. Eisenbrauns, 2000.

Caneday, Ardel B. "The Eschatological World Already Subjected to the Son: The οἰκουμένη of Hebrews 1.6 and the Son's Enthronement." Pages 28–39 in *A Cloud of Witnesses: The Theology of Hebrews in its Ancient Contexts*. Edited by Richard Bauckham, Daniel Driver, Trevor Hart, and Nathan MacDonald. T&T Clark, 2008.

Carlson, James M. "A Great High Priest How Has Passed Through the Heavens: In Quest of the Apocalyptic Roots of the Epistle to the Hebrews." PhD diss., Marquette University, May 2008.

Carlston, Charles Edwin. "Eschatology and Repentance in the Epistle to the Hebrews." *JBL* 78 (1959): 296–302.

Carlsson, Leif. *Round Trips to Heaven: Otherwordly Travelers in Early Judaism and Christianity*. VDM, 2008.

Carrell, Peter R. *Jesus and the Angels: Angelology and the Christology of the Apocalypse of John*. Cambridge University Press, 1997.

Charles, J. Daryl. "The Angels, Sonship and Birthright in the Letter to Hebrews." *JETS* 33.2 (June 1990): 171–178.

Charlesworth, J.H., et al, eds. *The Old Testament Pseudepigrapha, 2 vols.* Doubleday, 1983–1985.

Chester, Andrew. *Messiah and Exaltation*. WUNT 207. Mohr Siebeck, 2007.

Church, Philip. "Hebrews 1:10–12 and the Renewal of the Cosmos." *TynBul* 67.2 (2016): 269–286.

Church, Philip. "The Temple in the Apocalypse of Weeks and in Hebrews." *TynBul* 64.1 (2013): 109–128.

Clines, D.J.A. "The Image of God." *TynBul* 19 (1968): 53–103.

Cockerill, Gareth Lee. *The Epistle to the Hebrews*. NICNT. Eerdmans, 2012.

Cockerill, Gareth Lee. "Melchizedek or 'King of Righteousness.'" *EvQ* 63.4 (1991): 305–312.

Cockerill, Gareth Lee. "The Truthfulness and Perennial Relevance of God's Word in the Letter to the Hebrews." *BSac* 172 (April–June 2015): 190–202.

Cody, Aelred. *Heavenly Sanctuary and Liturgy in the Epistle to the Hebrews: The Achievement of Salvation in the Epistle's Perspective*. Grail, 1960.

Cole, Robert. "An Integrated Reading of Psalm 1 and 2." *JSOT* 98 (2002): 75–88.

Collins, Adela Yarbro. "Traveling Up and Away: Journeys to the Upper and Outer Regions of the World." Pages 135–166 in *Greco-Roman Culture and the New Testament: Studies Commemorating the Centennial of the Pontifical Biblical Institute*. Edited by David E. Aune and Frederick E. Brenk. Brill, 2012.

Collins, Adela Yarbro, and John J. Collins. *King and Messiah as Son of God: Divine, Human, and Angelic Messianic Figures in Biblical and Related Literature*. Eerdmans, 2008.

Collins, John J. *The Apocalyptic Imagination: An Introduction to Jewish Apocalyptic Literature*. 2nd ed. Eerdmans, 1998.

Collins, John J. *Apocalypse, Prophecy, and Pseudepigraphy: On Jewish Apocalyptic Literature*. Eerdmans, 2015.

Collins, John J. "A Throne in the Heavens: Apotheosis in Pre-Christian Judaism." Pages 43–58 in *Death, Ecstasy and Other Worldly Journeys*. Edited by John J. Collins and Michael Fishbane. State University of New York Press, 1995.

Compton, Jared M. "The Origin of ΣΩΜΑ in Heb 10:5: Another Look at a Recent Proposal." *TJ* 32 (2011): 19–29.

Compton, Jared M. *Psalm 110 and the Logic of Hebrews*. JSNTS 537. T&T Clark, 2015.

Compton, Jared M. Review of David M. Moffitt, *Atonement and the Logic of Resurrection in the Epistle to the Hebrews*. *TJ* 36 (2015): 133–135.

Cortez, Felix H. "'The Anchor of the Soul that Enters the Veil': the Ascension of the 'Son' in the Letter to the Hebrews." Ph.D Diss., Andrews University, January 2008. (Now published as *Within the Veil: The Ascension of the Son in the Letter to the Hebrews* [Fontes, 2020].)

Cortez, Felix H. "From the Holy to the Most Holy Place: The Period of Hebrews 9:6–10 and the Day of Atonement as a Metaphor of Transition." *JBL* 125 (2006): 527–547.

Craigie, Peter. *Psalms 1–50*. WBC 19. Thomas Nelson, 2004.

Creach, Jerome F.D. *The Destiny of the Righteous in the Psalms*. Chalice, 2008.

Creach, Jerome F.D. "Like a Tree Planted by the Temple Stream: The Portrait of the Righteous in Psalm 1:3." *CBQ* 61 (1999): 34–46.

Creach, Jerome F.D. *Yahweh as Refuge and the Editing of the Hebrew Psalter*. Sheffield Academic, 1996.

Croft, Steven J.L. *The Identity of the Individual in the Psalms*. Sheffield Academic, 1987.

Crowe, Brandon D. *The Last Adam: A Theology of the Obedient Life of Jesus in the Gospels*. Baker, 2017.

Crowe, Brandon D. *The Obedient Son: Deuteronomy and Christology in the Gospel of Matthew*. De Gruyter, 2012.

Cullmann, Oscar. *The Christology of the New Testament*. Translated by S.C. Guthrie and C.A.M. Hall. SCM, 1959.

Curtis, Edward Mason. "Man as the Image of God in Genesis in Light of Ancient Near Eastern Parallels." PhD diss., University of Pennsylvania, 1984.

Davies, J.D. *He Ascended into Heaven: A Study in the History of Doctrine.* Lutterworth, 1958.

Dawson, Gerrit Scott. *Jesus Ascended: The Meaning of Christ's Continuing Incarnation.* P&R, 2004.

Day, John. "The Canaanite Inheritance of the Israelite Monarchy." Pages 72–90 in *King and Messiah in Israel and the Ancient Near East: Proceedings of the Oxford Old Testament Seminar.* Edited by John Day. Bloomsbury T&T Clark, 2013.

Dean-Otting, Mary. *Heavenly Journeys: A Study of the Motif in Hellenistic Jewish Literature.* Judentum und Umwelt. Peter Lang, 1984.

De Conick, April D. "Heavenly Temple Traditions and Valentinian Worship: A Case for First-Century Christology in the Second Century." Pages 308–341 in *The Jewish Roots of Christological Monotheism: Papers from the St. Andrews Conference on the Historical Origins of the Worship of Jesus.* Edited by Carey Newman, James Davila, and Gladys Lewis. Brill: 1999.

De Jonge, M., and Van Der Woude, A.S. "11Q Melchizedek and the New Testament," *NTS*, 12.4 (1966): 301–326

De Wet, Chris L. "The Messianic Interpretation of Psalm 8:4–6 in Hebrews 2:6–9: Part II." Pages 113–125 in *Psalms and Hebrews Studies in Reception.* Edited by Dirk J. Human and Gert Jacobus Steyn. T&T Clark, 2010.

Dempster, Stephen. *Dominion and Dynasty: A Theology of the Hebrew Bible.* Intervarsity, 2003.

deSilva, David A. "Entering God's Rest: Eschatology and the Socio-Rhetorical Strategy of Hebrews." *TJ* 21 (2000): 25–43.

deSilva, David A. *Perseverance in Gratitude: A Socio-Rhetorical Commentary on the Epistle "to
the Hebrews."* Eerdmans, 2000.

Dey, Lala Kalyan Kumar. *The Intermediary World and Patterns of Perfection in Philo and Hebrews.* Scholars, 1975.

Docherty, Susan. *The Use of the Old Testament in Hebrews.* WUNT 2/260. Mohr Siebeck, 2009.

Dodd, C.H. *According to the Scriptures.* Fontana, 1965.

Donne, Brian K. "The Significance of the Ascension of Jesus Christ in the New Testament." *SJT* 30 (1977): 555–568.

Du Plessis, Paul Johannes. *Teleios: The Idea of Perfection in the New Testament.* Kok, 1959.

Dunn, James. *Christology in the Making.* 2nd ed. SCM, 1989.

Dunn, James. *The Epistle to the Colossians and Philemon.* NIGTC. Eerdmans, 1996.

Dunn, James. "Was Christianity a Monotheistic Faith from the Beginning?" *SJT* 35 (1982): 303–336.

Easter, Matthew. *Faith and the Faithfulness of Jesus in Hebrews.* SNTSMS 160. Cambridge University Press, 2014.

Eaton, John. *Kingship and the Psalms.* SCM, 1975.

Ebert, Daniel J., IV. "Wisdom in New Testament Christology with Special Reference to Hebrews 1:1–4." PhD diss., Trinity Evangelical Divinity School, 1998.

Ebert, Daniel J., IV. *Wisdom Christology: How Jesus Becomes God's Wisdom for Us.* P&R, 2011.

Ellingworth, Paul. *The Epistle to the Hebrews.* NIGTC. Eerdmans, 1993.

Ellingworth, Paul. "Jesus and the Universe in Hebrews." *EvQ* 58 (1986): 337–350

Enslin, Morton S. "The Ascension Story," *JBL* 47.1/2 (1928): 60–73.

Eskola, Timo. *Messiah and the Throne: Jewish Merkabah Mysticism and Early Christian Exaltation Discourse.* WUNT 2/124. Mohr Siebeck, 2001.

Farrow, Douglas. *Ascension and Ecclesia: on the Significance of the Doctrine of the Ascension for Ecclesiology and Christian Cosmology.* Eerdmans, 1999.

Farrow, Douglas. *Ascension Theology.* Bloomsbury T&T Clark, 2011.

Filtvedt, Ole Jakob. *The Identity of God's People and the Paradox of Hebrews.* WUNT 2/400. Mohr Siebeck, 2015.

Fitzmyer, Joseph. "The Ascension of Christ and Pentecost." *Theological Studies* 45.3 (1984): 409–440.

Fitzmyer, Joseph. "Further Light on Melchizedek from Qumran Cave 11" *JBL* 86 (1967): 25–41.

Fletcher-Louis, Crispin. *All the Glory of Adam: Liturgical Anthropology in the Dead Sea Scrolls.* Brill, 2002.

Fletcher-Louis, Crispin. "2 Enoch and the New Perspective on Apocalyptic." Pages 127–148 in *New Perspectives on 2 Enoch: No Longer Slavonic Only.* Edited by Andrei Orlov, Gabriele Boccaccini, and Jason Zurawski. Leiden, Brill, 2012.

Fletcher-Louis, Crispin. "God's Image, His Cosmic Temple and the High Priest." Pages 81–99 in *Heaven on Earth: The Temple in Biblical Theology.* Edited by T. Desmond Alexander and Simon Gathercole. Paternoster, 2004.

Fletcher-Louis, Crispin. *Christological Origins: The Emerging Consensus and Beyond.* Vol. 1 of *Jesus Monotheism.* Cascade, 2015.

Fletcher-Louis, Crispin. "King Solomon, Bearer of the Image of God, Incorporative Representative of God's People (1 Kings 3–4)." Paper presented at the St. Andrews "Son of God" Conference, June 6–8, 2016.

Fletcher-Louis, Crispin. "On angels, men and priests (Ben Sira, the Qumran Sabbath Songs and the Yom Kippur Avodah)." Paper presented at the "Gottesdienst und Engel" Conference. Zurich, January 2015. Accessed online 10/16/16 www.academia.edu/13408562/On_angels_men_and_priests_Ben_Sira_the_Qumran_Sabbath_Songs_and_the_Yom_Kippur_Avodah_

Fletcher-Louis, Crispin. "Some Reflections on Angelomorphic Humanity Texts among the Dead Sea Scrolls." *Dead Sea Discoveries* 7.3 (2000): 292–312.

Fletcher-Louis, Crispin. "The Temple Cosmology of P and the Theological Anthropology in the Wisdom of Jesus ben Sira." Pages 69–111 in *Of Scribes and Sages: Early Jewish Interpretation and Transmission of Scripture.* Edited by Craig A. Evans. Sheffield Academic, 2004. Also pages 1–57 in *Collected Works. Volume 1: The Image-Idol of God, the Priesthood, Apocalyptic and Jewish Mysticism.* Wipf & Stock/Whymanity, forthcoming.

Fletcher-Louis, Crispin. "The Worship of Divine Humanity as God's Image and the Worship of Jesus." Pages 112–128 in *The Jewish Roots of Christological Monotheism: Papers from the St. Andrews Conference on the Historical Origins of the*

*Worship of Jesus*. Edited by Carey C. Newman, James R. Davila, and Gladys S. Lewis. Brill, 1999.

Flusser, David. *Judaism and the Origins of Christianity*. Magness, 1988.

France, R.T. "The Writer of Hebrews as Biblical Expositor." *TynBul* 47 (1996): 245–276.

Franklin, Eric. "The Ascension and the Eschatology of Luke-Acts." *SJT* 23 (1970): 191–200.

Fuhrmann, Sebastian. "The Son, the Angels and the Odd: Psalm 8 in Hebrews 1 and 2." Pages 83–98 in *Psalms and Hebrews Studies in Reception*. Edited by Dirk J. Human and Gert Jacobus Steyn. T&T Clark, 2010.

Fuller, George C. "The Life of Jesus, after the Ascension (Luke 24:50–53; Acts 1:9–11)." *WTJ* 56 (1994): 391–398.

Gäbel, Georg. *Die Kulttheologie des Hebräerbriefes: Eine exegetisch-religionsgeschichtliche Studie*. WUNT 2/212. Mohr Siebeck, 2006.

Gaffin, Richard, Jr. "The Priesthood of Christ: A Servant in the Sanctuary." Pages 49–68 in *The Perfect Savior: Key Themes in Hebrews*. Edited by Jonathan Griffiths. Intervarsity, 2012.

Gao, Ming. "Heaven and Earth in Luke-Acts." PhD diss., Trinity International University, May 2015.

García Martínez, Florentino, and Eibert J. C. Tigchelaar, eds. *The Dead Sea Scrolls Study Edition*. 2 vols. Brill, 2000.

Gathercole, Simon. *The Preexistent Son: Recovering Christologies of Matthew, Mark, and Luke*. Eerdmans, 2006.

Gentry, Peter, and Stephen Wellum. *Kingdom Through Covenant: A Biblical-Theological Understanding of the Covenant*. Crossway, 2012.

Gheorghita, Radu. *The Role of the Septuagint in Hebrews: An Investigation of Its Influence with Special Consideration of the Use of Hab 2:3–4 in Heb 10:37–38*. WUNT 2/160. Mohr Siebeck, 2003.

Giles, K. "Ascension." Pages 46–50 in *Dictionary of Jesus and the Gospels*. Edited by Ralph P. Martin and Peter H. Davids. Intervarsity, 1992.

Gleason, Randall. "Angels and the Eschatology of Heb 1–2." *NTS* 49 (2003): 90–107.

Goldingay, John. *Old Testament Theology Volume 1: Israel's Gospel*. Intervarsity, 2003.

Goldingay, John. *Psalms, Volume 2: Psalms 42–89*. BCOTWP. Baker, 2007.

Goldsworthy, Graeme. *The Son of God and the New Creation*. Crossway, 2015.

Golitzin, Alexander. "Recovering the 'Glory of Adam': 'Divine Light' Traditions in the Dead Sea Scrolls and the Christian Ascetical Literature of Fourth-Century Syro-Mesopotamia." Pages 275–308 in *The Dead Sea Scrolls as Background to Postbiblical Judaism and Early Christianity: Papers from an International Conference at St. Andrews in 2001*. Edited by James R. Davila. Studies on the Text of the Desert of Judah 46. Brill, 2003.

Gooder, Paula. *Only the Third Heaven? 2 Corinthians 12.1–10 and Heavenly Ascent*. T&T Clark, 2006.

Grant, Jamie A. *The King as Exemplar: The Function of Deuteronomy's Kingship Law in the Shaping of the Book of Psalms*. Society of Biblical Literature, 2004.

Gray, Patrick. *Godly Fear: The Epistle to the Hebrews and Greco-Roman Critiques of Superstition*. Society of Biblical Literature, 2003.

*Greek Pseudepigripha*. Electronic Text. Entered by Craig A. Evans. Oak Tree Software, 2013.

Green, Douglas. "Psalm 8: What is Israel's King that You Remember Him?" Online Publication, *n.d.* www.academia.edu/7222228/Psalm_8_What_Is_Israels_King_That_You_Remember_Him

Grogan, Geoffrey. "Christ and His People: An Exegetical and Theological Study of Hebrews 2:5–18." *Vox Evangelica* 6 (1969): 54–71.

Griffiths, Jonathan. "The Word of God: Perfectly Spoken in the Son." Pages 35–48 in *The Perfect Savior: Key Themes in Hebrews*. Edited by Jonathan Griffiths. Intervarsity, 2012.

Guthrie, George, and Russell Quinn. "A Discourse Analysis of the Use of Psalm 8:4–6 in Hebrews 2:5–9." *JETS* 49.2 (June 2006): 235–246.

Hagner, Donald. "The Son of God as Unique High Priest: The Christology of the Epistle to the Hebrews." Pages 247–267 in *Contours of Christology in the New Testament*. Edited by Richard N. Longenecker. Eerdmans, 2005.

Hall, Robert G., "Pre-existence, Naming, and Investiture in the *Similitudes of Enoch* and in Hebrews." *Religion and Theology* 18 (2011): 311–333.

Hamerton-Kelly, R.G. *Pre-Existence, Wisdom, and the Son of Man*. Cambridge University Press, 1973. Repr., Wipf & Stock, 2000.

Haroutunian, Joseph. "The Doctrine of the Ascension: A Study of the New Testament Teaching." *Interpretation* 10 (1956): 270–281.

Harris, Murray J. *Jesus as God: The New Testament Use of Theos in Reference to Jesus*. Baker, 1992.

Harris, Murray J. "The Translation and Significance of Ὁ ΘΕΟΣ in Hebrews 1:8–9." *TynBul* 36 (1985): 129–162.

Harris, Murray J. "The Translation of *Elohim* in Psalm 45:7–8." *TynBul* 35 (1984): 65–89.

Harris, W. Hall, III. *The Descent of Christ: Ephesians 4:7–11 and Traditional Hebrew Imagery*. Baker, 1996.

Hart, Ian. "Genesis 1:1–2:3 As Prologue to the Book of Genesis." *TynBul* 46.2 (1995): 315–336.

Hay, David M. *Glory at the Right Hand: Psalm 110 in Early Christianity*. SBLMS 18. Abingdon, 1973.

Hayward, C.T.R. "The Figure of Adam in Pseudo-Philo's Biblical Antiquities." *JSJ* 23.1 (1992): 1–20.

Heiser, Michael. "Deuteronomy 32:8 and the Sons of God." *BSac* 158 (Jan.–March 2001): 52–74.

Hengel, Martin. *The Cross of the Son of God*. SCM, 1986.

Hengel, Martin. *Studies in Early Christology*. T&T Clark, 1995.

Herring, Stephen. *Divine Substitution: Humanity as the Manifestation of Deity in the Hebrew Bible and the Ancient Near East*. Vandenhoeck & Ruprecht, 2013.

Himmelfarb, Martha. *Ascent to Heaven in Jewish and Christian Apocalypses*. Oxford University Press, 1993.

Himmelfarb, Martha. "The Practice of Ascent in the Ancient Mediterranean World." Pages 123–137 in *Death, Ecstasy and Other Worldly Journeys*. Edited by John J.

Collins and Michael Fishbane. State University of New York Press, 1995.

Hoehner, Harold. *Ephesians: An Exegetical Commentary.* Baker, 2002.

Hoehner, Harold. "The Perfection of Christ in Hebrews." *Calvin Theological Journal* 9 (1974): 31–37.

Horbury, William. "Jewish and Christian Monotheism in the Herodian Age." Pages 16–44 in *Early Jewish and Christian Monotheism*. Edited by Loren T. Stuckenbruck and Wendy E.S. North. T&T Clark, 2004.

Hossfeld, Frank-Lothar, and Erich Zenger. *Psalms 2: A Commentary on Psalms 51–100*. Hermeneia. Fortress, 2005.

Hort, F.J.A. "Hebrews 1.8," 1894. Unpublished manuscript in the R.L. Bensly Collection. Cambridge University Library.

Horton, Michael. "Atonement and Ascension." Pages 226–250 in *Locating Atonement: Explorations in Constructive Dogmatics*. Edited by Oliver D. Crisp and Fred Sanders. Zondervan, 2015.

Hughes, Philip E. "The Christology of Hebrews," *Southwestern Journal of Theology* 28 (1985): 19–27.

Hughes, Philip E. *A Commentary on the Epistle to the Hebrews*. Eerdmans, 1977.

Hurst, L.D. "The Christology of Hebrews 1 and 2." Pages 151–164 in *The Glory of Christ in the New Testament: Studies in Christology in Memory of George Bradford Caird*. Edited by L.D. Hurst and N.T. Wright. Clarendon, 1987.

Hurst, L.D. *The Epistle to Hebrews: Its Background and Thought*. SNTS 65. Cambridge, 1990.

Hurtado, Larry. "First-Century Jewish Monotheism." *JSNT* 71 (1998): 3–26.

Hurtado, Larry. *How on Earth Did Jesus Become God? Historical Questions about Earliest Devotion to Jesus*. Eerdmans, 2005.

Hurtado, Larry. *Lord Jesus Christ: Devotion to Jesus in Earliest Christianity*. Eerdmans, 2003.

Hurtado, Larry. "Monotheism, Principal Angels, and the Background of Christology." Pages 547–565 in *The Oxford Handbook of the Dead Sea Scrolls*. Edited by John J. Collins and Timothy H. Lim. Oxford, 2010.

Hurtado, Larry. *One God, One Lord: Early Christian Devotion and Ancient Jewish Monotheism*. 2nd ed. T&T Clark, 1998.

Hurtado, Larry. "What Do We Mean by 'First-Century Jewish Monotheism'?" Pages 348–368 in *SBL 1993 Seminar Papers*. Edited by David Lull. Scholars, 1993.

Isaacs, Marie. *Sacred Space: An Approach to the Theology of the Epistle to the Hebrews*. JSNTS 73. Sheffield Academic, 1992.

Jamieson, R.B. "Hebrews 9.23: Cult Inauguration, Yom Kippur and the Cleansing of the Heavenly Tabernacle." *NTS* 62 (2016): 569–587.

Jamieson, R.B. *The Paradox of Sonship: Christology in the Epistle to the Hebrews*. InterVarsity, 2021.

Janse, Sam. *"You Are My Son": The Reception History of Psalm 2 in Early Judaism and the Early Church*. Peeters, 2009.

Jansen, John E. "The Ascension, the Church and Theology." *Theology Today* 16 (1959): 17–29.

Jeremias, Joachim. "Hbr 5,7–10." *ZNW* 44 (1952–53): 107–111.

de Jesús Legarreta-Castillo, Felipe. *The Figure of Adam in Romans 5 and 1 Corinthians 15: The New Creation and Its Ethical and Social Reconfiguration.* Fortress, 2014.

Jipp, Joshua. *Christ is King: Paul's Royal Ideology.* Fortress, 2015.

Jipp, Joshua. Review of *Atonement and the Logic of Resurrection in the Epistle to the Hebrews*, by David M. Moffitt. *BBR* 22.2 (2012): 298–299.

Jipp, Joshua. "The Son's Entrance into the Heavenly Word: The Soteriological Necessity of the Scriptural Catena in Hebrews 1.5–14." *NTS* 56 (2010): 557–575.

Jobes, Karen. "The Function of Paronomasia in Hebrews 10:5–7." *TJ* 13 (1992): 181–191.

Jobes, Karen. "Rhetorical Achievement in the Hebrews 10 'Misquote' of Psalm 40." *Biblica* 72 (1991): 387–396.

Johnson, Luke Timothy. *Hebrews: A Commentary.* Westminster John Knox, 2006.

Johnson, M.D. "Life of Adam and Eve: A New Translation and Introduction." Pages 249–295 in *The Old Testament Pseudepigrapha Volume 2.* Edited by J.H. Charlesworth. Doubleday, 1985.

Jones, Elaine. "Origins of 'Ascension' Terminology." *Churchman* 104.2 (1990): 156–161.

Joslin, Barry. "Christ Bore the Sins of Man: Substitution and the Atonement in Hebrews." *SBJT* 11.2 (2007): 74–103.

Käsemann, Ernst. *The Wandering People of God.* Translated by Roy A. Harrisville and Irving L. Sandberg. Augsburg, 1984.

Kaylor, Robert David. "The Ascension Motif in Luke-Acts, the Epistle to the Hebrews, and the Fourth Gospel." PhD diss., Duke University, 1964.

Kee, H.C. "Testaments of the Twelve Patriarchs: A New Translation and Introduction." Pages 775–828 in *The Old Testament Pseudepigrapha Volume 1.* Edited by J.H. Charlesworth. Doubleday, 1983.

Keener, Craig. *Acts: An Exegetical Commentary, Volume 2: 3:1–14:28.* Baker, 2013.

Keener, Hubert James. *A Canonical Exegesis of the Eighth Psalm: YHWH's Maintenance of the Created Order through Divine Reversal.* Eisenbrauns, 2013.

Kibbe, Michael. *Godly Fear or Ungodly Failure? Hebrews 12 and the Sinai Theophany.* BZNW 216. de Gruyter, 2016.

Kibbe, Michael. "Is It Finished? When Did it Start? Hebrews, Priesthood, and Atonement in Biblical, Systematic, and Historical Perspective." *JTS* 65.1 (2014): 25–61.

Kibbe, Michael. Review of *Atonement and the Logic of Resurrection in the Epistle to the Hebrews*, by David M. Moffitt. *Themelios* 37.1 (2012): 69–70.

Kim, Seyoon. *The Origins of Paul's Gospel.* Mohr Siebeck, 1981. Repr., Wipf & Stock, 2007.

Kim, Seyoon. *The Son of Man as the Son of God.* Eerdmans, 1985.

Kinzer, Mark Stephen. "'All Things Under His Feet': Psalm 8 in the New Testament and in Other Jewish Literature of Late Antiquity." PhD diss., University of Michigan, 1995.

Kirk, J.D. *A Man Attested by God: The Human Jesus of the Synoptic Gospels.* Eerdmans, 2016.

Kistemaker, Simon. "Atonement in Hebrews." Pages 163–175 in *The Glory of the Atonement: Biblical, Theological, and Practical Perspectives: Essay in Honor of Roger Nicole.* Edited by Charles E. Hill and Frank A. James III. Intervarsity, 2004.

Kistemaker, Simon. *Psalm Citations in the Epistle to the Hebrews.* Van Soest, 1961. Repr., Wipf & Stock, 2010.

Kline, Meredith. *Kingdom Prologue: Genesis Foundations for a Covenantal Worldview.* Two Age, 2000.

Knohl, Israel, "Melchizedek: A Model for the Union of Kingship and Priesthood in the Hebrew Bible, 11QMelchizedek, and the Epistle to the Hebrews." Pages 255–266 in *Text, Thought, and Practice in Qumran and Early Christianity.* Edited by Ruth A. Clements and Daniel R. Schwartz. Brill, 2009.

Knox, Wilfred. "The 'Divine Hero' Christology in the New Testament." *HTR* 41.4 (Oct. 1948): 229–249.

Koester, Craig R. *The Dwelling of God: The Tabernacle in the Old Testament, Intertestamental Jewish Literature, and the New Testament.* Catholic Biblical Association of America, 1989.

Koester, Craig R. *Hebrews: A New Translation with Introduction and Commentary.* AB 36. Doubleday, 2001.

Kraus, Joachim. *Psalms 1–59.* Translated by Hilton Oswald. Fortress, 1988.

Kuhn, Harold. "The Angelology of the Non-Canonical Jewish Apocalypses." *JBL* 67 (1948): 217–232.

Kurianal, James. *Jesus Our High Priest: Ps 110,4 As the Substructure of Heb 5,1–7,28.* Peter Lang, 1999.

Kwakkel, Gert. *According to My Righteousness: Upright Behavior as Grounds for Deliverance in Psalms 7, 17, 18, 26, and 44.* Brill, 2002.

Laansma, Jon. "The Cosmology of Hebrews." Pages 125–133 in *Cosmology and New Testament Theology.* Edited by Jonathan Pennington and Sean M. McDonough. T&T Clark, 2008.

Laansma, Jon. "Hidden Stories in Hebrews: Cosmology and Theology." Pages 9–18 in *A Cloud of Witnesses: The Theology of Hebrews in its Ancient Contexts.* Edited by Richard Bauckham, Daniel Driver, Trevor Hart, and Nathan MacDonald. T&T Clark, 2008.

Lane, William L. *Hebrews 1–8.* WBC 47A. Word, 1991.

Lane, William L. *Hebrews 9–13.* WBC 47B. Word, 1991.

Larkin, W.J., Jr. "Ascension." Pages 95–102 in *Dictionary of Later New Testament and Its Development.* Edited by Ralph P. Martin and Peter H. Davids. Intervarsity, 1997.

Laub, Franz. *Bekenntnis und Auslegung: Die paränetische Funktion der Christologie im Hebräerbrief.* Pustet, 1980.

Launderville, Dale. *Piety and Politics: The Dynamics of Royal Authority in Homeric Greece, Biblical Israel, and Old Babylonian Mesopotamia.* Eerdmans, 2003.

Lee, Aquila H.I. *From Messiah to Preexistent Son.* Wipf & Stock, 2005.

Levenson, Jon D. *Sinai and Zion: An Entry into the Jewish Bible.* Harper Collins, 1985.

Levenson, Jon D. *Resurrection and the Restoration of Israel: The Ultimate Victory of the God of Life.* Yale University Press, 2006.

Levenson, Jon D. "The Temple and the World." *The Journal of Religion* 64.3 (1984): 282–297.

Levison, J.R. *Portraits of Adam in Early Judaism: From Sirach to 2 Baruch.* Sheffield Academic, 1988.

Lightfoot, Neil R. "The Saving of the Savior: Hebrews 5:7ff." *Restoration Quarterly* 16 (1973): 166–173.

Lincoln, Andrew T. "Hebrews and Biblical Theology." Pages 313–338 in *Out of Egypt: Biblical Theology and Interpretation*. Edited by Craig Bartholomew, Mary Healy, Karl Möller, and Robin Parry. Zondervan, 2004.

Lindars, Barnabas. *The Theology of the Letter to the Hebrews*. Cambridge University Press, 1991.

Litwa, M. David. "The Deification of Moses in Philo of Alexandria." *The Studia Philonica Annual* 26 (2014): 1–27.

Longenecker, Bruce. *Eschatology and the Covenant: A Comparison of 4 Ezra and Romans 1–11*. Bloomsbury, 2015.

Longenecker, Richard. *Biblical Exegesis in the Apostolic Period*. 2nd ed. Eerdmans, 1999.

Lucass, Shirley. *The Conception of Messiah in the Scripture of Judaism and Christianity*. Bloomsbury T&T Clark, 2011.

Mackie, Scott D. "Ancient Jewish Mystical Motifs in Hebrews' Theology of Access and Entry Exhortations." *NTS* 58 (2011): 88–104.

Mackie, Scott D. "Confession of the Son of God in the Exordium of Hebrews." *JSNT* 30.4 (2008): 437–453.

Mackie, Scott D. "Confession of the Son of God in Hebrews." *NTS* 53 (2007): 114–139.

Mackie, Scott D. "Early Christian Eschatological Experience in the Warnings and Exhortations of the Epistle to the Hebrews." *TynBul* 63.1 (2012): 93–114.

Mackie, Scott D. *Eschatology and Exhortation in the Epistle to the Hebrews*. WUNT 2/223. Mohr Siebeck, 2007.

Mackie, Scott D. "Heavenly Sanctuary Mysticism in the Epistle to the Hebrews." *JTS* 62 (2011): 77–117.

MacLeod, David J. "The Cleansing of the True Tabernacle." *BSac* 152 (1995): 60–71.

MacLeod, David J. "The Finality of Christ: An Exposition of Hebrews 1:1–4." *BSac* 162 (2005): 210–230.

MacRae, George W. "Heavenly Temple and Eschatology in the Letter to the Hebrews." *Semeia* 12 (1978): 179–199.

Maier, Harry O. "'For Here We Have No Lasting City' (Heb 13:14a): Flavian Iconography, Roman Imperial Sacrificial Iconography, and the Epistle to the Hebrews." Pages 133–154 in *Hebrews in Contexts*. Edited by Gabriella Gelardini and Harold W. Attridge. Brill, 2016.

Maile, John F. "The Ascension in Luke-Acts." *TynBul* 37 (1986): 29–59.

Maré, Leonard. "The Messianic Interpretation of Psalm 8:4–6 in Hebrews 2:6–9: Part 1." Pages 99–112 in *Psalms and Hebrews Studies in Reception*. Edited by Dirk J. Human and Gert Jacobus Steyn. T&T Clark, 2010.

Marrevee, William H. *The Ascension of Christ in the Works of St. Augustine*. University of Ottawa Press, 1967.

Mason, Eric F. "'Sit at My Right Hand': Enthronement and the Heavenly Sanctuary in Hebrews." Pages 901–916 in *A Teacher for All Generations*. Edited by Eric F. Mason, Kelley Coblentz Bautch, Angela Kim Harkins, and Daniel A. Machiela. JSJSup 2/153. Brill, 2012.

Mason, Eric F. *'You Are a Priest Forever' Second Temple Jewish Messianism and the Priestly Christology of the Epistle to the Hebrews*. STDJ 74. Brill, 2008.

Matera, Frank J. *New Testament Christology*. Westminster John Knox, 1999.

Matthews, Kenneth A. *Genesis 1–11:26*. B&H, 1996.

McCready, Douglas. *He Came Down From Heaven: The Preexistence of Christ and the Christian Faith*. Intervarsity, 2005.

McCruden, Kevin B. "Christ's Perfection in Hebrews: Divine Beneficence as an Exegetical Key to Hebrews 2:1." *BR* 47 (2002): 40–62.

McCruden, Kevin B. "The Concept of Perfection in the Epistle to the Hebrews." Pages 209–229 in *Reading the Epistle to the Hebrews: A Resource for Students*. Edited by Eric F. Mason and Kevin B. McCruden. SBL, 2011.

McCruden, Kevin B. *Solidarity Perfected: Beneficent Christology in the Epistle to the Hebrews*. BZNW 159. de Gruyter, 2008.

McIver, Robert. "Cosmology as a Key to the Thought-World of Philo of Alexandria." *Andrews University Seminary Studies* 26.3 (1988): 267–279.

McRay, John. "Atonement and Apocalyptic in the Book of Hebrews." *ResQ* 23 (1980): 1–9.

Mealand, David. "The Christology of the Epistle to the Hebrews." *The Modern Churchman* 22.4 (1979): 180–187.

Meeks, Wayne. "Moses as God and King." Pages 354–371 in *Religions in Antiquity: Essays in Memory of E.R. Goodenough*. Edited by J. Neuser. Brill, 1968.

Meeks, Wayne. *The Prophet-King: Moses Traditions and Johannine Christology*. Brill, 1967.

Meier, John P. "Symmetry and Theology in the Old Testament Citations of Heb 1,5–14." *Biblica* 66 (1985): 504–533.

Merrill, Eugene. "Covenant and Kingdom: Genesis 1–3 as Foundation for Biblical Theology." *Criswell Theological Review* 1.2 (1987): 295–308.

Mettinger, Tryggve N.D. *King and Messiah: The Civil and Sacral Legitimation of the Israelite King*. Gleerup, 1976.

Metzger, Bruce. "4 Ezra: A New Translation and Introduction." Pages 517–559 in *The Old Testament Pseudepigrapha Volume 1*. Edited by J.H. Charlesworth. Doubleday, 1983.

Metzger, Bruce. *A Textual Commentary on the Greek New Testament*. 2nd ed. German Bible Society, 1994.

Michel, Otto. *Der Brief an die Hebräer*. 6th ed. KEK 13. Vendenhoeck & Ruprecht, 1966.

Middleton, J. Richard. *The Liberating Image: the Imago Dei in Genesis 1*. Brazos, 2005.

Milligan, William. *The Ascension and Heavenly Priesthood of Our Lord*. Macmillian, 1894. Repr., Wipf & Stock, 2006.

Moffatt, James. *The Epistle to the Hebrews*. T&T Clark, 1979.

Moffitt, David M. *Atonement and the Logic of the Resurrection in the Epistle to the Hebrews*. NovTSup 141. Brill, 2011.

Montefiore, Hugh. *A Commentary on the Epistle to the Hebrews*. HNTC. Harper & Row, 1964.

Moore, Nicholas J. review of *Atonement and the Logic of Resurrection in the Epistle to the Hebrews*, by David M. Moffitt. *JTS* 64 (2013): 675

Morales, L. Michael. *Who Shall Ascend the Mountain of the Lord? A Biblical Theology of the Book of Leviticus*. Intervarsity, 2015.

Moule, C.F.D. *The Birth of the New Testament*. London, 1962.

Moule, C.F.D. *An Idiom Book of New Testament Greek.* Cambridge University Press, 1959.

Moule, C.F.D. *The Origin of Christology.* Cambridge University Press, 1977.

Mowinckel, Sigmund. *The Psalms in Israel's Worship.* Translated by D.R. Ap-Thomas. Eerdmans, 2004.

Moyter, Stephen. "The Psalm Quotations of Hebrews 1: A Hermeneutic-Free Zone?" *TynBul* 50.1 (1999): 3–22.

Muir, Steven. "The Anti-Imperial Rhetoric of Hebrews 1.3: χαρακτήρ as a 'Double-Edge Sword.'" Pages 170–186 in *A Cloud of Witnesses: The Theology of Hebrews in its Ancient Contexts.* Edited by Richard Bauckham, Daniel Driver, Trevor Hart, and Nathan MacDonald. T&T Clark, 2008.

Needam, Nick. "Christ Ascended for Us: 'Jesus' Ascended Humanity and Ours.'" *Evangel* 25.2 (2007) 42–47.

Nelson, Richard D. "He Offered Himself: Sacrifice in Hebrews." *Interpretation* 57.3 (2003): 251–266.

Nickelsburg, George. *Jewish Literature Between the Bible and the Mishnah.* 2nd ed. Fortress, 2005.

Norman, Ralph. "Beyond the Ultimate Sphere: The Ascension and Eschatology." *Modern Believing* 42 (April 2001): 3–15.

Omark, Reuben E. "The Saving of the Savior: Exegesis and Christology in Hebrews 5:7–10." *Interpretation* 12 (1958): 39–51

Owens, Daniel. *Portraits of the Righteous in the Psalms: An Exploration of the Ethics of Book I.* Pickwick, 2013.

Oyetade, M.O. "Eschatological Salvation in Hebrews 1:5–2:5." *Ilorin Journal of Religious Studies* 3.1 (2013): 69–82.

Parsons, Mikeal Carl. "The Ascension Narratives in Luke-Acts." PhD diss., Southern Baptist Theological Seminary, 1985.

Parsons, Mikeal Carl. "Son and High Priest: A Study of the Christology of Hebrews." *EvQ* 60 (1988): 195–216.

Pate, Brian. "Who Is Speaking? The Use of Isaiah 8:17–18 in Hebrews 2:13 as a Case Study for Applying the Speech of Key OT Figures to Christ." *JETS* 59.4 (2016): 731–745.

Pate, Marvin C. *The Glory of Adam and the Afflictions of the Righteous: Pauline Suffering in Context.* Mellen Biblical, 1993.

Peeler, Amy. *You Are My Son: The Family of God in the Epistle to the Hebrews.* LNTS 486. Bloomsbury T&T Clark, 2014.

Peterson, David. *Hebrews and Perfection: An Examination of the Concept of Perfection in the "Epistle to the Hebrews."* SNTSMS 47. Cambridge University Press, 1982.

Peterson, Robert. *Salvation Accomplished by the Son: The Work of Christ.* Crossway, 2012.

Peuch, Emile. "Quelques aspect de la restauration du Rouleau des Hymns (1QH)." *JJS* 39 (1988): 38–55.

*Philo: Questions on Exodus.* Translated by Ralph Marcus. Loeb 401. Harvard University Press, 1953.

*Philo, Works of, Complete and Unabridged New Updated Version.* Translated by C.D. Yonge. Henderickson, 1993.

Philo, Works of: Greek Text with Morphology. The Norwegian Philo Concordance Project. Edited by Peder Borgen, Roald Skarsten, and Kare Fuglseth. 2005. Electronic edition. Oak Tree Software, 2009.

Pierce, Madison N. "Hebrews 1 and the Son Begotten 'Today.'" Pages 117–131 in *Retrieving Eternal Generation*. Edited by Fred R. Sanders and Scott W. Swain. Zondervan, 2017.

Pietersma, Albert, and Benjamin Wright, eds. *A New English Translation of the Septuagint* (NETS). Oxford University Press, 2007.

Playoust, Catherine Anne. "Lifted Up from the Earth: The Ascension of Jesus and the Heavenly Ascents of Early Christians." Th.D. diss., Harvard University, 2006.

Postell, Seth D. *Adam as Israel: Genesis 1–3 as the Introduction to the Torah and Tanakh*. Pickwick, 2011.

Purves, Andrew. *Reconstructing Pastoral Theology: A Christological Foundation*. Westminster John Knox, 2004.

Rahlfs, Alfred, and Robert Hanhart, eds. *Septuaginta*. Deutsche Bibelgesellschaft, 2006.

Rainbow, Paul. "Jewish Monotheism as the Matrix for New Testament Christology: A Review Article." *NovT* 33.1 (1991): 78–91.

Rainbow, Paul. "Melchizedek as a Messiah at Qumran." *BBR* 7 (1997): 179–194.

Rainbow, Paul. "Monotheism and Christology in I Corinthians 8. 4–6." D.Phil. thesis, University of Oxford, 1987.

Retieff, C. Wynand. "A Messianic Reading of Psalm 8." *OTE* 27.3 (2014): 992–1008.

Rhee, Victor. "Christology in Hebrews 1:5–14: The Three Stages of Christ's Existence." *JETS* 59.4 (2016): 717–729.

Rhee, Victor. "The Role of Chiasm for Understanding Christology in Hebrews 1:1–14." *JBL* 131.2 (2012): 341–62.

Ribbens, Benjamin. "Ascension and Atonement: The Significance of Post-Reformation, Reformed Responses to Socinians for Contemporary Atonement Debates in Hebrews." *WTJ* 80.1 (2018): 1–24.

Ribbens, Benjamin. *Levitical Sacrifice and Heavenly Cult in Hebrews*. BZNW 222. de Gruyter, 2016.

Richardson, Christopher. *Pioneer and Perfecter of Faith*. WUNT 2/338. Mohr Siebeck, 2012.

Robinson, William "Eschatology of the Epistle to the Hebrews: A Study in the Christian Doctrine of Hope." *Encounter* 22 (1961): 37–51.

Rooke, Deborah. "Kingship as Priesthood: The Relationship Between the High Priesthood and the Monarchy." Pages 187–208 in *King and Messiah in Israel and the Ancient Near East: Proceedings of the Oxford Old Testament Seminar*. Edited by John Day. Bloomsbury T&T Clark, 2013.

Rowland, Christopher. *The Open Heaven: A Study of Apocalyptic in Judaism and Early Christianity*. Wipf & Stock, 2002.

Rüpke, Jörg. "Starting Sacrifice: Flavian Innovations in the Concept of Priesthood and Their Reflections in the Treatise 'To The Hebrews.'" Pages 109–132 in *Hebrews in Contexts*. Edited by Gabriella Gelardini and Harold W. Attridge. Brill, 2016.

Schäfer, Peter. *The Origins of Jewish Mysticism*. Princeton University Press, 2009.

Schenck, Kenneth. "A Celebration of the Enthroned Son: The Catena of Hebrews 1." *JBL* 120 (2001): 469–485.

Schenck, Kenneth. "An Archaeology of Hebrews' Tabernacle Imagery." Pages 238–58 in *Hebrews in Contexts*. Edited by Garbiella Gelardini and Harold W. Attridge. Boston, 2016.

Schenck, Kenneth. *Cosmology and Eschatology in Hebrews*. SNTSMS 143. Cambridge University Press, 2007.

Schenck, Kenneth. "Keeping His Appointment: Creation and Enthronement in Hebrews." *JSNT* 66 (1997): 91–117.

Schenck, Kenneth. "Philo and the Epistle to the Hebrews: Ronald Williamson's Study after Thirty Years." *The Studia Philonica Annual* 14 (2002): 112–135.

Scholer, John M. *Proleptic Priests: Priesthood in the Epistle to the Hebrews*. JSNTSup 49. JSOT, 1991.

Schreiner, Thomas. *Commentary on Hebrews*. B&H, 2015.

Schrock, David. "Resurrection and Priesthood: Christological Soundings from the Book of Hebrews." *Southern Baptist Journal of Theology* 18 (2014): 89–114.

Schroeder, Christoph. "'A Love Song': Psalm 45 in Light of Ancient Near Eastern Marriage Texts." *CBQ* 58 (1996): 417–432.

Scott, J.M. "Heavenly Ascent in Jewish and Pagan Traditions." Pages 447–452 in *Dictionary of New Testament Background*. Edited by C. A. Evans and S. E. Porter. Intervarsity, 2000.

Segal, Alan F. "Heavenly Ascent in Hellenistic Judaism, Early Christianity and Their Environment." *ANRW* 23.2:1333–1394. Part 2, *Principat*, 23.2. Edited by H. Temporini and W. Haase. de Gruyter, 1980.

Silva, Moises. "Perfection and Eschatology in Hebrews." *WTJ* 39 (1976): 60–71.

Simisi, Seth M. "An Investigation into the Teleios ('Perfection') Motif in the Letter to the Hebrews and Its Contribution to the Argument of the Book." PhD diss., Dallas Theological Seminary, 2012. (Now published as *Pursuit of Perfection: Significance of the Perfection Motif in the Epistle to the Hebrews* [Wipf & Stock, 2016].)

Simpson, E.K. "The Vocabulary of the Epistle of Hebrews, Part 2." *EvQ* 18 (1946): 187–190.

Sleeman, Matthew. *Geography and the Ascension Narrative in Acts*. Cambridge University Press, 2009.

Smith, Gary. "Structure and Purpose in Genesis 1–11." *JETS* 20 (1977): 307–319.

Smith, Morton. "Ascent to the Heavens and the Beginning of Christianity." *Eranos-Jahrbuch* 50 (1981): 403–429.

Smith, Morton. "Two Ascended to Heaven: Jesus and the Author of 4Q491." Pages 290–302 in *Jesus and the Dead Sea Scrolls*. Edited by James H. Charlesworth. Doubleday, 1992.

Son, Kiwoong. *Zion Symbolism in Hebrews: Hebrews 12:18–24 as a Hermeneutical Key to the Epistle*. Paternoster, 2005.

de Souza, Elias Brasil. "The Heavenly Sanctuary/Temple Motif in the Hebrews Bible: Function and Relationship to the Earthly Counterparts." PhD. diss., Andrews University, 2005.

Spicq, Ceslas. *L'Épître aux Hébreux*. Gabalda, 1953.
Stanley, Steve. "Hebrews 9:6–10: The 'Parable' of the Tabernacle." *NovT* 38.4 (1995): 385–399.
Steyn, Gert. "Addressing an Angelomorphic Christological Myth in Hebrews?" *HvTSt* 59.4 (2003): 1107–1128.
Steyn, Gert. "The Eschatology of Hebrews as Understood within a Cultic Setting." Pages 429–450 in *Eschatology of the New Testament and Some Related Documents*. Edited by Jan G. Van Der Watt. WUNT 2/315. Mohr Siebeck, 2011.
Steyn, Gert. "Hebrews' Angelology in Light of Early Jewish Apocalyptic Imagery." *Journal of Early Christian History* 1.1 (2011): 143–164.
Steyn, Gert. "An Overview of the Extent and Diversity of Methods Utilised by the Author of Hebrews When Using the Old Testament." *Neot* 42.2 (2008): 327–352.
Steyn, Gert. *A Quest for the Assumed LXX Vorlage of the Explicit Quotations in Hebrews*. FRLANT 235. Vandenhoeck & Ruprecht, 2011.
Steyn, Gert. "The Vorlage of Psalm 45:6–7 (44:7–8) in Hebrews 1:8–9." *HvTSt* 60.3 (2004): 1086–1103.
Stewart, Alexander. "Cosmology, Eschatology, and Soteriology in Hebrews: A Synthetic Analysis." *BBR* 20.4 (2010): 545–560.
Strobel, August. "Die Psalmengrundlage der Gethsemane-Prallele Hebr 5:7ff." *ZNW* 45 (1954): 252–266.
Stuckenbruck, Loren T. "'Angels' and 'God': Exploring the Limits of Early Jewish Monotheism." Pages 45–70 in *Early Jewish and Christian Monotheism*. Edited by Loren T. Stuckenbruck and Wendy E.S. North. T&T Clark, 2004.
Stuckenbruck, Loren T. "Angels of the Nations." Pages 29–31 in *Dictionary of New Testament Background*. Edited by Craig A. Evans and Stanley Porter. Intervarsity, 2000.
Swete, H.B. *The Ascended Christ: A Study in the Earliest Christian Teaching*. Macmillan, 1910.
Swetnam, James. "The Crux at Hebrews 2,9 and Its Context." *Biblica* 91.1 (2010): 103–111.
Swetnam, James. "The Crux of Hebrews 5,7–8." *Biblica* 81 (2000): 347–361.
Swetnam, James. "Ἐξ ἑνός in Hebrews 2,11." *Biblica* 88 (2007): 517–525.
Swinson, L. Timothy. "Wind and Fire in Hebrews 1:7: A Reflection upon the Use of Psalm 104 (103)." *TJ* 28.2 (2007): 215–228.
Tabor, James D. *Things Unutterable: Paul's Ascent to Paradise in its Greco-Roman, Judaic, and Early Christian Contexts*. University Press of America, 1981.
Tate, Marvin. "An Exposition of Psalm 8." *Perspectives in Religious Studies* 28 (2001): 343–359.
Theophilos, Michael P. "The Numismatic Background of ΧΑΡΑΚΤΗΡ in Hebrews 1:3." *Australian Biblical Review* 64 (2016): 69–80.
Thompson, James. *The Beginnings of Christian Philosophy: The Epistle to the Hebrews*. Catholic Bible Association of America, 1982.
Thompson, James. *Hebrews*. Paideia. Baker, 2008.
Thompson, James. "Structure and Purpose of the Catena in Heb 1:5–13." *CBQ* 38.3 (1976): 352–363.
Thurston, Robert. "Philo and the Epistle to the Hebrews." *EvQ* 58.2 (1986): 133–143.

Toepel, Alexander. "Adamic Traditions on Early Christian and Rabbinic Literature." Pages 303–324 in *New Perspectives on 2 Enoch: No Longer Slavonic Only.* Edited by Andrei A. Orlov and Gabriele Boccaccini. Brill, 2012.

Toon, Peter. *The Ascension of Our Lord.* Thomas Nelson, 1984.

Toon, Peter. "Historical Perspectives of the Doctrine of Christ's Ascension Part 1: Resurrected and Ascended: The Exalted Jesus." *BSac* 140 (1983): 195–205.

Toon, Peter. "Historical Perspectives of the Doctrine of Christ's Ascension Part 2: The Meaning of the Ascension of Christ." *BSac* 140 (1983): 291–301

Toon, Peter. "Historical Perspectives of the Doctrine of Christ's Ascension Part 3: The Significance of the Ascension for Believers." *BSac* 141 (1984): 16–27

Toon, Peter. "Historical Perspectives of the Doctrine of Christ's Ascension Part 4: The Exalted Jesus and God's Revelation." *BSac* 141 (1984): 112–119

Urassa, Wenceslaus Mkeni. *Psalm 8 and Its Christological Re-Interpretations in the New Testament Context: An Inter-Contextual Study in Biblical Hermeneutics.* Peter Lang, 1998.

Vanhoye, Albert. *A Different Priest: The Epistle to the Hebrews.* Convivium, 2001.

Vanhoye, Albert. *The Letter to the Hebrews: A New Commentary.* Paulist, 2015.

von Rad, Gerhard. *Genesis.* Translated by John H. Marks. OTL. Westminster, 1961.

von Rad, Gerhard. *Old Testament Theology.* 2 vols. Prince, 1965.

Vos, Geerhardus. *Biblical Theology.* Eerdmans, 1948. Repr., Banner of Truth Trust 2000.

Vos, Geerhardus. "Hebrews, The Epistle of the Diatheke." Pages 161–233 in *Redemptive History and Biblical Interpretation.* Edited by Richard B. Gaffin, Jr. P&R, 1980.

Vos, Geerhardus. "The Idea of Biblical Theology." Pages 3–24 in *Redemptive History and Biblical Interpretation.* Edited by Richard B. Gaffin, Jr. P&R, 1980.

Vos, Geerhardus. "The Priesthood of Christ in Hebrews." Pages 126–160 in *Redemptive History and Biblical Interpretation.* Edited by Richard B. Gaffin, Jr. P&R, 1980.

Vos, Geerhardus. *The Teaching of the Epistle of Hebrews.* Eerdmans, 1956.

Wagner, James Benjamin. *Ascendit ad Coelos: The Doctrine of the Ascension in the Reformed and Lutheran Theology of the Period of Orthodoxy.* Keller, 1964.

Wallace, Daniel. *Greek Grammar Beyond the Basics.* Zondervan, 1996.

Wallace, David. "The Use of Psalms in the Shaping of a Text: Psalm 2:7 and Psalm 110:1 in Hebrews 1." *ResQ* 45 (2003): 41–50.

Walters, John R. *Perfection in New Testament Theology: Ethics and Eschatology in Relational Dynamics.* Mellen Biblical, 1995.

Waltke, Bruce. *Genesis: A Commentary.* Zondervan, 2001.

Webster, John. "One Who is Son: Theological Reflections on the Exordium to the Epistle to the Hebrews." Pages 69–94 in *The Epistles to the Hebrews and Christian Theology.* Edited by Richard Bauckham, Daniel R. Driver, Trevor A. Hart, and Nathan MacDonald. Eerdmans, 2009.

Weinfeld, Moshe. "Sabbath, Temple and the Enthronement of the Lord: The Problem of the *Sitz im Leben* of Genesis 1:1–2:3." Pages 501–512 in *Mélanges bibliques et orientaux en l'honneur de M. Henrie Cazelles.* Edited by A. Caquot and M Delcour. Butzon & Bercker, 1981.

Wenham, Gordon. *Genesis 1–15.* WBC 1. Word, 1997.

Wenham, Gordon. "Santuary Symbolism in the Garden of Eden Story." Pages 399–404 in *I Studied Inscriptions from Before the Flood: Ancient Near Eastern, Literary, and Linguistic Approaches to Genesis 1–11*. Edited by Richard S. Hess and David Toshio Tasumura. Eisenbrauns, 1994.

Wescott, Brooke Foss. *The Epistle to the Hebrews*. Macmillan, 1889.

Whitlark, Jason. "The God of Peace and His Victorious King: Hebrews 13:20–21 in Its Roman Imperial Context." Pages 155–178 in *Hebrews in Contexts*. Edited by Gabriella Gelardini and Harold W. Attridge. Brill, 2016.

Whitlark, Jason. *Resisting Empire: Rethinking the Purpose of the Letter to "The Hebrews."* JSNTS 484. Bloomsbury T&T Clark, 2014.

Whitley, C.F. "Textual and Exegetical Observations on Ps 45,4–7." *ZAW* 98.2 (1986): 277–282.

Wikgren, Allen. "Patterns of Perfection in the Epistle to the Hebrews." *NTS* 6 (1960): 159–167.

Williamson, Ronald. "The Background of the Epistle to the Hebrews." *ExpTim* 87 (1976): 232–237

Williamson, Ronald. *Philo and the Epistle to the Hebrews*. Brill, 1970.

Wright, J. Edward. *The Early History of Heaven*. Oxford University Press, 2000.

Wright, N.T. *The Climax of the Covenant*. Fortress, 1992.

Wright, N.T. *The New Testament and the People of God*. Fortress, 1992.

Wright, N.T. *The Resurrection of the Son of God*. Fortress, 2003.

Young, Norman. "The Gospel According to Hebrews 9." *NTS* 27 (1981): 198–210.

Zurawski, Jason. "The Two Worlds and Adam's Sin: The Problem of *4 Ezra* 7:10–14." Pages 97–106 in *Interpreting 4 Ezra and 2 Baruch: International Studies*. Edited by Gabriele Boccaccini and Jason M. Zurawski. LSTS 87. T&T Clark, 2014.

Zwiep, Arie W. *The Ascension of the Messiah in Lukan Christology*. Brill, 1997.

# Index

## Old Testament

**Genesis**

| | |
|---|---|
| 1–3 | 135 |
| 1–2 | 102 |
| 1 | 43n64, 96n33, 100n51, 108 |
| 1:2 | 102n60 |
| 1:11–12 | 157n40 |
| 1:26–28 | 27, 96, 97, 98, 100 |
| 1:26–27 | 98 |
| 1:26 | 96n34, 106 |
| 2:15 | 138n229 |
| 5:1 | 98n41 |
| 5:3 | 98n41 |
| 5:24 | 171 |
| 6:2 | 47n86 |
| 6:4 | 47n86 |
| 8:21 | 138n231 |
| 9:6 | 98n41 |
| 12:2 | 135n217 |
| 17:2 | 135n217 |
| 17:6 | 135n217 |
| 17:8 | 135n217 |
| 17:16 | 135n217 |
| 17:5 | 34, 35n23 |
| 22:18 | 135n217 |
| 25:31 | 55 |
| 26:3–4 | 135n217 |
| 26:24 | 135n217 |
| 28:3–4 | 135n217 |
| 28:14 | 135n217 |
| 31:7 (LXX) | 76n102 |
| 35:2 (LXX) | 76n102 |
| 35:11–12 | 135n217 |
| 41:14 (LXX) | 76n102 |
| 47:27 | 135n217 |
| 48:3 | 135n217 |
| 48:15–16 | 135n217 |
| 48:12–20 | 56 |
| 48:18 (LXX) | 55 |
| 49:3 | 55 |

**Exodus**

| | |
|---|---|
| 1:7 | 135n217 |
| 3:6 | 241n97 |
| 3:7 | 222, 224 |
| 3:8 | 128 |
| 3:9 | 222, 224 |
| 3:17 | 128 |
| 4:22–23 | 20, 58n9 |
| 4:22 | 34n20, 56 |
| 6:6–7 | 128 |
| 7:4–5 | 128 |
| 13:13 (LXX) | 76n102 |
| 15:1–21 | 62n41 |
| 19:18 | 147 |
| 24 | 191, 255 |
| 24:3 | 255 |

| | | | |
|---|---|---|---|
| 24:7 | 255 | 4:16 | 140 |
| 24:10 | 255n134, 256 | 6:22 | 140 |
| 24:12–15 | 256 | 7:27 | 117 |
| 24:16–17 | 256 | 8:21 | 117 |
| 24:17 | 255n134 | 8:25 | 117 |
| 25–40 | 139n232, 150n16 | 8:31 | 117 |
| 25:1–31:11 | 190n162 | 8:33 | 117 |
| 25:8–9 | 256 | 16 | 194 |
| 25:22 | 167 | 16:2 | 167 |
| 25:40 | 167, 193 | 16:32 | 117 |
| 26:1 | 167 | 20:8 | 130 |
| 26:33 | 167 | 21:10 | 117, 140 |
| 28:2 | 137 | 21:15 | 130 |
| 28:40 | 137 | 22:9 | 130 |
| 29:9 | 117 | 22:16 | 130 |
| 29:22 | 117 | 22:32 | 130 |
| 29:26 | 117 | 24:7 | 164 |
| 29:27 | 117 | 25:46 | 99 |
| 29:29 | 117 | 25:53 | 99 |
| 29:31 | 117 | 26:4 | 100 |
| 29:33 | 117 | 26:17 | 99 |
| 29:34 | 117 | 27:10 (LXX) | 76n102 |
| 29:35 | 117 | 27:27 (LXX) | 76n102 |
| 31:13 | 130 | 27:33 (LXX) | 76n102 |
| 33:9 | 206 | | |
| 33:11 | 206 | Numbers | |
| 33:19–20 | 206 | 3:3 | 117 |
| 34 | 160n51 | 4:7 | 164 |
| 34:29 | 206 | 11:14 | 42 |
| 34:35 | 206 | 12:13 | 70n75 |
| 35:30–39:43 | 190n162 | 13:20 | 161 |
| 38:9 | 164 | 15:3 | 138n231 |
| 39:17 | 164 | 15:10 | 138n231 |
| 40:1–33 | 190n162 | 15:13 | 138n231 |
| 40:18 | 190n162 | 15:14 | 138n231 |
| | | 15:24 | 138n231 |
| Leviticus | | 20:14–21 | 127n176 |
| 1:9 | 138n231 | 22:5 | 127n176 |
| 1:13 | 138n231 | 28:2 | 138n231 |
| 1:17 | 138n231 | 18:8 | 138n231 |
| 2:2 | 138n231 | 32:22 | 99 |
| 2:9 | 138n231 | 32:29 | 99 |
| 2:12 | 138n231 | 33:52 | 98 |
| 4:3 | 140 | | |
| 4:5 | 117, 140 | | |

*Index*

Deuteronomy
| | |
|---|---|
| 1:9 | 42 |
| 1:31 | 58n9, 212n14 |
| 2:4 | 241n97 |
| 7:13 | 135n217 |
| 8:5–6 | 212n14 |
| 8:5 | 58n9, 212n14 |
| 10:17 | 68n69 |
| 14:1–2 | 58n9, 212n14 |
| 21:17 | 55 |
| 26:19 | 58 |
| 28:1 | 58 |
| 28:4 | 100 |
| 28:11 | 100 |
| 28:12 | 100 |
| 32:1–44:1 | 62n41 |
| 32:1–20 | 212n14 |
| 32:4–6 | 58n9 |
| 32:8–9 | 56, 94n24 |
| 32:8 | 56 |
| 32:18–20 | 58n9 |
| 32:43 | 47n86, 58n9, 61, 62, 63, 63n45, 67, 212n14 |

Joshua
| | |
|---|---|
| 18:1 | 99 |
| 22:24 | 241 |

1 Samuel
| | |
|---|---|
| 1:34–35 LXX | 69n71 |
| 2:1–10 | 62n41 |
| 2:6–10 | 62n41 |
| 12:6 | 206 |
| 6:5 | 98 |
| 10:24 | 69n71 |
| 11–12 | 69n71 |
| 12:3 | 69n71 |
| 18:15 | 241, 241n97 |
| 18:29 | 241, 241n97 |
| 24:10 | 69n71 |
| 26:11 | 69n71 |

2 Samuel
| | |
|---|---|
| 1:14 | 69n71 |
| 7 | 48, 57 |
| 7:11 | 50 |
| 7:12–14 | 50 |
| 7:12 | 50 |
| 7:13 | 50, 73n87, 73n88 |
| 7:14 | 20, 32, 47, 50, 53, 58n9, 85, 211, 274 |
| 7:16 | 50, 73n87, 73n88 |
| 7:25 | 70n75 |
| 8:15 | 75n95 |
| 12:20 (LXX) | 76n102 |
| 22:7 | 222, 224, 225 |

1 Kings
| | |
|---|---|
| 2:4 | 212n12 |
| 2:45 | 73n87, 73n88 |
| 3–4 | 100n53 |
| 5:4 | 99 |
| 5:28 (LXX) | 76n102 |
| 6–8 | 150n16 |
| 7:45 (LXX) | 77n105 |
| 9:5 | 73n87, 73n88 |
| 10:9 | 75n95 |
| 21:25 (LXX) | 76n102 |
| 22:19 | 152, 158n46 |

2 Kings
| | |
|---|---|
| 5:5 (LXX) | 76n102 |
| 5:23 (LXX) | 76n102 |
| 11:18 | 98 |

1 Chronicles
| | |
|---|---|
| 16:35 | 70n75 |
| 17:12 | 73n87, 73n88 |
| 17:14 | 73n87, 73n88 |
| 17:27 | 73n87 |
| 20:5 | 222 |
| 22:10 | 73n87 |
| 22:20 | 73n88 |
| 28–29 | 150n16 |
| 28:2 | 147, 167 |
| 28:5 | 73n86 |
| 29:23 | 71n79, 73n86 |

2 Chronicles
| | |
|---|---|
| 2–7 | 150n16 |

| | | | |
|---|---|---|---|
| 9:8 | 71n79, 75n95 | 2:4 | 47, 147, 152 |
| 18:18 | 152, 158n46 | 2:5–9 | 102 |
| | | 2:6–7 | 20 |
| Ezra | | 2:6 | 33, 34n18, 48n91, 114n101, 152, 162, 246 |
| 6:11 (LXX) | 76n102 | | |
| 6:12 (LXX) | 76n102 | 2:7 | 32, 47, 50, 51, 52n104, 53, 57, 58n9, 110, 124, 124n164, 152, 153, 162, 165n67, 173, 173n104, 174, 199, 246, 247, 265, 276 |
| Nehemiah | | | |
| 5:19 | 70n75 | | |
| 6:14 | 70n75 | | |
| 9:6 | 80n121 | 2:8 | 34 |
| 9:9 | 222 | 2:9 | 48, 57 |
| 9:32 | 68n69 | 2:12 | 239 |
| 9:26 (LXX) | 76n102 | 3 | 235, 239 |
| 13:14 | 70n75 | 4:4 (LXX) | 170n86, 171 |
| 13:22 | 70n75 | 5:2–3 (LXX) | 228 |
| 13:29 | 70n75 | 5:8 | 228 |
| | | 5:11 (LXX) | 228 |
| Esther | | 5:11 | 70n75, 70n77, 215 |
| 13:9 | 44n71 | 5:13 (LXX) | 228 |
| 14:19 (LXX) | 44n71, 70n75 | 6 (LXX) | 228 |
| 16:18 (LXX) | 44n71 | 6:3 (LXX) | 228 |
| 16:21 (LXX) | 44n71 | 6:6 (LXX) | 228 |
| | | 6:7–9 (LXX) | 228 |
| Job | | 6:10 (LXX) | 228 |
| 1:6 | 47, 63n45, 65n56 | 7 | 235, 239n88 |
| 2:1 | 47, 63n45 | 7:1 | 215 |
| 13:25 | 241, 241n97 | 7:3–8 | 214 |
| 13:28 | 82 | 7:7–8 | 72n86 |
| 18:8 (LXX) | 77n105 | 8 | 21, 27, 51n102, 59, 65, 68n65, 69n69, 78n111, 88, 90, 93, 95, 96, 96n33, 96n34, 97n37, 100, 100n51, 100n53, 101, 101n57, 101n58, 102, 102N60, 103, 104, 105, 107n78, 108, 109, 110, 111, 112, 116n107, 120, 121, 125, 126, 129, 131, 136, 137, 139, 139n232, 141, 142, 165, 197, 216, 224, 226, 245, 260n160, 262, 270, 271, 272 |
| 19:29 | 241n97 | | |
| 37:32 | 75n97 | | |
| 38:4 | 78n111 | | |
| 38:7 | 63n45 | | |
| | | | |
| Psalm | | | |
| 1–2 | 101n57, 231 | | |
| 1 | 231, 239 | | |
| 1:3 | 231n63 | | |
| 2 | 29, 48, 48n91, 49, 68n65, 69n69, 85, 93, 142, 165, 173n104, 197, 226, 231, 233, 234, 239, 244, 245, 275 | | |
| | | 8:3 | 102 |
| 2:1 | 48, 50 | 8:4 (Eng. v.3) | 78n111 |

Index                                                                                     291

8:4–8              139
8:5–7 (Eng. v.4–6)  93, 95
8:5 (Eng. v.4) 23, 45, 95n28, 110,
8:6                44n71, 63, 94, 99n43, 110,
                   162
8:7 (Eng. v.6) 96, 98, 162
8:8–9              98
9:7                73n89
11:1               215
11:2 (LXX)         170n86, 171
11:4               147, 152, 158n45
12:1               171
15:10 (LXX)        170n86, 171
16 (LXX)           228
16:1 (LXX)         228
16:3–4 (LXX)       228
16:6 (LXX)         228
16:1               215
16:6               70n75
17                 226, 239n88
17:3               225
17:4–6 (LXX)       225
17:4               225
17:7 (LXX)         224, 225
17:21              225, 226
17:22              225, 226
17:25              225, 226
17:26 (LXX)        170n86
18–21              231
18                 235, 239n88
18:2               215
18:6               147, 222
18:20–24           214
18:26              171
18:30              215
21:5               101n55
21:15              69n69
21:25 (LXX)        227
21:26 (LXX)        227
22 (LXX 21)        133n206, 223n48, 226,
                   227, 227n57, 234n75, 270
22:22 (MT 22:23; LXX 21:23)   132, 221,
                   252
24:22              70n75
26                 239n88

26:1–3             214
26:9               70n75
27 (LXX)           229
27:2 (LXX)         229
27:6 (LXX)         229
27:7 (LXX)         229
27:8 (LXX)         229
27:9 (LXX)         229
29:1 (LXX 28:1)    47n86, 63n45
29:5 (LXX)         170n86
30 (LXX)           229, 233
30:6 (LXX)         233
30:10 (LXX)        229
30:11 (LXX)        229, 233
30:13 (LXX)        233
30:21 (LXX)        233
30:23 (LXX)        229, 233
30:24 (LXX)        170n86
31:6 (LXX)         170n86
32                 125
32:6               171
33:16 (LXX)        230
35:8               70n75
36:28 (LXX)        170n86
38:13 (LXX)        230
39 (LXX)           226, 230n39, 253, 254,
                   260, 264, 275
39:1 (LXX)         252
39:2 (LXX)         230
39:3 (LXX)         252
39:7–9 (MT 40:7-9; Eng. vv.6–8)
                   252
39:7 (LXX)         253, 253n124
39:9 (LXX)         253
39:10 (LXX)        252
41:1               70n75
41:2               70n75
41:4               70n75
42:1 (LXX)         170n86, 171
42:3               221
42:5–6             221
43:2               70n75
44                 239n88
45 (LXX 44)        55, 68, 69, 69n69, 85, 234,
                   269

| Reference | Page |
|---|---|
| 45:3 (Eng. 45:2) | 68n67 |
| 45:4 (LXX 44:4) | 68n68, 71n82 |
| 45:5 (Eng. 45:4) | 69n69 |
| 45:6 (LXX 44:6) | 69n69, 71n82, 73n86, 101n58 |
| 45:8 (Eng. 45:7) | 68n67, 69, 73n86 |
| 45:6–7 (LXX 44:7–8) | 67, 84n139, 224 |
| 45:7 (LXX 44:7) | 70n75, 214 |
| 46:1 | 68n67 |
| 46:7 | 68n67 |
| 46:10–11 | 68n67 |
| 47:2 | 68n67 |
| 47:5–8 | 68n67 |
| 47:10 | 70n75 |
| 47:11 | 70n75 |
| 49:5 (LXX) | 170n86 |
| 50:3 | 70n75 |
| 50:12 | 70n75 |
| 50:16 | 70n75 |
| 51 | 235 |
| 51:11 (LXX) | 170n86 |
| 52 | 235 |
| 53:3 | 70n75 |
| 53:4 | 70n75 |
| 54 | 235 |
| 54:2 | 70n75 |
| 54:24 | 70n75, 70n77 |
| 54:2 (LXX) | 230 |
| 55:8 | 70n75 |
| 55:13 | 70n75 |
| 56 | 235 |
| 56:2 | 70n75 |
| 56:6 | 70n75 |
| 56:8 | 70n75 |
| 57 | 235 |
| 58:2 | 70n75 |
| 58:10 | 70n75 |
| 58:18 | 70n75 |
| 59 | 235 |
| 59:3 | 70n75 |
| 59:12 | 70n75 |
| 60 | 235 |
| 60:2 | 70n75 |
| 60:6 | 70n75 |
| 60:2 (LXX) | 230 |
| 61:8 | 70n75 |
| 62 | 235 |
| 62:2 | 70n75 |
| 63:2 | 70n75 |
| 64:2 | 70n75 |
| 64:6 | 70n75 |
| 65:10 | 70n75 |
| 65:19 (LXX) | 230 |
| 66:4 | 70n75 |
| 66:6 | 70n75 |
| 67:8 | 70n75 |
| 67:10 | 70n75 |
| 67:11 | 70n75 |
| 67:25 | 70n75 |
| 67:29 | 70n75 |
| 68:2 | 70n75 |
| 68:6 | 70n75 |
| 68:7 | 70n75, 70n77 |
| 68:14 | 70n75, 70n77 |
| 68:20 | 70n75 |
| 68:30 (LXX) | 70 |
| 69:2 | 70n75, 70n77 |
| 69:6 | 70n75, 70n77 |
| 70:1 | 70n75 |
| 70:12 | 70n75 |
| 70:18 | 70n75 |
| 70:19 | 70n75 |
| 70:22 | 70n75 |
| 71:1 | 70n75 |
| 72:1–2 | 75n95 |
| 72:8–17 | 102N60 |
| 73:1 | 70n75 |
| 73:10 | 70n75 |
| 73:22 | 70n75 |
| 74:2 | 70n75 |
| 75:7 | 70n75 |
| 76:14 | 70n75, 71n78 |
| 76:17 | 70n75 |
| 78:1 | 70n75 |
| 78:2 (LXX) | 170n86 |
| 78:9 | 70n75, 70n77 |
| 79:1–2 | 171 |
| 79:4 | 70n75 |
| 79:8 | 70n75 |
| 79:15 | 70n75 |

Index                                                                                    293

| | | | |
|---|---|---|---|
| 81:8 | 70n75 | 102:13 (Eng. v.12) | 73, 73n89, 80n120 |
| 82 | 64n51 | 102:14 | 80n120 |
| 82:2 | 70n75 | 101:18 (LXX) | 230 |
| 82:21 | 45n77 | 102:20–21 (Eng. 19–20) | 77, 78n110 |
| 83:9 | 70n75, 70n77 | 102:23–24 | 79 |
| 83:10 | 70n75 | 102:24 | 79 |
| 84:5 | 70n75 | 102:25–27 (MT, LXX vv.26–28) | 68n68, |
| 84:7 | 70n75 | | 76, 78, 80, 84n139, 237 |
| 84:9 (LXX) | 170n86 | 102:25 | 80n120, 81 |
| 85:2 (LXX) | 170n86, 171 | 102:26 | 77, 78, 79n119, 81 |
| 85:6 (LXX) | 230 | 102:27 | 76, 76n102 |
| 85:14 | 70n75 | 102:28 | 80, 80n120 |
| 87:3 (LXX) | 230 | 103:6 | 75n97 |
| 89 (LXX 88) | 34, 34n21, 57, 73n87, | 103:19 | 147, 152, 158n46 |
| 89:4 | 73n87, 73n88 | 104 (LXX 103) | 40n48   , 82 |
| 89:6 (LXX 88:7) | 47n86, 63n45 | 104:1–2 (LXX 103) | 82 |
| 89:11 | 78n111 | 104:4 (LXX 103) | 82 |
| 89:14 | 75n97 | 104:7 (LXX 103) | 82 |
| 89:20 | 34n21 | 104:1 | 68n68 |
| 89:21 | 57 | 104:5 | 78n111 |
| 89:24 (Eng 23) | 57 | 105:20 (LXX) | 76n102 |
| 89:25 (Eng. 24) | 57 | 105:44 (LXX) | 230 |
| 89:26 (Eng. 25) | 34, 57 | 107:2 | 70n75 |
| 89:27–28 (LXX 88) | 233, 234 | 107:6 | 70n75 |
| 89:27 (Eng. 26) | 20, 34n21, 57 | 107:12 | 70n75 |
| 89:28 (Eng. 27) | 34, 57, 234 | 107:38 | 135n217 |
| 89:29 | 73n87, 73n88 | 108:1 | 70n75 |
| 89:30–33 | 212 | 110 (LXX 109) | 99n43, 133, 153, |
| 89:30 | 34, 34n21, 234 | | 154n29, 165, 197, 226, 233, |
| 89:31–35 | 58 | | 234, 244, 245, 275 |
| 89:36 | 73n87, 73n88 | 110:1 | 15, 33, 48n91, 68, 73n86, |
| 89:37–38 | 58n10 | | 85, 93, 95, 96, 114n101, |
| 90:2 | 73n90 | | 124n164, 142, 152, 153, 162, |
| 93:1 | 73n90 | | 174, 199,    247, 261, |
| 93:2 (LXX 92:2) | 73, 73n90 | | 262, 265, 276 |
| 96:6 | 69n69 | 110:4 | 72, 153, 166, 173n104, 199, |
| 96:10 (LXX) | 170n86 | | 209, 276 |
| 96:13 | 75n97 | 114–115 (LXX) | 243n103 |
| 97:2 | 75n97 | 114 (LXX) | 229 |
| 98:8 | 70n75, 70n77 | 114:1–4 (LXX) | 229, 230 |
| 98:9 | 75n97 | 114:1 (LXX) | 230 |
| 99:5 | 147 | 114:6–8 (LXX) | 230 |
| 102 (LXX 101) | 44n73, 55, 67, 78, 79, 82, | 114:7 (LXX) | 230 |
| | 84n140, 85, 157, 269 | 114:9 (LXX) | 230 |
| 101:1 (LXX) | 230 | 115:4 (LXX) | 230n61 |

| | | | |
|---|---|---|---|
| 115:6 (LXX) | 170n86, 230n61 | Isaiah | |
| 118:169 (LXX) | 230 | 1:2 | 58n9 |
| 118–119 | 231 | 5:1–9 | 62n41 |
| 119:91 | 44n71 | 5:16 | 75n97 |
| 121:4 (LXX) | 77n108 | 6:1–6 | 146 |
| 129:2 (LXX) | 230 | 6 | 150, 159 |
| 131:16 (LXX) | 170n86 | 6:1 | 147 |
| 132:7 | 147, 167 | 6:2–3 | 65n56, 68 |
| 132:11–12 | 73n87 | 8 | 270 |
| 132:12 | 73n88 | 8:17–18 | 132, 133n206, 220, 227 |
| 138:17 | 70n75 | 8:18 | 133 |
| 138:19 | 70n75 | 9 | 101n58 |
| 138:23 | 70n75 | 9:5 | 73n86 |
| 139:7 (LXX) | 230 | 9:7 | 75n95 |
| 139:9 | 171 | 10:21 | 68n69 |
| 139:16 | 171 | 16:5 | 75n95 |
| 140:1 (LXX) | 230 | 24:5 (LXX) | 76n102 |
| 141:3 (LXX) | 230 | 26:9 | 70n75 |
| 141:7 (LXX) | 230 | 28:4 | 161 |
| 142 | 235 | 30:19 | 222 |
| 142:1 (LXX) | 230 | 33:5 | 75n95 |
| 143:23 | 70n75 | 34:4 | 77, 77n105 |
| 144 | 101n57 | 37:16 | 78n112 |
| 144:10 (LXX) | 170n86 | 38:5 | 222 |
| 144:13 (LXX) | 170n86 | 38:10–20 | 62n41 |
| 144:17 (LXX) | 170n86 | 40:22 | 147 |
| 144:19 (LXX) | 230 | 40:26 | 80n121 |
| 145:13 | 73n89 | 40:28 (LXX) | 77n108, 80n121 |
| 148:14 (LXX) | 170n86 | 40:30 (LXX) | 77n108 |
| 149:1–2 | 171 | 40:31 (LXX) | 76n102 |
| 149:1 (LXX) | 170n86 | 41:1 (LXX) | 76n102 |
| 149:5 (LXX) | 170n86 | 42:5 | 78n112, 80n121 |
| 149:9 (LXX) | 170n86 | 42:6 | 64 |
| | | 42:8 | 40 |
| Proverbs | | 44:24 | 44n71, 78n112, 80n121 |
| 2:6–7 | 241n98 | 45:12 | 78n112, 80n121 |
| 2:6 | 241n98 | 45:15 | 70n75 |
| 2:8 | 241, 241n97 | 45:18 | 80n121 |
| 3:11–12 | 213, 274 | 48:11 | 40 |
| 3:12 | 213 | 48:13 | 78n111, 80n121 |
| 8:22ff | 38 | 49:6 | 64 |
| 8:25–26 | 38 | 50:9 | 82 |
| 8:25 | 38 | 51:2 | 135n217 |
| 28:14 | 241 | 51:5 | 82 |
| 30:5 | 241, 241n97 | 51:6 | 80n121, 82 |

*Index* 295

| | | | |
|---|---|---|---|
| 51:12 | 241, 241n97 | 28 | 109n80 |
| 51:13 | 78n111 | 28:11–19 | 139n232 |
| 51:16 | 78n111 | 28:12–16 | 138 |
| 53 | 198 | 34:4 | 64 |
| 53:12 | 35, 198 | 34:16 | 64 |
| 55:3 | 170 | 37 | 20 |
| 57:11 | 241n97 | 43:7 | 147 |
| 57:17 | 94n26 | 40–48 | 150n16 |
| 61:2 | 72n86 | | |
| 66:1 | 147, 152, 158n46, 180n133 | Daniel | |
| | | 3:26–45 | 62n41 |
| Jeremiah | | 3:52–56 | 62n41 |
| 2:11 (LXX) | 76n102 | 3:57–90 | 62n41 |
| 3–4 | 58n9 | 3:52–90 | 62n41 |
| 3:19 | 20 | 4:5 | 241n97 |
| 4:1 | 241n97 | 7 | 88, 101n55, 109, 110, 153, 257n140 |
| 5:22 | 241n97 | | |
| 9:24 | 75n97 | 7:14 | 35 |
| 10:16 | 44n71 | 11:39 | 96n34 |
| 13:23 (LXX) | 76n102 | 12:1–3 | 107 |
| 15:17 | 241, 241n97 | | |
| 22:25 | 241, 241n97 | Hosea | |
| 23:5 | 75n95 | 8:2 | 70n75 |
| 31:9 | 20, 56 | 13:4 (LXX) | 80n121 |
| 31:18 | 68n69 | | |
| 31:31–38 | 255 | Amos | |
| 31:32 | 191 | 5:8 LXX | 44n71 |
| 31:34 | 262 | 9:6 | 78n111 |
| 33:15 | 75n95 | 9:11 | 50 |
| 33:25 | 58n10 | | |
| 38:9 (LXX) | 56 | Jonah | |
| 51:19 | 44n71 | 2:2 | 222 |
| 52:33 (LXX) | 76n102 | 2:3–10 | 62n41 |
| | | | |
| Lamentations | | Micah | |
| 2:1 | 147 | 1:2 | 147, 158n45 |
| 5:19 | 73n89 | | |
| | | Nahum | |
| Ezekiel | | 1:17 | 241, 241n97 |
| 1 | 257n140 | | |
| 1:26–28 | 41n50 | Habakkuk | |
| 1:26 | 255n134 | 2:20 | 147, 158n45, 241n97 |
| 1:27 | 255m134 | 3:1–10 | 62n41 |
| 1:28 | 106, 255n134 | | |
| 4:14 | 70n75 | | |

Zephaniah
| | |
|---|---|
| 1:7 | 241n97 |
| 3:12 | 241n97 |

Haggai
| | |
|---|---|
| 2:6 | 77n107, 155n31 |
| 2:21 (Eng. 2:6) | 84n140 |

Zechariah
| | |
|---|---|
| 2:17 | 241n97 |
| 6:11 | 137 |
| 6:12–13 | 138 |
| 12:1 | 78n111 |

Malachi
| | |
|---|---|
| 3:16 | 241, 241n97 |

## New Testament

Matthew
| | |
|---|---|
| 11:27 | 44n71 |
| 13:32 | 60 |
| 17:12 | 244n108 |
| 18:35 | 244n108 |
| 23:28 | 244n108 |
| 24:33 | 244n108 |
| 26:38 | 221 |
| 26:39 | 221 |
| 27:50 | 221 |

Mark
| | |
|---|---|
| 3:14 | 206 |
| 4:15 | 61 |
| 4:16 | 61 |
| 4:29 | 61 |
| 4:31 | 61 |
| 4:32 | 61 |
| 9:42 | 218 |
| 13:29 | 244n108 |
| 14:34 | 221 |
| 14:36 | 221, 238n83 |

Luke
| | |
|---|---|
| 2:7 | 55 |
| 2:8–14 | 59 |
| 2:9 | 41n57 |
| 2:13–14 | 59n16 |
| 2:13 | 59n16 |
| 2:52 | 118n120 |
| 4:5 | 59 |
| 9:31 | 41n57 |
| 10:22 | 44n71 |
| 13:32 | 118 |
| 17:10 | 244n108 |
| 21:30 | 61 |
| 22:42 | 221 |
| 23:46 | 233 |
| 24:50–53 | 13n2 |

John
| | |
|---|---|
| 1:3 | 35, 44n71 |
| 1:14 | 41n57, 205 |
| 2:10 | 61 |
| 2:11 | 41n57 |
| 3:13–15 | 13n2 |
| 3:35 | 44n71 |
| 5:7 | 61 |
| 5:21 | 244n108 |
| 6:23 | 13n2 |
| 12:41–43 | 41n57 |
| 13:3 | 44n71 |
| 14:8 | 205 |
| 16:21 | 61 |
| 17:1 | 41n57 |
| 17:5 | 39n41 |
| 17:24 | 39n41 |
| 19:37 | 50 |
| 20:17 | 13n2 |

Acts
| | |
|---|---|
| 1:1–12 | 13n2 |
| 2:24–36 | 112 |
| 2:36 | 112, 154n28, 205 |
| 2:34 | 13n2 |
| 5:31 | 129n187 |
| 7:48–49 | 180n133 |
| 7:53 | 94 |
| 11:28 | 59 |
| 17:24 | 180n133 |

| | | | |
|---|---|---|---|
| 17:31 | 59, 73n86 | Colossians | |
| 24:5 | 59 | 1:16 | 35, 43n68 |
| 28:20 | 218 | 1L17 | 43n68 |
| Romans | | Hebrews | |
| 4 | 125 | 1–2 | 21, 23, 93, 123, 156 |
| 6:4 | 41n57 | 1 | 27, 51n102, 55, 67, 84n136, |
| 8:3 | 113n99 | | 85, 87, 90, 91, 111, 141, |
| 8:38 | 184 | | 142, 152, 154n28, 155, 157, |
| 9:33 | 33n16 | | 173n104, 215, 216, 240, |
| 5 | 88 | | 261, 268, 269, 270, 275 |
| 5:18–19 | 244n108 | 1:1–14 | 215 |
| 5:21 | 244n108 | 1:1–4 | 30, 38n39 |
| 15:10–12 | 50 | 1:1–5 | 29, 53 |
| | | 1:1 | 30 |
| 1 Corinthians | | 1:2–3 | 49, 72, 91, 112, 114, 268 |
| 3:20 | 50 | 1:2 | 30n3, 31n4, 35, 35n26, 43, |
| 3:22 | 184 | | 52, 72n83, 95, 112, 204, |
| 7:26 | 184 | | 205, 207, 269, 275 |
| 15 | 88, 99n43 | 1:3–4 | 18, 24, 61, 66, 95 |
| 15:23–25 | 73n86 | 1:3 | 36, 40, 41, 42, 44, 46, 49, |
| 15:27 | 60 | | 65, 71, 72n83, 83n135, 95, |
| 15:50 | 134, 219 | | 116, 137, 152, 153, 154, 162, |
| | | | 173,    174, 205, 206, |
| 2 Corinthians | | | 207, 247, 261 |
| 4:6 | 41n57 | 1:4 | 51, 60, 172, 173, 192, 216, |
| 9:13 | 113n99 | | 247n112, 268 |
| 12 | 14n2 | 1:5–6 | 61 |
| 12:2 | 173n103 | 1:5–12 | 21 |
| | | 1:5–14 | 24, 59 |
| Galatians | | 1:5 | 31n4, 47, 49, 52, 52n104, |
| 1:4 | 184 | | 53, 61, 91, 93, 95, 124, 162, |
| 3:19 | 94 | | 165, 204n2, 216, 247, 268 |
| | | 1:6–14 | 53, 85 |
| Ephesians | | 1:6 | 20, 34, 55, 58, 59, 60, |
| 1:10 | 43n68 | | 60n24, 61, 63, 72n83, 91, |
| 1:11 | 43n68 | | 93, 131, 234, 268 |
| 1:17 | 41n57 | 1:7 | 66, 67, 68 |
| 4:8–10 | 13n2 | 1:8–12 | 82 |
| | | 1:8–9 | 24, 55, 67, 162, 224, 268 |
| Philippians | | 1:8 | 43, 73n86, 74, 158 |
| 2:6–11 | 13n2 | 1:9 | 74, 75, 95, 263 |
| 3:4 | 210 | 1:10–12 | 24, 49, 76, 77, 84n140, |
| 3:4–5 | 210, 211 | | 205, 216, 237, 268 |
| | | 1:10–11 | 179n121, 180 |

| | | | |
|---|---|---|---|
| 1:10 | 72n83, 83, 154, 155, 205, 207 | 2:11 | 130, 132, 197 |
| | | 2:12 | 132, 221, 223n48, 227, 252 |
| 1:11–12 | 72n83 | 2:13 | 132, 220 |
| 1:12 | 76, 77n106 | 2:14–18 | 134 |
| 1:13 | 49, 66, 93, 95, 150, 153, 154, 162, 165, 261, 268 | 2:14–15 | 48n91, 132, 135, 155n35, 237 |
| 1:14 | 32n11, 66, 71 | 2:14 | 64n51, 113, 116, 131, 134, 166n69, 169, 170, 198, 217, 220, 221, 238, 254 |
| 2 | 45, 62, 64, 84n136, 87, 88, 89, 90, 90n12, 93, 109, 109n81, 109n83, 111, 116n107, 120, 128, 134, 136, 141, 142, 203, 226, 234, 252, 270, 271, 272 | | |
| | | 2:15 | 78n110, 116 |
| | | 2:16 | 135, 167, 224 |
| | | 2:17–18 | 120, 157 |
| | | 2:17 | 113, 134, 136, 153, 154, 157, 157n42, 166n69, 173, 217, 221, 238, 247n112, 254 |
| 2:1–4 | 111, 248, 260 | | |
| 2:2–3 | 123 | | |
| 2:2 | 91 | 2:18 | 157, 158, 220, 238 |
| 2:4 | 133 | 3 | 111 |
| 2:4–5 | 245 | 3:1–6 | 39, 135, 224, 260 |
| 2:5–18 | 90, 141 | 3:1–2 | 49 |
| 2:5–10 | 135, 162, 169 | 3:1 | 153, 154, 154n28, 162, 205 |
| 2:5–9 | 23, 73n86, 133, 270 | 3:2 | 154, 238 |
| 2:5–8 | 93, 239 | 3:3 | 206, 208 |
| 2:5 | 30n3, 60, 61, 91, 95, 184, 270 | 3:4 | 206 |
| | | 3:5 | 206, 207, 208, 209 |
| 2:6–18 | 271 | 3:6 | 31n4, 204, 205, 207, 208, 209, 275 |
| 2:6–10 | 173 | | |
| 2:6–9 | 221 | 3:14 | 123, 162 |
| 2:6–8 | 59, 60, 65, 93 | 3:18 | 239n90 |
| 2:6 | 93 | 4:3 | 254 |
| 2:7 | 94, 137, 206, 245 | 4:4 | 62 |
| 2:8–10 | 112 | 4:6 | 239n90 |
| 2:8–9 | 103 | 4:11 | 239n90 |
| 2:8 | 45, 95, 103, 112 | 4:14–16 | 20, 21, 27, 153 |
| 2:9–10 | 122, 154, 155n35 162, 219 | 4:14–15 | 217 |
| 2:9 | 94, 112, 113, 116, 122, 129, 131, 137, 165, 198, 206, 219, 245 | 4:14 | 31n4, 153, 155, 156, 179, 180, 245, 250 |
| | | 4:15 | 134, 156, 157, 170, 218, 219 |
| 2:10–18 | 136 | 4:16 | 155, 156, 158, 162, 167n72 |
| 2:10–16 | 120 | 5 | 272 |
| 2:10–11 | 125 | 5:1–10 | 154 |
| 2:10 | 31n4, 113, 114, 114n101, 116, 118, 121, 123, 126, 129, 130, 161, 197, 206, 210, 220, 246 | 5:1–4 | 136, 209, 217, 220, 236, 238, 244, 245, 251 |
| | | 5:1 | 136, 157, 166n69, 197, 217, 245 |
| 2:11–13 | 129 | 5:2 | 134, 217, 219 |

# Index

| | | | |
|---|---|---|---|
| 5:3 | 218, 254 | 7:1 | 166, 166n71 |
| 5:4 | 126, 141, 244, 245 | 7:3 | 31, 31n4, 52n104 |
| 5:4–5 | 137, 245 | 7:5 | 176, 210, 211 |
| 5:5–6 | 72, 136, 165, 173n104, 199, 244 | 7:6–7 | 166 |
| | | 7:6 | 166 |
| 5:5 | 31n4, 52n104, 114n101, 124, 126, 141, 155n35, 166n69, 173, 176, 245, 246, 247, 247n112, 249 | 7:7 | 166n70 |
| | | 7:11 | 167, 168, 169, 174, 176, 246 |
| | | 7:12 | 176 |
| | | 7:15–16 | 50 |
| 5:6 | 174, 247, 249 | 7:16–17 | 166, 174, 247, 247n112 |
| 5:7–10 | 27, 171n89, 203, 262, 273, 274, 276 | 7:16 | 50, 166n69, 168, 168n79, 169, 170, 173, 176 |
| 5:7–9 | 227, 263 | 7:17 | 166, 169, 169n82 |
| 5:7–8 | 113n99, 127, 220, 251 | 7:18 | 169, 169n82 |
| 5:7 | 27, 82, 103, 128, 128n181, 171, 214, 220n35, 221, 222, 225, 226, 227, 227n57, 234, 237, 238, 263, 274 | 7:19–20 | 209 |
| | | 7:19 | 116, 117, 118, 125, 154, 166, 167, 167n72, 168n77, 169, 246, 260 |
| | | 7:20–22 | 166 |
| 5:8–9 | 120, 237, 246 | 7:20 | 173n102, 209 |
| 5:8 | 52, 118, 118n120, 119, 204, 205, 208, 210, 211, 213, 216, 220, 237, 246, 249, 263, 270, 272, 275, 276 | 7:21–22 | 199, 209 |
| | | 7:21 | 169, 169n82, 174, 247 |
| | | 7:22 | 50, 169, 173, 192, 247n112, 260 |
| 5:9–10 | 244 | 7:23 | 166n69, 169, 169n82 |
| 5:9 | 113, 116, 121, 126, 131n200, 173, 221, 239n90, 247n112 | 7:24–25 | 198 |
| | | 7:24 | 169, 169n82, 174, 208 |
| 5:14 | 117, 246 | 7:25 | 167n72, 169, 169n82, 208 |
| 6:1 | 42, 117, 246 | 7:26–27 | 208 |
| 6:5 | 30n3, 184 | 7:26 | 27, 50, 155, 155n33, 157, 168, 170, 172, 173, 179, 180, 200, 208, 219, 247n112, 272 |
| 6:6 | 31n4, 123 | | |
| 6:9 | 123, 192 | | |
| 6:13–14 | 166 | | |
| 6:14 | 166, 166n71 | 7:27–28 | 154 |
| 6:17–20 | 124 | 7:27 | 170, 172, 188, 219, 254, 261 |
| 6:17 | 166 | 7:28 | 31n4, 116, 117, 118, 120, 121, 134, 137, 166n69, 169, 169n82, 170, 173, 176, 204, 208, 209, 218, 219, 246, 247, 275 |
| 6:18–20 | 160 | | |
| 6:18 | 154, 162, 163, 163n60, 165 | | |
| 6:19–20 | 20, 21, 27, 160, 200, 272 | | |
| 6:19 | 160, 162, 163, 163n60, 167 | | |
| 6:20 | 129, 160, 163, 164, 166, 168, 173, 247n112 | 8:1–6 | 27, 174, 175, 200, 272, 273 |
| | | 8:1–2 | 166, 174, 176 |
| 7 | 171n89, 272 | 8:1 | 18, 71, 155, 158, 164, 174 |
| 7:1–11 | 130 | 8:2 | 167, 180, 180n132, 186, 189 |
| 7:1–3 | 50 | 8:3 | 196n178 |

| | | | |
|---|---|---|---|
| 8:4 | 175, 176 | 9:24–28 | 21 |
| 8:5 | 167, 175, 180, 190, 193 | 9:24 | 21, 155, 179, 189, 192, 193, 197, 198, 199, 206 |
| 8:6 | 187, 192, 260 | | |
| 8:7–12 | 175 | 9:25–28 | 196n178 |
| 8:7–8 | 186 | 9:25 | 188, 189, 196, 197, 220n35 |
| 8:7 | 154, 176, 188, 255 | 9:26 | 30n3, 35n29, 62, 196, 197, 198, 254, 261 |
| 8:8–12 | 255 | | |
| 8:9 | 255, 272 | 9:27 | 198 |
| 8:11 | 255 | 9:28 | 198, 261 |
| 8:13 | 183, 186, 188 | 10 | 251 |
| 9:1–10 | 21 | 10:1–10 | 170n85 |
| 9:1 | 186, 188, 190 | 10:1 | 30n3, 33, 116, 117, 118, 124, 125, 159, 167n72, 193, 246, 251 |
| 9:2–3 | 185 | | |
| 9:2 | 180, 190, 190n162 | | |
| 9:3 | 180 | 10:2 | 154, 251, 260n162 |
| 9:4 | 189 | 10:3 | 252 |
| 9:6 | 180, 182, 184, 185 | 10:4 | 220n35, 252 |
| 9:7 | 188, 218, 220n35 | 10:5–14 | 27, 203, 262, 264, 273 |
| 9:8 | 182, 186, 189 | 10:5–10 | 275 |
| 9:9–10 | 185 | 10:5–9 | 230n62, 251 |
| 9:9 | 116, 118, 125, 154, 182, 184, 185, 246 | 10:5–7 | 103 |
| | | 10:5 | 52, 59, 62, 221, 223 |
| 9:10 | 184, 185, 220n35 | 10:7 | 70, 261 |
| 9:11–14 | 21, 27, 176, 200, 273 | 10:8 | 70, 255, 261 |
| 9:11–12 | 33, 178 | 10:9 | 188, 255 |
| 9:11 | 30n3, 177, 180, 180n132, 181, 192 | 10:10–14 | 260 |
| | | 10:10 | 260, 261 |
| 9:12–14 | 191 | 10:11–13 | 33 |
| 9:12 | 180, 180n132, 188, 190, 191, 220n35, 261 | 10:11 | 261, 262 |
| | | 10:12 | 261 |
| 9:13–14 | 188 | 10:14 | 246 |
| 9:13 | 185, 220n35 | 10:18–21 | 262 |
| 9:14 | 182, 185, 220n35 | 10:19–25 | 21 |
| 9:15 | 116, 188, 191, 255 | 10:19–22 | 248 |
| 9:16 | 42 | 10:26–31 | 159 |
| 9:17 | 123, 175 | 10:12 | 18, 71 |
| 9:18–21 | 191 | 10:14 | 116, 124, 125 |
| 9:18 | 188, 220n35, 264 | 10:19–22 | 159 |
| 9:19 | 220n35 | 10:19 | 220n35 |
| 9:20 | 220n35 | 10:23 | 154 |
| 9:21 | 180, 220n35 | 10:29 | 31n4, 130, 220n35 |
| 9:22 | 220n35 | 10:34 | 192 |
| 9:23–26 | 27, 33, 192, 200, 273 | 11 | 254 |
| 9:23 | 155, 179n125, 180, 192, 193, 194 | 11:3 | 46 |
| | | 11:7 | 62, 241, 254 |

*Index* 301

| | | | |
|---|---|---|---|
| 11:10 | 254 | 13:11 | 220n35 |
| 11:16 | 192 | 13:12 | 130, 220n35 |
| 11:12 | 155 | 13:13 | 42 |
| 11:21 | 31n4 | 13:14 | 83n135, 124n165 |
| 11:22 | 31n4 | 13:20–21 | 83n135 |
| 11:24 | 31n4 | 13:20 | 105n71, 199, 220n35 |
| 11:28 | 220n35 | | |
| 11:35 | 192 | 1 Timothy | |
| 11:38 | 62 | 2:7 | 33n16 |
| 11:40 | 116, 192, 246 | 3:16 | 41n57 |
| 12:1–23 | 154 | | |
| 12:1–2 | 164 | 2 Timothy | |
| 12:1 | 129, 218 | 1:11 | 33n16 |
| 12:2–3 | 238 | | |
| 12:2 | 71, 116, 127, 158, 161, 162, 240, 246 | 1 Peter | |
| | | 1:11 | 41n57 |
| 12:4–11 | 214 | 1:21 | 41n57 |
| 12:4 | 220n35 | 2:8 | 33n16 |
| 12:5–11 | 214 | 2:22 | 157n41 |
| 12:5–10 | 213 | 2:23 | 233n74 |
| 12:5 | 31n4 | 4:11 | 41n57 |
| 12:6 | 31n4, 213 | 4:19 | 233n74 |
| 12:7 | 31n4, 213 | | |
| 12:8 | 213 | 2 Peter | |
| 12:10 | 162 | 1:5–7 | 211 |
| 12:17 | 210, 211 | 1:12 | 210, 211 |
| 12:18–29 | 22 | | |
| 12:18–24 | 260 | 1 John | |
| 12:20–24 | 159 | 3:5 | 157n41 |
| 12:20–23 | 227 | | |
| 12:20 | 42 | Jude | |
| 12:21 | 159 | 7 | 164 |
| 12:22–24 | 48n91 | | |
| 12:22–23 | 132, 153, 247 | Revelation | |
| 12:22 | 162, 167n72 | 4–5 | 146 |
| 12:23 | 116, 127, 155, 227 | 4:4 | 73n91 |
| 12:24 | 192, 220n35 | 6:14 | 77, 77n106 |
| 12:25 | 155 | 12:5 | 13n2 |
| 12:26–27 | 77, 124n165 | 12:9 | 59 |
| 12:26 | 77n107, 155, 179n121, 180, 254, 258n152 | 19:10 | 66n57 |
| | | 21:23 | 41n57 |
| 12:28 | 48n91, 241 | 22:8–9 | 66n57 |
| 13:9 | 123 | | |
| 13:10 | 180 | | |
| 13:11–12 | 220n35 | | |

## Old Testament Apocrypha and Pseudepigraphs

*ALD*
| | |
|---|---|
| 4:4–6 | 190 |

*Apocalypse Of Abraham*
| | |
|---|---|
| 7:10 | 44n71, 80n121 |
| 8:1–9:4 | 40n47 |
| 10:3–4 | 91n17 |
| 10:4–15 | 40n47 |
| 12:10 | 39n46 |
| 14:1–5 | 39n46 |
| 15 | 39n46 |
| 15–20 | 190 |

*Apocalypse of Sedrach*
| | |
|---|---|
| 7:4 | 41 |

*Apocalypse of Zephaniah*
| | |
|---|---|
| 6:11–15 | 66n57 |

*Ascension of Isaiah*
| | |
|---|---|
| 7:21 | 66n57 |
| 8:5 | 66n57 |

*2 Baruch*
| | |
|---|---|
| 4 | 107, 149n14 |
| 4:1–2 | 149 |
| 4:3–6 | 149 |
| 4:3 | 149 |
| 4:4 | 149 |
| 4:5 | 149 |
| 5:21 | 107 |
| 14:13 | 240 |
| 14:17–19 | 107n79 |
| 14:18–19 | 107 |
| 14:19 | 107 |
| 15:7–8 | 243n103, 245n109 |
| 15:7 | 91n14 |
| 15:8 | 107, 115 |
| 21:4–11 | 82n132 |
| 21:4–6 | 83n134 |
| 21:6–7 | 67n61 |
| 21:6 | 39n45, 65n56 |
| 21:7 | 83n134 |
| 44:7 | 114 |
| 48:10 | 39n45, 65n56 |
| 48:49–50 | 243n103 |
| 48:50 | 114 |
| 51:1–2 | 243n103 |
| 51:2 | 107 |
| 51:5 | 107 |
| 51:7–12 | 172 |
| 51:11–15 | 243n103 |
| 51:11 | 39n45, 65n56 |
| 52:4–7 | 114 |
| 52:5–7 | 107 |
| 52:6–7 | 243n103 |
| 54:13 | 82n132 |
| 54:19 | 107 |
| 54:21 | 172n93, 243n103 |
| 59:3–4 | 149 |
| 59:3 | 258 |
| 59:4 | 149, 259 |
| 59:5–12 | 150 |
| 59:8 | 259 |
| 59:11 | 259 |

*3 Baruch*
| | |
|---|---|
| 11:4 | 74n91 |
| 11:6–8 [G] | 74n91 |

*Bel and the Dragon*
| | |
|---|---|
| 5 | 44n71, 80n121 |

*1 Enoch*
| | |
|---|---|
| 1:1–8 | 172 |
| 7:1 | 194n168 |
| 9:1–5 | 40n47 |
| 9:5 | 44n71 |
| 9:8 | 194n168 |
| 10:11 | 194n168 |
| 12:4 | 194n168 |
| 14 | 148 |
| 14:8–23 | 190 |
| 14:9 | 148 |
| 14:10 | 148 |
| 14:13 | 148 |
| 14:15–23 | 148 |

| | | | |
|---|---|---|---|
| 14:15 | 148 | 65:12 | 107 |
| 14:18 | 148 | 66:1–5 | 172n92 |
| 14:20 | 148 | 66:7 [J] | 172n92 |
| 14:16–25 | 152 | 71 | 148 |
| 14:18–24 | 39n45, 65n56 | 71:1 | 73n91, 172 |
| 14:18–20 | 146, 159n47 | 71:5–7 | 146, 159n47 |
| 14:20–21 | 40n47 | 71:5–6 | 148 |
| 14:21–25 | 148 | 71:5 | 172 |
| 14:25 | 148 | 71:7–8 | 148 |
| 15:1 | 172 | 71:15–16 | 172 |
| 15:3–4 | 194n168 | 71:29 | 148 |
| 17–36 | 39n46 | 75:1–3 | 73n91 |
| 18:2–3 | 148 | 79:6 | 73n91, 74n91 |
| 18:4 | 148 | 82:7 | 73n91, 74n91 |
| 18:8 | 148 | 82:11–12 | 74n91 |
| 19–21 | 73n91 | 83:3 | 83n134 |
| 20:1–7 | 74n91 | 84:2–3 | 40n47 |
| 25:3 | 148 | 84:3 | 44n71 |
| 25:4 | 148 | | |
| 39:3–5 | 148 | *2 Enoch* | |
| 39:7–8 | 148 | 3–22 | 190 |
| 39:12 | 39n45, 65n56 | 14:2 [J] | 39n45 |
| 40:1ff | 39n45, 65n56 | 19:1–5 | 74n91 |
| 47:1–4 | 146, 159n47 | 29:4–5 | 73n91 |
| 47:1–3 | 39n45, 65n56 | 47:3–4 | 80n121 |
| 48:2 | 64 | 65:10 [J] | 168n75 |
| 48:4 | 64 | 66:4 | 44n71, 80n121 |
| 48:5 | 64 | 67:1–3 | 172 |
| 49:2 | 64 | | |
| 50:1 | 107 | *1 Esdras* | |
| 51:3–5 | 107 | 4:28 | 241n97 |
| 51:3 | 64, 148, 153 | | |
| 52:4 | 64n50 | *Exagōgē of Ezekiel* | |
| 55:4 | 64, 148, 153 | 67–82 | 257 |
| 56:5–6 | 46n83 | 68 | 257 |
| 58:1–2 | 107 | 69 | 257 |
| 60:2 | 39n45, 65n56 | 74–75 | 257 |
| 61:8–9 | 148, 153 | 79–82 | 257 |
| 61:8 | 64 | 83–89 | 257 |
| 61:10 | 73n91 | 85–86 | 257 |
| 62:2 | 153 | | |
| 62:5 | 172n91 | *4 Ezra* | |
| 62:6 | 148, 153 | 2:20–32 | 243n103 |
| 62:15–16 | 84n136, 172 | 2:34–41 | 243n103 |
| 62:15 | 107 | 2:44–48 | 243n103 |

| | | | |
|---|---|---|---|
| 2:43 | 240 | 22:3 | 45n77 |
| 2:36 | 240 | 22:8 | 45n77 |
| 3:4–36 | 107n79 | | |
| 4:30 | 243n102 | *Jubilees* | |
| 6:7 | 35 | 1:25–2:1 | 39n46 |
| 6:53–59 | 107n79 | 2:2 | 67n61, 68 |
| 6:54–59 | 135n217 | 3:27 | 138 |
| 6:55 | 108 | 12:3–5 | 80n121 |
| 6:54 | 107 | 12:19 | 44n71 |
| 6:56 | 56, 107 | 15:31–32 | 46n83 |
| 6:58 | 56, 108 | 19:29 | 56 |
| 7:11 | 243n102 | 21:9 | 138n231 |
| 7:13–14 | 108 | 40:7 | 45n77 |
| 7:14 | 115 | | |
| 7:17–18 | 108 | *Judith* | |
| 7:17 | 115 | 9:14 | 70n75 |
| 7:46–48 | 243n102 | | |
| 7:50 | 35n30, 91n14 | *Ladder of Jacob* | |
| 7:88–98 | 243n103 | 7:35 | 78 |
| 7:89 | 108 | | |
| 7:91 | 108 | *Liber antiquitatum biblicarum* | |
| 7:92–98 | 108 | 11:15 | 258 |
| 7:98 | 108 | 12:1 | 258 |
| 7:113 | 35, 91n14 | 13:2–7 | 258 |
| 7:127–128 | 36n30 | 13:9–10 | 100 |
| 8:1 | 91n14 | 13:9 | 100 |
| 8:2 | 91n14 | 32:7–8 | 258n152 |
| 8:20–24 | 66 | 32:8–10 | 258 |
| 8:21–22 | 39n45 | | |
| 9–10 | 115 | *Life of Adam and Eve* | |
| 9:17ff | 107n79 | 3:2 | 74n91 |
| 10:15–16 | 115 | 13:2 | 74n91 |
| 10:20–24 | 115 | 13:3–14:3 | 65 |
| 10:24 | 115 | | |
| 10:44 | 115 | *1 Maccabees* | |
| 10:50 | 115 | 1:49 | 76n102 |
| 12:32–35 | 115 | 2:57 | 35 |
| 12:46–51 | 115 | 3:30 | 241n97 |
| 12:46–48 | 115 | 7:17 | 170 |
| 12:47 | 115 | 12:20 | 241n97 |
| | | 12:45 | 170 |

*Joseph and Aseneth*

| | | | |
|---|---|---|---|
| 12:1–2 | 80n121 | *2 Maccabees* | |
| 12:1 | 44n71 | 1:24 | 44n71, 80n121 |
| 15:11–12 | 66n57 | 2:8 | 41n57 |

*Index*

| | |
|---|---|
| 2:21 | 44n71 |
| 5:28 | 44n71 |
| 7:23 | 44n71 |
| 8:16 | 241n97 |
| 11:6 | 222, 235 |

*3 Maccabees*

| | |
|---|---|
| 1:16 | 222, 235 |
| 1:29 | 76n102 |
| 2:3 | 44n71 |
| 5:7 | 222, 236 |
| 5:25 | 222, 236 |
| 6:2 | 70n75 |

*4 Maccabees*

| | |
|---|---|
| 6:27 | 70n75 |
| 4:13–15 | 127 |
| 4:13 | 241n97 |
| 7:15 | 128 |
| 7:16 | 127, 128 |
| 7:20 | 127 |
| 7:19 | 127 |
| 7:22 | 127 |
| 12:3 | 218 |
| 14:1 | 240 |
| 15:4 | 41, 41n55, 157n40 |
| 17:5 | 241, 242 |
| 17:10 | 242 |
| 17:12 | 242 |
| 17:15 | 242 |
| 17:18 | 242 |
| 17:19–22 | 242 |

*Masık*

| | |
|---|---|
| 1:9–12 | 150 |

*Odes*

| | |
|---|---|
| 2:43 | 47n86, 63, 63n45 |
| 14:12 | 70n75 |

*Prayer of Manasseh*

| | |
|---|---|
| 2–3 | 44n71 |

*Psalms of Solomon*

| | |
|---|---|
| 2:10 | 70n75 |
| 2:15 | 70n75 |
| 2:25 | 70n75 |
| 5:4 | 70n75 |
| 5:8 | 70n75 |
| 5:11 | 70n75, 70n77 |
| 7:1 | 70n75 |
| 7:2 | 70n75 |
| 8:25 | 70n75 |
| 8:27 | 70n75 |
| 9:2 | 70n75 |
| 9:3 | 70n75, 70n77 |
| 9:6 | 70n75 |
| 9:8 | 70n75 |
| 13:9 | 56 |
| 14:1–5 | 243n103 |
| 15:1 | 70n75 |
| 15:2 | 70n75 |
| 16:5 | 70n75 |
| 16:6 | 70n75 |
| 16:7 | 70n75 |
| 16:14–15 | 221n37 |
| 17 | 48 |
| 17:1 | 70n75, 70n77 |
| 17:7 | 70n75 |
| 17:8 | 70n75 |
| 17:19–20 | 75n95 |
| 17:21 | 70n75, 70n77 |
| 17:22 | 75n95 |
| 17:23 | 35 |
| 17:26–27 | 75n95 |
| 17:32 | 75n95 |
| 17:34 | 75n95 |
| 17:36–42 | 243n103 |
| 17:37–38 | 75n95 |
| 17:39 | 243n103 |
| 17:40 | 243n103 |
| 17:43 | 75n95 |
| 18:4 | 56, 212 |
| 18:5 | 57 |
| 18:13 | 56n2 |

*Sibylline Oracles.*

| | |
|---|---|
| 3:20–23 | 44n71 |
| 5:228 | 218 |

*Sibylline Oracles Fragments*
| | |
|---|---|
| 1:5–6 | 80n121 |
| 1:17 | 44n71 |
| 1:35 | 44n71 |
| 3 | 80n121 |
| 5 | 80n121 |

*Sirach*
| | |
|---|---|
| 7:6 | 241n97 |
| 7:18 | 76n102 |
| 7:29 | 241n97 |
| 14:17 | 82 |
| 18:27 | 241, 241n97 |
| 22:22 | 241n97 |
| 23:4 | 70n75 |
| 23:18 | 241n97 |
| 26:5 | 241n97 |
| 29:7 | 241n97 |
| 33:21 | 76n102 |
| 34:14 | 241n97 |
| 41:3 | 241n97 |
| 43:33 | 44n71, 80n121 |
| 45:12 | 137 |
| 49:16–50:1 | 138 |
| 50 | 45n77, 139 |
| 50:11–13 | 139 |
| 50:12–13 | 139 |
| 50:16 | 139 |
| 51:2 | 235 |
| 51:5 | 235 |
| 51:6 | 235 |
| 51:8–11 | 235 |
| 51:8–9 | 235 |
| 51:10 | 221, 235 |
| 51:12 | 235 |

*Testament of Abraham*
| | |
|---|---|
| 1:4 | 74n91 |
| 13:10 | 74n91 |
| 13:13 | 74n91 |
| 20:11–14 | 172 |

*Testament of Job*
| | |
|---|---|
| 2:4 | 44n71, 80n121 |

*Testament of Isaac*
| | |
|---|---|
| 4:39 | 172n96 |
| 4:42 | 172n96 |
| 4:46–47 | 172 |
| 4:46 | 172n96 |
| 4:47 | 172n96, 243n103 |

*Testament of Levi*
| | |
|---|---|
| 2–5 | 190 |
| 2:5 | 148 |
| 2:7 | 148 |
| 2:8–9 | 149 |
| 2:9 | 149 |
| 2:20 | 149 |
| 3–4 | 172n98 |
| 3:1–10 | 172 |
| 3:2 | 149 |
| 3:3–9 | 73n91 |
| 3:3 | 149 |
| 3:4 | 66, 146, 149, 159n47 |
| 3:5 | 74n91 |
| 4:2 | 172, 172n94 |
| 4:5 | 39n45 |
| 4:6 | 172n94 |
| 5:1–2 | 39n46 |
| 5:1 | 146, 149, 152, 159n47 |
| 5:3–7 | 46n83 |
| 5:3 | 149 |
| 5:7 | 91n17 |
| 17:3 | 140 |

*Testament of Solomon*
| | |
|---|---|
| 2:4–7 | 74n91 |
| 7:7 | 74n91 |

*Tobit*
| | |
|---|---|
| 3:2 | 75n97 |
| 8:5 | 70n75 |
| 8:15 | 70n75 |
| 11:14 | 70n75 |
| 12:15 | 91n17 |
| 12:16–22 | 66n57 |

*Wisdom*
| | |
|---|---|
| 1:14 | 44n71 |

# Index

| | | | |
|---|---|---|---|
| 3:9 | 160n51 | 20 ii 22 | 150 |
| 4:11 | 76n102 | | |
| 4:15 | 160n51 | 4Q491C | |
| 5:5 | 47n86, 63n45 | Frag. 1 col.6 | 45n77 |
| 6:12 | 73n87 | | |
| 7:25 | 38 | 4Q504 | |
| 7:26 | 37n34, 38, 41n52 | | 71n79, 106 |
| 7:27–28 | 39 | | |
| 7:27 | 43, 43n68 | 4Q506 | |
| 8:1 | 44 | | 106 |
| 8:13 | 73n87 | | |
| 9:1–5 | 39 | 4QapGen ar | |
| 9:1 | 44n71, 70n75 | 20:13 | 44n71 |
| 9:4 | 153n25 | | |
| 9:6 | 44n71 | 4QDb | |
| 9:8 | 73n87, 147, 147n8, 148n8, 149n14 | 18:5–9 | 44n71 |
| 9:10 | 41n57, 153n25 | 4QDeutq | |
| 10:1–2 | 44n71 | 32:8 | 63n45 |
| 10:11 | 75n96 | 32:43 | 63 |
| 10:15–20 | 75n96 | | |
| 10:18 | 75n96 | 4QFlor | |
| 11:9–10 | 212 | 1:11–12 | 50 |
| 12:8 | 161 | | |
| 12:10 | 76n102 | 1QHa | |
| 12:13 | 44n71 | 4:14–15 | 106, 136, 243n103 |
| 17:8 | 241 | 4:15 | 105 |
| 18:15–16 | 43n65 | 5:20–26 | 106 |
| 18:15 | 43 | 5:23 | 106 |

## Dead Sea Scrolls

1QpHab
    114

4Q400
  1 i–ii    150
  1 i.9–13    150
  1 i.14    194n168
  1 i.19–20    150

1QM
  15    134n212

1QS
  3:15–16    105
  3:18    105
  3:20    105

4Q403
  1 i    150
  1 ii 10–16    146, 159n47

  4:7–8    105
  4:22    105
  4:23    105

4Q405
  14–15    150
  20 ii 21–22    146, 159n47

11 QMelchizedek
          45n77
  2.9     72n86
  2.10    72n86
  2.11    72n86
  2.13    64n51, 72n86
  2.17–18 72n86
  2.23    72n86

CD
  3:20    105

CD-A
  iii.12–20   243n103
  iii.20      243n103

## Josephus

*Ant.* (*Jewish Antiquities*)
  3.122–124   151
  3.123       151
  3.145       151
  3.180–181   151
  3.180       151
  3.181       151

*J.W.* (*Jewish War*)
  5.217   151
  5.218   44n71

## Philo

*Conf.* (*De confusione linguarum*)
  167   50n98

*Decal.* (*De decalogo*)
  155   42n63

*Det.* (*Quod deterius potiori insidari soleat*)
  83   41n53

*Ebr.* (*De ebrietate*)
  133   37n37
  134   151

  135–136   151

*Her.* (*Quis rerum divinarum heres sit*)
  1–29      237n79
  7         42n63
  2.122     50n98
  221–225   151

*Leg.* (*Legum allegoriae*)
  3:4   50n98

*Mos.* (*De vita Mosis*(
  1:158      259
  2.74–76    150
  2.80       151
  2.81–83    151
  2.102–105  151

*Mut.* (*De Mutatione nominum*)
  7   259

*Opif.* (*De opificio mundi*)
  146   37, 37n34
  148   97, 98

*Plant.* (*De plantatione*)
  18      41n53
  20      37n36
  36–37   37n35
  41      37n35
  44      37n35, 37n37, 41n53
  50      37, 37n34
  171     50n98

*Q.E.* (*Quaestiones et solutions in Exodus*)
  2:40      259
  2.69      151
  2.73–81   151
  2.83      151
  2.91–96   151
  2.91      151n22
  2.94      151

*Sobr.* (*De sobrietate*)
  8   50n98

Index

*Somn. (De somniis)*
  1.166       50n98

*Spec. Leg. (De specialibus legibus)*
  iv.123      37, 37n34

## Midrash

*Gen. Rab.*
  14.6        135n217
  99         69n72

## Babylonian Talmud

*Babli b. Shabbath*
  88–89       110

*b. Rosh Hash*
  21b        110

*b. Ned.*
  38a        110

## Early Christian Literature

*Barnabas*
  6:2        50n98
  6:4        50n98

*1 Clement*
  10:4       50n98
  10:6       50n98
  14:5       50n98
  15:3       50n98

*2 Clement*
  1:6        218

*Martyrdom of Polycarp*
  5:1        59

**Irenaeus**
*Against Heresies*
  I.x.1       14n5
  III.iv.2     14n5

**Tertullian**
*On Prescription Against Heresies*
  13        14n5

## Other Greek Literature

Euripides
*Iph. Aul. (Iphigenia aulidensis)*
  424       161

Heroditus
*Hist. (Historiae)*
  1.60.4     161
  7.203.1    161
  9.14.2     161

Polybius
*Hist.*
  12.20.7    161

Ps-Sophocles   44n71, 80n121

Theophrastus
*Hist. plant. (Historia plantarum)*
  5.1–5     161

www.ingramcontent.com/pod-product-compliance
Lightning Source LLC
Chambersburg PA
CBHW070722240426
43673CB00003B/106